TREATMENT OF FOREIGN LAW IN ASIA

How do Asian courts ascertain, interpret and apply a foreign law as the law governing the merits of the case? What should judges do if parties do not raise or disagree on the content of foreign law? This thematic volume in the Studies in Private International Law – Asia series analyses the treatment of foreign law before judicial authorities, that is, how the courts of Asian states deal with the proof of foreign law in court litigation involving cross-border elements.

The individual chapters cover 15 Asian jurisdictions: Mainland China, Hong Kong, Taiwan, Japan, South Korea, Singapore, Malaysia, Vietnam, Cambodia, Myanmar, the Philippines, Indonesia, Thailand, Sri Lanka, and India.

The Introduction and Conclusion examine similarities and differences in the approaches taken by the 15 Asian states with a view to assessing the extent to which those approaches are consistent or different from each other. The book also puts forward suggestions for harmonising differing approaches, especially between Asian common law and civil law states.

The book is a one-stop reference guide on the treatment of foreign law in Asia and will be indispensable to judges, practitioners, and scholars not just in Asia, but worldwide.

Volume 7 in the series Studies in Private International Law – Asia

Studies in Private International Law – Asia

Editors: Anselmo Reyes, Wilson Lui and Kazuaki Nishioka
Advisory Editor: Paul Beaumont

Much has been written about private international law in the EU and the US. Less is known about the conflict of laws in Asia. Thus, little attention has been paid so far to the modernisation of private international law codes and rules that has been taking place over the last decade all over Asia. That trend continues. Now is the time to take stock of those reforms that have already taken place and suggest further improvements for the future.

Published under the celebrated series *Studies in Private International Law*, this monograph sub-series provides a forum for discussion and analysis of private international law in Asia. The series is not solely a survey of jurisdictions for practitioners. Comprising in-depth thematic and country-specific studies, each volume considers the private international law of Asian countries from a variety of perspectives. An underlying assumption is that private international law in different jurisdictions follow broad discernible patterns. Each volume in this sub-series highlights those patterns and discusses how rules in different Asian jurisdictions are either converging with, or diverging from, the patterns identified. Such an analytical framework will assist academics, judges, lawyers and legislators to envisage ways in which laws affecting cross-border relationships can be harmonised across jurisdictions and be made more responsive to the needs of citizens in Asia and elsewhere.

Volume 1: Recognition and Enforcement of Judgments in Civil and Commercial Matters
Edited by Anselmo Reyes

Volume 2: Indonesian Private International Law
Afifah Kusumadara

Volume 3: Chinese Private International Law
Edited by Xiaohong Liu and Zhengyi Zhang

Volume 4: Direct Jurisdiction: Asian Perspectives
Edited by Anselmo Reyes and Wilson Lui

Volume 5: Japanese Private International Law
Kazuaki Nishioka and Yuko Nishitani

Volume 6: Indian Private International Law
Stellina Jolly and Saloni Khanderia

Volume 7: Treatment of Foreign Law in Asia
Edited by Kazuaki Nishioka

Treatment of Foreign Law in Asia

Edited by
Kazuaki Nishioka

•HART•
OXFORD • LONDON • NEW YORK • NEW DELHI • SYDNEY

HART PUBLISHING

Bloomsbury Publishing Plc

Kemp House, Chawley Park, Cumnor Hill, Oxford, OX2 9PH, UK

1385 Broadway, New York, NY 10018, USA

29 Earlsfort Terrace, Dublin 2, Ireland

First published in Great Britain 2023

A catalogue record for this book is available from the British Library.

A catalogue record for this book is available from the Library of Congress.

Library of Congress Control Number: 2023941459

ISBN: HB: 978-1-50995-655-5
ePDF: 978-1-50995-657-9
ePub: 978-1-50995-656-2

Typeset by Compuscript Ltd, Shannon
Printed and bound in Great Britain by CPI Group (UK) Ltd, Croydon CR0 4YY

MIX
Paper | Supporting responsible forestry
FSC® C013604

To find out more about our authors and books visit www.hartpublishing.co.uk. Here you will find extracts, author information, details of forthcoming events and the option to sign up for our newsletters.

SERIES EDITORS' PREFACE

One can only have sympathy for the Vietnamese judge who, in a workshop on judicial support for international arbitration a few years back, lamented that she occasionally had to determine the content of foreign law in applications for the enforcement of arbitral awards. One has a hard enough time deciding what principles of law to apply on a domestic matter, she complained. How was she, as a Vietnamese judge, supposed to discern the relevant Swiss law on an issue, when the parties adduced Swiss legal opinions coming to opposite conclusions?

The treatment of foreign law may seem a mundane and unpromising subject for a whole book. However, when one of the series editors was Representative of the Hague Conference's Regional Office for Asia and the Pacific (ROAP), the topic was a matter on which developing countries in Asia, especially civil law jurisdictions, were pressing the Hague Conference to come up with a convention or at least guiding principles. There was therefore disappointment when the Hague Conference's Council on General Affairs and Policy (CGAP) decided in March 2015 to remove the topic of accessing the content of foreign law from the Hague Conference's agenda, albeit 'with the understanding that this issue may be revisited at a later stage'.

What accounts for the widespread interest in Asia on the treatment of foreign law?

Given Asia's geographical circumstances, its diversity of laws, and the mobility of its populations, cases involving foreign elements will inevitably arise before Asian courts. The standard approach to such situations in many countries would be for judges dutifully to note the foreign elements calling for foreign law to be applied. But, in the course of analysis, for one reason or another, the courts would find in every single instance that it was appropriate to decide based on domestic law alone. This standard approach was long derided by Asian academics and the situation is gradually changing as a result. Nevertheless, the Vietnamese judge's query remains apposite: What in practical terms is a judge to do when presented with seemingly reasonable, but contradictory submissions on foreign law?

The starting point for civil law jurisdictions is the fiction that the court knows all the laws (*iura novit curia*). That includes foreign law. However difficult, the judge must inform oneself of the content of foreign law as best one can within a short time frame and then apply the same confidently to the matter at hand. The judge is duty-bound to apply foreign law whenever relevant, whether a party has asked for it or not. In contrast, the common law judge regards foreign law as purely a question of fact. The common law judge determines the content of foreign law by weighing the evidence on that law adduced by the parties. If neither party pleads foreign law, there is no obligation on the judge to raise it with the parties. If neither party adduces evidence on foreign law, the judge is entitled to assume that the relevant foreign law is identical to domestic law.

It might be imagined that the obvious answer to the Vietnamese judge's dilemma is to adopt the common law approach. In other words, just leave it to the parties to raise foreign law. Unfortunately, the matter cannot be so straightforward. The problem with the common law approach is that it can be costly. Even if a trial is conducted online rather than face-to-face, the parties' foreign law experts will both have to appear before the court at the same time to give evidence. Where the foreign law is contested, there will be oral examination of the experts. All this takes time and time is money. Not all cases can justify the expense. In cross-border family disputes, for instance, parties may simply not have the means to engage reliable foreign law experts. Worse, the common law approach can lead to a judgment being based on a capricious amalgam of foreign and domestic law, neither truly reflective of the one nor the other, merely because on some issues the parties have adduced expert evidence, while on others they have not.

The civil law approach is more flexible. Judges can inform themselves of the content of foreign law in various ways from (say) conducting private research over the internet to employing the common law method. The court can tailor the method used to what is reasonable and proportionate in the circumstances of a case, including the amount at stake and the gravity of the consequences of finding that foreign law is *x* as opposed to *y*. The constraint to what is possible is that the court must keep in mind the exigencies of due process and fairness. The parties must have a reasonable opportunity to comment on the appropriateness of the court's methodology and the correctness of the results obtained. In practice, this is easier said than done, since suitable safeguards will need to be built into the court procedure on a case-by-case basis depending on the method used to access the content of foreign law.

In summary, the theme of this book is how 15 Asian states balance the demands of cost-effectiveness, time-efficiency, and fairness in the ascertainment of foreign law; how their approaches can be improved; and how the ascertainment of Asian and other laws can be facilitated by regional, quasi-regional or international databases and institutions. Contrary to first impression, it is hoped that the book's subject-matter will make for an interesting and thought-provoking study.

The Editors
Kyoto
1 May 2023

ACKNOWLEDGEMENTS

Many people have been engaged in this book project. I am sincerely grateful for the contributors' efforts at elaborating comprehensive accounts of their jurisdictions despite the challenging circumstances and personal ordeals during the COVID pandemic. I would further express my gratitude to Adeline Chong, Akawat Laowonsiri, Anselmo Reyes, Lukas Rass-Masson, and Yuko Nishitani for their valuable comments on the tentative conclusion of this project at the Asian Private International Law Academy (APILA) conference in Kyoto in December 2022. My huge thanks also go to Hughes Tang for his editing support. Finally, I would like to thank my family and friends for their unfailing and unstinting support.

Kazuaki Nishioka
Kyoto
1 April 2023

CONTENTS

LIST OF CONTRIBUTORS

Tiurma M Pitta Allagan is a Lecturer of Private International Law at the Faculty of Law, Universitas Indonesia, Indonesia.

Sungjae Chun is a Counsel at Netflix Services Korea, South Korea.

Wasiq Abass Dar is an Associate Professor of Legal Practice, Jindal Global Law School, O.P. Jindal Global University, Sonipat, India.

Dixin Deng is Head of Academic Research and Development at Shanghai Arbitration Commission, People's Republic of China.

Mingchao Fan is Executive Vice President at Shanghai Arbitration Commission, People's Republic of China.

Ramesh Fernando is an Associate in the Disputes team of Afridi & Angell, Dubai. Until October 2022 he was a Junior Counsel in the Chambers of Geoffrey Alagaratnam, President's Counsel, in Sri Lanka.

Teh Wai Fung practises as a lawyer in Malaysia. He read law at Durham University. He has been called to both the Malaysian Bar and the Bar of England and Wales (Middle Temple). He is a Member of the Chartered Institute of Arbitrators.

Sai Ramani Garimella is an Assistant Professor at the Faculty of Legal Studies of South Asian University in India and Senior Research Associate at the Research Centre for Private International Law in Emerging Countries of University of Johannesburg in South Africa.

Ruian Guo is Head of Commission Affairs at Shanghai Arbitration Commission, People's Republic of China.

Trinh Nguyen Thi Hong is a Lecturer at College of Law, Hue University, Vietnam.

Chen Kuang is an Assistant Legal Counsel at Shanghai Arbitration Commission, People's Republic of China.

Afifah Kusumadara is an Associate Professor at the Faculty of Law, Brawijaya University, Indonesia.

Chun-Liang Lai is an Attorney-at-Law, Lai & Lai Law Firm, Taiwan.

Fuldien Li is an Emeritus Professor of Law, Chinese Culture University and Chairman, Chinese Arbitration Association, Taiwan.

Felice Fu-An Lu is an Associate at Point 101 Law PC, and a Bar Counsel at Point Bar Review, California.

Wilson Lui is a Pre-Doctoral Fellow and Lecturer at the Faculty of Law of the University of Hong Kong, Hong Kong.

Lemuel D Lopez is a Lecturer of Law, Royal Melbourne Institute of Technology University, Australia.

Kazuaki Nishioka is a Researcher at the Institute of Comparative Law in Japan, Chuo University, Japan.

Krisda Saengcharoensap is a Lecturer at the Faculty of Law of Rangsit University, Thailand.

Poomintr Sooksripaisarnkit is a Lecturer at Australian Maritime College, University of Tasmania, Australia, a Senior Research Associate, Research Centre for Private International Law in Emerging Countries, University of Johannesburg, and Fellow, The Chartered Institute of Arbitrators.

Ida Susanti is a Lecturer at the Faculty of Law, Parahyangan Catholic University, Indonesia.

Alvin Tan is an Associate of the Dispute Resolution Team at Schellenberg Wittmer Singapore, Singapore.

Nobumichi Teramura is an Assistant Professor at the Institute of Asian Studies at the University of Brunei Darussalam (UBD) and an Affiliate at the Centre for Asian and Pacific Law at the University of Sydney (CAPLUS).

Bui Thi Quynh Trang is a Lecturer at College of Law, Hue University, Vietnam.

Yuji Tsutsumi is an Attorney-at-law (Japan) and Management Partner of TNY International Law Firm, Japan.

Michael Weber is a PhD candidate and research assistant at the Faculty of Law of the University of Zurich, and holds an MLaw from the same university.

Andreas Wehowsky is an Associate of the Dispute Resolution Team at Schellenberg Wittmer, Switzerland.

Siyang Ye is an Assistant Legal Counsel at Shanghai Arbitration Commission, People's Republic of China.

LIST OF CASES

United Kingdom

United States

China

Dubai

Hong Kong

India

Indonesia

Japan

Malaysia

Myanmar

Philippines

Singapore

South Korea

Sri Lanka

Taiwan

Thailand

Vietnam

LIST OF STATUTES AND INSTRUMENTS

International Instruments

Bilateral Instruments

National Statutes, Rules and Other Instruments

Cambodia

China

European Union

Hong Kong

India

Indonesia

Malaysia

Myanmar

South Korea

Sri Lanka

Vietnam

1

Introduction

KAZUAKI NISHIOKA

I. Purpose

Private International Law traditionally deals with three questions.[1] First, there is the question of international (direct) jurisdiction: whether and under what conditions national courts can take jurisdiction to hear and determine a case involving foreign elements. Second, there is the question of applicable (or governing) law: what legal system will be applied to determine the merits of a case involving foreign elements? Third, there is the question of recognition and enforcement of foreign judgments: whether and under what conditions will they be recognised and enforced in other countries? This book considers some ancillary, but practically important aspects of the second question.[2] It will do so by looking at the issue of treatment of, and access to, foreign law across 15 Asian states. It comes after the two thematic books in the *Studies in Private International Law: Asia series*. The first volume deals with recognition and enforcement of judgments in civil and commercial matters in the same 15 Asian states.[3] Volume One thus considered the third question. The second volume considered direct jurisdiction (that is, the first question) in the same 15 Asian states.[4]

In a globalised world, people, goods, capital and services frequently go beyond national boundaries, with the result that the number of international business transactions and incidental cross-border disputes is rapidly increasing worldwide. In this connection, national courts are often faced with a challenge of ascertaining and applying foreign law to decide cross-border disputes. The application of foreign law has been regarded as the crux of the

[1] See, eg, Lord Collins of Mapesbury (ed), *Dicey, Morris and Collins on Conflict of Laws* 15th edn, vol 1 (London, Sweet and Maxwell, 2012) para 1-003. Nowadays, international arbitration is often regarded as part of private international law.

[2] Note that each chapter of this book is not intended to analyse choice of law rules in the respective state. For a detailed analysis of choice of law rules in family matters within the Asian states, see A Reyes, W Lui and K Nishioka (eds), *Choice of Law and Recognition in Family Law* (Oxford, Hart Publishing, forthcoming). More generally, see the country volumes in Hart Publishing's *Studies of Private International Law in Asia* series. To date, four volumes have been published: A Kusumadara (ed), *Indonesian Private International Law* (Oxford, Hart Publishing, 2021); X Liu and Z Zhang (eds), *Chinese Private International Law* (Oxford, Hart Publishing, 2021), K Nishioka and Y Nishitani, *Japanese Private International Law* (Oxford, Hart Publishing, 2021), and S Jolly and S Khanderia, *Indian Private International Law* (Oxford, Hart Publishing, 2021).

[3] A Reyes (ed), *Recognition and Enforcement of Judgments in Civil and Commercial Matters* (Oxford, Hart Publishing, 2019).

[4] A Reyes and W Lui (eds), *Direct Jurisdiction: Asian Perspectives* (Oxford, Hart Publishing, 2021).

conflict of laws (private international law).[5] How do national courts treat foreign law in court proceedings? As that issue stands at the intersection of private international law and domestic procedural law, it may be grounded on different theoretical foundations and practical conceptions in different legal systems. To date, some academic research on this topic has been done. However, the focus has primarily been on rules and practices in western states.[6] It remains unknown how national courts in a majority of Asian states approach this issue,[7] despite the application of foreign law by national courts being an important question in private international law. In practice, this situation may diminish the certainty of an applicable law and constitute an impediment to citizens' access to justice. Under these circumstances, this volume aims to shed light on the current law and practice in the 15 Asian states examined in this book, with a view to assessing whether Asian approaches are consistent with (or different from) each other. It will also put forward suggestions for improving the situation in Asia with regard to the treatment of and access to foreign law. Note that this book refers to earlier discussions and developments at international and regional levels. However, it is not intended to analyse and discuss them in detail. Instead, the plan is to examine the current situation and discuss how to improve it in practical ways.

This volume first will look into the treatment of foreign law before judicial authorities in Asia, that is, how the courts of Asian states deal with foreign law in court proceedings. For instance, is a foreign law considered a matter of law or fact? Does the *iura novit curia* ('the court knows the law') principle apply? Or do the parties have to plead foreign law and prove its contents? Who bears the burden of proving the contents of relevant foreign law? How do the courts ascertain, interpret and apply a foreign law as the law governing the merits of a case? What should national courts do if the parties or the courts cannot ascertain the contents of foreign law? If the courts erroneously apply the foreign law applicable to the merits of a case, can the parties appeal or seek some form of judicial review? As many chapters show, there are no (or few) black-letter rules on these questions in most of the Asian states surveyed. These questions are considered in individual chapters dealing with the law and practice in each of the 15 Asian jurisdictions.

In general, there is a difference of approach between civil and common law jurisdictions.[8] It is well-known that common law courts (such as those in India and Singapore) regard foreign law as a matter of fact and so the parties need to plead foreign law and prove its contents. In contrast, civil law jurisdictions (most Asian states) treat the ascertainment of foreign law as a question of law. Therefore, courts are required to ascertain and apply foreign

[5] R Fentiman, *Foreign Law in English Courts: Pleading, Proof and Choice of Law* (Oxford, Clarendon Press Oxford, 1998) 1.

[6] For instance, Swiss Institute of Comparative Law (ed), *The Application of Foreign Law in Civil Matters in the EU Member States and its Perspectives for the Future* (JLS/2009/JCIV/PR/0005/E4, 2011, available at ec.europa.eu/) Part I: Legal Analysis; Part II: Empirical Analysis; Synthesis Report with Recommendations; C Esplugues, JL Iglesias, and G Paolo (eds), *Application of Foreign Law* (Munich, Sellier, 2011); Y Nishitani (ed), *Treatment of Foreign Law – Dynamics towards Convergence?* (Cham, Springer, 2017). On the HCCH's work, see section II.

[7] The existing volumes of Hart's country series (n 2) deal with this topic. However, there is scant literature or any regional study comprehensively looking into the current position in Asian states. Professor Yuko Nishitani's 2017 study (n 6) covers only Japan and Macau among Asian jurisdictions.

[8] See, eg, C Esplugues and G Palao, 'Foreign Law, Application and Ascertainment' in J Basedow, G Rühl, F Ferrari and P de Miguel Asensio (eds), *Encyclopedia of Private International Law* (Cheltenham, Edward Elgar, 2017) 769–78.

law for themselves. In addition, a hybrid nature approach has been argued and adopted in some countries, that is, foreign law considered as a matter of law, albeit not of the same kind as domestic law. Beyond such general perception of the divide between the common and civil law, it is unclear or unknown how exactly national courts in practice approach those issues.

Second, this book will look into the treatment of foreign law before other bodies, such as administrative authorities, arbitrators and mediators in the respective Asian jurisdictions, in particular, whether such institutions treat foreign law in the same way as the courts.

Furthermore, each chapter provides detailed accounts on the current system or framework for access to the relevant jurisdiction's legislation and court decisions with a view to promoting access to its law, especially for foreign users. Each chapter also elaborates on the channels and methods national courts use to ascertain the contents of foreign law. At the international level, there has so far been no framework for access to foreign law, except for the International Hague Network of Judges (IHNJ)[9] for cross-border child abduction cases under the Hague convention and the Judicial Insolvency Network (JIN)[10] for cross-border insolvency disputes.[11] Hence, national courts typically ascertain the contents of foreign law through channels available to them under their domestic laws or through bilateral or multilateral arrangements.

The heart of this book then are the 15 chapters that follow after this Introduction. Each will describe and analyse how national courts or other instances treat foreign law and provide its system or framework for access to both its law and foreign law. The respective Asian states are China, Hong Kong, Taiwan, Japan, South Korea, Singapore, Malaysia, Vietnam, Cambodia, Myanmar, Philippines, Indonesia, Thailand, Sri Lanka and India.[12] The chapters, however, are not mere national reports. Contributors were invited to argue how treatment of (and access to) foreign law should and can be developed in Asia. This concerns a fourth question of private international law mentioned in the previous volume of this thematic series, that is, the harmonisation of private international law rules. To what extent is it possible, desirable, or worthwhile to harmonise the various rules of different states on cross-border matters? Contributors were encouraged to identify recent developments and potential infrastructure enabling judges and citizens easily to access and ascertain the contents of foreign law.

[9] See www.hcch.net/en/instruments/conventions/specialised-sections/child-abduction/ihnj. Each Member State designates one or more members of the judiciary to act as a channel of communication and liaison with their National Central Authorities, with other judges within their jurisdictions and judges in other Contracting States to deal with the 1980 Hague Child Abduction Convention cases.

[10] See jin-global.org/jin-guidelines.html.

[11] For preceding international and regional developments, see section II.

[12] The word 'Asia' has no precise widely accepted definition. The concept of 'Asia' may encompass the massive geographical area and refer to the continent that is to the east of Europe, the west of the Pacific Ocean, and the north of the Indian Ocean. The 15 jurisdictions surveyed here cannot be said to be representative of the diversity of the whole of Asia so defined. Thus, at best, the expression 'Asia' as used in this book merely refers to a sampling of Asian states.

II. An Overview of International and Regional Developments

Since 2006 the Hague Conference on Private International Law (HCCH) has been engaged in a study on cross-border treatment of foreign law with a view to setting up a legal instrument providing for international cooperation on the treatment of foreign law.[13] Initially, the HCCH's work focused on the feasibility of a new international instrument dealing with the differences of approach as to the treatment of foreign law before national courts. However, its interest and focus shifted to a more feasible (or narrower) topic, that is, the facilitation of access to foreign law. Indeed, an Experts Meeting in 2007 concluded:[14]

> [T]here should be no attempt to comprehensively harmonise the different approaches to the treatment of foreign law, as there is no need or likelihood of success for harmonisation. Several experts, nevertheless, recognised the need to develop an instrument, which effectively improves access to foreign law, accommodates the different approaches taken by legal systems in this subject matter and at the same time fits into their procedural framework. The experts indicated that according to their practice, there is a need to obtain information on foreign law mostly in the areas of family law, the law of successions and commercial law. They were of the view that there were no compelling reasons to exclude, at this point, any areas of civil, commercial and procedural law.

Following the latter conclusion, a Note of 2009 drawn by the HCCH's Permanent Bureau stated:[15]

> The Experts' Meeting [...] concluded that it would be pointless to 'attempt to comprehensively harmonise the different approaches to the treatment of foreign law, as there [was] no need or likelihood of any success for such harmonisation'. Yet, the Experts agreed that there was 'clearly a need to facilitate access to foreign law' and 'they supported the Permanent Bureau's continued work in the area'. These conclusions were shared by the Council on General Affairs and Policy in 2007. Consequently, the focus of the feasibility study shifted from the *legal status of foreign law*, in particular in civil and commercial proceedings, to the need for *cross-border administrative and legal co-operation* for the purpose of accessing the content of foreign law. Further work the revealed the increasing practical importance of *information on (foreign) Law* available online.

The HCCH has since focused on the topic of access to foreign law, conducting some research and monitoring the same. In particular, it has examined: (1) facilitating access to online legal information on foreign law; (2) cross-border administrative or judicial co-operation; and (3) the feasibility of a global network of institutions and experts for more complex questions. To date, however, the HCCH has not produced any instrument in this regard, other than some provisions in the existing Hague conventions.[16]

[13] For an overview of the HCCH's previous work, see, eg, P Lortie and M Groff, 'The Evolution of Work on Access to Foreign Law at the Hague Conference on Private International Law' in Y Nishitani (ed), *Treatment of Foreign Law – Dynamics towards Convergence?* (Cham, Springer, 2017) 615–38.

[14] Preliminary Document No 21 A of March 2007, 'Feasibility Study on the Treatment of Foreign Law: Report of the Meeting of 23–24 February 2007', 3. Available at the HCCH's archive.

[15] Preliminary Document No 11 A of March 2009 – Accessing the Content of Foreign Law and the Need for the Development of A Global Instrument in this Area – A Possible Way Ahead', para 1. Available at assets.hcch.net/docs/ec2804c3-f55c-427d-9761-e0fa4eac41a7.pdf.

[16] Although not legally binding in effect, the HCCH developed in 2008 the Guiding Principle and, in 2012, released, together with the European Commission, the Conclusions and Recommendations on Access to Foreign

At the international level, organisations or institutions such as the United Nations Educational, Scientific and Cultural Organization (UNESCO) and the International Federation of Library Associations and Institutions (IFLA) have also been addressing the improvement of online access to (possibly free) legal information.[17] They have not so far established any legal platform or framework for direct access to foreign law.

Looking at the regional level, there are some multilateral frameworks on access to foreign law in Europe (the European Convention of 7 June 1968 on Information on Foreign Law[18] and the European Judicial Network in Civil and Commercial Matters (the London Convention[19])),[20] in Latin America (the Inter-American Convention on Proof and Information of Foreign Law[21]), and in the Commonwealth of Independent States (CIS) (the Convention on Legal Aid and Legal Relations in Civil, Family and Criminal Cases (the Minsk Convention)[22]). There exists no equivalent framework in Asia.[23] This means that the national courts of Asian states are left to ascertain the contents of foreign law through whatever channels may be available to them under domestic law and other arrangements.

Due in part to a lack of international or regional framework on access to foreign law, national courts in many Asian states (particularly, in civil law countries within the region) seemingly often land into difficulties when ascertaining the contents of foreign law. This indicates that there is a need to improve the situation. This can be done domestically, for instance, by establishing a national institute or network to assist courts in accessing and ascertaining foreign laws.[24] But, there is a limit to what a single state can do. It is highly unlikely that state A's judiciary will comprehensively understand and have full information on the whole of state B's legal system and its development in timely fashion without assistance. In reality, legislative texts often do not give a clear-cut answer to a legal question. Instead, one needs to look into court decisions and publications in local languages. In this regard, assistance and cooperation from state B and foreign law experts will be needed. In the Asian context, what can (or should) be done? As the experts at the HCCH concluded, there is no doubt that we should aim for an international or regional framework which can serve concerned parties (including courts and citizens). What kind of framework would be a preferable and feasible approach to cater for the real needs in this region? Should we aim for a rigid approach (such as a convention) or a soft system (such as a cooperative network among judiciaries without any legal obligations)?

Law in Civil and Commercial Matters (available at assets.hcch.net/docs/b093f152-a4b3-4530-949e-65c1bfc9cda1.pdf). For details of the HCCH's work, see, eg, Lortie and Groff (n 13) 615–38.

[17] For details of their activities, see Lortie and Groff (n 13) 626–27.

[18] ETS No. 62. Available at rm.coe.int/1680072314.

[19] e-justice.europa.eu/content_european_judicial_network_in_civil_and_commercial_matters-21-en.do.

[20] Furthermore, a group of European scholars drafted the so-called 'Madrid Principles' as a starting point to establish a common set of rules pertaining to treatment of foreign law within the EU. See, eg, CE Mota, 'Harmonization of Private International Law in Europe and Application of Foreign Law: the "Madrid Principles" of 2010' (2011) 13 *Yearbook of Private International Law* 273. However, there has been no EU instrument in this regard so far.

[21] See www.un.org/ruleoflaw/files/volume-1439-I-24393-English.pdf.

[22] Adopted in Minsk on 22 January 1993. See www.unhcr.org/protection/migration/4de4edc69/convention-legal-aid-legal-relations-civil-family-criminal-cases-adopted.html.

[23] Although there is no equivalent platform in Asia, there are some bilateral arrangements and memorandums of understanding on the treatment of, or access to, foreign law. See, eg, the chapters of South Korea (6) and Singapore (7).

[24] See ch 2.

III. Scope: Treatment of and Access to Foreign Law in Asia

This section identifies four categories of issues that will be considered in succeeding chapters: (A) status of choice of law rules, (B) foreign law before judicial authorities, (C) foreign law before other instances (administrative or non-judicial authorities and ADR service-providers), and (D) access to local and foreign law. Each category highlights key issues. The issues are simply meant to serve as springboards for ideas and contributors have been invited to add, discuss, and consider related matters as they see fit.

A. Status of Choice of Law Rules

The first category of issues is the status of choice of law rules. In particular, each chapter will handle the following two issues: (1) is the application of choice of law rules mandatory or facultative? and (2) do choice of law rules lead to the application of foreign law? Concerning the first question, the obvious (and well-known) difference of approach between common law and civil law has been described. While courts in civil law jurisdiction are typically required to apply choice of law principles as mandatory rules,[25] courts in common law jurisdiction will not normally introduce foreign law unless a party seeking the application of foreign law pleads the same and proves its contents. Readers might find the second question nonsensical or self-evident. It is, however, not entirely clear whether national courts in some Asian jurisdictions have choice of law rules leading to the application of foreign law or apply a foreign law in practice.[26]

B. Foreign Law before Judicial Authorities

The second category of issues is the treatment of foreign law before judicial authorities. This is the key part of this book. This will entail a discussion by contributors of features of their respective states, rooted in theoretical foundations from the common law or civil law, but with modifications based on their own legal system and current surrounding situation. The first sub-category of issues is the nature of foreign law, namely, is foreign law considered to be a matter of law or fact or of a hybrid nature? The second sub-category is the ascertainment and confirmation of foreign law. How do national courts ascertain foreign law? Does the *iura novit curia* principle apply? Or do the parties have to prove the content of foreign law? What kind of means are used to ascertain foreign law (for instance, documents, internet

[25] Most states surveyed in this book belong to the civil law family. From historical circumstances or other reasons, however, they have been influenced by common law and some of them adopt the common law approach as to the treatment of foreign law. For example, Thailand has a predominantly civil legal system, but it treats foreign law as a matter of fact. See ch 14.

[26] See ch 11. It is generally said that Myanmar was and remains a member of the common law family even after its independence. If this is the case, the relevant common law conflict of law rules might conceivably apply. Furthermore, as some chapters (eg, ch 13 Indonesia) report, their courts do not apply foreign law in certain matters, such as labour law cases.

sources, assistance of the parties, expert witnesses, enquiry to domestic or foreign judicial and non-judicial institutions, direct communications with judges, or any other methods)? Do individuals or institutions that provide legal information need specific qualifications? Is the legal information provided binding upon judicial authorities? Is there any mechanism to examine the reliability of the legal information provided? Who bears the costs of ascertaining the contents of foreign law? How do national courts guarantee due process in the ascertainment of the contents of foreign law? The third sub-category is the interpretation and application of foreign law. When, and under what conditions, is foreign law applied before judicial authorities? Ex officio, at a party's request, or under any other conditions? How do national courts interpret and apply foreign law? Do they do it the same way as the courts of the country of origin? How do national courts fill a gap in foreign law? The fourth sub-category is the failure to establish foreign law. How do national courts approach the situation where foreign law cannot be ascertained? In other words, what will the court do if the parties are (or the court is) unable to establish the contents of the foreign law applicable to a case? Will the court simply apply the lex fori? Why do national courts adopt such a solution? What is the underlying rationale and policy? The fifth sub-category is judicial review and appeal. When national courts erroneously apply choice of law rules (that is, they apply the law of state A instead of the designated law of state B), can the parties file an appeal to higher courts including the supreme court? If yes, under what conditions can they do so? Why do national courts adopt this solution? What is the underlying rationale and policy? Where national courts erroneously apply a designated foreign law, can the parties file an appeal to higher courts including the supreme court? If yes, under what conditions can they do so? Why do courts adopt this solution? What is the underlying rationale and policy? Each chapter gives not only an overview, but also an analysis of actual practice before judicial authorities in a jurisdiction.

C. Foreign Law before Other Instances

The third category will deal with the treatment of foreign law before other adjudicative bodies, for instance, administrative or quasi-judicial authorities,[27] as well as arbitral tribunals or mediators. The application of foreign law is not limited to courts. Foreign law is often applied, or taken into consideration, by non-judicial authorities, such as public notaries and civil or family registrars. This book poses several questions in connection with this common situation: (1) how is foreign law applied and ascertained before administrative or quasi-judicial authorities in a given jurisdiction? and (2) how is foreign law applied and ascertained in arbitration, mediation or other alternative dispute resolution process in a given jurisdiction? Will administrative tribunals, arbitrators, and mediators approach issues of foreign law in the same way as national courts? If yes, do the approaches have to be the same? If not, what would be the reasons supporting any differences? For administrative or quasi-judicial authorities as governmental organisations analogous to the judiciary, one

[27] For example, a Chinese and a Korean living in Japan can marry by submitting a marriage notification to a local authority. The officers at the relevant authority would then be required to check if by the couple's respective national laws the two persons can marry. Accordingly, administrative authorities are occasionally required to apply foreign laws.

might be tempted to take a similar approach to that taken by the courts. But arbitrators and mediators often have to follow the regulations of a specialised professional association[28] or rules based on the parties' agreement. Such regulations and rules are typically tailored to their specific purposes. They will usually involve more informal, less technical, procedures. It is submitted that differences of this nature should be considered when deciding how foreign law is to be established in a proceeding. But when compared to section B, there has been little discussion with regard to these differences in the respective state. What appears from this is that there is still much room for development and improvement.

D. Access to Local and Foreign Law

The fourth category will look into infrastructure for access to local and foreign law in a jurisdiction. Each contributor was encouraged to identify useful legal sources (including databases and electronic materials) available in languages other than the local one.

There are not many English legal materials in Asian jurisdictions (except for the jurisdictions where English is spoken as an official language). In some jurisdictions, legislation and court decisions may be available in other languages (primarily English). But this is the exception rather than the rule in Asia. The paucity of English language materials is certainly a major reason why Asian law has been not readily accessible to foreign users.[29]

Each contributor was further requested to discuss future developments on the treatment of and access to foreign law in one's jurisdiction. In light of a lack of an international or regional framework in Asia and the paucity of English language materials, a national system may not be satisfactory. What can be done to improve the situation? Contributors were encouraged to put forward proposals on the following matters:

(1) Is their state a party to an international or regional instruments on the treatment of or information on foreign law?
 (1a) if yes, is the instrument's mechanism useful?
(2) Is there need to improve access to foreign law?
 (2a) if yes, how?
 (2b) Is there need for a regional or international instrument or scheme to facilitate access to foreign law?
(3) Is there need for a regional or international institution that can assist national courts and citizens in ascertaining the contents of foreign law by providing information (for

[28] Eg, F De Ly, MW Friedman and LG Radicati di Brozolo, 'International Law Association International Commercial Arbitration Committee's Report and Recommendations on "Ascertaining the Contents of the Applicable Law in International Commercial Arbitration"' (2010) 26(2) *Arbitration International* 193.

[29] If there were sufficient materials in foreign languages, that would help foreign parties to understand, or at least grasp, the relevant laws of an Asian state. That said, as there is no perfect translation (it being difficult to translate concepts, nuances, connotations or implications), references to materials in their original language may still be required.

example, the Swiss Institute of Comparative Law[30] and the International Juridisch Instituut[31])?

(4) Is there need for a regional or international instrument unifying the treatment of foreign law?

IV. Summary

The treatment of foreign law stands at the intersection of private international law and domestic procedural law. Consequently, it is grounded on different theoretical foundations and practical conceptions in different legal systems. The Conclusion in chapter seventeen will look into similarities and differences in the approaches taken by the 15 Asian states with a view to assessing the extent to which those approaches are consistent with or different from each other. It will also put forward suggestions for improving the situation in Asia with regard to treatment of foreign law.

[30] This is a national institute in Switzerland that is intended to assist Swiss courts in ascertaining the contents of foreign law by conducting research and providing information of foreign laws. Some jurisdictions in Asia (such as mainland China) have such national institutes, whether inside the judiciary or not. See ch 2.

[31] www.iji.nl/en/. This private institution is 'a knowledge centre for private international law and foreign law,' advising legal practitioners in those fields.

2

China

MINGCHAO FAN, DIXIN DENG, RUIAN GUO,
CHEN KUANG AND SIYANG YE

I. Introduction

China has been increasingly active in global dynamics. This process has also placed higher demands on the legislation on China's treatment of foreign laws. This chapter introduces the Chinese conflict of laws system, with a special focus on the Law of the People's Republic of China on Choice of Law for Foreign-related Civil Relationships ('2010 Conflicts Statute') and the Interpretations of the Supreme People's Court on Several Issues Concerning Application of the Law of the People's Republic of China on Choice of Law for Foreign-Related Civil Relationships (I) ('2012 Interpretations'). Then, based on Article 10 of the 2010 Conflict Statute, we provide an in-depth explanation of the subjects and methods of determining the applicable law in disputes concerning foreign civil legal relationships. Meanwhile, the chapter also discusses the controversial issues in the process of determining the applicable law in light of the Chinese conflict law and cases.

After around 40 years of rapid growth under its reform and opening-up policy, China has developed to become a truly global economic power.[1] According to the WTO World Trade Statistical Review in 2021, Chinese trade exports were ranked fourth in the world, while its imports were ranked in the second position.[2] With ever stronger links to the rest of the world comes an increasing number of private international law cases adjudicated in Chinese courts.[3]

This chapter aims to provide a high-level overview of the treatment of foreign laws in China, including the general review of the Chinese conflict of laws regime, how the content of foreign laws is determined, and a brief discussion on the threshold of 'failing to ascertain foreign laws'. The latest academic trends and judicial practices will also be covered.

II. The Chinese Conflict of Laws Regime

The conflict of laws is one of the branches of law that regulates foreign-related civil relations. When there are different provisions in civil laws of several countries with respect to

[1] L Zhu, 'Conflict of laws in the People's Republic of China' (2017) 25 *Asia Pacific Law Review* 199.

[2] World Trade Organization, *Word Trade Statistical Review 2021*, (World Trade Organization, 22 July 2022), www.wto.org/english/res_e/statis_e/wts2021_e/wts2021chapter05_e.pdf.

[3] Zhu (n 1) 199.

one foreign-related civil legal relationship, conflict of laws can specify which one should be applied to that particular legal relationship. The conflict of laws is an indirect legal norm that invokes the direct legal norm that determines the rights and obligations of the parties.[4]

China has a long history of addressing conflict issues between different legal systems, while the legislation on conflict of laws, without a clear structure or statement of their hierarchy and effectiveness, is scattered among various legal sources.[5] Therefore, before getting into the core issue of the treatment of foreign laws, a brief review of the conflict of laws regime in China helps understand the landscape.

A. The Source of Legislation for the Chinese Conflict of Laws

The source of legislation for the Chinese conflict of laws includes piecemeal legislation and interpretations and 'Guiding Cases' issued by courts. Among them, there are two main legal instruments.

First, the 2010 Conflicts Statute sets a straightforward rule for the application of foreign laws. According to Article 10 of the 2010 Conflicts Statute,

> foreign laws applicable to foreign-related civil relations shall be ascertained by the people's court, arbitral authority or administrative organ. If any party chooses the applicable foreign laws, he or she shall provide the laws of this country. If foreign laws cannot be ascertained or there are no provisions in the laws of this country, the laws of the People's Republic of China shall apply.[6]

Second, the 2012 Interpretations provide further directions to judiciaries and practitioners on conflict of laws issues, giving more concrete legislative guidance for them.

While the high-level legislation structure is roughly in place, judiciaries are accumulating experiences from practice to promote the entire regime. Meanwhile, an in-depth understanding of foreign-related civil legal relations can help them to apply better conflict of laws in resolving foreign-related civil disputes.

B. The Definition and Judgement Principles of Foreign-related Civil Relationship

According to Article 1 of the 2012 Interpretations,[7] a 'foreign-related civil relationship' is a civil legal relationship in which one or both parties are foreign citizens, foreign legal persons or other organizations or stateless persons; or the subject is within the territory of a foreign country; or the legal facts that lead to establishment, change or termination of the relationship of civil rights and obligations occur in a foreign country.

[4] Y Zou, *Dictionary of Jurisprudence* (China University of Political Science and Law Press,1991).

[5] S Zhu, *Chinese Conflicts of Law: A Restatement and Legisprudence Proposal,* (2017) SJD Dissertations.

[6] Art 10 of the Law of the People's Republic of China on Choice of Law for Foreign-related Civil Relationships, Standing Committee of the National People's Congress, 28 October 2010.

[7] Art 1 of the Interpretations of the Supreme People's Court on Several Issues Concerning Application of the Law of the People's Republic of China on Choice of Law for Foreign-Related Civil Relationships (I), Supreme People's Court Judicial Committee, 10 October 2012.

The 2010 Conflicts Statute regulates foreign-related civil relationships in six aspects: the rights and responsibilities of parties to the relationship; marriage and family; inheritance; property rights; creditors' rights; and intellectual property rights.[8] General principles of the conflict of laws regarding foreign-related civil relationships include the following:[9]

- The principle of party autonomy – the parties to a foreign-related civil relationship have the right to choose the law applicable to the foreign-related civil relationship expressly in accordance with the relevant Chinese laws and regulations.[10]
- The principle of the most significant relationship – if there are no provisions in Chinese laws and regulations regarding the specific applicable law for a foreign-related civil relationship, then the laws with the closest relationship to this foreign-related civil relationship shall be applied.[11]

In conclusion, although the source of the Chinese conflict of laws allocates in various legal instruments, we can still summarise the definition and judgment principles of its core adjustment object – foreign-related civil relationships – by mainly focusing on the 2010 Conflicts Statute and 2012 Interpretations. In the following sections, we will remain focused on these two instruments to figure out the treatment of foreign laws in China.

III. Ascertainment of Foreign Laws

The ascertainment of foreign laws is also called the proof of foreign laws. When the conflict of laws regime of one country provides to apply foreign laws in a dispute, the courts need to confirm the existence and determine the content of the applicable foreign law.[12]

Generally, in the dispute of a foreign-related civil relationship, if foreign law counts as 'fact', it has to be pleaded by the parties, and the proof of its content should be provided by the parties as evidence to establish the 'fact'. By contrast, if it counts as 'law', it becomes the primary responsibility of the court to ascertain foreign laws.[13]

Interestingly, according to the 2010 Conflicts Statute, especially Article 10(1), foreign laws seem to be comprehended as either 'law' or 'fact', since it seems that in Chinese judicial practices, both courts and parties can bear the obligation to ascertain foreign laws.[14] The vague legal definition of foreign laws leads to the following questions on its establishment.

[8] Arts 21–50 of the 2010 Conflicts Statute.

[9] Art 41 of the 2010 Conflicts Statute.

[10] Y (Lee) Li and W Yan, 'PRC Law on the Application of Laws to Foreign-Related Civil Relationships' (*Faegre Drinker*, 1 February 2011), www.faegredrinker.com/en/insights/publications/2011/2/prc-law-on-the-application-of-laws-to-foreignrelated-civil-relationships.

[11] ibid.

[12] Y Guo, 'The Theory and Practice of Ascertainment and Application of foreign law in China in Recent Years' (2007) 2 *Wuhan University International Law Review* 1.

[13] X Song, 'Foreign Law: The Difference between "Fact" and "Law"' (2010) 1 *Global Law Review* 14.

[14] Art 10(1) of the 2010 Conflicts Statute.

A. Subjects of Ascertaining Foreign Laws

When it comes to a situation where foreign laws are applicable, the introduction of foreign laws into the court is necessary. The first question to be resolved is the ascertainment of the applicable subject to establish foreign laws, which means we have to figure out who should find out foreign laws and take the responsibility of ascertaining them.

In 2005, the Supreme People's Court issued *the Second Conference Summary of the National Symposium on Foreign-Related Commercial and Maritime Trial Work* ('Second Meeting Minutes'). It provides that when the law that should be applied in commercial disputes belongs to a foreign country, in principle, it should be ascertained by the parties; only in cases of genuine difficulty should it be ascertained by the court.[15] The Second Meeting Minutes established the principle of ascertaining foreign laws by parties, especially in commercial disputes, which still has a great impact on today's judicial practice.[16]

Article 10 of the 2010 Conflicts Statute[17] attempts to clarify that the responsibility for establishing foreign laws should be mainly carried by courts, arbitration institutions, and administrative agencies. Meanwhile, parties should find out foreign laws when they agree on its application.[18] However, in practice, there are lots of controversial issues regarding the application of this article.

First, from a comparative law perspective, it is hard to find other countries in the world providing for the ascertainment of foreign laws by arbitral tribunals and even fewer by administrative agencies.[19] This is because the characters and functions of arbitral tribunals and administrative agencies are quite different from those of courts. Take the arbitral tribunal as an example. In the arbitration process, the agreement of parties is far more important than in the litigation, so the parties will always take the obligation of ascertainment. If there are no agreements between the parties, then the arbitrator can even choose other countries' conflict of laws to ascertain foreign laws. However, in the litigation process, the party autonomy is not so significant as in the arbitral process; and the Chinese courts are forbidden to apply foreign conflict of laws. Because of the dispute of taking arbitration institutions and administrative agencies as subjects of ascertaining foreign laws, in this article, we will mainly discuss courts.

Second, because of the vague expression of the 2010 Conflicts Statute and the impact of the Second Meeting Minutes, the allocation of responsibility for the ascertainment of foreign laws remains unclear. In practice, the obligation of parties is not limited to 'finding out' foreign laws but rather 'ascertaining' them, which places a heavier burden on them.[20]

[15] The Second Conference Summary of the National Symposium on Foreign-Related Commercial and Maritime Trial Work, the Supreme People's Court, 26 December 2005, at §5(51).

[16] J Deng, 'The Practical Dilemma of Foreign Law Ascertainment in China and the Path of Breaking it–An Empirical Analysis Based on 43 Maritime Cases' (2021) 2/2021 *Jiangxi Social Science* 182.

[17] Art 10(1) of the 2010 Conflicts Statute.

[18] Y Lin and Y Huang, 'Why Foreign Laws is Difficult to Ascertain an Empirical Analysis Based on Article 10 of the Law on the Legal Application of Foreign-related Civil Relations' (2014) 10 *Legal Science Monthly* 116.

[19] Y Jiao, 'A Review of the New Regulations on the Ascertainment of Foreign Laws in China: A Review of Article 10 of the Law on the Legal Application of Foreign-related Civil Relations' (2013) 2 *Tsinghua Law Review* 163.

[20] 'Ascertaining' is different from 'finding out'. The former requires proof that the foreign laws can be used as the applicable law in a particular case. In China the distinction between them is quite vague. Some researchers argue that in China the foreign laws are considered as 'law' in foreign-related civil relationship. Therefore, it is necessary

In Chinese judicial practice, the parties often submit their findings on foreign laws to facilitate the proceedings, as the Chinese courts are overloaded with cases, and the parties are unwilling to wait. So actually, foreign laws' ascertainment is mainly led by the parties.[21] Submissions regarding foreign laws are usually made in the form of a written memo by experts or lawyers from relevant countries.

For example, in a mortgage contract dispute, *Industrial and Commercial Bank of China Limited Ningbo Branch v Hengfu shipping limited*, both parties in the trial agreed on the application of Panamanian law. However, since the defendant could not provide the relevant Panamanian law, the copy provided by the plaintiff of the Panamanian maritime law could not be confirmed due to a lack of authenticity and legality. Consequently, the Court directly ascertained that, in this case, foreign laws could not be ascertained. Therefore, according to the principle of most significant relationship, the Court confirmed that Chinese laws should be applied to the case.[22]

However, with the implementation of the Belt and Road Initiative, the Supreme People's Court attempts to encourage more active involvement by the courts and arbitral institutions to lighten the burden on the parties. According to Article 8 of the Opinions of the Supreme People's Court on Providing Judicial Guarantee for the Building of Pilot Free Trade Zones (which is limited to Free Trade Zone cases), the Supreme People's Court requested courts to improve the system of judicial review and confirmation; and ask arbitral institutions to further explore the mechanism for resolving disputes.[23]

An example could be found in *the Series Dispute of Angelic Power Ship's Crew Labour Contract*, which is the National Typical Cases of Maritime Trials in 2021 issued by the Supreme Court. In this case, per the 2010 Conflict Statute, the Court fully respected the parties' autonomy, ascertained the applicable law according to the different legal relationships, and combined various ways, such as the Court's ascertainment and the expert opinion provided by the parties. Consequently, the Court accurately established Greek and Philippine law and safeguarded foreign crew member's legitimate rights and interests.[24]

B. Approaches to Ascertain Foreign Laws

After having a grasp of the subject of foreign laws' ascertainment, ascertainment approaches are also an important topic that should be focused on. The 2010 Conflicts Statute is the programmatic statute governing the foreign-related civil relationship. However, it fails to provide the appropriate means to ascertain foreign laws concretely. Nevertheless, a variety of methods of ascertaining foreign laws are provided sporadically.

to distinguish 'ascertaining foreign laws' and 'finding out foreign laws'. The parties only need to 'find out' foreign laws, while the court has the responsibility to 'ascertain' it. See Jie Deng, 182.

[21] J Hu, J Xu and L Wang, 'Research and Analysis over Discerning and Applying Foreign Law – from the Perspective of Judicial Practice of Ningbo Maritime Court' (2019) 1 *Chinese Journal of Maritime Law* 42.

[22] Industrial and Commercial Bank of China Limited Ningbo Branch v Hengfu shipping limited, China Judgements Online, Ningbo Maritime Court, 21 February 2012.

[23] The Opinions of the Supreme People's Court on Providing Judicial Guarantee for the Building of Pilot Free Trade Zones (which is limited to Free Trade Zone cases), the Supreme People's Court, 15 May 2017, at §4(8).

[24] Series Dispute of Angelic Power Ship's Crew Labour Contract, China Judgements Online, the Supreme People's Court, 24 December 2021.

From the party's perspective, according to the Second Meeting Minutes, parties may find out about foreign laws with the help of 'legal experts, legal service agencies, industrial associations, international organizations, or the Internet' to 'provide the relevant legal writings, legal introduction materials, and legal opinions ….'[25]

For courts, Article 8 of the Provisions of the Supreme People's Court on Several Issues concerning the Establishment of International Commercial Courts ('2018 Provisions') provides that if foreign laws should be applied to the case tried by an international commercial court, the court may ascertain it through the following ways:

> (1) Provided by the parties; (2) Provided by Chinese and foreign legal experts; (3)Provided by law ascertaining service institutions; (4) Provided by expert members of an international commercial committee; (5) Provided by the central organ of the opposite party who has concluded judicial assistance convention with China; (6) Provided by Chinese embassy in the corresponding country; (7) Provided by the embassy of the foreign country in China; (8)Other reasonable ways.[26]

The above-mentioned regulations provide for a wide range of approaches for ascertaining foreign laws and do not provide a strict limitation for it. In the above provisions, the expressions like 'other reasonable ways' suggest that other ascertainment approaches can also be adopted as long as they do not violate other legal provisions, leaving the court with a margin of discretion.[27]

In practice, potential sources of ascertaining foreign laws include

> (1) The parties provide notarized legal opinions issued by lawyers practicing outside the territory; (2) The parties or courts entrust foreign laws' ascertainment platform to provide a report; (3) The parties provide legal provisions or public publications in which relevant foreign laws are included; (4) Courts seek ex officio access to provisions, publications, and relevant judicial precedent.[28]

Among them, foreign laws' ascertainment platform, as an emerging and efficient way of establishing foreign laws, has attracted people's attention.

The Supreme People's Court's foreign laws' ascertainment platform was launched on the website of the International Commercial Court[29] on 29 November 2019. It is a significant achievement from a joint effort of the Supreme People's Court, the China-ASEAN Legal Research Centre of Southwest University of Political Science and Law, the Benchmark Chambers International Centre, and the ECUPL Center For Proof of Foreign Law, etc. The establishment of a unified platform has provided courts and parties with a more convenient and authoritative means for ascertaining foreign laws and has released the pressure on courts to establish foreign laws.[30]

[25] Second Meeting Minutes, at §5(51).

[26] Art 8 of the Supreme People's Court on Several Issues concerning the Establishment of International Commercial Courts, the Supreme People's Court, 27 June 2018.

[27] J Tan, 'The Predicament and Perfection of China's Foreign Laws' Ascertainment System' (2021) *Beijing Jiaotong University* 2021.

[28] J Gu, 'Study on the Legal Aspects of the Free Trade Area (II): Ascertaining Recent Practices in Foreign Laws – Cross-border Guardianship' (*Tiantong Law Firm*, 24 April 2020), www.sohu.com/a/390883403_159412.

[29] http://cicc.court.gov.cn.

[30] Gu (n 28).

C. Certification of Foreign Laws in Judicial Practice

In Chinese judicial practice, compared with other ascertainment approaches, the most common method is to achieve proof documents from parties. However, due to the limitation of parties' professional legal knowledge, law ascertainment skills, and financial ability, it is difficult to guarantee the quality of proof documents. So the court's standards for ascertaining foreign laws submitted by parties will be more stringent. How can one make foreign laws submitted by parties more likely to be certified by the court? The answer is to treat the submitted materials to ascertain foreign laws as evidence.

It means that the submitted materials, in whatever form they might be, must conform to the same standards of authenticity, relevance, and legitimacy as other evidence. Take authenticity as an example. Notarisation of the legal opinion drafted by a foreign lawyer can always be essential for submission to consist with this criterion. Article 11 of Some Provisions of the Supreme People's Court on Evidence in Civil Procedures (amended in 2019) provides that:

> Where the official documentary evidence provided by a party is created outside the territory of the People's Republic of China, the evidence shall be certified by the notary office of the country where the evidence comes, or the certification procedures as outlined in the relevant treaty concluded between the People's Republic of China and the country shall be performed.[31]

Meanwhile, the court has the right to review the submitted evidence. Article 16 of the 2012 Interpretations provides that the court shall examine and confirm the foreign laws provided by the parties and has the judicial power to make a final decision:

> The people's court shall hear the views of the parties on the content of foreign laws to be applied and its understanding and application, and if the parties do not object to the content of foreign laws and its understanding and application, the people's court may confirm it; If the parties have objections, the people's court shall review and determine.[32]

In judicial practice, notarisation and authorisation of materials on foreign laws can be decisive in the ascertainment of foreign laws. For instance, in *Evergreen Marine (Singapore) Pte. Ltd. v Evergreen Marine Corp* case, during the first trial, Evergreen did not notarise the legal opinion provided by the foreign legal expert, so the court of the first instance did not ascertain the submitted law. During the second trial, Evergreen's relevant Mexican legal provisions were notarised and authenticated, so the Court of Re-examination confirmed them as the applicable law.[33]

However, with the in-depth construction of China's foreign-related law regime and the increasing number of foreign-related civil and commercial disputes, the standard of proof for the materials submitted by the parties to determine the applicable law is also changing. Article 11 of Some Provisions on Evidence in Civil Procedures (2001) provided that all the official documentary evidence created outside the territory of China should be authenticated

[31] Art 16 of Some Provisions of the Supreme People's Court on Evidence in Civil Procedures (amended in 2019), the Supreme People's Court, 25 December 2019.

[32] Art 16 of the 2012 Interpretations.

[33] Evergreen Marine (Singapore) Pte. Ltd. v Evergreen Marine Corp, China Judgements Online, the Supreme People's Court, 28 June 2019.

by the embassy or consulate of China.[34] However, in 2019, the Decision of the Supreme People's Court to Amend Some Provisions on Evidence in Civil Procedures deleted this regulation, except for the official documentary evidence related to status relationships.[35]

Nevertheless, the trend of judicial practice needs further observation. At present, notarisation and authentication might still be the best practice to guarantee the authenticity of legal opinions or memoranda of foreign laws.

IV. The Threshold of 'Failing to Ascertain Foreign Laws'

Article 10(2) of the 2010 Conflicts Statute provides that 'if foreign laws cannot be ascertained or there are no provisions in the laws of this country, the laws of the People's Republic of China shall apply.'[36] It means that where the law of that country is unregulated, Chinese law could be applied. But the question is: what counts as a failure to prove the chosen law, or put it in another way, what is the threshold of Article 10(2)? The question might be solved by examining the following three issues.

A. Three Theoretical Issues on the Threshold of 'Failing to Ascertain Foreign Laws'

First of all, when a court is ascertaining foreign laws according to Article 10(1), does the court have to exhaust all possible means before it applies the law in China? If we turn back to the 1990s, Article 193 of the Supreme People's Court on Several Issues concerning the Implementation of the General Principles of the Civil Law of the People's Republic of China ('1988 Opinion') provided that if the applicable foreign laws cannot be proved even after using the five enumerated methods, the Chinese law should be applied.[37] However, it is unlikely that the 1988 Opinion expected the courts to exhaust all methods as it would be devastating to the court proceedings. Nevertheless, the provision seems to encourage the judges to try their best.

According to Article 15(1) of the 2012 Interpretations,

> where a people's court fails to obtain the content of foreign laws by such reasonable means as the provision by the parties, methods as set forth in the international treaties binding upon the People's Republic of China, and provision by Chinese and foreign legal experts, the people's court may determine that foreign laws cannot be ascertained.[38]

[34] Art 1 of Some Provisions of the Supreme People's Court on Evidence in Civil Procedures, the Supreme People's Court, 21 December 2001.

[35] Art 17 of Decision of the Supreme People's Court to Amend the Some Provisions on Evidence in Civil Procedures (2019), the Supreme People's Court, the Supreme People's Court, 25 December 2019.

[36] Art 10(2) of the 2010 Conflicts Statute.

[37] Invalid now. See Art 193 of the Supreme People's Court on Several Issues concerning the Implementation of the General Principles of the Civil Law of the People's Republic of China (For Trial Implementation), the Supreme People's Court, 2 April 1988.

[38] Art 15(1) of the 2012 Interpretations.

Focusing on three means that frequently appeal in judicial practice, Article 15(1) provides a suggestion for courts on applicable laws' ascertainment. Nevertheless, the list is not exhaustive. The phrase 'reasonable means' provides the courts with discretion. So, Article 15(1) still aims at encouraging the courts to be more diligent and make reasonable attempts before it declares 'foreign laws cannot be ascertained'.

Second, when a party is obliged to provide the court with the content of foreign laws according to Article 10(1), to what point can the court declare that foreign laws are not ascertainable? According to Article 15(2) of the 2012 Interpretations, a party shall provide any foreign laws; however, if one fails to provide them within the reasonable time limit designated by the court without justifiable cause, the court *may* determine that foreign laws cannot be ascertained.[39] In this provision, it seems that the obligation of ascertaining foreign laws mainly belongs to the parties. However, the word 'may' provides the courts with discretion. It remains ambiguous whether the court should ex officio try to ascertain the content of foreign laws through other approaches as suggested by Article 15(1).

Last, when both parties have provided foreign laws to the court according to Article 10(1) and their submissions conflict with each other, whether it means that foreign laws cannot be ascertained or not? The answer is negative. According to Article 16 of the 2012 Interpretations,

> the people's courts shall listen to the opinions of the parties on the content of foreign laws that shall be applicable and the understanding and application thereof, and if the parties have no objection to the content of them and the understanding and application thereof, the people's court may confirm the same; and if the parties have any objection, the people's court shall examine such objection and then determine the applicable law.[40]

As mentioned above, the court has the judicial power to make the final decision, provided that the parties have a conflict regarding the contents of foreign laws.

For example, in the *Super Auto Investments Limited v Keep Bright Limited* case, the High People's Court of Guangdong held that the Hong Kong law provided by the parties could not be ascertained due to the different cases cited in their legal opinions and their inconsistent conclusions. However, the Supreme People's Court held that it is expected that parties have different opinions on the application of the law, so it is up to the court to make the final decision on the contents of the applicable law. Therefore, in the end, the Supreme Court accepted the appellant's argument that Hong Kong law should be applied in this case.[41]

Based on the theoretical analysis above, the sole reliance on the context of the provisions, the criteria of 'unable to ascertain foreign laws' appears to be quite vague and even less reliable, and the determination of this standard depends largely on the court's discretion. Meanwhile, before making the decision that foreign laws cannot be ascertained, courts are encouraged to make reasonable attempts, including using the principle of most significant relationship to establish other foreign laws – in the event that the party-agreed applicable law cannot be ascertained, this practice is introduced based on an underlying

[39] Art 15(2) of the 2012 Interpretations.

[40] Art 16 of the 2012 Interpretations.

[41] Super Auto Investments Limited v Keep Bright Limited, China Judgements Online, the Supreme People's Court, 22 March 2019.

assumption that applying another foreign law that has the most significant relationship with the parties and the dispute is a better practice than simply applying the domestic law of that forum.

B. The Threshold of 'Failing to Ascertain Foreign Laws' in Chinese Judicial Practice

However, in judicial practice, Article 10(2) of the 2010 Conflicts Statute is often abused by the courts. Jie Deng, a professor of law at Shanghai Normal University, searched 32 maritime cases in China relating to the ascertainment of foreign laws in the last five years; he found that among them, 21 cases were judged as 'failing to ascertain foreign laws'.[42] On the one hand, when parties give up the right to provide foreign laws, judges always abuse the principle of most significant relationship to apply Chinese laws. On the other hand, if parties agreed on using foreign laws but failed to provide it, judges will easily turn to Article 10(2) of the 2010 Conflicts Statute to apply Chinese laws.

For example, in the case of *America steamship owners' mutual protection and indemnity association, Inc. v Diamond cruise international Co. Limited*, although the parties to the contract had agreed that the applicable law was the law of the State of New York, the plaintiff stated at the trial that the law of the People's Republic of China was applicable, given that the vessel was probably the only property owned by the defendant and was currently being auctioned in China. The court supported the pleading of the plaintiff without the parties' agreement or any other reasonable approaches for ascertaining foreign laws.[43]

However, with the rapid implementation of the Belt and Road Initiative overseas, the courts have become more and more cautious in applying Article 10(2) of the 2010 Conflicts Statute. In practice, after the implementation of the 2010 Conflicts Statute, common grounds for 'unable to ascertain' include: (1) the law or precedent is not comprehensive; (2) the law or precedent is not notarised; (3) the legal opinion provided is not directly on point; (4) there exists other reasonable interpretations of the law, etc.[44]

In conclusion, although courts are not mandated to use all the possible methods of ascertaining foreign laws, they still should take a case-by-case approach. However, in practice, some courts abuse Article 10(2) of the 2010 Conflicts Statute without giving the parties a reasoned explanation of what attempts have been made to ascertain foreign laws. Promisingly, the situation is improving because of the implementation of the Belt and Road Initiative.

[42] Deng (n 16) 182.

[43] America steamship owners' mutual protection and indemnity association, Inc. v Diamond cruise international Co. Limited, China Judgements Online, Shanghai Maritime Court of PRC, 27 December 2019.

[44] W Xu and J Yao, 'The Improvement of the System of Ascertainment of Foreign Laws by Experts under the Belt and Road Initiative – an Empirical Analysis of 134 Cases in China since the Implementation of the Law on the Legal Application of Foreign-related Civil Relations ('一带一路"倡议下专家查明外国法制度的完善 —— 基于《涉外民事法律关系适用法》施行以来全国134件案件的实证分析') (2019) *A Study on Comprehensive Reform of the Judicial System and Criminal Trials* 2011.

V. Possible Future Development on Treatment of Foreign Law in China

In general, the current route of foreign law ascertainment in foreign-related civil relations in China is not ideally straightforward, which is the main obstacle for courts to reasonably apply foreign laws and effectively handle foreign-related civil cases.[45] Based on the above analysis, this situation is reflected in the fact that the law is unclear as to who, the courts or the parties, are responsible for the ascertainment and the criteria for 'unidentifiable'. Besides, the simplex approach of ascertaining foreign laws is a practical reflection of the current situation of foreign law ascertainment in China.[46] Thus, this chapter provides suggestions for future development on the treatment and ascertainment of foreign law in China by outlining the root causes of these typical reflections.

A. Clarification of the Subject in Foreign Law Ascertainment

Article 10 of the 2010 Conflict Statute seems to provide four subjects in foreign law ascertainment. Contextually, it appears to provide that foreign law should, in principle, be ascertained by the courts, arbitral institutions, and administrative authorities. However, the Second Meeting Minutes provides that, in principle, the foreign law in international commercial disputes should be ascertained by the parties; only in cases that encounter 'genuine difficulties' should be ascertained by the court. Vague regulations have led to confusion in judicial practice in determining the subject of foreign law ascertainment. Moreover, arbitration institutions and administrative organs are rarely regulated as foreign ascertainment subjects under the comparative law perspective and should be removed, as mentioned above.

In practice, the primary debate centers on whether the subject of identification should be the court or the parties. One of the main causes of this confusion is that the current legislation in China has not defined the nature of foreign laws in cases of foreign-related relations.[47]

There have been two different theories on the nature of foreign law in the international community – the 'legal theory' and the 'factual theory'. Respectively, there are two different modes of identification, namely, ex officio identification by the court and proof by the parties.[48]

However, neither the factual nor the legal theory has found a one-size-fits-all solution. There seems to be no standard answer to the question of whether foreign law is factual or legal. It could be interpreted by each country on a case-by-case basis.[49] In mainland China, there is no unified interpretation of either theory.

[45] J Zhong, 'A Study on the Identification of Foreign Law in the Practice of Foreign-related Civil and Commercial Judgment in China' [2021] *Guilin University of Electronic Science and Technology* 5.
[46] Deng (n 16) 183.
[47] ibid 184.
[48] T William, *International Conflict of Laws: Common Civil and Maritime* (Montreal, Blais, 1994) 512–21.
[49] Song (n 13) 14–21.

B. Routes to Ascertain Foreign Laws

Article 8 of the 2018 Provisions provides that the approaches for ascertaining foreign laws include submission by parties, Chinese and foreign legal experts, law ascertaining service institutions, expert members of an international commercial committee, embassy, etc.[50] However, in judicial practice, only the approaches of 'provided by parties' and 'provided by legal experts' are commonly used.

From a legal economics perspective, the provision of foreign law by parties and professionals is consistent with the comparative advantages of economics.[51] Parties tend to have stronger incentives to provide foreign law because they have a stake in the sound adjudication of the case. Experts in foreign law, in most cases, have a deeper comprehension of foreign law than domestic courts and greater access to and experience in identifying foreign law and are, therefore, able to ascertain foreign law more efficiently.

However, to some extent, such limited approaches have limited the development of the foreign law ascertainment system in China. Besides, even the more commonly used means of ascertainment in practice, information provided by the parties and legal experts, are always unable to play a practical role because the courts do not recognise them in many cases.[52] This phenomenon is attributed to two reasons: objectively, many of the means of identification of foreign law currently provided are not accompanied by supporting systems, meaning institutional support is inadequate. Second, the application of foreign law is generally complex and tricky, especially in circumstances where the judge has no previous exposure, which tends to make judges cautious about applying foreign law and even make them try their best to avoid using it. In response to these two issues, this chapter makes the following recommendations.

The first proposal is to set up institutional supporting systems. For example, a foreign law database can significantly reduce the cost of foreign law ascertainment and increase its efficiency and accuracy. Moreover, it is necessary to clarify the standard of 'foreign law expert' and establish a list of experts with the required knowledge. From a comparative law perspective, both English and US courts have provided for the qualifications of foreign law experts.[53] Furthermore, a list could provide a legal standard of 'foreign law expert' and bind the court, which means that the court cannot randomly deny an opinion on the application of the law issued by an expert on the list.

The second is to establish incentives and exemptions for foreign law ascertainment. Several Chinese scholars have proposed specific solutions that can be drawn upon in this regard: on the one hand, the number of cases tried by judges on the reasonable application of foreign law should be counted in the judges' assessment system. The excellent cases should also be commended and publicised in order to motivate judges to identify and apply foreign law at their own initiative. On the other hand, the procedure for the ascertainment

[50] Art 8 of the 2018 Provisions.

[51] H Wang and W Shen, 'Fixing the Failure of Ascertainment of Foreign Law An Empirical and Economics Study' (2016) 5 *Journal of the University of International Business and Economics* 135–49.

[52] Zhong (n 45) 13–14.

[53] The English courts have held that foreign judges or practising lawyers are ex officio legal experts; the US Federal Rules of Evidence provide that a person possessing the requisite knowledge and skill, training or education is an expert. See Wang and Shen (n 51) 135–49.

of foreign law should be clearly defined so that after the judges have done their reasonable duty of ascertainment in accordance with the procedure, they may be excused even in the event of an error in the ascertainment and application of foreign law.[54] However, it is undeniable that the application of foreign law carries greater risks and that the wrong application of the law is detrimental to justice and the interests of both parties. How and to what extent an exemption regime is established is, therefore, still a matter for further inquiry.

C. Specification on the Threshold to 'Fail to Ascertain Foreign Laws'

Article 10(2) of the 2010 Conflict Statute provides that 'where the law of a foreign country cannot be identified or is not provided for in the law of that country, the law of the People's Republic of China shall apply'.[55] In practice, this article has been somehow overused, if not abused. In this regard, the following suggestions are made to tackle the problem.

The first is to promote legislation. A more specific standard of 'fail to ascertain foreign laws' could be provided in the interpretation of the 2010 Conflict Statute. According to Article 15 of the 2012 Interpretations, the 'standard' seems to be 'after researching through reasonable approaches' and 'within a reasonable period of time specified by the People's Court'. However, the two standards currently give judges too much discretion, which may not be the best legislative option for a country where the application of foreign law by the courts is not yet a fixed practice. The legislator could consider the current state of judicial practice, assess the time normally required to ascertain foreign law and the necessary means of ascertainment, and define more clearly the preconditions for 'fail to ascertain foreign law'.

The second is to develop a review mechanism so that judges should have fulfilled their due diligence to ascertain foreign laws. For example, when it comes to foreign-related cases, the judges should provide a narrative of the process of ascertaining foreign law, which will be reviewed internally.

D. An Erroneous Application of Choice of Law Rules and Foreign Law – Is it a Ground for Judicial Review?

Again, in Mainland China, the foreign law has not been strictly categorised as 'fact' or 'law'. This, however, would not necessarily have impacts on how foreign laws are treated in courts, as the appeal court will review both facts and the applicable law according to Article 168 of Civil Procedure Law. In *Woodtrans Navigation Corporation & Sanwai Navigation S. A. v Angang Group International Economic Trade Co.*,[56] a retrial case of disputes over the delivery of goods without Bill of Lading in carriage of goods by sea, the Supreme People's Court rejected Sanwai Navigation's argument that the lower court has erroneously applied Panama law. In this case, the Supreme People's Court reviewed and agreed the lower court's application of Panama law.

[54] Zhong (n 45) 148.
[55] Art 10(2) of the 2010 Conflict Statute.
[56] SPC Gazette, Issue 1, 2002 (Total No. 75).

Bearing in mind that courts do not, by principle, follow precedents, nevertheless, the 'guidance' shows that upper courts' judgments are significant in practice. By the same token, it can be assumed that the case of erroneous application of choice of law rules and/or foreign law might be appealed.

VI. Access to Chinese Law

English translations of national legislation and other legal instruments are available in various databases, whether official or private. Official ones include the State Council of the People's Republic of China (official database of law and regulations)[57] and the National People's Congress of The People's Republic of China (official database of law and regulations).[58] There are also other comprehensive English databases, with legal news, case summaries of court judgments and decisions, law and regulations, and law journals available; while this chapter does not mean to provide an exhaustive list, instrumental platforms include Chinalawinfo Database,[59] PKULAW,[60] Westlaw China,[61] LexisNexis China,[62] and Wolters Kluwer info China.[63]

[57] english.www.gov.cn/archive/lawsregulations?utm_source=wechat_session&utm_medium=social&utm_oi=914993972622036992.
[58] en.npc.gov.cn.cdurl.cn/laws.html.
[59] www.lawinfochina.com/.
[60] www.pkulaw.com/english/.
[61] www.thomsonreuters.cn/zh/products-services/legal/westlaw-china.html.
[62] www.lexisnexis.com.cn/.
[63] law.wkinfo.com.cn/.

3

Hong Kong

WILSON LUI*

I. Introduction

The proof of foreign law is a fundamental and important issue in legal disputes and proceedings, particularly for cross-border commercial cases.[1] At times, establishing foreign law also directly establishes the parties' legal rights and duties.[2] Approaches towards the proof of foreign law may affect the parties' choice of forum, their readiness to settle, the cost and duration of proceedings, and the way in which a case is argued. There may be a higher litigation risk for parties if the proof of foreign law in a particular jurisdiction introduces considerable uncertainty.[3]

Hong Kong aims to position itself as the leading centre for international legal and dispute resolution services in the Asia-Pacific region, and Hong Kong courts – chosen by parties for reasons of neutrality and expertise – frequently hear disputes which may not be closely connected with Hong Kong and which may be governed in substance by foreign law; under the common law, a judge may be called upon to apply foreign law.[4] While matters of procedure are governed by domestic law, or the *lex fori*, which is Hong Kong law, matters of

* I thank Mr Michael Chung for his helpful research assistance.

[1] Proof of foreign law is also important for non-commercial cases. For example, in Hong Kong, where a surrogacy arrangement and/or birth took place outside Hong Kong, expert evidence should be adduced to show, at least, whether or not surrogacy is permitted in that foreign jurisdiction, how the law defines the legal relationship amongst the surrogate mother, her husband, the child and the commissioning parents; this would assist the court on the issue of whether there has been abuse of public policy: *Re A and B* [2019] 5 HKLRD 366, [2019] HKCFI 1749. In cases involving the Law of the People's Republic of China on Safeguarding National Security in the Hong Kong Special Administrative Region (the National Security Law, NSL), it was thought that the relevant substantive law of Mainland China may inform the construction of the NSL or a particular NSL provision: *HKSAR v Lui Sai Yu* [2023] 1 HKLRD 751, [2022] HKCA 1780 [87]–[89]. This was rejected by the Court of Final Appeal: *HKSAR v Lui Sai Yu* [2023] HKCFA 26 [43]–[48].

[2] R Fentiman, 'Laws, Foreign Laws, and Facts' (2006) 59(1) *Current Legal Problems* 391, 404.

[3] Adopting the risk analysis in R Fentiman, *International Commercial Litigation*, 2nd edn (Oxford, Oxford University Press, 2015).

[4] A Mills, 'Arbitral Jurisdiction and the Mischievous Presumption of Identity of Foreign Law' [2008] *Cambridge Law Journal* 25, 25; A Briggs, *Private International Law in English Courts*, 2nd edn (Oxford, Oxford University Press, 2023) 26.

substance are governed by the law to which the court is directed by its choice of law rules, or the *lex causae*, which may or may not be Hong Kong law.[5]

Most of the choice of law rules in Hong Kong originated from the common law. The application of choice of law rules may lead to the application of foreign law in certain circumstances. Unless there are overriding mandatory provisions, the Hong Kong court does not have a particular preference as to whether it will apply foreign law or not.[6] As will be seen below, in Hong Kong, questions of foreign law are questions of fact (albeit being described as special questions of fact) which a party is at liberty to raise or not to raise, and any foreign law pleaded by the parties is usually proved by expert evidence. A Hong Kong court is generally not allowed to introduce or apply foreign law on its own motion.[7]

For the purposes of Hong Kong, Mainland (or PRC) law[8] and Macau law[9] are both considered to be foreign law. Chinese customary law could be directly applied to Chinese persons domiciled in Hong Kong as it is incorporated into Hong Kong domestic law through Article 8 of the Basic Law,[10] but a Hong Kong court can and usually will rely on expert evidence when parties plead and prove Chinese customary law.[11] However, it is not always necessary to adduce expert evidence to determine questions of fact pertaining to Chinese customary law.[12]

[5] The distinction between substance and procedure is not always easy to make. See, eg, Lord Collins of Mapesbury and others (eds), *Dicey, Morris and Collins on the Conflict of Laws*, 16th edn (London, Sweet and Maxwell, 2022) ch 4. For example, issues of limitation periods are considered to be matters of procedure in Hong Kong and are governed by the *lex fori*: *Peregrine Fixed Income Ltd v JP Morgan Chase Bank* [2005] 3 HKLRD 1 [31]–[32]; *China Agri-Products Exchange Ltd v Wang Xiu Qun* [2021] HKCFI 137 [516]–[517].

[6] Examples of overriding mandatory provisions include s 17 of the Control of Exemption Clauses Ordinance (Cap 71) (for consumer contracts) and s 70 of the Employment Ordinance (Cap 57) (for employment contracts). The latter is not definitively settled: see the contrasting views in *HSBC Bank plc v Wallace* [2008] 1 HKLRD 613 and *Cantor Fitzgerald Europe v Boyer* (unreported, HCA 1160/2011 and HCA 44/2012, 29 February 2012). For a detailed analysis of issues of choice of law in Hong Kong, see W Lui and A Reyes, *Hong Kong Private International Law* (Oxford, Hart Publishing, 2024).

[7] For an interesting historical account on how English courts 'ascertain' foreign law as law (not as fact), and by consultation or certification (not by sworn expert evidence), see JH Baker, 'Ascertainment of Foreign Law: Certification to and by English Courts Prior to 1861' (1979) 28(1) *International and Comparative Law Quarterly* 141–51.

[8] *Ding Shu Ju v Chu Sai Keung* [2021] HKCA 626 [42.1] ('This is because the PRC and Hong Kong have different legal systems, and as such, PRC law is regarded as foreign law which has to be proved by expert evidence.'). There had been some confusion in an early post-handover case: *Nan Tung Bank Ltd, Zhu Hai v Wangfoong Transportation Ltd* [1999] 2 HKC 606 [13] ('In fact, Mainland law can no longer be strictly said to be foreign law after the resumption of the exercise of sovereignty over Hong Kong.'). In a similar vein, a Mainland judgment is considered a foreign judgment and will be enforced or recognised in Hong Kong only if it fulfils the conditions under the Mainland Judgments (Reciprocal Enforcement) Ordinance (Cap 597), the Mainland Judgments in Civil and Commercial Matters (Reciprocal Enforcement) Ordinance (Cap 645), the Mainland Judgments in Matrimonial and Family Cases (Reciprocal Recognition and Enforcement) Ordinance (Cap 639), or common law. For a detailed analysis of recognition and enforcement of foreign judgments in Hong Kong, see Lui and Reyes (n 6).

[9] *MGM Grand Paradise Ltd v Wong Sing Wa* (unreported, HCA 2140/2011, 21 May 2012) [17]; *MGM Grand Paradise Limited v Chiu Tak Wah* (unreported, HCA 259/2012, 8 October 2012) [57]–[59]; *Venetian Macau Limited v Chen Mei Huan* (unreported, HCA 1440/2012, 27 January 2014) [50].

[10] Art 8 reads: 'The laws previously in force in Hong Kong, that is, the common law, rules of equity, ordinances, subordinate legislation and customary law shall be maintained, except for any that contravene this Law, and subject to any amendment by the legislature of the Hong Kong Special Administrative Region.'

[11] *Suen Toi Lee v Yau Yee Ping* (2001) 4 HKCFAR 474 [28]–[38]. See also *Tang Tak Sum v Tang Kai Fong* [2015] 1 HKLRD 286 [24]–[27]; W Lui, 'Hong Kong' in A Reyes, W Lui and K Nishioka (eds), *Choice of Law and Recognition in Asian Family Law* (Oxford, Hart Publishing, 2023) 51–80.

[12] *Wong Zhong Lan Xiang v Wong Frank* [2003] 4 HKC 609 [41]–[43]; *Fung Ying Cheung v Yip Woon Yung* [2019] HKCFI 1818 [20]–[28].

II. Foreign Law before Judicial Authorities

A. Nature of Foreign Law

As stated by the Hong Kong Court of Final Appeal, 'expert evidence of foreign law, although a matter of fact, will be treated differently to other, ordinary, findings of fact'.[13] It is well established that foreign law is treated as a question of fact by the courts of Hong Kong and is therefore usually ascertained by a process of pleading and proof involving expert witnesses, usually examined and cross-examined at trial.[14]

The question of foreign law is addressed only if a party chooses to plead it. The burden of proving foreign law lies on the party who bases a claim or defence upon it.[15] The party must show that it has a good claim or defence under that foreign law.[16] However, this does not mean that whenever a claim is governed by foreign law, it is necessary for the claimant to plead and prove the material content of that law (or indeed, as a logically prior matter, to plead a case as to governing law at all).[17] If no foreign law is pleaded at all, then a case with foreign elements would be decided as though it were a purely domestic case, through applying the 'default rule'. This is different from the situation where the parties pleaded but failed to (sufficiently) prove foreign law, where a 'presumption' of similarity between the foreign law and the *lex fori* might apply. The distinction between failing to plead foreign law at all, and pleading but not proving foreign law, is discussed in more detail in section II.C below.

B. Ascertainment of Foreign Law

i. *How Can the Court Ascertain Foreign Law?*

A court is generally not qualified to decide an issue of foreign law without the assistance of a foreign law expert.[18] There is no principle of *iura novit curia* (the court knows the law) in Hong Kong. Therefore, Hong Kong courts cannot take judicial notice of foreign law, even if it is notorious law.[19] A court also cannot introduce issues of foreign law on its own motion.[20]

[13] *Zhang Hong Li v DBS Bank (Hong Kong) Ltd* (2019) 22 HKCFAR 392, [2019] HKCFA 45 [97(c)].

[14] *Zhang Hong Li* (n 13) [95], citing G Johnston and P Harris, *The Conflict of Laws in Hong Kong*, 3rd edn (Hong Kong, Sweet and Maxwell, 2017) para 2.060. See also, eg, *Szeto Wing Hong v Maintown Industries Ltd* [2021] HKCFI 179 [63].

[15] *Wang Qian Wei v 郭文雨* [2019] 1 HKC 413, [2018] HKCFI 2253 [35].

[16] *Brownlie v FS Cairo (Nile Plaza) LLC* [2021] UKSC 45, [2022] AC 995 [116].

[17] *Iranian Offshore Engineering and Construction Co v Dean Investment Holdings SA* [2018] EWHC 2759 (Comm), [2019] 1 WLR 82 [3].

[18] *Kaefer AG v Winfield Marine Services Co Ltd* [2021] HKDC 656 [93].

[19] *Lazard Brothers & Co v Midland Bank Ltd* [1933] AC 289, 297–98; approved in *Hong Jing Co Ltd v Zhuhai Kwok Yuen Investment Co Ltd* [2013] 1 HKLRD 441 [73]. But see *Saxby v Fulton* [1909] 2 KB 208, 211 ('… it is notorious that at Monte Carlo roulette is not an unlawful game.'). The English courts seem to welcome the idea of taking judicial notice of decisions of foreign courts (and perhaps academic writings) in deciding what the relevant foreign law is: *Morgan Grenfell & Co Ltd v SACE – Istituto Per I Servizi Assicurativi Del Commercio* [2001] EWCA Civ 1932 [53]; HM Courts & Tribunals Service, *The Commercial Court Guide* 11th edn (2022), para H3.3(d), available online: www.judiciary.uk/wp-content/uploads/2022/06/Commercial-Court-Guide-11th-edition-1.pdf.

[20] *Caspian Resources Development Pte Ltd v Fortune Oil plc* [2015] 5 HKLRD 836 [31]. As for the rationale behind such a policy, Johnston and Harris (n 14) para 2.061 noted that: 'There is simply no established machinery for the

It is considered wrong for the court to conduct its own research into issues of foreign law, regardless of whether they have or have not been raised by the parties.[21] As the court is not at liberty to introduce foreign law, there is currently no mechanism for Hong Kong courts to ascertain the content of foreign law through making enquiries to domestic or foreign institutions, whether judicial or non-judicial, or through the direct communication of judges. Moreover, it is not possible and indeed incorrect for parties to fill the evidentiary vacuum of foreign law by way of counsel submissions in Hong Kong.[22] Whether there is a future possibility for Hong Kong to depart from these practices is discussed in section V below.

It was recently suggested by Lord Leggatt in the UK Supreme Court case of *Brownlie v FS Cairo (Nile Plaza) LLC* (*Brownlie (No 2)*, simply known as *Brownlie* in this chapter) that there can be more flexibility in the nature of procedures available to ascertain the content of foreign law:[23]

> The old notion that foreign legal materials can only ever be brought before the court as part of the evidence of an expert witness is outdated. Whether the court will require evidence from an expert witness should depend on the nature of the issue and of the relevant foreign law. In an age when so much information is readily available through the internet, there may be no need to consult a foreign lawyer in order to find the text of a relevant foreign law. On some occasions the text may require skilled exegesis of a kind which only a lawyer expert in the foreign system of law can provide. But in other cases it may be sufficient to know what the text says.

Whether this approach will be adopted in Hong Kong is untested, not least because at the time of writing, no Hong Kong case has addressed this aspect of *Brownlie*. However, the English courts have enthusiastically embraced Lord Leggatt's suggestion. For instance, the Privy Council recently approved the Cayman Court of Appeal's approach to directly consider the text of the foreign legislation and case law in discerning the content of the applicable foreign law.[24] The English Court of Appeal even suggested that the examples given in *Brownlie* – foreign legal texts and online translations of foreign legal materials – are not 'exhaustive of the sources of evidence on which a court might draw' in working out the content of the applicable foreign law.[25] The latest edition of the Commercial Court Guide edited by the judges of the Commercial Court of England and Wales also provides detailed guidance on their current approach towards expert evidence on foreign law, which is clearly influenced by *Brownlie*.[26]

There is indeed much to be said in favour of Lord Leggatt's approach;[27] after all, the Hong Kong courts already recognise that they are 'entitled, indeed bound, to contribute [their] own legal skill and experience in reaching [their] conclusions on foreign law'.[28] With

ascertainment of points of foreign law which the parties have not raised, and it seems most unjust for the court to raise a point which it has (or thinks it has) identified and demand that the parties address it.'

[21] *Bumper Development Corp v Commissioner of Police of the Metropolis* [1991] 1 WLR 1362, 1371.

[22] *Lim Yi Shenn v Wong Yuen Yee* [2012] 3 HKLRD 505 [60].

[23] *Brownlie* (n 16) [148], applied in eg, *Suppipat v Narongdej* [2022] EWHC 1806 (Comm).

[24] *Gol Linhas Aereas SA v MatlinPatterson Global Opportunities Partners (Cayman) II LP* [2022] UKPC 21, [2022] 2 All ER (Comm) 841 [46]–[47].

[25] *Soriano v Forensic News LLC* [2021] EWCA Civ 1952, [2022] QB 533 [64].

[26] Commercial Court Guide (n 19). See also section V below.

[27] Contrast the scepticism expressed in Briggs (n 4) 38–39.

[28] *MCC Proceeds Inc v Bishopgate Investment Trust plc* [1999] CLC 417 [13]; *Shenzhen Development Bank Co Ltd v New Century International (Holdings) Ltd* (unreported, HCA 2976/2001, 31 July 2002) [25]–[27]; *Hong Jing* (n 19) [110].

the increasing ease by which foreign legal materials could be accessed in light of technological advances, there is no reason to impose an absolute bar on judges consulting such materials in the absence of expert evidence. This is all the more so if the foreign legal issues concerned are of a nature familiar to Hong Kong courts, such as those of other common law systems. Such an approach also has the additional benefit of reducing the time and costs associated with litigation. While the *Brownlie* approach is conceptually neat, it may be difficult to identify the cases where 'skilled exegesis of a kind which only a lawyer expert in the foreign system of law' is genuinely necessary in practice. To alleviate these practical concerns, a rebuttable presumption – under which the Hong Kong courts may consult foreign law materials without the assistance of expert witnesses *as long as the parties are given reasonable notice and do not object to such an exercise* – might be adopted in the future.

ii. Expert Evidence

With the appropriate assistance of expert evidence, the courts of Hong Kong are in a position to apply foreign law.[29] The approach which the Hong Kong courts adopt in assessing expert evidence of foreign law is essentially the same as other types of expert evidence. They are subject to the control of the relevant civil procedure rules, as well as examination and cross-examination in the usual way. In particular, experts owe an overriding duty to the court; they should not be biased or act as a 'hired gun'.[30] Moreover, as long as foreign law evidence is filed pursuant to the court's directions and the counterparty had ample opportunity to respond to the same, there cannot be any complaint of unfairness.[31] Delays in adducing foreign law evidence and relying on foreign law are frowned upon.[32]

In the context of interlocutory applications, points of foreign law would have to be determined without pleading.[33] For interlocutory matters, evidence of foreign law can be properly given by way of an affidavit of the expert. This is because

> [i]n practice, the Hong Kong courts are more relaxed because of the interlocutory nature and urgency. The courts often rely for interlocutory purposes upon unsworn letters or opinions exhibited to an affidavit of the adducing party's solicitor. However, evidence in that form may, in the court's discretion, be given somewhat lesser weight in cases of doubt.[34]

As these pieces of evidence are not subject to cross-examination, some judges have encountered difficulties in resolving issues of foreign law.[35] Failure to plead foreign law in the

[29] *Mehta v Mehta* [2007] 2 HKLRD 520 [39], applied in *China Shanshui Cement Group Ltd v Tianrui (International) Holding Co Ltd* [2020] HKCFI 3043 [65(d)]. Professor Adrian Briggs once lamented that '[t]here is more than a trace of irony in the fact that although the judge has no knowledge of foreign law, he is required to determine which of two witnesses, each with an expertise which he does not share, has ascertained and stated with greater accuracy the content and meaning of foreign law': A Briggs, *Private International Law in English Courts* (Oxford, Oxford University Press, 2014) para 3.31. However, with respect, this view not only applies with equal (or even greater) force to other forms of expert evidence, but it also ignores the legal dimensions of questions of foreign law, where judges (with legal training and practice) will be more competent and comfortable in evaluating the evidence of foreign law: see n 102 below. Briggs subsequently toned down his criticism in the second edition: Briggs (n 4) 34.

[30] Rules of the High Court (Cap 4A), Ord 38, r 35A.

[31] *China NPL Holdings Pte Ltd v Mo Haidan* [2021] 1 HKLRD 344, [2020] HKCA 1014 [96].

[32] *Universal Entertainment Corp v Kazuo Okada* [2020] HKCFI 1406 [38]–[41].

[33] *China NPL Holdings* (n 31) [96]. For the English practice, see, eg, Commercial Court Guide (n 19) para F8.10.

[34] *Agritrade Resources Ltd v Ashok Kumar Sahoo* [2021] HKCFI 685 [26].

[35] See, eg, *The Polessk* [1996] 2 Lloyd's Rep 40; *The Spirit of Independence* [1999] 1 Lloyd's Rep 43.

statement of claim when it is plain and obvious that foreign law should apply constitutes a material non-disclosure which would justify a discharge of the ex parte leave, but does not necessarily lead to the setting aside of the claim.[36]

Moreover, for cases that involve foreign law, the procedure contained in Order 14A of the Rules of the High Court (Cap 4A) is not appropriate. Order 14A concerns the Court's power to summarily dispose of an action by determining a point of law without a full trial of the action. This is because the Court cannot rely on expert opinion on foreign law, which is a question of fact, to make a determination on a point of law. The parties would have to file expert reports on foreign law, and it is simply impossible for the Court to determine these issues summarily.[37] When the plaintiff is plainly disputing the applicability and/or the force of the foreign law, the Court cannot simply determine the application on the assumed facts and would need to resolve the conflicts in the expert evidence.[38] It would be embarrassing if, in the course of the Order 14A procedure, it is found out that the Court would have to listen to oral evidence to determine questions of fact or foreign law. The Court cannot ignore such potential risks and it would be safer for the Court to conduct the trial in the conventional manner.[39]

Under Hong Kong law, there are no particular requirements as to the formal qualifications required from an expert. Section 59(1) of the Evidence Ordinance (Cap 8) provides that:

> A person who is suitably qualified to do so on account of his knowledge or experience is competent to give, in civil proceedings, expert evidence as to the law of any country or territory outside Hong Kong, irrespective of whether he has acted or is entitled to act as a legal practitioner there.

The burden is on the party seeking to adduce that person's evidence to prove that the person is 'suitably qualified to do so on account of his knowledge or experience'.[40] Thus, despite the broad formulation of section 59(1), parties will usually appoint experts that are sufficiently competent and credible to give evidence on foreign law, considering their qualifications and achievements as appropriate to their cases. This is usually a lawyer, an academic, or a person *peritus virtute officii* (the holder of an official position which requires and therefore implies legal knowledge). Moreover, the evidence on foreign law must be given in the capacity as an expert. In the context of criminal law, the Court of Appeal held that whether gambling was unlawful in Myanmar is a question of foreign law which must be proved by expert evidence. The second prosecution witness, a police officer, was not tendered or regarded as an expert, and his opinion on the illegality issue therefore could not support the conviction.[41]

In trials, when there is a dispute as to the foreign law, a party would have to seek expert evidence to prove or dispute the contested points. In Hong Kong, it is still prevalent to appoint separate experts for matters of foreign law, but the courts have actively encouraged

[36] *Tremendous Success Holdings Ltd v Sinosoft Technology Group* (unreported, HCA 2345/2013, 11 July 2016) [19]–[47].

[37] *Nativivat v Nativivat* [2012] 3 HKLRD 747 [27]–[28]; *Nagravision SA v Zhuhai Gotech Intelligent Technology Co Ltd* [2020] HKCFI 1422 [20]–[21].

[38] *G H Property Holdings Ltd v Able Profit Investment Ltd* [2018] HKCFI 2480 [26].

[39] *Nagravision SA* (n 37) [28].

[40] *TJB v DMT* [2022] HKCA 1223 [15.2].

[41] Criminal Procedure Ordinance (Cap 221), s 65DA; *HKSAR v Tam Hung* (unreported, CACC 127/2010, 27 July 2011) [19]–[28].

the use of a single joint expert after the Civil Justice Reform, seeing this as 'the growing trend' and 'the mainstream in modern litigation'.[42] The task of a foreign law expert is to provide assistance on matters of foreign law. The functions of the expert are:[43]

(1) to inform the court of the relevant contents of the foreign law; identifying statutes or other legislation and explaining where necessary the foreign court's approach to their construction;
(2) to identify judgments or other authorities, explaining what status they have as sources of the foreign law; and
(3) where there is no authority directly on point, to assist the judge in making a finding as to what the foreign court's ruling would be if the issue was to arise for decision there.

It is the third function that gives scope for opinion evidence. The purpose is to predict the likely decision of a foreign court, rather than to press upon the judge the witness's personal views as to what the foreign law might be. In fact, where there is authority directly in point (or if the court is satisfied that the foreign law point could not have escaped the attention of the foreign court or the parties), then there is little room for experts to give evidence to determine the likely outcome of the foreign court applying the foreign law, 'unless if there are conflicting decisions in the foreign court or where it is clear that a piece of relevant legislation had not been considered'.[44]

A foreign law expert is obliged to set out not only their conclusion, but also the source materials, legal principles, and process of reasoning leading to that conclusion.[45] Opinions on foreign law simply consisting of assertions for which no basis is established on the face of the opinion or its attachments are unlikely to carry any serious weight.[46] Similarly, no weight is given to suggestions that the opinion is correct through inquiring and confirming with some unspecified person.[47]

There is a difference in the expert's role in relation to foreign legislation and an instrument or document governed by foreign law. While an expert is entitled to give an opinion on the foreign legislation, it is the court which applies the foreign legislation and determines the interpretation, effect, and/or validity of the instrument or document, based on submissions from the parties. The expert's role in the latter case is simply to give an opinion as to the relevant foreign rules governing the dispute.[48]

In addition to expert reports, the court is entitled, and indeed bound, to draw on its knowledge of the common law and of the rules of statutory construction insofar as it may

[42] *Peace Mark (Holdings) Ltd (in liq) v Chau Cham Wong Patrick* (unreported, HCA 2371/2009, 2 November 2017) [35]–[64].

[43] *MCC Proceeds* (n 28) [23]–[24]. See also *Guangzhou Green-Enhan Bio-Engineering Co Ltd v Green Power Health Products International Co Ltd* [2004] 3 HKLRD 223 [2(a)]; *Hung Fung Enterprises Holdings Ltd v Agricultural Bank of China* [2012] 3 HKLRD 679 [58].

[44] *National Bank of Egypt International Ltd v Oman Housing Bank SAOC* [2002] EWHC 1760, cited in *Guangzhou Green-Enhan Bio-Engineering* (n 43) [2(b)], [2(d)], [3].

[45] *Newmark Capital Corp Ltd v Coffee Partners Ltd* [2007] 1 HKLRD 718 [47].

[46] *GM Commercial Consultants Corp v Euro-Asia Zhong Ji (HK) Ltd* [2021] HKCFI 1378 [64]–[65]. See also Johnston and Harris (n 14) para 2.067.

[47] *The Adhiguna Meranti* [1986] HKLR 487 [72]–[73], where the expert claimed to have 'made inquiries at the Supreme Court of the Republic of Indonesia and have been advised that my opinion on this issue is correct'.

[48] *The Adhiguna Meranti* (n 47) [31].

have a bearing on the resolution of dispute, even though it is an issue of foreign law.[49] Moreover, as a common law jurisdiction and as stated in Article 84 of the Basic Law, Hong Kong is at liberty to refer to other common law authorities as persuasive authorities when deciding matters of Hong Kong law. In these references, no expert evidence is required to 'prove' foreign law. Legal representatives can directly cite these authorities, preferably in an official reported format, to support their propositions. What weight (if any) is to be given to these authorities is a matter for the court to decide.

Of course, if foreign law is pleaded by one party and admitted by the other party or parties, then this constitutes an admission, and no further evidence is admissible in relation to the question of foreign law. It was also suggested that if all parties agree, and the trial court does not consider it inappropriate, then the court may apply foreign statutes directly without any expert evidence, or directly refer to law reports and even textbooks.[50] In these 'consent' cases, it is much more difficult for an appellate court to interfere with the findings on foreign law.

iii. The Effect of Expert Evidence on Judicial Authorities

The court is not bound to accept all of the (expert) evidence adduced in relation to foreign law. 'Even if uncontradicted, the court will examine the content of any expert opinion evidence as to foreign law and will reject it as unsatisfactory if the circumstances so warrant.'[51] 'The consequence of such a rejection depends on the context. Where the rejected evidence is put forward to resist an application for summary judgment, the basis of any defence reliant upon that evidence falls away.'[52] The Court of Final Appeal approved the approach set out in *Dicey and Morris*:[53]

> If the evidence of the expert witness as to the effect of the sources quoted by him is uncontradicted, 'it has been repeatedly said that the court should be reluctant to reject it', and it has been held that where each party's expert witness agrees on the meaning and effect of the foreign law, the court is not entitled to reject such agreed evidence, at least on the basis of its own research into foreign law. But while the court will normally accept such evidence it will not do so if it is 'obviously false', 'obscure', 'extravagant', or 'patently absurd', or if 'he never applied his mind to the real point of law', or if 'the matters stated by [the expert] did not support his conclusion according to any stated or implied process of reasoning'; or if the relevant foreign court would not employ the reasoning of the expert even if it agreed with the conclusion. In such cases the court may reject the evidence and examine the foreign sources to form its own conclusion as to their effect. Or, in other words, a court is not inhibited from 'using its own intelligence as on any other question of evidence'. Similarly, the court may reject an expert's opinion as to the meaning of a foreign statute if it is inconsistent with the text or the English translation and is not justified by reference to any

[49] See n 28 above. For example, in *Re Lee Yang, Shiu Chuen Joyce* [2021] 4 HKLRD 252, [2021] HKCFI 2468 [20], after the party failed to adduce evidence of BVI law, the judge referred to s 220(1) of the Business Companies Act 2004 (BVI) to establish the principle that the Attorney-General of the BVI should be joined as the respondent, and the failure to do so is a procedure irregularity. See also the deduction process in *Lim Yi Shenn* (n 22) [61]–[69].

[50] *Celltech Chiroscience Ltd v Medimmune Inc* [2002] EWHC 2167 (Patents) [8]; Johnston and Harris (n 14) para 2.070, citing *Jabbour v Custodian of Absentee's Property of State of Israel* [1954] 1 All ER 145.

[51] *Zhang Hong Li* (n 13) [97(d)].

[52] *Traffic Stream Infrastructure Co Ltd v Full Wisdom Holdings Ltd* (2004) 7 HKCFAR 442 [22].

[53] *Traffic Stream Infrastructure* (n 52) [21], citing L Collins and others (eds), *Dicey and Morris on the Conflict of Laws*, 13th edn (London, Sweet and Maxwell, 2000) para 9-016. The paragraph in the current edition is almost identical: *Dicey, Morris and Collins* (n 5) para 3-015. This paragraph was also approved in *Zhang Hong Li* (n 13) [96].

special rule of construction of the foreign law. It should, however, be noted in this connection that quite simple words may well be terms of art in a foreign statute.

In studying the validity of any opinion based on foreign law, the court does not simply accept any stated conclusions as being correct, even where there may be no legal opinion contradicting them. The court is entitled to (and indeed must) look at the basis of the legal reasoning in determining what weight, if any, should be attached to the legal opinion.[54] In the situation where the expert failed to make available crucial documents that forms the basis of the foreign law opinion, there is no opportunity for the opposing party to instruct experts to make a reply, and no weight is placed on that.[55]

There is no specific mechanism to examine the reliability of the legal information provided. The court will usually make an assessment based on each case, 'drawing on methodologies derived from its own law, or from universal standards of reasoning and argumentation'.[56] A court is not bound to accept the evidence of a foreign law expert 'if he never applied his mind to the real point of law', or 'if the matters stated by the expert did not support his conclusion according to any stated or implied process of reasoning'.[57]

iv. *Foreign Law Based on a Court Decision*

In addition to expert evidence, a finding of foreign law based on a court decision can also be evidence of foreign law. However, a decision by a Hong Kong or English court as to foreign law is not binding as a precedent before a later decision of the Hong Kong court. This is because questions of foreign law are questions of fact which can be disputed in each case.[58] There can also be changes in the foreign law over time. However, if the High Court of Hong Kong or England (or the appellate courts of these two jurisdictions) have determined any question of foreign law, that determination is admissible as evidence in a later case to establish foreign law, unless the contrary is proved.[59] In Hong Kong, section 59 of the Evidence Ordinance (Cap 8) provides that:

> (2) Where any question as to the law of any country or territory outside Hong Kong with respect to any matter has been determined (whether before or after the commencement of this Part) in any such proceedings as are mentioned in subsection (4), then in any civil proceedings (not being proceedings before a court which can take judicial notice of the law of that country or territory with respect to that matter)—
>
> (a) any finding made or decision given on that question in the first-mentioned proceedings shall, if reported or recorded in citable form, be admissible in evidence for the purpose of proving the law of that country or territory with respect to that matter; and

[54] See, eg, *Full Wisdom Holdings Ltd v Traffic Stream Infrastructure Co Ltd* [2004] 2 HKLRD 1016 [23]; *Zhang Hong Li* (n 13) [96]; *GM Commercial Consultants* (n 46) [64].

[55] *Employees for whom Zhang Caikui is holding shares in China Shanshui Investment Co Ltd v Zhang Caikui* [2017] 5 HKLRD 240 [40]–[41].

[56] R Fentiman, 'Foreign Law in National Courts: A Common Law Perspective' in M Andenas and D Fairgrieve (eds), *Courts and Comparative Law* (Oxford, Oxford University Press, 2015) 97.

[57] *Newmark Capital* (n 45) [49].

[58] *Seridom Servicios Integrados Idom SAU v Heng Wen Trade Co Ltd* [2019] HKCFI 85 [116], citing Johnston and Harris (n 14) para 2.060.

[59] One might question why English courts' decisions are still a valid source after the handover. However, there does not seem to be any basis for disapplying this rule: Johnston and Harris (n 14) para 2.074. See also *Monat Investment Ltd v All Person(s) in Occupation of Part of the Remaining Portion of Lot No 591 in Mui Wo DD 4* [2023] 2 HKC 627, [2023] HKCA 479 [52.1]–[52.5].

(b) if that finding or decision, as so reported or recorded, is adduced for that purpose, the law of that country or territory with respect to that matter shall be taken to be in accordance with that finding or decision unless the contrary is proved:

Provided that paragraph (b) shall not apply in the case of a finding or decision which conflicts with another finding or decision on the same question adduced by virtue of this subsection in the same proceedings.

(3) Except with the leave of the court, a party to any civil proceedings shall not be permitted to adduce any such finding or decision as is mentioned in subsection (2) by virtue of that subsection unless he has in accordance with rules given to every other party to the proceedings notice that he intends to do so.

(4) The proceedings referred to in subsection (2) are the following, whether civil or criminal, namely—

(a) proceedings at first instance in the High Court or in the Supreme Court of England as constituted by section 1 of the Courts Act 1971 (1971 c. 23 U.K.);
(b) appeals arising out of proceedings as are mentioned in paragraph (a);
(c) proceedings before the Court of Final Appeal.

(5) For the purposes of this section a finding or decision on any such question as is mentioned in subsection (2) shall be taken to be reported or recorded in citable form if, but only if, it is reported or recorded in writing in a report, transcript or other document which, if that question had been a question as to the law of Hong Kong, could be cited as an authority in legal proceedings in Hong Kong.

The Rules of the High Court (Cap 4A), Order 38, rule 7 provides that:[60]

7. Evidence of finding on foreign law (O. 38, r. 7)

(1) A party to any cause or matter who intends to adduce in evidence a finding or decision on a question of foreign law by virtue of section 59 of the Evidence Ordinance (Cap. 8) shall—

(a) in the case of an action to which Order 25, rule 1, applies within 28 days after the pleadings in the action are deemed to be closed, and
(b) in the case of any other cause or matter, within 21 days after the date on which an appointment for the first hearing of the cause or matter is obtained,

or in either case, within such other period as the Court may specify, serve notice of his intention on every other party to the proceedings.

(2) The notice shall specify the question on which the finding or decision was given or made and specify the document in which it is reported or recorded in citable form.

(3) In any cause or matter in which evidence may be given by affidavit, an affidavit specifying the matters contained in paragraph (2) shall constitute notice under paragraph (1) if served within the period mentioned in that paragraph.

The failure of a party to give notice of their intention to rely on foreign case law as required by section 59(3) of the Evidence Ordinance (Cap 8) and Order 38, rule 7 of the Rules of the High Court (Cap 4A) is usually fatal.[61] An extension of time may be granted retrospectively

[60] The Rules of the District Court (Cap 336H), Ord 38, r 7 contains an identical provision.

[61] See, eg, *Lesnina H DOO v Wave Shipping Trade Co Ltd* [2022] 2 HKLRD 727, [2022] HKCFI 1070 where one out of four Hong Kong decisions was excluded because the notice of intention was only filed a week before the hearing. That line of decisions (notably *DBS Bank (Hong Kong) Ltd v Pan Jing* [2020] 4 HKC 395, [2020] HKCFI

upon application, although a late application is usually disallowed, particularly in light of the Civil Justice Reform and the unfairness it would inflict on the other party. One way of circumventing this requirement might be to adduce a legal opinion of foreign law,[62] which may be allowed at the court's discretion based on considerations of fairness.[63]

The section 59 mechanism provides an effective and economical way of proving foreign law in a case where there is or can be no substantial dispute as to foreign law. However, where there is a real dispute as to foreign law, expert evidence is usually employed, and this provision is seldom relied upon.

In addition to the judgments of the Hong Kong and English courts, Hong Kong courts have accepted the judgments of the courts in the Mainland as conclusive evidence of Mainland law.[64] However, the effect of these judgments is subject to proof to the contrary by the other party. Indeed, Hong Kong courts are frequently required to apply Mainland law. For instance, Hong Kong still retains the 'double actionability rule', that is, in order for acts or omissions on the part of defendant(s) to give rise to tortious liability, the matter must be actionable under both the *lex fori* and *lex loci delicti*. Therefore, it is important to ascertain whether tortious liabilities can be established under Mainland law. The operation of this rule, and its exception developed under *Red Sea Insurance*, has led to different outcomes in Hong Kong courts.[65] Moreover, the non-existence or non-equivalence of concepts between Hong Kong and the Mainland often causes difficulties in applying Mainland law as foreign law. For example, the concepts of beneficial ownership and trust assets as understood in common law jurisdictions do not exist under Mainland law.[66] There are no concepts equivalent to dishonest assistance and constructive trust under Mainland law.[67] The economic tort of conspiracy does not exist under Mainland law.[68]

268 and *TTI Global Resources Hong Kong Ltd v Hongkong Myphone Technology Co Ltd* [2021] HKCFI 306) is frequently adduced by s 59 of the Evidence Ordinance, which concerns 'underground banking' or 'underground money exchange transaction' in breach of Art 45 of the PRC Administrative Regulations on Foreign Exchange and Arts 30 and 39 of the PRC Foreign Exchanges Measures for Individuals.

[62] *Jessop & Baird (Hong Kong) Ltd v Neo Hwee Khim* [2020] HKCFI 2264 [69] ('The short answer is that apart from relying on the findings on relevant PRC law in the cases, Robert has adduced a PRC legal opinion dated 27 October 2016 by Guangdong Sun Law Firm that the trust of the Subject Properties alleged by JBHK did not fulfil a numbers of requirements of a valid trust (e.g. the requirement of writing) under the Law of Trusts of the PRC. I accept the opinion expressed in such report, especially in the absence of a contrary view. In other words, on the PRC law evidence before me, under the law governing JBHK's interest in the Subject Properties, the beneficial ownership asserted by JBHK is not sustainable.').

[63] See, eg, *Tokić DOO v Hong Kong Shui Fat Trading Ltd* [2022] HKCFI 217 [25]–[35].

[64] *Shenzhen Development Bank (n 28)* [33]–[36]; *First Laser Ltd v Fujian Enterprises (Holdings) Co Ltd* (unreported, HCA 4414/2001, 12 December 2002) [56]; *Guangzhou Green-Enhan Bio-Engineering* (n 43) [2(c)].

[65] In *Xiamen Xinjingdi Group v Eton Properties Ltd* [2016] 2 HKLRD 1106 [270]–[272], the plaintiff's cause of action in conspiracy was found to be not actionable in Hong Kong due to the non-existence of trusts concepts under Mainland law. In *China Agri-Products Exchange* (n 5) [499]–[523], the dishonest assistance claim was found to be actionable under the Tort Liability Law in Mainland China. See also *China International Fund Ltd v West China Cement Ltd* [2020] HKCFI 2976 [42].

[66] See, eg, *Xiamen Xinjingdi Group* (n 65) [270]–[272]; *Jessop & Baird (Hong Kong)* (n 62) [65]; *GM Commercial Consultants* (n 46) [66].

[67] *China Agri-Products Exchange* (n 5) [500].

[68] *Jessop & Baird (Hong Kong)* (n 62) [67].

There is also no concept of estoppel of convention.[69] In these cases, it is difficult to rely on the presumption of similarity to plead (say) a proprietary claim based on trust assets under Mainland law.[70]

v. Costs of Ascertaining Foreign Law

As Hong Kong courts predominantly ascertain foreign law through the use of experts appointed by both parties, the costs are usually subsumed as part of the parties' costs. Following the general rule that 'costs follow the event', the costs of experts may be recovered as part of the parties' costs after determination of the dispute.

C. Failure to Establish Foreign Law

For questions of fact generally, the party which has the burden of proof or disproof has to satisfy such burden. To plead but not to prove a fact leaves a gap. In these cases, the court will proceed on the basis that the fact does not occur.

For questions of foreign law, the burden of proving foreign law lies on the party who bases a claim or defence upon it. 'Any principle of foreign law or foreign legislative provision upon which a party's case is based must be clearly identified and the basis of its application explained.'[71] However, as discussed, this does not mean that whenever a claim is governed by foreign law, it is necessary for the claimant to plead and prove the material content of that law. Nonetheless, the court cannot proceed if there is a gap in questions of foreign law, and an action cannot be dismissed simply because the content of the foreign law and the elements of the cause of action are not established.[72] It is here where it is crucial to distinguish between failing to plead foreign law at all, and pleading but not proving foreign law.

A neat summary of the current position in Hong Kong can be found in the authoritative English text on private international law, *Dicey, Morris and Collins on the Conflict of Laws*. Rule 2 of the latest edition provides that:[73]

(1) Where a party relies on foreign law, that law must be pleaded and proved as a fact to the satisfaction of the court by evidence or sometimes by other means.
(2) In a case involving a foreign element in which foreign law is not pleaded, the court will apply English law.
(3) Where foreign law is recognised to be applicable, but there is no evidence, or insufficient evidence, of the content of the foreign law, it will in general be presumed to be the same as English law.

[69] *First Laser Ltd v Fujian Enterprises (Holdings) Co Ltd* (2012) 15 HKCFAR 569.
[70] See, eg, *Peng Yingzhen v Absolute Skill Holdings Ltd* [2022] HKCFI 3328 [125].
[71] Commercial Court Guide (n 19) para C1.3(f).
[72] *Iranian Offshore* (n 17) [11].
[73] *Dicey, Morris and Collins* (n 5) para 2–001. This appears differently in Lord Collins of Mapesbury and others (eds), *Dicey, Morris and Collins on the Conflict of Laws*, 15th edn (London, Sweet and Maxwell, 2012) para 9R–001.

The Hong Kong courts have consistently applied the substance of the rule, but rarely stated it in very clear terms.[74] The courts either considered the proposition too trite to cite an authority, or consistently cited a paragraph in a practitioners' text.[75] However, none of these cases and legal authorities in Hong Kong have explicitly adopted the crucial distinction between rule 2(2) (failing to plead foreign law) and 2(3) (pleading but not proving foreign law), which is unsatisfactory.[76]

If foreign law is pleaded but not proved, that is, when no evidence is produced as to the content of the foreign law, there is a presumption, or an evidential assumption, that foreign law is the same as Hong Kong law. In other words, in the absence of sufficient proof of foreign law after it is pleaded, the Hong Kong courts will apply Hong Kong law *in place of* the foreign law. This may be called a 'presumption' of similarity that the foreign law is the same as Hong Kong law; described in *Dicey, Morris and Collins*, rule 2(3) above. It is well established that this 'presumption' only applies when foreign law has been pleaded but not proved.[77] It has no application unless and until a party has specifically pleaded or relied on foreign law.

The other situation is when there is no allegation as to the application of foreign law, that is, when foreign law is not pleaded at all. As the parties are entitled to raise (or not raise) foreign law as matters of fact as they see fit, there can be situations where even though a claim is theoretically governed by foreign law, the claimant need not plead a case as to the content of that foreign law.[78] In these cases, Hong Kong law applies as a natural consequence. A case with foreign elements would be decided as if it were a purely domestic case. This may be called the 'default rule', described in *Dicey, Morris and Collins*, rule 2(2) above. It is not necessary for a claimant to plead the existence of, or an intention to rely at trial upon, the default rule. 'It goes without saying that it will apply—otherwise it would not be the default rule that it is—unless reason not to apply it be demonstrated.'[79] This default rule is applicable at trial and also in pre-trial or interlocutory proceedings.[80] Where the 'default rule' applies, there is no scope for the 'presumption' of similarity to operate.

The distinction above has been recently endorsed by the UK Supreme Court in *Brownlie v FS Cairo (Nile Plaza) LLC*, where Lord Leggatt summarised the position as follows:[81]

> [It is] preferable in the interests of clarity not to treat the terms 'presumption' and 'default rule' as interchangeable and to recognise that there are two different rules which are conceptually quite

[74] See, eg, *Sera Ltd v Excelling Profit Investments Ltd* [1992] 2 HKC 262, 268H; *Li Yuen Ling v Tang Kwong Wai Thomas* [2010] 1 HKLRD 522 [26]; *Ding Shu Ju* (n 8) [42.1]; *China Metal Recycling (Holdings) Ltd v Chun Chi Wai* [2021] HKCFI 378 [71].

[75] Johnston and Harris (n 14) para 2.075, which simply states '[a]bsent proof of foreign law, the court will ordinarily apply Hong Kong law'.

[76] For example, in *Caspian Resources Development* (n 20) [30], 'the default rule concerns proof of foreign law and only applies when foreign law has been pleaded but not proved'. This should now be known as the 'presumption of similarity'. Johnston and Harris (n 14) para 2.075 also referred to the 'presumption of similarity' (in the *Brownlie* sense) as the 'default rule'. See Lui and Reyes (n 6) for a revised discussion on proof of foreign law in Hong Kong.

[77] *Caspian Resources Development* (n 20) [30].

[78] *Iranian Offshore* (n 17) [20].

[79] *Iranian Offshore* (n 17) [11(i)]. See also *Dicey, Morris and Collins* (n 5) para 3–025.

[80] *GDH Ltd v Creditor Co Ltd* [2008] 5 HKLRD 895 [33]–[37].

[81] *Brownlie* (n 16) [112]. Before *Brownlie* was decided, *Dicey, Morris and Collins*, 15th edn (n 73) para 9R–001 subsumed both the presumption of similarity and the default rule under a single rule. The rule is updated after *Brownlie*: *Dicey, Morris and Collins* (n 5) para 3R–001. See also W Day, 'Pleading and Proving Foreign Law' (2022) 81(1) *Cambridge Law Journal* 24, 25.

> distinct. So too are their respective rationales. The presumption of similarity is a rule of evidence concerned with what the content of foreign law should be taken to be. By contrast, the 'default rule' … is not concerned with establishing the content of foreign law but treats English law as applicable in its own right where foreign law is not pleaded.

It is suggested that a clear distinction must also be made in Hong Kong between the 'default rule' and the 'presumption' of similarity.

The presumption of similarity can be applied in most cases, although it is subject to a number of exceptions.[82] An English authority stated that the presumption of similarity may not be applicable where: (1) it is not in the interests of justice to apply the same; (2) the foreign law is not based on the common law; (3) the domestic law alters the common law; (4) it is inherently improbable that foreign law is the same; and (5) fairness requires it.[83] Lord Leggatt in *Brownlie* reiterated that the application of the presumption is fact-specific, but proceeded to make a few observations: (1) the presumption is more likely to be appropriate where the applicable foreign law stems from a common law system rather than one based upon the civil law; (2) the presumption is less likely to be appropriate where the relevant domestic law is contained in a statute (depending on the nature of the statute and the relevant statutory provisions); (3) the procedural context should also be considered, with more scope for reliance at an early stage of proceedings versus at trial; and (4) whether the presumption can be relied on may often be uncertain, but this is not problematic given that the reliance on the presumption is always a matter of choice by the parties.[84]

For the presumption of similarity to apply, there has to be 'some degree of universality' between the foreign law statute and the *lex fori* statute,[85] or in other words, they have to be 'materially similar'.[86] For example, Hong Kong courts have considered foreign companies law to be different across jurisdictions, approving *Shaker* where the English Court of Appeal held that certain accounting provisions under the Companies Act were not applicable to a Pennsylvanian company because: (1) the UK Companies Act only applies to companies incorporated under it; and (2) it cannot be expected of the Pennsylvanian company to comply with the accounting provisions under the Companies Act.[87] Another example is foreign taxation law, where there is great reluctance in applying the presumption of similarity.[88] The Hong Kong Court of First Instance refused to assume that Taiwanese tax laws[89] and Russian tax laws[90] are the same as Hong Kong tax laws, which are likely to vary significantly across different legal systems with different local economic, financial, and societal conditions.

[82] *Belhaj v Straw* [2014] EWCA Civ 1394, [2015] 2 WLR 1105 [157].

[83] *Balmoral Group Ltd v Borealis UK Ltd* [2006] EWHC 1900 (Comm) [428], [2006] 2 CLC 220, 347E–F, citing *Damberg v Damberg* (2001) 52 NSWLR 492.

[84] *Brownlie* (n 16) [144]–[147]. See also Day (n 81).

[85] *Capsian Resources Development* (n 20) [30]–[37], citing *Shaker v Al-Bedrawi* [2002] EWCA Civ 1452, [2003] Ch 350. See also *The Ship "Mercury Bell" v Amosin* (1986) 27 DLR (4th) 641. It seems that the notion of 'universality' is unduly uncertain and imprecise.

[86] *Brownlie* (n 16) [126].

[87] *Shaker* (n 85) [67]–[68].

[88] *Damberg* (n 83) [162].

[89] *Igal Dafni v CMA CGM SA* [2013] 2 HKLRD 73 [42]–[48].

[90] *Autonomous Non-Commercial Organization "Organizing Committee etc of 2014 Sochi Winter Olympics" v Pico Projects (International) Ltd* [2021] 2 HKLRD 246, [2021] HKCFI 606 [18], not pursued on appeal: [2021] 5 HKLRD 754, [2021] HKCA 1798.

Some criticisms have been made against the presumption of similarity, on the ground that it unfairly reverses the burden of proof.[91] Fentiman argued that the presumption is

> unacceptable … [allowing] a party to seek the application of foreign law and at the same time, with luminous inconsistency, to invite the court to apply [Hong Kong] law by declining to offer evidence of any other. It is also potentially unfair that one party should (in effect) be made to prove (or disprove) a matter which another has introduced.[92]

D. Appeal

The appellate courts do have the power to interfere with finding of facts of lower courts, including issues of foreign law which are treated as facts by the courts of Hong Kong and are ascertained by a process of pleading and proof, including expert evidence. However, it was suggested that issues of foreign law are treated as facts 'of a peculiar kind', in the sense that an appellate court's power to interfere with ordinary findings of fact do not apply to the same extent; rather, the appellate courts may be more prepared than usual to question and interfere with the assessment of the trial judge on such evidence.[93] The UK Supreme Court noted that:[94]

> the notion that the resolution of a dispute as to foreign law involves a factual finding rather than a legal conclusion is somewhat artificial, and in any event, the Judge did not hear any oral evidence from the expert foreign law witnesses. We are therefore in as good a position as he was to analyse the effect of the evidence as to foreign law.

Whether or not the English position is applicable in Hong Kong is more ambivalent. Although there is Court of Appeal authority to the effect that appellate courts should be slow to interfere with a trial judge's finding on foreign law,[95] the same Court adopted a more nuanced view in another case:[96]

> The Court of Appeal should in appropriate cases be more ready to question the judge's conclusions on an issue of foreign law than it is on other questions of fact. But it should be extremely reluctant to substitute its own views where questions of credibility are concerned, since the judge has had the benefit of seeing and hearing the witnesses.

In fact, the Hong Kong appellate courts have shown readiness to question the judge's conclusions on foreign law.[97] For example, the Court of Final Appeal in *Zhang Hong Li* held that it was not precluded from reaching conclusions contrary to the courts below on the foreign law issues of whether the trustees owed certain equitable duties under Jersey law.[98]

[91] A Gray, 'Choice of Law: The Presumption in the Proof of Foreign Law' (2008) 31(1) *UNSW Law Journal* 136–57.

[92] R Fentiman, *Foreign Law in English Courts* (Oxford, Oxford University Press, 1998) 152–53.

[93] *Parkasho v Singh* [1968] P 233, 250, 254; *Bumper Development* (n 21) 1370 (Purchas LJ).

[94] *Actavis UK Ltd v Eli Lilly & Co* [2017] UKSC 48, [2018] 1 All ER 171 [93].

[95] See, eg, *Mok Hing Chung v Wong Kwong Yiu* [2019] HKCA 452 [53].

[96] *Waddington Ltd v Chan Chun Hoo Thomas* [2016] HKCA 200 [139], citing *Grupo Torras SA v Sheik Fahad Mohammed Al Sabah* [1995] CLC 1025, 1037.

[97] See, eg, *Nomura Funds Ireland plc v The Collector of Stamp Revenue* [2021] 3 HKLRD 744, [2021] HKCA 1040 [32]–[45]. See also *Li Xiao Yun v China Gas Holdings Ltd* [2015] 5 HKLRD 845 [9.1]–[9.2].

[98] *Zhang Hong Li* (n 13) [91]–[101].

It is submitted that it will be inappropriate to lay down a universal proposition that appellate courts should be slow to interfere with findings on foreign law. After all, given the nature of foreign law as 'quasi-legal' findings of fact, judges, whether sitting as trial judges or at the appellate level, should be able to

> use [their] legal training where it has a bearing in determining such [issues], especially where the concepts are not very different from Hong Kong law, and where appropriate may form his own view as to the meaning of the statutes of another jurisdiction.[99]

There should be less reluctance in interfering, especially when the 'advantages enjoyed by a trial judge who received the evidence on such an issue at first-hand'[100] in proof of foreign law issues is usually far less potent than (say) issues pertaining to the credibility of witnesses. Briggs made similar observations in the English context:

> But where this is expert evidence of foreign law, and the texts of the foreign law are in English and the concepts of the foreign law are similar to those of English law, the judge's professional expertise as a lawyer may allow him or her to be more active and less passive in the evaluation of the evidence; and an appellate court may be more willing to reverse the judge on such foreign law than on other issues of fact on which they might be inclined to disagree with him.[101]

III. Foreign Law in Other Instances

A. Arbitration

It might be thought that foreign law in arbitral proceedings must be proved as fact by adducing expert evidence, similar to most court proceedings in common law systems. However, this is clearly not a pragmatic and efficient approach in the context of international arbitration. It is suggested that:[102]

> … in almost all international arbitrations, 'law' is treated as 'law'. The relevant provisions of that law are then identified and substantiated either in written submissions by counsel (or by a lawyer experienced in that law acting as co-counsel), or by way of expert testimony in the form of an expert opinion by legal experts on the law in issue, with the possibility that those experts may be called as witnesses to explain their reasoning and conclusions.

Similar observations have been made in Hong Kong, where 'it is common in arbitrations for some parties to seek to submit expert evidence of foreign law, while others assert that foreign law may be the subject of legal submissions by a party's advocate'.[103] Section 47(3)

[99] *Relevant employees whose shares in China Shanshui Investment Co Ltd were held by Zhang Caikui on trust v Zhang Caikui* [2018] HKCFI 195 [51].

[100] *Ting Kwok Keung v Tam Dick Yuen* (2002) 5 HKCFAR 336 [42].

[101] Briggs (n 4) 35 (footnotes omitted).

[102] N Blackaby, C Partasides and A Redfern, *Redfern and Hunter on International Arbitration*, 7th edn (Oxford, Oxford University Press, 2022) para 6.152.

[103] G Ma and D Brock (eds), *Arbitration in Hong Kong: A Practical Guide*, 5th edn (Hong Kong, Sweet and Maxwell, 2021) para 8.152.

of the Arbitration Ordinance (Cap 609) provides arbitral tribunals with great flexibility to receive evidence. It states:

> When conducting arbitral proceedings, an arbitral tribunal is not bound by the rules of evidence and may receive any evidence that it considers relevant to the arbitral proceedings, but it must give the weight that it considers appropriate to the evidence adduced in the arbitral proceedings.

In practice, arbitral proceedings seated in Hong Kong will 'increasingly allow the parties to determine for themselves whether [the proof of foreign law] should be done through oral and written legal submissions from counsel, or via expert legal witnesses'.[104] This approach is not only sensible following the Civil Justice Reform, especially since *the* objective of the new Arbitration Ordinance is to facilitate 'the fair and speedy resolution of disputes by arbitration without unnecessary expense',[105] but it also accords with the position of Hong Kong as a leading centre for international legal and dispute resolution services, especially when Mainland legal issues are often thrown up in arbitral proceedings. This is because

> where PRC lawyers are involved, counsel for each party can argue their interpretation of the law before the tribunal and the tribunal can make its decision based on this. The role of expert witnesses is, therefore, redundant.[106]

The section 59 mechanism for adducing evidence of decisions of foreign courts is also applicable to civil proceedings before any tribunal as well as arbitral proceedings. Section 60(1) of the Evidence Ordinance (Cap 8) provides that:

> (1) In this Part, unless the context otherwise requires, civil proceedings ... includes, in addition to civil proceedings in any court—
> (a) civil proceedings before any tribunal, being proceedings in relation to which the strict rules of evidence apply; and
> (b) an arbitration or reference, whether under an enactment or not, but does not include civil proceedings in relation to which the strict rules of evidence do not apply.

The relevant provisions of the Rules of the High Court (Cap 4A) are also applicable *mutatis mutandis*.[107]

B. Non-Judicial and Administrative Authorities

There may be occasions where non-judicial and administrative authorities in Hong Kong have to deal with issues of foreign law. For instance, before a marriage takes place in Hong Kong to which a party had been previously married in a foreign jurisdiction, a sealed certified copy of the foreign court's decree of the dissolution of the former marriage must be produced to the Registrar of Marriages. This effectively requires the Registrar to determine the validity of the foreign court's decree under the foreign law.

[104] ibid para 21.062.
[105] Arbitration Ordinance (Cap 609), s 3(1).
[106] Ma and Brock (n 103) para 21.063.
[107] Evidence Ordinance (Cap 8), s 60(3).

Decisions made by non-judicial and administrative authorities in relation to foreign law are subject to some judicial oversight, most commonly in the guise of judicial review applications. A recent example in this respect is *QT v Director of Immigration*,[108] which arose because the Director of Immigration refused to grant the applicant, who had entered into a same-sex civil partnership in England with a spouse who was offered employment in Hong Kong, a spousal visa on the ground that the relevant immigration policy in Hong Kong only recognised parties to monogamous marriages as dependants. The Court of Final Appeal ruled that the policy was unconstitutional as it unduly infringed upon the applicant's rights under the Basic Law and the Hong Kong Bill of Rights. A similar outcome was reached in *Leung Chun Kwong v Secretary for Civil Service*,[109] where the Court of Final Appeal struck down the impugned administrative decisions of the Secretary for the Civil Service and the Inland Revenue which discriminated against same-sex couples lawfully married in New Zealand.

C. Relationship between Foreign Law and *forum non conveniens*

There is some relationship between foreign law and the discretionary exercise to establish a jurisdiction as the appropriate forum for trial (*forum conveniens*). The ease or difficulty of establishing foreign law is often considered as an element in determining the *forum conveniens*, and the *forum conveniens* enquiry itself often depends on establishing facts about foreign law. However, it is not sufficient for the applicant to simply point to the applicability of foreign law in the context of an application of a stay on the ground of *forum non conveniens* ground. The *forum non conveniens* doctrine does not automatically turn away any dispute involving foreign law, because litigants would be unduly denied legal redress and access to justice in the forum of their choice. The question of the whole inquiry remains to be this: whether there is some other available forum which is the appropriate forum for the trial of an action, for the interests of all the parties and the ends of justice.[110]

As a popular forum for international litigation, Hong Kong courts commonly receive, and are accustomed to dealing with and applying evidence of foreign law from experts. It is therefore trite that there is little risk of injustice in resolving issues of foreign law with the assistance of experts, and the need to ascertain foreign law will therefore rarely be a decisive factor in favour of a stay of proceedings.[111] In *Rambas Marketing Co LLC v Chow Kam Fai David*, it was held that:[112]

> In cases where substantial and difficult issues of foreign law are involved, the court may well be compelled to stay the proceedings where there is an appreciable risk that justice will not be done. This risk may in certain circumstances be attributable to factors such as expense, but in the

[108] *QT v Director of Immigration* (2018) 21 HKCFAR 324, [2018] HKCFA 28.
[109] *Leung Chun Kwong v Secretary for Civil Service* (2019) 22 HKCFAR 127, [2019] HKCFA 19.
[110] *SPH v SA* (2014) 17 HKCFAR 364 [51]; *DP World Djibouti Fzco v China Merchants Port Holdings Co Ltd* [2020] 1 HKC 224, [2019] HKCFI 3104 [85]; *China Shanshui Cement Group* (n 29) [65(c)]. See also *Spiliada Maritime Corp v Cansulex Ltd* [1987] 1 AC 460, 477; *VTB Capital plc v Nutritek International Corp* [2013] UKSC 5, [2013] 2 AC 337 [46]–[47].
[111] See, eg, *Rambas Marketing Co LLC v Chow Kam Fai David* [2001] 3 HKC 250, 266F–266I; *China International Fund Ltd* (n 65) [47].
[112] *Rambas Marketing* (n 111) 266F–267A.

> usual case would arise where the court was somehow concerned with the possibility that it might reach a wrong conclusion on an important aspect of foreign law. ... The courts in Hong Kong (particularly the Commercial Court and the Admiralty Court), given the international identity and nature of the type of commercial litigation and litigants here, are often accustomed to dealing with aspects of foreign law. It does not therefore follow at all that once it is shown that issues of foreign law arise, that this will necessarily be a powerful, much less a decisive, factor in favour of a stay. On the other hand, however, it is unrealistic not to acknowledge the fact that complicated issues of foreign law may arise with which the Hong Kong courts will not feel itself confident to deal. It is all a question of degree ...

It is incumbent on the defendant to show that the relevant issues of foreign law are so 'substantial or difficult' that the Hong Kong court 'will not feel itself confident to deal' with them. The 'novelty' of a point of foreign law is a factor to be taken into account in the court's assessment of the difficulty of dealing with it and the likelihood of its reaching the right conclusion, but the existence of a novel point of foreign law does not in itself call for a different approach.[113] Even where the novel point involves foreign public policy, the party has to identify some specific public policy (as distinguished from general notions of public policy), and the court has to consider the nature of such public policy and assess whether the Hong Kong court would feel confident to deal with it at trial with expert evidence.[114]

Therefore, when asking for a stay based on issues of foreign law:[115]

> ... it is incumbent on the defendant as the applicant for stay to identify and articulate what the disputed issue of foreign law is, why there is an issue, so that the court can decide whether the issue is indeed as substantial or difficult as [contended], to compel a stay of the action on the basis that there is an appreciable risk that justice will not be done, as the Court might reach a wrong conclusion on an aspect of foreign law.

IV. Access to Hong Kong Law

Hong Kong law is easily accessible through official means, while some unofficial means are also available. Most legal sources in Hong Kong are available in both Chinese and English, which are both official languages of Hong Kong.[116]

Hong Kong legislation is available online through the Hong Kong e-Legislation database,[117] with its official status accorded by statute.[118] A copy of a database instrument that is published on or printed directly from an approved website, and bears an official verification mark, is a verified copy of the instrument; such verified copy is presumed, unless the contrary is proved, to correctly state the instrument as at the date specified in the copy.[119] All legislation is available in both official languages, and they are equally authentic; where there are differences in meaning which the rules of statutory interpretation ordinarily applicable

[113] *DP World Djibouti Fzco v China Merchants Port Holdings Co Ltd* [2022] HKCA 1330 [26].
[114] *DP World Djibouti Fzco* (CA) (n 113) [27].
[115] *DP World Djibouti Fzco* (CFI) (n 110) [85].
[116] Official Languages Ordinance (Cap 5), s 3.
[117] www.elegislation.gov.hk.
[118] Legislation Publication Ordinance (Cap 614), s 3.
[119] ibid, s 5.

do not resolve, the meaning which best reconciles the two texts, having regard to the object and purposes of the particular legislation, shall be adopted.[120]

Most judgments in Hong Kong are available through the Legal Reference System operated by the Judiciary.[121] Judgments are delivered in the language in which the case is heard (English or Chinese); a translated version may be available, but they have no legal status as a judgment. In addition, there are various Law Reports published by commercial publishers. The most common Law Reports include the Hong Kong Court of Final Appeal Reports (HKCFAR), the Hong Kong Law Reports & Digest (HKLRD), and the Hong Kong Cases (HKC). In practice, practitioners should cite and only cite the Law Reports if the case is published in the Law Reports. Only if that case does not appear in the Law Reports should other law reports or publications be cited. Where neutral citations of local cases are available (from 1 January 2018 onwards), they should also be given.[122] Unreported judgments can be downloaded from the Legal Reference System, in which the original Word format is preferred over the online format.[123]

Some judgments are accompanied by press summaries or case summaries in both Chinese and English. These usually include all cases from the Court of Final Appeal, as well as cases at other court levels which have generated significant public attention.[124] However, these are not part of the judgments and therefore have no official status. The Department of Justice also prepares summaries of 'notable judgments' for selected cases which involve important or significant legal principles or issues, issues of public interest, issues that attract strong media or public interest, and/or for educational purposes.[125] Again, these summaries have no legal effect and are not intended to be cited as authorities of any kind.

Another notable, unofficial means to access Hong Kong law is the Hong Kong Legal Information Institute (HKLII).[126] HKLII is a free access legal information system developed and jointly operated by the Department of Computer Science and Faculty of Law of the University of Hong Kong. The website has been accessed more than 17 million times since its establishment on 11 November 2011.

V. Reforms and Future Directions

Although Hong Kong is not a party to any international or regional instruments on the treatment and/or information of foreign law, section IV above shows that Hong Kong law is generally accessible to anyone – within or outside Hong Kong – who is interested in the content of Hong Kong law. It is also common for Hong Kong lawyers to be engaged in providing advice or expert evidence on Hong Kong or foreign law. Moreover, although there might be problems with the disproportionate time and cost spent on adducing expert

[120] Interpretation and General Clauses Ordinance (Cap 1), s 10B. Needless to say, the attempt to reconcile bilingual legal discrepancies is a difficult task: see, eg, *T v Commissioner of Police* (2014) 17 HKCFAR 593.
[121] legalref.judiciary.hk/lrs/common/ju/judgment.jsp.
[122] Practice Direction 5.5, para 5.
[123] Practice Direction 5.5, para 6.
[124] legalref.judiciary.hk/lrs/common/ju/ps.jsp?L1=FA.
[125] www.doj.gov.hk/en/notable_judgments.
[126] www.hklii.hk.

evidence on foreign law, Hong Kong generally has an effective and efficient framework to facilitate the adducing of foreign law in Hong Kong proceedings.

There is a recent trend in Hong Kong to codify or reformulate common law principles through statutory enactments or amendments. A relatively recent example in private international law is the Domicile Ordinance (Cap 596), which consolidates and reforms the law for determining the domicile of individuals. Similarly, one can propose that it is mature for Hong Kong to codify some of its rules in relation to proof of foreign law. This can be done on various fronts.

In relation to the more welcoming attitude (as reflected in Lord Leggatt's statement in *Brownlie*) towards the different kinds of legal materials that can be adduced as evidence of foreign law suggested above, reference may be made to section 144 of the New Zealand Evidence Act 2006, which provides for a range of legal materials that can be adduced as evidence of foreign law:[127]

> (1) A party may offer as evidence of a statute or other written law, proclamation, treaty, or act of State, of a foreign country—
>
> (a) evidence given by an expert; or
>
> (b) a copy of the statute or other written law, proclamation, treaty, or act of State that is certified as a true copy by a person who might reasonably be supposed to have the custody of the statute or other written law, proclamation, treaty, or act of State; or
>
> (c) any document containing the statute or other written law, proclamation, treaty, or act of State that purports to have been issued by the government or official printer of the country or by authority of the government or administration of the country; or
>
> (d) any document containing the statute or other written law, proclamation, treaty, or act of State that appears to the Judge to be a reliable source of information.
>
> (2) In addition, or as an alternative, to the evidence of an expert, a party may offer as evidence of the unwritten or common law of a foreign country, or as evidence of the interpretation of a statute or other written law or a proclamation of a foreign country, a document—
>
> (a) containing reports of judgments of the courts of the country; and
>
> (b) that appears to the Judge to be a reliable source of information about the law of that country.
>
> (3) A party may offer as evidence of a statute or other written law of a foreign country, or of the unwritten or common law of a foreign country, any publication—
>
> (a) that describes or explains the law of that country; and
>
> (b) that appears to the Judge to be a reliable source of information about the law of that country.
>
> (4) A Judge is not bound to accept or act on a statement in any document as evidence of the law of a foreign country.
>
> (5) A reference in this section to a statute of a foreign country includes a reference to a regulation, rule, bylaw, or other instrument of subordinate legislation of the country.

The New Zealand framework provides for more potential sources of foreign law (while remains as an exhaustive list of sources), including any reports of judgments of the courts of a country (not limited to Hong Kong or the UK as currently stated in section 59 of the Evidence Ordinance (Cap 8)), or any publications that describe or explain the law of that

[127] Evidence Act 2006 (New Zealand), ss 144(1)–144(5).

jurisdiction. For instance, academic writings may be highly significant in ascertaining the content of legal principles in civil law jurisdictions.[128] The weight to be given to such evidence is another matter, and a judge is certainly not bound to accept or act on those as provided in section 144(5); this note of caution may also be expressly provided in the proposed statute.

In addition to provisions advocating for a broader range of sources of foreign law, further statutory codifications will also be welcomed in relation to: (1) how the court would fill the 'gap' in foreign law, by employing the distinction between the 'presumption' of similarity and the 'default rule' as decided in *Brownlie* and reflected in the latest edition of *Dicey, Morris and Collins*; and (2) the appeal mechanisms based on grounds of foreign law. Clarifications from the higher levels of courts on these issues will also be helpful.

In contrast, the issue of whether courts can receive counsel submissions on foreign law directly might be considered to be more controversial in Hong Kong, as this goes against common practice. However, it should be noted that some common law courts had invited and/or determined foreign law issues by way of counsel submissions, or are at least prepared to do so.[129] The Singapore International Commercial Court has explicit provisions allowing the question of foreign law to be determined on the basis of submissions instead of proof.[130] The Dubai International Financial Court also adopted an 'international approach' which allows counsel to make legal submissions on all applicable or relevant law, including foreign law.[131]

There might also be potential in Hong Kong for direct court-to-court cooperation or interaction regarding proof of foreign law. *Dicey, Morris and Collins* has illustrated such trends in other (common law) jurisdictions:[132]

> [T]here are signs that direct court-to-court co-operation may provide an avenue for the ascertainment of foreign law, with the result in a court in one jurisdiction may be asked to, and may, entertain proceedings whose purpose is to obtain an authoritative statement of foreign law for use in local proceedings. An English court has given such a judgment in response to proceedings brought before it to ascertain English law for the purpose of proceedings before the courts in Singapore; and the courts in New South Wales may refer cases directly to courts in certain other countries for a ruling on a question of foreign law.

Such arrangements to ascertain foreign law by reference 'may not always be more cost effective than proof by expert evidence … [but a] reference will always … provide a more accurate answer, indeed, an authoritative answer, than expert evidence'.[133] This may be particularly attractive between Hong Kong and Mainland China, given the ever-increasing levels of

[128] *Dicey, Morris and Collins* (n 5) para 3.019.

[129] *Celltech Chiroscience* (n 50) [8]; I Fletcher, 'Review of Forum Law in English Courts' (1999) 115 *LQR* 518, 520, citing *Robinson v Bland* (1760) 96 ER 129, 141; J Hogan-Doran and D Hogan-Doran, 'New and Alternative Approaches to Proof of Foreign Law: A Practitioners' Perspective' in M Douglas and others (eds), *Commercial Issues in Private International Law: A Common Law Perspective* (Oxford, Hart Publishing, 2019) 243–44 on examples from the US to grant foreign lawyers a right of appearance *pro hac vice* to make submissions as to foreign law, and to be available for questions from and arguments before the bench; Commercial Court Guide (n 19) para H3.5: '[In the England and Wales Commercial Court, the] parties will often have retained foreign lawyers … It will not always be necessary to instruct a separate foreign law expert to provide the expert evidence.'

[130] Singapore International Commercial Court Rules 2021, Ord 16, r 8.

[131] *Fidel v Felecia* [2015] DIFC CA 002 [48]–[76].

[132] *Dicey, Morris and Collins* (n 5) para 3–023 (footnotes omitted).

[133] JJ Spigelman, 'Proof of Foreign Law by Reference to the Foreign Court' (2011) 127 *LQR* 208, 213.

economic interaction between Hong Kong and Mainland China. There have been many efforts in recent years to harmonise other aspects of private international law across the border.[134] More generally, there are calls to develop an interregional framework of private international law.[135] The concept of cross-border judicial cooperation is not alien at all to Hong Kong as a special administrative region established under Article 31 of the Constitution of the People's Republic of China, and the only common law jurisdiction in China.

If Hong Kong adopts direct court-to-court communication, this might indeed be contrary to the traditional common law position that there is no principle of *iura novit curia*. However, improvements may also take the form of facilitating access to foreign law in interregional cases: for example, under some co-operation or mutual assistance arrangements, parties may be able to prove foreign law by ascertaining its content through a competent authority of the other jurisdiction. Currently, in the Mainland, the Supreme People's Court has established a procedure known as the 'ascertainment of foreign law process', and the China International Commercial Court also permits various methods to be used to answer foreign legal questions as stated in 'Several Provisions of the SPC on Establishing China International Commercial Court'.[136] However, determining the entity which should be made the competent authority in Hong Kong under such arrangements might be a problem.

Arrangements to facilitate access to foreign law are also seen in other jurisdictions. For example, the Singapore International Commercial Court has explicit provisions to refer issues of foreign law to specified foreign courts (in the New South Wales, Dubai and Bermuda), or to request for opinions on questions of foreign law (from China).[137] However, it is also important to note the potential disadvantages of these processes. For example, despite the British Law Ascertainment Act 1859 allowing an English court to remit contested questions of foreign law to the courts of other Commonwealth countries, the process has seldom been employed because of the delay, increased cost and inherent unpredictability.[138] Similar criticisms have been made against the 1968 European Convention on Information on Foreign Law.[139] More time is required to see how these arrangements might work out in the Greater China or the Asian region.

More generally, there may be room for courts to be given a broad, discretionary power to determine the procedure by which foreign law issues will be best resolved. Academics have suggested that any procedure may be adopted, subject only to 'proper notice … given by the party raising the matter to the court and other parties'.[140] In more concrete and

[134] The most recent example is the Mainland Judgments in Civil and Commercial Matters (Reciprocal Enforcement) Ordinance (Cap 645), which follows closely the 2019 HCCH Convention on the Recognition and Enforcement of Foreign Judgments in Civil and Commercial Matters.

[135] See, eg, J Huang, *Interregional Conflict of Laws* (Taipei, Perennial Culture Publishing Inc, 1996); G Tu, 'Inter-regional Private Law among Mainland China, Hong Kong and Macau after the Handovers: Achievements, Reflections and Prospects' (2021) 8(2) *Chinese Review of International Law* 115–128; W Lui, 'Researching and Teaching Asian and Hong Kong Private International Law' (2023) 20(2) *Indonesian Journal of International Law,* Article 2; Lui and Reyes (n 6).

[136] Nevertheless, it was observed that 'although protocols have been introduced in the Mainland to facilitate Mainland courts determining issues of foreign law, courts generally have little experience of doing so': *Citicorp International Ltd v Tsinghua Unigroup Co Ltd* [2022] 2 HKLRD 1225, [2022] HKCFI 1558 [10].

[137] Singapore International Commercial Court Rules 2021, Ords 15 and 15A.

[138] Fentiman *(n 92)* 238–39. See also *International Energy Group Ltd v Zurich Insurance plc* [2013] EWCA Civ 39; *Dicey, Morris and Collins* (n 5) para 3–022.

[139] Hogan-Doran and Hogan-Doran (n 129) 251.

[140] ibid 254.

practical terms, paragraph H3.3 of the Commercial Court Guide in the UK provides for a (non-exhaustive) range of mechanisms that parties should discuss with the Court during a case management conference:[141]

(a) The Court can direct an exchange (simultaneous or sequential) of expert reports, an experts' meeting and joint memorandum, and (if strictly required) supplemental reports following the joint memorandum, from experts to be called to give oral evidence at trial if their evidence is not agreed.
(b) The Court can direct such an exchange of reports (etc), but on the basis that the experts will not give evidence at trial although their evidence is not agreed, or do so only on some of the matters covered by their reports although their evidence on other matters is also not agreed, with the advocates making submissions at trial by reference to the reports and foreign law materials filed.
(c) The Court can limit the expert evidence to identification of the relevant sources of foreign law, and of any legal principles as to the interpretation and status of those sources, with the advocates making submissions at trial as to the relevant content of foreign law by reference to the sources thus identified.
(d) In some cases, the Court may be prepared to take judicial notice, or accept the agreement of the parties, as to the nature and importance of sources of foreign law, and have the advocates make submissions at trial as to the relevant content of foreign law by reference to the sources thus identified, providing the source materials from their own researches.

Paragraph H3.4 further provides a list of factors relevant to the Court's decision in determining the appropriate approach to adopt:[142]

(a) How much of the content of the relevant foreign law is in issue (as distinct from its application to the facts of the case, which is for argument not evidence).
(b) How important those points of difference are to the issues to be determined at trial.
(c) The time and cost efficiency of different approaches (particularly having regard to the amount in issue in the proceedings which is affected by the issues of foreign law).
(d) The nature of the issues and the legal sources in issue. For example, the approach in H3.3(c) or H3.3(d) may be more appropriate when the foreign law issues relate to a common law system or a system of law with which the Court has familiarity from other cases.
(e) Whether there is already an English law decision on the relevant point of foreign law (which is admissible under s.4 CEA 1972 [being the equivalent of Evidence Ordinance (Cap 8), section 59]).

In line with the more liberal and flexible attitude towards the proof of foreign law as suggested above, Hong Kong may seriously consider implementing similar proposals.[143]

[141] Commercial Court Guide (n 19) para H3.3.
[142] Commercial Court Guide (n 19) para H3.4.
[143] For how the UK implemented these proposals, see *Suppipat v Narongdej* (n 23).

VI. Conclusion

To conclude, the processes to plead and prove foreign law in Hong Kong courts follow the 'traditional' or 'orthodox' views and approaches in common law closely. These processes have been reinforced and supplemented by a wealth of local and overseas authorities in recent years. There might be room for these processes to be further refined or expanded. As argued above, some relaxation from the traditional strictures in favour of a more malleable framework on the sources and methods of proving foreign law is not only normatively compelling but also practically sensible. However, it is unlikely that these adjustments will radically change the current regime, or impact greatly on the popularity of Hong Kong as a forum for litigation. Moreover, while an international or regional instrument unifying the treatment of foreign law might be useful, it is unclear how the position in Hong Kong can be reconciled with those in some other civil law jurisdictions in Asia and elsewhere, where a more active and aggressive approach in ascertaining foreign law is taken. Rather, inter-regional approaches within the Greater Bay Area or Greater China to access and ascertain foreign law might be worth exploring.

Whatever the rules might be, the proof of foreign law should conform with the tenets of achieving justice, cost efficiency and expediency. This is not least because of the objectives of the Civil Justice Reform to increase the cost-effectiveness of the system of civil procedure and to eliminate delays in litigation.[144] The eventual solution chosen by the court in each case may well be different, but must always be reasonable and proportionate.

[144] Rules of the High Court (Cap 4A), Ord 1A, r 1; *Wing Fai Construction Co Ltd v Yip Kwong Robert* (2011) 14 HKCFAR 935 [31].

4

Taiwan

CHUN-LIANG LAI, FULDIEN LI AND FELICE FU-AN LU

I. Treatment of Foreign Law

A. Mandatory Character of Choice of Law Rules

In 1953, the 'Application of Law Act' (法律適用條例) promulgated in 1918 to deal with the choice of law rules of matters involving foreign property and foreign personal status was greatly amended and was renamed the 'Act Governing the Choice of Law in Civil Matters Involving Foreign Elements' (涉外民事法律適用法) (Choice of Law Act). In 2010, the Choice of Law Act was again substantially amended, amounting to 63 Articles in total. Since the Choice of Law Act is a law that has been approved by the Legislative Yuan, it shall bind upon all courts and institutions of Taiwan. Judgments have shown that in Taiwan's legal practice, the court shall apply the Choice of Law Act to determine the applicable law while hearing cases involving foreign matters, or else the judgment it makes will be in contravention of the laws and regulations.[1] These judgments further indicate that if the administrative agencies, including but not limited to household registries and land administration offices, when carrying out their administrative duties, do not apply the Choice of Law Act while they should, the administrative rulings they make will also be in contravention of the laws and regulations.[2] For example, when a foreign spouse applies to enter or reside in Taiwan according to Articles 18 and 22 of the Immigration Act, or when a foreigner applies to marriage registration according to Article 9 of the Household Registration Act, the administrative agencies shall apply the Choice of Law Act when determining the effect of these applications. If not, it will constitute a violation of Article 147 of the Administrative Procedure Act.[3] Taipei High Administrative Court Judgment Su-Tzu No 14 of 2020[4] ruled that it is an unlawful administrative ruling when a household registry overruled the application of the

[1] G-P Wu, 'Fa Guan Ying Yi Zhi Quan Shi Yong She Wai Min Shi Fa Lu Shi Yong Fa' [Should the Courts Apply the "Statute Governing the Application of Laws to Civil Matters" Ex Officio?] in *Er Shi Yi Shi Ji Fa Xue Fa Zhan Xin Jing Jie – Ke Ze Dong Jiao Shou Qi Zhi Hua Dan Zhu Shou Lun Wen Ji [Collected Papers For Professor Tse-Tung Ke's 70th Birthday Celebration (2008)]*, 415–16 (Taipei, Angle Publishing, 2008).

[2] ibid.

[3] Taiwan High Court Tainan Branch Civil Judgment Chia-Shang-Tzu No 67 of 2013, Ministry of Home Affairs Letter Tai-Nei-Hu-Tzu No 1050439179 dated October 27, 2016.

[4] The judgment is available at: judgment.judicial.gov.tw/FJUD/data.aspx?ty=JD&id=TPBA,109%2c%e8%a8%b4%2c14%2c20210506%2c1.

same-sex marriage registration between a Macau resident and a citizen of the Republic of China because it failed to apply the Laws and Regulations Regarding Hong Kong & Macao Affairs and Choice of Law Act. From this point of view, the Choice of Law Act has a mandatory character.

Several judgments ruled by the Supreme Court of Taiwan have reconfirmed the mandatory character of the Choice of Law Act.[5] The Supreme Court Civil Judgment Tai-Shang-Tzu No 1021 of 2010[6] pointed out,

> Civil matters that are related to any foreign elements are deemed civil matters involving foreign elements. The Choice of Law Act should be applied to determine the applicable laws, whether internal or foreign laws. The so-called 'involving foreign elements' refers to those facts that constitute the civil matters, including the connecting factors that have something to do with foreign states like parties, the place where the juridical act is done, or the place where the fact occurs. Here, the appellee is an Italian. The appellee requested the appellant, according to the agreement in dispute, to give the above-mentioned property as well as half of the balance of the account receivable/payable of the wine sale calculated by the accountant. As previously stated, the court shall determine the applicable law according to the Choice of Law Act. In this case, the original court entered the judgment without following the process of choosing applicable law and did not explain the rationale of applying the internal law. Thus, the original court had violated the law because it did not provide reasons for its judgment.

This judgment shows that the choice of law rules have a mandatory character.

Article 71 of Taiwan's Civil Code provides: 'A juridical act which violates an imperative or prohibitive provision of the act is void except voidance is not implied in the provision.' Therefore, in Taiwan, when a law is deemed mandatory, it cannot be altered by the parties, or the legal acts between the parties will become invalid. Despite the mandatory character of Taiwan's Choice of Law Act, there are still many rules incorporating the principle of party autonomy. For example, Article 20 stipulates that the applicable law regarding the formation and effect of a juridical act that results in a relationship of obligation is determined by the intention of the parties; Article 31 states that where the parties with respect to an obligation that arises otherwise than from a juridical act agree to the application of the law of the Republic of China (ROC)/Taiwan after a suit has been brought on the obligation in a court of the ROC, the law of the ROC is applied; Article 48 allows the spouses to agree upon the applicable law that applies to their matrimonial property regime in writing; Article 50 provides that the parties are able to mutually agree to divorce by the applicable law.

The mandatory character of the Choice of Law Act should also be further examined from the perspective of the principles of litigation procedures. There are different litigation structures corresponding to different matters in the litigation system of Taiwan. The property cases are matters subject to the parties' own measures, and an adversary system is adopted. In contrast, identity matters and non-contentious matters involve the identity

[5] Wu (n 1) 415–16. The Article refers to the following judgments that infer the mandatory character of the Choice of Law Act. These judgments include Supreme Court Civil Judgments Tai-Shang-Tzu No 1765 of 2005, Tai-Shang-Tzu No 1721 of 2005, Tai-Shang-Tzu No 1416 of 2005, Tai-Shang-Tzu No 687 of 2005, Tai-Shang-Tzu No 2121 of 2004, Tai-Shang-Tzu No 491 of 2004, Tai-Shang-Tzu No 5 of 2004, Tai-Shang-Tzu No 150 of 2003, Tai-Shang-Tzu No 525 of 2002, and Tai-Shang-Tzu No 95 of 2002.

[6] The judgment is available at judgment.judicial.gov.tw/FJUD/data.aspx?ty=JD&id=TPSV,109%2c%e5%8f%b0%e4%b8%8a%2c1021%2c20210304%2c1.

or status of a third-party. Good examples for identity matters are family litigation matters, including matters concerning the determination of invalidity of marriage, or the existence or non-existence of marriage relation, and matters concerning the determination of the existence or non-existence of a parent-child relation. Other examples for non-contentious matters include matters concerning maintenance between relatives, and matters concerning the approval of an adoption or termination of an adoption by a court, or approval of terminating an adoption by a court. These cases are not subject to the parties' own measures, and therefore the principle of ex officio is adopted. If the principles of litigation procedures adopted by the cases are different, the mandatory character of the Choice of Law Act will also more or less be affected.

In the property cases involving foreign elements that adopt the adversary system, the court shall not enter a judgment based on a claim that the parties did not make. It is the so-called 'burden of claim'. In the civil proceedings in Taiwan, for the litigations that adopt the adversary system, a party bears the burden of claim with regard to the facts which one alleges in its favour. The court shall not take any facts that the party did not claim into consideration.[7] Therefore, some scholars propose that the Choice of Law Act should be considered optional rather than mandatory when it comes to matters subject to the parties' own measures to protect the procedural and substantial interests of the parties.[8] Other scholars also propose that, since these matters are subject to the parties' own measures, Article 31 of the Choice of Law Act can be applied, and the parties are allowed to mutually agree upon the applicable law.[9] Although this opinion has its rationale in both substantive law and procedural law, the mandatory character of the Choice of Law Act does not merely exist in civil litigation proceedings but also exists in other administrative litigations or administrative proceedings like registration of rights. The above-mentioned view of the Taiwan Supreme Court shows that even in property cases adopting the adversary system, the Choice of Law Act should be applied no matter whether the parties have claimed it or not. Therefore, as legal practice in Taiwan, the Choice of Law Act is still mandatory, regardless of whether the parties claim to apply it. The mandatory character is even more explicit in family matters and non-contentious matters that adopt the principle of ex officio, for the Choice of Law Act is applied without doubt no matter whether the parties claim to apply it or not.

B. Choice of Law Rules of Taiwan – The Two-sided Rules

The legislative types of the choice of law rules are categorised as the one-sided rule and two-sided rule. The one-sided rule merely stipulates the law of the forum shall apply. The two-sided rule involves abstract connecting factors, and appoints an applicable law, whether internal or foreign laws, for matters involving foreign matters.

All the choice of law rules in the Choice of Law Act of Taiwan adopts the legislative type of the two-sided rule. However, some choice of law rules scattering in other laws adopt

[7] S-M Chiang, *Min Shi Su Song Fa (Xia) [Civil Procedure II]* 3 (Taipei, New Sharing Culture Enterprise, 2014).

[8] Wu (n 1) 446–47.

[9] E-W Lin, 'Wai Guo Fa Shi Yong Wen Ti Zhi Yan Jiu: Tai Wan Si Fa Shi Wu Pan Jue Yu Bi Jiao Fa Shang De Yi Xie Si Kao' ['A Study on the Application of Foreign Law: Some Reflections on Taiwan Judicial Practice Judgment and Comparative Law'] (2019) 58 *Tunghai University Law Review* 103, 138.

the one-sided rule. For example, Article 94 of the Maritime Law states, 'Collision of ships, regardless of the place of the collision, shall be governed by the provisions of this Chapter.'

II. The Status of Foreign Law

A. Nature of Foreign Law: 'Law' or 'Fact,' or of a Hybrid Nature?

The wording 'the law of a foreign State is applicable' in the Choice of Law Act refers to the situation when the court shall apply the Choice of Law Act when hearing cases involving foreign matters, and the law of a foreign state becomes applicable in those matters. This includes the situation where the choice of law rules appoint a foreign law as the applicable law on the merits,[10] and the situation where the law of a foreign state shall be applied to determine whether a bankruptcy trustee of a company has the standing in a lawsuit.[11] To elaborate, in cases where Taiwanese courts determine whether a bankruptcy trustee of a company has the standing in a lawsuit, the court needs to examine whether a foreign law bestows such standing to the bankruptcy trustee, and therefore there are chances to apply the foreign law. Other situations include when petitioning for litigation aid or claim for state compensation, the court should first determine whether there is mutual reciprocity in foreign laws.[12] To be more specific, when the Taiwanese litigation aid agency decides whether to financially aid a foreigner in Taiwanese lawsuits, it will consider whether the Taiwanese will also be treated equally and receive litigation aid in that country. Therefore, it is necessary to review the relevant litigation aid regulations in the foreign law.

Some treaties that Taiwan has signed with other countries have already been passed by the Legislative Yuan and therefore become national legislation. Take the 'Convention on the Territorial Sea and the Contiguous Zone' of the United Nations for example. Once it is passed as a treaty Bill and 'Law on the Territorial Sea and the Contiguous Zone' is promulgated as an internal law, it is no longer a foreign law. However, in recent years, there are several conventions related to human rights being introduced into Taiwan as implementation acts one after another, including the International Covenant on Civil and Political Rights 1966, International Covenant on Economic, Social and Cultural Rights (ICESCR), the Convention on the Elimination of all Forms of Discrimination Against Women (CEDAW), the Convention on Rights of Persons with Disabilities (CRPD), United Nations Convention Against Corruption, and the Convention on the Rights of Children (CRC). They have been consecutively introduced into Taiwan as the 'Act to Implement the International Covenant on Civil and Political Rights and the International Covenant on Economic, Social and

[10] H-P Ma and Chun-Liang Lai, *Guo Ji Si Fa: Zong Lun Ge Lun [Private International Law: General Principles and Special Provisions]*, 4th edn (Taipei, self-publishing, 2022) 221.

[11] According to Art 82 of Bankruptcy Act of Taiwan, 'the properties belonging to a bankrupt is deemed the bankrupt estate, except those exclusively belong to the bankrupt and those cannot be seized'. Para 1, Art 174 further provides, 'When a party is adjudicated bankrupt, the proceeding of all actions concerning the bankruptcy estate shall be stayed automatically until a qualified person assumes the action pursuant to the Bankruptcy Act or the bankruptcy proceeding is concluded.' Therefore, whether the properties of the bankrupt (ie, claims of damages or family support) shall be included in the bankrupt estate and whether the bankruptcy trustee has standing may be determined by examining foreign laws.

[12] Supreme Court Civil Judgment Tai-Kang-Tzu No 11 of 2008.

Cultural Rights' promulgated on 22 April 2009, 'Enforcement Act of Convention on the Elimination of All Forms of Discrimination against Women' promulgated on 8 June 2011, 'Act to Implement the Convention on the Rights of Persons with Disabilities' promulgated on 20 August 2014, 'Act to Implement United Nations Convention against Corruption' promulgated on 20 May 2015, and 'Implementation Act of the Convention on the Rights of the Child' promulgated on 19 June 2019.

These soft laws with the international law nature cannot be self-executed into national laws through normal process like signing a treaty. The reason for this situation is known to the public – Taiwan is not a Member State of the United Nations. The legislative agencies can only proclaim the contents of the treaties by promulgating the implementation acts by its legislative procedure. These implementation acts are therefore effective as internal laws and are no longer international conventions. Given that the contents of the treaties have become internal legislation, they can be cited by the courts as a source of internal laws.

In theories of private international law, it has always been argued whether the applicable foreign law should be regarded as fact or should be regarded as law. In the theory that regards the applicable foreign law as fact, the foreign law has no legal effect within the state's boundary of the forum. It is, therefore, merely a fact. The theory that regards the foreign law as law, however, is influenced by the German scholar, von Savigny. He advocated a theory stating that internal laws and foreign laws are equal. He claimed that the foreign law should be deemed to have the same effect as the law of the forum and is thus law in its nature.

When it comes to the debate on whether the applicable foreign law should be deemed as fact or law, the answer changes with time. During times affected by analytical legal philosophy,[13] people considered the law as orders of the commander.[14] In view of legal positivism, clearly identifying the origin of law will assist with legal application and research. Foreign law is not an order from the commander of the state, and as a matter of course is not law in its nature. In China, traditional ideology is influenced by a concept from Confucianism (儒家) – unity of man and nature (天人合一). Natural law (天道) is the governing principle of law, and humanity (人道) is the realisation of law. Natural law and humanity merge and blend, and form a system of trinity – science, society, and man. This is to effectuate the legal philosophy of the trinity of the three forces – heaven, earth and man (天、地、人三才一體).[15] When determining the legal legitimacy of law, this ideology does not distinguish internal law makers from foreign ones. Instead, it determines whether the law has been in accordance with the natural law pursuant to 'following the nature to govern (the country)' (法天而治) and 'following the order of the nature' (人副天數). The concept was formed in an important book *Records of the Grand Historian* (史記) in 90 BC. In *Li Shu Di Yi* (禮書第一), it says at the very beginning 'We formulate the rules of etiquette based on human nature, and create the ceremonies in accord with humanity' (緣人情而制禮，依人性而作儀). It also says

> manners come from man … we formulate the manners and righteousness to satisfy human's desire and respond to human's requests. Thus, man will not be discontent because of the

[13] H-P Ma, *Xi Yang Fa Lu Si Xiang Lun Ji [Essays on Western Legal Thoughts]* (Taipei, Han Lin Publishing, 1977) 51–108.

[14] J Austin, *The Province of Jurisprudence Determined* (Xing Liu tr, China Legal System Publishing House, 2002) 17.

[15] Y-S Huang, *Zhong Guo Fa Shi Dao Lun [The Introduction of the Legal History of China]* (Taipei, New Sharing Culture Enterprise, 2012) 78–79.

> shortage of resources, and the resources will not be exhausted due to man's desire (禮由人起 … 制禮義以養人之欲，給人之求，使欲不窮於物，物不屈於欲).

During 618–907 AD, the *Tang* dynasty, foreigners came to the land of *Tang* for business, and many Chinese literary works were translated into Sogdian or Arabic by Manichaeism.[16] According to *Ancient accounts of India and China* (蘇萊曼遊記) written by an Arabic businessman, the dispute between Muslims were resolved and judged by Muslims. Muslims served as judges and constituted a special court to hear the câse. In those cases, the Muslims' national law should apply.[17] Muslims' national law would not be disqualified as an applicable law simply because it was the law of the foreigners. However, contemporary scholars point out that the distinction between internal and foreign law in the untamed[18] legal systems was totally different from now. Foreign law was actually a mixture of imperialism – all lands belong to the emperor – and the concept of the social hierarchy of Chinese and foreigners.[19] The earliest record of private international law in legal history can be traced back to *Yong Huei* (永徽) 2 (651 AD) in *Tang Ley Su Yi* (唐律疏義), which says 'for the dispute between the people from the same gens, their respective customary law shall apply; for the dispute between gentes, the *Tang*'s law shall apply. (諸化外人，同類自相犯者，各依本俗法。異類相犯者，以法律論。)'[20]

> *Su Yi* says, the untamed are those in barbarian states with their own governors, different customs and law systems. If the dispute arises between the untamed from the same barbarian state, ask for their national law and their common national law applies. If the dispute arises between the untamed from different barbarian states, like Goryeo people and Baekje people, then the Tang's law shall apply. (疏義曰，化外人謂蕃夷之國別立君長者，各有風俗法制不同。其有同類自相犯者，須問本國之制，依其俗法斷之。異類相犯者，若高麗之與百濟相犯之類，皆以國家法律論定刑名。)[21]

There is no clear distinction between civil and criminal matters in the Chinese legal system. Although *Tang Ley Su Yi* is silent on the conflict of civil laws, it clearly specifies that the foreign law shall apply to the dispute between foreigners from the same state. *Song Xing Tong* (宋刑統) is a verbatim adoption of the Tang Code.[22] The *Ming* dynasty was influenced by the way Mongolian treated barbarians in the *Yuan* dynasty. The liberal *Tang* regulations were thus altered. A provision in *Da Ming Lu* (大明律) says, 'When the untamed commit crimes, the Ming's law shall apply', switching from *Jus sanguinis* (the Nationality Principle) to *Jus soli* (the Territoriality Principle).[23] Following the Ming Code, *Da Qing Lu Li*

[16] A Mazahéri, *La Route De La Soei 315* (Sheng Geng tr, China Tibetology Publishing House, 2014).

[17] H-J Pak, *Da Tang Di Guo De Yi Chan: Hu Han Tong He Ji Duo Min Zu Guo Jia De Xing Cheng [Legacy of the Great Tang Empire: Han-barbarian Integration and the Form of Multi-ethnic State]* (Taipei, Gūsa Press, 2020) 64–65, 79, 83; J-H Yen, 'Lun "Hua Wai Ren" Yu Wen Hua Ren Tong – Yi Ba Shi Ji De Du Tang Ri Ben Ren Wei Li' ['A Study on "Persons beyond the Pale of Civilization" and Their Cultural Identification: Using Japanese Who Went to China in the 8th Century as Example'] in M-S Kao (eds), *Tang Lu Yu Guo Jia Zhi Xu [Tang Code and National Order]* (Taipei, New Sharing Culture Enterprise, 2013) 312.

[18] 'The untamed' refers to both foreigners outside the nation and the minority inside the nation at that time.

[19] W-H Tang and Y Huang, *Qing Dai Guang Zhou She Wai Si Fa Wen Ti Yan Jiu 1644–1840 [Research on Juridical Questions Involving Foreign Elements in Guangzhou in Qing Dynasty 1644–1840]* (Beijing, China Social Sciences Press, 2009) 209.

[20] Z Wuji, *Tang Ley Su Yi* (653) 14.

[21] ibid.

[22] *Song Xing Tong* provides: 'When it comes to the barbarian, for the dispute arising between themselves, their laws are applicable; for the dispute between Chinese and barbarian, Song's law is applicable.'

[23] *Da Ming Lu* (Ming Code) provides that 'Whenever barbarians commit crimes, Ming Code shall apply.'

(大清律例) also provides that, 'Whenever the untamed commit crimes, the Qing's law shall apply.' The next time this provision was changed again was at the end of the *Qing* dynasty and the beginning of the ROC.

Private international law is a subject that has always been valued from the *Qing* dynasty to the beginning of the ROC.

In 1918, the Application of Law Act was promulgated by the Beijing Government. It is the earliest legislation of private international law in the ROC. It is divided into general principles, provisions regarding man, family, succession, property, the formality of juridical acts, and appendix. There were seven chapters with 27 Articles in total. At that time, the legislation in other countries usually incorporated private international law into their civil codes. In France, private international law was first promulgated at the beginning of the Civil Code in the eighteenth century, with three Articles in one chapter. The legislation was followed by several countries in Europe after that. There were four Articles for private international law in Spain, and six Articles each in Austria, Holland, and Portugal. It was provided in the implementation act of the civil code in Germany with 25 Articles. In Japan, there was an individual act called *Hou-Rei* (法例) with 30 Articles. Article 1 provided the effect of the announcement and enforcement of the act, and Article 2 provided the effect of the custom. These were the general principles of civil code. There were 28 Articles related to private international law. Compared to other countries, the Application of Law Act of the ROC was indeed the most complete and detailed legislation at that time.

Most Taiwanese scholars support the opinion that foreign laws should be deemed as law, rather than simply facts, for several reasons. Some suggest that Taiwanese courts apply foreign laws because those laws are chosen by the choice of law rules in the Choice of Law Act, not subject to the parties' own measures. The foreign laws, therefore, have the nature of law. Others refer to syllogism, claiming that there should be a valid law as the major premise, and then we can conclude that it is applicable. The phase one of dealing with matters involving foreign elements is to use syllogism to conclude that the foreign law should apply in those cases. In phase two of reviewing matters involving foreign elements, the foreign law is used as the major premise, the facts as the minor premise, and then the conclusion is therefore structured. From the process above, a foreign law should have the nature of law, or it cannot be the major premise.[24] Some scholars further explain that applying foreign laws should be purposeful. The foreign laws should be deemed principles of law in accordance with the national public policy so that they can fit in the democratic system and be in line with the principle of *jus soli* (the principle of territoriality).[25]

Article 283 of the Taiwan Code of Civil Procedure (TCCP) provides,

> A party has the burden of proof with regard to customs, local ordinances, and foreign laws which are unknown to the court. Notwithstanding, the court may investigate on its own initiative.

Given that the Article is placed in the evidence section of the civil procedural law, it is inevitably disputable that the foreign laws are viewed as a fact in the Taiwan legal system. Nevertheless, according to the main idea of the original legislative explanation, the contents of the foreign laws are unknown to domestic courts, and thus the parties should provide

[24] Y-C Su, *Guo Ji Si Fa [Private International Law]*, 5th edn (Taipei, Wu-Nan Book, 2008) 93–94.
[25] Lin (n 9) 114.

evidence to the court. The methods to prove the foreign laws were not limited. The court could also investigate the contents of the foreign law itself by sending inquiry letters to institutions of the Ministry of Justice.[26] Moreover, the provision clearly stated that the parties would need to provide evidence for the foreign laws only when the court has no knowledge of them. The provision does not confine the court to review a case based only on the parties' submitted foreign law. Foreign law, in legal practice in Taiwan, is not only a 'fact' that the parties should prove.

Supreme Court Civil Judgment Tai-Kang-Tzu No 81 of 2005 deals with a matter regarding intercountry adoption. It points out that 'the foreign law does not lose its nature'. It is inclined to confirm that foreign law should be regarded as law rather than a mere fact.

In conclusion, from the scholars' point of view and legal practice in Taiwan, it is shown that foreign law is not regarded as a pure fact. Instead, it is regarded as law, and the parties should assist in investigating its contents.

B. Confirmation of Foreign Law

i. Proof and Confirmation of Foreign Law: 'iura novit curia' *or 'the Party's* onus probandi'

When hearing matters involving foreign elements, is it the court that should confirm the contents of the foreign law, or should the parties bear the burden of proof? It depends on the matters' nature. The procedure which applies will vary based on the nature of the matters involving foreign elements. Foreign-related property and identity matters are processed by the adversary system. Take international marriage matters and paternity litigation matters for example. In these matters, the polemic doctrine in the Civil Procedure Law shall apply, and the parties shall be responsible for the collection of evidence.[27] In contrast, in foreign-related family identity lawsuits and non-contentious cases that adopt the principle of ex officio, the court shall investigate the foreign laws at its discretion just like it collects other facts and evidence in accordance with the procedural principles of law and the parties simply bear the duty of cooperation. As for the property lawsuits where the adversary system applies, there are different opinions on how to prove or confirm the foreign laws as discussed below.

Regarding the dispute of who shall bear the duty to prove the foreign law, there are two theories. One is that the parties shall bear the burden of proof, and the other is the judge shall confirm the foreign law at its discretion. The former deems that the foreign law has the nature as a fact, and the parties shall bear the burden of proof regarding the facts. The latter

[26] ibid 123.

[27] Take the Taiwan Supreme Court Civil Judgment Tai-Shang-Tzu No 1305 of 1997 for example. The appellant claimed that the contract in dispute was formed and signed in Hong Kong, and thus Hong Kong law shall apply. However, the court ruled that based on the Choice of Law Act, Taiwanese laws shall apply when the accident happened in Taiwan. This ruling is affirmed later in the Taiwan Supreme Court Civil Judgment Tai-Zai-Tzu No 118 of 1997. The cases demonstrate that parties are responsible to investigate the foreign laws and present such laws in court, where the court has the discretion to interpret and apply the Choice of the Law Act and determine the applicable law.

considers the foreign law to be a law, and thus the judge shall be responsible for confirmation of the foreign law because of the principle of *iura novit curia*.[28] Article 283 of TCCP provides, 'A party has the burden of proof with regard to customs, local ordinances, and foreign laws which are unknown to the court. Notwithstanding, the court may investigate on its own initiative.' Literally, it does not provide that the parties shall bear the burden of proof concerning the foreign law, and it does not insist that judges know all the contents of the foreign law. Therefore, the scholars mostly support that the court shall or may investigate the foreign law at its discretion, and the parties shall cooperate to prove the contents of the foreign law.[29]

Although there is a dispute between theories regarding the burden of proof of foreign law, there are many decisions stating that the court shall investigate the contents of foreign law at its discretion. This is an embodiment of the principle of *iura novit curia*. The Supreme Court Civil Judgment Tai-Kang-Tzu No 81 of 2005 deals with intercountry adoption. When applying a foreign law, it states that 'foreign law does not lose its nature'. The Supreme Court Civil Judgment Tai-Shang-Tzu No 2192 of 1990 deals with a dispute of international transaction, where the court applied the Sale of Goods Act of UK. Lower courts (both High Court and District Court) were instructed by the Supreme Court to investigate the contents of the Sale of Goods Act of UK at its discretion. Another example is Taiwan High Court Civil Decision Kang-Tzu No 1293 of 2000 concerning the approval of an adoption. The court applied the Adoption Act of Malaysia. The lower court (ie the District Court) was also asked by the Taiwan High Court to investigate into the contents of the Adoption Act of Malaysia at its discretion.[30]

As can be seen, Taiwan in principle follows *iura novit curia* and it is the court that shall investigate and confirm the foreign law.

ii. Investigation of Foreign Law

There are two issues regarding the investigation of foreign law. One is the rules of evidence, and the other is the methods used for investigation.

For the rules of evidence, there is a distinguishment between strict proof and free proof in the civil procedure in Taiwan. Strict proof is based on a structure of confrontational legal system. It means that the court shall only render a judgment based on the evidence and the facts proved by such evidence. The facts and the evidence, including witnesses and documents, can only become case-in-chief evidence after being presented and debated or confronted in court. When handling evidence, the parties and the court shall follow the provisions and investigation procedures expressly set out by law. On the other hand, free proof is based on a non-confrontational structure. It usually applies to non-contentious matters, where the court has much discretion to determine how to handle evidence and the investigation procedure. How the evidence is used and investigated is not provided in law, but at the court's discretion. There is no limit to what kind of evidence could be admitted,

[28] Ma (n 10) 225; T-Z Liu and J-C Chen, *Guo Ji Si Fa [Private International Law]*, 6th edn (Taipei, San Min Book, 2018) 199–201.

[29] Ma (n 10) 225–26; Liu and Chen (n 28) 201. See also H-K Tsai, *Guo Ji Si Fa Shi Li Yan Xi [Case Study on Private International Law]* (Taipei, San Min Book, 2018) 11.

[30] Tsai (n 29) 11.

and there is no required investigation procedure regarding presentation or confrontation. Therefore, when the court adopts the free proof procedure to investigate the evidence and determine the facts, it can call the parties or witnesses by phone or investigate the documents at its discretion, and then render a judgment based on such evidence.[31]

Strict proof applies to civil litigation proceedings and family litigation matters due to the litigation structure adopted, namely the adversary system. As for family non-contentious matters, the scholars tend to think the free proof procedure is adoptable because the non-contentious matters proceedings are deemed to be more flexible, efficient, prospective, purposeful, and are at the court's discretion, especially in those cases that the court takes the initiative. In addition, free proof is also adoptable for the procedural requirements in non-litigation proceedings.[32] Other scholars believe that it depends on the needs of the types of family non-contentious matters. For matters that need speedy resolution, free proof should apply.[33]

Foreign law can be investigated by questioning witnesses or examining documents. If strict proof is adopted, the investigation procedure provided in the TCCP, namely provisions starting from Article 298 or those starting from Article 341, shall apply. Article 320 grants the parties the right to conduct an examination. The court can determine the authenticity of a foreign public document at its discretion according to Article 356. If free proof is adopted, the court can conduct any investigation method that it deems appropriate, including searching the contents of the foreign law on the internet itself. Some other scholars point out that since the contents of the foreign law are not known to the domestic courts, it should be provided by the parties.[34] In this situation, the ways to prove are not restricted. The court can send letters of inquiry to judicial institutions to investigate the contents of the foreign law on its own initiative.[35]

Article 283 is placed in the evidence chapter of the TCCP. Thus, in Taiwan's practice, strict proof like investigating foreign laws by examining expert witnesses, and free proof like reading books and documents on its own, are both adopted. Taiwan has referred to German legislation in its judicial practice. Article 293 of the German Code of Civil Procedure provides that when the court investigates a foreign law, the legal evidence is not limited to the evidence provided by the parties. The means to investigate the evidence should be determined by the court based on the discretion in accordance with the procedural obligation of the court ('*pflichtmäßig*') to adopt strict proof or free proof. The wording 'discretion in accordance with the procedural obligation of the court' means the contents of the foreign law could be proved and confirmed by adopting such a method of proof. The free proof is adopted in the investigation procedure of this evidence. It is not required that the probative value of the evidence acquired this way reach preponderance of the evidence. The contents of the foreign law can be admitted once the evidence is obvious.[36] After the court exercises its discretion to determine whether to adopt strict proof or free proof procedures, it

[31] S-M Chiang, *Fei Song Shi Jian Fa Xin Lun [New Theory of Non-Contentious Matter Law]*, 2nd edn (Taipei, New Sharing Culture Enterprise, 2013) 142.

[32] ibid 153–54.

[33] K-L Shen, 'Cheng Xu Bao Zhang Yu Dang Shi Ren' ['Procedural Guarantees and Parties'] in *Min Shi Su Song Fa [Civil Procedure]* (Taipei, Angle Publishing, 2012) 39.

[34] Lin (n 9) 123.

[35] ibid.

[36] H Prütting and M Gehrlein (eds), *ZPO Kommentar*, 5th edn (Köln, Luchterhand Verlag, 2013) 872.

shall then follow the evidence investigation procedure. If the court rules that it will adopt strict proof procedure including witnesses' investigation, the formal evidence investigation procedure shall apply, and the parties shall be given the right to examine or argue.[37] If the court decides to adopt free proof, there is no need to apply the above-mentioned procedure. The Taiwan Supreme Court Civil Judgment Tai-Shang-Tzu No 2393 of 2005 can be an example for free proof procedure. It states that

> … Lodgment Guide provides that when the beneficiary of the security has consented to the return of the lodgment, a consent form submitted by the beneficiary of the security and a seal certificate shall be provided. For legal persons or organizations, relevant evidentiary documents or the identity certification of its representative or administration shall also be provided. Absent such consent form, one can go to the public lodgment office with the beneficiary of the security along with her National ID Card, and jointly make written records of consent. This rule is intended to ensure that the beneficiary of the security has indeed agreed to return the lodgment. Free proof procedure shall apply. Therefore, by ruling that the fact that Tsai-Yun Zhuo provided the appellant and its representative's seal certificates issued by Taipei City Government Economic Affairs Bureau had already verified the identity of the appellant and its representative … the original judgment did not violate the law.

There are several methods to investigate foreign law:

Expert and Specialist Consultation – there are regulations regarding experts in the TCCP, but no expert witnesses. The chapter starting from Article 324 is specifically for experts. The court can choose a specialist in foreign law as an expert and investigate the foreign law by examining the expert's statement. There is a system of expert witnesses provided in Article 17 of the Commercial Case Adjudication Act. Article 1 of the 'Working Guidelines for Expert Consultation' promulgated by the Judicial Yuan in 2000 provides,

> The working guidelines are promulgated in order to improve the correctness of the court's judgment in terms of determining facts and applying laws, to conduct enforcement proceeding speedily, to protect parties' interests, and to increase the citizens' reliance on the judicial system.

Article 2 provides that in specific matters, the court can conduct expert consultation at its discretion. When reviewing all types of matters, the court can ask an expert to assist with confirming the contents of the foreign law based on provisions about expert witnesses and expert consultation system provided in the guidelines.

The expert witness system is adopted in some courts' practices. The Supreme Court Civil Judgment Tai-Shang-Tzu No 1201 of 2018 states that the second instance court had an expert witness to confirm the contents of adoption laws in Japan. It said

> … There are regular adoptions and special adoptions in the Japanese adoption system. Only in special adoptions, the rights and duties between an adopted child and his or her natural parents are terminated. This regulation has been enforced since 1988 and is found in Article 817-2 of the Civil Code of Japan. According to the expert witness Xue-Ren Deng's statement,[38] regular adoptions in Japan do not terminate the rights and duties between the adopted person and his or her biological parents, including the right to inherit or support obligations. The adopted person is obliged to support both the adoptive parents and the biological parents. However, if the adopted

[37] ibid 873f.

[38] Xue-Ren Deng is a professor at Central Police University.

person is a minor, the adoptive parents have the priority to exercise parental rights over the biological parents. Here, no matter applying Taiwanese law or Japanese law, the adopted person's national law ie Japanese law shall apply to the relationship regarding adoption. Where either the husband or the wife terminates the adoption, the adoption relationship remains effective between the other spouse and the adopted person. The above is confirmed by Xue-Ren Deng.[39]

Legal opinion – confirming the contents of foreign law by free proof is a method allowed by the Taiwan Code of Civil Procedure. A legal opinion is not a document that records facts but a document to prove the foreign law. Therefore, a legal opinion is not a document provided in Article 341 of the TCCP.[40] The legal opinion can be submitted by the foreign law experts like professors at school, lawyers, or any national law experts that are familiar with foreign law. The legal opinion is not required to be verified since the free proof is adopted.

In practice, there was once a legal opinion submitted by a foreign law firm to confirm the contents of the foreign law. The Taiwan Hsinchu District Court Civil Judgment Zhong-Su-Tzu No 44 of 2007 involves German regulations regarding limited liability companies.[41] According to the judgment, the plaintiff once submitted two legal opinions provided by a lawyer in a German law firm to prove the regulations in Germany. The court states that the plaintiff had already submitted the legal opinion, and that the defendant simply argued that the legal opinion should not be admitted but did not state substantively why it should not be admitted. The legal opinions were ruled to be admitted as the reference of the case.

Taiwan Supreme Court Civil Judgment Tai-Shang-Tzu No 447 of 2009 involves a distribution agreement where Israeli law is applied.[42] The parties mutually agreed that Israeli law would apply but were having a dispute about whether Israeli law provides that the interpretation of a contract should be subject to the real intention of the parties. One party submitted a legal opinion provided by an Israeli lawyer to prove that Israeli law provides that the interpretation of a contract should be referred to the parties' real intention. The judgment said,

[39] The judgment is available at: judgment.judicial.gov.tw/FJUD/data.aspx?ty=JD&id=TPSV,107%2c%e5%8f%b0%e4%b8%8a%2c1201%2c20181205%2c1. The quoted contents are between lines 71–80.

[40] Art 341 of the TCCP provides, 'A document must be produced when it is identified to be introduced as documentary evidence.'

[41] In this case, the plaintiff claimed that it is the debt clearing administrator of the German company, since the German company had started the debt clearing procedure, but it had made payment to the defendant. Therefore, it asked the defendant to return such payment. The issues in this case include: 1. Which country's law is applicable? 2. Does the plaintiff have the legal standing to file the suit on behalf of the German company? 3. Shall the court apply the German regulations regarding limited liability companies? 4. Has the defendant violated the German regulations regarding limited liability companies? 5. Is the plaintiff entitled to €1,727,969.88 based on Arts 30, 31, 32 of German regulations regarding limited liability companies? The judgment is available at: judgment.judicial.gov.tw/FJUD/data.aspx?ty=JD&id=SCDV,96%2c%e9%87%8d%e8%a8%b4%2c44%2c20090930%2c5.

[42] The plaintiff claimed that: 'the parties entered into a business plan contract (Business Proposal) on June 30, 2005, and then signed License and Distribution Agreement in August of the same year. They agreed that the plaintiff will give authorization of sets of software to the appellee. According to Article 1.4, 3.1 of Appendix A – Business Engagement, the appellee shall assure to obtain at least 100,000 sets of computer software authorization … and according to Article 4.3 of License and Distribution Agreement, the appellee shall make the payment to the plaintiff within 30 days after the plaintiff issues an invoice.' The first instance court dismissed the plaintiff's claim. The plaintiff appealed. After being reviewed by High Court and Supreme Court, the case was remanded to the Taiwan High Court. Taiwan High Court Civil Judgment Shang-Geng-Erh-Tzu No 22 of 2010 ruled that the defendant shall make the payment to the plaintiff, and the Supreme Court Civil Judgment Tai-Shang-Tzu No 131 of 2011 affirmed the High Court's decision. The judgment is available at: judgment.judicial.gov.tw/FJUD/data.aspx?ty=JD&id=TPSV%2c98%2c%e5%8f%b0%e4%b8%8a%2c447%2c20090319.

> Here, in Article 13.2 of the distribution agreement between the parties, there is an agreement that the Israeli law shall apply to this agreement (Choice of Law. The parties agree that this Agreement shall be governed by the laws of the State of Israel.) The original court also confirmed that the Israeli law applies to this case. The dispute seemed to arise from the interpretation of the contract between the parties, and the original court admitted the legal opinion provided by an Israeli lawyer Erez Tikolsker submitted by the appellate. In the original court, the section D of the legal opinion provided by an Israeli lawyer Gilad Wekselman ....

The Supreme Court affirms that this method of proof is valid but only further requested that the parties provide the Israeli Supreme Court's judgments cited in the legal opinion.

Entrust the investigation to the Ministry of Foreign Affairs – where the evidence is to be taken in a foreign country, the evidence-taking may, according to Article 295 of the TCCP, be entrusted to be conducted by the competent jurisdictional authorities of that foreign country or the relevant Taiwanese ambassador, minister envoy or consul, or other institution or organisation in that foreign country authorised to do so. This provision may also apply to the investigation of foreign law. The former part of Article 103 of the Directions for Civil Litigations states:

> To entrust the investigation to competent jurisdictional authorities of such country or the relevant ROC ambassador/minister envoy/consul or other institution or organization in that country authorized to do so, one should report the request to the Taiwan High Court for referral to the Ministry of Foreign Affairs.

Thus, when the court is to entrust the investigation of foreign law to the authorities of foreign affairs, it should report the request to the Taiwan High Court, which would then transfer it to the Ministry of Foreign Affairs. The Ministry of Foreign Affairs will then require the relevant ROC ambassador/minister envoy/consul or other institutions or organisations to assist with the investigation. As for the investigation of the content of Mainland China law, since the 'Cross-Strait Joint Crime-Fighting and Judicial Mutual Assistance Agreement' is promulgated, the court should refer the investigation to the Department of International and Cross-Strait Legal Affairs under the Ministry of Justice according to the Agreement.[43] As for the investigation of the content of Vietnam law, the 'Agreement between the Taipei Economic and Cultural Office in Vietnam and the Vietnam Economic and Cultural Office in Taipei on Judicial Assistance in Civil Matters' was signed. To investigate Vietnamese law, the court should request the Ministry of Justice, the executive authorities in the Agreement, to assist with the communication.[44]

There is no required form regarding the methods to present the contents of a foreign law through the relevant ROC ambassador/minister envoy/consul or other institution or organization in that country authorised to do so. Taiwan Supreme Court Civil Judgment Tai-Shang-Tzu No 2064 of 1986 held that

> Article 295, Paragraph 1 of Taiwan Code of Civil Procedure provides that where the evidence is to be taken in a foreign country, the evidence-taking shall be entrusted to be conducted by the competent jurisdictional authorities of such country or the relevant ROC ambassador/minister envoy/consul. The entrustment of the evidence-taking to the relevant ROC ambassador based

[43] Judicial Yuan Letter Shao-Chia-Erh-Tzu No 1060017706 dated 9 August 2017.
[44] Judicial Yuan Letter Mi-Tai-Ting-Shao-Chia-Erh-Tzu No 1020000165 dated 17 January 2013.

> on this provision is valid no matter what methods are adopted. The investigation report made by the ambassador/minister envoy/consul, the documents provided by witnesses, the records of the examination of the witnesses who failed to sign an affidavit to tell the truth, etc. can all be admitted as evidence and the free evaluation of such is decided by the court. For the countries without diplomatic ties, the court can also entrust the investigation of the evidence to the relevant ROC authorities in those countries.

The contents of the foreign law provided by the parties – another method for the parties to prove the contents of foreign law is to provide the writings or publications of a foreign scholar. The Supreme Court Civil Judgement Tai-Shang-Tzu No 1201 of 2018 deals with a dispute regarding the right to inheritance. The plaintiff claimed that he was born to an ancestor and was adopted by a Japanese couple on 28 May 1979. He was deprived of Taiwanese nationality on 4 February 1998, and acquired Japanese nationality by naturalisation on 7 April of the same year. On 18 February 2000, the adoptive relationship between him and the adoptive father was terminated, while the adoptive relationship between him and the adoptive mother still existed. According to Article 18 (current Article 54) of the Choice of Law Act at that time, the Japanese Civil Code applied. The application of Articles 809 and 810 of the Japanese Civil Code and the contents in the publication *Essential of the Civil Code* authored by a famous legal scholar Ume Kenjiro showed that the relationship between the plaintiff and his natural parents would not be affected by adoption. The Supreme Court vacated the original judgment, reasoning that, 'according to *Essential of the Civil Code* authored by Ume Kenjiro, a well-known Japanese jurist, the relationship between an adopted child and his or her natural parents is not terminated after the adoption'. However, while the Supreme Court introduced and explained the contents of Japanese law, it did not use the foreign scholar's book submitted by the party to evidence such contents. The book was not cited in the judgment.

Taiwan High Court Civil Judgment Zhong-Shang-Geng-Erh-Tzu No 64 of 2019 deals with a matter where the plaintiff seeks damages. The plaintiff claimed that Chuan Hsiang Company violated the agreement between it and the plaintiff, and the plaintiff sued it in the US District Court of Northern District of Illinois Eastern Division, where the court ruled that Chuan Hsiang Company should pay US$4,394,676 to the plaintiff. Chuan Hsiang Company was dissolved on 30 April 2012. The appellee was the liquidator of Chuan Hsiang Company. He violated Articles 84 and 334 of the Taiwanese Company Act and did not recover the debt of 34,477,878 NTD from the third party, Grand Land International Ltd (GL). It then caused damages to the plaintiff since his claims on Chuan Hsiang Company's estate were not satisfied. The court further recognised the contents of a foreign law provided by the parties and cited it in the judgments. The judgment said,

> The appellee provided the former Article 113 of Samoa Companies Act amended on April 7, 2014: 'Accounts to be kept – (1A) An international company shall keep such accounts and records as the directors consider necessary or desirable in order to reflect the financial position of the company.' From this article, we can infer that when GL was founded, the then Samoa Companies Act required the company to reserve the accounts and records that the directors consider necessary or desirable to reflect the financial status of the company. Therefore, GL should prepare the records and documents that can reflect the financial status of the company as a matter of course.

The Investigation Ex Officio by Court – the court can investigate the contents of foreign law at its discretion. The investigation methods include reviewing the books in all courts' libraries and entering the Judicial Yuan's website to look up the database of foreign laws constructed by the Judicial Yuan. This database provides Mandarin translations of foreign laws in the section 'Translation of Foreign Laws.'

Some foreign laws that the court investigates on its own initiative are obvious or have already been known to the court and are therefore admitted as evidence. In Taiwan, these laws are admitted as evidence according to Article 283 of the TCCP. However, to protect the parties' right to be heard, the court shall afford the parties an opportunity to be heard regarding the foreign laws investigated ex officio by the court.

iii. Institutions or Organisations Authorised to Investigate Foreign Laws

The institutions and organisations that investigate foreign laws are mainly research institutes or universities and colleges. The professors that are familiar with foreign laws and Chinese law are hired in the institute of law in Academia Sinica[45] and law schools in universities and colleges. However, there is no research or academic organisation focusing on comparative law. The Chinese Comparative Law Association was formed in 1970, which was an academic organisation, and was registered as a corporation. Yet the corporation was renamed the 'Taiwan Law Society' in 1994 and completed its registration in 1999. From then on, there are no organisations focusing on comparative law. Nevertheless, there are systems for people to look up foreign laws in the Chinese Arbitration Association (CAA), China International Economic and Trade Arbitration Commission (CIETAC) under the China Council for the Promotion of International Trade (CCPIT), and the Arbitration Center Across the Straits (ACAS) in Pingtan County.

To make it more convenient for judges to investigate foreign laws, the Judicial Yuan has posted on its website all the foreign laws that judges have ever inquired about by letter (under digital library/a list of foreign laws that have been requested) for all judges' reference.[46]

iv. The Binding Force of the Investigation of Foreign Laws in Court

Foreign laws are matters that can be proved by evidence. Whether the evidence is sufficient to confirm the contents of the foreign law is determined by the judge case by case. In practice, the contents of foreign laws are determined by the evidence provided by the parties or the court that investigates it ex officio.

Hsinchu District Court Civil Judgment Zhong-Su-Tzu No 44 of 2007[47] dealt with a case regarding an unjust enrichment of a German company. Since whether the party had the standing (whether the party was an eligible party) was at issue, German law needed to be inspected. Though the applicable law was Taiwanese, German law should apply to the standing issue.[48] Each instance court reviewed the contents of the German law through the evidence obtained by investigation. The judgment said,

[45] See www.sinica.edu.tw.

[46] See www.judicial.gov.tw/tw/cp-1954-22-dfce6-1.html.

[47] Please refer to fn 37 for the details of this case.

[48] Art 14 of Choice of Law Act provides: 'The following internal affairs of an alien legal person are governed by its national law: .... (5) The representative of the legal person and the limitation on his/her power of representation. ...' Therefore, whether the party is the eligible representative here should be determined by German law.

> The Der Deutsche Bundestag has passed the new German Insolvency Law and its enforcement law on April 21, 1994, which has come into effect since January 1, 1999. The German Insolvency Law replaced the old laws (ie the Bankruptcy Law and the Settlement Law), which was a two-tier system including bankruptcy and settlement legislation. The united insolvency procedure is hereby adopted. According to Section 80, Paragraph 1 of the German Insolvency Law, 'Upon the opening of the insolvency proceedings the debtor's right to manage and transfer the insolvency estate shall be vested in the insolvency administrator.' Thus, the insolvency administrator has the power to dispose of or manage another person's property based on his qualification bestowed by the German Insolvency Law, and as a matter of course, he has standing. Therefore, after the German company Gi-XXX commenced the insolvency procedure, it lost the right of disposition and management to the insolvent foundation's property, and the insolvency administrator (similar to the bankruptcy administrator in Taiwan's Bankruptcy Law) should be the plaintiff or defendant in the suits against the insolvent foundation. As such, though the plaintiff is not the subject in the privity of the subject matter, he has the power to dispose of or manage another person's property based on his qualification bestowed by the German Insolvency Law and hence has standing. In conclusion, the plaintiff is verified to have validly filed the suit as the German company Gi-XXX's insolvency administrator.

The case was appealed but affirmed by Taiwan High Court Civil Judgment Zhong-Shang-Tzu No 683 of 2009. It agreed with the Hsinchu District Court's opinion and only revised the translation of the title of the law, saying '… The Der Deutsche Bundestag has passed the new Bankruptcy Law (*Insolvenzordung*, also translated as "German Insolvency Law") and its enforcement law on April 21, 1994.'

The Taiwan Supreme Court Civil Judgment Tai-Shang-Tzu No 447 of 2009[49] involves a distribution agreement where Israeli law was mutually agreed to be applied. The issue was whether the real intention of the parties should be sought in terms of the interpretation of the contracts according to Israeli law. Although the parties submitted a legal opinion provided by an Israeli lawyer to prove the contents of the Israeli law, the Supreme Court deemed there was a need to further investigate Israeli law and remanded the case back to the Taiwan High Court, asking for further investigation. The judgment states,

> … the paragraph 15 of part (D) legal analysis in the legal opinion submitted by the Israeli lawyer Gilad Wekselman provided that: according to the Israeli law, in the interpretation of a commercial contract, the parties' real intention must be sought (referring to Article 25(a) of the Contract law). The parties' real intention refers to the common goals, purposes, benefits, and plans that the parties intend to achieve (*The State of Israel v. Apropim Shikun Veyezum (1991) Ltd*). In paragraph 25, it said: regarding the relationship between the Israel law and the appellee's interpretation of Article 4.2, the Israel Supreme Court's opinions are cited. The Associate Justice H. Cohen stated in *Marcaz Wolobelski and others v. Hàopotropos Lénechasei Nefkadim and others* that … , and the Associate Justice Berenzon stated in *Israel Halevi Segal v. Georgini Magi Ltd* that …. These laws and judicial cases that can apply in this case have already been provided. The original court erred when it did not investigate whether the laws and the cases are real but, using them as the basis, directly rendered the judgment that is unfavorable to the appellate.

Therefore, we can conclude that the legal opinion submitted by a lawyer is not absolutely binding.

[49] Please refer to fn 38 for the details of this case.

v. Credibility Confirmation System after Investigation of Foreign Laws

There are no restrictions on the methods of the investigation of foreign laws. It can be conducted by parties providing documents, by experts providing legal opinions, by the court appointing expert witnesses or entrusting organisations or associations to investigate. There is no order of precedence between the legal effects of these methods of proof.[50] However, to ensure the parties' right to be heard, for the evidence being investigated through strict proof, the procedure set out in the Code of Civil Procedure should be followed. That is, to give the parties opportunities to review documents, examine the experts and make arguments. For the evidence obtained by free proof, the parties should still have the opportunities to review documents and argue. The court should also use these methods of proof to review the contents of the foreign laws repeatedly so that the correctness of the investigation can be ensured.

vi. Bearing of Investigation Expenses of Foreign Laws

The basic principle regarding the bearing of litigation expenses in civil procedure in Taiwan is set forth in the Supreme Court Civil Decision Tai-Kang-Tzu No 520 of 2012,[51] which said,

> The parties ask the court to exercise the public authority to protect their private rights. When it comes to the court rulings, the non-gratuitous principle is adopted, and the parties shall bear the litigation expenses. The litigation expenses are divided as court costs and costs other than court costs. The costs other than court costs are, as a general rule, calculated as actual out-of-pocket expenses.

Article 78 of the TCCP provides that the losing party shall bear the litigation expenses. The expenses of foreign law investigations are part of the litigation expenses. Though it should be paid in advance by the party requesting the investigation, the losing party shall in principle bear the costs after the judgment is rendered. Besides, Article 79 of the TCCP provides that, in cases of a partial victory or a partial defeat, the court may, in its discretion, order the litigation expenses to be borne by both parties in a certain proportion; or by a particular party alone, or order both parties separately to bear the litigation expenses they incurred respectively.

The losing party shall, as a rule of thumb, bear the costs to investigate foreign laws that are deemed as litigation expenses. However, if the costs to investigate foreign laws are incurred due to inappropriate litigation acts of the prevailing party, the court may order the prevailing party to bear the litigation expenses. Therefore, Article 81 of the TCCP provides that

> The court may, in its discretion, order the prevailing party to bear the litigation expenses incurred in full or in part for the following: 1. An act performed by the prevailing party which is unnecessary for asserting or defending its rights; 2. An act performed by the defeated party which is necessary for asserting or defending its rights in accordance with the phase of the proceedings reached at the time.

[50] Liu and Chen (n 28) 206.

[51] This decision deals with the litigation expenses sharing between the parties. The decision is available at: judgment.judicial.gov.tw/FJUD/data.aspx?ty=JD&id=TPSV,101%2c%e5%8f%b0%e6%8a%97%2c520%2c20120627.

Article 82 further provides,

> Where a party has failed timely to present means of attack or defense, or to meet a specified date or period, or otherwise delayed the proceeding by reason of whatever cause imputable to such party, the court may order such party to bear the litigation expenses incurred from the delay, in full or in part, irrespective of his/her victory.

Whether the costs to investigate foreign laws are part of the litigation expenses specified in Article 78 of the TCCP depends on the nature of the method of evidence. If those are not deemed as litigation expenses, the expenses shall be borne by the party that initiates the investigation. Whether the costs are deemed as litigation expenses concerns Article 77-23 of the TCCP, which shall include 'taxable fees for photocopies, video recording, transcripts, translation, daily fees, travel expenses of witnesses and expert witnesses, and other fees and disbursements necessary for the proceeding items'. The court can appoint an expert witness to investigate foreign laws, and the expert witness may claim daily fees, travel expenses, and reasonable compensation according to Article 338 of the TCCP. Therefore, the daily fees, travel expenses and compensation are all considered litigation expenses. Translation fees are listed as an example of litigation expenses in Article 77-23 of the TCCP.[52] According to the same article, if the translation of the contents of foreign laws is necessary for the legal proceedings, it should still be deemed as litigation expenses. In practice, the legal opinions submitted by scholars or experts are means of attack or defence employed by the parties, and the fees incurred therefrom are not litigation expenses.

The Judicial Yuan promulgated the 'Outlines for Compensations for Witness and Expert Witness Received for Their Services, Travels and Testaments'[53] and 'Outlines for Compensations for Photocopies, Video Recording, Transcripts and Translation' to standardise the regulations of the bearing of the costs.[54] Article 3 of the former outlines stipulates, 'The daily fees for witnesses and expert witnesses are five hundred NT [New Taiwan] dollars per trip.' Article 4 provides,

> The transportation fees for witnesses and expert witnesses are compensated depending on the means of transportation. The means of transportation refers to buses and metro system in cities, and trains, Taiwan High-Speed Rail, buses, steamships for long-distance trips. If there are multiple travel classes, the fees of the median class are compensated. However, people with disabilities or physically challenged may take taxis in cities. Where the witnesses and expert witnesses live in outlying islands or foreign countries and have to take flights, where there are obstacles for transportation by water or land, or where the trial date is closely approaching, they are allowed to travel in economy class.

Article 5 of the latter outlines provides,

> For translation from Mandarin to English and Japanese, three hundred and fifty NT dollars are compensated for every hundred words. For translation to Spanish, French, or German, four hundred and fifty NT dollars are compensated for every hundred words. For all other languages, six hundred and fifty NT dollars are compensated for every hundred words. The words shall be

[52] See the conclusion of the Civil Case Proposal No 44 of the law seminar held by the Taiwan High Court and its Subordinate Courts in 2016.

[53] The regulations are available at: law.moj.gov.tw/LawClass/LawAll.aspx?PCODE=B0010021.

[54] The regulations are available at: law.moj.gov.tw/LawClass/LawAll.aspx?pcode=B0010034.

counted by Mandarin characters. For the word counts of less than a hundred words, it should be rounded up to a hundred words.

C. Interpretation and Application of Foreign Laws

i. Procedural Conditions to Initiate the Application of Foreign Laws

Regarding the application of foreign laws, there is a question of whether the court should decide the issue only after the parties claim it or the court can decide it at its discretion. The answer first depends on the mandatory nature of the choice of law rules, and second depends on the principles of the procedural law that apply in matters involving foreign elements (see section I.A.).

ii. Methods to Interpret and Apply Foreign Laws

Where the Choice of Law Act provides that the law of a foreign state is applicable, it is disputed whether the application of the foreign law should be interpreted using the Taiwanese court's methods of interpretation or following the foreign court's methods of interpretation. Taiwanese scholars believe that the foreign court's methods of interpretation, rather than the local court's methods of interpretation, should be followed.[55] The same principle also applies to situations when the foreign choice of law rules should be applied and interpreted due to remission.[56]

The Taiwan Supreme Court Civil Judgment Tai-Shang-Tzu No 447 of 2009[57] involves a distribution agreement where the parties mutually agreed to apply Israeli law, and there was a dispute on how to apply Israeli law providing that the interpretation of a contract should be subject to the real intention of the parties. The Supreme Court points out that according to the interpretation of Israeli law, it should follow Israeli law and the opinion of the Israeli Supreme Court. The judgment said as follows:

> Paragraph 15 of part (D) legal analysis in the legal opinion submitted by the Israeli lawyer … provided that: according to the Israeli law, in the interpretation of a commercial contract, the parties' real intention must be sought (referring to Article 25(a) of the Contract law). According to the principle of contract interpretation prescribed in *The State of Israel v. Apropim*, the process of contract interpretation is not simply investigating the words showing the parties' real intention. The words in the contract and all the external circumstances should also be taken into consideration. Only in this way can the real intention of the parties be determined … the paragraph 15 of part (D) legal analysis in the legal opinion submitted by the Israeli lawyer … in the original court provided that: according to the Israeli law, in the interpretation of a commercial contract, the parties' real intention must be sought …. The parties' real intention refers to the common goals, purposes, benefits, and plans that the parties intend to achieve (*The State of Israel v. Apropim ShikunVeyezum(1991)Ltd*). In paragraph 25, it said: regarding the relationship between the Israeli law and the appellee's interpretation of Article 4.2, the Israeli Supreme Court's opinions are cited.

[55] Su (n 24) 96–97.
[56] ibid.
[57] Please refer to fn 38 for the details of this case.

> The Associate Justice H. Cohen stated in *Marcaz Wolobelski and others v. Hàopotropos Lénechasei Nefkadim and others*: the contract between the parties should be interpreted as a whole and single document. One should not separate one sentence from the others and interpret it to have a separate meaning, being irrelevant to other articles. The Associate Justice Berenzon stated in *Israel Halevi Segal v. Georgini Magi Ltd*: when interpreting a legal document, do not separate one clause or article from its chapter and interpret it solely, making it irrelevant to other clauses. As the rule of the thumb, interpreting a legal document should be based on the whole document and consider the background already known in that event in order to seek the real intention of the parties …. It seems that the laws and judicial cases that can apply in this case have already been provided. The original court erred when it did not investigate whether the laws and the cases are real but, using them as the basis, directly rendered the judgment that is unfavourable to the appellate.

In the Supreme Court Civil Judgment Tai-Shang-Tzu No 113 of 2010,[58] the following judgment of the Supreme Court Civil Judgment Tai-Shang-Tzu No 447 of 2009, further points out that '… the Israel law shall apply to this case … therefore, the relevant regulations in the Israel law shall apply to the interpretation of the contract at dispute.'

iii. Filling Loopholes when Applying Foreign Laws

Sometimes there are loopholes when applying foreign laws. The loopholes are formed either from the conflict inside the foreign law system or from the conflict between the contents of the foreign law and the public policy in Taiwan. According to Article 8 of the Civil Code, courts in Taiwan can refuse to apply such foreign laws.

Article 8 of the Choice of Law Act provides, 'Where this Act provides that the law of a foreign state is applicable, if the result of such application leads to a violation of the public order or *boni mores* of the ROC, that law of the foreign State is not applied.' Therefore, when the result of the application of the foreign law leads to a violation of the public order or *boni mores* of the ROC, courts in Taiwan will exclude its application, and loopholes are formed. When it comes to the condition of Article 8's application, it is the result of the application of the applicable foreign law that violates the public order or *boni mores* of the ROC, not the regulations of the foreign law itself that violate the public order or *boni mores* of the ROC. Hence, the exclusion of foreign laws' applications should be deemed as an exception.[59] It should be reviewed and decided by judges case by case.[60] The Supreme Court Civil Judgment Tai-Shang-Tzu No 883 of 2012[61] said,

> The parties agree to apply the Holland law. If the Holland law provides that there can be an interest rate of 20% a month, whether Philip Corp. requests Princo Corp. to pay interests based on their agreement violates the public policy or *boni mores* of Taiwan is doubtful.

The Court tends to think that though the regulation regarding an interest rate of 20 per cent a month in the Holland law violates Article 205 of the Civil Code in Taiwan, it does not violate the public order of the ROC.

[58] The judgment is available at: judgment.judicial.gov.tw/FJUD/data.aspx?ty=JD&id=TPSV,99%2c%e5%8f%b0%e4%b8%8a%2c113%2c20100121.

[59] Liu and Chen (n 28) 225 –27.

[60] Ma (n 10) 241.

[61] This judgment deals with a licence agreement between the parties. The dispute arose when one party stopped paying loyalties. The issue was how much interests the other party could collect. The judgment is available at: judgment.judicial.gov.tw/FJUD/data.aspx?ty=JD&id=TPSV,101,%E5%8F%B0%E4%B8%8A,883,20120614.

Where the application of the foreign law is excluded because of a violation of the public order or *boni mores* of the ROC, there are two theoretical opinions regarding how to choose an applicable law. Some advocate that the foreign law should be replaced by the law of the forum,[62] while others claim that other general regulations in that foreign state shall apply.[63]

D. When the Contents of Foreign Law are Unclear

i. Solution to Situation when Foreign Law is Unclear

Both the Choice of Law Act and the TCCP are silent on how to apply a foreign law when it remains unclear after the parties' submission of evidence or after the court's investigation of its contents ex officio according to Article 283. Article 283 of the TCCP provides that the contents of foreign law can be proved by evidence and should be proved by the parties or investigated by the court ex officio. Therefore, a situation when the foreign law is unclear refers to the situation where the foreign law remains unclear even after adequate and careful evidence investigation procedure. Only under this situation can a substitute solution be sought. In Taiwanese judicial practice, the contents of foreign law can be found through evidence investigation, either by the parties providing the contents of the regulations that the foreign governments publicise online or by research documents. Courts can also obtain the contents of a foreign law through diplomatic channels. Although the contents are not perfectly accurate, there has never been a situation where foreign law is unclear, and the court needs to find an alternative solution in practice.

In academic circles, various theories from different countries are introduced to address this issue. They are Request Overruled Theory, Similar Law Application Theory, the Law of the Forum Application Theory, and the Jurisprudence Theory. Request Overruled Theory claims that since the contents of the foreign law cannot be proved, the party's claims based on such contents of the foreign law should be deemed groundless due to the lack of proof, and therefore should be dismissed. Similar Law Application Theory advocates that though the contents of the foreign law cannot be proved, laws in countries with similar legal systems to that foreign country should be sought. The Law of the Forum Application Theory considers that given the contents of the foreign law cannot be proved, and that the plaintiff's claim should not be dismissed promptly, the law of the forum that the court is most familiar with should be applied as the legal basis.[64] Those supporting the jurisprudence theory deem that Article 1 of the Civil Code should be taken into consideration. That is, if there is no applicable law for a civil case, the case may be decided according to customs and jurisprudence (general principles of law).[65]

Scholars in Taiwan have different opinions about this issue. Some think the law of the forum should be applied,[66] while others think a similar law should be applied.[67]

[62] Lin (n 9) 125–26; See also Tsai (n 29) 69.

[63] Ma (n 10) 243; Liu and Chen (n 28) 227; Tse-Tung Ke (G-P Wu (ed)), *Guo Ji Si Fa [Private International Law]* (Taipei, Angle Publishing, 2020) 165.

[64] Ma (n 10) 228–29.

[65] ibid.

[66] Liu and Chen (n 28) 211–12; Lin (n 9) 125.

[67] Ma (n 10) 230; Ke (n 63) 78.

E. Appeal Relief Proceedings

i. Relief Proceedings for Misapplying the Choice of Law Act and the Policy Reasons

The civil and family matters trial system in Taiwan adopts the trial practices of the three-level courts and trials. The first trial is conducted by district courts or district summary courts. The second trial is conducted by high courts or district court collegiate panels. The third trial, in principle, is conducted by the Supreme Court, while civil non-contentious matters are reviewed by high courts. The second instance trial is generally a trial of post facto, which means the reviewing process after the first instance trial, further investigating the evidence that has not been investigated and reviewing the legal claims and defences already submitted. Therefore, the second instance courts have the authority to review whether the first instance courts have applied laws correctly. The third instance trial is a trial of law, meaning only when the second instance court judgment is in contravention of the laws and regulations can the appeal be taken to the third instance court (Article 467 of the TCCP). In December 2021, the Judicial Yuan proposed the Amendment draft to the TCCP. It is a reform of the third instance review system, aiming at adopting a much stricter trial of law system so that the third instance court may 'devote' itself to cases with three elements – cases that are necessary for the continued development of the laws (ie, the continued interpretation of law), to ensure the coherence of decisions, and involve legal opinions that are significant in principle. Only when these three conditions are satisfied can the appeal be taken to the third instance court.

The Choice of Law Act has mandatory nature, which has already been fully explained in section I.A. When the first instance court applies the Choice of Law Act incorrectly, the second instance court has the authority to remand and correct the wrong after the case is appealed. If the second instance court applies the Choice of Law Act incorrectly, it is also deemed to be in contravention of the laws and regulations, and the appeal is allowed to be taken to the third instance court. The third instance court can correct the mistakes of the application made by the second instance court after the case is admitted.

ii. Relief Proceedings for Misapplying a Foreign Law and the Policy Reasons

There are many reasons why a foreign law can be misapplied. If the first or second instance court misapplies the Choice of Law Act and therefore refers to a wrong foreign law, it is deemed as a mistake of the application of the Choice of Law Act. This can be a reason for the appeal to be taken to the third instance court, as stated in section II.E.i. If the first or the second instance court misapplies Article 283 of the TCCP, and there are mistakes regarding the evidence investigation procedure or the burden of proof, the parties can appeal for relief. If the first or second instance court knows the contents of a foreign law, but the dispute arises when interpreting the foreign law, the second instance court can correct the mistake of misapplying foreign laws made by the first instance court based on the court review system in Taiwan. The problem at issue is whether the appeal can be taken when the second instance court misapplied the foreign law, and whether the third instance court can correct the mistake of misapplying foreign laws made by the second instance court.

Influenced by the traditional legal culture and the countries adopting civil law legal systems, Taiwan is inclined to think that foreign law has a nature of law both in academic circles and in legal practice. Details have been explained in section II.A.i. Given that foreign law has the nature of law, when it is misapplied, the appeal should be able to be taken to the third instance court. However, whether the appeal can be taken when the second instance court misapplies the foreign law, and whether the third instance court can correct the mistake of misapplying foreign laws made by the second instance court remains unsolved because Taiwanese scholars have different hypotheses with regard to the powers and functions of the third instance court. Some scholars consider the application of foreign law as the result of applying the domestic private international law, and therefore the misapplication of the foreign law indirectly violates the domestic private international law. This leads to a violation of laws, and the appeal to the third instance court should be granted.[68] Other scholars deem that from the view of deductive reasoning, the Supreme Court should have the review power to unify the interpretation of the application of laws.[69] Still, others claim that the Supreme Court is not only the one applying internal laws but also a guardian of legal order and substantive justice. Any mistakes that occur in the judgment as a major premise in the syllogism should be monitored by the Supreme Court. The application of foreign law, the major premise, should also be reviewed by the Supreme Court.[70] Few scholars advocate that the Supreme Court only holds the power to unify the interpretation of internal laws and has no power over reviewing the misapplication of foreign law. Therefore, the appeal cannot be taken to the third instance court based on the misapplication of the foreign law.[71] Nevertheless, most scholars still support the view that the Supreme Court can review the misapplication of a foreign law made by the second instance court.[72]

III. Application of Foreign Law in Other Matters Involving Foreign Elements

A. Application and Confirmation of Foreign Law in Administrative Courts and Other Courts

The application of foreign laws not only happens when the applicable law is foreign. Where a party cites a foreign law to prove an administrative regulation exists to ensure a document exists, the issue of proving the foreign law is also involved.

The Supreme Court Civil Judgment Tai-Shang-Tzu No 90 of 2019[73] pointed out,

> A party has the burden of proof with regard to customs, local ordinances, and foreign laws which are unknown to the court. Notwithstanding, the court may investigate on its own initiative. Where

[68] Ma (n 10) 223.
[69] Lin (n 9) 129.
[70] Liu and Chen (n 28) 215–16.
[71] Ke (n 63) 79.
[72] Lin (n 9) 129.
[73] The judgment is available at: judgment.judicial.gov.tw/FJUD/data.aspx?ty=JD&id=TPSV,108%2c%e5%8f%b0%e4%b8%8a%2c90%2c20190403%2c1.

> a document identified to be introduced as documentary evidence is in a third person's possession, a party may move the court either to order such third person to produce such document or to designate a period of time within which the party who intends to introduce it as evidence shall produce such document. These regulations are provided explicitly in Article 283 and Paragraph 1, Article 346 of TCCP. Furthermore, Paragraphs 1 and 3 of Article 222 provide, in making a judgment the court shall, taking into consideration the entire import of the oral argument and the result of evidence-taking, determine the facts by free evaluation. The court shall not violate the rules of logic and experience in finding the facts by free evaluation. It is common that a corporation, as a for-profit legal association, should prepare logbooks, tables and documents for the inspection of the authorities concerned, for shareholders' review and supervision, and for engaging in business activities. The party claimed that an offshore company does not need to produce logbooks, tables and documents according to the law of that foreign country. Then the party shall bear the burden of proof of this abnormal fact that in the country where the company is registered, the companies do not need to produce logbooks, tables and documents.

Though the judgment addressed the issue of foreign law application and the bearing of burden of proof, this case is about the liability of damages of a liquidator liquidating assets in Taiwan. The court holds that this case involves a tort claim, and therefore it is governed by the law of the place where the tort was committed, namely the law of the forum, Taiwan law, not the law of the country where the corporation is registered, Samoa law. In this case, to confirm the corporation's assets, the defendant's liquidator was requested to provide balance sheets, financial statements, and other business records and documents to prove the financial status of the corporation. The defendant referred to Samoa law, and claimed that he did not need to set up those logbooks, tables, and documents, and that he could not confirm the corporation's assets. Since he was not able to liquidate the assets and recover the debts, he did not violate the provisions of any law and regulations in the performance of his duties, and thus was not liable for any damages. The Supreme Court addressed the defendant's defence and held that it was the defendant that should bear the burden of proof regarding the claimed Samoa law. According to the Supreme Court's opinion, the burden of proof regarding a foreign law not only exists when the applicable law is a foreign law and the party claims that foreign law should apply, but also exists when there is a dispute whether a duty of care exists in the foreign law. Article 283 of the TCCP also applies.

Taipei High Administrative Court Judgment Su-Tzu No 14 of 2020[74] heard a case involving a household registry in Taiwan dealing with a same-sex marriage registration between a Macau resident and a citizen of the ROC. It also involved the application of the choice of law rules. The judgment pointed out,

> … the defendant claims that the plaintiffs' marriage is established between two same-sex people. Since the plaintiff … is the resident of Macau, and according to Article 46 of the Act Governing the Choice of Law in Civil Matters Involving Foreign Elements, the formation of a marriage is governed by the national law of each party, when determining whether the substantial essentials of a marriage between two people are satisfied, the Macau Civil Code should apply. Given that the Macau Civil Code explicitly forbids same-sex marriage, the substantial essentials of the marriage between two plaintiffs are not satisfied. Moreover, the six-month period of a valid affirmation/affidavit of marital status has expired. The plaintiffs thus have violated Article 5 of the above-mentioned Regulations Governing the Processing of Marriage Registration by the Household

[74] See n 4 above.

> Registration Office. The defendant, therefore, rendered the original administrative ruling that denied the plaintiffs' application. However, in terms of whether the plaintiffs' marriage is valid, the law of the ROC should apply to the determination of the substantial essentials of a valid marriage due to remission according to Article 6 of the Act Governing the Choice of Law in Civil Matters. Article 2 of the Act for Implementation of J.Y. Interpretation No. 748 of the Republic of China further provides that two persons of the same sex may form a permanent union of intimate and exclusive nature for the purpose of living a common life. That is to say, the relationship of same-sex marriage is unambiguously protected by the law enacted by the legitimate authorities in our country, providing that two persons of the same sex may form a marriage relationship. Accordingly, the law of the ROC should be applied to determine the formal and substantial essentials of whether the plaintiffs' marriage is valid. The plaintiffs form a same-sex marriage relationship in our country, and there is no defect lacking any substantial essential here. The original administrative ruling did not consider the application of 'remission' in Article 6 of the Act Governing the Choice of Law in Civil Matters, and erred when it did not apply the applicable law and promptly denied the marriage registration application based on the reasons above.

In addition, the Ministry of Justice Letter Fa-Lu-Tzu No 12554 of 1981[75] points out that when the administrative agencies render administrative rulings where foreign laws should apply, Article 283 of the TCCP may also be employed and the parties will bear the burden of proof regarding any foreign laws unknown to the compensating authority. The letter states,

> … in state compensation cases, where the claimant is a foreigner, and the national law or customs of that foreign state is unknown to the court or the compensating authority, the foreign claimant shall bear the burden of proof, while the court or the compensating party may also investigate on its own initiative. Explanations: … 2. Article 15 of State Compensation Law provides: 'The provisions of this Law shall be applicable to a foreign claimant only to the extent that the people of the ROC, according to a treaty, law, or custom of that foreigner's country, enjoy the same rights in that country.' Where the claimant is a foreigner, except for the treaties, the claimant namely the plaintiff has to prove the existing laws, local ordinances, or customs of that foreigner's country which are unknown to the court. Notwithstanding, the court may investigate on its own initiative (Article 283 of TCCP).

B. Application and Confirmation of Foreign Law in Arbitration, Mediation, and Other Alternative Dispute Resolution Methods

Arbitrations for matters involving foreign elements may be referred to the Chinese Arbitration Association in Taiwan. The parties can follow the arbitration rules set by the Chinese Arbitration Association in terms of the arbitration procedure. Article 19 of the Arbitration Law of the ROC provides,

> In the absence of an agreement on the procedural rules governing the arbitration, the arbitral tribunal shall apply this Law. Where this Law is silent, the arbitral tribunal may adopt the Code of Civil Procedure mutatis mutandis or other rules of procedure which it deems proper.

In an arbitral proceeding, where a foreign law should apply based on the parties' agreement or the Choice of Law Act, the provisions of the TCCP may apply mutatis mutandis to the

[75] The Letter is available at: mojlaw.moj.gov.tw/LawContentExShow.aspx?type=e&id=FE074841.

investigation of the foreign law. Therefore, the evidence rules and the bearing of the burden of proof provided in Article 283 of the TCCP may also apply mutatis mutandis.

In other alternative dispute resolution methods like village, township, and city-administered mediations, the parties may mutually agree to the proposed mediation resolution. Thus, the investigation of the contents of foreign law may be decided by the parties' agreement and not subject to the court's review.

IV. Foreign Languages' Translations of National Laws

The laws of the ROC are numerous and complicated, governed by the different authorities concerned. So far, the foreign languages' translations database has been actively established and has been deemed fairly effective. English translations of the laws of the ROC can be found on the internet.[76] The Judicial Yuan set up a legal data retrieval system where one can look up the laws of the ROC and JY Interpretations by surfing the Judicial Yuan/Legal Data Retrieval System website and entering keywords of a law.[77] The Ministry of Justice has also set up a national law and regulations database, 'Laws and Regulations Database of the Republic of China (Taiwan)', where one can look up English translations of all laws and regulations. Furthermore, each institution has created a legal search section on its website where one can look for that institution's regulations. Some important laws and regulations have also been translated into English for inquiries. In addition, one can also look for English versions of the laws of the ROC on the 'Law Bank' website operated by a private company.

V. Approaching Foreign Laws: The Future Development of Asia

A. Improvement of Foreign Law Investigation System

There are many legal traditions in Asia. From the perspective of comparative law scholars, law systems are classified into the Romanistic law system, Germanic law system, common law system, Far East law family, and religious law family. The Far East law family further includes Chinese law and Japanese law, while the religious law family includes different legal systems like Islamic law and Hindu traditional law.[78] Although they all follow the civil law system, German, Chinese, Japanese, and Korean law have already developed different legal paths of their own. Korea sticks to the German tradition, using articles of law like an encyclopaedia. Japan has started to develop its own civil law system. China is now making a reform, approaching pragmatism, and promulgated its own civil code.[79] In Indonesia, though there are state laws promulgated by the nation, Islamic law and local custom legal

[76] English translations of laws/regulations are available at: law.moj.gov.tw/ENG/Index.aspx.

[77] The Judicial Yuan Law and Regulations Retrieving System: lawsearch.judicial.gov.tw/.

[78] K Zweigert and H Kötz, *Einführung in die Rechtsvergleichung*, 3rd edn (Türbingen, Mohr Siebeck, 1996).

[79] Z Kitagawa, 'Development of Comparative Law in East Asia' in M Reimann and R Zimmermann (eds), *The Oxford Handbook of Comparative Law* (Oxford, Oxford University Press, 2006) 259.

system 'adat' still exist. These two are not only deemed national laws but are also legal systems that are practiced effectively and independently.[80]

Taiwan is located in East Asia, belonging to a region where the economy develops fast. Taiwan has profuse economic activities and social interactions with its neighbouring countries and areas. Nonetheless, regarding investigating the legal systems, there is no mechanism to effectively research in or communicate with the neighbouring regions. Taiwan lacks the local view in terms of comparative law. This, indeed, needs urgent improvement.

B. The Function of International and Regional Organisations in the Integration of Foreign Law Research

Taiwan has been actively participating in conversations about foreign laws through non-governmental organisations and academic organisations. For example, the Chinese Arbitration Association has been holding the Taipei International Conference on Arbitration and Mediation since 2007. As for non-governmental academic organisations, Kajo Press in Japan has engaged in three-nation meetings about New Asia family law since 2010. They discuss individual issues in the meetings and compare the differences between the countries' legal systems. The meetings are rather productive. However, since there are no complete, thorough, stable international activities, the research on the integration of foreign laws is still insufficient. Exchanges between international organisations will more effectively integrate different research on foreign laws and help shed light on the study.

VI. Conclusion

The Choice of Law Act should apply to the civil matters involving foreign elements accepted by Taiwanese courts to determine the applicable law. The Choice of Law Act is mandatory, and all instances of courts have the duty to apply the Choice of Law Act to determine the applicable law. When a foreign law shall be applied as a result of applying the Choice of Law Act, the foreign law is deemed as law as well, and the courts shall in principle apply the contents of the foreign law ex officio. However, Article 283 of the TCCP also provides that the parties shall bear the burden of proof regarding the investigation of foreign laws. The contents of foreign laws are deemed as a matter that can be proved. The methods of proof include entrustment, expert opinions, foreign publications, and internet regulations information. The investigation of evidence should be conducted in accordance with the procedural principles of law applicable to matters involving foreign elements. Taiwan is an open society. With abundant information, the courts and the parties both have the capacity to investigate the basic contents of foreign laws. Nevertheless, the lack of long-term, complete communication activities makes the investigation of foreign law an exhausting matter in the court hearing process. Therefore, establishing an international and regional cooperative system to integrate the investigation of foreign laws will effectively resolve the problems of reviewing matters involving foreign elements.

[80] K O'Shaughnessy, *Gender, State and Social Power in Contemporary Indonesia: Divorce and Marriage Law* (New York, Routledge, 2009) 26.

5

Japan

KAZUAKI NISHIOKA AND MICHAEL WEBER

I. Introduction: Status of Choice of Law Rules

A. Choice of Law Rules in Japan

Choice of law rules in Japan are mainly contained in national legislation. The Act on General Rules for Application of Laws ('AGRAL')[1] contains the main rules on choice of law issues. AGRAL was enacted in 2006 and entered into force on 1 January 2007.[2] By Article 2 of its supplementary provisions, AGRAL is also applicable to cases that occurred before 1 January 2007, with the exception of the cases listed in Article 3 of the supplementary provisions.[3] Furthermore, specific issues are covered in the Act on the Law Applicable to Maintenance Obligation,[4] the Act on the Law Applicable to the Forms of Wills,[5] the Negotiable Instrument Act[6] and the Check Act.[7] These acts contain choice of law rules for specific issues and do not state any rules pertaining to the problem of ascertaining and applying foreign law. Thus, these acts will not be discussed further.

In addition, Japan is a party to various international agreements and conventions which contain choice of law rules. Major international agreements and conventions in this sense

[1] Act No 78 of 21 June 2006.

[2] For the history and development of Japanese Private International Law, see, eg, M Dogauchi, 'Historical Development of Japanese Private International Law' in J Basedow et al. (eds), *Japanese and European Private International Law in Comparative Perspective* (Tübingen, Mohr Siebeck, 2008) 23; Y Sakurada, 'The Origin and Evolution of Private International Law in Japan' (2013) 56 *Japanese Yearbook of International Law* 164; J Yokoyama, *Private International Law in Japan*, 2nd edn (Alphen aan den Rijn, Kluwer Law International, 2020); K Nishioka and Y Nishitani, *Japanese Private International Law* (Oxford, Hart Publishing, 2021).

[3] The former Code of Japanese Private International Law ('Horei') is still applicable to certain matters that occurred prior to 1 January 2007: (1) the capacity to act; (2) an order for commencement of guardianship, curatorship or assistance; (3) the adjudication of disappearance; (4) the formation and effect of a juridical act; (5) the formation and effect of a claim arising from management without mandate and unjust enrichment; (6) the formation and effect of a claim arising from a tort for which the result of the wrongful act occurred prior to 1 January 2007; (7) the effect of an assignment of a claim; (8) the formalities for a juridical act concerning a family relationship (excluding the family relationships prescribed in Horei Arts 14 through 21); and (9) the ruling of appointment of a guardian, curator or assistant or any other ruling concerning guardianship, etc. based on a petition filed prior to 1 January 2007.

[4] Act No 84 of 12 June 1986.

[5] Act No 100 of 10 June 1964.

[6] Act No 20 of 15 July 1932.

[7] Act No 57 of 29 July 1933.

are the Convention of 24 October 1956 on the Law Applicable to Maintenance Obligations towards Children; the Convention of 5 October 1961 on the Conflicts of Laws Relating to the Form of Testamentary Dispositions; the Convention of 2 October 1973 of the Law Applicable to Maintenance Obligations; the Convention of 25 October 1980 on the Civil Aspects of International Child Abduction; the Convention relating to the Status of Refugees of 28 July 1951; and the Convention on Supplementary Compensation for Nuclear Damage of 12 September 1997. Choice of law rules in most of these conventions are implemented through domestic acts. Therefore, Japanese courts apply choice of law rules as found in those implementation acts. These international sources and implementation acts contain choice of law rules regarding specific issues, but do not state any rules pertaining to the matter of ascertaining and applying foreign law. These sources will therefore not be discussed further.

Apart from national legislations and international conventions, court decisions are also counted among the sources of choice of law rules. Although the Japanese legal system generally belongs to the civil law family and thus statutes are the main source of law, court decisions provide legally non-binding guidelines on the interpretation of the law and may constitute a precedent for future cases. This is especially so with regards to decisions from the Japanese Supreme Court.[8]

Lastly, choice of law rules can also come from *jori* or general principles of law. *Jori* can be drawn from scholarly writings, which often draw from cases and theories from foreign jurisdictions like the US or European countries. Scholarly writings, however, are usually not cited by the courts in their decisions or judgments.[9] Regarding the ascertainment of application of foreign law, *jori* are mainly used to fill legal loopholes in cases where neither an explicit rule, nor previous case law can be found.[10]

B. Nature of Choice of Law Rules

The application of choice of law rules in Japan is considered mandatory by academia[11] and followed by court decisions[12] in cases with a cross-border element ('internationality'). This follows from the understanding that choice of law rules are part of domestic law and thus have to be applied ex officio by the court. The application of choice of law rules should not depend on the parties' intention.[13]

To apply choice of law rules properly, judges need to define and verify the connecting factor specified by the relevant choice of law rules. In a contractual dispute, for instance, judges will need to determine what the parties intended when choosing the law applicable to the contract and whether this was a tacit choice and and *dépeçage* (that is, the laws of different states may be applied to different issues in the same contract) (Article 7 of AGRAL). In a tortious dispute,

[8] Nishioka and Nishitani (n 2) 3.

[9] ibid.

[10] Nishioka and Nishitani (n 2) 3; Y Sakurada, *Kokusai Shiho*, 7th edn (Tokyo, Yuhikaku, 2020) 25; T Sawaki and M Dogauchi, *Kokusai Shiho Nyumon*, 8th edn (Tokyo, Yuhikaku, 2018) 11.

[11] Eg, S Nakano, 'Japan: Proof of and Information About Foreign Law in Japan' in Y Nishitani (ed), *Treatment of Foreign Law – Dynamics towards Convergence?* (Cham, Springer, 2017) 530; Y Nishitani, 'Treatment of and Access to Foreign Law in Japan' (2018) 23(46) *Journal of Japanese Law (Zeitschrift für Japanisches Recht)* 69, 71. Although not supported, the theory of 'facultative conflicts rules' advocated by Flesser has been also discussed in Japan. See, eg, H Sano, 'Nin'i-teki Teishokuho no Riron' (2000) 49(3–4) *Okayama Law Journal* 781.

[12] There is one exceptional case in which the court dismissed the claim by applying Japanese law on the ground that the claimant failed to submit and prove that foreign law was applicable. Judgment of Osaka District Court, 12 April 1960, *Kaminshu* 11(4), 817.

[13] Nakano (n 11) 530–31; Nishitani (n 11) 71–72.

judges will be required to define and determine the *locus damni* as the place where a tortious act has its effects, and whether it includes the place of mental suffering (Article 17, 1st sentence of AGRAL). As far as legal notions are concerned, judges exercise their authority ex officio.

To the contrary, there is some dispute as to whether a court has the duty to investigate the facts underlying the connecting factor or can simply rely on the parties' submissions in accordance with adversarial procedure rules. The traditional and majority view is that the parties are required to plead and prove them and the court is not obliged to look into underlying facts beyond those raised by the parties.[14] In other words, the duty to present the fact lies with the parties, unless the procedural rules explicitly provide for a more wide-ranging investigation by the judge.[15] Recently, however, some authors have argued that a judge is not confined to the facts as presented, but may need to probe further. They argue that a broad investigation is a necessary condition for the correct application of mandatory choice of law rules, since it would make it harder for the parties to manipulate the facts and thereby the operative connecting factor. Such manipulation, it is suggested, would give the parties a de facto choice of law.[16]

C. Treatment of Foreign Law in General

Choice of law rules in Japan generally follow the principle of the closest connection.[17] In other words, the basic principle of Japanese choice of law rules is reference to the law of the state that is most closely connected with the legal relationship at hand. By characterising the law of the state of closest connection as the most appropriate law to govern a legal relationship, Japanese choice of law rules aim to realise international harmony of decisions. Therefore, Japanese choice of law rules can lead to the application of Japanese law as well as foreign law.[18]

Under AGRAL, domestic and foreign law are – in general – treated equally.[19] The connecting factors in AGRAL follow the principle of the closest connection, which means that they are designed in a way that should lead to the application of the law (domestic or foreign) that is most closely connected to the matter (and thus considered to be best suited to govern it).[20] As an exception, AGRAL also contains some rules which can only lead to the application of domestic law (that is, Japanese law).[21]

[14] Y Nakanishi et al., *Kokusai Shiho*, 2nd edn (Tokyo, Yuhikaku, 2018) 62–63.

[15] In contrast, courts may examine it ex officio in family and personal status matters. For example, Art 20 of PLSA provides that '[I]n personal status litigation, the court may take facts which are not asserted by the parties into consideration and examine evidence by its own authority. In this case, the court shall hear the opinions of the parties regarding such facts and the results of the examination of the evidence.'

[16] Nishitani (n 11) 73; K Yamamoto, 'Renketsuten no Shucho Rissho' in Y Sakurada and M Dogauchi (eds), *Chushaku Kokusai Shiho Vol 2* (Tokyo, Yuhikaku, 2011) 369.

[17] Nishioka and Nishitani (n 2) 7.

[18] ibid.

[19] Nishioka and Nishitani (n 2) 8–9; Nishitani (n 11) 76.

[20] Nishioka and Nishitani (n 2) 7; eg, Art 13 of AGRAL (rights in rem): '(…) the law of the place where the subject property is located'; Art 17 (torts): '(…) the law of the place where the results of the infringing act are produced'; Art 24 (requirements for formation of marriage): '(…) the national law of each spouse respectively' (para 1), '(…) the law of the place of the ceremony' (para 2), or Art 36 (succession): '(…) the national law of the decedent'.

[21] Eg, Art 5 of AGRAL (order for commencement of guardianship etc.): 'A court may issue an order for commencement of guardianship, curatorship or assistance (…) under Japanese law if the ward or person under curatorship or assistance is domiciled or resident in Japan or has Japanese nationality'; Art 6 (adjudication of disappearance): 'A court may issue an order for commencement of guardianship, curatorship or assistance (…) under Japanese law if the ward or person under curatorship or assistance is domiciled or resident in Japan or has Japanese nationality' (para 1).

It follows that in principle, foreign law should be equally likely to be applied as domestic law. However, amendments to AGRAL in 2006 have led to there being fewer cases overall in which foreign law is applied in Japan.[22] This is especially the case in choice of law rules regarding tort. Although Article 17 AGRAL[23] maintains the *lex loci delicti commissi* principle which would equally likely lead to the application of foreign law as domestic law, the exception in Article 20 (so-called escape clause)[24] as well as the choice of law clause in Article 21[25] may favour in effect the application of domestic law.[26]

II. Foreign Law before Judicial Authorities

A. Nature of Foreign Law

Foreign law is nowadays considered to be 'law' and not 'fact' by the majority of academics[27] as well as court decisions.[28] This follows from the principle that domestic and foreign law are to be treated equally (that is, foreign law has the same value as domestic law when designated by relevant choice of law rules), and from the fact that the process of applying foreign law does not differ – in substance – from the process of applying domestic law, that is, the finding of relevant rules and their subsequent application to the facts of a case.[29]

[22] Nakano (n 11) 530.

[23] Art 17 of AGRAL (Tort): 'The formation and effect of a claim arising from a tort is governed by the law of the place where the result of the wrongful act occurred; provided, however, that if the occurrence of the result at the relevant place was ordinarily unforeseeable, the law of the place where the wrongful act was committed is govern.'

[24] Art 20 of AGRAL (Exception for Cases Where Another Place Is Obviously More Closely Connected): 'Notwithstanding the provisions of the preceding three Articles, the formation and effect of a claim arising from a tort are governed by the law of the place with which the tort is obviously more closely connected than the place indicated in the preceding three Articles, in light of that the parties had their habitual residence in the places governed by the same law at the time of the occurrence of the tort, that the tort was committed in breach of the obligation under a contract between the parties, or any other circumstances concerned.'

[25] Art 21 of AGRAL (Change of Governing Law by the Parties): 'The parties to a tort may, after the tort occurs, change a law applicable to the formation and effect of a claim arising from the tort; provided, however, that if the change prejudices the rights of a third party, it may not be duly asserted against the third party.' Where the parties put forward their claims without referring to the applicable law, it can be deemed a parties' implicit agreement of Japanese law. In this regard, the presiding judge is able, or required, to ask questions of a party or ask a party to give proof with regard to a factual or legal matter to clarify a matter that is related to the litigation.

[26] Nakano (n 11) 530.

[27] Nakano (n 11) 531; Nishioka and Nishitani (n 2) 18; Nishitani (n 11) 74; Sakurada (n 10) 126; Sawaki and Dogauchi (n 10) 52. There are some differing opinions advocating foreign law be treated as a matter of fact or as of a hybrid nature. See A Mikazuki, 'Gaikokuho no Tekiyo to Saibansho' in T Sawaki and Y Aoyama (eds), *Kokusai Minji Soshoho no Riron* (Tokyo, Yuhikaku, 1987) 252, 260; H Sakai et al., *Kokusai Minji Tetsuzukiho*, 2nd edn (Tokyo, Yuhikaku, 2012) 166.

The former Art 219 of the 1890 CCP set out that 'Regional customary law, commercial customs, bylaw, or foreign law in force are to be proven. Courts can make necessary investigations *ex officio* whether or not the parties prove it.' On this provision, see Nishitani (n 11) 74.

[28] *Cf* Judgment of Supreme Court, Second Petty Bench, 20 July 1984, *Minshu* 38(8), 1051 (28 *Japanese Annual of International Law* 221). To the contrary, some court decisions in 1960s subjected the ascertainment of foreign law to the parties' pleading and proving it. See, eg, Judgment of Fukuoka District Court, Kokura Branch, 22 January 1962, *Kaminshu* 13(1), 64; Judgment of Osaka High Court, 6 April 1962, *Kaminshu* 13(4), 653.

[29] K Yamamoto, 'Gaikokuho no Tekiyo' in Y Sakurada and M Dogauchi (eds), *Chushaku Kokusai Shiho Vol 2* (Tokyo, Yuhikaku, 2011) 352.

B. Ascertainment of Foreign Law

i. General Principle

The court has a duty to ascertain and apply domestic law, which is summarised in the *iura novit cura* principle (ie, the principle that the judge is supposed to know all the law). Since foreign law and domestic law are to be treated equally, it also lies in the responsibility of the court to ascertain the designated foreign law ex officio.[30] The *iura novit cura* principle thus also applies to foreign law.[31] This helps to mitigate differences in the ability of the parties to identify the relevant law and ensures a uniform application of the law, as the onus to ascertain the (domestic or foreign) law ultimately lies with the court.[32] The parties are therefore not obligated to plead, invoke, or present the foreign law to the court. However, this does not hinder the parties from assisting the court in the ascertainment of the foreign law and from submitting relevant documents.[33] The parties can even agree on the content of the applicable law and propose this to the court, although this proposal is – according to the ex officio-principle – not binding on the court.[34] Occasionally courts seem to adopt and apply the proposed contents if they are not disputed by a party.[35]

ii. Means of Ascertainment

In theory, the courts have a variety of means at hand to ascertain foreign law. These include research by a judge, seeking assistance from the parties, seeking expert opinions, and assistance via diplomatic channels. In family and personal matters, the family department of the Supreme Court can be called on for advice. However, not all means are utilised equally – or utilised at all.

First, the court cannot free itself from the task of ascertaining the designated law by delegating it to the parties, since the onus to ascertain the designated law lies with the court. However, the court can ask the parties to assist in the task and submit relevant documents.[36] Even so, the responsibility to ascertain the law does not shift to the parties and they are free to adopt or to deny. If the correct ascertainment of the foreign law is in the interests of a party, compliance will be more likely. This is especially so in commercial issues.[37] One might also argue that this is due to the higher expertise in cross-border litigation of the mandated lawyers or law firms in such cases.

Apart from assistance by the parties, the court will mainly obtain its information from published materials (books, journals etc) or internet sources.[38] When researching, the judge is free to use their own knowledge and any experience of the foreign law, the foreign

[30] Nakano (n 11) 531; Nishioka and Nishitani (n 2) 18; Nishitani (n 11) 71–72; Sakurada (n 10) 127; Sawaki and Dogauchi (n 10) 51.

[31] Nakano (n 11) 532; Nishioka and Nishitani (n 2) 18; Nishitani (n 11) 75.

[32] Nakano (n 11) 532; Nishitani (n 11) 75; Yamamoto (n 29) 354.

[33] Nishioka and Nishitani (n 2) 18; Nishitani (n 11) 71–72.

[34] Nishitani (n 11) 75.

[35] Sawaki and Dogauchi (n 10) 50.

[36] Nakano (n 11) 532; Nishioka and Nishitani (n 2) 19; Nishitani (n 11) 75; Sawaki and Dogauchi (n 10) 51.

[37] Nishioka and Nishitani (n 2) 19; Nishitani (n 11) 79.

[38] Nakano (n 11) 532; Nishitani (n 11) 79. Eg, Judgment of Tokyo District Court, 28 December 2015, 2015WLJPCA12288002.

language in which such law is stated, or the use of IT, which the judge may have gained in the past through their own studies, etc.[39]

The court may also consult relevant departments of the Supreme Court.[40] In family and personal matters, the family department of the Supreme Court replies based on documents published by the General Secretariat of the Supreme Court, the Ministry of Justice, or the Parliamentary Library.[41] This method of ascertaining information about foreign law is, however, limited to family and personal status matters. The civil department of the Supreme Court has no specific expertise in foreign law regarding other civil or commercial matters.[42]

Occasionally the courts may also seek an expert opinion from a court-appointed expert (Articles 212–217 of CCP[43]). Japanese courts, however, do not often take advantage of this method.[44] Possible explanations for this are that the exercise is time-consuming and costly – the costs are typically to be borne by the losing party[45] – or that opinions from party-appointed experts are often submitted by the parties anyway. Furthermore, although not expressly stated, it is presumed that the courts cannot call for an expert ex officio, but only at the request of a party.[46] The court may, however, suggest that the parties make such a request (Article 149 of CCP[47]).[48]

Pursuant to Article 218 of CCP,[49] theoretically it would be possible for courts to ask foreign institutions such as the Max Planck Institute for Comparative and International Private Law,[50] the Swiss Institute of Comparative Law[51] and the International Juridisch Instituut[52] to provide information on a specific law. To the authors' knowledge, however,

[39] Yamamoto (n 29) 356–57.

[40] Nakano (n 11) 532; Nishioka and Nishitani (n 2) 19.

[41] Nishitani (n 11) 80.

[42] ibid.

[43] Art 213 of CCP provides that '[A]n expert is designated by the court in charge of the case, authorised judge or a commissioned judge.' According to Art 212, '[a] person who has the relevant knowledge and experience necessary to give expert testimony bears the obligation to give expert testimony.'

[44] Nishioka and Nishitani (n 2) 19; Nishitani (n 11) 79.

[45] Art 61 of CCP (Principle of Burden of Court Costs) stipulates that '[t]he defeated party bears the court costs.' Note that the term 'court costs' does not include attorney fee.

[46] Nishitani (n 11) 79. Some argue that the courts can call for an expert ex officio (eg, H Matsuoka, 'Gaikoku Ho no Tekiyou to Saibansho' in A Takakuwa and M Dogauchi (eds), *Shin Saiban Jitsumu Taikei 3 (Kokusai Minji Sosho Ho (Zaisan Ho kankei))* (Tokyo, Seirin Shoin, 2002) 280–81).

[47] Art 149(1) of CCP (Authority to Ask for an Explanation) stipulates that '[T]he presiding judge, on a date for oral arguments or on any other date, may ask questions of a party or call for a party to give proof with regard to a factual or legal matter, in order to clarify a matter that is related to the litigation.'

[48] Nishitani (n 11) 79.

[49] Art 218 of CCP (Commissioning of Expert Testimony) stipulates as follows:

(1) If the court finds it to be necessary, it may commission a government agency or public office, a foreign government agency or public office, or a corporation that has adequate equipment to give expert testimony. In such a case, the provisions of this Section, except for those concerning swearing under oath, apply mutatis mutandis.

(2) In the case as referred to in the preceding paragraph, when the court finds it to be necessary, it may have a person designated by the government agency, public office, or corporation give an explanation of written expert testimony.

[50] www.mpipriv.de/home.

[51] www.isdc.ch/en/.

[52] www.iji.nl/en/.

there has been no such case. Obviously, the information provided is not binding on the courts. The courts are rather required to assess the reliability of the information provided ex officio (see II.B.iii).

Regarding opinions by party-appointed experts, individuals and institutions that provide legal information do not need any specific qualifications. In cases where the amount of dispute is significant, it is common for the parties to submit expert opinions at their own expense due in part to a certain unpredictability of an opinion from a court-designated expert. This can be detrimental to the other party, since such private expert opinions are nothing more than party assertions and the other party has thus no possibility to cross-examine the expert (in particular, to dispute their eligibility) if the expert opinion is only submitted as a written document. Nevertheless, if the party-appointed expert also appears as a witness in an oral trial, cross-examination becomes possible. In any event, the courts are not bound by these opinions, but are required to assess their reliability (see II.B.iii).

Judicial assistance via diplomatic channels is, in principle, also available,[53] but is usually not used due to the time required on the one hand and the uncertainty regarding the usefulness of the results on the other.[54] In addition, the courts normally do not inquire directly to foreign judicial or non-judicial authorities or consult directly with foreign judges on the matter.[55] Access to legal information via bilateral or multilateral channels is also not often used, since Japan has not ratified a treaty which would allow that.[56]

Therefore, the courts mainly obtain their information from published media, internet sources and party submissions. Where the courts exercise authority to seek information under the doctrine of discovery thorough ex officio, whatever the source of information may be, the judge is obliged to present their view on the matter to the parties early enough to ensure the parties' opportunities to express their opinions in this regard.[57] Only in this way the fairness of the trial can be ensured.[58]

iii. Free Judicial Assessment of the Provided Information

It is the duty of the court to ascertain the designated law; at the same time, the court is free in its assessment of the information on the foreign law. This holds true regardless of whether the parties submit information on the applicable law to the court, whether they agree on the applicable law or whether the court itself commissions a third party to submit information on the subject.[59]

[53] Eg, Decision of Sapporo Family Court, 23 July 1974, *Katei Saiban Geppo* 27(5), 146.

[54] Nishitani (n 11) 83.

[55] Nakano (n 11) 532. Although direct judicial communications are available through the International Hague Network of Judges, Japanese judges are not allowed to discuss the merits of specific cases.

[56] Nakano (n 11) 532. However, Japan has recently concluded a memorandum of understanding with Singapore. See below section V.

[57] *Cf* Art 20 of the Personal Status Litigation Act: 'In personal status litigation, the court may take facts which are not asserted by the parties into consideration and examine evidence by its own authority. In this case, the court shall hear the opinions of the parties regarding such facts and the results of the examination of the evidence.' The underlying principles should apply where the courts exercise authority to seek information. See also Yamamoto (n 29) 354.

[58] Yamamoto (n 29) 354.

[59] Nakano (n 11) 532–33; Nishitani (n 11) 75; Sawaki and Dogauchi (n 10) 52.

The court is not bound by any of the provided information on the foreign law.[60] Mechanisms to examine the reliability of the provided information do not exist.[61] It thus boils down to the discretion and judgment of the court to validate the reliability of the provided information.

iv. Costs

The costs of ascertaining foreign law (including for a court-designated expert opinion) are, as part of the court costs, placed upon the defeated party (Article 61 of CCP). Costs for party-appointed expert reports and the like are borne by the commissioning party.[62]

C. Interpretation and Application of Foreign Law

i. Conditions for the Application of Foreign Law

First, foreign law is only applied in cases with at least one cross-border element ('internationality'), since only in cases with a cross-border element choice of law rules will become relevant.[63] That cross-border element might, for example, be the nationality of a person, the business location of a company or even just a choice of law clause in a contract between two Japanese companies declaring that foreign law applicable.

Second, the applicable law is designated by a connecting factor which is stated in the relevant choice of law rule.[64] The court is obliged to apply the choice of law rules and the law that they designate ex officio.[65] If the choice of law rule designates a foreign law, the designated foreign law has to be treated equally as the domestic law and its application is thus also mandatory.[66] There is no room for the court to deviate from the designated law at this stage. Conversely, the parties have no duty to invoke the application of a particular foreign law before the court, although they are allowed to submit to the court that foreign law should be applied.[67]

Third, a condition for the application of the designated foreign law is that it is in line with the *ordre public* of the forum within the meaning of Article 42 of AGRAL.[68] If the designated foreign law conflicts with Japanese *ordre public*, the application of foreign law will be excluded. However, this leads to the question of which law should be applied as a substitute. Some academics suggest that by branding the foreign law as inapplicable, a lacuna is created that should be filled by the application of Japanese law.[69] Others suggest that the application

[60] Nakano (n 11) 533.
[61] ibid.
[62] Nakano (n 11) 533.
[63] Nishioka and Nishitani (n 2) 7; Nishitani (n 11) 72.
[64] Nishioka and Nishitani (n 2) 7; Nishitani (n 11) 70–71.
[65] Nakano (n 11) 531; Nishioka and Nishitani (n 2) 18; Nishitani (n 11) 71–72.
[66] Nakano (n 11) 531; Nishioka and Nishitani (n 2) 18; Nishitani (n 11) 71–72.
[67] Nishioka and Nishitani (n 2) 18; Nishitani (n 11) 71–72.
[68] See Nishioka and Nishitani (n 2) 22–24; Sakurada (n 10) 137–47; Sawaki and Dogauchi (n 10) 56–62. Art 42 of AGRAL (Public Policy): 'In cases where a foreign law is [to be] govern[ed], if the application of those provisions of the foreign law is against public policy, those provisions do not apply.'
[69] Eg, Sakurada (n 10) 140.

of *ordre public* itself is enough to decide the case, since the unwanted result (which the application of the foreign law would bring) is being avoided.[70] In the case of a foreign law not allowing compensation for damages, the former opinion would lead to the application of Japanese law instead, whereas the latter would only allow the smallest possible sum compatible with the *ordre public*.[71] The case law is not clear on this. The application of the *ordre public* doctrine to one question does not, however, lead to the complete exclusion of foreign law, as preliminary and follow-up questions need to be assessed separately.[72]

ii. Interpretation and Application of Foreign Law by the Courts

Japanese courts have to apply foreign law in the way courts of the country of origin would apply their law.[73] In other words, Japanese courts should not interpret the foreign law according to Japanese case law or doctrinal style. The methods of application and interpretation of the foreign law as practiced in the country of origin have thus to be determined and adopted by the Japanese court. This includes ways of filling apparent gaps in foreign law, that is, when the foreign law seemingly does not deal with the issue before the Japanese court.[74] This does not mean that Japanese courts have to follow foreign case law to the letter, even if a clear practice on the issue in question exists. Rather, it means that the Japanese court has to put itself in the position of the foreign court deciding the case. Depending on the jurisdiction, the Japanese court may also differ in its decision from established jurisprudence, if it does so according to the ways of legal interpretation of the concerned jurisdiction.[75]

D. Failure to Establish Foreign Law

There is no clear rule on how the court should proceed if it is unable to ascertain foreign law.[76] On this, the courts and academia have developed a variety of methods, depending on the circumstances of a case. Five approaches have been advocated.

First, if foreign law can be regarded as a matter of fact, the judge can dismiss a claim on the basis of a failure to establish fact. This view is, only supported by a minority of academics and has not been reflected in recent court practice.[77] Following the majority of academics

[70] Eg, Sawaki and Dogauchi (n 10) 59–60.

[71] ibid 60.

[72] ibid.

[73] Eg, Judgment of Fukuoka High Court, 10 February 2009, *Hanrei Jiho* 2043, 89. Nakano (n 11) 533; Nishitani (n 11) 78–79; Sawaki and Dogauchi (n 10) 53; Yamamoto (n 29) 357–58.

[74] Decision of Osaka High Court, 22 April 2003, *Kasai Geppo* 56(5), 124. Nakano (n 11) 533.

[75] Yamamoto (n 29) 358.

[76] It must be noted that such a scenario does not extend to situations where a specific legal system does not exist in the foreign jurisdiction concerned. Suppose that in a case of a divorce between a Japanese man and a Filipina, the law applicable to their divorce is the law of the Philippines. Since the Philippines' law does not have divorce as a legal system, there are no legal rules on divorce. As a result, the court would not be able to 'ascertain' the rules on divorce in the Philippines. However, the court could still find out that divorce is not allowed in the Philippines. Such a situation must be distinguished from situations where the court is unable to ascertain the contents of a foreign law due to, for instance, the fact that they have no access to the law.

[77] Judgment of Fukuoka District Court, Kokura Branch, 22 January 1962, *Kaminshu* 13(1), 64; S Atobe, *Kokusai Shihoron, Vol 1* (Kyoto, Kobundo Shobo, 1925) 418.

and established court practice, foreign law is regarded as a matter of law and the duty of establishing foreign law lies with the court.[78] For the sake of fairness and justice, it is therefore not permissible for the judge to dismiss a case on the ground that the applicable foreign law is unascertainable.

Second, the court can fall back on the *lex fori*. Since this would run contrary to the general principle of the Japanese private international law (ie, the equality of domestic and foreign law),[79] this approach should not be taken prematurely,[80] as some courts did in early decisions.[81]

Third, the court can determine the merits of the case based on *jori* (natural reasoning), as the majority of court decisions have done. Several variations of this approach have been broached. The court may fall back on *jori*, while taking into account relevant statutory provisions and case law of the designated legal order (also known as the 'reasonableness' test).[82] This has been done by looking at the characteristic and fundamental principles of a foreign legal system, including its social and cultural background.[83] While some courts have relied on the general reasonableness test to deduce foreign norms by taking into account the fundamental principles of that foreign legal system and the appropriateness of a solution to the relevant circumstances,[84] others have referred to the reasonableness test under Japanese law[85] or the presumed foreign law.[86]

[78] See above section II.B.

[79] Nishitani (n 11) 81; Sakurada (n 10) 130.

[80] Nishitani (n 11) 81.

[81] Judgment of Nagoya District Court, Handa Branch, 20 May 1952, *Kaminshu* 3(5), 676 (North Korea); Judgment of Tokyo District Court, 28 September 1954, *Kaminshu* 5(9), 1640 (North Korea); Judgment of Osaka District Court, 27 November 1956, *Kaminshu* 7(11), 3393 (South Korea); Decision of Nagoya High Court, Kanazawa Branch, 25 March 1980, *Hanrei Jiho* 970, 163 (North and South Korea); Judgment of Tokyo High Court, 26 September 1984, *Katei Saiban Geppo* 37(9), 87 (South Korea); Decision of Yamaguchi Family Court, Shimonoseki Branch, 28 July 1987, *Katei Saiban Geppo* 40(3), 90 (North Korea); Judgment of Kyoto District Court, 30 September 1987, *Hanrei Jiho* 1275, 107 (North Korea).

[82] Nishioka and Nishitani (n 2) 19–20; Nishitani (n 11) 81.

[83] Eg, Decision of Nagano Family Court, 12 March 1982, 35 (1) *Katei Saiban Geppo* 105; Judgment of Osaka District Court, 27 September 1985, *Hanrei Jiho* 1179, 94.

[84] Eg, Judgment of Tokyo District Court, 12 August 1958, Kaminshu 9(8), 1573 (North Korea); Decision of Utsunomiya Family Court, 10 August 1959, *Katei Saiban Geppo* 11(11), 134 (North Korea); Judgment of Kobe District Court, 6 October 1959, *Kaminshu* 10(10), 2099 (English Law); Decision of Kobe Family Court, 14 September 1960, *Katei Saiban Geppo* 12(12), 101 (North Korea); Decision of Urawa Family Court, 31 August 1961, *Katei Saiban Geppo* 13(12), 65 (North Korea); Decision of Urawa Family Court, 5 June 1962, *Katei Saiban Geppo* 14(12), 154 (North Korea); Judgment of Tokyo District Court, 13 January 1966, *Katei Saiban Geppo* 19(1), 43 (North Korea); Decision of Kyoto Family Court, 10 March 1975, *Katei Saiban Geppo* 27(11), 61 (China); Judgment of Tokyo High Court, 13 July 1981, *Katei Saiban Geppo* 34(9), 72 (China); Judgment of Osaka District Court, 27 September 1985, *Hanrei Jiho* 1179, 94 (North Korea).

[85] Eg, Judgment of Nagoya District Court, 29 May 1954, *Kaminshu* 5(5), 788 (North Korea); Judgment of Shizuoka District Court, 12 February 1971, *Kaminshu* 22(1–2), 160 (North Korea); Decision of Osaka Family Court, 26 March 1979, *Katei Saiban Geppo* 34(2), 160 (China); Decision of Nagano Family Court, 12 March 1982, *Katei Saiban Geppo* 35(1), 105 (North Korea); Judgment of Kobe District Court, 30 March 1983, *Hanrei Jiho* 1092, 114 (India).

[86] Eg, Judgment of Tokyo High Court, 8 August 1959, *Hanrei Jiho* 227, 34 (North Korea); Judgment of Tokyo District Court, 25 October 1962, *Kaminshu* 13(10), 2146 (China); Decision of Sapporo Family Court, 23 July 1974, *Katei Saiban Geppo* 27(5), 146 (Malaysia); Decision of Tokyo Family Court, 27 December 1974, *Katei Saiban Geppo* 27(10), 71 (Malaysia and Chinese customary law); Judgment of Nagoya District Court, 7 October 1975, *Kaminshu* 26(9–12), 910 (North Korea); Judgment of Kofu District Court, 29 October 1976, *Hanrei Jiho* 852, 103 (North Korea); Judgment of Sapporo District Court, 26 June 1984, *Katei Saiban Geppo* 37(7), 65 (29 *Japanese Annual of International Law* 260) (Zimbabwe); Judgment of Hiroshima District Court, 30 January 1986, *Katei Saiban Geppo* 38(6), 43 (Laos); Judgment of Tokyo District Court, 28 August 1987, *Hanrei Jiho* 1278, 97 (China).

Fourth, the court can take an approach similar to the third one by referring to or applying related, sister legal systems (particularly socialist regimes).[87] Following this approach, it may be assumed that the rules of the other legal system to which reference is made are similar to the designated law. This approach has been suggested to avoid arbitrary decisions and provide for concrete criteria.[88] In several cases lower courts have referred, for example, to the law of South Korea or the former Soviet Union to establish North Korean family law.[89] To ascertain Chinese adoption law, the Nagoya Family Court referred to the laws of the Soviet Union, East Germany, Poland, Rumania and Hungary.[90] To determine the rules on tort and unjust enrichment in Myanmar, the Tokyo District Court took English law as a reference for its considerations based on *jori*.[91] Although widely supported,[92] this way of referring to the similar legal system must be used with caution so as not to reach the wrong conclusions. One of the problems of using this approach is that, to assess the similarity of a legal system, the court needs to make several initial assumptions about the nature of the original designated law and legal system. One may criticise this approach for courts as one of 'ascertaining' the content of the original designated law based on a set of rules of a similar legal system. In other words, this approach might be better classified as a method of determining the content of the original designated law.[93]

Fifth, the court can make a supplementary or 'second-closest' reference.[94] This idea is aimed at achieving the ultimate goal of private international law, that is, referring a case to the legal order which has the closest connection to it. However, this solution is rarely used and runs contrary to choice of law rules by substituting the originally designated foreign law with something else.[95]

Although there have been a variety of proposed solutions, judges should first try to ascertain the contents of foreign law by following the third or fourth approaches, as these are most in conformity with the objective of private international law, and only fall back on the *lex fori* (Japanese law) as a last resort if they genuinely cannot find out the content of foreign law within a reasonable time and at a proportionate cost.[96] Since the 1990s, there has been a drastic decrease in the number of court decisions declaring the content of foreign law to be unascertainable. Reasons for this include improvements in the means of ascertaining

[87] Eg, Judgment of Fukuoka District Court, 14 January 1958, *Kaminshu* 9(1), 15 (North Korea); Decision of Osaka Family Court, 22 August 1962, *Katei Saiban Geppo* 15(2), 163 (North Korea); Decision of Tokyo Family Court, 13 June 1963, Katei Saiban Geppo 15(10), 153 (North Korea); Judgment of Osaka District Court, 17 March 1964, *Hanrei Times* 162, 197 (North Korea); Decision of Yokohama Family Court, 2 October 1973, *Katei Saiban Geppo* 26(6), 52 (Taiwan); Decision of Naha Family Court, 17 January 1975, *Katei Saiban Geppo* 28(2), 115 (Taiwan). For this approach, see, eg, S Ikehara, *Kokusai Shiho Soron* (Tokyo, Yuhikaku, 1973) 243; R Yamada, *Kokusai Shiho* 3rd edn (Tokyo, Yuhikaku, 2004) 136. As some court decisions also referred to *jori*, one may be able to regard this type of approach as one variation of the second – *jori* – approach. See Sakurada (n 10) 132.

[88] Nishitani (n 11) 81.

[89] Cases with reference to South Korean Law: eg, Decision of Fukuoka District Court, 14 January 1958, *Kaminshu* 9(1), 15; Decision of Osaka Family Court, 22 August 1962, *Katei Saiban Geppo* 15(2), 163. Cases with reference to the law of the socialist states such as the former Soviet Union: eg, Judgment of Chiba District Court, Matsudo Branch, 11 August 1965, *Katei Saiban Geppo* 18(9), 53 (North Korea); Decision of Tokyo Family Court, 13 June 1963, *Katei Saiban Geppo* 15(10), 153; Judgment of Tokyo District Court, 19 March 1976, *Kaminshu* 27(1–4), 125.

[90] Decision of Nagoya Family Court, 30 November 1983, *Katei Saiban Geppo* 36(11), 138 (China).

[91] Judgment of Tokyo District Court, 28 December 2015, 2015WLJPCA12288002 (Myanmar).

[92] Eg, Yamamoto (n 29) 360.

[93] Nakano (n 11) 533–34; Sawaki and Dogauchi (n 10) 55.

[94] Yamamoto (n 34) 364; T Kanzaki, 'Junkyo Gaikokuho no Fumei o megutte' (1990) 107(6) *Hogaku Kyokai Zasshi* 1039.

[95] Nishioka and Nishitani (n 2) 20.

[96] Nishioka and Nishitani (n 2) 20; Sakurada (n 10) 132; Sawaki and Dogauchi (n 10) 55–56.

the content of foreign law, especially the improved availability of information which at least partly goes back to increased digitalisation of legal information, and rapid legal development (especially codification) in neighbouring countries such as China and North and South Korea.[97]

E. Judicial Review/Appeal

In the context of the application of foreign law, two grounds of appeal must be distinguished: the application of 'wrong' foreign law (in other words, incorrect application of choice of law rules)[98] and the incorrect application of 'correct' foreign law.

i. Application of 'Wrong' Foreign Law/Incorrect Application of Choice of Law Rules

Since choice of law rules are part of domestic law, any incorrect application of those rules will constitute a ground of appeal. The parties have a right to appeal to a high court (first-level appeal) and subsequently to file a petition for a final appeal to the Supreme Court. Article 312(3) CCP provides that 'A final appeal to the high court may [...] be filed on the grounds of a violation of law and regulation that has clearly influenced the judgment.'[99] Regarding petition for acceptance of final appeal to the Supreme Court, the requirements of Article 318(1) CCP need to be fulfilled. Article 318(1) CCP stipulates that

> With regard to a case in which the judgment in prior instance contains a determination that is inconsistent with precedents rendered by the Supreme Court (or precedents rendered by the former Supreme Court or those rendered by high courts as the final appellate court or the court of second instance, if there are no precedents rendered by the Supreme Court) or any other case in which the judgment in prior instance is found to involve material matters concerning the construction of laws and regulations, where the court with which a final appeal shall be filed is the Supreme Court, the Supreme Court, upon petition, by an order, may accept such case as the final appellate court).

Therefore, if no prior case law of the Supreme Court exists, only 'material matters concerning the construction of laws and regulations' are granted certiorari. In general, the incorrect application of choice of law rules is considered materially important by the Supreme Court.[100]

ii. Incorrect Application of 'Correct' Foreign Law

If the court applies the law of the 'correct' state as designated by the choice of law rules but applied that (foreign) law incorrectly, the parties are also entitled to judicial review

[97] Nishitani (n 11) 82.

[98] This may happen where a Japanese court misidentified important facts pertaining to the connecting factor (such as nationality) or misinterpreted and erroneously applied relevant choice of law rules.

[99] Yamamoto (n 34) 365. See also Nakano (n 11) 534; Nishitani (n 11) 77.

[100] Eg, Judgments of Supreme Court, 26 September 2002, *Minshu* 56(7), 1551 (US patent infringement); 29 October 2002, *Minshu* 56(8), 1964 (ownership of a German car stolen in Italy and found in Japan); 17 October 2006, *Minshu* 60(8), 2853 (employee invention). See Nakano (n 11) 534; Nishitani (n 11) 77; Yamamoto (n 34) 365.

(including one by the Supreme Court).[101] This follows from the equality of foreign law and domestic law.[102] As stated above, the parties have a right to appeal to a higher court. If a party subsequently appeals to or files a petition for acceptance of final appeal to the Supreme Court, the requirements of Article 312(3) or Article 318(1) CCP need to be fulfilled. As foreign law has the same value as a domestic law, foreign law is considered part of 'laws and regulations' within the meaning of Articles 312(3) and 318(3). Hence, incorrect application of the designated foreign law will be a ground for final appeal or petition for acceptance of final appeal. Note that for petition for acceptance of final appeal under Article 318, the judgment in prior instance must involve important matters concerning the interpretation of laws and regulations. In this regard, the court should consider the frequency the law in question is applied in Japan and its general importance for Japanese cases to decide whether the judgment involves important matters.[103] Accordingly, if the parties of two cases concerning the same question regarding the correct application of the designated foreign law (eg, whether the respective law of succession was applied correctly), but where the applicable law differs (eg, South Korean law in one case and the law of state A that is not often applied by Japanese courts, in the other) were to file a petition for acceptance of final appeal to the Supreme Court, the Supreme Court may only decide to hear the South Korean law and reject a petition for the appeal concerning the law of state A according to its (lack of) importance based on the frequency of the cases in which the law of state A is applied in Japan.[104]

III. Foreign Law in Other Instances

A. Administrative Authorities

Japanese law requires Japanese nationals to notify a change in their family status (for instance, as a result of the birth of a child, marriage, divorce, an acknowledgment of paternity, adoption, etc) to the local authority, with a view to updating a person's personal particulars in the family register (*Koseki*).[105] Accordingly, officials of the relevant local authority are required to assess the legal validity of such juridical acts under the respective law(s) applicable to them before accepting parties' notifications.[106] Furthermore, the acquisition of Japanese nationality upon certain judicial acts such as an acknowledgement

[101] Judgment of Supreme Court, 2 July 1981, *Minshu* 35(5), 881; Judgment of Supreme Court, 25 February 1997, *Kagetsu* 49(7), 56 (41 *Japanese Annual of International Law* (1998), 111); Judgment of Supreme Court, 18 March 2008, *Shumin* 227, 571; Nakano (n 11) 534–535; Nishitani (n 11) 77.

[102] See above section II.A. Nakano (n 11) 534–35; Nishitani (n 11) 77.

[103] Yamamoto (n 29) 367.

[104] ibid.

[105] See ch 4 of the Family Register Act.

[106] For details of Japanese choice of law rules in family law matters, see Nishioka and Nishitani (n 2). For instance, Art 24 (Formation and Formalities of Marriage) reads as follows:

(1) The formation of a marriage is governed by the national law of each party.
(2) The formalities for a marriage are governed by the law of the place where the marriage is celebrated (lex loci celebrations);
(3) Notwithstanding the preceding paragraph, the formalities that comply with the national law of either party to a marriage are valid; provided, however, that this does not apply where a marriage is celebrated in Japan and either party to the marriage is a Japanese national.

of paternity may entail the application of foreign law by the officials of a relevant authority to validate the acknowledgement.[107]

When the administrative authorities are required to apply a foreign law, they normally refer to publications in Japanese.[108] If they are not able to collect relevant information from sources available to them, they eventually refer to the Civil Affairs Bureau of the Ministry of Justice. For instance, in the case of marriage between a Japanese woman and a man from state A, where it is unclear how the law of state A regulates that marriage and the local authority to which the couple submitted a marriage notification makes reference on whether they should accept a marriage notification, the Ministry of Justice normally reverts to the local authority with a concrete answer (that is, whether the authority can accept a marriage notification).[109]

B. Arbitration, Mediation and Legal Services by Practitioners

Foreign law often has to be applied to determine the merits of a case in international commercial arbitration. According to Article 36 of the Japanese Arbitration Act, the arbitral tribunal shall 'decide the dispute in accordance with such rules of law as are agreed by the parties as applicable to the substance of the disputes'; absent such agreement, the arbitral tribunal 'shall apply the substantive law of the State with which the civil dispute subject to the arbitral proceedings is most closely connected'.[110] In the arbitration context, there is no equivalent rigorous reference system as in Japanese court proceedings. Therefore, arbitrators normally require the parties to tender evidence of and make submissions on the foreign

[107] Article 3 of the Nationality Act stipulates that:

(1) In cases where a child acknowledged by the father or mother is under twenty years of age (excluding a child who was once a Japanese citizen) and the acknowledging father or mother was a Japanese citizen at the time of the birth of the child, Japanese nationality may be acquired through notification to the Minister of Justice if that father or mother is currently a Japanese citizen or was so at the time of death.
(2) The person making notification under the preceding paragraph will acquire Japanese nationality at the time of the notification.

[108] Nakano (n 11) 535. One of the most often-used literature is M Kimura et al. (eds), *Zentei Shinban-Shogai Koseki no tameno Kakkoku Horitsu to Yoken* (Tokyo, Nihon Kajo Syuppan, 2017). This literature consists of 6 volumes and provides detailed information on the legislation and practice in 192 jurisdictions.

[109] Eg, Answer No. 751 of Director of the Civil Affairs First Division, Civil Affairs Bureau, Ministry of Justice on 9 June 2015. Available at (2016) 923 *Koseki.*

[110] Art 36 of the Japanese Arbitration Act reads as follows:

(1) The law which the Arbitral Tribunal should comply with in making an Arbitral Award shall be as provided by the agreement of the parties. In this case, if laws and regulations of a given State have been designated, such designation shall be deemed as designating the laws and regulations of the State which shall be directly applied to the case and not the laws and regulations of the State providing the application of conflicting domestic and foreign laws and regulations, unless a contrary intention has been clearly indicated.
(2) If an agreement set forth in the preceding paragraph has not been reached, the Arbitral Tribunal shall apply the laws and regulations of a State which has the closest relationship to the civil dispute that has been referred to the arbitration procedure and which should be directly applied to the case.
(3) Notwithstanding the provisions of the preceding two paragraphs, if a clearly indicated request has been made by both of the parties, the Arbitral Tribunal shall decide *ex aequo et bono.*
(4) An Arbitral Tribunal shall decide in accordance with the terms of the contract pertaining to the civil dispute which has been referred to the arbitral procedure, if said contract exists, and take into account the usages applicable to the relevant civil dispute, if any usages exist.

law applicable to a case, much as judges in common law jurisdictions. Parties therefore often submit experts reports on the law applicable to their dispute.

In commercial mediation, the governing law normally does not play an important role, as legal evaluation is, in principle, not required to settle a dispute. In complex commercial disputes, nevertheless, an analysis of law may be the key to an effective mediation. In addition, the governing law may play an important role in family law or succession law disputes before the court-connected mediation in Japan.[111] In case of cross-border family or succession disputes, family court mediators and officers need to ascertain the contents of the law applicable to the merits of a case. In succession cases, the contents of the applicable law typically mean a lot to the parties to a dispute (particularly, statutory portion). In ascertaining the contents of the applicable law, mediators normally refer to publications in Japanese.[112]

Without any doubt, a lawyer may be also required to ascertain the contents of foreign law in their daily advisory work, for instance, counselling in cross-border divorce or succession cases and negotiating or drafting an international contract. Practitioners normally refer to various legal sources written in not only Japanese, but also other languages. In addition, major law firms often engage foreign-registered lawyers (*gaikokuho jimu bengoshi*) who are authorised to give foreign law-related legal services in Japan such as representing a party in international mediation and arbitration (subject to certain conditions).[113] Other legal specialists including patent attorney (*benrishi*),[114] certified public tax accountant (*zeirishi*), and judicial scrivener (*shiho shoshi*)[115] may be also required to ascertain the contents of foreign law in their service. They do so in a similar way to that of lawyer.

IV. Access to Japanese Law

A. Translation of Japanese Laws and Regulations

The Ministry of Justice provides English translations of most (but not all) Japanese laws, ancillary regulations, and rules on the website 'Japanese Law Translation Database System'.[116] However, the English translations provided there are not official and, in some

[111] Nakano (n 11) 536.

[112] ibid.

[113] Act on Special Measures concerning the Handling of Legal Services by Foreign Lawyers.

[114] Art 4(1) of the Patent Attorney Act read as follows: 'A patent attorney shall, in response to the request of others, engage in the business of representing others regarding procedures with the Japan Patent Office as pertaining to patents, utility models, designs or trademarks, or international applications or international applications for registration, and procedures with the Minister of Economy, Trade and Industry with regard to application an objection or to an award pertaining to patents, utility models, designs or trademarks, giving expert opinions and handling other affairs pertaining to the matters relating to the said procedures.'

[115] According to Art 1 of the Judicial Scrivener Act, '[t]he mission of judicial scriveners is to protect the rights of the people as specialists in the registrations, deposits with official depositories, litigation, and other legal services that comprise their services pursuant to the Judicial Scriveners Act, and to hereby contribute to the formation of a free and fair society.' The main task of judicial scriveners is to draft an official document submitted to relevant authorities. In addition, they are also authorised to represent a party only before a summary court (subject to certain conditions).

[116] www.japaneselawtranslation.go.jp.

cases, may only be tentative (that is, subject to revision[117]). Further, the English translations are not necessarily of the most up-to-date version of a law.[118] Accordingly, users must check whether an English translation is of the current text of a statute or other instrument. Further, the website makes it clear that the Japanese Government 'is not responsible for the accuracy or reliability' of any English translations. Some regulatory authorities (for instance, the Japan Fair Trade Commission[119] and Financial Services Agency[120]) provide unofficial or provisional English translations not just of relevant laws, but also of guidelines on their websites.

According to Japan's Response to the 2008 Questionnaire of Hague Conference on the Treatment of Foreign Law, '[e]ach ministry usually responds to written or oral requests for information on the law of which the ministry takes charge'; '[m]inistries can respond to written requests in English'; and '[m]inistries provide such service for free'.[121]

There are some translations by academics of Japanese laws.[122] Although unofficial, such translations may be available in languages other than English, (in particular, German).[123] Some associations also publish unofficial English translations of relevant laws.[124]

B. Translation of Court Decisions

The website of the Japanese Supreme Court provides information on Japanese court decisions (from those of the lower courts to those of the Supreme Court) in Japanese.[125] The website only provides English translations of recent Supreme court decisions.[126] The Intellectual Property High Court also provides English summaries and translations of court decisions involving intellectual property rights, whether civil or administrative proceedings.[127] For

[117] It is unfortunately unclear whether and when the finalised translation will be uploaded.

[118] In the context of private international law, for example, available English translations of both the Personal Status Litigation Act and Domestic Relations Case Procedure Act that provide jurisdictional rules in status and family matters are that of the previous Act (prior to 2019 amendment). An unofficial English translation is available at (2019) 62 *Japanese Yearbook of International Law* 486–95.

[119] www.jftc.go.jp/en/legislation_gls/index.html.

[120] www.fsa.go.jp/en/laws_regulations/index.html.

[121] This Response used to be available at www.hcch.net/upload/wop/genaff_pd09jp.pdf.

[122] For instance, Z Kitagawa, *Doing Business in Japan* (LexisNexis, 1980 – to date); B Huber and H Nakamura, *Die japanische ZPO in deutscher Sprache* (Köln, Heymanns Verlag, 2006). In the field of private international law, for example, K Anderson and Y Okuda, 'Japan's Private International Law: Act on the General Rules of Application of Laws [Ho no Tekiyo ni Kansuru Tsusokuho], Law No 10 of 1898 (as newly titled and amended 21 June 2006)]' (2006) 8(1) *Asian-Pacific Law & Policy Journal* 160; K Takahashi, 'Japan's Newly Enacted Rules on International Jurisdiction: with a Reflection on Some Issues of Interpretation' (2011) 13 *Japanese Yearbook of Private International Law* 146; Y Okuda, 'Translation of New Rules on International Jurisdiction of Japanese Courts in Family Matters' (2020) 25 *Journal of Japanese Law (Zeitschrift für Japanisches Recht)* 235–46.

[123] For instance, H Kansaku, A Kimura, G Koziol, M Lentz, F Nagano, M Nakamura, T Spiegel, A Katharina Suzuki-Klasen, H Tanaka and K Wada, 'Übersetzung des novellierten Zivilgesetzes 2020' (2018) 23 *Journal of Japanese Law (Zeitschrift für Japanisches Recht)* 183.

[124] For instance, Certified Public Tax Accountant Act by Japan Federation of Certified Public Tax Accountants' Associations (www.nichizeiren.or.jp/eng/pdf/Zeirishi_Act.pdf).

[125] www.courts.go.jp/app/hanrei_jp/search1. Also, there are some databases provided by private companies such as 'Westlaw Japan', 'LEX/DB' and 'D1-Law.com'.

[126] www.courts.go.jp/app/hanrei_en/search?

[127] www.ip.courts.go.jp/app/hanrei_en/search?reload=1.

lower court decisions in other cases (that is, non-intellectual property rights cases), there is no summary or English translations provided by the Japanese courts. But unofficial English translations (sometimes with commentary) of key court decisions in the fields of private and public international law are available in the *Japanese Yearbook of International Law*[128] and other publications.[129] *The Journal of Japanese Law* provides an overview of some of the most important decisions of the Japanese Supreme Court in the area of private law each year (in German).[130]

Furthermore, court decisions on international child abduction (typically with summaries and commentary in English) are available on the 'International Child Abduction Database (INCADAT)' of the Hague Conference on Private International Law.[131]

V. Access to Foreign Law: Future Developments in Asia

Japan has not so far concluded any bilateral or multilateral treaties on the proof of, or providing information on, foreign law. Japanese courts therefore have to ascertain the contents of foreign law through their own means (see II.B). For cross-border child-abduction cases, Japan joined the International Hague Network of Judges (IHNJ) in 1985.[132] IHNJ judges are able to liaise with IHNJ judges of other states through this network. Since August 2021 there have been three Japanese judges on the members' list of IHNJ. Japan is not a member of the European Judicial Network for civil and commercial matters.[133] Japan has not joined any other comparable framework,[134] there being no other international or regional frameworks facilitating access to foreign law.

As a result, the current situation in Japan on access to foreign law is not satisfactory. This means that the process of ascertaining the contents of foreign law is time-consuming and costly, and can lead to unpredictable results.[135] Many judges and officials of local authorities normally refer to publications in Japanese because they have not received the training necessary to utilise resources in non-Japanese languages. However, literature and other sources in Japanese are not necessarily reliable as, for instance, they might not provide up-to-date information on relevant laws. Consequently, the parties will often be asked to submit expert reports on foreign law, which can be expensive. Considering the current situation, we can

[128] www.ilajapan.org/jyil/.

[129] For instance, M Bälz, M Dernauer, C Heath and A Petersen-Padberg (eds), *Business Law in Japan – Cases and Comments: Intellectual Property, Civil, Commercial and International Private Law* (Alphen aan den Rijn, Kluwer, 2012). For arbitration cases, see, K Ogawa, 'Introduction to Japanese Arbitration Act with Court Cases', available at idrc.jp/en/.

[130] www.zjapanr.de/index.php/zjapanr.

[131] www.incadat.com/en. Most of English Translations on INCADAT are provided by the Hague Convention Division of the Consular Affairs Bureau of the Ministry of Foreign Affairs of Japan.

[132] www.hcch.net/en/instruments/conventions/specialised-sections/child-abduction/ihnj. Each Member State designates one or more members of the judiciary to act as a channel of communication and liaison with their National Central Authorities, with other judges within their jurisdictions and judges in other Contracting States to deal with the 1980 Hague Child Abduction Convention cases.

[133] e-justice.europa.eu/content_european_judicial_network_in_civil_and_commercial_matters-21-en.do.

[134] Eg, Inter-American Convention on Proof of and Information on Foreign Law on 8 May 1979. The text of this convention is available at www.un.org/ruleoflaw/files/volume-1439-I-24393-English.pdf.

[135] Nakano (n 11) 538.

see an obvious need to improve access to foreign law. There should be a more efficient and easy-to-use mechanism for judicial and administrative authorities.[136]

A recent notable development is that Japan has concluded a memorandum of cooperation ('MOC') with some countries in Asia, for instance, Singapore,[137] Thailand[138] and Vietnam.[139] According to paragraph 1 of the MOC with Singapore,

> [t]he Participants will cooperate on matters of mutual interest, including but not limited to the following fields: (a) International commercial dispute resolution; (b) People-to-people exchanges in the legal sector; and (c) Other areas decided by the Participants.

Paragraph 2 (Forms of Cooperation) stipulates that

> [t]he Participants may cooperate in the fields mentioned in Paragraph 1 (Scope of Cooperation) in the following means: (a) Exchanging of legal publications; (b) Exchanging visits and study trips; (c) Organising and holding meetings, conferences and dialogues; and/or (d) Other forms of cooperation as may be decided by the Participants.

Although the MOC is a notable development in the field of international commercial dispute resolution in Japan, it does not directly deal with 'access to foreign law'. According to paragraph 6.1, '[e]ach Participant will ensure the confidentiality of information and knowledge obtained in the course of the cooperative activities under this MOC and use them solely for the purpose of implementing this MOC'. Thus, the MOC, by itself, is unlikely to facilitate the access to foreign law in Japan. To improve the situation on the access to foreign law in Japan, concrete measures will be needed.

There may still be cases where courts will be unable to ascertain the contents of foreign law applicable to the merits of a case and need to apply some other law out of necessity. This would be despite a perceptible decrease since the 1990s in the number of court decisions declaring that the content of some foreign law cannot be ascertained. Considering the underlying thrust of choice of law in private international law (that is, application of the law that is most closely connected to a case), the application of some other law due to an inability to discern foreign law should be resisted as much as possible. It is preferable (and necessary) to set up an international or regional mechanism to enable judiciaries to access and ascertain foreign law readily.[140] Such mechanism will serve the parties' interests, as it will enable them to reduce the cost, time and unpredictability of court proceedings.

[136] ibid.
[137] www.moj.go.jp/content/001353708.pdf.
[138] www.moj.go.jp/content/001312005.pdf.
[139] www.moj.go.jp/content/001331839.pdf.
[140] The HCCH has been making their best efforts for this. However, their project has not so far brought any product.

6

South Korea

SUNGJAE CHUN*

I. Introduction

Throughout 2021, South Korea's total amount of trade reached US$1.2 trillion, marking the highest record ever.[1] As a nation with an export-oriented economy, it is inevitable for Korean companies to face disputes with international elements and for Korean courts to review and adjudicate the same. For this reason, the issue on the treatment of foreign law at Korean courts indeed deserves genuine attention.

A. Mandatory Nature of the Application of the Choice of Law Rules

To begin with, it should be noted that Korean law has a statute dedicated to regulating the issues regarding choice of law rules, titled the Act on Private International Law ('KAPIL'). As the Korean jurisprudence is categorised among the civil law system, KAPIL is considered as the quintessential source of law, while judgments rendered by the Supreme Court of Korea hold substantial value in practice.

This said, the Korean court's position on whether the application of choice of law rules would be mandatory or facultative should be checked. In this regard, the Supreme Court of Korea examined this issue back in 1982, in a case concerning a dispute between a Korean citizen and a Japanese company over a joint and several guarantee contract. In this case, the Supreme Court ruled that, even if the parties did not make any arguments on the issue of governing law, it is mandatory for the court to consider choice of law rules in a case involving international factors.[2]

In a more recent case regarding a dispute between a Korean company and a Dutch company, the Supreme Court ruled that, in a case involving international factors, the court should actively exercise the right to elucidation and request the parties to submit an opinion and/or materials on the potential application of foreign laws.[3]

* This chapter represents the author's personal view and is not related to the company.

[1] San-up-tong-sang-ja-won-bu [Ministry of Trade, Industry and energy] '2021-nyun soo-chool-aek, moo-yuk-aek 'sa-sang choi-dae" (Dae-han-min-guk Jeong-chaek-briefing [Korea Policy Briefing] 4 January 2022), available online: www.korea.kr/news/visualNewsView.do?newsId=148897615(accessed 10 February 2022).

[2] Judgment of the Supreme Court, 24 August 1982, 81Da684.

[3] Judgment of the Supreme Court, 13 January 2022, 2021Da269388.

Gathering from the above, it is understood that the court views that the application of choice of rules under Korean law as mandatory and that the court should apply the said rules regardless of whether a party brings forward an argument about the above issues.[4] Likewise, the majority of scholars in Korea also supports the mandatory nature of choice of law rules.[5]

B. Choice of Law Rules and the Application of Foreign Law

KAPIL Article 45, paragraph 1 (Party's Autonomy) stipulates:

> (1) A contract shall be governed by the law which the parties choose explicitly or implicitly: Provided, That the implicit choice shall be limited to the case in which the implicit choice can be reasonably recognized by the content of the contract and all other circumstances.

The aforementioned provision provides for a general principle of party autonomy, upholding the parties' legitimate expectations of stability in international transactions.[6] In this regard, there are several precedents in which the Korean courts applied foreign law as per the choice of law rules.

One example would be a recent case between foreign companies (one in the US and the other in Japan) and a Korean company. In this case, the engineering contract (which was the basis of the claimants' request for monetary compensation) stipulated that the governing law of the contract was the Illinois State law of the US. Based on the above, the court ruled that the choice of law rules should be applied to ascertain the applicable law and that upon the application of the choice of law rules, Illinois law applied.[7]

C. Application of Mandatory Provisions

KAPIL Article 20 (Mandatory Application of Acts of the Republic of Korea) states:

> In the light of the purpose of legislation, irrespective of the applicable laws, the mandatory provisions of the Republic of Korea shall govern the corresponding legal relations even if foreign laws are designated as applicable laws thereof under this Act.[8]

Here, the KAPIL does not explicate the detailed meaning and the scope of what constitutes a mandatory provision. In practice, the court will peruse relevant provisions and their legislative history and determine their legal nature on a case-by-case basis. A recent notable decision rendered by the Korean court on this issue is as follows:

> The claimant (a Korean company) filed a lawsuit against the defendant (a Canadian company), seeking compensation under Article 56, Paragraph 1 of the Korean Monopoly Regulation and Fair

[4] KH Suk, *Guk-je-sa-bub Hae-sol [Commentary on Private International Law]* (Seoul, Pakyoungsa, 2013) 128.

[5] Suk (n 4) 128.

[6] KH Suk, *Guk-je-sa-bub-gwa Guk-je-so-song Je-6-kwon [Private International Law and International Litigation Vol 6]* (Seoul, Pakyoungsa, 2019) 93.

[7] Judgment of the Supreme Court, 24 December 2019, 2016Da222712.

[8] 'Act on Private International Law' (National Law Information Center), available online: law.go.kr/engLsSc.do?menuId=1&subMenuId=21&tabMenuId=117#.

Trade Act ('Monopoly Regulation Act').[9] In this case, the Seoul High Court ruled that, although the contract between the parties stipulates that the governing law is the laws of Ontario, Canada, the Monopoly Regulation Act is applicable.

Here, the court focused on the very first provision of the Monopoly Regulation Act, which stipulates its purpose as:

> to promote fair and free competition, encourage thereby creative business activities, protect consumers, and strive for balanced development of the national economy, by preventing business entities from abusing their market-dominant positions and any excessive concentration of economic power and by regulating illegal cartel conduct and unfair trade practices (Article 1).

Considering the above, the court recognised that based on the legislative purpose of the Monopoly Regulation Act it should be mandatorily applied, regardless of applicable foreign law as agreed by between the parties.[10]

Other examples of mandatory rules under Korean law include the Foreign Trade Act, the Foreign Exchange Transaction Act and the Cultural Heritage Protection Act.[11]

D. Exceptions to the Mandatory Application of Foreign Law

KAPIL Article 23 (Provisions of Foreign Law Contrary to Social Order) provides:

> In case a foreign law shall govern, if the application of provisions of the foreign law shall evidently violate good customs and other social order of the Republic of Korea, the law shall not apply.

Based on Article 23 of the KAPIL, the court shall not apply foreign law in case the result incurred by applying the foreign law violates the social order of Korea.[12] Here, it should be noted that the issue at hand is the 'result' of the application of foreign law and not the 'content' of the foreign law itself and the social order denotes 'international public policy'.[13]

Whilst it is understood that there does not yet exist a clear precedent in which Article 23 of the KAPIL was actually triggered, the majority of scholars view that, in a case where the foreign law is not applicable due to Article 23 of the KAPIL, Korean law would be applied alternatively in that particular case.[14]

[9] For reference, the former Art 56, para 1 of the Monopoly Regulation and Fair Trade Act corresponds to Art 109, para 1 of the same Act. The said provision states:

> Article 56 (Liability for Compensation) (1) Where a person sustains damage because a business entity or trade association violates any provision of this Act, the business entity or trade association shall be liable to compensate for the damage: Provided, That the foregoing shall not apply where the business entity or trade association verifies that the damage was caused neither by intention nor by negligence.

[10] Judgment of the Seoul Hight Court, 11 February 2010, 2009Na31323.
[11] Suk (n 6) 96.
[12] Suk (n 4) 174.
[13] Suk (n 4) 175–76.
[14] Suk (n 4) 179.

II. Foreign Law before Judicial Authorities

A. Nature of Foreign Law as 'Law'

At the outset, the Civil Procedure Act of Korea applies the so-called inquisitorial proceeding principle, in which each party is, in principle, required to present its arguments and to submit evidentiary materials which support the said argument, and the court shall only consider the said arguments and materials during the proceedings.[15]

However, there are certain exceptions to this principle. With regards to the issues that need to be examined as objectively as possible, the court shall gather evidentiary materials under its own responsibility and consider the said materials as a basis for the judgment.[16] Examples could be materials related to foreign law and customary law.[17] On an additional note, the Administrative Litigation Act (Article 26) and Family Litigation Act (Article 17) allow the court to examine issues that the parties have not presented and to examine evidentiary materials *ex officio*.[18]

There are varying opinions among scholars on the nature of foreign law. Some view foreign law as a matter of 'fact' in which the burden of proof would lie on the parties, some others consider that foreign law becomes a part of domestic law, but the majority opinion recognises foreign law as 'law' which is entirely separate from domestic law.[19] In this regard, foreign law would be applied and treated equally as domestic law.

As explained above, it is understood that the Korean court's position and that of the majority of scholars interpret the nature of foreign law as 'law' rather than 'fact'.[20] For this reason, the court has ruled that the ascertainment and interpretation of foreign law should accurately reflect how it is being actually applied in that country.[21]

Further, it is also understood that the common law countries tend to treat foreign law as a matter of 'fact' whereas civil law countries such as Germany, Austria, Switzerland and Japan regard foreign law as a matter of 'law', in which the court is required to investigate on its own.[22]

B. Ascertainment of Foreign Law

i. *The Application of* 'iura novit curia' *Principle*

KAPIL Article 18 (Application of Foreign Law) states:

> A court shall investigate and apply, on its own initiative, the contents of the foreign law designated by this Act and may request a party's cooperation for the purpose.

[15] SY Lee, *Shin-min-sa-so-song-bub [New Civil Procedure Act]*, 12th edn, (Seoul, Pakyoungsa, 2018) 326.
[16] ibid 334.
[17] ibid 326.
[18] ibid 326.
[19] KH Suk, *Guk-je-min-sa-so-song-bub [International Civil Litigation Law]* (Seoul, Pakyoungsa, 2012) 326.
[20] ibid; Judgment of the Supreme Court, 25 March 2010, 2008Da88375.
[21] Judgment of the Supreme Court, 25 March 2010, 2008Da88375.
[22] AR Han, 'Jun-ge-bub-in Eo-guk-bub-ui Jo-sa-e Gwan-han So-go' ['A Study on the Investigation of the Foreign Law as the Governing Law'] (2019) *Guk-je-sa-bub-yeon-gu [Korea Private International Law Journal]* 33, 35–37.

The aforementioned provision was introduced when KAPIL was fully revised in 2001.[23] It is understood that Article 18 of the KAPIL is similar to Article 16, paragraph 1 of the Swiss Private International Law.[24]

Based on the literal interpretation of Article 18 of the KAPIL, it is understood that the principle of *iura novit curia* is applied to obligate the court to investigate and confirm the contents of the foreign law that is applicable in the handling case. In this regard, the court should, in principle, make use of all available resources to analyse and scrutinise the applicable foreign law, regardless of the parties' arguments being presented.[25] Further, since foreign law is treated as 'law' rather than 'fact' under Korean law, the court may not put the same level of burden of proof on the parties to prove the contents of foreign law as that of the 'facts'.[26]

This is the reason why Article 18 of the KAPIL merely stipulates that the court may ask for a party's cooperation rather than require a party to search the contents of the applicable foreign law. Here, 'cooperation' connotes that the parties may provide precedents or other sources of foreign law that may be difficult for the court to be aware of.[27]

Meanwhile, there is an issue on whether the court would be required to investigate and confirm the contents of foreign law, even in cases of provisional measures. The said issue stems from a concern that cases on provisional measures are usually reviewed and processed very quickly and that any unnecessary delay may defeat the purpose of the application of a provisional measure. Nonetheless, a prevailing opinion among the scholars is that the applicable foreign law should be applied in principle even in cases of provisional measures.[28] However, the level of proof required is lowered to 'vindication' (疎明), in which the judge would only be required to establish a firm understanding.[29]

In this regard, vessel arrest can be a good example of a provisional measure in which foreign law may apply.

On this, Article 94, subparagraph 1 of the KAPIL provides that the issues regarding maritime lien shall be ruled by the law of the flag state. It is widely understood that shipping companies usually establish a special-purpose company (SPC) in a foreign country such as Panama and the Marshall Islands to register their vessels in the flag of convenience.

As a result, Korean courts would be required, in principle, to analyse and examine the laws of the aforementioned countries in case of a vessel arrest based on maritime lien. In practice, the applicant would usually acquire an expert opinion from a law firm of that country and submit the same and its translation as evidence. Whilst the court may request the applicant to submit further evidence on the applicable foreign law, the court does, in fact, often render a decision to proceed with the arrest of the vessel.

[23] ibid 38.
[24] ibid 38.
[25] Suk (n 4) 125.
[26] Han (n 22) 39.
[27] Suk (n 4) 126.
[28] KH Suk, 'Han-guk-bub-won-e-seo je-gi-deon joong-guk-bub-ui jaeng-jum – gye-yak-bub, bul-bup-haeng-wi-bup, hon-in-bup-gwa oi-guk-pan-gyul-ui seung-in jip-haeng-eul joong-sim-ui-ro' ['Several Chinese Law Issues raised before Korean Courts: With Emphases on Laws on Contract, Tort, Marriage and Recognition and Enforcement of Foreign Judgments'] (2010) 51(3) *Seoul-dae-hak-kyo-bup-hak [Seoul Law Journal]* 181, 184.
[29] IY Min, 'Ju-seok Min-sa-so-song-bup' ['Commentary on Civil Procedure Act'] (2018) *Han-guk-sa-bub-haeng-jong-hak-hoi [Korea Private Law Administration Academy]* 196.

ii. Means to Ascertain the Contents of Foreign Law

At the outset, the KAPIL is silent about the method which can be used by the court to ascertain the contents of foreign law.[30]

In practice, it is understood that there is no particular limit as to the means and resources that the court may use to ascertain foreign law. Thus, the court is not obligated to obtain expert testimony or a fact-finding inquiry from government agencies and educational institutions.[31] In light of this, it is possible that individual judges may work with reliable legal databases on foreign law or even ask other judges or research judges (ie, an official at the judiciary branch dedicated to research works on complex legal disputes ongoing at Korean courts) about the contents and legal principles relevant to the applicable foreign law.[32]

There may be a due process concern with regards to whether the court should provide each party a chance to review and present its opinion with regards to the court's finding of foreign law. In practice, the court is likely to clarify the core issues of the case, especially if the case deals with complex foreign law. By doing so, each party is often provided with a chance to review and present its argument on the same, which ultimately helps the court to adjudicate the handling case in an accurate manner.

On the other hand, the court may request the parties to submit relevant materials to explain the contents of the applicable foreign law.[33] It is possible that one party may face disadvantages in case the court does not clearly understand the contents of foreign law. In this case, that party may submit to the court the relevant materials on the interpretation and application of relevant foreign law (such as private expert opinions), and the court may take the said materials into account if it is found to be reliable.[34]

iii. Provision of Legal Information

At the outset, it is understood that there is no provision under Korean law which requires specific qualifications for an individual or an institution to provide legal information. However, in practice, the court may request the parties to submit legal information on foreign law prepared and written by a legal professional holding a licence in that country.

It is understood that in a case where the parties have designated foreign law (especially US law) as the governing law, there is a practice for a party to procure an affidavit testimony from an attorney licensed in that country and submit the same to the court to shed light on the interpretation of the foreign law.[35] Here, in practice, the affidavit testimony is often considered as having equal weight as that of evidence rather than reference materials.[36]

Some scholars raise a concern about the said practice, pointing out that the parties tend to submit affidavit testimony that is advantageous to themselves and that in case the parties' affidavit testimonials are contradictory, it may create some confusion and may lead

[30] Suk (n 28) 184.
[31] Judgment of the Supreme Court, 10 April 1990, 89Daka20252.
[32] Han (n 22) 52.
[33] ibid 43.
[34] ibid 40.
[35] ibid 53.
[36] ibid 54.

to a wrongful interpretation of foreign law.[37] The fact that the Korean courts tend to briefly explain the interpretation of foreign law on judgment makes it even harder for relevant precedents to be accumulated.[38]

Meanwhile, it is rare for the court to directly seek a legal professional in foreign law nor appoint an expert witness to investigate the contents of foreign law.[39]

iv. The Issue of Binding Force of Legal Information Provided

As explained above, the court bears the main responsibility to ascertain the substance of foreign law to be applied in a particular case. Thus, in principle, the parties are not obligated to present an argument on the foreign law, nor is the court bound by the parties' assertion or arguments about the application and/or contents of foreign law.[40]

In light of this, the legal information provided would not be binding upon the judicial authorities, and the court may take into account the said information only if the court considers it to be appropriate and accurate.[41] Note that a concrete set of criteria or mechanisms to evaluate the credibility of legal information does not exist. In this regard, the Supreme Court of Korea ruled that, since there is no specific restriction under the Civil Procedure Act on the procedures and/or evidentiary materials related to the applicable foreign law, the court has complete discretion in ascertaining the contents of applicable foreign law.[42]

v. Examination of the Reliability of the Legal Information Provided

Article 202 of the Civil Procedure Act of Korea (Principle of Free Evaluation of Evidence) provides:

> A court shall determine, by its free conviction, whether or not an allegation of facts is true, taking account of the whole purport of pleadings and the results of examination of evidence, on the basis of the ideology of social justice and equity in accordance with the principles of logic and experiences.[43]

Based on the above provision, Korean courts have a wide range of discretion in terms of evaluating the evidentiary materials. In light of this, it is understood that there is no particular mechanism to examine the reliability of the legal information provided.

[37] Suk (n 28) 185.

[38] ibid.

[39] Han (n 22) 55–56.

[40] ibid 41; Lee (n 15) 334–35.

[41] Han (n 22) 40.

[42] Judgment of the Supreme Court, 28 July 1992, 91Da41897. For reference, it is understood that the concept of 'free proof' has been first developed in Germany, which was accepted in Japanese legislation and finally affected the Korean jurisprudence [Jeong Han Kim, 'Jeung-geo-jae-pan-ju-ui-ui ui-mi-wa um-gyuk-han jeung-myung, ja-yu-ro-un jeung-myung' ['The Reconsideration of "Principle of Trial by Evidence", and Strict Proof, Free Proof'] (2010) 17(1) *Chosun-dae-bup-hak-non-chong [The Legal Studies Institute of Chosun University]* 459, 469.

[43] It is understood that Art 202 of the Civil Procedure Act has been derived from the German law concept of 'Freie Beweiswürdigung', in which the court is given full discretion on reviewing the evidentiary materials (Lee (n 15) 530).

vi. Cost of Ascertaining Foreign Law

Article 98 of the Civil Procedure Act (Principle of Bearing Costs of Lawsuit) expounds that the costs of a lawsuit shall be borne by the losing party.

Here, it is understood that the meaning of the 'costs' includes the costs that the court has spent discretionally on reviewing the case.[44] In this regard, any cost that the court may have paid in the course of ascertaining the contents of applicable foreign law shall be, in principle, borne by the losing party. However, if the court has undertaken unofficial research on foreign law, then it can be said that relevant costs shall be borne by the judiciary.[45]

In the meantime, Article 116 of the Civil Procedure Act (Prepayment of Costs) states:

(1) In regard to the litigation incurring costs, the court may have the party make a prepayment of such costs.
(2) When the costs have not been prepaid, the court may refuse to do such litigation.

Based on the above provision, it is understood that the court may order a party who may benefit from applying foreign law to make a prepayment of costs that can be incurred for researching materials related to the applicable foreign law.[46]

C. Interpretation and Application of Foreign Law

i. Ex officio *Application of Foreign Law*

As explained above, foreign law is treated as 'law' rather than 'fact'. In this regard, in principle, foreign law is applied *ex officio* by the court. However, in practice, the court may request each party to submit its opinion on the governing law and its contents when foreign law can potentially be applied.

ii. The Interpretation and Application of Foreign Law by Korean Courts

Whilst KAPIL is silent on how the court should interpret and apply foreign law, the Supreme Court of Korea ruled that foreign law should be interpreted in the same way applied in the country of origin.[47] Further, the Supreme Court ruled that the interpretation of the highest court of that country shall be upheld unless there exist special circumstances.[48] Thus, the courts may not interpret or apply foreign law under the lens of Korean jurisprudence.

On the other hand, an additional issue arises as to how that foreign law could be interpreted in a case where there does not exist sufficient materials to figure out or clarify its appropriate interpretation. The Supreme Court of Korea held that, in a case where parties fail to submit materials to explain the contents of the applicable foreign law to the court's satisfaction, the court should apply the general principle of interpretation of law to ascertain its contents.[49]

[44] Han (n 22) 56.
[45] ibid 57.
[46] ibid 57.
[47] Judgment of the Supreme Court, 9 February 1996, 94Da30041.
[48] Judgment of the Supreme Court, 28 June 2007, 2006Da5130.
[49] Judgment of the Supreme Court, 22 February 1991, 90Daka19470.

The court does not explain what constitutes 'the general principle of interpretation of law'. Some scholars view that the general principle of interpretation of law includes literal interpretation, structural interpretation, historical interpretation and teleological interpretation.[50]

iii. A Gap in Foreign Law

As explained above, the Korean court's position is that the contents of foreign law should be interpreted and applied in the same manner as in that country. However, in the case where the contents of foreign law have certain flaws or the parties have failed to provide relevant materials so that the court cannot check and ascertain the contents of the applicable foreign law, then the court has to, based on the basic principle of Korean civil law, apply the customary law of that country. If it is impossible to check and ascertain the contents of the customary law of that country, then the court would ultimately apply sound reasoning.[51]

Here, it is understood that 'sound reasoning' denotes natural reasoning or the general legal principle of law. In a case involving a dispute over bills of exchange and promissory notes in which the governing law (ie, Chinese law) did not have relevant provision at the time of the occurrence of the said dispute, the Korean court ruled that, based on sound reasoning, it is reasonable to apply the newly revised Chinese law on bills of exchange which was formulated after the occurrence of the said dispute.[52]

iv. Failure to Establish Foreign Law

There are various opinions among Korean scholars about which law should be applied when the contents of foreign law cannot be clarified. Some view that domestic law should be applied, taking other foreign law provisions as examples – such as Swiss law and Austrian law.[53] However, others opined 'sound reasoning' can be applied, since allowing an exception to apply domestic law may let courts choose to apply domestic law too easily.[54]

The Korean courts held that 'the general principle of law' can be applied in cases where the contents of foreign law cannot be clarified at all due to a lack of evidentiary materials to explain the contents of applicable foreign law.[55] However, while stating this general principle of applying the general principle of law, the Supreme Court actually reversed and remanded the appeal court's decision in this case.[56] Here, the case involved the interpretation of a letter of indemnity under English law. The Supreme Court ruled that the appeal court had erred in recourse to the general principle of law without fully analysing the requirements under English law in establishing a contract based on the letter of indemnity.

However, some scholars criticised the court's stance as being inconsistent. In some cases, courts: (i) apply domestic law and the general principle of law;[57] (ii) gather up relevant

[50] Suk (n 15) 188.
[51] Judgment of the Supreme Court, 8 July 2021, 2017Da218895.
[52] Judgment of the Supreme Court, 9 June 2000, 98Da35037.
[53] Suk (n 19) 335.
[54] ibid 335.
[55] Han (n 22) 45.
[56] Judgment of the Supreme Court, 25 March 2010, 2008Da88375.
[57] Judgment of the Supreme Court, 24 December 2001, 2001Da30469.

materials on foreign law and make their interpretation of foreign law;[58] (iii) consider other countries' precedents which interpret the applicable foreign law;[59] or (iv) simply proceed to make a literal interpretation of the foreign law.[60]

Based on recent judgments, it is understood that the lower courts' position is close to position (iii) in the above, as position (iii) seems to be the most recent ruling by the Supreme Court on this issue.[61] Whilst the Supreme Court's judgments do not have a binding effect in principle, these judgments have a significant influence in interpreting Korean law in practice.

D. Judicial Review/Appeal

Article 390, paragraph 1 of the Civil Procedure Act of Korea (Object of Appeal) stipulates:

> An appeal may be filed against a final judgment rendered by a district court in the first instance: Provided, That the same shall not apply where both parties have agreed not to file an appeal subsequent to the final judgment, by withholding the right to file an appeal in the second instance.

At the outset, the Civil Procedure Act does not restrict the grounds for appeal on the judgment rendered by the court of the first instance.[62] In this regard, a party may submit an appeal if the court of the first instance has wrongfully applied or interpreted foreign law.

Further, Article 423 of the Civil Procedure Act of Korea (Grounds for Appeal to Supreme Court) states:

> An appeal to the Supreme Court may be filed only when stating as the grounds therefor that there has been a violation of the Constitution, Acts, administrative decrees, or regulations, which has affected the judgment.[63]

Within the context of the application of foreign law, two instances should be separately considered.

[58] Judgment of the Supreme Court, 31 January 2008, 2004Da26454.

[59] Judgment of the Supreme Court, 12 May 2016, 2015Da49811.

[60] Judgment of the Supreme Court, 29 June 2007, 2006Da5130.

[61] Judgment of the Seoul High Court, 16 September 2021, 2018Nu64025; Judgment of the Seoul Administrative Court, 26 March 2021, 2019Guhap89555.

[62] Lee (n 15) 861.

[63] For reference, the Art 424 of the Civil Procedure Act of Korea stipulates a set of 'absolute' grounds for appeal to the Supreme Court as follows:

> (1) When there exists in a judgment any one ground of the following subparagraphs, it shall be deemed that there exists a justifiable ground in the appeal to the Supreme Court:
>
> 1. When an adjudicating court has not been constituted in compliance with the provisions of Acts;
> 2. When a judge, who is ineligible to take part in a judgment pursuant to the provisions of Acts, has participated in the judgment;
> 3. When the provisions as to an exclusive jurisdiction have been violated;
> 4. When there is any defect in granting a legal representation right, powers of attorney, or a special authority for the litigation by a representative;
> 5. When the provisions for opening the pleadings to the public have been violated;
> 6. When the grounds for a judgment are not clarified, or contain any contradiction.

First, the appeal court may wrongfully apply the KAPIL (ie, in the case in which the court applies the law of country A, while the correct law to be applied is the law of country B under the conflict of laws rule). In this case, a party will be able to file an appeal to the Supreme Court since the appeal court has erred in interpreting and applying the KAPIL (ie, a violation of the Act).[64]

Second, it is possible that the appeal court has applied a correct foreign law but erred in the interpretation of that foreign law. Here, the majority view among the scholars is that a party may lawfully submit an appeal to the Supreme Court.[65] The reasoning is that the Supreme Court is the institution that can correctly interpret and apply foreign law and that such interpretation and application would have a significant impact on Korean jurisprudence.[66]

Even further, some scholars argue that, since the court has an obligation and responsibility to correctly interpret and apply law, even if a party did not present an argument on the wrongful interpretation of foreign law, the Supreme Court has to review the contents of the foreign law to check whether the appeal court had made any errors in the application and interpretation of applicable foreign law.[67,68]

III. Access to Korean Law

At the outset, a government institution named the Korea Legislation Research Institute ('KLRI') provides English translations of Korean law on its website. Although the said website does not provide every single provision under Korean jurisprudence, as of March 2022, 14,321 English translations of various statutes and enforcement decrees are being provided.[69] In addition, KLRI publishes an English-only law journal on Korean law on its website.[70]

In the meantime, the Supreme Court provides English and Chinese translations of selected judgments on its website.[71] Also, the Constitutional Court of Korea regularly updates English translations of selected decisions on its website.[72] Further, major law firms in Korea provide up-to-date information on current issues on their websites and regularly issue newsletters on various topics under Korean jurisprudence.

[64] Suk (n 4) 134.
[65] ibid 134.
[66] Suk (n 19) 339.
[67] Han (n 22) 44.
[68] It is understood that how other administrative bodies and/or arbitral tribunals in Korea treat foreign law would not be so much different from that of the courts, it is difficult to find any material to ascertain the position of other administrative bodies and/or arbitral tribunals.
[69] elaw.klri.re.kr/kor_service/lawStatistics.do (accessed 3 March 2022).
[70] www.klri.re.kr/eng/engpub/list.do.
[71] library.scourt.go.kr/kor/judgment/eng_judg.jsp.
[72] english.ccourt.go.kr/site/eng/main.do.

IV. Access to Foreign Law

The Korean Government has entered into bilateral treaties with multiple countries on judicial assistance in civil and commercial matters, namely Australia, China, Mongolia, Uzbekistan and Thailand.[73]

Based on the said treaties, each country may request the other country to provide information about legal proceedings. However, it is understood that, in practice, it is rare for Korean courts to request the other country's judicial branch to provide legal information based on the said treaties, due to the time-consuming procedure.[74]

V. Conclusion

On 4 January 2022, the KAPIL was thoroughly revised. Whilst the revised version is essentially the same in terms of choice of law rules, the revised statute introduces detailed criteria for determining whether the Korean courts have jurisdiction in a case with international elements, along with a set of general provisions on international jurisdiction.[75] The revised version of the KAPIL has entered into force on 5 July 2022.

In light of the above, it is understood that the legislative branch is aware of the importance of conflict of law rules, thereby putting substantial efforts to ameliorate the relevant statute. However, mere revision of legal provisions would not be effective, if it does not receive as much attention in practice. Hopefully, the revised KAPIL will serve as an impetus among the legal scholars and practitioners in the field of conflict of laws, which will contribute to the promotion of the rule of law under Korean jurisprudence.

[73] Han (n 22) 52. For reference, the links to the conventions are as follows: (i) Korea-Australia: www.law.go.kr/LSW/trtyBInfoP.do?trtySeq=1122, (ii) Korea-China: law.go.kr/trtySc.do?menuId=1&subMenuId=25&tabMenuId=135&query=%EB%AF%BC%EC%82%AC%EC%82%AC%EB%B2%95%EA%B3%B5%EC%A1%B0#licTrty965 (Chinese version available as attachment in the above website); (iii) Korea-Mongolia: law.go.kr/trtySc.do?menuId=1&subMenuId=25&tabMenuId=135&query=%EB%AF%BC%EC%82%AC%EC%82%AC%EB%B2%95%EA%B3%B5%EC%A1%B0#licTrty2515; (iv) Korea-Uzbekistan: law.go.kr/trtySc.do?menuId=1&subMenuId=25&tabMenuId=135&query=%EB%AF%BC%EC%82%AC%EC%82%AC%EB%B2%95%EA%B3%B5%EC%A1%B0#licTrty7737 (English version available as attachment in the above website); (v) Korea-Thailand: law.go.kr/trtySc.do?menuId=1&subMenuId=25&tabMenuId=135&query=%EB%AF%BC%EC%82%AC%EC%82%AC%EB%B2%95%EA%B3%B5%EC%A1%B0#licTrty10797 (English version available as attachment in the above website).

[74] Suk (n 19) 335.

[75] 'Act on Private International Law' (National Law Information Center), available online: www.law.go.kr/LSW//lsInfoP.do?lsiSeq=238791&ancYd=20220104&ancNo=18670&efYd=20220705&nwJoYnInfo=N&efGubun=Y&chrClsCd=010202&ancYnChk=0#0000.

7

Singapore

ANDREAS WEHOWSKY AND ALVIN TAN

I. Introduction

Singapore has long been an international business hub and has over the past few decades fortified its position as the major dispute resolution centre in South-East Asia, notwithstanding fierce competition from other jurisdictions.[1] It is thus no surprise that foreign law plays a vital part in the legal practice in Singapore. Not only that, with the establishment of the Singapore International Commercial Court ('SICC'), Singapore has even dedicated a specific judicial forum for the resolution of international disputes, in which foreign law regularly features.[2]

The application of (foreign) law in the common law jurisdiction of Singapore has been influenced by English court cases[3] and by means of statutory provisions the common law of England (including the principles and rules of equity) to a certain extent still forms part of the law of Singapore.[4] Yet, as will be seen in the following, Singapore has developed its own approach and body of authorities on the application of foreign law.

This chapter will provide an overview of how courts and other judicial authorities apply foreign law in Singapore. Section II starts by exploring the status of choice of laws rules in Singapore. Building on that, section III explains the treatment of foreign law by Singapore courts. Section IV describes the procedure of establishing foreign law before the Singapore courts, with an added focus on the practice of the Singapore International Commercial Court. Section V then focusses on the judicial review of foreign law in appeal procedures. Section VI separately examines the application of foreign law before other authorities, such as administrative bodies and arbitral tribunals and other authorities in the ADR context, and

[1] Queen Mary University of London and White & Case LLP, '2021 International Arbitration Survey, Adapting Arbitration to a Changing World', 6, https://arbitration.qmul.ac.uk/media/arbitration/docs/LON0320037-QMUL-International-Arbitration-Survey-2021_19_WEB.pdf (accessed 29 March 2023); see further A Yeap, K Poon and A Pang 'The rise of arbitration in the Asia-Pacific' in *The Asia-Pacific Arbitration Review 2022* (Global Arbitration Review, 2022) 29.

[2] J Landbrecht, 'The Singapore International Commercial Court (SICC) – an Alternative to International Arbitration?' (2016) 34(1) *ASA Bulletin* 112, 112–25; see in detail below section IV.B.

[3] W Lui, 'Singapore' in A Reyes and W Lui (eds), *Direct Jurisdiction, Asian Perspectives* (Oxford, Hart Publishing, 2021) 127.

[4] Specifically, English common law which formed part of Singapore law immediately before 12 November 1993 shall continue to apply so far as it is applicable to the circumstances of Singapore and its inhabitants and subject to such modifications as those circumstances may require. See Application of English Law Act 1994 Rev Edn, s 3.

section VII discusses access to law in Singapore in general and to foreign law in particular. Finally, section VIII concludes the chapter with a summary of the most significant points.

II. Status of Choice of Laws Rules

Unlike civil law jurisdictions, Singapore has not passed an act or statute that predetermines in an abstract manner the rules on the application of foreign law. Instead, the Singapore courts determine the applicable choice of law rules on a case-by-case basis. In every case, the courts consistently adopt a systematic approach, which is described in further detail below.[5]

In addition, Singapore has ratified a comparatively small number of international conventions that lead to the determination of the applicable law in specific instances involving foreign and international elements. Examples include the Hague Convention of 18 March 1970 on the Taking of Evidence Abroad in Civil or Commercial Matters[6] and the Hague Convention of 30 June 2005 on Choice of Court Agreements.[7]

The Singapore courts treat foreign law as an issue of fact that the parties must invoke, plead and prove. The burden of proof falls on the party that asserts the application of foreign law.[8] The judicial authorities have no duty to apply foreign law by their own volition. This is consistent with the general principle of Singapore civil litigation that the parties' pleadings define the boundaries of a dispute, including the applicable points of law.[9] Hence, there is no principle of *iura novit curia* (ie, the principle that the judge is supposed to know the law), known in civil law jurisdictions.[10]

As a consequence, the parties have to prove the foreign law and its content.[11] If the parties are unable to sufficiently prove to the satisfaction of the court the content of the foreign law they consider applicable to a case, the courts will apply Singapore law, that is, the *lex fori*.[12] This principle is premised on the notion that the court lacks knowledge of foreign law and must be informed of its content by evidence from the parties.[13]

Notably, however, the courts may sometimes apply a public policy exception against the application of foreign law, even if the latter is proved. Under this exception, the courts will not apply foreign law if its result would be repugnant to the overriding public policy of the *lex fori*, viz. Singapore.[14] When assessing whether public policy is impinged, the court, as the master of its own forum, will apply its own mind to the circumstances and is fully

[5] See in detail below section III.
[6] See, eg, Art 9 of the convention.
[7] See, eg, Art 5(1) of the convention.
[8] *The 'Chem Orchid'* [2015] 2 SLR 1020 (HC), 153, 157.
[9] *V Nithia (co-administratrix of the estate of Ponnusamy Sivapakiam, deceased) v Buthmanaban s/o Vaithilingam and another* [2015] 5 SLR 1422 (CA), 34–36.
[10] D Girsberger and N Voser, *International Arbitration: Comparative and Swiss Perspectives*, 4th edn (Baden-Baden, Schulthess, 2021) para 1419; A Staehelin, D Staehelin, P Grolimund and E Bachofner, *Zivilprozessrecht, Unter Einbezug des Anwaltsrechts und des internationalen Zivilprozessrechts*, 3rd edn (Baden-Baden, Schulthess, 2019) ch 10, para 18.
[11] *The 'Chem Orchid'* [2015] 2 SLR 1020 (HC), 153, 157.
[12] ibid 159.
[13] *EFT Holdings, Inc and another v Marinteknik Shipbuilders (S) Pte Ltd and another* [2014] 1 SLR 860 (CA), 57; *The 'Chem Orchid'* [2015] 2 SLR 1020 (HC), 159.
[14] *TQ v TR and Another Appeal* [2009] 2 SLR(R) 961 (CA), 87.

entitled to re-characterise a transaction according to the law and logic of the *lex fori*, so as not to allow local public policy concerns to be easily circumvented by 'forum-shopping'.[15] Hence, this public policy exception may result in an overriding choice of law rule in favour of domestic law,[16] which will be illustrated by an example below.[17]

Another situation in which foreign law may have no effect in Singapore is where the so-called forum non conveniens doctrine applies. According to this doctrine, the court may consider the appropriateness of the exercise of its jurisdiction in light of the existence of other potentially more appropriate fora.[18] Should a Singapore court, when seized with a dispute (potentially) involving foreign law, hold that Singapore is not the appropriate forum, it will decline jurisdiction and thereby also prevent the application of foreign law in Singapore.

III. Foreign Law before Judicial Authorities

As already introduced, the Singapore courts determine the applicable choice of law rules on a case-by-case basis. The first step of this choice of law analysis is to characterise the legal issues that the parties have raised (this is also sometimes referred to as 'classification').[19] This classification will determine whether the application of choice of law rules is mandatory or facultative and whether the choice of law rules lead to the application of foreign law.

For the purpose of a choice of law analysis, legal issues may be divided into two broad categories: issues of procedure or issues of substance. The Singapore courts apply the traditional common law test of whether the issue in question concerns the 'existence of a right' or the 'enforcement of a right'.[20] A question concerning the former is considered substantive, while the latter is deemed procedural.

If the issue in question is deemed to be one of procedure, the law of the forum (ie, Singapore law) mandatorily applies to that issue, and there would be no need to proceed further in the choice of law analysis.[21] This is due to the underlying principle that the court of the forum will apply only its own procedure, and not foreign procedure.[22] Where a substantive issue is involved, the court would then enter the second step, which is to apply the choice of law rules applicable for that particular type of legal issue.[23] For example,

[15] *Star City Pty Ltd (formerly known as Sydney Harbour Casino Pty Ltd) v Tan Hong Woon* [2002] 1 SLR(R) 306 (CA), 27–29.

[16] K Ching, 'A Theoretical Perspective of the Public Policy Doctrine in the Conflict of Laws' (2018) 14(1) *Journal of Private International Law* 130.

[17] Below, section III (specifically the case of *Star City Pty Ltd (formerly known as Sydney Harbour Casino Pty Ltd) v Tan Hong Woon* [2002] 1 SLR(R) 306 (CA).

[18] *Rappo, Tania v Accent Delight International Ltd* [2017] 2 SLR 265 (CA).

[19] *JIO Minerals FZC and others v Mineral Enterprises Ltd* [2011] 1 SLR 391 (CA), 76–79; *Baker, Michael A (executor of the estate of Chantal Burnison, deceased) v BCS Business Consulting Services Pte Ltd and others* [2020] 4 SLR 85 (HC(I)), 200.

[20] *CIFG Special Assets Capital I Ltd (formerly known as Diamond Kendall Ltd) v Polimet Pte Ltd and others* [2016] 1 SLR 1382 (HC), 39–40.

[21] ibid.

[22] 'Halsbury's Laws of Singapore' (2021) 6(2) LexisNexis, (accessed 29 March 2023) 75.255.

[23] *Baker, Michael A (executor of the estate of Chantal Burnison, deceased) v BCS Business Consulting Services Pte Ltd and others* [2020] 4 SLR 85 (HC(I)), 200.

a three-step choice of law analysis applies to claims on the basis of contract and trust, while a so-called double-actionability rule applies to claims on the basis of tort.[24]

Given that the most common example of a substantive issue is contractual claims, the choice of law analysis applicable to them is discussed here. Where a conflict of laws issue arises in respect of a contractual claim, the court takes a three-step choice of law analysis to determine the applicable governing law of the contract:

> First, the court will examine the contract itself to determine whether it states expressly what the governing law is. In the absence of an express statement, the court considers whether the intention of the parties as to the governing law can be inferred from the circumstances. If that cannot be done, the court then identifies the system of law with which the contract has its closest and most real connection: in essence, this is an objective analysis undertaken from the perspective of a reasonable person in the position of the parties at the time of the contract. The court may bypass the second stage and move to the third stage where neither party addressed their mind to the question of which law is to govern.[25]

When engaging in the second stage of this analysis (ie, determining whether there is an implied agreement by the parties on the governing law), the focus is on whether the evidence supports an inference of the parties' common intention. To this end, the court may consider factors or circumstances such as:

- if the contracting parties agreed that the courts of a given country shall have jurisdiction in any matter arising out of a contract;
- if they agree that arbitration shall take place in a given country;
- the language or terminology used in the contract (though the use of English in an international commercial contract is not strongly indicative of any choice of law given that English is the *lingua franca* of international business);
- the form of the documents involved in the transaction;
- a connection with a preceding transaction;
- the currency of the contract or the currency for payment;
- the places of residence or business of the parties; or
- the commercial purpose of the transaction.[26]

The court may also look at the parties' course of dealing to find inferences of the parties' common intention as to the governing law. Where parties have established a course of dealing through a series of transactions with each other and continue to transact without always spelling out all the terms but on the basis of that established course of dealing, that earlier course of dealing can be relevant for inferring the parties' intentions as to later transactions (in the absence of evidence that the parties intend to transact on different terms). For example, in one case where four prior written agreements between the parties expressly

[24] *JIO Minerals FZC and others v Mineral Enterprises Ltd* [2011] 1 SLR 391 (CA), 88. This means that the tort must be actionable under both the law of the forum and the law of the place in which the tort was committed.

[25] *JIO Minerals FZC and others v Mineral Enterprises Ltd* [2011] 1 SLR 391 (CA), 79; *Baker, Michael A (executor of the estate of Chantal Burnison, deceased) v BCS Business Consulting Services Pte Ltd and others* [2020] 4 SLR 85 (HC(I)), 203.

[26] *Pacific Recreation Pte Ltd v S Y Technology Inc* [2008] 2 SLR 491 (CA), 37–38.

stipulated for Swiss law to govern those agreements, the Singapore Court of Appeal held that it was unlikely that the parties would have intended a different law to govern a subsequent transaction if there was no evidence or conceivable reason for the latter.[27] It also bears noting that an implied choice of law may possibly be ascertained from the circumstances even in the case of an oral contract (where there is no written agreement).[28]

Where the circumstances do not clearly point to one governing law that can be inferred as the common intention of the parties, the court would then move to the third stage of the analysis (ie, determining *the system of law with which the contract has its closest and most real connection).*[29] The aim of the third stage is no longer to infer what the parties *had intended* in the circumstances, but to determine what 'just and reasonable persons *ought to have intended* if they had thought about the matter at the time when they made the contract'. Therefore, the 'closest and most real connection' test is applied from the perspective of the objective, reasonable person. As such, while the factors of consideration at the third stage are not different from those at the second stage, the weight that the court may place on each factor may differ.[30]

Notably, claims under trust entail similar choice of law rules as claims under contract. Thus, in a trust case the court would look at whether there is an express or implied choice of law by the trustee, and if not, it would determine the system of law to which the trust has the closest connection.[31]

As can be seen from the overall approach described above, the application of choice of law rules in Singapore does not always lead to the application of foreign law, since different choice of law rules may apply depending on the type of issues arising in each particular case, which may ultimately lead to the application of Singapore law.

In addition to the general approach outlined above, it should be noted that there can be instances where mandatory provisions of Singapore law apply to a foreign cause of action brought in the Singapore courts, which parties cannot avoid by contracting out of.[32] For example, in a case where an action was brought in Singapore to enforce money owed under a gaming contract governed by the law of New South Wales (and said contract was valid under that foreign law), the Singapore Court of Appeal held that section 5(2) of the Civil Law Act mandatorily applied so as to prohibit the enforcement of such a contract in Singapore. This mandatory provision of Singapore law was premised on Singapore's public policy that the courts should not act as gambling debt collectors for foreign casinos.[33] Another example would be that a contract for the transfer of Singapore real estate may be subject to foreign law, but the real estate as such is subject to Singapore law (for example, the law governing the succession of real estate situated in Singapore must be Singapore law).[34]

[27] *Rappo, Tania v Accent Delight International Ltd and another and another appeal* [2017] 2 SLR 265 (CA), 79–81.

[28] *Baker, Michael A (executor of the estate of Chantal Burnison, deceased) v BCS Business Consulting Services Pte Ltd and others* [2020] 4 SLR 85 (HC(I)), 204.

[29] *Pacific Recreation Pte Ltd v S Y Technology Inc* [2008] 2 SLR 491 (CA), 46–47.

[30] ibid 48–49.

[31] *Baker, Michael A (executor of the estate of Chantal Burnison, deceased) v BCS Business Consulting Services Pte Ltd and others* [2020] 4 SLR 85 (HC(I)), 203.

[32] *Star City Pty Ltd (formerly known as Sydney Harbour Casino Pty Ltd) v Tan Hong Woon* [2002] 1 SLR(R) 306 (CA), 29.

[33] ibid 31–32.

[34] *State of Johor and another v Tunku Alam Shah ibni Tunku Abdul Rahman and others* [2005] 4 SLR(R) 380 (HC), 26.

Conversely, Singapore legislation occasionally expressly provides that some significant provisions of Singapore law shall be inapplicable to the extent that foreign law applies. For example, where any matter affecting the validity of a marriage would fall to be determined (in accordance with the rules of private international law) by reference to the law of a country other than Singapore, the grounds on which marriage is void or voidable according to Singapore law shall not preclude the determination of the matter according to foreign law.[35]

IV. Establishment of Foreign Law in the Singapore Courts

This section will examine the establishment of foreign law in Singapore courts. For this purpose, it will first address the general approach and principles governing this issue (sub-section IV.A). Subsequently, two special approaches will be examined, namely the additional mechanism of the Singapore International Commercial Court (sub-section IV.B) and the mechanism of referral of questions of foreign law to a foreign court, available to the Singapore High Court, Court of Appeal, and the Singapore International Commercial Court (sub-section IV.C).

A. General Approach

i. General Principles

As explained above, Singapore courts treat foreign law as an issue of fact which a party must prove. There are two methods of proving foreign law before the Singapore courts.

First, a party may directly adduce raw sources of foreign law as evidence.[36] Such sources include foreign court decisions, law reports and books (with translations into English, if required), which may be cited as evidence of the foreign law. A party who relies on this method would first bear the costs of doing so, subject to it obtaining a costs order in its favour should it ultimately prevail on its case.[37]

Second, in specific circumstances, a party could adduce the opinion of an expert on foreign law as expert evidence of foreign law, in accordance with the procedure set out in the Singapore Rules of Court 2021 (which came into force on 1 April 2022). In order to do so, a party must first seek the court's approval by satisfying the court that the expert evidence will contribute materially to the determination of an issue in the case, and that the issue cannot be resolved by an agreed statement of facts between the parties or by submissions based on mutually agreed materials.[38] Further, the rules require that, as far as possible, parties must agree on the appointment of one common expert.[39] Given this joint appointment

[35] Women's Charter 2020 Rev Edn, s 108(a).

[36] *Pacific Recreation Pte Ltd v S Y Technology Inc* [2008] 2 SLR 491 (CA), 54. See also Evidence Act 1997 Rev Edn, ss 40 and 47.

[37] *The 'Chem Orchid'* [2015] 2 SLR 1020 (HC), 153.

[38] Rules of Court 2021, Ord 12, r 2(1)-(3).

[39] Rules of Court 2021, Ord 12, r 3.

mechanism, parties will likely have to first jointly remunerate the expert, subject later to the court's discretion to allocate such costs in a costs order at the conclusion of the matter.[40]

At the time of writing, these limitations on the use of expert evidence for proving foreign law are a relatively recent development in the Singapore framework, and constitute a departure from the earlier Rules of Court 2014 (Revised Edition) which allowed each party to appoint their own foreign law expert, and without the need to obtain approval from the court. Under the old framework, both parties would typically appoint an expert who supports their respective positions. While this old framework has now been revoked and replaced by the new provisions of the Rules of Court 2021 beginning from 1 April 2022, it should be noted that the latter contains transitional provisions which provides that the 2014 rules would remain applicable to civil proceedings commenced before 1 April 2022.[41]

ii. *Expert Evidence on Foreign Law*

Notwithstanding the differences between the old and new frameworks governing the use of expert evidence in the Singapore courts, some principles relating to such expert evidence remain the same.

Under both frameworks, a foreign law expert is defined as a person who has the relevant 'scientific, technical or other specialised knowledge based on training, study or experience'.[42] Further, an expert's fundamental duty remains to be to assist the court, and this duty 'overrides any obligation to the person from whom the expert has received instructions or by whom the expert is paid.'[43]

The three main duties of a foreign law expert are:

> (1) to inform the court of the relevant contents of the foreign law; identifying statutes or other legislation and explaining where necessary the foreign court's approach to their construction;
> (2) to identify judgments or other authorities, explaining what status they have as sources of the foreign law; and
> (3) where there is no authority directly in point, to assist the … judge in making a finding as to what the foreign court's ruling would be if the issue was to arise for decision there.[44]

Under both frameworks, a foreign law expert must also give their evidence in the form of a written report (sworn or affirmed).[45] In order to maximise the reliability of legal information provided by an expert, both versions of the Rules of Court set out a list of requirements of an expert report, for example, to include details of the expert's qualifications, a statement that they understand their fundamental duty to assist the court, and a list of materials they relied on in making the report, etc.[46]

Both versions of the Rules of Court also provide mechanisms to further examine the reliability of expert reports. For example, a party may, with the court's permission, direct written questions to an expert about their report.[47] In cases where there is more than one

[40] Rules of Court 2021, Ord 12, r 3(6).
[41] Rules of Court 2021, Ord 1, r 2.
[42] Evidence Act 1997 Rev Edn, s 47(1); Rules of Court 2021, Ord 12, r 1(1).
[43] Rules of Court 2014 Rev Edn, Ord 40A, r 2(1)-(2); Rules of Court 2021, Ord 12, r 1(3).
[44] *The 'Chem Orchid'* [2015] 2 SLR 1020 (HC), 160.
[45] Rules of Court 2014 Rev Edn, Ord 40A, r 3(1); Rules of Court 2021, Ord 12, r 5.
[46] Rules of Court 2021, Ord 12, r 5(2); Rules of Court 2014 Rev Edn, Ord 40A, r 3(2).
[47] Rules of Court 2014 Rev Edn, Ord 40A, r 4(1); Rules of Court 2021, Ord 12, r 6(3).

expert, the court may also in its discretion order that some or all of the expert witnesses testify as a panel (ie, give concurrent expert evidence).[48]

It bears noting that since the court has the discretion to determine whether foreign law is sufficiently proven by a party, it is not bound by any information provided by an expert. Indeed, the court has the power to 'disregard or even draw an adverse inference against expert evidence' if it finds that the expert opinion exceeds the boundaries of coherence, rationality and impartiality.[49]

iii. Interpretation and Application of Foreign Law

When interpreting foreign law, the Singapore courts aim to interpret it in the same way as the courts of the country of origin. Where there is a gap in foreign law (ie, a point that has not been addressed or settled in the law), an expert may give an opinion on what a foreign court would likely decide.[50] Indeed, this is one of the three main duties of a foreign law expert as outlined above.

B. Additional 'Submissions' Mechanism of the Singapore International Commercial Court

As introduced above, the Singapore International Commercial Court is a Court dedicated to resolving international commercial disputes.[51] It goes without saying that foreign law may often be relevant in the cases before the Court, which is confirmed by the fact that the SICC Rules[52] contain a specific and comprehensive section on the application of foreign law.[53]

The default approach of the Singapore International Commercial Court mostly follows the general approach outlined above (similarly, with a change since 1 April 2022 towards allowing expert evidence only with the Court's permission, with the exception that there is no rule for parties to as far as possible jointly appoint a common expert in the SICC).[54] That said, the SICC has, in deviation from ordinary court practice, an additional mechanism for the parties to establish foreign law not on the basis of proof, but on the basis of submissions. The Court may, upon the application of a party, order that a question of foreign law be determined in this manner, specifying one or more persons who may make submissions on the question of foreign law. The Court may also make such further orders and directions as may be appropriate with regard to such determination. Before making such an order, the court must be satisfied that each party is or will be represented by a counsel, restricted registration foreign lawyer or registered law expert who is suitable and competent to make submissions on the relevant question of foreign law.[55]

[48] Rules of Court 2014 Rev Edn, Ord 40A, r 4(6); Rules of Court 2021, Ord 12, r 7.

[49] *Pacific Recreation Pte Ltd v S Y Technology Inc* [2008] 2 SLR 491 (CA), 71.

[50] *Pacific Recreation Pte Ltd v S Y Technology Inc* [2008] 2 SLR 491 (CA), 82.

[51] Singapore International Commercial Court, 'Establishment of the SICC' www.sicc.gov.sg/about-the-sicc/establishment-of-the-sicc (accessed 29 March 2023).

[52] Singapore International Commercial Court Rules 2021.

[53] Singapore International Commercial Court Rules 2021, Ord 16, r 8.

[54] Singapore International Commercial Court Rules 2021, Ord 14.

[55] Singapore International Commercial Court Rules 2021, Ord 16, r 8(1) and (2).

In addition to considering the parties' submissions, the Court may have regard to the following when determining the relevant questions of foreign law:[56]

(a) the legislation of the foreign country;
(b) the decisions of the courts of the foreign country;
(c) any relevant judgment of the Singapore courts on similar questions of foreign law.

These provisions not only show the significance of foreign law before the International Commercial Court, but also its special approach towards it (aimed at incorporating international best practices in international commercial dispute resolution).[57] They also document the high standards that the Court requires for the correct establishment of foreign law. Adding further to the quality of the proceedings also with respect to foreign law is the fact that the Court's bench consists of regular Supreme Court judges as well as international judges, which may come from different backgrounds, in particular foreign jurisdictions.[58]

C. Referral of Questions of Foreign Law to a Foreign Court by the Singapore High Court, Court of Appeal, and Singapore International Commercial Court

As mentioned, the Singapore courts mostly employ the general approach described under sub-section IV.A. Yet, there exists an additional mechanism for the establishment of foreign law, applicable to the Singapore High Court, Court of Appeal, and Singapore International Commercial Court.[59] This mechanism allows the court to refer questions of foreign law arising in its proceedings to a foreign court for the latter's determination, and is contained in Order 29 of the Rules of Court 2021[60] (for the High Court and Court of Appeal) and Order 15 of the SICC Rules 2021 (for the SICC).

An introduction to the background of this mechanism is apposite. In the 2009 Singapore Court of Appeal case *Westacre Investments Inc v The State-Owned Company Yugoimport SDPR*,[61] a question of foreign law arose before the court, namely whether as a matter of English law, an English court judgment was enforceable without the leave of an English court. The parties' legal experts came to completely differing conclusions. The Court of Appeal then adjourned the proceedings and directed the appellant to seek declaratory relief from an English court on the question of English law.[62] The appellant proceeded as

[56] Singapore International Commercial Court Rules 2021, Ord 16, r 8(8).

[57] Singapore Judiciary, 'Singapore International Commercial Court introduces standalone SICC Rules 2021 to incorporate international best practices and facilitate international dispute resolution' www.judiciary.gov.sg/news-and-resources/news/news-details/media-release-singapore-international-commercial-court-introduces-standalone-sicc-rules-2021-to-incorporate-international-best-practices-and-facilitate-international-dispute-resolution (accessed 29 March 2023).

[58] See generally on the composition of the bench Landbrecht (n 2) 121–22.

[59] See generally on this topic GS Teo and HD Wong, 'Referring Questions of Foreign Law to the Court of the Governing Law: No Longer "Lost in Translation"' (2011) 23(1) *Singapore Academy of Law Journal* 227, *passim*.

[60] Previously Ord 101 of the Rules of Court 2014 Rev Edn.

[61] *Westacre Investments Inc v The State-Owned Company Yugoimport SDPR (also known as Jugoimport-SDPR)* [2009] 2 SLR(R) 166.

[62] *Westacre Investments Inc v The State-Owned Company Yugoimport SDPR (also known as Jugoimport-SDPR)* [2009] 2 SLR(R) 166, 10.

indicated and eventually submitted the English court's judgment[63] as evidence before the Singapore Court of Appeal.[64]

Based on this innovative approach,[65] the Supreme Court of Singapore signed three memoranda of understanding of references of questions of law with the Dubai International Financial Centre Courts on 19 January 2015,[66] Supreme Court of New South Wales on 6 August 2015[67] and the Chief Judge of the State of New York on 21 December 2015.[68] On 6 September 2017, the Supreme Court of Singapore signed another memorandum of understanding with the Supreme Court of Bermuda.[69] The preamble of all four of these memoranda refers to the innovative approach adopted by the Singapore court. Each of the memoranda of understanding provides that it will be terminated five calendar years after the date of signing at which time it is anticipated that the procedures herein referred to will be sufficiently well established not to require a succeeding agreement.

Since then, Singapore has indeed incorporated the practices established under the memoranda of understanding with the Dubai International Financial Centre Court, the Supreme Court of New South Wales and the Supreme Court of Bermuda into its legislation, in the form of Order 29 of the Rules of Court 2021 and Order 15 of the SICC Rules 2021.

Pursuant to these Orders, where in any proceedings before the courts there arises any question relating to the law of any specified foreign country (meaning New South Wales, Australia; Dubai, United Arab Emirates; and Bermuda)[70] or to the application of such law, the court may, on the application of one or more of the parties, order that proceedings be commenced in a specified court in that specified foreign country seeking a determination of such question.[71] The court may give such directions as it thinks fit for the preparation of a statement of the issue from which the question arises for inclusion with the question of law to be determined by the specified court in the specified foreign country.[72]

In addition and notably, under both Orders the court may, on its own motion, order that proceedings be commenced in any court of competent jurisdiction in any foreign country (not being a specified foreign country) seeking a determination of any question relating to the law of that foreign country or to the application of such law.[73]

The approach set forth in these Orders is an innovative and successful implementation of the memoranda of understanding into legislation.[74] In particular the determination of foreign law by a court of the jurisdiction whose law may be relevant may be a significant advantage over expert evidence described in sub-section IV.A.ii. There have been concerns as to whether or not expert witnesses on foreign law, at least when appointed by the parties,

[63] *Westacre Investments Inc v The State-Owned Company Yugoimport SDPR* [2008] EWHC 801 (Comm).

[64] *Westacre Investments Inc v The State-Owned Company Yugoimport SDPR (also known as Jugoimport-SDPR)* [2009] 2 SLR(R) 166, 16.

[65] Teo and Wong (n 59) 229.

[66] www.judiciary.gov.sg/docs/default-source/who-we-are-docs/references_of_questions_of_law_dubai_2015.pdf. (accessed 29 March 2023).

[67] www.judiciary.gov.sg/docs/default-source/who-we-are-docs/references_of_questions_of_law_australia_2015.pdf. (accessed 29 March 2023).

[68] www.sicc.gov.sg/docs/default-source/guide-to-the-sicc/usa-2015-mou---cj-and-chief-judge-of-the-state-of-new-york-(21-december-2015)8ab63033f22f6eceb9b0ff0000fcc945.pdf. (accessed 29 March 2023).

[69] www.sicc.gov.sg/docs/default-source/guide-to-the-sicc/mou-with-bermuda-(6sep2017)74b63033f22f6eceb9b0ff0000fcc945.pdf. (accessed 29 March 2023).

[70] Rules of Court 2021, Ord 29, r 6; Singapore International Commercial Court Rules 2021, Ord 15, r 7.

[71] Rules of Court 2021, Ord 29, r 2(1); Singapore International Commercial Court Rules 2021, Ord 15, r 3(1).

[72] Rules of Court 2021, Ord 29, r 2(3); Singapore International Commercial Court Rules 2021, Ord 15, r 3(3).

[73] Rules of Court 2021, Ord 29, r 3; Singapore International Commercial Court Rules 2021, Ord 15, r 4.

[74] Teo and Wong (n 59) 229.

may not be entirely impartial.[75] On the other hand, a foreign court can most likely be considered to provide an impartial account of its own law. Even when compared to the opinion of a jointly-appointed common expert under the Rules of Court 2021, the court's determination will presumably be of a higher authoritative value.[76]

In addition to the referral mechanism under Order 29 of the Rules of Court 2021 and Order 15 of the SICC Rules 2021, there exists a special referral mechanism with respect to specifically the courts of the People's Republic of China (PRC). Under Order 29A of the Rules of Court 2021 and Order 15A of the SICC Rules 2021, where there arises any question relating to the law of the PRC, a Singapore court may, on the application of one or more of the parties or on its own motion, transmit to the PRC courts a request for an opinion on that question, if all of the parties consent to the transmission of this request. This is a separate mechanism specifically with regard to the PRC and is the result of the implementation of a Memorandum of Understanding between the Supreme Court of Singapore and the Supreme People's Court of China on cooperation on information on foreign law, signed in December 2021.

V. Judicial Review/Appeal

The application of foreign law is not only relevant in first instance proceedings in Singapore but also in appeal proceedings. A party may appeal to higher courts, including the Court of Appeal, on the basis that the lower court erroneously applied choice of law rules. In some cases (where the amount in dispute is not more than SGD$250,000 or if the case falls under the Fifth Schedule of the Supreme Court of Judicature Act), the party would need to first apply for leave of court before filing an appeal.[77]

This approach is consistent with the high-quality control of the Singapore judiciary.[78] At the same time, the requirement to seek leave for amounts in dispute not exceeding SGD$250,000 promotes the efficiency of the court processes.

It should be noted that given that a lower court's decision on foreign law continues to be treated as a question of fact on appeal, the applicable standard of review by an appellate court differs from the standard which applies to questions of law. While an appellate court will readily intervene on an issue of law, it will be slow to reverse findings of fact, and will do so only if the findings are plainly wrong or against the weight of the evidence.[79] The appellate court will also be slow to re-assess the credibility of the witnesses (ie, the foreign law experts giving evidence on foreign law) as it recognises that the lower court was in a better position to do that. However, an appellate court may re-assess a witness's credibility in two situations: where such assessment is based on inferences drawn from the internal consistency in the content of the witness's testimony and the external consistency between the content of the witness's evidence and the extrinsic evidence.[80]

[75] ibid 230.

[76] ibid 231.

[77] Supreme Court of Judicature Act 2007 Rev Edn, s 29A.

[78] In general on the high quality, see World Justice Project, 'Rule of Law Index 2020', 28 worldjusticeproject.org/sites/default/files/documents/WJP-ROLI-2020-Online_0.pdf (accessed 29 March 2023).

[79] *Yeo Chong Lin v Tay Ang Choo Nancy and another appeal* [2011] 2 SLR 1157 (CA), 42.

[80] *Sandz Solutions (Singapore) Pte Ltd and others v Strategic Worldwide Assets Ltd and others* [2014] 3 SLR 562 (CA), 39.

The appellate court may ultimately decide on the correct application of foreign law and render a new judgment which varies or reverses the decision of the lower court.[81]

Foreign law may be relevant also in an appeal from a judgment or an order of the International Commercial Court. In such instances, the Court of Appeal may determine any question of foreign law on the basis of submissions if the question of foreign law has been ordered by the Singapore International Commercial Court to be determined on the basis of submissions; or if the question of foreign law has been ordered by the Singapore Court of Appeal, on its own motion or on an application by a party, to be determined on the basis of submissions.[82]

VI. Foreign Law before Other Authorities

A. Recognition of Foreign Law by Administrative or Other Non-judicial Authorities in Singapore

In Singapore, administrative or non-judicial authorities may recognise foreign law on the basis of documentary evidence from a foreign competent authority. For example, an overseas marriage will be recognised in Singapore if it was registered according to the law of the place in which the marriage was contracted (the so-called *lex loci celebrationis*).[83] Accordingly, a marriage certificate which was issued by a competent authority of the relevant country could be accepted as evidence of a marriage, unless there is reason to doubt the validity of said marriage.[84]

Generally, foreign public documents would need to be legalised in order to be recognised in Singapore. However, since the Hague Convention of 5 October 1961 Abolishing the Requirement of Legalisation for Foreign Public Documents ('Apostille Convention') entered into force for Singapore on 16 September 2021, Singapore authorities will recognise apostilles in place of legalisation for incoming foreign public documents from contracting parties of said convention.[85]

B. Foreign Law in Arbitration, Mediation and Other Forms of Alternative Dispute Resolution

Arbitral tribunals seated in Singapore regularly apply foreign law in order to determine the merits of the dispute submitted to them. The legislative framework, within which they do so,

[81] 'Halsbury's Laws of Singapore' (2021) 4 LexisNexis, (accessed 29 March 2023) 50.394.

[82] Singapore International Commercial Court Rules 2021, Ord 16, r 8(9).

[83] *Cf* on this concept in general LV Chan, 'Taming the Unruly Public Policy Horse in Private International Law in Family Law: A Pragmatic Singaporean Approach to the Recognition of Foreign Same-Sex Marriages and Divorces' (2021) 35(1) *International Journal of Law, Policy and the Family* 1, 4.

[84] Singapore Registry of Marriage, Section Q 'Married Overseas': va.ecitizen.gov.sg/cfp/customerpages/msf/rom/explorefaq.aspx (accessed 29 March 2023).

[85] Ministry of Law Singapore, 'Singapore Accedes to the Apostille Convention' (19 Jan 2021) www.mlaw.gov.sg/news/press-releases/2021-01-19-singapore-accedes-to-the-apostille-convention (accessed 29 March 2023).

differs. International arbitrations are subject to the International Arbitration Act,[86] which declares the UNCITRAL Model Law on International Commercial Arbitration to have the force of law.[87] Domestic arbitrations are governed by the Arbitration Act.[88]

The International Arbitration Act incorporates the provision of the UNCITRAL Model Law on International Commercial Arbitration which stipulates that the arbitral tribunal shall decide the dispute in accordance with such rules of law as are chosen by the parties as applicable to the substance of the dispute, and failing any designation by the parties, the arbitral tribunal shall apply the law determined by the conflict of laws rules which it considers applicable.[89] The Arbitration Act provides for a solution similar to the one of the UNCITRAL Model Law on International Commercial Arbitration, as it states that the arbitral tribunal shall decide the dispute in accordance with the law chosen by the parties as applicable to the substance of the dispute. If or to the extent that the parties have not chosen the law applicable to the substance of their dispute, the arbitral tribunal shall apply the law determined by the conflict of laws rules.[90]

Apart from these principles, however, the Singapore legislation does not regulate the application and treatment of foreign law in arbitral proceedings any further. Therefore, it would be up to the parties to agree on the procedure in terms of establishing foreign law in their arbitration. Failing which, the tribunal would decide on the applicable method.[91] Whether the tribunal would adopt the traditionally common law approach of having the parties prove foreign law as an issue of fact (similar to the Singapore courts' approach, as described above) may well depend on the legal background and preferences of the arbitrators, as well as other factors such as the legal backgrounds of the parties and procedural rules.

There is no clear rule on whether arbitral tribunals seated in Singapore have to apply foreign mandatory norms ex officio, but it has been suggested in commentary that a tribunal in Singapore may need to consider foreign mandatory laws such as those of a party's place of incorporation or the law of the likely place of enforcement.[92]

Courts generally do not have the authority to review the award on the basis of whether or not the arbitral tribunal applied foreign law correctly since judicial review of the merits of the award is excluded.[93] The only possible exception arises where the application of foreign law is relevant for the narrow grounds for the setting aside of an award.[94] This differs from the approach described above regarding appeals on the application of foreign law in litigation.

For other forms of ADR, such as mediation, expert determination or adjudication, the Singapore legislation does not provide specific guidance on whether and how to

[86] International Arbitration Act 2002 Rev Edn.

[87] ibid, s 3.

[88] Arbitration Act 2002 Rev Edn.

[89] International Arbitration Act 2002 Rev Edn, First Schedule, Art 28(1)-(2).

[90] International Arbitration Act 2002 Rev Edn, s 24 and First Schedule, Art 34; Arbitration Act 2002 Rev Edn, s 47.

[91] International Arbitration Act 2002 Rev Edn, First Schedule, Art 19.

[92] J Choong, M Mangan and N Lingard, *A Guide to the SIAC Arbitration Rules*, 2nd edn (Oxford, Oxford University Press, 2018) para 5.20; in general N Blackaby, C Partasides, A Redfern and M Hunter, *Redfern and Hunter on International Arbitration*, 6th edn (Oxford, Oxford University Press, 2015) paras 3.128–3.130.

[93] International Arbitration Act 2002 Rev Edn, First Schedule, Art 34; Arbitration Act 2002 Rev Edn, s 48.

[94] See on this in general International Arbitration Act 2002 Rev Edn, s 24 and First Schedule, Art 34; and Arbitration Act 2002 Rev Edn, s 48.

apply foreign law. Recent developments such as the adoption of the Singapore Mediation Convention have not related to the application of foreign law but rather to the enforcement of international mediation agreements.[95] In any event, to a certain degree the law in general, and with it foreign law as well, may be of less importance with these forms of ADR. For example, mediation is described to focus on interests whereas arbitration focuses on rights.[96]

VII. Access to Law

The previous sections have shown how different legal institutions apply foreign law in Singapore. This section will focus on the general access to Singapore and foreign law. It will also take into account potential future improvements and debate whether developments on an international or regional level should be considered.

A. Singapore Law

The Singapore legal system features a high degree of accessibility, which is inter alia exhibited by the easy availability of legislation and case law. The Singapore Government provides a state-of-the-art website with a comprehensive database of the jurisdiction's legislation.[97] In addition, several regularly updated databases archive Singapore court judgments, making them open to anyone.[98]

Moreover, the entire legislation and case law is in English, thereby offering easy access to users both inside and outside of Singapore. However, the statutes and judgments are not translated into any other languages.

B. Access to Foreign Law and Future Developments

Consistent with Singapore's status as an international business hub, the country has signed several instruments on the treatment and information of foreign law in court proceedings, in addition to the memoranda described above.[99]

Recently in July 2021, Singapore and Japan signed a Memorandum of Understanding to further strengthen legal cooperation. By means of this memorandum, the two countries will work together on matters such as international commercial dispute resolution and people-to-people exchanges in the legal field.[100] Paragraph 1 of the memorandum sets forth that

[95] See generally N Alexander and S Chong, *The Singapore Convention on Mediation: A Commentary* (London, Wolters Kluwer, 2019) paras 0.41–0.52.

[96] L Kirchhoff, *Constructive Interventions: Paradigms, Process and Practice of International Mediation* (Alphen aan den Rijn, Kluwer Law International, 2008) 122, with further references.

[97] sso.agc.gov.sg/ (accessed 29 March 2023).

[98] www.judiciary.gov.sg/judgments (accessed 29 March 2023); www.singaporelawwatch.sg/Judgments (accessed 29 March 2023).

[99] See above section IV.C.

[100] Singapore Ministry of Law, 'Singapore and Japan to Strengthen Legal Cooperation' (29 July 2021) www.mlaw.gov.sg/news/press-releases/2021-07-29-singapore-and-japan-to-strengthen-legal-cooperation (accessed 29 March 2023).

Singapore and Japan will cooperate on matters of mutual interest. Paragraph 2 concerns the specific forms of cooperation and provides that the countries may: (a) exchange legal publications; (b) exchange visits and study trips; (c) organise and hold meetings, conferences and dialogues; and/or (d) engage in other forms of cooperation.

Although this memorandum is definitely a valuable addition to the toolbox of Singapore's judiciary, it does not per se facilitate the access to foreign law in Singapore, which, as has been seen, is for the parties to invoke and prove.[101] Moreover, according to paragraph 6.1, the information and knowledge obtained in the course of the cooperative activities under the memorandum of understanding are confidential and may solely be used for the purpose of implementing the memorandum. Thus, one may query the overall effect the memorandum has on the access to foreign law specifically in court proceedings.[102]

Going one step further, in December 2021 the Supreme Court of Singapore and the Supreme People's Court of China signed a memorandum of understanding on cooperation on information on foreign law. This memorandum establishes a mechanism between these two courts to determine questions of foreign law in international civil and commercial cases. This should enable the courts to obtain accurate and authoritative information on the foreign laws of Singapore and the People's Republic of China.[103] Compared to the previous memorandum of understanding concluded with Japan, this memorandum of understanding with the People's Republic of China to a certain degree seems to have more impact on the access to foreign law in Singapore. Indeed, the mechanism in this memorandum has now been entered into legislation in the form of Order 29A of the Rules of Court 2021 and Order 15A of the SICC Rules 2021, as discussed above.

In addition to the above, it would also be worthwhile to contemplate other mechanisms to improve access to foreign law. One proposal would be the launch of an independent centre or institute dedicated to the establishment of foreign law. There already exist such centres in other jurisdictions, for example the Institute of Comparative Law in Lausanne, Switzerland.[104] This type of institute typically employs legal professionals from a variety of jurisdictions, being fluent in several foreign languages.[105] Thanks to these qualities, these professionals are in an ideal position to research and present the content of the foreign law in question. Should the establishment of such an institution be considered, Singapore could attract talented foreign researchers that would be tasked as experts in court proceedings to assist with the establishment of foreign law on a certain issue. Additional memoranda between Singapore and other jurisdictions could provide for a regular assignment of legal professionals from these jurisdictions to this centre.

[101] Above section II.

[102] Whether Japanese courts, for their part, could in their own court proceedings rely on information about Singapore law ascertained in the course of the cooperative activities is unclear given that Paragraph 6.1 of the Memorandum states that the information received under the Memorandum is confidential.

[103] Singapore Supreme Court, 'Supreme Court of Singapore and Supreme People's Court of China sign Memorandum of Understanding on cooperation on information on foreign law' (3 December 2021) www.judiciary.gov.sg/news-and-resources/news/news-details/supreme-court-of-singapore-and-supreme-people%27s-court-of-china-sign-memorandum-of-understanding-on-cooperation-on-information-on-foreign-law (accessed 29 March 2023).

[104] www.isdc.ch/de/ (accessed 29 March 2023); further AK Schnyder and M Liatowitsch, *Internationales Privat- und Zivilverfahrensrecht*, 4th edn (Zurich, Schulthess, 2017) para 250.

[105] See, eg, the Institute of Comparative Law in Lausanne www.isdc.ch/de/sir/mitarbeitende (accessed 29 March 2023).

This idea does not seem that far-fetched considering that Singapore has for decades attracted lawyers from many different jurisdictions across the globe to practise in Singapore's prestigious law firms. At the same time, this existing influx of foreign lawyers already enables legal practitioners in Singapore to more easily access the law of the home jurisdictions of these foreign professionals – either via these lawyers in Singapore or via their contacts. The proposal has further benefits considering that Singapore is currently not a member of an international or regional framework to facilitate access to foreign law.

Further strengthening the access to foreign law in Singapore is the fact that court proceedings may be conducted virtually.[106] Therefore, in case an expert on foreign law is required, the expert does not even need to be physically present in Singapore in order to establish foreign law.

As a result, it may be concluded that Singapore does offer fairly easy access to foreign law. Yet, there is still some room for improvement.

C. Effect of An International or Regional Instrument Unifying the Treatment of Foreign Law

Whether an international or regional instrument unifying the treatment of foreign law would be beneficial to Singapore is debatable but on balance, the benefits seem to prevail. International and regional instruments unifying the treatment of foreign law already exist in other parts of the world, like the European Convention on Information on Foreign Law.[107] The convention does have sufficient appeal to have prompted even states outside of Europe, such as Costa Rica, Mexico and Morocco, to ratify it.[108] An essential aspect of the convention is the duty of the contracting parties to supply one another with information on their law and procedure in civil and commercial fields as well as on their judicial organisation.[109]

Building on this convention and paying special regard to the innovative approach of the Singapore Supreme Court as established in the *Westacre Investments Inc v The State-Owned Company Yugoimport SDPR* case, an interesting option for Singapore would be to either first conclude memoranda of understanding with numerous jurisdictions and, after a period of successful cooperation, transform the memoranda into treaties or directly conclude such treaties. Unlike the singular memoranda of understanding that Singapore has concluded in sequence, an international or regional instrument could consist of the simultaneous conclusion of several memoranda or treaties. Like the approach of Order 29 of the Rules of Court 2021 and Order 15 of the SICC Rules 2021, these memoranda of understanding or treaties could provide for the possibility to submit a question on foreign law to a court of that foreign jurisdiction. This would establish a similar mechanism as the European Convention on Information on Foreign Law.

Notwithstanding these benefits, some caution may be warranted as to whether a unification of the treatment of foreign law by means of an international or at least regional instrument is necessary. In particular, Singapore's international approach comprised of,

[106] Rules of Court 2021, Ord 13, r 14; Rules of Court 2014 Rev Edn, Ord 39A.
[107] CETS 062.
[108] rm.coe.int/1680072314 (accessed 29 March 2023).
[109] ibid.

amongst other things, the referral mechanisms under the Rules of Court 2021 and the SICC Rules 2021, and the specialised International Commercial Court are strong indicators that foreign law will usually be established in an efficient and sophisticated manner.[110] It is to be expected that Singapore will continue its international approach. In addition, due to the at least historically strong influence of English common law,[111] there exists already some unity in approach as regards jurisdictions that are also rooted in the tradition of English common law. Nonetheless, the easy access to foreign law in Singapore should not prevent the implementation of additional instruments to promote a unified approach towards the access to foreign law.

VIII. Conclusion

Based on the foregoing overview of the application of foreign law in Singapore by various judicial authorities, the approach adopted by the Singapore courts follows the common law tradition in that foreign law is treated as a fact that the parties need to prove. The Singapore courts have developed specific choice-of-law principles under Singapore law. In order to establish foreign law in court proceedings, expert evidence may play a role. Of particular interest in the future will also be the practice of the Singapore International Commercial Court, with its innovative approach towards foreign law.

In line with Singapore's status as an international business and also dispute resolution hub, foreign law is frequently also of great significance before other judicial authorities, such as arbitral tribunals. While their approach towards foreign law to a certain degree resembles the one followed by courts, the particularities of arbitration need to be considered.

Last, it has been established that Singapore offers easy access to its law and also follows an international-oriented approach with regard to foreign law. The conclusion of multiple memoranda of understanding with foreign jurisdictions and the implementation of many of these mechanisms into legislation emphasise this. Nevertheless, Singapore may consider further improving access to foreign law, inter alia by the establishment of a centre dedicated to the establishment of foreign law.

[110] Above sections IV.B and IV.C.
[111] Above, section I.

8

Malaysia

TEH WAI FUNG

I. Introduction

Malaysia is a Commonwealth nation with Islam as 'the religion of the Federation', and the freedom for other religions to be 'practised in peace and harmony'.[1] Malaysia has been judicially described as practising 'federal parliamentary constitutional democracy'.[2] The Federal Constitution, the 'supreme law' of the Federation of Malaysia,[3] generally allocates legislative power between Parliament and individual state legislatures through three lists: a Federal List, enumerating matters exclusive to Parliament;[4] a State List, enumerating matters exclusive to state legislatures;[5] and a Concurrent List, enumerating matters on which both Parliament and state legislatures may legislate,[6] with some differences for the States of Sabah and Sarawak.[7]

The structure and the diverse heritage of the Malaysian legal system[8] have several consequences for the treatment of foreign law in Malaysia.[9] First, English law retains a particular influence on both Malaysian legislation and case law especially in the realm of the conflict of laws.[10] This influence manifests itself at times through wholesale application[11] or direct adoption[12] of English law, and at others through the persuasiveness of English judgments.[13]

[1] Federal Constitution, Art 3(1).

[2] *Datuk Seri Anwar Ibrahim v Kerajaan Malaysia & Anor* [2021] 6 MLJ 68 (FC) [28]; SS Faruqi, *Our Constitution* (London, Sweet & Maxwell, 2019) 40–41.

[3] Federal Constitution, Art 4(1).

[4] ibid, Art 74(1), sch 9, List 1.

[5] ibid, Art 74(2), sch 9, List 2, but note Art 76.

[6] ibid, Art 74(1), (2), sch 9, List 3.

[7] ibid, Art 95B.

[8] SA Aziz, 'The Malaysian Legal System: The Roots, The Influence and The Future' (2009) 3 *Malayan Law Journal* xcii.

[9] For more historical details, see RH Hickling and MA Wu, *Conflict of Laws in Malaysia* (Singapore, Butterworths Asia, 1995) 1–16.

[10] ibid 19; D McClean and V Ruiz Abou-Nigm, *Morris on The Conflict of Laws*, 9th edn (London, Sweet & Maxwell, 2016) para 1–004.

[11] Civil Law Act 1956, s 3(1), which requires the Malaysian courts to apply the common law and rules of equity of England as they were prior to Malaysia's independence, and s 5, on the application of English law in commercial matters; but note also *Danaharta Urus Sdn Bhd v Kekatong Sdn Bhd* [2004] 2 MLJ 257 (FC) [14].

[12] Courts of Judicature Act 1964, s 24(b), which essentially directly imports certain sections of English admiralty legislation into Malaysian law.

[13] On some of the issues this may cause, see MF Rutter, 'The Applicable Law in Singapore and Malaysia' [1989] *Malayan Law Journal* pt II; TAH Mohamad and A Trakic, 'The Reception of English Law in Malaysia

Second, the law of other Commonwealth jurisdictions is also influential. For instance, Malaysia's Contracts Act 1950 and – importantly for questions of foreign law – Evidence Act 1950 are modelled on their Indian counterparts.[14] The case law of these other jurisdictions too is often cited before and by the Malaysian courts. Third, in certain areas of law, such as marriage and divorce, there are differences in the laws applicable to Muslims (Syariah law), non-Muslims, and natives of Sabah and Sarawak, which within themselves may also vary according to state legislation.

It is in this context that the sections below discuss the treatment of foreign law in Malaysia. At the outset, it is recalled that the issue of proper law is, strictly, a separate question from that of jurisdiction;[15] the focus of this chapter is on the former.

II. Status of Choice of Laws Rules

A. General

There appear to be no Malaysian judicial pronouncements thus far specifically and expressly on whether the application of choice of law rules by the Malaysian courts, in general, is mandatory or facultative. Neither is Malaysia currently party to any regional or international instruments on the topic, such as the Rome I and Rome II Regulations of the European Union (EU),[16] which expressly refer to 'mandatory provisions' of the forum.[17] Absent specific indications that such rules are mandatory as a matter of general application, and given the influence of English law on the Malaysian approach to conflict of laws,[18] it might be argued, based on views propounded in the context of English law,[19] that the application of such rules in Malaysia is facultative rather than mandatory. This would also be consistent with the High Court's power (but not obligation) on its own motion to appoint an independent expert on questions of foreign law,[20] which, in Malaysia, are treated as questions of fact.[21]

However, the absence of a 'blanket' general position should not be taken to mean that choice of law rules are applied facultatively in all cases in Malaysia. A few areas of law are addressed in turn below.

and Development of the Malaysian Common Law' (2015) 44 *Common Law World Review* 123; A Phang BL, 'Of "Cut-Off" Dates and Domination: Some Problematic Aspects of the General Reception of English Law in Singapore' (1986) 28 *Malaya Law Review* 242.

[14] Contract Act 1872 (India); Evidence Act 1872 (India); *Looi Wooi Saik v PP* [1962] MLJ 337 (CA) 339E-I; *Meelamchan v PP* [1962] 1 MLJ 213 (CA) 215 on the weight given to Indian judgments on Indian statutory provisions in pari materia with Malaysian ones.

[15] *YK Fung Securities Sdn Bhd v James Capel (Far East) Ltd* [1997] 2 MLJ 621 (CA) 666.

[16] Regulation (EC) No 593/2008 on the law applicable to contractual obligations 2008; Regulation (EC) No 864/2007 on the law applicable to non-contractual obligations 2007.

[17] Rome I, Art 9; Rome II, Art 16; See also *YK Fung Securities* (CA) (n 15) 666E–G.

[18] Hickling and Wu (n 9) 19; McClean and Ruiz Abou-Nigm (n 10) para 1–004.

[19] See R Fentiman, *Foreign Law in English Courts* (Oxford, OUP, 1998) 70–76 for discussion of similar ambiguities in English law.

[20] Rules of Court 2012, Ord 40, r 1(1).

[21] Evidence Act 1950, s 45(1).

B. Tort

For the purposes of ascertaining jurisdiction and liability in respect of a tort committed outside the jurisdiction,[22] the Malaysian courts apply the 'double actionability' rule: the tort must be actionable under both the law of the foreign country where it was committed (*lex loci delicti*), and Malaysian law had it been committed in Malaysia.[23] This rule necessarily requires both Malaysian law and the foreign *lex loci delicti* to be ascertained and applied. In this implied sense, the application of choice of law rules to tortious claims might be described as being mandatory. However, where a tort involves foreign elements but is nevertheless deemed to have been committed within the jurisdiction,[24] Malaysian law exclusively is applied to determine liability.

C. Contract

The general Malaysian position on the governing law of a contract mirrors that of English law. The courts will generally uphold an express choice of law in a contract (as distinct from an exclusive jurisdiction clause[25]), although 'floating proper law' clauses are treated as invalid and unenforceable.[26] If there is no choice of law, the courts look for an implied choice from the terms or form of contract or surrounding circumstances. Absent an implied choice, the courts adopt the system of law with which the transaction has the closest and most real connection.[27] This supplies the substantive law of the contract, which governs questions of liability. Where an act is illegal by the law only of a foreign country and not Malaysian law, the Malaysian courts will nevertheless apply public policy in recognising such foreign illegality.[28] For the purposes of quantum, Malaysian law as the *lex fori* applies

[22] Courts of Judicature Act 1964, s 23(1)(b).

[23] *Attorney General of Hong Kong v Zauyah Wan Chik* [1995] 2 MLJ 620 (CA) 633E, 635I; *Jupiters Ltd v Lim Kin Tong* [2006] 5 CLJ 277 (HC) [32]–[36]; *Scandinavian Bunkering (Singapore) Pte Ltd v MISC Bhd* [2012] 4 MLJ 105 (HC) [22]; *Scandinavian Bunkering (Singapore) Pte Ltd v MISC Bhd* [2015] 3 MLJ 753 (FC) [36]; TAG Beazley, 'Jurisdiction and Choice of Law in Tort Conflicts: Chan Kwon Fong & Anor v Chan Wah' (1977) 19 *Malaya Law Review* 391, 391, 394–400; Hickling and Wu (n 9) 183–84; NV Nadkarni and WF Teh, 'Malaysia' in A Reyes and W Lui (eds), *Direct Jurisdiction: Asian Perspectives* (Oxford, Hart, 2021) 162–63.

[24] Rules of Court 2012, Ord 11, r 1(1)(H); Courts of Judicature Act 1964, s 23(1)(a).

[25] *American Express Bank Ltd v Mohamed Toufic Al-Ozeir & Anor* [1995] 1 MLJ 160 (SC) 168E.

[26] *Q2 Engineering Sdn Bhd v PJI-LFGC (Vietnam) Ltd & Ors* [2012] 8 CLJ 1005 (HC) [46]. See also *Apex Marble Sdn Bhd & Anor v Leong Tat Yan* [2018] 7 MLJ 84 (HC) [55], [73]. However, note *KNM Process Systems Sdn Bhd v Ceca Gold Company Ltd & Ors* [2023] 1 MLJ 814 (CA) [49]–[54], where the Malaysian Temporary Measures for Reducing the Impact of Coronavirus Disease 2019 (COVID-19) Act 2020 was held to afford a party relief under a contract which designated Singapore law as its governing law. The Court of Appeal held that one country's laws can be applied even where a contract contains an express choice of another country's laws, where 'the justice and facts of the case' so require.

[27] *James Capel (Far East) Ltd v YK Fung Securities Sdn Bhd* [1996] 2 MLJ 97 (HC) 109F-110E, upheld on appeal in *YK Fung Securities* (CA) (n 15); *Bonython v Commonwealth of Australia* [1951] AC 201 (UKPC) 209; *Amin Rasheed Shipping Corpn v Kuwait Insurance Co, The Al Wahab* [1984] AC 50 (UKHL) 61–62; see also, eg, *United Overseas Bank Ltd v United Securities Sdn Bhd (in liq) & Ors* [2021] 9 CLJ 593 (CA) [18]–[19]; *Dhaneshvaran S Baskaran & Ors v Singapore Airlines Ltd* [2022] 3 CLJ 624 (HC) [21]–[22].

[28] *ABDA Airfreight Sdn Bhd v Sistem Penerbangan Malaysia Bhd* [2001] 3 MLJ 641 (HC) 701C–G.

regardless of the substantive law,[29] quantum being a procedural question. Malaysian law appears to recognise the principle of *dépeçage*.[30]

The distinction between the applicable substantive or governing law, on the one hand, and the applicable procedural law, on the other, was demonstrated in a High Court judgment on a claim for debts under a gaming credit agreement.[31] One submission by the debtor was that the Civil Law Act 1956, section 26(1) and (2) and the Contracts Act 1950, section 31(1) of Malaysia, the *lex fori*, required the Malaysian courts to refuse to entertain actions based on gambling transactions.[32] Rejecting this argument, the High Court held these Malaysian statutory provisions to concern matters of substantive law, not procedural law. Rather, the applicable substantive law was Macanese law as the express governing law of the agreement. As Macanese law contained no such prohibitions, the High Court declined to dismiss the action on the grounds argued by the debtor.[33]

D. Family Law

i. Non-Muslims

The Law Reform (Marriage and Divorce) Act 1976 applies only to 'all persons in Malaysia and to all persons domiciled in Malaysia but [who] are resident outside Malaysia' who, loosely, are not Muslim or native/aborigine,[34] a minority of the population. For Muslims in Malaysia, the majority of the population, the applicable Islamic family laws vary between states.[35] Conflicts often arise too between civil (secular) law and (state) Islamic or Syariah law.[36] For brevity, and as Malaysian cases on cross-border conflicts of law tend to come before the secular rather than the Syariah courts, these latter topics are discussed only summarily further below.[37]

Under the Law Reform (Marriage and Divorce) Act 1976's provisions on marriages abroad or in foreign embassies in Malaysia,[38] the application of the *lex domicilii* to capacity

[29] *Scandinavian Bunkering (Singapore) Pte Ltd v MISC Bhd* (n 23) [37].

[30] *Thai-Lao Lignite Co Ltd v Government of the Lao People's Democratic Republic* [2017] 9 CLJ 273 (FC) [155]–[156].

[31] *Wynn Resorts (Macau) SA v Poh Yang Hong* [2019] MLJU 2003 (HC).

[32] ibid [5].

[33] ibid [138]–[145]; see also CN Chen, 'Recovery of Gambling Debts in Malaysia and Singapore' (2001) 1 *Malayan Law Journal* i and *2WTrade LLP v Zepto Express Bhd* [2023] MLJU 386 (HC).

[34] Law Reform (Marriage and Divorce) Act 1976, ss 3(1), 3(3); see also *AJS v JMH* [2022] 1 MLJ 778 (FC) [30]–[31].

[35] R Reddy, 'Marriage and Divorce Regulation and Recognition in Malaysia' (1995) 29 *Family Law Quarterly* 613, 619; M Mohamad, 'The Islamic Divorce Contract and a Flawed Axiom of Masculine Protectionism' (2011) 39 *Asian Journal of Social Science* 821, 828; *Muhammad Faizz Amin bin Roslee v Maidatul Sarah bt Mior Rosli* [2013] 2 SHLR 98 (Shariah Subordinate Court, Terengganu).

[36] Eg, *Loh Siew Hong v Nagahswaran a/l Muniandy (Majlis Agama Islam dan Adat Istiadat Melayu Perlis (MAIPs), Proposed Intervener))* [2022] 5 AMR 882 (HC); *Indira Gandhi a/p Mutho v Pengarah Jabatan Agama Islam Perak* [2018] 1 MLJ 545 (FC); YN Foo and K Dhaliwal, 'Dissolution of Marriage: Jurisdiction and Forum' in SS Lee (ed), *Law and Practice of Family Law in Malaysia* (London, Sweet & Maxwell, 2019) 62–66; T Moustafa, 'Liberal Rights versus Islamic Law? The Construction of a Binary in Malaysian Politics' (2013) 47 *Law & Society Review* 771.

[37] For a comparison of some of the differences between Syariah and secular law on marriage and divorce in Malaysia, see N Ibrahim, 'The Right of Wife to Apply for the Division of Matrimonial Property on Dissolution of Marriage: The Malaysian Perspective' [2007] *The Law Review* 13.

[38] Law Reform (Marriage and Divorce) Act 1976, ss 26(1), 28(4), 104, 105.

and of the *lex loci celebrationis* to formalities would appear to be mandatory. Meanwhile, section 72 preserves the application of foreign law to the ascertainment of the validity of a marriage under common law ('apart from this Act') where required by 'the rules of Private International Law'. For matters prior to the coming into force of the Act on 1 March 1982,[39] the position at common law would appear likewise to be that the application of each contracting party's *lex domicilii* is mandatory.[40] In respect of divorce, section 47 directly imports 'the principles on which the High Court of Justice in England acts and gives relief in matrimonial proceedings' as they currently stand,[41] not as foreign law, but as part of Malaysian law itself. Other than the above, the Act would appear not to expressly address or involve questions of foreign law or choice of law, and instead to focus on matters of jurisdiction.[42]

As regards matters relating to children, the Guardianship of Infants Act 1961, which applies to non-Muslims in Peninsular Malaysia,[43] has been remarked to have 'augmented' the 'inherent jurisdiction' of the High Court.[44] Before the Guardianship of Infants Act 1961, the Civil Law Act 1956, section 27 stipulated that the law applicable to the custody and control of infants was to be the same as that in England as of the effective date of the Civil Law Act 1956, thus importing English law (as it stood on 7 April 1956[45]), again, not as foreign law but as part of Malaysian law itself.

ii. Muslims

For Muslims in Malaysia, the majority of the population, the applicable Islamic family laws vary between states.[46] The Islamic Family Law (Federal Territories) Act 1984, applicable in Kuala Lumpur and Labuan,[47] is used here as an example. The Act permits four categories of marriages abroad.[48] Loosely, these are: (1) marriages solemnised in Malaysian embassies abroad;[49] (2) foreign marriages solemnised abroad other than in Malaysian embassies;[50] (3) foreign marriages with the prior permission of the Registrar of Marriages, Divorces and *Ruju*';[51] and (4) foreign marriages without the prior permission of the Registrar of Marriages, Divorces and *Ruju*'.[52] As regards foreign law (insofar as the Act's provisions address it), the common thread would appear to be that each party must have capacity to marry according

[39] ibid, s 1; PU(B) 73/1982.

[40] *In re Maria Huberdina Hertogh; Inche Mansor Adabi v Adrianus Petrus Hertogh and Anor* [1951] 1 MLJ 164 (CA) 167–68; *In re Suzie Teoh; Teoh Eng Huat v Kadhi of Pasir Mas Kelantan and Majlis Ugama Islam dan Adat Istiadat Melayu, Kelantan* [1986] 2 MLJ 228 (OCJ) 233F–H. See also R Daw, 'Some Problems of Conflict of Laws in West Malaysia and Singapore Family Law' (1972) 14 *Malaya Law Review* 179, 183–84 and 191–92.

[41] *In re Divorce Petitions No 18, 20 and 24 of 1983* [1984] 2 MLJ 158 (HC) 162B–C.

[42] On which see Nadkarni and Teh (n 23) 167–69.

[43] Guardianship of Infants Act 1961, ss 1(2), 1(3).

[44] *W v H* [1987] 2 MLJ 235 (HC) 237; on the implications of this, see Hickling and Wu (n 9) 151–52.

[45] PU(A) 424/1971.

[46] Reddy (n 35) 619; Mohamad (n 35) 828; *Muhammad Faizz Amin bin Roslee v Maidatul Sarah bt Mior Rosli* (n 35).

[47] Islamic Family Law (Federal Territories) Act 1984, s 1(1).

[48] NM Zin et al, *Islamic Family Law in Malaysia* (London, Sweet & Maxwell, 2016) 43–46.

[49] Islamic Family Law (Federal Territories) Act 1984, s 24.

[50] ibid, s 108(1).

[51] ibid, ss 17 and 20.

[52] ibid, s 31.

to both *Hukum Syarak* (principles of Islamic law[53]) and the law of the (foreign) place where the party is resident, while the formalities must be in a form required or permitted by the *lex loci celebrationis*,[54] suggesting that application of these rules is mandatory. Upon divorce, although the Act is silent on the question, it would appear that in practice the Syariah courts do not consider the *lex situs* of immovable property in dividing matrimonial assets.[55]

E. Property

Where a trust affects immovable property, rights under the trust and the validity of the trust, insofar as the trust concerns the immovable property, are governed by the *lex situs*, even where the land is sold and converted into money.[56] In contrast, a trust affecting movable property is governed by the personal law of the testator, that is, the *lex domicilii*.[57]

F. Law of Corporations and Insolvency

Malaysia has not adopted the UNCITRAL Model Law on Cross-Border Insolvency,[58] despite the Model Law having been given legal force in neighbouring Singapore[59] and applied by the Singapore courts in considering parallel Malaysian winding-up proceedings.[60] Additionally, unlike the Insolvency Act 1967,[61] the Companies Act 2016 seems not to stipulate any elements of reciprocity or mutual aid and assistance in matters of insolvency between Malaysian courts and their foreign counterparts.[62]

In relation to the *Gibbs* rule,[63] where a proposed scheme of arrangement in Malaysia involves the discharge or modification of contractual rights governed by laws of a foreign

[53] Zin et al (n 48) xiii; Islamic Family Law (Federal Territories) Act 1984, s 134A; see as an example, *Fernando Vadillo & Anor v Alawiyah bt Abdul Rahman* [2012] 4 SHLR 38 (Syariah HC) [16]–[17].

[54] Islamic Family Law (Federal Territories) Act 1984, ss 24(2), 108(1). However, in *Fernando Vadillo* (n 53), the Syariah High Court validated a foreign marriage despite certain requirements seemingly not having been strictly observed.

[55] Zin et al (n 48) 251–52.

[56] *Re Syed Shaik Alkaff (decd)* [1923] 2 MC 38 (HC); *Re Huey Yet Tin Dredging Ltd* [1935] 1 MLJ 34 (OCJ); *Re Shaik Abubakar bin Mohamed Lajam Decd* [1935] 1 MLJ 137 (OCJ); see also *Charles Priya Marie v Koshy Cherian* [2010] 6 CLJ 693 (HC) [35]–[36] and *Yii Chee Ming v Teo Ah Khing @ Teo Cho Teck & Anor* [2005] 5 MLJ 354 (HC) [30]–[32].

[57] *Re Syed Shaik Alkaff (decd)* (n 56).

[58] UNCITRAL Model Law on Cross-Border Insolvency 1997; S Atkins and J Martin, 'The Model Law on Cross-Border Insolvency Turns 25' (*Norton Rose Fulbright*, May 2022) www.nortonrosefulbright.com/en/knowledge/publications/87d4ce21/the-model-law-on-cross-border-insolvency-turns-25 (accessed 11 May 2023).

[59] Insolvency, Restructuring and Dissolution Act 2018 (Singapore), s 252 and sch 3; but note that Singapore appears not to impose a condition of reciprocity, unlike certain other jurisdictions: SC Mohan, 'Cross-Border Insolvency Problems: Is the UNCITRAL Model Law the Answer?' (2012) 21 *International Insolvency Review* 199.

[60] *United Securities Sdn Bhd (in receivership and liq) and anor v United Overseas Bank Ltd* [2021] SGCA 78, [2021] 2 SLR 950 [49]–[76]. The parallel Malaysian proceedings are reported in (amongst others) *United Overseas Bank* (n 27).

[61] Insolvency Act 1967, s 104.

[62] PJ Omar, 'Cross-Border Jurisdiction and Assistance in Insolvency: The Position in Malaysia and Singapore' [2008] *Potchefstroomse Elektoniese Regsblad* 1. However, note that the provision on mutual aid and assistance in the Insolvency Act 1967, s 104(1) refers to 'all matters of bankruptcy and insolvency', which may arguably encompass corporate insolvency.

[63] *Antony Gibbs & Sons v Société Industrielle et Commerciale des Métaux* (1890) 25 QBD 399 (EWCA).

state, this will not prevent the Malaysian courts from approving the scheme.[64] This is despite the Malaysian courts having acknowledged that foreign courts may not accept a discharge or modification approved by the Malaysian courts, just as the Malaysian courts are likewise unlikely to recognise a foreign court's discharge or modification of contractual rights whose proper law (in the view of the Malaysian courts) is Malaysian law.[65]

Both the Companies Act 2016 and its predecessor, the Companies Act 1965, allow (or allowed) 'foreign companies'[66] to be wound up.[67] One notable change between the Acts, however, is the addition of the ground that 'the company is being used for unlawful purposes or any purpose prejudicial to or incompatible with peace, welfare, security, public interest, public order, good order or morality *in Malaysia*' as a ground for a foreign company to be wound up,[68] a ground previously available only in respect of domestic companies.[69] As there appear to be no reported cases to date on the winding up of foreign companies under the Companies Act 2016, it remains to be seen whether this ground encompasses a purpose which is unlawful only by the law of a foreign state.[70]

G. Bankruptcy

The Insolvency Act 1967, section 104 contains various '[r]eciprocal provisions relating to Singapore and designated countries', which at the date of writing are the UK and Australia.[71] These include, for instance, a requirement that the High Court 'act in aid of and be auxiliary to' the courts of those countries 'in all matters of bankruptcy and insolvency',[72] and a stipulation that an order by the courts of those countries seeking aid with a request to the High Court shall enable the High Court to exercise (in essence) the same jurisdiction that it would have had locally,[73] a discretion to be exercised 'hav[ing] regard to the rules of private international law'.[74] However, there is little judicial guidance on the precise effect of these provisions on the treatment of foreign law.[75] In a case before the Kuala Lumpur High Court, the successful party made submissions on both the reciprocity provisions in the Insolvency Act 1967, section 104 and matters of Singapore law,[76] and the High Court's judgment was expressed to be based on 'the Bankruptcy Laws of both Singapore and Malaysia',[77] but the judgment did not state whether the High Court specifically considered potential questions of choice of law in reaching its decision.

[64] *Airasia X Bhd v BOC Aviation Ltd & Ors* [2021] 10 MLJ 942 (HC) [313].
[65] ibid [314]–[315]; *RHB Bank Bhd v First Omni Sdn Bhd & Anor* [2021] 8 MLJ 43 (HC) [30]–[32] (obiter).
[66] Defined in the Companies Act 2016, s 2(1) and the Companies Act 1965, s 4(1).
[67] Companies Act 2016, s 545 (read with s 544); Companies Act 1965, s 315 (read with s 314).
[68] Companies Act 2016, s 545(1)(c)(iv) (emphasis added).
[69] Companies Act 1965, ss 218(1)(m) and 315(1)(c); KPK Foo and S Lee, *Companies Act 2016: The New Dynamics of Company Law in Malaysia* (Selangor, CLJ Publication, 2017) 519–20.
[70] See discussion above of *ABDA Airfreight* (n 28) 701C–G.
[71] Insolvency Act 1967, s 104(1); PU(B) 2/1989.
[72] Insolvency Act 1967, s 104(1).
[73] ibid, s 104(2).
[74] ibid, s 104(2A).
[75] It has been suggested that this may be because the Insolvency Act 1967, s 104 is not widely known: Omar (n 62) 37.
[76] *Bangkok Bank Company Ltd v Thye Nam Loong Holdings Sdn Bhd & Anor* [2005] 6 CLJ 457 (HC).
[77] ibid 462d–e.

H. Admiralty

The Courts of Judicature Act 1964, section 24(b) confers on the High Court 'the same jurisdiction and authority in relation to matters of admiralty as is had by the High Court of Justice in England under the United Kingdom Supreme Court Act 1981', which is now the Senior Courts Act 1981.[78] Additionally, by the Civil Law Act 1956, section 5(1), English law on 'carriers by air, land and sea [and] marine insurance' as it stood prior to Malaysia's independence applies, where and insofar as Malaysian legislation is silent.[79] The effect of these provisions is that the admiralty provisions of the English Senior Courts Act 1981, as they stand today, and (to a lesser extent) English common law, as it stood in 1956 – including English case law on them[80] – continue to apply or feature heavily in Malaysia, not as foreign law in the strict sense, but as part of Malaysian law. The Senior Courts Act 1981, section 20(7)(c) expressly envisages that mortgages or charges created under foreign law may come before the Malaysian courts.[81]

On questions of priority, the Malaysian courts have adopted the Privy Council's definition of a maritime lien from *The Bold Buccleugh*.[82] However, it remains to be seen whether they will eventually also follow the majority of the Privy Council in *The Halcyon Isle*, by recognising foreign maritime liens only where the same events, had they occurred within Malaysian territory, would have created a maritime lien in Malaysian law, that is, as a procedural matter governed by the *lex fori*, as opposed to a question governed by the *lex causae*.[83]

I. Arbitration

The primary statute on arbitration in Malaysia is the Arbitration Act 2005. The Act is based primarily on the UNCITRAL Model Law on International Commercial Arbitration,[84] with significant similarity to New Zealand's Arbitration Act 1996.[85]

The Act envisages three categories of arbitration: domestic arbitrations where the seat is in Malaysia, international arbitrations where the seat is in Malaysia, and international

[78] *Pacific Bunkers Pte Ltd v Owners of The Ships or Vessels 'Geniki Sarawak' and 'Geniki Johor' (No 2)* [2015] 11 MLJ 145 (HC) [48]. The retention of s 24(b) has been criticised: S Selvaratnam, 'Maritime Reform: Arrest for Arbitration' (2005): https://www.tommythomas.net/upload/staticpage/download/Maritime%20Reform%20-%20Arrest%20for%20Arbitration.pdf (accessed 11 May 2023); S Selvaratnam, 'The Right of Arrest – Are We Making It Too Difficult? A Common Law Perspective' paras 15, 33: www.aiac.world/news/209/Sitpah-Selvaratnam:-The-Right-of-Arrest-%E2%80%93-Are-we-making-it-too-difficult-?-A-Common-Law-Perspective (accessed 11 May 2023).

[79] *Owners of Cargo Carried in the Ship 'Gang Cheng' v Owners and/or Persons Interested in the Ship 'Gang Cheng'* [1998] 6 MLJ 468 (HC) 474–75.

[80] *The Fordeco Nos 12 and 17; The Owners of and All Other Persons Interested in the Ships Fordeco No 12 and Fordeco No 17 v Shanghai Hai Xing Shipping Co Ltd, The Owners of the Ship MV Xin Hua 10* [2000] 1 MLJ 449 (FC) 457–61.

[81] *Nassau Maritime Holdings Designated Activity Co v The owners of the ship or vessel 'Cape Lambert' of the Port of Marshall Islands* [2020] 11 MLJ 561 (HC) [14].

[82] *Harmer v Bell, The Bold Buccleugh* [1843–60] All ER Rep 125 (UKPC) 128; *Pemunya Kapal MV Brihope v Emmanuel E Okwuosa* [1997] 1 MLJ 453 (CA) 487C–F; *Lee Wong Yu v The Owners of The Ship or Vessel 'MV Hua Hong Satu'* [1999] 6 CLJ 197 (HC) 203A–D.

[83] *The 'Halcyon Isle' Bankers Trust International Limited v Todd Shipyards Corporation* [1980] 2 MLJ 217 (UKPC) 221D, 222C–I.

[84] UNCITRAL Model Law on International Commercial Arbitration 1985, with amendments as adopted in 2006.

[85] *Master Mulia Sdn Bhd v Sigur Rus Sdn Bhd* [2020] 12 MLJ 198 (FC) [28].

arbitrations where the seat is not in Malaysia (referred to here, for convenience, as foreign-seated arbitrations).[86] Under section 22, if parties have not agreed on the seat – and hence curial law or *lex arbitri* – of arbitration,[87] the seat must be determined by the arbitral tribunal 'having regard to the circumstances of the case, including the convenience of the parties'.[88] However, section 22 (unlike, for instance, section 10[89]) is not expressly stipulated to apply to foreign-seated arbitrations. It is therefore not clear whether section 22 applies where the choice to be made is between Malaysian curial law and a foreign curial law.[90]

Meanwhile, section 30(1) requires the arbitral tribunal to 'decide the dispute in accordance with such rules of law as are chosen by the parties as applicable to the substance of the dispute'. Section 30(3) stipulates that '[a]ny designation of the law or legal system of a given State shall be construed, unless otherwise expressed, as directly referring to the substantive law of that State and not to its conflict of laws rules'. If there is no designation, section 30(4) requires the arbitral tribunal to 'apply the law determined by the conflict of laws rules which it considers applicable', suggesting that the arbitral tribunal is granted a rather wide discretion as to which choice of law rules apply in determining the applicable substantive law.[91] Where there is a conflict between the parties' chosen applicable law and mandatory rules of the *lex arbitri*, the mandatory rules of the *lex arbitri* will prevail.[92] An error by an arbitral tribunal in identifying the applicable substantive law (including interpretation of a contractual designation of it) is not a ground for the setting aside of an arbitral award.[93] In particular, the Malaysian courts regard an arbitral tribunal's identification of applicable limitation laws as a question of admissibility, not jurisdiction, which the courts thus will not review.[94]

As regards the law governing the arbitration agreement – that is, its validity, interpretation and effect – the Arbitration Act 2005 would appear to be silent.[95] The current leading Malaysian case on this point is the Federal Court's judgment in *Thai-Lao Lignite* in 2017.[96] Based on *Thai-Lao Lignite*, where an arbitration agreement is silent on the law which governs it, the law of the stipulated seat will 'usually [be] decisive' in this respect '[u]nless it is shown to the contrary', taking precedence over the governing law of the

[86] Arbitration Act 2005, ss 2(1), 3.

[87] ibid, s 22(1).

[88] ibid, s 22(2).

[89] ibid, s 10(4).

[90] *Aras Jalinan Sdn Bhd v Tipco Asphalt Public Company Ltd & Ors* [2008] 5 CLJ 654 (HC) [20], not affected on this point by *Aras Jalinan Sdn Bhd v Tipco Asphalt Public Co Ltd & Ors* [2012] 1 MLJ 510 (CA); *Envac Scandinavia AB v Muhibbah Engineering (M) Bhd* [2020] MLJU 2092 (HC) [26]; B Premaraj, 'The Choices of Law – Better Safe Than Sorry: The Malaysian Arbitration Perspective' 15–16: beldenlex.com/training/publications/The%20Choices%20of%20Law%20-%20Better%20Safe%20Than%20Sorry.pdf (accessed 11 May 2023); see also *Masenang Sdn Bhd v Sabanilam Enterprise Sdn Bhd* [2021] 6 MLJ 255 (FC) which examined s 22 in detail, but in relation to domestic arbitrations.

[91] See also Premaraj (n 90) 25–29.

[92] *Thai-Lao Lignite* (n 30) [157].

[93] *Hindustan Oil Exploration Company Ltd v Hardy Exploration & Production (India) Inc* [2022] 6 CLJ 81 (HC) [30(iii)]; Arbitration Act 2005, s 37(1).

[94] *Hindustan Oil Exploration Company* (n 93) [33]–[34], applying *BBA v BAZ* [2020] SGCA 53, [2020] 2 SLR 453, affirmed on appeal in *Hindustan Oil Exploration Company Limited v Hardy Exploration & Production (India) Inc* [2023] MLJU 795 (CA) [44]–[77].

[95] *Thai-Lao Lignite* (n 30) [162]–[163]; S Subramaniam, 'Determining the Law to Govern an Arbitration Agreement' (2020) 47 *Journal of Malaysian and Comparative Law* 1, 15.

[96] *Thai-Lao Lignite* (n 30); see also *The Government of India v Cairn Energy India Pty Ltd* [2011] 6 MLJ 441 (FC).

overall contract.[97] Interestingly, despite recognising that 'New York [not Malaysian] law governed the substance of the dispute', the Federal Court based its reasoning on the law governing the arbitration agreement on sections 30(2) and 30(4) as they then stood (pre-amendment) which, by contrast, referred to the law applicable to the 'substance of the dispute'.[98] While this may give the impression that Malaysian law treats these two choices of law as synonymous in every case, the Federal Court itself earlier in *Thai-Lao Lignite* had in fact rightly[99] recognised these choices as separate and distinct.[100] In addition, *Thai-Lao Lignite* was decided before both the amendment in 2018 of the Arbitration Act 2005, s 30,[101] and the UK Supreme Court's landmark judgment in 2020 on these issues in *Enka v Chubb*.[102] Since then, there have been no reported cases which meaningfully address the updated wording of section 30(4), and *Enka v Chubb* appears to have received only passing reference by the Malaysian courts.[103] It remains to be seen what influence, if any, these developments may have on existing Malaysian jurisprudence. Where a party opposes a stay pending arbitration[104] on the ground that the arbitration agreement is null and void, inoperative or incapable of being performed under its foreign governing law, the onus lies on that party to prove this with the necessary evidence of that foreign law.[105]

III. Foreign Law before Judicial Authorities

A. Nature of Foreign Law in Malaysia

By the Evidence Act 1950, section 45, the general position is that foreign law before a 'court' is a 'pure' question of fact,[106] upon which the evidence of 'experts' is relevant:

> **45.** (1) When the court has to form an opinion upon a point of foreign law … the opinions upon that point of persons specially skilled in that foreign law … are relevant *facts*.
> (2) Such persons are called experts.[107]

Here, 'court' means a court established by or under the Federal Constitution, Part IX, and includes a judge, a Sessions Court judge, a Magistrate, and every person legally authorised

[97] *Thai-Lao Lignite* (n 30) [244].
[98] ibid [186]–[187].
[99] Tan Sri Dato', C Abraham and AA Amirudin, 'Interaction of Laws in International Arbitration' in Tun Arifin Zakaria, Datuk Professor S Rajoo and P Koh (eds), *Arbitration in Malaysia: A Practical Guide* (London, Sweet & Maxwell, 2016) para 3.019.
[100] *Thai-Lao Lignite* (n 30) [153].
[101] Previously, s 30(2) upheld arbitral parties' agreed choice of applicable substantive law, and s 30(4) provided that '[f]ailing any agreement under subsection (2), the arbitral tribunal shall apply the law determined by the conflict of law rules.' With the Arbitration (Amendment) (No 2) Act 2018, s 9, s 30(2) of the main Act was repealed, whereas s 30(4) was amended to its current wording.
[102] *Enka Insaat ve Sanayi AS v OOO Insurance Company Chubb* [2020] UKSC 38, [2020] 1 WLR 4117.
[103] *Masenang* (n 90) [148]; *Hindustan Oil Exploration Company* (HC) (n 93) [24].
[104] Arbitration Act 2005, s 10.
[105] *Hew Choong Jeng & Ors v Kok Low Kau* [2022] MLJU 1738 (HC) [21]–[23].
[106] *Mak Sik Kwong v Minister of Home Affairs, Malaysia (No 2)* [1975] 2 MLJ 175 (HC) 180C, cited with approval in *The 'Lung Yung' & 'Thai Yung' Owners & Ors v Sadit Timber Sdn Bhd & Ors* [1984] 1 MLJ 29 (FC) 45C.
[107] Emphasis added.

to take evidence, except an arbitrator.[108] There are certain exceptions to this general position, such as in the case of statutes of the UK. These are addressed further below.

B. Ascertainment of Foreign Law

i. Ascertainment and Proof of Foreign Law and Non-applicability of 'iura novit curia'

As it is not open to Malaysian courts simply to take judicial notice of foreign laws without admissible evidence of them (such as expert evidence),[109] '*iura novit curia*' is arguably inapplicable to proceedings before Malaysian courts. Rather, the starting point is that the burden of proving foreign law lies on the party whose claimed relief depends on the existence of such foreign law.[110] Neither may Malaysian courts rely on foreign law proved before the Malaysian courts (or indeed foreign courts) in a previous case; as a question of fact, foreign law must be proved afresh on each occasion.[111] In practice, however, it has been remarked that Malaysian courts would be unlikely to disagree with a statement of the law of a foreign country given by a superior court of that foreign country.[112]

ii. Sources of Foreign Law

a. Experts

Foreign law may be proved, first, by experts, under the Evidence Act 1950, s 45(1). An expert on foreign law plays two roles. The expert may first give factual evidence on the existence of the relevant foreign legislation or law and any judicial pronouncements on such legislation or law by the relevant foreign courts. The expert must be able to point to a specific law; a bare assertion will not suffice.[113] If the expert goes further by propounding how such legislation or law should be interpreted or applied to the facts at hand, the Malaysian courts will treat this as 'mere opinion evidence which the court may or may not accept'.[114] The procedures for court- and party-appointed experts in court proceedings are in the Rules of Court 2012, Orders 40 and 40A respectively.

Where a foreign law expert tenders a witness statement and opinion, but fails to attend court to give direct oral evidence as required by the Evidence Act 1950, section 60(1), the witness statement and opinion are inadmissible.[115] However, a hearing may proceed on expert evidence by affidavit alone without oral examination of the experts where all parties

[108] Evidence Act 1950, s 3.

[109] *Mak Sik Kwong* (n 106) 180C; *The 'Lung Yung'* (n 106) 180C; *Sivagami Achi v PRM Ramanathan Chettiar & Anor* [1959] 1 MLJ 221 (OCJ) 223G.

[110] Evidence Act 1950, s 101; see also s 102.

[111] *Re M Meyer, Deceased* [1938] 1 MLJ 190 (OCJ) 193.

[112] Hickling and Wu (n 9) 46; see, eg, *Ng Chee Meng v Wynn Resorts (Macau) SA* [2021] MLJU 1808 (HC) [27]–[29].

[113] *The Taveechai Marine* [1995] 1 MLJ 413 (HC) 430H–433D.

[114] *YK Fung Securities* (CA) (n 15) 663C–F.

[115] *PT Adhiyasa Saranamas v Kumpulan Guthrie Bhd & Ors* [2014] 1 MLJevi 91 (HC) [15]–[16].

to the action so agree[116] (apart from the non-applicability of the Evidence Act 1950 to affidavits[117]). It would appear that a foreign law expert being a party to the action being tried or having an interest in its outcome does not, in itself, necessarily render his evidence inadmissible for lacking independence.[118] Where one party but not the other calls expert evidence of foreign law, it is open to the latter party to establish its reliance on that foreign law by cross-examination of the former party's expert, without calling its own expert (although practically this may affect the latter party's ability to challenge the expert's evidence).[119]

Specifically on an application for a grant in non-contentious probate proceedings, the Rules of Court 2012, Order 71, rule 16 permits the Registrar to accept, as evidence of a foreign law where required for the application, the affidavit of either: (1) any person who practises or has practised as a barrister or advocate in that country, and who is conversant with its law; or (2) in special circumstances, any other person lacking these qualifications but whom the Registrar is satisfied nevertheless has knowledge of that country's law.

b. Collections of Laws and Reports of Judgments

The Evidence Act 1950, s 38 provides as follows:

> **Relevancy of statements as to any law contained in law books**
>
> **38.** When the court has to form an opinion as to a law of any country, any statement of that law contained in a book purporting to be printed or published under the authority of the Government of that country, and to contain any such law, and any report of a ruling of the courts of that country contained in a book purporting to be a report of such rulings, is relevant.

Section 38 can be read with section 84:[120]

> **Presumption as to collections of laws and reports of decisions**
>
> **84.** The court shall presume the genuineness of every book purporting—
>
> *(a)* to be printed or published under the authority of the Government of any country and to contain any of the laws of that country; or
>
> *(b)* to contain reports of decisions of the courts of that country.

To meet these requirements, a book must contain an express indication that it purports to be printed or published under the authority of the government in question.[121] Additionally, it would appear that the condition of authority requires a book to have been printed or published *by* a government, whereas law reports may be published either officially or privately.[122] The effect of the obligation ('shall') in section 84 is that the courts must regard the genuineness of such books as proved unless and until it is disproved.[123]

[116] *Tan Kui Lim & Anor v Lai Sin Fah* [1980] 1 MLJ 222 (FC) 224D.

[117] Evidence Act 1950, s 2.

[118] *Portcullis Trustnet (Singapore) Pte Ltd v George Pathmanathan a/l Michael Gandhi Nathan & Ors* [2017] MLJU 223 (HC) [137]–[143]; *Spind Malaysia Sdn Bhd v Justrade Marketing Sdn Bhd* [2018] 4 MLJ 34 (FC) [136].

[119] *EG Tan & Co (in liq) v Tan Chong San* [1998] 6 MLJ 583 (HC) 590A–C, 593G.

[120] *Atico Overseas Ltd v Procast Furniture Industry Sdn Bhd* [2014] 1 MLJevi 15 (HC) 23A–C.

[121] *Goh Tat Eng v Goh Eng Loon* [1911] 1 LNS 3 (HC).

[122] *Atico Overseas* (n 120) [8(d)]; note, however, *B v Comptroller of Inland Revenue* [1974] 2 MLJ 110 (FC) 112D–113B which has been criticised because the book in question was not one published under governmental authority: Hickling and Wu (n 9) 44.

[123] Evidence Act 1950, s 4(2).

c. Acts, Ordinances and Statutes of Commonwealth Countries

The Evidence Act 1950, s 78(2) provides as follows:

> Copies of Acts, Ordinances and Statutes passed by the legislature of any part of the Commonwealth and of orders, regulations and other instruments issued or made under the authority of any such Act, Ordinance or Statute, if purporting to be printed by the Government Printer, shall be received in evidence by all courts in Malaysia without any proof being given that the copies were so printed.

'[T]he Commonwealth' means collectively the Commonwealth countries, any part of British Crown dominions not being a Commonwealth country, any territory under the protection of a Commonwealth country and any territory administered by the government of a Commonwealth country under the trusteeship system of the United Nations.[124] In turn, a 'Commonwealth country' means any country recognised by the Yang di-Pertuan Agong to be a Commonwealth country.[125] 'Government Printer' means the printer purporting to be the printer authorised to print the Acts, Ordinances or Statutes of the legislature of a Commonwealth country, or otherwise to be the Government Printer of that territory.[126]

d. Documents Forming or Recording Acts of Foreign Countries

Read together, the Evidence Act 1950, ss 74(a) and 78(1)(f) allow documents forming or recording the acts of certain branches of a foreign country's government to be proved if three conditions are met, that is:[127]

> … by the original or by a copy certified by the lawful keeper thereof, with a certificate under the seal of a notary public or of a consular officer of Malaysia that the copy is duly certified by the officer having the lawful custody of the original and upon proof of the character of the document according to the law of the foreign country.

The recognised branches of government are the sovereign authority, official bodies and tribunals, and public officers, whether legislative, judicial or executive.[128]

Specifically for foreign judicial records of non-Commonwealth countries, section 86 gives Malaysian courts the following discretion entailing two requirements:[129]

> The court may presume that any document purporting to be a certified copy of any judicial record of any country not being a part of the Commonwealth is genuine and accurate if the document purports to be certified in any manner which is certified by any representative of the Yang di-Pertuan Agong in or for such country to be the manner commonly in use in that country for the certification of copies of judicial records.

The effect of the discretion ('may') in section 86 is that the courts may either regard the genuineness and accuracy of such documents to be proved unless and until they are disproved, or may call for proof of them.[130]

[124] Interpretation Acts 1948 and 1967, s 66.
[125] ibid; Federal Constitution, Art 160(2).
[126] Evidence Act 1950, s 78(3).
[127] *Edmund Ming Kwan @ Kwaun Yee Ming, Edmund v Extra Excel (Malaysia) Sdn Bhd & Ors (Part 2)* [2007] 7 MLJ 276 (HC) [10].
[128] Evidence Act 1950, s 74(a).
[129] *Edmund Ming Kwan* (n 127) [10].
[130] Evidence Act 1950, s 4(1).

e. Statutes, Proclamations, Orders and Regulations of the United Kingdom

Peculiarly to laws of the UK, the Evidence Act 1950, section 57(1)(b) requires Malaysian courts to take judicial notice of 'all public Acts passed or hereafter to be passed by the Parliament of the United Kingdom, and all local and personal Acts directed by it to be judicially noticed'. This does not extend, however, to taking judicial notice of opinions on English law by (for instance) former judges, practitioners and academicians of English law; such opinions must be tendered as expert evidence in accordance with section 45(1).[131] The effect of judicial notice is that a fact need not be proved,[132] although the courts if called upon by any person to take judicial notice of any fact may refuse to do so unless and until the person produces such books or documents as the courts consider necessary to enable them to do so.[133]

Meanwhile, by section 78(1)(c), proclamations, orders or regulations issued by the Crown in the UK or by the Privy Council or by any minister or department of the Crown may be proved by copies or extracts contained in the *London Gazette* or in the *Gazette* or in any state *Gazette* or purporting to be printed by Her (or His) Britannic Majesty's Printer.

f. Treatises

The Evidence Act 1950, s 60(2) provides as follows:

> The opinions of experts expressed in any treatise commonly offered for sale and the grounds on which such opinions are held may be proved by the production of the treatise if the author is dead or cannot be found or has become incapable of giving evidence or cannot be called as a witness without an amount of delay or expense which the court regards as unreasonable.

A mere essay, pamphlet, summary or compilation on or of a foreign law, which contains or condenses the notes or opinions of others rather than of the author, does not amount to a treatise within the meaning of section 60(2).[134] The expertise of the author – including qualifications, training and experience – should also be stated in the putative treatise.[135]

iii. Whether Individuals or Institutions must have Qualifications to Provide Legal Information

As with any expert under the Evidence Act 1950, section 45, a person must be 'specially skilled' or 'peritus' in a foreign law to give expert evidence on it.[136] The Rules of Court 2012, Order 40, rule 1(5) further specifies that a court-appointed expert must have 'such knowledge or experience of or in connection with [any question arising in a cause or matter] that his opinion on it would be admissible in evidence'.[137] In practice, the courts determine the question of 'special skill' with 'considerable laxity'.[138] An expert needs only to be skilled and

[131] *Ranjeet Singh Sidhu & Anor v Zavarco Plc & Ors* [2016] 2 CLJ 975 (HC) [42(g)–(i)].
[132] Evidence Act 1950, s 56.
[133] ibid, s 57(3).
[134] *Goh Tat Eng* (n 121).
[135] ibid.
[136] Evidence Act 1950, s 45(1); *PP v Muhamed bin Sulaiman* [1982] 2 MLJ 320 (FC) 322–23.
[137] Rules of Court 2012, Ord 40A on party-appointed experts does not contain a similar stipulation.
[138] *PP v Muhamed bin Sulaiman* (n 136) 322H.

to possess adequate knowledge. The expert can acquire this skill and this knowledge in any way, so long as they have had sufficient (practical) experience to do so.[139] The expert does not necessarily need to have done so professionally or through special study, or even to be legally trained or qualified, which may affect the weight but not the admissibility of their evidence.[140] Neither does the expert need to have given expert evidence on the foreign law concerned before, or to have written any publications on it.[141]

As examples, Malaysian courts have previously accepted foreign law expert evidence from practising lawyers qualified and registered in the relevant foreign jurisdictions;[142] practising solicitors familiar with the laws of the foreign country, but whose qualifications relate to a neighbouring or related jurisdiction;[143] on the laws of a particular state of the US, a lawyer practising in a different state of the US;[144] a legally untrained and unqualified retired customs officer of long standing and experience, on the practical aspects of the foreign country's customs laws;[145] a pupil in chambers with postgraduate qualifications and practical experience all in relation to the foreign law and country concerned;[146] a university lecturer with undergraduate and postgraduate qualifications on local Chinese customs;[147] and a headman and registrar of customary marriages, on Chinese marriage customary law.[148]

The requirements in relation to the publishers or authors of collections of laws, reports of judgments, books, treatises and other official documents relating to foreign law have been explained above.

iv. Whether Information on Foreign Law Binding on Courts

As with any type of expert evidence,[149] expert evidence on foreign law is not binding upon Malaysian courts; rather, after the experts submit propositions of foreign law for the courts' consideration, as assistance and guidance, the courts themselves must then make their own findings on what the foreign law is.[150] This includes application of the courts' own mind to the text of the foreign law itself to choose between competing interpretations proffered by party-appointed experts.[151] In particular, a bare or unreasoned assertion by an expert will

[139] ibid 322–23.

[140] ibid 322H.

[141] *ABDA Airfreight* (n 28) 698C–F.

[142] *Aldar for Construction and Architecture v Majlis Agama Islam Negeri Johor* [2019] MLJU 1502 (HC) [40]–[45]; *ABDA Airfreight* (n 28) 689B, 693F, 694C; *Portcullis Trustnet* (n 118) [140]–[141].

[143] *Ng Chee Meng* (n 112) [26] where a solicitor qualified in Hong Kong was held to have the required familiarity with certain points of the law of Macau.

[144] *Playboy Enterprises International Inc v Zillion Choice Sdn Bhd & Anor* [2011] 2 MLJ 59 (HC) [30].

[145] *ABDA Airfreight* (n 28) 689C, 693F.

[146] *PP v Forster Frank Edald Heinrich* [1988] 2 MLJ 594 (OCRJ) 599.

[147] *Beh Lee Liang v Chew Sah Suak* [1995] 4 MLJ 397 (HC) 409–10.

[148] *Kong Nen Siew v Lim Siew Hong* [1971] 1 MLJ 262 (OCJ) 263D.

[149] *Dr Shanmuganathan v Periasamy s/o Sithambaram Pillai* [1997] 3 MLJ 61 (FC) 85B; *Wong Swee Chin v PP* [1981] 1 MLJ 212 (FC) 213I–214B.

[150] *YK Fung Securities* (CA) (n 15) 663D; *The H156* [1999] 3 SLR 756 (SGHC) [27], applied in *Best Re (L) Ltd v Hanwha General Insurance Co Ltd* [2014] 9 MLJ 125 (HC) [35]; see also the dissenting judgment of David Wong CJSS in *Jabatan Pendaftaran Negara & Ors v A Child & Ors (Majlis Agama Islam Negeri Johor, intervener)* [2020] 2 MLJ 277 (FC) [210].

[151] *NV De Bataafsche Petroleum Maatschappij v The War Damage Commission* [1956] 1 MLJ 155 (SGCA) 166.

not suffice.[152] At the same time, in reaching their own conclusions, the courts must actually consider the expert evidence; ignoring and disregarding expert evidence may amount to a substantial miscarriage of justice which invites appellate interference.[153] If the courts find themselves at a 'deadlock' after competing expert evidence has been given, a court-appointed expert may be appointed under the Rules of Court 2012, Order 40, rule 1.[154]

Similarly, documentary or 'raw' sources of foreign law, such as collections of laws, are not automatically binding upon the courts. While they will be admissible if they satisfy the requirements in the Evidence Act 1950 (as explained above), even if unaccompanied by expert opinion, the courts must still determine the evidentiary weight to be given to them.[155]

v. Examination of Reliability of Information on Foreign Law Provided

Expert evidence on foreign law may be tested through cross-examination by the parties' counsel, whether the expert is appointed by the courts[156] or parties.[157] Questions can also be put to expert witnesses by the courts themselves.[158] However, this power should generally be exercised sparingly and only where necessary, as the courts in posing questions must be careful not to descend into the arena of the dispute.[159]

As for the various categories of documentary evidence of foreign law recognised by the Evidence Act 1950, the manner in which the genuineness and accuracy of such evidence are to be tested (or indeed presumed) varies depending on the particular section of the Act under which the evidence is put.[160] Subject to the minutiae of those individual sections, the courts in reviewing such documentary evidence may themselves review the 'raw' material cited by foreign law experts, such as legislation and case law.[161]

vi. Costs of Ascertaining Foreign Law

Where a foreign law expert is appointed by the courts, the expert's remuneration is fixed by the courts and the parties are jointly and severally liable for payment.[162] However, where one party opposes the appointment of a court-appointed expert, the courts may impose a condition that the other party applying for the appointment give such security for the expert's remuneration as the courts think fit.[163] Otherwise, there would appear to be no rule

[152] *The Taveechai Marine* (n 113) 430H–433D.
[153] *Asean Securities Paper Mills Sdn Bhd v CGU Insurance Bhd* [2007] 2 MLJ 301 (FC) 314G.
[154] *Ernest Cheong Yong Yin v KM Engineering & Development Sdn Bhd* [1996] 4 MLJ 438 (HC) 451D.
[155] *Pacific Recreation Pte Ltd v Technology Inc* [2008] SGCA 1, [2008] 2 SLR 491 [55], [60], applied in *Atico Overseas* (n 120) [9].
[156] Rules of Court 2012, Ord 40, r 4.
[157] ibid, Ord 40A, r 4.
[158] Evidence Act 1950, s 165.
[159] *Abuchi Ngwoke v PP* [2016] 2 MLJ 623 (CA) [29]–[30]; *Teng Boon How v PP* [1993] 3 MLJ 553 (SC) 563D–F, applying *Jones v National Coal Board* [1957] 2 QB 55 (EWCA) 63–65.
[160] Evidence Act 1950, ss 38, 57(1)(b), 60(2), 74(1)(a), 78(1)(c), 78(1)(f), 78(2), 84, each discussed above.
[161] *Playboy Enterprises International* (n 144) [35]–[36]; *Pacific Recreation* (n 155) [55], [60], applied in *Atico Overseas* (n 120) [9].
[162] Rules of Court 2012, Ord 40, r 5; see also *Wong Chin Chaw v Sri Melinger Sdn Bhd* [2015] 1 LNS 799 (HC) [12].
[163] Rules of Court 2012, Or 40, r 5(2).

as to costs peculiar to the ascertainment of foreign law, whether through party-appointed experts or documentary evidence, such that these costs are governed by the general rules on costs.[164]

C. Interpretation and Application of Foreign Law

i. Conditions for Application of Foreign Law before Malaysian Courts

Malaysian courts apply foreign law only if pleaded by at least one party to an action; if no party so pleads, the courts apply a rebuttable presumption that the relevant foreign law is the same as Malaysian law, and the fact that foreign law is involved will not in itself necessarily amount to a triable issue which bars the grant of summary judgment.[165] However, this does not extend to Malaysian statutes specifically stated to apply only in Malaysia.[166] Another exception to this is the 'double actionability' rule applicable to a tort committed outside the jurisdiction: if no evidence of the foreign *lex loci delicti* is led, the claim will fail.[167]

ii. Interpretation and Application of Foreign Law by Malaysian Courts

The sections above have discussed whether evidence of foreign law is binding upon the courts and how the reliability of this evidence is examined. Those considerations aside, there would appear to be no particular rules as to how the Malaysian courts interpret and apply foreign law.

iii. Gaps in Foreign Law

Where there is no foreign judgment or authority directly on point in respect of foreign legislation, or the law there is unsettled, it is open to an expert witness to assist Malaysian courts in making a finding as to what the foreign courts' ruling would be, were the decision to arise there; in so doing, the expert must explain their analytical process.[168] Otherwise, it is open to the Malaysian courts to presume (rebuttably) that the relevant foreign law is the same as Malaysian law,[169] except where a Malaysian statute expressly applies only in Malaysia,[170]

[164] See, eg, ibid, Ord 59.
[165] *Elders Keep Ltd v Luen Mei Plastic Industries Sdn Bhd & Ors* [1989] 1 CLJ Rep 517 (HC) 520e–f; *Sutures (M) Sdn Bhd v Worldwide Holdings Bhd & Ors* [2015] 8 MLJ 659 (HC) [44]; *Union De Banques Arabes Et Francaises Singapore Branch v Prodimex Resources Sdn Bhd* [2021] MLJU 2767 (HC) [72]–[74]. However, note *Lin Securities (Pte) v Noone & Co Sdn Bhd* [1989] 1 MLJ 321 (HC) where the High Court allowed an application to set aside summary judgment on the ground that whether and how Singapore law applied raised 'too many questions' to be dealt with at that stage. Note also *Wu Der Haw v Unsur Pancar Sdn Bhd & 3 Ors* [2001] 1 LNS 41 (HC) where the High Court refused to make a finding that a trust existed, on the ground that no evidence had been produced that the law of trusts in Taiwan, the country concerned, was the same as that in common law countries.
[166] *Ontrade Finance Limited v Landmark Enterprise Sdn Bhd & Ors* [1993] MLJU 165 (HC) 8–9.
[167] *Chan Kwon Fong v Chan Wah* [1977] 1 MLJ 232 (FC) 234G.
[168] *Atico Overseas* (n 120) [9], citing *Pacific Recreation* (n 155).
[169] *Elders Keep* (n 165) 520e–f.
[170] *Ontrade Finance* (n 166) 8–9.

or where the cause of action requires conditions to be fulfilled under both Malaysian law and the foreign law.[171]

Where the existence of foreign legislation *in pari materia* with or very similar to Malaysian law has been duly ascertained by expert evidence, it would appear that the Malaysian courts will 'safely assume', absent judicial decisions of the foreign jurisdiction to the contrary, that the foreign courts would decide the matter as the Malaysian courts would, such that the Malaysian courts will effectively apply Malaysian law.[172] However, it should be noted that the cited authority, *YK Fung Securities*, concerned the application of Singaporean law; although not expressed in the judgment, one might speculate that the Court of Appeal's decision on this point may well have been partly influenced by the similarities and intertwined heritage which Singaporean law and Malaysian law share.

D. Failure to Establish Foreign Law

Where no or no satisfactory evidence of foreign law is before the courts, the courts will generally apply a rebuttable presumption that the relevant foreign law is the same as Malaysian law, and thus decide a case according to Malaysian law as the *lex fori*.[173] However, in a case where a contract was stipulated to be governed by a foreign law, both parties submitted based on Malaysian law while omitting to tender admissible evidence of the content of that foreign law; the High Court refused to grant summary judgment on the ground that the differences between Malaysian law and that foreign law on the substantive issue in question were 'at least a triable issue'.[174] Reported case law appears not to contain substantial judicial discussion of the background and policy surrounding the former presumption, save that the presumption originates from English law.[175]

E. Judicial Review and Appeals

i. *Judicial Review and Appeals Generally*

An application for judicial review generally may be made against any 'person or authority'[176] for illegality, irrationality, procedural impropriety and possibly proportionality, grounds which have been held to permit review of the merits of the impugned decision.[177] A 'person or authority' may include an inferior tribunal that exercises a quasi-judicial function, if the legislation governing the tribunal does not provide for appellate (as opposed to supervisory)

[171] *Chan Kwon Fong v Chan Wah* (n 167) 234D.
[172] *YK Fung Securities* (CA) (n 15) 663C–F.
[173] *Elders Keep* (n 165) 520e–f; *Portcullis Trustnet* (n 118) [144]–[146].
[174] *Dhaneshvaran S Baskaran* (n 27) [26], [31].
[175] *Portcullis Trustnet* (n 118) [144]–[146].
[176] Courts of Judicature Act 1964, s 25(2), sch, para 1.
[177] *R Rama Chandran v The Industrial Court of Malaysia & Anor* [1997] 1 MLJ 145 (FC) 187; *Ketua Pengarah Hasil Dalam Negeri v Alcatel-Lucent Malaysia Sdn Bhd & Anor* [2017] 1 MLJ 563 (FC) [71].

review.[178] One example is the Malaysian Competition Appeal Tribunal, which has exclusive jurisdiction to review decisions of the Competition Commission.[179]

Meanwhile, under the Courts of Judicature Act 1964, a party may appeal in civil cases to the High Court against a decision of a subordinate court where, broadly, the value of the dispute exceeds 10,000 ringgit, or the appeal is on a question of law.[180] In turn, a party may appeal to the Court of Appeal against a decision of the High Court, whether the High Court has exercised its original or appellate jurisdiction.[181] Last, an appeal may lie to the Federal Court, Malaysia's apex court, only against decisions of the Court of Appeal in respect of decisions by the High Court in the exercise of the High Court's original jurisdiction which involve a question of general principle decided for the first time, or a question of importance upon which further argument and a decision of the Federal Court would be to public advantage.[182] In general, an appellate court will not interfere with factual findings of a trial judge except where those findings are 'plainly wrong', such as where there has been insufficient judicial appreciation of evidence.[183] Other grounds warranting appellate interference include where a court at first instance takes into account irrelevant considerations, fails to take into account relevant considerations, fundamentally misdirects itself or asks itself the wrong question, or decides a case based on an incorrect premise of fact or law.[184]

ii. Erroneous Application of Choice of Law Rules

There appears to be no prominent reported Malaysian case law which specifically discusses whether erroneous application of choice of law rules is amenable to judicial review or appellate interference. However, the cases discussed earlier in this chapter on choice of law rules include appeals allowed against decisions at first instance, and decisions of the Court of Appeal allowing appeals which have been upheld by the Federal Court.[185] It will also be evident from the sections above that the Malaysian courts' approach to choice of law rules is treated as a question of law, rather than one of fact. It is therefore respectfully submitted that erroneous application of choice of law rules by a court at first instance as a misdirection in law is amenable, at the very least, to one round of appellate interference. However, existing case law would appear not to offer any indications of whether such an error can give rise to judicial review, whether through the route of illegality, irrationality, or otherwise.

[178] *Rama Chandran* (n 177) 191.

[179] Competition Act 2010, ss 35, 39, 40, 44. See, eg, *MyEG Services Bhd & Anor v Competition Commission & Anor* [2020] 3 CLJ 363 (HC). Following the Industrial Relations (Amendment) Act 2020, s 24 which inserted the new Industrial Relations Act 1967, s 33C, challenges to awards of the Industrial Court are now by way of appeal to the High Court, and no longer through applying for judicial review.

[180] Courts of Judicature Act 1964, ss 27, 28.

[181] ibid, s 67(1).

[182] ibid, s 96(a).

[183] *Ng Hoo Kui & Anor v Wendy Tan Lee Peng (administratrix for the estate of Tan Ewe Kwang, deceased) & Ors* [2020] 12 MLJ 67 (FC) [62].

[184] *Nor Azlina Abdul Aziz v Expert Project Management Sdn Bhd* [2017] 5 CLJ 58 (CA) [19]–[20].

[185] See, eg, *A-G of Hong Kong v Zauyah Wan Chik* (n 23) 638A–C; *Scandinavian Bunkering (Singapore) Pte Ltd v MISC Bhd* (n 23) [38].

iii. Erroneous Application of Foreign Law

In contrast, as discussed earlier, the Malaysian courts treat foreign law as a question of fact.[186] Appellate interference is therefore warranted only where there has been insufficient judicial appreciation of evidence given on foreign law, such as where the court of first instance has ignored and disregarded expert evidence,[187] provided that the threshold of 'plainly wrong' is met.[188] Meanwhile, it is again not apparent from existing case law whether erroneous application of foreign law is amenable to judicial review. Hypothetically, one might perhaps argue that it is, on the premise that the ground of irrationality for judicial review mirrors that of insufficient judicial appreciation of evidence in appeals, but this proposition seemingly has yet to be tested before the courts.

IV. Foreign Law in Other Instances

A. Administrative and Non-judicial Authorities

The proceedings of administrative bodies – such as consumer tribunals, labour tribunals, and in-house disciplinary inquiries – are not 'judicial proceedings' within the meaning of the Evidence Act 1950, section 2, such that they are not subject to the Evidence Act 1950.[189] Despite this, the Industrial Court, for example, will still take cognisance of the Act's underlying principles.[190] Nevertheless, it would appear that the Industrial Court considers itself to lack the 'extraterritorial jurisdiction' necessary to hear claims governed by foreign law,[191] such that the question of how foreign law is to be applied and ascertained before it is unlikely to come up for consideration.

B. Alternative Dispute Resolution

i. Arbitration

The Evidence Act 1950, section 45, which characterises foreign law as a question of fact in court proceedings, does not apply to arbitral proceedings.[192] Apart from the provisions of

[186] *Mak Sik Kwong* (n 106) 180.

[187] *Asean Securities Paper Mills* (n 153) 314G although note that here, the Federal Court's comments about insufficient judicial appreciation of the evidence were directed at the Court of Appeal, not the High Court with which the Federal Court agreed; see also *Dr Shanmuganathan* (n 149) 82H-83B, albeit that the expert evidence there was not on foreign law.

[188] But note *MacMillan Inc v Bishopsgate Investment Trust plc (No 4)* [1999] CLC 417 (EWCA), [1998] Lexis Citation 1465, which reported Malaysian decisions have yet to discuss.

[189] *Rosli Yahya v Affin Bank Berhad* [2007] 3 ILR 474 (IC) [20]–[21]; *Zulkifli bin Ab Razak v CIMB Bank Bhd & Anor* [2020] MLJU 2667 (HC) [37]; H Omar, SB Marimuthu, and M Mahali, *Law of Evidence in Malaysia*, 2nd edn (London, Sweet & Maxwell, 2018) para 1.030.

[190] *Rosli Yahya* (n 189) [21].

[191] *Niall Atholl Murray v Baker Hughes (Malaysia) Sdn Bhd & Anor* [2018] 3 ILR 126 (IC) [68]; *Lee Suh Mun v K Strategic Management Sdn Bhd* [2020] 4 ILR 387 (IC) [11]. However, it is respectfully submitted that these awards did not take into account the distinction between jurisdiction and applicable law.

[192] Evidence Act 1950, ss 2, 3.

the Arbitration Act 2005, section 30 discussed above, the Arbitration Act 2005 does not prescribe any particular methods by which foreign law should be ascertained in arbitration. As such, especially in international arbitrations, it is arguably open to arbitral tribunals subject to the Arbitration Act 2005 to ascertain foreign law as 'law' through the means which they deem suitable, whether through tribunal-appointed foreign law experts,[193] party-appointed foreign law experts, submissions by counsel or the tribunals' own knowledge and expertise.[194]

ii. Adjudication under Construction Industry Payment and Adjudication Act 2012

The Construction Industry Payment and Adjudication Act 2012 applies to contracts for construction work 'wholly or partly within the territory of Malaysia',[195] even if only a 'minute part' of such work is within Malaysia and a 'substantial part' is performed outside Malaysia.[196] It therefore seems conceivable that the governing law of such contracts could be foreign, which would arguably suggest that an adjudicator under the Act has jurisdiction over such contracts – although there are no reported cases to this effect.[197] Neither is there clarification in the Act or case law of how an adjudicator under the Act should address foreign law, and the Construction Industry Payment and Adjudication Act 2012, section 12(9) provides that the Evidence Act 1950 is inapplicable to statutory adjudication proceedings. As with arbitrators, therefore, it is presumably open to adjudicators under the Act to ascertain foreign law through the means which they deem suitable, such as through experts[198] or by drawing on their own knowledge and expertise.[199]

iii. Mediation

The Mediation Act 2012 (which applies only to certain mediations[200]) is silent on the question of foreign law. However, as mediators do not conduct 'judicial proceedings' within the meaning of the Evidence Act 1950, section 45 presumably does not apply to mediations.[201] As a mediator does not make any rulings or decisions,[202] binding determinations on questions of foreign law are highly unlikely to arise in mediations.

[193] Arbitration Act 2005, s 28; Hamid Sultan bin Abu Backer, *International Arbitration with Commentary to Malaysian Arbitration Act 2005* (Kuala Lumpur, Amirudeen bin Hamid Sultan ed, Janab, 2016) 308.

[194] Arbitration Act 2005, s 21(3)(b); N Blackaby et al, *Redfern and Hunter on International Arbitration*, 6th edn (Oxford, OUP, 2015) paras 6.143–6.145.

[195] Construction Industry Payment and Adjudication Act 2012, s 2.

[196] *TH Heavy Engineering Bhd v Innovative Synergy Solutions Sdn Bhd* [2018] MLJU 31 (HC) [94].

[197] *Cf* the English Housing Grants, Construction and Regeneration Act 1996, s 104(7) which states that Pt II of that Act applies whether or not the law of England or Wales or Scotland is otherwise the applicable law in relation to a contract; see also *Motacus Constructions Ltd v Paolo Castelli SPA* [2021] EWHC 356 (TCC), 196 ConLR 159 [3].

[198] Construction Industry Payment and Adjudication Act 2012, s 25(e).

[199] ibid, s 25(d).

[200] Mediation Act 2012, s 2.

[201] Evidence Act 1950, s 2.

[202] G Dhillon and SL Lee, 'Alternative Dispute Resolution Methods and Processes in Malaysia – A Review' (2015) 2 *Malayan Law Journal* viii, xii–xiii.

V. Access to Malaysian Law

A. Legislation

Under the National Languages Act 1963/67, section 6, all Acts of Parliament and subsidiary legislation issued by the Federal Government (amongst other texts) must be in both the national language of Malaysia (Bahasa Malaysia, the Malay language) and the English language, with the former generally being authoritative.[203] The most authoritative online source of Malaysian legislation is LawNet,[204] an online library operated by Percetakan Nasional Malaysia Berhad, the Malaysian national printing company.[205] Legislation can also be accessed for free through the Attorney General's Chambers' website,[206] or the databases of LexisNexis, CLJ or Westlaw Asia through paid subscriptions.

B. Case Law

The National Languages Act 1963/67, section 8 requires all proceedings before the courts of Peninsular Malaysia,[207] other than the giving of evidence by a witness, to be in the national language of Malaysia. This is subject to the courts' discretion to order, of its own motion or on the application of any party, that proceedings be partly in the national language and partly in English.[208] In practice, many reported judgments are written in English,[209] and the headnotes of reported judgments accessible on LexisNexis, CLJ and Westlaw Asia are often provided in both languages. The grounds of judgment of decided cases, where issued, can also be accessed for free through the website of the Office of the Chief Registrar of the Federal Court of Malaysia.[210]

[203] Except where otherwise prescribed, such as the authoritative English text of the Companies Act 2016: PU(B) 408/2016.

[204] Percetakan Nasional Malaysia Berhad, 'About Us' (*LawNet*) www.lawnet.com.my/home/aboutus (accessed 11 May 2023).

[205] Percetakan Nasional Malaysia Berhad, 'Welcome to Malaysia's National Printer' (*Percetakan Nasional Malaysia Berhad*) www.printnasional.com.my/ (accessed 11 May 2023).

[206] Attorney General's Chambers of Malaysia, 'Federal Legislation Portal': lom.agc.gov.my/ (accessed 11 May 2023).

[207] The Federal Court, the Court of Appeal, the High Court and any Subordinate Court.

[208] Note also that the Rules of Court 2012, Ord 92, r 1(1) requires broadly that all cause papers be filed in the national language, although they may be accompanied by an English translation, in Peninsular Malaysia. By the Rules of Court 2012, Ord 92, r 1(2), the position in Sabah and Sarawak is the opposite, in that filing in English is mandatory and the filing of translations in the national language is optional.

[209] S Lee, 'The National Language in the Courts' (*Of Counsel*, 20 April 2008) leeshih.com/2008/04/20/the-national-language-in-the-courts/ (accessed 11 May 2023); Nallini Pathmanathan JCA, 'Managing and Enhancing Quality in Judicial Performance and the Writing of Judgments' (2015) paras 38–41: www.kehakiman.gov.my/sites/default/files/YA-Datuk-Nallini-1.pdf (accessed 11 October 2022); R Powell and A Hashim, 'Language Disadvantage in Malaysian Litigation and Arbitration' (2011) 30 *World Englishes* 92.

[210] Pejabat Ketua Pendaftar Mahkamah Persekutuan Malaysia, 'EJudgment Management System': cms2.kehakiman.gov.my/CommonWeb/ejudgment/SearchPage.aspx?JurisdictionType=ALL (accessed 11 May 2023).

VI. Access to Foreign Law: Future Developments in Asia

A. International or Regional Instruments on Foreign Law

Malaysia is not currently party to any international or regional instruments on treatment of foreign law or information on foreign law. For instance, although Malaysia has been a member of the Hague Conference on Private International Law since 2002, Malaysia remains neither a contracting party nor a signatory of any of its instruments.[211]

Acceding to such instruments and perhaps even agreeing a model choice of law regime with other countries[212] would arguably improve the Malaysian courts' ability to achieve decisional harmony with their foreign counterparts, thus minimising the risk of regulatory conflict, discouraging forum shopping, improving certainty for litigants, and ultimately improving the efficiency of dispute resolution where disputes involve elements of foreign law.[213]

At the same time, the potential risks of harmonisation must be acknowledged. For countries to reach consensus on the content of such instruments, compromise is likely to be required, and the Malaysian courts may ultimately find themselves 'worse off' than if they or the Malaysian legislature simply implement unilateral measures or unilaterally develop the Malaysian common law.[214] Neither is harmonisation a complete answer, for its success would depend on systematic application by both the Malaysian courts and foreign courts. Realising this ideal across borders is not always straightforward where national courts of different countries have distinct legal traditions.[215] Even within the Association of Southeast Asian Nations (ASEAN), there is considerable diversity amongst the legal systems of the bloc's component countries.[216]

A possible middle ground may be for Malaysia to agree on the harmonisation of foreign law with key trading partners or neighbouring countries,[217] such as Singapore. For example, the Malaysian judiciary might consider entering into memoranda of understanding with foreign judiciaries on references of questions of law, as has been done between the Supreme Courts of Singapore and a number of foreign courts.[218] In this eventuality, however, the courts would need to guard against possible 'fragmentation' of the rules applicable within Malaysia, depending on which foreign country's law is involved.[219]

[211] 'Malaysia' (*Hague Conference on Private International Law*) www.hcch.net/en/states/hcch-members/details1/?sid=52 (accessed 11 May 2023); Hickling and Wu (n 9) 27.

[212] YN Lim, 'Towards a Uniform Conflict of Laws Regime in ASEAN Governing International Commercial Transactions: Uniformization of Choice of Law Rules in Contract and Tort' (Montreal, McGill University, 2000).

[213] A Mills, 'Private International Law and EU External Relations: Think Local Act Global, or Think Global Act Local?' (2016) 65 *ICLQ* 541, 549–50; DP Stewart, 'New Directions in Private International Law' [2009] *Agenda Internacional* 255, 256.

[214] Mills (n 213) 554.

[215] A Fiorini, 'Rome III – Choice of Law in Divorce: Is the Europeanization of Family Law Going Too Far?' (2008) 22 *International Journal of Law, Policy and the Family* 178.

[216] Lim (n 212) 2–3.

[217] Mills (n 213) 558–59.

[218] Singapore Courts, 'References of Questions of Law between Singapore and Foreign Courts': www.judiciary.gov.sg/who-we-are/references-questions-of-law-singapore-foreign-courts (accessed 11 May 2023); GS Teo and HD Wong, 'Referring Questions of Foreign Law to the Court of the Governing Law: No Longer "Lost in Translation"' (2011) 23 *Singapore Academy of Law Journal* 227.

[219] Mills (n 213) 560.

B. Access to Foreign Law

As the discussion earlier in this chapter shows, formal access to foreign law before the Malaysian courts remains, in practice, highly dependent on the evidence of party-appointed foreign law experts, even to the extent of accepting foreign law evidence from a witness with an obvious interest in the outcome of the proceedings.[220] Even accounting for the overriding duty of an expert to assist the courts,[221] the reality is that expert testimony will inevitably favour the party who has engaged the expert.[222] Finding a credible and capable foreign law expert can also be challenging,[223] quite apart from the typically considerable costs of engaging such experts. While the alternative of a court-appointed expert may alleviate some of these issues, parties may hesitate to agree to such an expert because of the adversarial tradition of the Malaysian courts; even where they do, they can still call their own experts to challenge the opinions of the court-appointed expert.[224]

To improve access, measures suggested and, in certain cases, implemented in other jurisdictions should be considered in the Malaysian context. These might include authorising or encouraging judges to conduct their own research when confronted with questions of foreign law,[225] compilation (by database providers such as LexisNexis) of Malaysian cases which have addressed questions of foreign law as points of reference,[226] and, through that compilation, providing a means of identifying and assessing potential foreign law experts based on their past work product.[227] Such initiatives can take advantage, in particular, of advances in technology which can be used to create 'open knowledge' or 'open data' sources of Malaysian law, for users outside Malaysia, and foreign law, for users within it.[228]

VII. Conclusion

While Malaysian law on the choice of laws is anything but nascent, there is certainly room for continued development and sophistication. For instance, it would seem that the Malaysian courts and more recent Malaysian literature have yet to engage in substantial discussion of the finer questions of the choice of laws, such as whether choice of laws rules are mandatory or facultative. Additionally, most reported judgments on this topic have addressed conflicts between foreign law and secular Malaysian (federal) laws; there are fewer indications of how the Syariah courts, for example, would approach conflicts between foreign law and personal or religious (state) laws. Other potential areas for legislative development or

[220] *Portcullis Trustnet* (n 118) [137]–[143]; *Spind Malaysia* (n 118) [136].

[221] Rules of Court 2012, Ord 40A, r 2.

[222] Tun Tengku Maimun Tuan Mat and Gopal Sri Ram (eds), *Malaysian Civil Procedure 2021* (London, Sweet & Maxwell, 2021) para 40/0/2.

[223] L Turner, 'Buried Treasure: Excavating Foreign Law from Civil Pleadings Filed in US Federal Courts' (2019) 47 *International Journal of Legal Information* 22, 40–41.

[224] Rules of Court 2012, Ord 40, r 6; Teo and Wong (n 218) para 11.

[225] Turner (n 223) 42.

[226] ibid 45–46.

[227] ibid 50.

[228] R Ward, 'Building Free Access to Law in Africa: Some Examples of Successful Projects' (2014) 14 *Legal Information Management* 290, 291.

judicial clarification in relation to the choice of laws have been discussed above, including admiralty law and international arbitration.

In contrast, Malaysian law on the treatment of foreign law would appear to be slightly more developed, perhaps due in part to the more structured framework and foundation of the Evidence Act 1950 around which case law has evolved. Nevertheless, the heavy reliance in practice on party-appointed experts on foreign law presents a possible area for improvement, innovation or at least reflection. Similar remarks might be made on the consequences of Malaysian law's current strict treatment of foreign law as a question of 'fact', as opposed to 'law', in light of the limited extent of appellate intervention presently permitted.

As mentioned, one way for Malaysia to bring itself further in line with international practice and developments would be to accede to international or regional instruments of harmonisation or unification, like those of the Hague Conference on Private International Law, or to implement international model laws, like the UNCITRAL Model Law on Cross-Border Insolvency. The difficulty in reality of achieving such objectives, however, is acknowledged. Short of attempting steps of such magnitude, progress might still be achieved through more incremental or gradual measures, such as memoranda of understanding between the Malaysian judiciary and foreign judiciaries, or even simply affording greater prominence to the topics of the choice of laws and foreign law in the discourse of legal practitioners and academics. It is hoped that the contributions of this chapter will assist in the latter respect.

9

Vietnam

NGUYEN THI HONG TRINH AND BUI THI QUYNH TRANG

I. Introduction: Status of Choice of Laws Rules

In general, the application of the choice of law rules is a binding obligation of the national courts in Vietnam when dealing with civil cases which include foreign elements.[1] As a matter of principle, when dealing with a civil case which has foreign elements, the relevant authorities have to apply the appropriate choice of law rules given in Vietnamese national laws or in the international treaties to which Vietnam is a party.[2]

With regards to national legislation, the choice of law rules are largely covered by the Civil Code (CC)[3] and are also scattered in various legislative documents such as the Law on Marriage and Family, Law on Adoption, Law on Investment, and Commercial Law.[4] This means that the choice of law rules have been codified in the national legislative system of Vietnam. Therefore, they have legal values and are recognised as a source of national law.

Academics also support the view requiring the mandatory application of choice of law rules in Vietnam. However, choice of law rules deserve a better representation in the practices of the courts and the non-judicial state authorities in the country. Most of the judgments and decisions in cases with foreign elements do not cite or apply choice of law rules, nor do the judgments ever try to explain why the cases do not call for the application of choice of law rules. In some random judgments, jurisdictional rules are cited and applied, but they are hardly ever interpreted for their way of application. Therefore, in general, private international law rules, and especially choice of law rules, are largely undermined by either being ignored, applied without explanation or not being mentioned at all in judicial and administrative practices in Vietnam, although they are embodied in an increasing number of articles in many national legal documents.

[1] Foreign elements are defined in Art 464(2) of the Civil Procedure Code 2015 (CPC) to mean the presence in a case of one or more of the following: (a) a foreign party; (b) a material connection with a foreign country (for example, a contract concluded abroad); or (c) a foreign subject matter (for example, property located abroad).

[2] Institute of Legal Science (Ministry of Justice), Special Issue of Legal Information and Sciences 'Some issues in the application of foreign law in civil trials at Vietnamese Courts', 2020.

[3] Part V of the Civil Code (CC) 2015 provides for general principles in determining the applicable law to civil relations involving foreign elements (Art 664) and principles in determining the applicable law for various specified civil relations (Arts 672–86).

[4] Currently, Vietnam does not have a private international law code, thus the provisions of the Vietnamese private international law, including the choice of law rules, are embodied in the Civil Code and in numerous documents.

Vietnamese choice of law rules include not only unilateral but bilateral rules. Thus, many of them do not solely mandate Vietnamese laws to apply but also point to the laws of other countries. Therefore, the choice of law rules under the regime of Vietnamese private international law shall lead to the application of foreign laws based on the connecting factors. There are various connecting factors that have been learned from the international experiences and laws of other countries, such as the nationality of individuals and organisations, the country having the closest connection with the contract, and the place where the damage occurred.

Among these, nationality is the most popular connecting factor for determining the applicable law in civil cases with foreign elements.[5] The choice of law rules based on nationality have attempted to apply the foreign law where the subjects bear foreign nationalities.

In another example, in contractual or tort matters involving foreign elements, the parties are free to choose the applicable law, including foreign laws. In the case where there is no agreement on the applicable laws, the choice of law rules lead to the law of the state most closely connected to the contract, being Vietnamese laws or foreign laws, depending on the facts of the case. Similarly, in tort cases, the law applicable in the absence of a choice of the parties is the law of the place of damage. Where the damages occur abroad, it shall lead to the application of foreign laws.

II. Foreign Law before Judicial Authorities

A. Nature of Foreign Law

Before 2015, Vietnamese law did not have any specific regulations on the nature of foreign law, and there was no clear opinion on whether foreign law was regarded as a matter of 'law' or 'fact' (among Vietnamese scholars).[6] At that time, however, this issue was also mentioned in several legal documents. But they did not directly regulate it. Varied positions on the nature of foreign law can be interpreted from these statutory provisions. Circular No 11-TAND of the Supreme People's Court in 1974[7] considered foreign law as 'law',[8] while

[5] Nationality plays the role of a connecting factor in choice of law rules regarding the matters below: legal capacity to hold rights and obligations; civil capacity to act; civil procedure capacity to hold rights and obligations and procedural capacity to act; determination of persons as having no, having lost, or having been restricted in civil act capacity; determination of persons as missing or dead; heir-at-law inheritances involving foreign elements; testamentary inheritance; marriage; and adoption.

[6] DM Tuan, 'Xác định nội dung pháp luật nước ngoài để giải quyết tranh chấp dân sự quốc tế bởi tòa án' [Ascertaining the content of foreign law for resolving international civil disputes by courts] (2014) 40 *Tạp chí Kinh tế Đối ngoại [Journal of International Economics and Management]*, available online: tinyurl.com/2p9ec3ds.

[7] This Circular has a legally binding effect. It was promulgated on 12 July 1974 guiding some matters as to principles and procedures in solving divorce disputes with foreign elements (no longer in force).

[8] Whenever there is a demand for reference to foreign law, local courts are bound to report to, and get advice from, the Supreme Court on the merits of each case. The Supreme Court will ascertain the content of the foreign law through the relevant central authorities in order to guide the local courts in its efficient application. In other words, this Circular regards the ascertainment of foreign law as being the work of the courts.

Article 5 of Decree No 138/NĐ-CP dated 15 November 2006[9] gives another particular illustration, where this decree seemed to treat foreign law as 'fact'.[10]

Vietnamese legal sciences during this period tended to favour the view that foreign law should be considered as 'law' instead of 'fact'. Accordingly, judicial agencies and courts are responsible for ascertaining the content of the foreign law that needs to be applied. That said, the parties are allowed to provide the courts with information on the contents of that foreign law. However, their role is limited to assisting the courts because the duty to ascertain the contents of foreign law lies with the courts.[11]

Since the new CPC was promulgated in 2015 and came into effect on 1 July 2016, Vietnam has taken a specific approach to the nature of foreign law. According to Article 481 of the CPC 2015, where the parties are allowed to choose the applicable law,[12] they need to plead the chosen foreign law. The court's task is to consider the application of the pleaded foreign law. On the other hand, where the conflict rules refer to foreign law (meaning in matters such as family relations where the parties are not allowed to choose the applicable law or where they are allowed but have not done so), the courts must ascertain it. Therefore, Vietnamese legislation treats foreign laws as having a hybrid nature. This is a kind of 'mixed approach' requiring cooperation between the courts and the parties to ascertain the contents of foreign law efficiently.[13]

B. Ascertainment of Foreign Law

Before 2015, Vietnamese law did not contain any general statutory provisions on the question of whether the courts apply foreign law *ex officio* or only upon the parties' application. The most relevant document was Circular No 11-TAND of the Supreme People's Court in 1974, which provided for the *ex officio* application of foreign law and that the duty of ascertaining the foreign law lies with the courts. It stated that:

> whenever there is demand for reference to foreign law, local courts are bound to report to and get advice from the Supreme Court on the merits of each case. The Supreme Court will ascertain the content of the foreign law through the relevant central authorities in order to guide local courts in its efficient application.

[9] Decree No 138/NĐ-CP dated 15 November 2006 detailing the implementation of the Civil Code's provisions on civil relations involving foreign elements (currently in force).

[10] Art 5 [Involved parties' burden of proof for law application requests] of Decree No 138/NĐ-CP dated 15 November 2006: 'In case of application of laws to stateless persons or foreigners with two or more foreign nationalities under Article 760 of the Civil Code or application of laws of foreign countries with different legal systems under Clause 3, Article 4 of this Decree, the involved parties are obliged to prove to Vietnamese competent agencies their closest relations regarding citizens' rights and duties to the legal system requested for application. When the involved parties fail to prove their closest relations regarding citizens' rights and duties to the legal system requested for application, Vietnamese laws shall be applied.'

[11] Hanoi Law University, *Giáo trình Tư pháp quốc tế [Textbook on Private International Law]* (Hanoi, Nhà xuất bản Công an Nhân dân [People Police Publishing House], 2013), 61–62; DV Dai and M H Quy, *Tư pháp quốc tế Việt Nam* [*Vietnamese Private International Law*] (Hanoi, Nhà xuất bản chính trị quốc gia [National Political Publishing House], 2010) 228.

[12] According to the CC 2015, in contractual or tort matters involving foreign elements, the parties are allowed to choose applicable law (may be foreign laws).

[13] CE Mota, 'Application of Foreign Law – Harmonisation of Private International Law in Europe and Application of Foreign Law: "The Madrid Principles" of 2010' (2011) 13 *Yearbook of Private International Law* 273, 294.

Vietnamese scholars have advocated the *ex officio* ascertainment of the contents of foreign law with assistance from the parties, meaning that the courts are obliged to ascertain the foreign law under the principle of *iura novit curia* and that the parties are allowed to provide the courts with evidence of the foreign law to protect their rights.[14]

Since the CPC 2015 came into force, Vietnamese law has had a specific regulation on the ascertainment of the contents of foreign law when dealing with international civil disputes. Article 481 reads as follows:

> Article 481. Determination and provision of foreign laws for the Court to apply in the settlement of civil cases involving foreign elements
>
> If the Vietnamese courts apply a foreign law to settle a civil case involving a foreign element according to the provisions of Vietnamese law and/or of an international treaty to which the Socialist Republic of Vietnam is a signatory, the responsibility for determining and providing the foreign laws shall be performed as follows:
>
> 1. If the involved party of a civil case is allowed to choose a foreign law to be applied, he/she shall provide the foreign law he/she has chosen for the Court being in charge of such a case. The involved party shall be responsible for the accuracy and legitimacy of the foreign law he/she provides for the Court.
>   If the involved parties fail to agree with each other about the foreign law to be chosen, or in necessary cases, the Court shall request the Ministry of Justice, Ministry of Foreign Affairs, consular offices of the Socialist Republic of Vietnam in foreign countries or request the diplomatic missions of foreign countries in Vietnam (via the Ministry of Foreign Affairs) to provide the foreign laws;
> 2. If Vietnamese law and/or international treaties to which the Socialist Republic of Vietnam is a signatory provide that foreign laws shall be applied, the involved parties may provide the foreign laws for the Court or the Court shall request the Ministry of Justice, the Ministry of Foreign Affairs or consular offices of the Socialist Republic of Vietnam in foreign countries to provide it with the foreign laws;
> 3. The Court may request agencies, organizations and individuals who are professionals in foreign laws to provide it with information about the foreign laws;
> 4. Past the 6-month time limit from the date of request for the provision of foreign laws as provided for in this Article, if there is no response, the Court shall apply Vietnamese law to settle the civil case.

The Vietnamese approach to foreign law has changed as a result of the CPC 2015's introduction. The parties are now responsible for pleading and proving foreign law and its contents to the courts' satisfaction, where they are allowed to choose the applicable law and do it. Notably, they shall also be responsible for the accuracy and legitimacy of the contents of the foreign law that they provide.

Accordingly, if the parties choose a foreign law to govern their legal relationship,[15] Vietnamese law requires them to plead and prove the contents of the chosen foreign law to

[14] NN Dien, 'Chế định Ly hôn trong Tư pháp quốc tế' [Divorce in Vietnamese Private International Law] in B Audit (ed) *Material of Conference on Private International Law* (Hanoi, Vietnamese – French Publishing House, 2005) 70; Dai and Quy (n 11) 228.

[15] Currently, Vietnamese private international law rules allow the parties to agree to choose the applicable laws, possibly foreign law, in contract and tort matters involving foreign elements.

the court. It is mandatory for the parties to do so. The reason behind this new regulation is that the application of foreign law is ultimately to ensure the interests of the litigants, and they cannot stand aside from this work for their sake.[16] Considering that the parties themselves can choose a foreign law, they should research and understand more or less the contents of the foreign law. Thus, it is not too difficult for the parties to provide their content.[17]

However, the parties may but are not obliged to provide the foreign law where Vietnamese law or rules in international treaties to which Vietnam is a party requires the application of foreign law. Instead, the courts are responsible for ascertaining the contents of foreign law, and they shall request the Ministry of Justice, Ministry of Foreign Affairs or Vietnamese consular offices in foreign countries to provide it with information on the foreign law.[18]

The legislator explained that this regulation was based on Article 22(2) of Decree 138/2006/ND-CP dated 15 November 2006 *Guiding the Civil Code 2005 on civil relations involving foreign elements*,[19] which provides that the Ministry of Foreign Affairs and Ministry of Justice are responsible for assisting the courts and state agencies in determining the applicable laws and for providing the applicable foreign legal documents.[20]

Scholars also support this approach due to its consistency with the Vietnamese courts' function of adjudicating and settling cases. The courts have various instruments and are in a better position to perform this work.[21] This also shows consistency with the state's obligation to apply foreign law. When a state promulgates a conflict rule leading to the application of foreign law, it is responsible for the state to find the content of foreign law through specialised agencies, including the courts and the judges.

Alongside the above provisions on the responsibilities of ascertaining the contents of foreign law, the legislators were also concerned about how the courts would acquire the contents of foreign law within a reasonable time. Therefore, the regulation in Article 481(3) of the CPC 2015 enables the courts to request agencies, organisations and individuals who are professionals in foreign law to provide them with information on foreign law to decide the cases.[22]

i. Means of Ascertainment

With the regulations in Article 481 of the CPC 2015, Vietnamese law has provided basic provisions on how to ascertain the contents of foreign law. However, it is undeniable that they are still incomplete compared to other countries in the world.

[16] Institute of Legal Science (n 2) 19.

[17] ibid.

[18] Art 481(2) of the CPC 2015.

[19] This Decree is still in force. Although the CC 2005 has been replaced by the CC 2015, there has been no new Decree to replace this Decree.

[20] 'When requested by courts or state agencies competent to settle affairs or disputes arising from civil relations involving foreign elements, the Ministry of Foreign Affairs and the Ministry of Justice shall assist the requesting agencies in determining applicable laws and provide applicable foreign legal documents.'

[21] Dai and Quy (n 11) 228.

[22] LM Hung, 'Vấn đề áp dụng pháp luật nước ngoài trong giải quyết các vụ việc dân sự tại Tòa án Việt Nam [The application of foreign law in civil cases in Vietnamese courts]' [2021] *Tạp chí Tòa án điện tử [Online People's Court Journal]*, available online: tinyurl.com/4e7xkv9n (accessed 20 February 2022).

First, with regard to the courts taking the main responsibility for ascertaining the contents of foreign law, there are three channels through which they can request assistance:

1. Domestic authorities. The courts can request the assistance of the Ministry of Foreign Affairs, Ministry of Justice or the Overseas Representative Missions of the Socialist Republic of Vietnam in providing the contents of foreign law. This method has been set out in all three relevant legal documents. Circular No 11-TAND prescribed the method of ascertaining foreign laws with the assistance of authorised agencies of Vietnam as follows: 'Whenever there is demand for reference to foreign law, local courts are bound to report to and get advice from the Supreme Court on the merits of each case. The Supreme Court will ascertain the content of foreign law through relevant central authorities in order to guide local courts in its efficient application.' Decree No 138/2006/NĐ-CP also provides: 'When requested by courts or state agencies competent to settle affairs or disputes arising from civil relations involving foreign elements, the Ministry of Foreign Affairs and the Ministry of Justice shall assist the requesting agencies in determining applicable laws and provide applicable foreign legal documents.' Article 481(2) of the CPC 2015 also provides that the: 'Court shall request the Ministry of Justice, the Ministry of Foreign Affairs or consular offices of the Socialist Republic of Vietnam in foreign countries to provide it with foreign laws'.
2. Experts or expert institutes. The CPC 2015 has just recognised the method of ascertaining foreign laws with assistance from experts on foreign law. Article 481(3) of the CPC 2015 stipulates: 'The court may request agencies, organizations and individuals who are professionals in foreign laws to provide it with information about the foreign laws.'
3. Foreign authorities. This is a method of determining foreign laws through diplomatic channels. This method is not currently mentioned in the CPC but is set out in mutual legal assistance agreements. Accordingly, the Vietnamese courts can request assistance from relevant authorities of the partner country only if such an agreement apply.[23]

Second, in cases where the parties are responsible for providing information on the contents of foreign law, the CPC does not impose any specific regulations on the methods of ascertaining it. When formulating Article 481(1) of the CPC 2015, which grants parties an opportunity to plead foreign law, it was suggested that it was necessary to specify that the involved parties can request individuals, agencies and organisations with expertise in foreign law, such as experts, Vietnamese or overseas law firms, and law offices to provide information on the contents of foreign law. However, the majority opinion was that such a regulation was unnecessary. Because this is the obligation of the parties involved, they have the full right to decide on the measures to search and identify the contents of the foreign law. Therefore, the parties have a variety of means at hand to search and identify the contents of the foreign law. For instance, they can search and identify the legal contents through individuals, agencies or organisations, regardless of whether they are Vietnamese citizens,

[23] Vietnam has signed mutual legal assistance agreements with many countries. As of 17 March 2021, there are 60 such agreements. However, only some have regulations on the exchange and providing information of foreign laws, such as mutual legal assistance agreements with Poland, Russia and Laos. Take one example, Art 13 of the Mutual Legal Assistance Agreement between Vietnam and Russia stipulates: 'The Ministry of Justice and the Federal Procuracy of the Soviet Socialist Republic, the Ministry of Justice and the Supreme People's Procuracy of the Socialist Republic of Vietnam, at the request of each party, will notify each other of legal documents currently in force or formerly in force in their respective countries and of the application of such documents by judicial authorities.' (Authors' translation as we could not find the English version of this agreement).

foreigners, or Vietnamese or foreign agencies and organisations, provided that the contents of such laws are accurate and legitimate.[24]

When parties bear the obligation of pleading foreign laws, as prescribed in Article 481(1) of the CPC 2015, there are no regulations on the qualifications of the experts who provide information on foreign law. That means that foreign law firms, experts or agencies can do this. This was implied by the fact that Article 481(1) of the CPC 2015 was guided by the Draft Resolution 2019[25] with regard to the criteria of the documents containing information on foreign law which are submitted to the courts. According to Article 14.1 of the Draft Resolution 2019, the parties must submit to the courts a document containing information on foreign law along with a notarised Vietnamese translation[26] or a Vietnamese translation with the certified translator's signature.[27] If an authorised foreign agency submits a document containing information on foreign law, besides a notarised or certified Vietnamese translation, the parties need to have such a foreign document legalised in accordance with Vietnamese law.

Where the court needs to ascertain the contents of foreign law, Article 481 of the CPC 2015 allows the court to request the assistance of the Ministry of Foreign Affairs, Ministry of Justice or Overseas Representative Missions or agencies, or even private organisations and individuals who are professionals in foreign laws. In terms of qualifications, the current laws provide no regulations. In the course of formulating Article 481 of the CPC 2015, there was a suggestion that it should specify the criteria and qualifications of those individuals and organisations who can provide the courts with information on foreign law. However, the majority opinion preferred leaving the courts with discretion to decide how to collect information on relevant foreign law according to the circumstances of individual cases.[28] On the other hand, the Draft Resolution 2019 provides guidelines for interpreting Article 481(3) of the CPC 2015, stating that those experts qualified in foreign laws only include foreign law firms that are allowed to operate in Vietnam, domestic law firms, law offices, and lawyers and legal experts with a professional knowledge of foreign laws directly related to civil cases.[29]

ii. Binding Effect of the Provided Information?

Currently, there is no clear answer to this question. The statutes do not explicitly provide whether or not the information provided shall be binding upon judicial authorities. Neither have the courts provided guidance in any cases or documents.

Based on Article 481 of the CPC 2015, whether the foreign legal information provided shall be binding on the judicial authorities depends on who collected it. Where the parties

[24] Hung (n 22). Notably, the author, Le Manh Hung (Deputy Director, Department of International Cooperation, Supreme People's Court), was assigned to prepare the content of Art 481 in the project revising the Civil Procedure Code. The preparation and related documents of the draft code did not explain clearly the intention of the drafters. Le Manh Hung later explained and analysed Art 481 in two continuous articles published on the *Online People's Court Journal* in 2021.

[25] Draft Resolution 2019 *Guiding the Implementation of the Civil Procedure Code Regarding the Competence and Procedures for Settlement of Civil Cases Involving Foreign Elements*. This Draft Resolution was formulated in 2019, but it has not taken effect. A Resolution issued by the Judges' Council of the Supreme Court is binding on courts of all levels. This Draft Resolution consists of the provisions explaining several Articles of the CPC 2015 (such as Artis 469, 470, and 472) concerning jurisdiction and procedures for settling civil disputes involving foreign elements before the courts.

[26] Accoriding to Art 61 of the Vietnamese Notary Law 2014, this can be done at notarial practice organisations including notary bureaus belonging to Judicial Department of Provinces in Vietnam and notary offices.

[27] This is done at a District-level Judicial Office in accordance with Vietnamese laws on certification.

[28] Hung (n 22).

[29] Draft Resolution 2019, Art 14(3).

plead the application of a foreign law and provide information on that foreign law, the provided information is not binding upon the judicial authorities since it is considered a matter of fact. The courts shall consider and evaluate the information in the same way they deal with other evidence in a civil proceeding in accordance with the laws. The courts shall accept or refuse the information provided on foreign law and its application for the resolution on the merits of a case. It can be assumed that the courts can freely assess the reliability of the information provided and can accept or refuse its application as a whole or in part. There is, however, no regulation or cases on this. Therefore, the practical application of the courts remains to be seen.

Where the courts ascertain the contents of foreign law, they shall request competent agencies or qualified experts to provide the information on foreign law. There is no regulation on whether the courts can assess the reliability of the information provided, but it can be assumed that the courts should be entitled to do so. When the courts are convinced of the reliability of the information provided, the application of foreign laws is binding on them because foreign law in this case is considered as law.

Vietnamese law currently has no mechanism specifically designed to examine the reliability of the information on foreign law provided by foreign or domestic agencies or experts. However, there are some relevant provisions from which ideas on this matter can be drawn.

When a party pleads the application of a particular foreign law and provides the court with a document containing information on that foreign law, the Draft Resolution 2019 requires that such a document has to be translated into the Vietnamese language by a licensed organisation if it is made by private experts; if competent foreign agencies execute it, such document has to be translated into the Vietnamese language by a licensed organisation and legalised.[30] These regulations aim to ensure the quality of the translations and the authenticity of the documents submitted by competent foreign agencies. They do not intend to guarantee the reliability of the legal information provided. To investigate the reliability of the legal information provided by the parties, in case the involved parties disagree with each other about the foreign law, the court can request the Ministry of Justice, Ministry of Foreign Affairs, Vietnamese consular offices in foreign countries or the diplomatic missions of foreign countries in Vietnam (through the Ministry of Foreign Affairs) to provide information on the foreign laws.[31] Where the courts have requested the Ministry of Justice, Ministry of Foreign Affairs or the Vietnamese consular offices in foreign countries to provide information on foreign law under Article 481(2) of the CPC 2015, pursuant to Article 481(3), they may further request agencies, organisations and individuals who are professionals in foreign laws to provide them with information on foreign laws. In doing so, they may be able to examine the reliability of the information provided. In all situations, of course, the judges can conduct their own research to examine the reliability of the information on foreign law at hand.

iii. Costs

Where the involved parties are responsible for providing information on foreign law, the information is evidence that the parties must submit to the court. Therefore, each party will bear any expenses incurred in the evidence.

[30] Draft Resolution 2019, Art 14(1).
[31] CPC 2015, Art 481(1).

When the parties fail to agree with each other about the contents of foreign law and the court requests relevant ministries and other authorities to provide the foreign law in accordance with Article 481(1) of the CPC 2015, there is no clear regulation on who shall bear the costs. As the court costs stipulated in the CPC 2015 do not include this kind of cost, the parties might have to bear this cost jointly. Detailed regulation should come in the future.

Vietnamese laws currently do not stipulate who bears this cost, where the court is responsible for ascertaining the contents of foreign law. However, the regulations in the CPC 2015 concerning court costs may provide some guidance. When the courts request competent authorities (ie, Ministry of Justice, Ministry of Foreign Affairs or Vietnamese consular offices in foreign countries) to provide information on foreign law as stipulated in Article 481(2) of the CPC 2015, the state of Vietnam must bear the costs, and such costs should not be included in the court costs.[32] The detailed rules on this question should be formulated in the future.

On the other hand, when the court requests experts on foreign laws to provide information under Article 481(3) of the CPC 2015, the Draft Resolution 2019 stipulates that the involved parties must bear any payments for the expenses to the agencies, organisations or individuals with expertise in foreign laws.[33]

C. Interpretation and Application of Foreign Law

Although it is not totally clear, one can infer from the regulations in the CC, CPC and other relevant laws that the first condition for foreign laws to be applied before Vietnamese judicial authorities is that the conflict rules must refer to foreign law.

Even when a choice of law rule points to a foreign law, that foreign law will not be applied in these two situations where: (a) the consequences of their application are not consistent with the fundamental principles of the laws of Vietnam; or (b) the contents of the foreign law are not identifiable, despite the necessary measures prescribed by procedural law being taken.[34] The concept of 'the fundamental principles of the laws of Vietnam' is interchangeable with the notion of 'public policy' in private international law.[35] This notion is explained in a number of national laws. For example, in the case of civil law in general, the five basic principles are set out in Article 3 of the CC.[36] The fundamental principles in other legal fields are stipulated in more detail, and frequently they appear in a particular

[32] Court costs as provided for by the CPC 2015 include court fees, charges and other procedural expenses (Chapter IX). Other procedural expenses do not include the cost of ascertaining foreign laws done by the courts.

[33] Draft Resolution 2019, Art 14(4).

[34] CPC 2015, Art 670(1).

[35] TN Quang, *Pháp luật về Hợp đồng [Laws on Contracts]* (Nhà xuất bản Dân Trí [Dan Tri Publisher], 2020) 765.

[36] CPC 2015, Art 3 [Basic principles of civil law]: '(1) Every person shall be equal in civil relations, may not use any reason for unequal treatment to others, and enjoy the same protection policies of law regarding moral rights and economic rights. (2) Each person establishes, exercises/fulfills and terminates his/her civil rights and obligations on the basis of freely and voluntarily entering into commitments and/or agreements. Each commitment or agreement that does not violate regulations of law and is not contrary to social ethics shall be bound by contracting parties and must be respected by other entities. (3) Each person must establish, exercise/ fulfill, or terminate his/her civil rights and/or obligations in the principle of goodwill and honesty. (4) The establishment, exercise and termination of civil rights and/or obligations may not infringe national interests, public interests, lawful rights and interests of other persons. (5) Each person shall be liable for his/her failure to fulfill or the incorrect fulfillment of any such civil obligations.'

code or law in the 'General Provisions' section.[37] The Supreme Court once explained this concept in Resolution No 01/2014/NQ-HDTP dated 20 March 2014 of the Judges' Council of the Supreme People's Court on Guiding Some Provisions of the Law on Commercial Arbitration, stating that the 'fundamental principles of the law of the Socialist Republic of Viet Nam' are 'the basic rules which have an overall effect in the development and application of Vietnamese law'… [so that the infringement of these principles] 'severely violates the interests of the state, the rights and legitimate interests of one or all of the involved parties or a third party'.[38]

However, the authors cannot find any case in which the courts relied on the notion of the fundamental principles of the law to refuse the application of foreign law.

The CC 2015 has only recently introduced the principle of the application of foreign law. According to Article 667, '[w]here the application of the foreign law is subject to different interpretations, the application must follow the interpretation of the competent authority in that foreign country'. This implies that the courts must apply foreign laws the same way as the courts in the country of origin do. The purpose of introducing this new principle on the application of foreign laws in the CC 2015 was to require Vietnamese judges to avoid interpreting foreign laws from the perspective of domestic laws.[39] Even before the CC 2015 included this provision, scholars had proposed a similar principle.[40]

The issue of filling a gap in foreign laws during the process of applying and interpreting them is not regulated or explained clearly in Vietnamese law. However, as a consequence of the general principles employed in the application and interpretation of foreign laws just mentioned, filling a gap in foreign laws should be done in tune with the principles required by the laws of that country (the country of origin) to ensure the integrity and cohesion of the system of foreign laws being applied.

So far, there has been no case law to illustrate the method of filling a gap in foreign laws by Vietnamese courts. However, in some cases, the courts have applied Vietnamese laws for issues that are not governed by an international convention (eg, the United Nations Convention on Contracts for the International Sale of Goods (CISG)) and international practices (eg, the Uniform Customs and Practice (UCP) for Documentary Credits).[41] Vietnamese arbitration has reported that they have resorted to international soft law instruments like the Principles of International Commercial Contracts (UNIDROIT Principles or PICC) to fill gaps when they apply the CISG. Nevertheless, the arbitrators noted that they did not indicate or cite clearly in the arbitral awards that they had applied the PICC to fill gaps in the CISG but that they did search for the solution there and had written the awards based on that. In many other cases, the arbitrators have applied Vietnamese laws to fill gaps in the applicable international commercial practices.

[37] For example, the Law on Commercial Arbitration, Marriage and Family Law, Maritime Code and Commercial Law.

[38] Draft Resolution 2019, Art 14(2)(dd).

[39] PH Huong and HN Bich, 'An Overview of Vietnamese Private International Law' (2016/2017) 18 *Yearbook of Private International Law* 341, 344.

[40] BQ Tuan, 'Áp dụng và giải thích pháp luật nước ngoài trong tư pháp quốc tế [Application and Interpretations of Foreign Law in Vietnamese Private International Law]' (2017) 3 *Tạp chí Nghiên cứu lập pháp [Journal of Legislative Reseach]* 3; D Nang, *Một số vấn đề lý luận cơ bản về Tư pháp quốc tế [Some Basic Theoretical Issues about Private International Law]* (Nhà xuất bản Chính trị quốc gia [Vietnamese National Political Publishing House] 2001).

[41] Possibly because the law governing those parts is Vietnamese law, although the judgments do not expressly address so.

D. Failure to Establish Foreign Law

Where the contents of foreign law cannot be ascertained, Vietnamese law shall be applied in accordance with the provisions of Article 481(4)[42] of the CPC 2015 and Article 670(2)[43] of the CC 2015. This approach was also provided for in Article 5 of Decree No 138/2006/ND-CP dated 15 November 2006.[44]

It is worth noting that this regulation is not intended to encourage the courts to immediately apply Vietnamese law in place of unascertainable foreign laws. Instead, the courts have to make efforts to identify and apply the contents of foreign law and applying Vietnamese law is only the ultimate solution where all of these efforts have been unsuccessful. With this purpose in mind, the CPC 2015 fixed a deadline of six months for the provision of information on foreign law by the parties or by the requested agencies. After this time limit, the courts can apply Vietnamese law.

This regulation gives clear guidance for the courts not to dismiss a case where the parties have failed to prove the contents of foreign law, but instead to apply Vietnamese law to determine the case. Before having this regulation in the two codes, the approaches taken by the courts were slightly different depending on whether the courts had to ascertain the content of foreign laws[45] or where they had asked the parties to provide them, but the parties failed to respond.[46] In the former case, the court applied Vietnamese law, but in the latter, the court dismissed the case. The regulations in the CPC and CC 2015 now mandate the courts to apply Vietnamese law in both situations. However, illustrative cases are missing.

The legislators considered that where the parties chose foreign law to apply in their cases, it was not until disputes occurred that the parties were then obliged to search for and provide the contents of the foreign law to the court. They must do so since they have chosen that law to govern their legal relationships. However, in order for the involved parties to have more time to fulfil their obligations to provide the court with the contents of the chosen foreign law, Article 481(4) of the CPC 2015 allows the involved parties an additional six months. In addition, to have a basis for the determination of the civil case, it stipulates that the legal consequence of the failure of the involved parties to provide the court with the contents of foreign law is that the court shall apply Vietnamese law to determine the

[42] 'Past the 6-month time limit from the date of the request for the provision of the foreign laws as provided for in this Article, if there is no response, the Court shall apply Vietnamese law to settle the civil case.'

[43] 'In the case where the foreign law is not applied as prescribed in Clause 1 of this Article, Vietnamese law shall apply.'

[44] 'When the involved parties fail to prove their closest relations regarding citizens' rights and duties to the legal system requested for application, Vietnamese laws shall be applied.'

[45] In this case, Vietnamese workers sued a Vietnamese labour export company for damages due to their loss of work in Malaysia. The Malaysian employer ran out of finances and the Vietnamese workers were sent back before the contracted return date. As the Vietnamese court lacked knowledge of Malaysian labour laws, thus could not ascertain the content of the Malaysion laws, it applied Vietnamese law to force the Vietnamese labour export company to compensate the workers. See NV Cuong, Tranh chấp của người lao động và công ty xuất khẩu lao động [Dispute of Employees with Labor Export Companies]' (2006) 11 *Tạp chí Tòa án nhân dân [The People's Court Journal]* 18.

[46] See Decision No 01/QĐ dated 21 September 2001, Hanoi People's Court. In this case (regarding recognition and enforcement of a foreign arbitral judgment), the Court required a Vietnamese company to prove that a Japanese company's branch in Singapore lacked the capacity to sign a contract according to Singapore law. The Vietnamese party failed to do that, and, as a result, the Court dismissed the Vietnamese party's application to the Court, asking the Court not to recognise a decision of Singapore arbitration.

merits of a case.[47] This Regulation (the time limit of six months under Article 481(4)) was developed to promote a sense of responsibility in the litigants about their case and the spirit of cooperation of the state. The legislators explained as follows:

> A review of the mutual legal assistance agreements to which Vietnam is a member showed that the cases where the courts had to apply the laws of an agreement member country all arose where one of the parties was either a citizen or an organization of that country. For example, cases concerning the law applicable to movable inheritance located in the territory of Vietnam; or the personal and property relations of the spouses of citizens of a member country of an agreement, in which one spouse resides permanently in Vietnam and the other resides permanently in that member country. In this context, the litigants in the case would find out for themselves that the content of their country's law which is acquired in time by Vietnamese court is an important basis for them to protect their legitimate rights and interests. Therefore, the litigants will consider themselves more responsible in using their rights to assist the Vietnamese courts in obtaining the content of their country's law.[48]

For a member country of an agreement, the prompt provision of the contents of its laws at the request of the Vietnamese courts is also one of the effective ways to contribute to the protection of the legitimate rights and interests of its citizens and organisations. Therefore, it is unlikely that this country would refuse to cooperate or comply with a request by a Vietnamese court to provide the contents of its law, especially where that country acknowledges the legal consequences of the failure to comply, being that the court will apply Vietnamese law to decide the dispute.[49]

The time limit of six months, as fixed by Article 481(4) of the CPC 2015, should not be understood solely as a means to open the way for Vietnamese courts to apply Vietnamese law in place of foreign laws where they have not taken full responsibility and actively participated in the task of ascertaining the foreign laws.[50] The drafters further explained that the provisions had been formulated to harmonise the approach with international standards and that the application of Vietnamese law was ultimately to protect the rights and interests of the parties.[51] Academic research and international experiences have also been referred to as other influences. The principle of 'presumption of similarity' was employed, which means that where the contents of foreign law cannot be ascertained, the principle allows the presumption that they do not substantially differ from Vietnamese law. The drafters explained that this was also the approach taken in the laws of many countries, such as in England, Australia and Germany.[52]

E. Judicial Review/Appeal

Choice of law rules are embedded in the CC and other laws. The courts are obliged to apply them to determine the applicable laws to resolve a dispute. If the court makes an error in

[47] Hung (n 22) 7.
[48] ibid.
[49] ibid.
[50] ibid.
[51] ibid.
[52] ibid.

applying relevant choice of law rules (that is, the courts applied the laws of the incorrect country), a party can file an appeal to higher courts (appellate courts including the High Court and the Supreme Court) according to the appellate procedure,[53] or the cassation procedure.[54] This is because such an error consequently affects the rights and interests of the involved parties.

According to Articles 35 and 37 of the CPC 2015, the provincial courts have the jurisdiction to hear cases with foreign elements as the first instance. If the first-instance court has made an error in applying the law, the High Court shall review this issue at the request of a party through the appellate procedure.

Even if a judgment has become final (ie, the parties no longer have the right to appeal), the parties still have the right to use the judgment review mechanism of the High Court or the Supreme Court through the cassation procedures.[55] However, the parties cannot appeal directly to the High Court or the Supreme Court. Instead, if it is found that the first-instance court has improperly applied the rules defined in the applicable law, the parties must file an application requesting the competent agency (the Chief Justice of the Supreme People's Court and the Chairperson of the Supreme People's Procuracy)[56] to lodge an appeal for review.

In practice, the courts usually do not explain why they have applied Vietnamese law in the judgments. Therefore, it is difficult to know whether they have applied the choice of law rules correctly or not. Furthermore, the courts typically do not mention or cite relevant provisions, and they just apply Vietnamese law as if the cases were solely domestic. Therefore, it is hard to see whether, in fact, the appeal procedure proceeds, as described above.

Where foreign law is considered a matter of 'law' (that is, the court is responsible for ascertaining the contents of foreign law), the following process applies. As in the case where a court applies a wrong applicable law, when a court erroneously applies the contents of foreign laws in the process of settling civil cases involving foreign elements, the unsuccessful parties have the right to file an appeal to a higher court through the appellate procedure or to propose a review through the cassation procedures which are processed by the High Court or the Supreme Court.

Where foreign law is considered a matter of 'fact' (that is, the parties need to invoke, plead foreign law and prove its contents), the following process applies. If a court has made errors in applying foreign law, it can be understood as an error in the process of accessing and evaluating the evidence. In practice, the fact that a first-instance court has considered and assessed evidence incompletely and unobjectively, leading to the delivery of a wrong decision, is one of the common mistakes that lead to appellate trial procedures. Thus, the parties are fully entitled to file an appeal to higher courts, including the High Court or Supreme Court. However, unlike in cases where the foreign law is considered a matter of 'law', the review procedure in the High Court and Supreme Court in this situation is a reopening procedure.

[53] CPC 2015, Art 270.

[54] CPC 2015, Art 326 (1)(c); CPC 2015, Art 337.

[55] CPC 2015, Art 326. Under the cassation procedures, a seriously flawed application of law can form the basis of an application to annul the whole judgment, decision, or part of the judgment.

[56] CPC 2015, Art 331.

III. Foreign Law before Other Instances

A. Foreign Law before Administrative and Other Non-judicial Authorities

There are a number of cross-border matters which administrative and other non-judicial authorities are required to apply foreign laws to deal with (typically, the national law of a party). For example, in a case of marriage between a Vietnamese national and a foreigner, the district-level People's Committee is obliged to examine whether the marriage conditions under both laws are satisfied.[57] Another example is where a foreigner (not a resident in Vietnam) wants to adopt a Vietnamese person. In such a case, the competent authority must examine whether the adoption requirements under both Vietnamese law and the law of the country where that adoptive person permanently resides are met.[58]

While the competent agencies are supposed to ascertain the foreign laws, in practice, they rely on the documents issued by foreign countries certifying that their nationals meet the requirement of their laws. For example, as provided for in Article 30(1)(b) of the Decree No 123/2015/NĐ-CP on Guidelines for the law on civil status,[59] the Judicial Department of the district-level People's Committee can request a document certifying the marital status of a foreigner which has been issued by a foreign competent authority or an equivalent document issued by a competent foreign authority certifying the holder's eligibility for marriage as prescribed in the law of such country. Similarly, in the case of intercountry adoptions, as provided for in Article 18(1) of the Decree No 19/2011/NĐ-CP dated 21 March 2011,[60] the Department of Child Adoption (Ministry of Justice) should request documents issued by the competent agencies in the countries where the adopting persons permanently reside certifying that they meet enough conditions to adopt under their country's laws. Under Vietnamese law, there are currently no provisions on how administrative and non-judicial authorities should ascertain and apply foreign law. There are neither case laws nor academic publications on this matter.

B. Foreign Law in Arbitration, Mediation and Other Alternative Dispute Resolution Methods

In Vietnam, arbitral tribunals can deal with only cross-border disputes arising from commercial activities,[61] mainly disputes involving contracts with foreign elements. Vietnam

[57] Law on Marriage and Family 2014, Art 126.

[58] Law on Adoption 2010, Art 29.

[59] 'A document certifying marital status of a foreigner is a document which is issued by a foreign competent authority, remains valid, and certifies that the holder is being single. If the foreign country does not issue a document certifying marital status, an equivalent document issued by the foreign competent authority certifying the holder's eligibility for marriage as prescribed in law of such country is required.'

[60] '1. After receiving enough dossiers of adopting persons, the Department of Child Adoption, consider and appraise dossiers to define:

a) The adopting persons ensured by the competent agencies of the country in which they permanently residing that they meet enough conditions to adopt under such country's regulations of laws;'.

[61] Law on Commercial Arbitration 2010, Art 2(1).

has promulgated the Law on Commercial Arbitration 2010, which includes provisions on the laws applicable to the merits of disputes to be resolved at arbitration. Specifically, for disputes involving foreign elements, the arbitral tribunal shall apply the law chosen by the parties; if the parties do not agree on the applicable law, the arbitral tribunal shall apply the law that it considers most appropriate.[62] Thus, the arbitrators may apply foreign laws to settle a dispute if the parties agree, or they can apply a foreign law which they deem appropriate to the relationship between the disputing parties. This provision gives great freedom to the arbitrator and is in line with the current developments in arbitration law around the world.[63]

However, Vietnamese arbitration law still does not contain specific provisions on the ascertainment and application of foreign law in arbitration proceedings. In practice, the arbitral tribunals have applied foreign law.[64] According to the statistics produced by the Vietnamese International Arbitration Centre (VIAC) from 2014 to 2019, there were six cases in which arbitral tribunals applied foreign laws (three Russian, two English and one Korean) and four cases where tribunals applied both Vietnamese and foreign laws (two Vietnamese and English laws, and two Vietnamese and Korean laws).[65]

Arbitration proceedings often involve regulations on confidentiality. Therefore information related to how the foreign laws were determined and interpreted in the process of settling disputes at Vietnamese arbitration centres is often not publicly available. It is thus difficult to identify the practices related to this issue.

The settlement of cross-border civil disputes through mediation and other alternative dispute resolution methods is growing rapidly in Vietnam (in 2021, at the Vietnam Mediation Centre (VMC), 50 per cent of 10 mediation cases involved foreign elements).[66] However, at present, Vietnamese law does not have any provisions related to the ascertainment and application of foreign law in mediation and other alternative dispute resolution methods.

IV. Access to Vietnamese Law

There are a number of official and unofficial websites and services that provide information on Vietnamese law (in non-Vietnamese languages) as follows:

- *Official website*: Primary Database on Legal Normative Documents (website: vbpl.vn). This database was established in accordance with the provisions of Decree No 52/2015/ND-CP on the National Database of Laws issued by the government on 28 May 2015.

[62] ibid, Art 14.

[63] NQ Chien and NH Anh, 'Trọng tài thương mại quốc tế và vấn đề luật áp dụng [International Commercial Arbitration and applicable law]' (2021) 1 *Tạp chí Nghiên cứu lập pháp số [Journal of Legislative Research]*.

[64] For example, in a case settled by the VIAC in 2012, the parties chose Vietnamese law to govern an insurance contract, and for those issues not covered by Vietnamese law they chose English maritime insurance law to apply. See DV Dai, 'Pháp luật trọng tài thương mại Việt Nam [Arbitration law in Vietnam]' 1 (2018) Nhà xuất bản Hồng Đức [Hong Duc Publishing House] 582.

[65] PT Dat (Vice Chief Secretary of VIAC), Áp dụng CISG trong Trọng tài thương mại quốc tế [Application of CISG in international Commercial Arbitration] Power Point Presentation at Conference on CISG (2020).

[66] Báo cáo Thường niên VIAC và VMC 2021 [Annual Report of VIAC and VMC 2021], available online: www.viac.vn/.../VIAC_Bao-cao-thuong-nien-2021.pdf (accessed 23 February 2022).

Currently, the system provides a database of the legal documents of the central government and 63 databases of local legal documents in Vietnamese. In addition, an English version of the system has also been built, which provides English translations of most of the current legal documents (made by the Vietnam News Agency[67]).

- *Non-official services*: In addition to the national legal database, many unofficial websites also provide a service of looking up legal documents in English, and English translations of most laws and regulations, for example, the Information Law Library (thuvienphapluat.vn), Vietnam Law information page (luatvietnam.vn), etc.
- *Mutual legal assistance activities*: Vietnam has signed bilateral agreements on mutual legal assistance with other countries, which contain provisions on legal information. When there is a request from the competent authorities of another contracting party, Vietnam (in particular the Ministry of Justice) will provide relevant legal information, including documents and publications on legal issues, case laws, and as the law enforcement practices in Vietnam.[68]
- *Memoranda on legal and judicial cooperation*: Vietnam has signed a number of memoranda of understanding on cooperation in the field of justice and law with countries such as Singapore (2008), Lao People's Democratic Republic (2015) and Japan (2020). Within the scope of cooperation based on these memoranda of understanding, Vietnam will provide and exchange legal information, documents and publications in the legal field for their partners. The language used in the process of cooperation and exchange is usually English so that the parties can access specific content more easily. In addition, cooperation activities can also be organised in the form of conferences, seminars, and training courses in the field of justice and legal affairs.[69] This can be a forum for stakeholders to approach the practical application of Vietnamese legal regulations.

V. Access to Foreign Law: Future Developments in Asia

Vietnam is not a party to any international or regional instruments on the treatment of foreign law or information on foreign law. The country became a member of the Hague Conference in 2013 and has taken part in the activities of the Conference regarding this issue.

The application of foreign law in Vietnam is a practical and objective demand for the purposes of broadening and strengthening the relationships with foreign countries. The application of foreign law is also necessary to protect the legal rights of parties in a dispute. Moreover, this application also ensures the recognition and enforcement of judgments in foreign countries and the harmony of decisions and uniformity of outcomes.

[67] The Vietnam News Agency is an agency directly under government control and is currently the agency performing the task of translating Vietnamese legal documents into English. Translations by this agency are the official translations recognised by the government (According to Art 102(2) of Decree No 34/2016/ND-CP).

[68] Art 12 Agreement on mutual legal and legal assistance in civil and criminal matters between Vietnam and Czechoslovakia, later inherited by the Czech Republic and Slovakia (Effective from 16 April 1984); Art 15 of the Agreement between Vietnam and the Republic of Belarus (2001); Art 14 of the Agreement on mutual legal assistance between Vietnam and Taiwan (2010).

[69] Para 3, Memorandum of Cooperation between the Ministry of Justice of Japan and the Ministry of Justice of the Socialist Republic of Vietnam on Legal and Judicial Fields, 2020.

However, the challenges for the judiciary in applying foreign law are enormous in Vietnam. Admittedly, Vietnamese courts rarely apply foreign law. However, the Vietnamese courts and judges are not hostile to foreign law. The judges have had difficulties in applying foreign law for various reasons. The biggest obstacle is the access to and interpretation of foreign law. The language barrier has created a lot of challenges for judges in accessing foreign legal documents, especially where their laws are not written in common languages like English. In addition, it is even more difficult to apply foreign law when the judges cannot understand the general spirit of foreign law due to the differences in the legal policies and values.[70] This is the situation not only in Vietnam but also in many other developing countries around the world.[71]

To cater for the parties' needs (in particular, where they need to invoke, plead foreign law and prove its contents), it is also necessary to improve the situation on access to foreign law. Unlike competent authorities, the parties must search by themselves and provide the contents of the law to the court despite not being able to request support from state agencies such as the Ministry of Justice or diplomatic agencies.

Moreover, it is submitted that having better access to foreign law contributes to the further development of the Vietnamese legal system.

There are several ways to improve the current situations:

- *Building international or regional instruments with information on foreign laws*: Some scholars believe that Vietnam should propose to the ASEAN Economic Community (AEC) member countries to develop an agreement on the issue of providing foreign legal information, noting specific proposals including: (i) establish or designate a national agency to receive legal information requests from foreign countries and to transfer the necessary information to the competent authorities of the foreign countries; (ii) create a process and method of providing content of foreign law; (iii) propose a time limit and the cost of providing foreign legal information.[72]
- *Building a network of connections between judges*: The proposed model is similar to the Hague Judicial Network but the scope is wider. Accessing (searching, looking up) foreign legal documents is the first step, however, in order to apply foreign laws in a dispute settlement process, judges must understand the interpretations of the contents of the foreign laws in their original sense. Therefore, a network between judges can be an important information channel providing precedents or interpretations related to foreign laws.[73]

Aside from these, another way to build the judicial capacity to apply foreign law is to invest in human resources. Admittedly, this is a long-term policy, but it will have a better effect on the future by: (i) promoting comparative legal studies through education in universities

[70] In some cases, although the courts and judges have access to foreign legal documents, they cannot accurately interpret the provisions of that legal system. This requires the competent authority to consider the application and interpretation of foreign laws in that country through relevant case law, the views of scholars, etc. However, accessing an appropriate interpretation of the laws of that country is a huge challenge if the authorities do not receive support from the relevant experts or individuals of its own country. This leads to a great need to build a network of judges to connect and exchange the necessary legal information.

[71] Institute of Legal Science (n 2).

[72] Institute of Legal Science (n 2).

[73] ibid.

and colleges; (ii) equipping educational institutions with resources and materials related to foreign laws, and (iii) offering with foreign universities courses to students, which may offer an opportunity to gain the knowledge on foreign law.[74]

The reason behind this is that the need to access foreign laws today is significant, not only in the settlement of disputes with foreign elements but also in comparative law research. However, access to foreign law has long faced a number of obstacles that such an international or regional instrument unifying the treatment of foreign laws may help remove.

The first obstacle is the language barrier. Since the English language is not the official language or a working language in many countries, it can be very difficult to access the laws of some countries (especially small countries which use little-used native languages). The development of an international or regional instrument on access to foreign law could therefore be the impetus for countries to 'transform' their laws into a common language, probably English.

Such an instrument would also help remove barriers to foreign legal information. The internet is considered a vast store of knowledge, including information on foreign law. Still, it is undeniable that accessible information there is not enough, namely judges cannot find detailed information on the laws of all countries on the internet. In addition, it should be noted that information on the internet may not be official. An international or regional instrument on access to foreign law would enable countries to obtain legal information from official sources. Hence, their accuracy will be better guaranteed.

Such an instrument may also help ensure the correct interpretation of foreign law. The application of foreign law requires competent authorities, judges or parties to explain how the foreign law is applied in the country of origin. This is also one of the most serious difficulties. With an international or regional instrument on access to foreign law, countries could seek assistance from other Member States to find out how a foreign law should be applied in the country of origin. For example, countries could build a network of judges to assist each other in interpreting and applying foreign law. In addition, countries could also develop a reporting system of precedents that can be accessed and consulted on how to interpret and apply their laws in practice.

VI. Conclusion

The integration of Vietnam into the international market has given rise to cross-border disputes before the national courts and authorities and consequently to practical demands to apply foreign laws. The country has developed rules to meet such demands, notably Article 481 of the CPC 2015 and Article 670 of the CC 2015, which have provided the basic principles and methods for the courts and non-judicial authorities to follow to ascertain, designate and apply foreign law. Nevertheless, many issues related to the practical application of these provisions need more explanation relating to concrete cases, which will eventually come in the future.

[74] ibid.

10

Cambodia

NOBUMICHI TERAMURA*

I. Introduction: Status of Choice of Law Rules

Choice of law rules are only at an early stage of development in the Kingdom of Cambodia. As discussed elsewhere, Cambodian private law is largely based on Japanese law thanks to the Legal Technical Assistance Project (the Project) by the Japan International Cooperation Agency (JICA), in which experienced Japanese legal experts guided Cambodian legal elites in drafting the main codes and laws regulating civil matters.[1] Nevertheless, the Project did not result in establishing a set of conflict-of-law rules like Japan's 2006 Act on General Rules for Application of Laws (AGRAL). The Cambodian legal experts were passionate at first about a plan for codifying choice of laws rules in the Civil Code of Cambodia 2007 (CC), and the Japanese advisors agreed to materialise that plan.[2] The Khmer lawyers' idea was to establish a comprehensive framework of choice of laws based on private international law (PIL) norms that arguably existed in the country before the Khmer Rouge period.[3] However, the Khmer lawyers ultimately dismissed the plan due to alleged time constraints.[4]

It is curious that those Khmer legal elites insisted on adopting such old choice of law norms. First, the Communist Party of Kampuchea's persistent persecution and execution of legal professionals during the Khmer Rouge period turned the country into a legal vacuum with few lawyers and the near-total destruction of legal documents.[5] Consequently, when the new Cambodian Government was established in 1993, only a limited amount of literature was available for the surviving Cambodian lawyers to investigate the pre-Khmer Rouge

* For editorial assistance, this author thanks Caitlin Turner, a research assistant for the Transnational Law and Policy Centre at the University of Wollongong, Australia.

[1] N Teramura, 'Cambodia' in A Reyes and W Lui (eds), *Direct Jurisdiction* (Oxford, Hart Publishing, 2021); N Teramura, 'Japan as a Source of Legal Ideas: A View from the Mekong Subregion of ASEAN' (2021) 13 *New Voices in Japanese Studies* 19; Y Kaneko, 'Japan's Civil Code Drafting Support for Socialist Reform Countries: Diversity of Normative Choice' in Y Kaneko (ed), *Civil Law Reforms in Post-Colonial Asia: Beyond Western Capitalism* (Cham, Springer, 2019).

[2] Industrial Development and Public Policy Department at JICA, *Legal Technical Assistance for Cambodia: The History and Methodology of the Assistance of JICA in Drafting the Civil Code and the Civil Procedure Code [in Japanese]* (2012) 9.

[3] ibid 10–11.

[4] ibid.

[5] M Vickery, *Kampuchea: Politics, Economy and Society* (London, Frances Pinter, 1986) 120; K Phallack, 'Overview of the Cambodian Legal and Judicial System and Recent Efforts at Legal and Judicial Reform' in H Peng, K Phallack and J Menzel (eds), *Introduction to Cambodian Law* (Phnom Penh, Konrad-Adenauer-Stiftung, 2012) 8; DA Donovan, 'Cambodia: Building a Legal System from Scratch' (1993) 27 *The International Lawyer* 445.

statutory norms such as the old Civil Code and the old Code of Civil Procedure.[6] Thus, the government requested the JICA to help rebuild its legal infrastructure.[7] Second, a few commentators suggested in the early 1970s that certain French legal principles applied to choice of law issues in Cambodia as the Kingdom did not have relevant legislation.[8] However, they did not clarify the source of such principles.[9] Third, it would be more appropriate to draft choice-of-law legislation based on inspirations from Japanese PIL because the CC and the Code of Civil Procedure of Cambodia 2006 (CCP),[10] as well as other main bodies of private law, are built upon Japanese legal concepts and principles, and because, '[i]n contrast to France, which has no codified private international law, Japan [has] modern legislation in the field'.[11] In the end, virtually no traditional PIL principles are available to supplement the lack of codification of Cambodian choice of law rules. In contrast, Japanese PIL doctrines may play a gap-filler role for Cambodian PIL because of Japanese private law's role as the foundation of modern Cambodian civil law.

One may find that Cambodia's sources of choice of law rules are scattered in various codes and laws. For instance, Article 3 of the CC (recognising the principle of party autonomy in private legal relationships) is regarded by practitioners as the basis of parties' rights to designate the governing law of a contract.[12] Likewise, Article 36 of the Commercial Arbitration Law of Cambodia (CAL) confers the parties freedom to agree on the rules of law to be applied to the merits of the dispute, allowing the arbitral tribunal to choose the appropriate applicable law voluntarily in case the parties are unable to reach such an agreement. Article 46 of the CAL confers the Appeal Courts of Cambodia with the power to refuse the recognition and enforcement of a foreign arbitral award that has not yet become binding on the parties under the law of which the award was made.[13] Moreover, the Law on the Marriage and Family sets out in Articles 79–81 a couple of conflict of laws rules pertaining to marriage between Khmer citizens in a foreign country and that between a Cambodian citizen and a foreign national in Cambodia. Hence, the legal system of Cambodia indeed contains norms on conflict of laws, but these are not as comprehensive and systematic as the AGARL.

Nevertheless, the fact that those choice of law rules constitute some parts of the Cambodian legal system implies the significance of the treatment of foreign law for the

[6] Teramura (n 1) 201–03; I Sakano, 'Reflection on the Legal and Judicial Development Project for Drafting the Civil and Civil Procedure Codes of Cambodia [in Japanese]' (2003) *ICD NEWS* 91, 97.

[7] Teramura (n 1) 26–27.

[8] J Menzel, 'Cambodian Law: Some Comparative and International Perspectives' in H Peng, K Phallack and J Menzel (eds), *Introduction to Cambodian Law* (Phnom Penh, Konrad-Adenauer-Stiftung, 2012) 490.

[9] ibid.

[10] Unless otherwise stated, this chapter relies on the unofficial English translation of the CC and CCP prepared by the JICA through the Legal Technical Assistance Project, which is available at (respectively): www.jica.go.jp/project/cambodia/0701047/04/ku57pq00001spnva-att/01_02e.pdf; www.jica.go.jp/project/english/cambodia/0701047/materials/c8h0vm000000zsb2-att/01_01e.pdf.

[11] ibid 490–91.

[12] Bun & Associates, 'Governing Law and Dispute Resolution [in Japanese]', (*Bun & Associates Newsletter*, August 2017).

[13] Art 46(1)(e) of the CAL. Note that the Appeal Courts may refuse the enforcement/recognition of an award only where the party against whom the enforcement/recognition is invoked requests the refusal, furnishing proof that the ground of refusal has been met.

Khmer justice system. Because the judges have the duty to observe the legal procedures and laws in force in the country,[14] and those PIL rules form parts of the domestic law of the Kingdom, the application of the rules in the courts is not facultative but mandatory. Thus, Cambodian judges would need to consider how to treat foreign law (if the choice of law rules apply to their proceedings) as the PIL rules in the national law may lead to the application of foreign legal norms.

Nonetheless, examining features of Cambodian treatment of foreign law is more complicated than it seems. For example, in contrast to the situation in other Southeast Asian jurisdictions such as Singapore and Brunei Darussalam, where past judgments are publicly available,[15] it is difficult (and probably pointless) for commentators to try discerning judicial reasoning behind the application of foreign law in Cambodia. The reason for this is that Khmer lawyers, including judges, do not regard the doctrine of precedent as being significant or convincing, as seen from their reluctance to perceive judgments as sources of law and their lack of passion for publishing judgments.[16] However, one may still obtain useful information from relevant statutes and other vital legal documents, such as official commentaries and textbooks, as well as notes and reports prepared by those legal experts involved in the drafting process of codes and laws. A great deal of these secondary authorities on Cambodian private law is written only in Khmer and/or Japanese.[17] Thus, this chapter explores the treatment of foreign law in Cambodia, taking into consideration relevant documents written not only in English but also in Japanese. In case such materials fall short of needed information, the chapter will recourse to the PIL concepts and principles of Japanese law because modern Cambodian private law has its roots in Japanese civil law.

II. Foreign Law before Judicial Authorities

A. Nature of Foreign Law

Whether a court characterises foreign law as 'law' or 'fact' may determine how the court treats foreign law.[18] Characterising foreign law as 'law' means that the court regards foreign law as part of or equivalent to domestic law, and that arguably leads to the mandatory application of foreign law by judges.[19] Characterising foreign law as 'fact' means that the court treats foreign law like other facts, so it will apply foreign law facultatively, relying primarily

[14] Art 129 of the Constitution of Cambodia.

[15] State Judiciary Department: Brunei Darussalam, 'Judgments Search' (2020) www.judiciary.gov.bn/SJD%20Site%20Pages/Judgment%20Search.aspx (accessed 6 May 2023); Singapore Courts: The Judiciary, 'Judgments' (2022) www.judiciary.gov.sg/judgments (accessed 6 May 2023).

[16] Teramura (n 1) 201–03; and the author's interview with local practitioners.

[17] Teramura (n 1) 202; Teramura (n 1) 28; S Leng, 'Problems in Translating Cambodian Civil Code and Civil Procedure Code and Future Prospects [in Japanese]' (2016) *ICD NEWS* www.moj.go.jp/content/001298242.pdf.

[18] Y Nishitani, 'Treatment of Foreign Law: Dynamics Towards Convergence? – General Report' in Y Nishitani (ed), *Treatment of Foreign Law – Dynamics towards Convergence?* (Cham, Springer, 2017) 17.

[19] ibid.

on evidence provided by parties.[20] Accordingly, which classification the court takes will influence how foreign law is introduced, examined and applied in legal proceedings.[21]

The classification of foreign law under Cambodian law is not clear-cut. In explaining the rules of evidence under the CCP, the official commentary states as follows:

> In civil lawsuits, the major subjects of proof are facts. However, *depending on the circumstances*, empirical principles and *legal norms may also be the subjects of proof*. … Since judges are experts of law, they have the authority to apply laws and regulations based on their expertise, and they shall exercise such power in most cases. Nevertheless, *foreign law, local government ordinances and customs are not always clear and unambiguous to judges, so that the contents of these norms may have to be identified [by parties] based on evidence*.[22] [emphasis added]

This comment suggests as a basic rule categorising foreign law as 'law' provided that the law is clear to judges. However, it does not eliminate the possibility to treat foreign legal norms as 'facts' because the contents of these norms may be based on evidence. Therefore, foreign law is likely to be categorised as 'tertium genus' or of 'hybrid nature' in Cambodia.

B. Ascertainment of Foreign Law

i. Who Owes the Duty to Ascertain Foreign Law?

One might argue that a hybrid categorisation of foreign law is unusual for Cambodia which follows a civil law system. Based on comparative research mainly targeting Europe, the Americas and Northeast Asia, Nishitani claims that almost all civil law jurisdictions, including Japan, consider foreign law as 'law'.[23] Indeed, not a few Japanese PIL academics, as well as some judges, justify the characterisation of foreign law as 'law', relying on a thesis that foreign law is treated equally as domestic law (ie, it can be applied without incorporation to Japanese law) so as to ensure international harmony of judicial decisions – arguably the main objective of Japanese PIL.[24] Thus, they claim that judges owe a professional obligation to investigate and apply foreign law. However, the central authority on Japanese civil procedure, Mikazuki, disagrees. He correctly points out that most Japanese judges are not trained in foreign law and are unlikely to have sufficient expertise in foreign legal systems to deal with random cross-border issues in litigation.[25] For better procedural efficiency

[20] ibid.

[21] ibid.

[22] JICA, 'Commentary on Cambodian Code of Civil Procedure: Judgment Procedure [in Japanese]' (n.d.), 58ff www.moj.go.jp/content/000122394.pdf [This author's translation].

[23] Nishitani (n 18) 17. Among the countries investigated by the comparative research, other civil law countries adopting a hybrid categorisation of foreign law are Macau and Spain only, although the Spanish approach is different from Cambodia's as parties have the primary duty of proving foreign law (ibid 19); CA Monzonís, 'Spain: The Application of Foreign Laws in Spain – Critical Analysis of the Legal Novelties of 2015' in Y Nishitani (ed), *Treatment of Foreign Law – Dynamics towards Convergence?* (Cham, Springer, 2017) 331; G Tu, 'Macau: Proof and Information About Foreign Law in Macau' in Y Nishitani (ed), *Treatment of Foreign Law – Dynamics towards Convergence?* (Cham, Springer, 2017) 543.

[24] Y Nishitani, 'Treatment of and Access to Foreign Law in Japan' (2018) 23 *Journal of Japanese Law* 69, 75.

[25] A Mikazuki, 'The Application of Foreign Law and the Court [in Japanese]' in T Sawaki and Y Aoyama (eds), *Theories of International Civil Procedure Law* (Tokyo, Yuhikaku Publishing, 1987) 250–53. Some French commentators also state that the strict application of the *iura novit curia* principle to foreign law is deemed to be unrealistic:

and economy, Mikazuki refuses to impose on judges a duty to investigate the content of foreign law, suggesting that courts are only entitled to ascertain foreign law based on, but not limited to, the evidence submitted by parties.[26] According to Nishitani and Nakano, Mikazuki's practical approach that allegedly draws on common law is likely to be a minority view in Japan.[27] Nevertheless, his thesis is compatible with the Cambodian categorisation of foreign law advocated by the official commentary of the CCP.[28]

Moreover, the Cambodian judicial system may not underestimate the procedural efficiency and economy Mikazuki emphasises. This is because the strict extension of the principle of *iura novit curia* to the ascertainment of foreign law may pose an additional burden on the Khmer judicial officers who are already overwhelmed by their daily case management tasks. For example, as part of the Legal Technical Assistance Project, the JICA closely reviewed 14 first-instance judgments on divorce and loan refund cases issued between 2016 and 2017.[29] The salient challenge the Japanese legal experts found in the judgments was that some judges did not manage to apply major codes and laws of Cambodia properly, although these had been established about a decade ago.[30] According to Shinoda, a Long-term JICA Legal Expert stationed in the Ministry of Justice of Cambodia (MOJC), some courts in loan refund cases failed to reflect in their judgments the precise understanding of interest and late payment damage/interest.[31] Under Cambodian law, interest is the monetary charge for borrowing money.[32] On the other hand, a party is entitled to claim damage/interest for late payment if the other party has paid back borrowed money after considerable delay.[33] The distinction between interest and late payment damage/interest has practical consequences for parties as the annual interest rate cap for interest on borrowed money is 18 per cent, while the same for late payment damage/interest is 27 per cent.[34] Nevertheless, the courts sometimes ordered a party to pay 'interest' on borrowed capital that was overdue and other times described late payment damage/interest as 'fine' (ie, criminal penalty).[35] In other cases, the courts voluntarily decided on non-ex-officio matters not claimed by the parties despite Article 182(2) of the CCP prohibiting the court from adjudicating issues that the parties did not raise.[36] Such struggle of Khmer judges with applying domestic law and Cambodia's international reputation of being a state with limited legal

S Corneloup, 'France – The Evolving Balance Between the Judge and the Parties in France' in Y Nishitani (ed), *Treatment of Foreign Law – Dynamics towards Convergence?* (Cham, Springer, 2017) 170.

[26] Mikazuki (n 25) 259–65 (pointing out that applying the *iura novit curia* principle to foreign law may overburden national courts that are unlikely to have sufficient capacities and resources, as well as time, to thoroughly investigate foreign legal systems).

[27] Nishitani (n 24); S Nakano, 'Japan: Proof of and Information about Foreign Law in Japan' in Y Nishitani (ed), *Treatment of Foreign Law – Dynamics towards Convergence?* (Cham, Springer, 2017).

[28] JICA, 58ff.

[29] Y Shinoda, 'Report on the Investigation of Cambodian Court Judgments (1) [in Japanese]' (2019) *ICD NEWS* 60.

[30] ibid.

[31] ibid.

[32] Arts 578 and 583 of the CC.

[33] Arts 389 and 390 of the CC.

[34] Arts 1 and 2 of the Prakas (Ministerial Ordinance) No 128 MoJ.PK/11 of the Ministry of Justice on the Maximum Interest Rate.

[35] Shinoda (n 29) 68.

[36] ibid 65ff.

certainty and a weak rule of law,[37] will not warrant the strict inclusion of foreign law into the *iura novit curia* doctrine in the Cambodian courts. Because of the hybrid status of foreign law, Cambodian judges may investigate and apply foreign legal norms based on but not bound by evidence submitted by parties.[38]

ii. Means for the Ascertainment of Foreign Law

As discussed above, Khmer judges treat foreign law as law and evidence (fact). The legal aspect allows the judges to investigate foreign legal systems *sua sponte*, while no discernible legal texts on Cambodian law define the authority of the judges in such a context. The factual aspect is highly likely to lead the application of the rules of evidence to the ascertainment of foreign law. Then, the courts will find the following evidence of foreign law admissible: documentary evidence, including documents comprised of transcriptions of tape recordings or other recording media;[39] objects equivalent to documents 'such as drawings, photographs, audio and video tapes, or other items that are not documents but were created in order to express information';[40] expert witnesses designated by the court upon request by a party;[41] and evidence located abroad (that would be examined by an institution commissioned by the court to conduct the investigation, like a competent government agency of the foreign country or an embassy, that is, an ambassador, minister or counsel, of Cambodia stationed in the foreign country).[42] Also, the courts may request competent foreign administrative institutions and Cambodia's diplomatic missions to conduct evidence investigation abroad,[43] while Cambodia is not a party to the 1970 Hague Convention on the Taking of Evidence Abroad in Civil or Commercial Matters.[44] In addition, it is uncertain whether Cambodian judges are

[37] The Rule of Law Index 2022 ranked Cambodia 139th across 140 countries, and the Corruption Perception Index 2022 ranked Cambodia 150th across 180 states: World Justice Project, *Rule of Law Index® 2022* (World Justice Project, 2022) 62; Transparency International, 'Corruption Perception Index 2022' (2022) www.transparency.org/en/cpi/2022 (accessed 6 May 2023).

[38] This view is compatible with Arts 46(1)(a) and (e) of the CAL. The Articles provide the Appeal Courts with the power to decide the enforceability and recognisability of a foreign arbitral award where: (1) a party proves that the original arbitration agreement is not valid under the law applicable to the agreement; and (2) the award has not become binding on the parties under the law of which the award was made. In other words, the Articles allow the Appeal Courts to determine the enforceability/recognisability based on but not limited to the party's proof of the foreign law applicable to the arbitration agreement/award.

[39] Arts 148 and 159 of the CCP.

[40] Art 158 of the CCP.

[41] Arts 143 and 144 of the CCP. The expert witness is to testify matters specified by the parties and court.

[42] Art 129(1) of the CCP. The Article suggests in its official note (in Japanese) that the court intending to undertake the examination of evidence abroad needs to obtain permission from the host country based on international conventions and/or bilateral agreements (if any). Nevertheless, Art 129(2) of the CCP provides that '[a]n examination of … evidence conducted in a foreign [country], even [if] it contravenes [the] laws of [that country], [is still valid] if it does not contravene [the CCP]. It is unclear whether the host country will permit an institution commissioned by the court to undertake such illegal evidence taking.

[43] Art 130 of the CCP. However, the Article provides in its official note (in Japanese) that the court may commission a (foreign) government agency to conduct the necessary evidence examination only where the purpose of the examination is to ascertain an objective fact that may not lead to any fairness concern. For example, the note raises commissioning to a foreign meteorological bureau to investigate past weather in the country. Thus, the court is unlikely to rely on this Article to investigate controversial or complicated foreign legal issues, while it may request a foreign government agency to send non-contentious legal information such as statutes and judgments.

[44] HCCH, 'Status Table: Convention of 18 March 1970 on the Taking of Evidence Abroad in Civil or Commercial Matters' (2023) www.hcch.net/en/instruments/conventions/status-table/?cid=82 (accessed 6 May 2023).

able to communicate directly with foreign judges on official channels because none of the Khmer judicial officers have participated in the International Hague Network of Judges.[45] Moreover, in the age of information technology, it is hard to assume that Khmer judges and attorneys hesitate to rely on accessible internet sources and electronic documents – foreign statutes, commentaries, textbooks and other publications – in searching for relevant information.[46] In fact, many courts in civil law countries utilise internet sources.[47] However, as webpages and e-documents can be easily modified and even forged,[48] it might not always be appropriate for Khmer lawyers to depend on internet sources in ascertaining foreign law. Nonetheless, no statutory provisions in Cambodian law explicitly require judges to rely on authentication in determining the admissibility of internet sources.

Further, that foreign law is subject to proof in legal proceedings means that parties need to provide voluntary assistance to the court with examining the content of relevant foreign law, as per the evidence procedures under the CCP. Thus, following the principle of evidence-based decision-making, the court owes the duty to examine evidence offered by parties.[49] To support their argument and persuade the court, a party who intends to make a claim based on applicable foreign law needs to submit to the court evidence demonstrating the content of the foreign law. Then, the court may examine the evidence by its authority,[50] but the examination is to be conducted on evidence submitted by the parties only – the court is not allowed to undertake evidence collection on its motion.[51] Moreover, if a party submits as evidence a document written in a foreign language, the party shall attach the translation of the part of the document for which examination is sought.[52] The counterparty having any opinion on the accuracy of the translation shall express the opinion to the court in writing.[53] In addition, a party may file a request for the court to order the person (or party) possessing an evidentiary document to submit it to the court.[54] If the party does not comply with the document submission order, the court may find the other party's allegations on the document to be true.[55] Hence, those who rely on foreign law in Cambodian legal proceedings are advised to submit and/or specify evidence showing the content of the law.

Despite the evidence procedure under the CCP, the hybrid nature of foreign law may enable Khmer judges to determine the law's substance without being bound by evidence submitted by parties. For example, the judges may adopt any other means to investigate foreign law independently, such as inquiries to (foreign) judicial/administrative

[45] HCCH, 'International Hague Network of Judges (IHNJ)' (2022) assets.hcch.net/docs/665b2d56-6236-4125-9352-c22bb65bc375.pdf.

[46] See, eg, Nishitani (n 18) 23.

[47] For example, German and Japanese courts: O Remien, 'Germany: Proof of and Information about Foreign Law – Duty to Investigate, Expert Opinions and a Proposal for Europe' in Y Nishitani (ed), *Treatment of Foreign Law – Dynamics towards Convergence?* (Cham, Springer 2017) 193; Nakano 532.

[48] H Brander, 'Fake or Fact? (1) Digital Docs Manipulation and How to Spot It', (*Counsel*, 15 January 2021) www.counselmagazine.co.uk/articles/fake-or-fact-digital-docs-manipulation-how-to-spot-it-(1) (accessed 6 May 2023).

[49] Arts 123–125 of the CCP.

[50] Art 124(2) of the CCP.

[51] Art 124(1) of the CCP.

[52] Art 149(1) of the CCP. See also Art 5 of the Constitution of Cambodia stating that '[t]he official language and script [of Cambodia] are Khmer'.

[53] Art 149(2) of the CCP.

[54] Art 148(1) of the CCP.

[55] Art 153(1) of the CCP.

institutions,[56] without being restricted to the result they obtained.[57] Indeed, ambiguity exists between the court's right to call for the assistance of the parties in the ascertainment of foreign law and the parties' obligation (or willingness) to satisfy such a request.[58] However, the court is unlikely to be deterred from exercising such a right, and the parties shall endeavour to fulfil the assistance request expeditiously. This is because Article 4 of the CCP provides the court's general duty to proceed with civil actions fairly and speedily, mandating the parties to participate in such actions honestly and in good faith. Timely ascertainment of foreign law may help both judges and parties satisfy their obligations imposed by that Article. However, the assistance request does not force the judges to be bound by evidence offered by the parties since the court may determine the reliability of the legal information by itself.[59] In the end, it is at the judges' discretion whether to adopt in their judicial reasoning the evidence of foreign law submitted by the parties. Nevertheless, no discernible statutory provisions in Cambodian law set out rules for the courts' examination of the legal information submitted by the parties.

iii. Qualifications to Provide Foreign Legal Information

In accordance with Article 144 of the CCP, the court shall appoint as an expert witness a person with the knowledge and experience needed to provide expert testimony on foreign law matters. However, the Article prohibits the following persons from serving as expert witnesses:

- a person whose expert testimony may lead to the criminal prosecution, conviction, reputational cost or family breakdown of the person, their spouse or another relative;[60]
- a (former) public officer, if they are required by the court to testify about matters related to their professional secret unless their supervisory government agency has approved them to provide the witness testimony;[61]
- an attorney at law, doctor, dentist, birth assistant, nurse, pharmacist, clergyman or any other person, if the witness testimony they are required by the court to provide is related to their professional secret or any fact that they learned in the course of their professional duties;[62] and
- any other person, if they are asked by the court to testify matters on their technological or professional secret.[63]

[56] Art 130 of the CCP. See also Mikazuki (n 25) 264–65.

[57] ibid 259–63; Nishitani (n 24) 75 (discussing Mikazuki's thesis).

[58] Mikazuki (n 25) 264.

[59] Art 124(2) of the CCP provides that '[t]he court may conduct an examination of the evidence on its own authority in cases where it finds that it cannot reach a conclusion on whether or not the factual allegations made by a party are true on the basis of the evidence offered by the parties, or in any other case where the court finds such examination necessary'.

[60] Art 144(3)(a) of the CCP.

[61] Art 144(3)(b) of the CCP (noting that '[t]he supervisory government agency may not refuse to [grant] approval, except where such approval is likely to harm the public interest or significantly hinder the performance of public duties').

[62] Art 144(3)(c) of the CCP.

[63] Art 144(3)(d) of the CCP.

Moreover, a party may challenge the expert witness if there are circumstances that could prevent the witness from giving expert testimony in good faith.[64] Unless one of these grounds exists, the court may appoint as an expert witness any specialist who is knowledgeable about the disputed topic.

iv. Who Bears the Costs of Ascertaining Foreign Law?

Under Cambodian law, parties are primarily responsible for bearing the costs of ascertaining foreign law. For example, Article 62 of the CCP requires the parties or other persons related to the case to compensate for:

> (a) an amount [of cost for] the court to investigate … evidence, serve documents, and conduct any other procedural act during the civil action; and
>
> (b) an amount [of cost] equivalent to … travel and lodging costs for a judge and a court clerk should [they need to carry out] the investigation of evidence, investigation of facts, or other act … carried out outside of the courtroom.

As these provisions demonstrate, judges may order parties to pay their costs of ascertaining foreign law, and the unsuccessful party usually bears such costs.[65] Moreover, each party to a lawsuit shall pay its own attorney's fees.[66] In practice, it is common among Cambodian lawyers to claim the time they spent to investigate foreign legal systems as part of their billable hours.[67]

C. Interpretation and Application of Foreign Law

A corollary of judges' obligation to apply choice of law rules under Cambodian law is that Khmer judges are required to apply foreign law *ex officio* if the applicable choice of law rules lead to the application of such law.[68] The judges also have the power to ascertain the content of foreign law *ex officio* because of the hybrid nature of foreign law in the Cambodian legal system.[69] Requesting the application of foreign law, the parties may indeed plead and prove the content of foreign law as per the evidence rules in the CCP, and the judges take into account suggestions by the parties.[70] However, without being fully bound by the parties' pleadings and proof, the judges may exercise their professional right and authority to examine, determine and apply relevant foreign legal norms.[71]

There are no evident laws or regulations that define how judicial officers shall interpret and apply foreign law in the Cambodian civil courts. In Japan, the prevailing PIL theory suggests that judges shall interpret and apply foreign law in the ways courts of the country

[64] Art 145 of the CCP.
[65] Art 64 of the CCP.
[66] The official note on Art 63 of the CCP [in Japanese].
[67] The author's interview with Cambodian practitioners.
[68] See section I above.
[69] See sections II.A and II.B.i above.
[70] See section II.B.ii above.
[71] ibid.

of origin take.[72] It also claims that the doctrine is extended to situations where there is a gap in foreign law, that is, where the applicable foreign law fails to cover issues submitted to the courts.[73] No noticeable evidence points out that the Japanese legal theory has been incorporated into the Cambodian legal system. However, comparative research justifies the Cambodian courts to follow the doctrine. Investigating the treatment of foreign law in 29 major common and civil law jurisdictions, Nishitani concludes that 'it is generally accepted that foreign law ought to be interpreted and applied in accordance with the rules of interpretation established in the country of origin'.[74] Nishitani upholds this principle, invoking the purpose of the conflict of laws as follows:

> Where conflicts rules designate foreign law as the applicable law, it ought to be interpreted and applied correctly – in the same manner that a judge in that country would – to achieve international harmony and respect the parties' interests.[75]

Nishitani further claims that the general principle is naturally extended to gaps in foreign law, suggesting these are 'filled pursuant to the criteria in the country of origin to ensure the coherence of the foreign legal system'.[76] Because the majority of civil law countries including Japan opt for the approach elucidated by Nishitani,[77] and because Cambodia adopts a civil law system based on Japanese law,[78] it will not be unreasonable for Khmer judicial officers to put on the shoes of the judges of the country of origin when they interpret foreign legal norms and fill their gaps.

However, mandating Cambodian judges to follow Nishitani's thesis is likely to be impractical, given the current situation of the Cambodian judiciary. The reason for this is that Khmer judicial officers are trained in adjudicating disputes under Cambodian domestic law. In the Kingdom, most new judges are appointed from judge students (sometimes referred to as 'judge trainees') who have passed 'the examination for the selection of judge students' and have completed the professional training organised by the MOJC.[79] The institution responsible for conducting the professional training is the Royal School for Judges and Prosecutors (RSJP),[80] which was established by the Government of Cambodia in 2002.[81] The objective of the RSJP is to provide judge students with opportunities to

[72] Nakano (n 27) 533; Y Tameike, *Lecture on Private International Law* [in Japanese] (Tokyo, Yuhikaku Publishing, 2005) 244; R Yamada, *Lectures on Private International Law* [in Japanese], 3rd edn (Tokyo, Yuhikaku Publishing, 2004) 133.

[73] Tameike (n 72) 250; S Ikehara, H Egawa and R Yamada, *The General Theory of Private International Law and Nationality Law [in Japanese]* (Tokyo, Yuhikaku Publishing, 1973) 240; Yamada (n 72) 134.

[74] Nishitani (n 18) 31, noting that 23 of the 29 jurisdictions investigated and the Inter-American Convention on General Rules of Private International Law support that principle. Note, however, that the 23 jurisdictions are civil law jurisdictions, and the signatories of and parties to the Inter-American Convention are South and Central American countries that follow the civil law tradition: www.oas.org/juridico/english/sigs/b-45.html (accessed 6 May 2023). Thus, the principle is generally accepted among civil law countries.

[75] ibid.

[76] ibid.

[77] ibid.

[78] See section I above.

[79] Arts 19ff of the Law on the Status of Judges and Prosecutors.

[80] Also sometimes referred to as the Royal School for Magistracy (RSM): V Phun, 'Country Factsheet 2: Judicial Training in Cambodia' in A Nababan and others (eds), *Judicial Training in ASEAN: A Comparative Overview of Systems and Programs* (Phnom Penh, Konrad-Adenauer-Stiftung, 2014) 31.

[81] M Ito, 'The History of JICA's Legal Technical Assistance in Cambodia [in Japanese]' (2021) 87 *ICD News* 47, 50; C Huot and S Rith, 'Hope of Justice Lies in School for Judges', (*The Phnom Penh Post*, 21 November 2003) www.phnompenhpost.com/national/hope-justice-lies-school-judges (accessed 6 May 2023).

learn about Cambodian judicial proceedings to adjudicate domestic disputes.[82] Thus, the RSJP's training curriculum for judge students focuses on the Cambodian legal system.[83] In fact, major private law subjects taught in the RSJP are (Cambodian) civil proceedings, judgment writing, family law and land law, among others.[84]

The judicial training curriculum does not systematically cover foreign-law-related topics like the ASEAN legal framework, international law, comparative law or conflict of laws.[85] During the RSJP's one-year practical judicial traineeship,[86] some selected trainees are reportedly placed at courts abroad based on the frameworks of international cooperation that Cambodia concluded with foreign donors.[87] In addition, some donor countries offer special training programmes for senior judges and instructors teaching at the RSJP. For example, the JICA has trained Khmer judicial elites for many years as part of the Legal and Judicial Development Project. It has sent elite legal officers (including those working for the RSJP) to Japan to enrol them in special capacity-building programmes on Japanese judicial proceedings, which have been taught by senior Japanese judges, experienced lawyers and famous professors.[88] This initiative aims to help those elite officers make use of the practical knowledge of Japanese law to enrich their understanding of the Cambodian justice system. However, the duration of the programmes is normally several weeks. Thus, whether junior or senior, ordinal Khmer judges are unlikely to have opportunities to study foreign legal systems comprehensively and systematically.

Certainly, chosen some might be able to have intensive training on foreign judicial proceedings in Cambodia and abroad. However, such special programmes organised by Cambodia's official development assistance (ODA) partners are optimised for guest students who learn about specific topics on foreign law on a short-term basis. The programmes are not designed to let Khmer trainees undergo 'real' professional training for judges who are expected to handle disputes under the foreign legal system. This is legitimate for these kinds of cooperation projects, most of which have small budgets and are delivered based on agreements between Cambodia and donor countries whose official languages are different.[89] Demanding Cambodian trainees to pass a professional training course whose participants

[82] A Misawa, 'Supporting the Training of Judges and Prosecutors in Cambodia [in Japanese]' (2004) 18 *ICD News* 1, 7; M Ito, 'Professional Legal Education at the Royal School for Judges and Prosecutors (Cambodia)' [in Japanese] (2022) 90 *ICD News* 47, 49.

[83] Phun (n 80) 34.

[84] Misawa (n 82) 7; Ito (n 82) 48–50.

[85] Phun (n 80) 34.

[86] The judicial training program of the RSJP consists of: (1) in-class training on legal theory for eight months; (2) practical judicial traineeship for one year; and (3) specialised training for four months: ibid 33.

[87] ibid 33.

[88] See, eg, Social Development Department at JICA, *The Final Evaluation Report on the Project for the Improvement of Training on Civil Matters at the Royal School for Judges and Prosecutors of the Royal Academy for Judicial Professions [in Japanese]* (2008); Public Policy Department at JICA, *The Ex-ante Evaluation Report on the Project for the Improvement of the Training on Civil Matters at the Royal School for Judges and Prosecutors of the Royal Academy for Judicial Professions (Phase 2) [in Japanese]* (2009); Public Policy Department at JICA, *The Mid-term Review Report on the Project for the Improvement of the Training on Civil Matters at the Royal School for Judges and Prosecutors of the Royal Academy for Judicial Professions (Phase 2) [in Japanese]* (2010); Industry Development and Public Policy Department at JICA, *The Final Evaluation Report on the Project for the Improvement of the Training on Civil Matters at the Royal School for Judges and Prosecutors of the Royal Academy for Judicial Professions (Phase 2) [in Japanese]* (2012).

[89] P Nicholson and T Kuong, 'Japanese Legal Assistance: An East Asian Model of Legal Assistance and Rule of Law?' (2014) 6 *Hague Journal on the Rule of Law* 141.

are expected to be equipped with specialist (non-Khmer) language skills and expertise is unreasonable at best and unrealistic at worst.

In the end, the situation of the judicial training in Cambodia confirms Mikazuki's thesis – judges of a certain legal system are not trained in adjudicating disputes based on foreign legal norms.[90] Thus, Cambodian judges may be required to interpret and apply foreign law in the manner adopted by courts of the country of origin, following their reasonable knowledge and investigation of such treatment. However, it is likely to be impractical for the judges to replicate foreign judicial reasonings in Cambodian judgments.

D. Unascertainable Foreign Law

No noticeable materials suggest how Cambodian courts cope with a case in which the parties and the judges are unable to establish the content of the foreign law applicable to the case. In Japan, the courts and academics are divided on how to fill such a legal vacuum reasonably and effectively.[91] For example, many courts have handed down decisions referring to the *lex fori*[92] (ie, Japanese law) in filling a gap in applicable foreign law.[93] On the other hand, a significant number of judgments rely on the so-called reasonable test approach that seeks to deduce and apply relevant norms presumably in force in the country of origin, considering the fundamental principles of the foreign legal system and appropriate solutions for the case at hand.[94] However, judicial and academic opinions have not been settled as to whether the reasonable deduction of the content of applicable foreign law is based on the *lex fori*,[95] the presumed foreign law,[96] or the general reasonableness test.[97] Further, several judges and scholars recommend relying on the legal system most similar to the applicable foreign law in presuming the non-ascertainable content of the law.[98] For instance, the Tokyo District Court determined in 2015 the rules of tort and unjust enrichment in Myanmar, relying on UK law.[99]

[90] Mikazuki (n 25) 251ff.

[91] Nishitani (n 24) 80; Nakano (n 27) 533–34.

[92] *Lex fori* means the law of the jurisdiction or authority seized with a case.

[93] See, eg, *Takechi v Hayashi* [1987] Yamaguchi Family Court (Shimonosoki Branch) Showa 62 (Ka) No 163 Kateisaiban Geppo [in Japanese] 40/3, 90; *XX v YY* [1987] Kyoto District Court Showa 61 (Wa) No 2444 Hanrei Jiho [in Japanese] 1275, 107; *Kin v Gen* [1984] Tokyo High Court Showa 59 (Ne) No 58 Kaiteisaiban Geppo [in Japanese] 37/9, 87. See also Nishitani (n 24) 81.

[94] Nishitani (n 24) 81.

[95] *Tokio Marine Fire Insurance Co Ltd v The Shipping Corporation of India Ltd* [1983] Kobe District Court Showa 51 (Wa) No 908 Hanrei Jiho [in Japanese] 1092, 114; *Tei v Pak* [1982] Nagano Family Court Showa 51 (Ka) No 131 Kateisaiban Geppo [in Japanese] 35/1, 105.

[96] *XX v YY* [1987] Tokyo District Court Showa 58 (Wa) No 7218 / Showa 60 (Wa) No 162 / Showa 61 (Wa) No 1748 Hanrei Jiho [in Japanese] 1278, 97; *Son Phong v Champassak* [1986] Hiroshima District Court Showa 60 (Ta) No 18 Kateisaiban Geppo [in Japanese] 38/6, 43. See also Nishitani (n 24) 81.

[97] *XX v YY & others* [1985] Osaka District Court Showa 60 (Ta) No 4 Hanrei Jiho [in Japanese] 1179, 94; *Doihara v The Superintending Prosecutor of the Tokyo High Public Prosecutors Office* [1981] Tokyo High Court Showa 55 (Ne) No 1051 Kateisaiban Geppo [in Japanese] 34/9, 72.

[98] *Takahara v Ryu* [1983] Nagoya Family Court Showa 58 (Ka) No 1493 Kateisaiban Geppo [in Japanese] 36/11, 138; *XX v YY* [1975] Naha Family Court Showa 49 (Ka I) No 21 / Showa 49 (Ka I) No 22 Kateisaiban Geppo [in Japanese] 28/2, 115; Ikehara, Egawa and Yamada (n 73) 243; Yamada (n 72) 136; Nakano (n 27) 533–34; Nishitani (n 24) 81.

[99] *XX v YY* [2015] Tokyo District Court Heisei 25 (Wa) No 32882 LEX/DB [in Japanese] No 25532655, 1.

This diversity of opinions among Japanese judges and scholars will likely spark controversy among the Cambodian legal profession when the issue of unascertainable foreign law has caught more attention from Khmer lawyers. In the age of the internet, Cambodian judges will probably seldom declare foreign law as unascertainable because many countries have improved means of ascertaining their laws by publishing their legislation and cases online. Nevertheless, the judges may not eliminate the possibility as Cambodia is surrounded by countries whose legal systems do not strictly follow the doctrine of precedent and publish only a small number of judgments.[100]

E. Judicial Review/Appeal

i. Erroneous Application of Choice of Law Rules

In Cambodia, choice of law rules form part of domestic law.[101] Thus, a court's erroneous application of such rules may constitute an error on a question of law that may become a cause for reversal by a higher court, provided that the judgment has not yet become final and binding.[102] Those who intend to challenge a court's holding on choice of law need to prepare an *Uttor* appeal and/or *Satuk* appeal.[103] Parties may file an *Uttor* appeal against a judgment rendered by a court of first instance[104] within one month from the day when service of the written judgment was made to the parties.[105] Such an appeal is permissible where the parties have not agreed in writing to exclude their right to appeal to an *Uttor* appellate court,[106] and where the judgment was handed down on a civil or commercial matter whose value exceeded 5,000,000 Riel (= around US$1,230).[107] Then, the parties may request a second instance court to re-examine both legal and factual determinations in a judgment rendered at the first instance.[108] Incidentally, the parties may apply to the Supreme Court in Phnom Penh for a *Satuk* appeal on a judgment issued by an *Uttor* appellate court.[109] The parties may file the appeal only 'on the grounds of a violation of the Constitution, laws, or regulations that influence the judgment'.[110] Thus, they are not allowed to request the Supreme Court to review a lower court's factual determinations.[111] The Supreme Court only re-examines

[100] N Sakai and S Kamata, 'The Doctrine of Precedent in Vietnam [in Japanese]' (2017) *ICD News* 29; A Ito, 'Legal Education and Professional Legal Training in Laos: Towards the Birth of Lao Jurisprudence [in Japanese]' (2020) *ICD News* 40, 47.

[101] See section I above.

[102] Art 259ff of the CCP.

[103] Art 259(1) of the CCP.

[104] Art 259(1)(a) of the CCP.

[105] Art 264 of the CCP.

[106] Arts 260(1)(a), 260(2), 263 of the CCP.

[107] Arts 260(1)(b) of the CCP.

[108] JICA, 127.

[109] Art 283 and Arts 259(1)(a)–(b) of the CCP. Note that the parties may file a *Satuk* appeal against a judgment rendered by a first instance court if they have agreed not to have an *Uttor* appeal but have agreed to reserve the right to file a *Satuk*/final appeal: Arts 259(1)(a) and 260(1) of the CCP.

[110] Arts 284 of the CCP; JICA, 129. The Supreme Court shall transfer a claim of unconstitutionality to the Constitutional Council, except where it deems the claim is inadmissible: Art 19 of the Law on the Organisation and the Functioning of the Constitutional Council 2018.

[111] Note that parties must file a *Satuk* appeal within one month of receiving the written judgment by an appeal court: Art 286 of the CCP.

an *Uttor* judgment's specific legal issues – including matters on choice of law – raised by the parties because the Court is bound by the facts lawfully determined in the original judgment.[112] Therefore, when a Cambodian court misapplied the choice of law rules, the parties would be allowed to file an appeal to a higher court.

ii. Erroneous Application of Foreign Law

A party would possibly consider an option to challenge a judgment when the court that issued the decision correctly applied conflict of law rules and nevertheless misinterpreted the foreign law applicable to the dispute. As discussed in section II.A, Cambodian law perceives foreign law as a question of fact and law. The hybrid nature of foreign law does not prevent the party from appealing against a judgment rendered by a first instance court because they may file an *Uttor* appeal to request for review of both factual and legal issues in that judgment.[113] One might argue that the hybrid nature will pose a difficulty to the party when they plan to undertake a *Satuk* appeal. However, the Supreme Court is unlikely to reject such an appeal by emphasising the factual aspect of foreign law. Article 297 of the CCP provides that judges in a *Satuk* appeal case are not obliged to follow facts determined in the original judgment when they intend to examine *ex officio* matters.[114] Accordingly, the Supreme Court is not constrained by the determination of foreign law in the previous instance (even where the decision emphasises the factual aspect of the foreign law) because Khmer judges have the authority to investigate the content of foreign law on their own motion.[115] Hence, the Cambodian legal system is likely to allow the appellate courts and the Supreme Court to review the erroneous application of foreign law.

III. Foreign Law in Other Instances

A. Administrative and Non-judicial Authorities

Local government officials and diplomats at Cambodian embassies/consulates are sometimes required to ascertain foreign law as part of their daily duty. For instance, the Sub-Decree No 103 S-D/BK on Civil Status (the Civil Registration Sub-Decree) mandates in Article 3 all Khmer citizens to register their civil status in Civil Status Books.[116] Each commune/sangkat shall keep the Books to record the birth, marriage and death of Khmer

[112] Arts 295–96 of the CCP; K Phallack, 'Overview of Contemporary Civil Procedures of Cambodia' in H Peng, K Phallack and J Menzel (eds), *Introduction to Cambodian Law* (Phnom Penh, Konrad-Adenauer-Stiftung, 2012) 166.

[113] See section II.E.i above.

[114] Art 296 of the CCP.

[115] See section II.B.i above.

[116] The unofficial English translation of the Sub-Decree is available at: www.skpcambodia.com/storage/uploads/files/Nationality_Immegration_Civil%20Registration/Sub-dree%20No103%20on%20Civil%20Registration-Eng.pdf (accessed 6 May 2023).

citizens and foreigners living in the jurisdiction.[117] The Chief of the commune/sangkat,[118] as the Registrar of the administrative division,[119] has the professional obligation to maintain the Books for the commune/sangkat.[120] The Registrar has to examine and record essential facts related to the birth, marriage and death of those registered in the Books.[121] To keep records on Cambodian national residents in foreign countries, the embassies and consulates of Cambodia also keep the Books,[122] and each embassy/consulate must have one officer who takes the role of Registrar to update the Books upon nomination by the Ministry of Foreign Affairs and International Cooperation.[123] Hence, Cambodian Registrars, particularly those working at diplomatic missions overseas, will have to discern foreign law when they undertake civil registrations involving foreign elements.

In fact, the Registrars, whether working at local governments or diplomatic offices, are required to investigate foreign law in handling marriages performed overseas. On Registrars at embassies/consulates, Article 79 of the Law on the Marriage and Family provides:

> [A] [m]arriage between [Cambodian citizens] or between a Cambodian citizen and [a] foreigner living in a foreign country must be held before the [R]egistrar of the embassy or consulate of the State of Cambodia which is located in the [foreign] country where both part[ies] reside. … [A] [m]arriage between [Cambodian citizens] or [between a] Cambodian citizen and [a] foreigner, which is formally held [in accordance with] marriage procedure[s] described by the law of the marriage [in the foreign country where both parties reside], shall be recognized as being valid in the [Kingdom] of Cambodia as long as such a marriage is not against … the laws of the [Kingdom] of Cambodia. A marriage certificate or a copy of the marriage certificate must be registered in a [Civil Status Book kept at] the embassy or consulate of the [Kingdom] of Cambodia [in the foreign country].[124]

Accordingly, the Registrars must examine whether the marriage has complied with thc law of the foreign country where the couple resides. On Registrars in communes/sangkats, Article 79 states that:

> [t]he [Kingdom] of Cambodia shall enter the marriage certificate [issued by the authority of the country where the couple held the marriage] or [a] copy of the marriage certificate in the [Civil Status Book] of the [c]ommune or [sangkat] where both [parties] reside.[125]

[117] Art 12 of the Civil Registration Sub-Decree.

[118] The sub-national administration of Cambodia consists of: (1) capital city/province; (2) district/municipality/khan; and (3) sangkat/commune. As of 6 May 2023, Cambodia has 1,390 communes and 262 sangkats: National Committee for Sub-National Democratic Development, 'Gazetteer Database Online' (n.d.) db.ncdd.gov.kh/gazetteer/view/index.castle (accessed 6 May 2023). Each commune/sangkat has a commune council consisting of a president (also called commune/sangkat chief), a few deputies and other members. All members of the council are elected directly by Khmer citizens living in the commune/sangkat: OpenDevelopment Cambodia, 'Administration' (2015) opendevelopmentcambodia.net/topics/administration/#ref-79177-3 (accessed 6 May 2023).

[119] Art 8 of the Civil Registration Sub-Decree.

[120] Arts 9 and 15 of the Civil Registration Sub-Decree.

[121] ibid.

[122] Art 14 of the Civil Registration Sub-Decree.

[123] Art 11 of the Civil Registration Sub-Decree (noting that the Ministry of Interior shall be informed of the nomination of Registrar).

[124] The unofficial English translation of the Law on the Marriage and Family is available at: /www.ilo.org/dyn/natlex/docs/ELECTRONIC/86095/96933/F1861658608/KHM86095.pdf. See also Art 32 of the Civil Registration Sub-Decree.

[125] www.ilo.org/dyn/natlex/docs/ELECTRONIC/86095/96933/F1861658608/KHM86095.pdf (accessed 6 May 2023).

Then, the local Registrars possibly have to discern whether the marriage and its certificates comply with the matrimonial law of the state where the marriage took place and the document was issued.[126]

B. Alternative Dispute Resolution

The two types of arbitration popular in Cambodia are international commercial arbitration (ICA) and labour arbitration.[127] Because ICA is a means of solving cross-border business disputes, international arbitrators are used to dealing with issues on conflict of laws and application of foreign law. The CAL recognises party autonomy to choose the rules of law governing the merits of the dispute, mandating the arbitral tribunal to designate and apply the rules it considers appropriate where the parties are unable to agree on the governing law.[128] Cambodia's top ICA institution, the National Commercial Arbitration Centre (NCAC), also articulates such norms in its Arbitration Rules.[129] In contrast, the main aim of labour arbitration in Cambodia is to settle differences between employers and employees following domestic labour law. In fact, the mission of the Arbitration Council – Cambodia's flagship labour arbitration body established in 2003 with the support of the Ministry of Labour[130] – is to facilitate parties to settle collective employment disputes in Cambodia, in accordance with the Labour Law of the Kingdom.[131] Thus, both conflict of laws and ascertainment of foreign law may rarely arise in labour arbitration held in Cambodia, while arbitrators are expected to come across such issues in ICA proceedings.

The complexity is that no discernible legal instruments and materials define how international arbitrators ascertain foreign legal norms under Cambodian law. The ambiguity is exacerbated by a widely accepted theoretical justification of international arbitration. The thesis suggests that international arbitration is not anchored in any municipal legal system, claiming that international arbitration is underpinned by the autonomous arbitral order that exists outside states.[132] Adopting the thesis, arbitrators will regard any applicable national

[126] Moreover, Art 34 of the Civil Registration Sub-Decree allows a couple between immigrants/foreigners living lawfully in the territory of Cambodia to have a marriage in accordance with the law on marriage of the couple's country, provided that the Registrar of the couple's commune/sangkat has approved the marriage. Following the marriage, the couple may request either the embassy/consulate of their home country to Cambodia or the Registrar of their commune/sangkat to record the marriage in the Civil Status Book. Then, the Registrar may need to study the foreign law applied to the marriage. Other instances where the Registrar may be expected to investigate foreign law include the registration of the birth of a child between Khmer parents or between a Khmer citizen and a foreign national living abroad, as well as the registration of the death of a Khmer citizen who was residing in a foreign country. See Arts 26 and 41 of the Civil Registration Sub-Decree.

[127] The author's interview with Cambodian practitioners while working at a top Cambodian law firm in 2020.

[128] Art 36 of the CAL.

[129] Art 32 of the 2021 NCAC Arbitration Rules.

[130] The Arbitration Council, 'The Arbitration Council: Background' (n.d.) www.arbitrationcouncil.org/about-ac/the-arbitration-council/ (accessed 6 May 2023); S Tamagaki, 'The Arbitration Council in Cambodia: Impacts of the 2016 Law on Trade Unions and Prakas No. 303 by the Ministry of Labour and Vocational Training [in Japanese]' (2019) *ICD NEWS* www.moj.go.jp/content/001306610.pdf (accessed 6 May 2023).

[131] The Arbitration Council, 'Law' (n.d.) www.arbitrationcouncil.org/resources/laws-regulations/law/ (accessed 6 May 2023) (noting that '[t]he Labour Law is pivotal to all decision making by the Arbitration Council').

[132] E Gaillard, *Legal Theory of International Arbitration* (Leiden, Martinus Nijhoff Publishers, 2010); N Teramura, *Ex Aequo et Bono as a Response to the 'Over-Judicialisation' of International Commercial Arbitration* (Alphen aan

law as foreign law. They will unlikely distinguish Cambodian law from other legal systems in that respect even where the seat of their arbitration is in Cambodia. This is because the arbitration will be presumed to be independent of the Cambodian legal order, and both Cambodian and other foreign legal norms will be equally foreign to the arbitrators. Thus, pondering international arbitrators' treatment of 'foreign law' under 'Cambodian law as domestic law' is theoretically complex and difficult.

In the context of the general practice of international arbitration, commentators are inclined to discuss arbitrators' duty to ascertain the content of the applicable law without drawing a sharp line between domestic and foreign laws.[133] The Arbitration Committee of the International Law Association (ILA) supports the lack of distinction, suggesting that '[u]nlike before national courts where there is a distinction between national and foreign law, in arbitration one can only speak of applicable law'.[134] Applying this to the context of Cambodia, international arbitrators in the Kingdom have to identify their approach to assessing the 'applicable law' instead of the applicable foreign law. However, no harmonised rules have yet been established to regulate such a field of arbitration practice.[135]

The Arbitration Committee of the ILA has recognised the need for guidance and development of best practices for arbitrators to investigate the contents of the applicable law.[136] In 2010, the Committee published *the Report on Ascertaining the Contents of the Applicable Law in International Arbitration* to set out basic principles that international arbitrators are encouraged to follow in discerning the substance of the applicable law.[137] Taking into account various arbitration acts, institutional rules and arbitral awards, the Report comments that arbitrators who decide a matter based on a legal norm not invoked by the parties may be subject to the accusation from the parties of exceeding their mandate, even where such an approach would have been acceptable in a court adopting the *jura novit curia* doctrine.[138] The reason for this comment is that arbitrators are not allowed to stray beyond their mandate agreed by the parties.[139] In addition, the Report articulates what it calls 'the most acceptable general approach' for arbitrators to determine the content of the applicable law as follows:

> Arbitrators should primarily rely on the parties to articulate legal issues and to present the law, and disputed legal issues. They should give parties appropriate directions in relation thereto and should give appropriate weight to information so obtained. Arbitrators must through the

den Rijn, Wolters Kluwer, 2020) 153ff; N Teramura, 'Ex Aequo et Bono and Arbitration Theories: an Arbitrator's Subjective Perspective of Fairness as the Final 'Gap-Filler'' (2020) 38 *ASA Bulletin* 350.

133 GB Born, *International Commercial Arbitration*, 3rd edn (Alphen aan den Rijn, Wolters Kluwer, 2020) 2141; N Blackaby and others, *Redfern and Hunter on International Arbitration*, 6th edn, (Oxford, Oxford University Press, 2015) 219; G Kaufmann-Kohler, 'The Arbitrator and the Law: Does He/She Know It? Apply It? How? And a Few More Questions' (2005) 21 *Arbitration International* 631.

134 F De Ly, MW Friedman and LG Radicati di Brozolo, 'International Law Association International Commercial Arbitration Committee's Report and Recommendations on Ascertaining the Contents of the Applicable Law in International Commercial Arbitration' (2010) 26 *Arbitration International* 193, 206.

135 P Baysal and M Atar, 'A Comparative Analysis of Content-of-Laws Inquiry and Its Importance for International Commercial Arbitration', (*Kluwer Arbitration Blog*, 25 January 2020) arbitrationblog.kluwerarbitration.com/2020/01/25/a-comparative-analysis-of-content-of-laws-inquiry-and-its-importance-for-international-commercial-arbitration/ (accessed 6 May 2023).

136 Blackaby and others (n 133) 219.

137 Ly, Friedman and Brozolo (n 134) 193.

138 ibid 214.

139 ibid.

> proceeding develop a sufficient understanding of the applicable law that they can fulfill their mandate to decide the dispute according to law. Arbitrators who attempt to develop legal issues in a strict application of *iura novit curia* approach risk taking the arbitration from the parties and appearing partial. Yet arbitrators who completely fail to seek clarification of legal issues in a strict *laissez faire* approach risk not having sufficient guidance when they go to render an award, or risk making an award that is incorrect on the legal issue in question. Accordingly, arbitrators should inquire about the applicable law within the general parameters of the arbitration defined by the parties and, considering costs, time and relevance of issues, may conduct their own research, provided the parties are given an opportunity to be heard on material that goes meaningfully beyond the parties' submissions.[140]

International arbitrators in Cambodia are possibly willing to adopt this balanced approach when researching applicable law. They are keen to follow the international best practice of arbitration,[141] and global legal experts perceive the approach advocated by the ILA's Report as part of the best practice.[142] Hence, compared with Khmer judges, international arbitrators in Cambodia are with limited authority to invoke their independent investigation in the application of municipal law.

IV. Access to Cambodian Law

Some government ministries and departments whose duties are related to the activities of foreign companies have websites that provide, in English, information on the laws and regulations of Cambodia. For example, the Council for the Development of Cambodia (CDC) has a webpage that aims at helping foreign investors access business-related legislation and government orders.[143] Noting that the translation is unofficial,[144] the page offers in English a comprehensive set of such legislation and orders in the fields of: agriculture, fisheries, general business, construction, customs, development, education, environment, finance, forestry, government, industry, infrastructure, intellectual property rights, investment, labour and employment, land, mining, society special economic zones, tax and accounting, telecommunications, tourism, trade, transportation and logistics, among others. Moreover, the Consumer Protection Competition and Fraud Repression (CCF) Directorate-General of the Ministry of Commerce has a webpage that lists the English language versions of laws, regulations and other legal documents related to its roles and functions. Such laws include the Law on Consumer Protection, Law on the Management of Quality and Safety of Products and

[140] ibid 217–18.

[141] S Sarath, 'Arbitration Rules Under Review', (*Khmer Times*, 28 July 2020) www.khmertimeskh.com/50749327/arbitration-rules-under-review/ (accessed 6 May 2023).

[142] S Loizou, 'Revisiting the "Content-of-Laws" Enquiry in International Arbitration' (2018) 78 *Louisiana Law Review* 811; CP Alberti and DM Bigge, 'Ascertaining the Content of the Applicable Law and Iura Novit Tribunus: Approaches in Commercial and Investment Arbitration' (2015) 70 *Dispute Resolution Journal* 1; J Waincymer, 'International Arbitration and the Duty to Know the Law' (2011) 28 *Journal of International Arbitration* 201.

[143] CDC, 'Laws and Regulations' (2017) cdc.gov.kh/laws-and-regulations/ (accessed 6 May 2023).

[144] Art 5 of the Constitution provides that '[t]he official language and script [of the Kingdom of Cambodia] are Khmer'.

Services, Law on E-Commerce, Law on Trademark and Acts of Dishonest Competition and the Law on Competition.[145] The CDC and the CCF Director-General regularly update their websites to assist foreign businesses in obtaining the latest Cambodian legal instruments.

The ODA partners of Cambodia also maintain websites collecting the non-Khmer language versions of principal legislative documents. For example, the Ministry of Justice of Japan (MOJJ) has a page dedicated to the Legal and Technical Assistance Project implemented by its International Cooperation Department (ICD) and JICA.[146] The unofficial Japanese translation of many laws and regulations of various fields is available on the Japanese language website. In addition, the JICA has a webpage exhibiting materials that Japanese and Cambodian legal experts prepared through the Legal Technical Assistance Project.[147] Such materials include the unofficial Japanese and English versions of the CCP, CC and other relevant bodies of law.[148] Thus, the websites of the ICD and JICA are valuable tools for Japanese investors to learn about Cambodia's statutory documents.

While many online platforms introduce the laws and regulations of the Kingdom in non-Khmer languages, scant platforms touch upon the decisions of the Cambodian courts. A database of the Asian Legal Information Institute (AsianLII), which was developed by the Australasian Legal Information Institute (AustLII), provides the English translation of judgments rendered by the Constitutional Council of Cambodia between 2003 and 2009.[149] Moreover, some project reports authored by JICA legal experts present selected civil court judgments in Japanese.[150] However, the vast majority of court decisions are not available in foreign languages because the courts in Cambodia are not expected to publish their rulings.[151] It was only around the end of 2020 that the MOJC started publishing some judicial decisions as points of reference, thanks to the JICA's long-term support.[152] However, the MOJC's new database contains only a handful of verdicts from civil litigation cases, and these decisions are not regarded as sources of law.[153] In the end, the most plausible method for foreign entities to access Cambodian court decisions is likely to seek assistance from local law firms that maintain close connections with Khmer judicial officers and have the capacity to provide legal services in English.[154]

[145] CCF Director-General, 'Laws & Regulations: Laws, Regulations and Other Legal Documents Related to the Roles and Functions of the CCF Directorate-General' (2021) www.ccfdg.gov.kh/en/laws-regulations/ (accessed 6 May 2023).

[146] MOJJ, 'Cambodia [in Japanese]' (n.d.) www.moj.go.jp/housouken/houso_houkoku_cambo.html (accessed 6 May 2023).

[147] JICA, 'The Legal and Judicial Development Project (Phase 3): Materials' (n.d.) www.jica.go.jp/project/english/cambodia/0701047/materials/index.html (accessed 6 May 2023).

[148] ibid.

[149] Asian Legal Information Institute, 'Constitutional Council of Cambodia' (2006) www.asianlii.org/kh/cases/KHCCl/ (accessed 6 May 2023).

[150] A Kamiki, 'Report on the Investigation of Cambodian Court Judgements [in Japanese]' (2011) *ICD News* 25; Shinoda (n 29).

[151] See section I above.

[152] N Chheng, 'Courts' Decisions Now Published as Reference Source', (*The Phnom Penh Post*, 4 January 2021) www.phnompenhpost.com/national/courts-decisions-now-published-reference-source (accessed 6 May 2023).

[153] ibid.

[154] Teramura (n 1) 218. In contrast, the Arbitration Council has published many past arbitral awards: The Arbitration Council, 'Arbitral Awards' (n.d.) www.arbitrationcouncil.org/arbitral-decision/arbitral-award/ (accessed 6 May 2023).

V. Conclusions and Recommendations: Future Developments in Cambodia and Asia

Cambodian legal norms on the ascertainment and treatment of foreign law have not yet fully developed. This is somewhat inevitable since the Kingdom has no comprehensive set of choice of law rules, and many Khmer lawyers are unfamiliar with PIL. Thus, there has been little discussion on how the courts in Cambodia investigate and apply foreign law in cross-border disputes. Fortunately, however, the treatment of foreign law is not a complete legal vacuum under Cambodian law. As this chapter has demonstrated, the CCP and other statutes regulate how judges are expected to manage major legal issues related to the ascertainment of foreign law. The judges can deal with the complicated and theoretical problems by referring to the official commentaries of the principal statutes and relevant Japanese legal principles on which the statutes are based.

The lack of international insights (apart from those imported via Japanese law) in the treatment of foreign law is possibly due to Cambodia's reluctance to adopt international frameworks governing that area of law. In fact, the country has not signed any international instruments on administrative cooperation for the facilitation of access to foreign law, including but not limited to the European Convention on Information on Foreign Law ('the London Convention 1968'),[155] Inter-American Convention on Proof of and Information on Foreign Law ('the Montevideo Convention 1979')[156] and Convention on Legal Aid and Legal Relations in Civil, Family and Criminal Cases ('the Minsk Convention 1993').[157] Cambodia's lack of interest in these multilateral agreements is not absurd because the country has no territorial links with them. While being open to any country for participation, these Conventions are by-products of regional institutions such as the Council of Europe, the Organisation of American States (OAS) and the Commonwealth of Independent States (CIS), all of which are in the far distance from the Mekong subregion. It is unreasonable to criticise Cambodia for having little interest in those regional arrangements that are not well-known even among legal practitioners based within the geographical reach of those regional organisations.[158] After all, the dearth of globally harmonised rules is linked to Khmer lawyers' lack of passion for pursuing internationally accepted principles on the treatment of foreign law. If so, new formal instruments by the Hague Conference (if any) might change the mindset of Cambodian legal experts, provided the Eurocentric institution could overcome the curious exclusion of Southeast Asian nations from its Access to Foreign Law in Civil and Commercial Matters Conference in 2012.[159] Otherwise, Khmer lawyers will

[155] Council of Europe, 'Treaty Office: Chart of Signatures and Ratifications of Treaty 062' (2023) www.coe.int/en/web/conventions/full-list?module=signatures-by-treaty&treatynum=062 (accessed 6 May 2023).

[156] OAS: Department of International Law, 'Multilateral Treaties: Inter-American Convention on Proof of and Information on Foreign Law' (n.d.) www.oas.org/juridico/English/sigs/b-43.html (accessed 6 May 2023).

[157] UNHCR, 'Convention on Legal Aid and Legal Relations in Civil, Family and Criminal Cases, Adopted in Minsk on 22 January 1993 (The Minsk Convention)' (2022) www.unhcr.org/protection/migration/4de4edc69/convention-legal-aid-legal-relations-civil-family-criminal-cases-adopted.html (accessed 22 November 2022).

[158] Nishitani (n 18) 49–50.

[159] European Commission and Hague Conference on Private International Law, 'Access to Foreign Law in Civil and Commercial Matters: Conclusions and Recommendations' (2012) assets.hcch.net/docs/b093f152-a4b3-4530-949e-65c1bfc9cda1.pdf (accessed 6 May 2023).

find ASEAN-focused instruments on the information on foreign law more useful to absorb external perspectives on the topic, although no such legal documents are available yet.

Probably, the first step for ASEAN to establish new uniformed frameworks for access to the treatment of foreign law is to improve the regional networks currently available. For instance, the Council of ASEAN Chief Justices (CACJ) accredited by the ASEAN Charter 'provides a regular forum for the *Chief Justices* to discuss and exchange views on common issues facing the ASEAN Judiciaries' and 'facilitates judicial cooperation and collaboration to enhance economic growth [in the region]'.[160] However, the CACJ does not aim to promote direct and general communications between judges in different Member States, unlike the International Hague Network of Judges. Moreover, the ASEAN Law Association aspires to be the framework for regional cooperation in exchanging and disseminating information on the laws of the ASEAN states.[161] Nonetheless, its Standing Committee on Legal Information has yet to issue noticeable recommendations on access to foreign law.[162] New initiatives addressing those gaps in the existing regional frameworks will hopefully build the foundation of legal instruments that improve and harmonise the treatment of foreign law in ASEAN. Active participation in such initiatives will help Cambodia shake off its stereotypical reputation for having limited legal certainty and a weak rule of law.[163]

[160] Council of ASEAN Chief Justice, 'About CACJ: Mission Statement' (n.d.) cacj-ajp.org/about-cacj/mission-statement/ (accessed 6 May 2023) (emphasis added).

[161] ASEAN Law Association, 'About ALA: Objectives' (2019) www.aseanlawassociation.org/about-ala/#1571425345512-313f5198-86e5 (accessed 6 May 2023).

[162] ASEAN Law Association, 'About ALA: Standing Committees' (2019) www.aseanlawassociation.org/about-ala/#1572932443790-bff759c2-d61d (accessed 6 May 2023).

[163] World Justice Project (n 37).

11

Myanmar

YUJI TSUTSUMI AND KAZUAKI NISHIOKA

I. Introduction

This chapter will deal with the treatment of foreign law in Myanmar. It will provide an overview of how courts and other judicial authorities apply foreign law in Myanmar. When going through this chapter, it should be kept in mind that the Myanmar legal system inevitably remains in a state of development[1] because it has only emerged from a long period of military rule and initiated a process of opening up to the rest of the world about a decade ago. Furthermore, on 1 February 2021, the military again took over Myanmar's government and declared a state of emergency. According to the military, the state of emergency is to be followed by fresh elections by August 2023. Under these circumstances, the extent to which the laws and practices described in this chapter will continue to apply in Myanmar during the state of emergency and beyond is unknown at this moment. Even if the laws and practices described will remain generally applicable, it may be difficult to say with certainty how tribunals and authorities in Myanmar handle foreign law.

This section first provides an overview of the Myanmar legal and judicial system since it is still unknown, and readers might not be familiar with it. In terms of governance, the Union of Myanmar is divided into seven States (Chin, Kachin, Kayah, Kayin, Mon, Rakhine, and Shan States), seven regions (Ayeyarwady, Bago, Magway, Mandalay, Sagaing, Tanintharyi and Yangon Regions), five self-administered zones (Danu, Kokang, Naga, Pa'O and Pa Laung Self-Administered Zones), one self-administered division (that is, Wa Self-Administered Division) and the Naypyidaw Union Territory.

The legal system of Myanmar is a unique combination of the customary law of the family, codified English common law and recent Myanmar legislation. The principles of English common and statutory law were implanted in Myanmar by the British law codes of the pre-independence India Statutes. These statutes, based on and incorporating English common and statutory law of the time, include the Contract Act, the Evidence Act, and the Transfer of Property Act. Where there is no statute regulating a particular matter, the courts are to apply Myanmar's general law, which is based on English common law adopted and moulded

[1] On a detailed account of the Myanmar legal system, see, eg, NY Kham, 'An Introduction to the Law and Judicial System of Myanmar' CALS Myanmar Working Paper, No 1 March 2014, available at law1.nus.edu.sg/pdfs/cals/working_papers/Myanmar/MWPS001.pdf; Z Thura, 'Myanmar' in A Reyes (ed), *Recognition and Enforcement of Judgments in Civil and Commercial Matters* (Oxford, Hart Publishing, 2019).

by Myanmar case law and embodies the rules of equity, justice and good conscience. Where there is no relevant statutory general law on point, the Myanmar courts must decide the matter according to justice, equity and good conscience.

Courts of the Union consist of: (a) Supreme Court of the Union, High Courts of the Region, High Courts of the State, Courts of the Self-Administered Division, Courts of the Self-Administered Zone, District Courts, Township Courts and the other Courts constituted by law; (b) Courts-Martial; and (c) Constitutional Tribunal of the Union.[2]

II. Private International Law in Myanmar

Private international law traditionally deals with three questions: (direct) jurisdiction,[3] applicable law and recognition and enforcement of foreign judgments.[4] As Professor Briggs wrote in 2015, little of the private international law is to be found in Myanmar legislation.[5] There has been since no noticeable development. Regarding the choice of law rules, there are only a few provisions in specific legal fields, such as company law.[6]

The question arises where other choice of law rules are to be found. One might argue that Myanmar still belongs to the common law family even after the independence, and therefore, the private international law principles in other common law jurisdictions (especially England and India) are applicable in Myanmar. On this, Professor Briggs wrote that 'in the years before the independence, it was more common for judges to make express reference to English law' and that even after the independence, Myanmar courts confirmed, in effect, that the common law rules of private international law were part of Myanmar law.[7] Furthermore, the Union Attorney General of the day, Dr Tun Shin, stated in 2013 that Myanmar law was part of the common law family and that the legal maxims and principles of the common law are part of Myanmar law.[8] If this is the case, the principles in other common law jurisdictions will be applicable or at least provide guidelines. As most court decisions are not public and there are few cases involving foreign elements before the Myanmar courts, however, it is hard – or more or less impossible – to answer whether that is still the case. From one of the authors' own practical experiences, the reality seems to be slightly different from what has been argued.[9] It seems that most judges

[2] Constitution of 2008, s 293.

[3] On this topic, see Thura (n 1).

[4] On the law of foreign judgments, see Z Thura, 'Myanmar' in A Reyes and W Lui (eds), *Direct Jurisdiction: Asian Perspectives* (Oxford, Hart Publishing, 2021).

[5] A Briggs, *Private International Law in Myanmar* (Oxford, Oxford University Press, 2015) 11.

[6] The Myanmar Companies Act 1914 (as amended in 1955) states that the law by which a company may be established under Myanmar law, and provides that the rules which set out the powers and responsibilities of the various organs of a company formed under Myanmar law.

[7] Briggs (n 5) 11. He referred to several judgments, for instance, *Ramaswamy Iyengar v Velayudhan Chettiar BLR* (1952) SC 25; *State Bank of India v Collector of Rangoon BLR* (1961) HC 336. Burma Law Reports (BLR) is available on the website of the Myanmar Law Library (www.myanmar-law-library.org).

[8] Reported in *The New Light of Myanmar*, Vol 20, No 296, 10 February 2013. Note that he made this statement in general context and he did not specifically refer to private international law.

[9] Note that recent Myanmar courts do not necessarily follow the principles in other common law jurisdictions in other legal fields (such as tort law) and one can see a deviation from it in a daily practice. Considering this development, one may say that a Myanmar court does not follow the common law principles anymore.

do not consider the common law principles and preceding case laws, not only case laws in other common law jurisdictions but also cases in Myanmar. Nevertheless, from a practical perspective, one is still well-advised to consider relevant principles in other common law jurisdictions just in case. This chapter will not go further in regard to each choice of law rule in Myanmar.[10]

Regarding arbitration, Myanmar is a signatory to the Geneva Protocol on Arbitration Clauses of 1923[11] and the Geneva Convention on the Execution of Foreign Arbitral Awards of 1927[12] as well as a party to the New York Convention on the Recognition and Enforcement of Foreign Arbitral Awards 1958[13] which includes a few choice of law rules. It has translated the New York Convention legal instrument into the domestic and private international law of Myanmar.[14] Apart from these, Myanmar has not ratified international conventions that lead to the determination of the applicable law in specific instances involving foreign and international elements.

III. Status of Choice of Law Rules

There is no provision or court decision on the status of choice of law rules in Myanmar. Unlike civil law jurisdictions, common law jurisdictions traditionally do not pass an act or statute that predetermines the rules on the application of foreign law. Instead, their courts determine the applicable choice of law rules on a case-by-case basis. If Myanmar remains in the common law family (it seems to be the case), the principles in common law jurisdictions are applicable in Myanmar (that is, the Myanmar courts treat foreign law as a matter of fact). Hence, the parties must invoke and plead the foreign law and prove its contents. The judicial authorities have no duty to apply foreign law on their own motion.

Nevertheless, it is very difficult to say whether Myanmar courts of the moment, in practice, apply a relevant choice of law rule in cross-border cases. The reason is that there is no written guidance for the courts. However, it does not mean that one cannot choose foreign law. Instead, one may choose and apply foreign law in an international commercial contract to govern the contract, and such a choice will be respected in the arbitration (see section V).

[10] In this case, each chapter of Briggs (n 5) will be helpful.

[11] Protocol on Arbitration Clauses (Treaty No 3 of 3 July 1928). This instrument deals with the recognition of the validity of an arbitration agreement by contracting states and does not directly deal with recognition and enforcement of a foreign arbitral award. Art 3 simply provides: 'Each Contracting State undertakes to ensure the execution by its authorities and in accordance with the provisions of its national laws of arbitral awards made in its own territory under the preceding articles.'

[12] Convention on the Execution of Foreign Arbitral Awards of 26 September 1927 (Treaty No 11 of 18 August 1952).

[13] Convention on the Recognition and Enforcement of Foreign Arbitral Awards of 10 June 1958 (Treaty No 10 of 14 July 1961).

[14] Arbitration Law No 5/2016 (Arbitration Law). An unofficial English translation of this act is available at www.myanmarlegalservices.com/wp-content/uploads/2021/01/Myanmar-Arbitration-LawUnofficial-English-Translation-140116_1827166_1.pdf. See also section V.

IV. Foreign Law before Judicial Authorities

A. Nature of Foreign Law

The nature of foreign law has not been expressed until now in Myanmar. It is thus unclear how Myanmar courts treat foreign law. In this regard, the very important question is again whether Myanmar remains in the common law family. As well-known, the common law regards foreign law as a matter of fact. If Myanmar remains in the common law family, the parties seeking to rely on foreign law need to invoke, plead and prove the contents of foreign law.[15] Then, based on the parties' pleadings, Myanmar courts will make a finding on this. In this case, there is no principle of *iura novit curia* (ie, the principle that the judge knows the law) known in civil law jurisdictions.[16]

As above-mentioned, the parties must prove the contents of foreign law. Suppose that the parties fail to sufficiently prove the contents of a particular foreign law to the court's satisfaction. In this case, the Myanmar courts are highly likely to apply the Myanmar law (namely, the *lex fori*) as other common law jurisdictions.[17] This is because the judge has neither the power nor the duty to apply foreign law *ex officio*. In other words, the courts are unfamiliar with foreign law and must be informed by the parties of its contents.

If Myanmar courts followed the civil law approach (that is, treat foreign law as a matter of law), the courts would be called upon to ascertain and apply foreign law on their own motion. Nevertheless, the parties are allowed to submit documents as to the contents of foreign law, and courts can request them to do so. After all, parties would play an important role in ascertaining the contents of foreign law, regardless of whether foreign law is treated as a matter of fact or law.

B. Ascertainment of Foreign Law

As mentioned above, the Myanmar courts make a finding based on evidence adduced by the parties if they follow the common law approach. The parties must plead the foreign law and prove its contents in accordance with Myanmar procedural laws. Myanmar Evidence Act, section 38 is relevant. It stipulates that:

> When the Court has to form an opinion as to a law of any country, any statement of such law contained in a book purporting to be printed or published under the authority of the Government of such country and to contain any such law, and any report of a ruling of the Courts of such country contained in a book purporting to be a report of such rulings, is relevant.

It is evident from the wording of section 38 that the rule extends only to laws and law reports but will not extend to textbooks or articles.[18]

[15] Briggs (n 5) 73.

[16] See other chapters of most civil law jurisdictions in the book.

[17] Briggs (n 5) 72. Dicey, Morris and Collins, *Conflict of Laws Vol 1*, 14th edn (London, Sweet and Maxwell, 2006) 255. See other chapters of common law jurisdictions in the book.

[18] Briggs (n 5) 73.

Furthermore, section 45 of the Evidence Act provides that:

> When the Court has to form an opinion upon a point of foreign law, or of science, or art, or as to identity of handwriting or finger impressions, the opinions upon that point of persons specially skilled in such foreign law, science or art, or in questions as to identity of handwriting or finger impressions, are relevant facts. Such persons are called experts.

When the parties plead a foreign law and adduce evidence about that foreign law, such as expert opinions, the judges will evaluate such evidence. Both institutions and individuals can provide legal information. In respect of qualification, there is no explicit regulation under Myanmar law. If legal information is provided by individuals and institutions such as law firms, it does not bind the judicial authorities. To the contrary, it is understood that legal information provided by government departments binds the courts in practice.

Courts can freely assess the reliability of the information on foreign law provided by institutions or individuals because there is no written mechanism, procedure or guideline for this purpose.

C. Costs

The Code of Civil Procedure, section 35 sets out that:

> (1) Subject to such conditions and limitations as may be prescribed, and to the provisions of any law for the time being in force, the costs of and incident to all suits shall be in the discretion of the Court, and the Court shall have full power to determine by whom or out of what property and to what extent such costs are to be paid, and to give all necessary directions for the purposes aforesaid. The fact that the Court has no jurisdiction to try the suit shall be no bar to the exercise of such powers.
>
> (2) Where the Court directs that any costs shall not follow the event, the Court shall state its reasons in writing.
>
> (3) The Court may give interest on costs at any rate not exceeding six per cent. per annum, and such interest shall be added to the costs and shall be recoverable as such.

Accordingly, the Myanmar courts will decide who and to what extent bears the costs.

D. Interpretation and Application of Foreign Law

No provision stipulates how courts should interpret and apply foreign law. Furthermore, to the authors' knowledge, there has been, since the independence, no published case law in which Myanmar courts applied foreign law. It is thus unclear how Myanmar courts interpret and apply foreign law. Generally speaking, the judges are unfamiliar with foreign law as they are trained according to the Myanmar legal system. That said, when interpreting foreign law, the Myanmar courts will interpret it the same way as the courts of the country of origin. Hence, expert evidence can be especially helpful. Where there is a legal lacuna in foreign law (namely, a point that has not been addressed or settled in the law), a party may prove what a foreign court would likely decide. A foreign expert is expected to show how the courts of that foreign country should handle such a point. As above-mentioned, if the parties fail to prove to the satisfaction of the judges the contents of foreign law, Myanmar courts will apply

Myanmar law following the traditional common law approach (ie, assuming that foreign law is the same as the *lex fori*).

E. Judicial Review/Appeal

The application of foreign law is not only relevant in first-instance proceedings but also appeal proceedings. Per Myanmar procedural law, Code of Civil Procedure, sections 96 to 112, a party may appeal to higher courts (including the Supreme Court) on the basis that the lower court erroneously applied choice of law rules. An appeal may lie from an original decree passed ex parte.[19] No appeal shall lie from a decree passed by the court with the parties' consent.[20] To file a second appeal (appeals from appellate decrees), one must satisfy the requirements in sections 96–99. For instance, one needs to have any of the grounds in section 100.[21] Section 100 provides that:

> (1) Save where otherwise expressly provided in the body of this Code of by any other law for the time being in force, an appeal shall lie to the High Court from every decree passed in appeal by any Court subordinate to the High Court, on any of the following grounds, namely: -
>
> (a) the decision being contrary to law or to some usage having the force of law; the decision having failed to determine some material issue of law or usage having the force of law;
>
> (b) a substantial error or defect in the procedure provided by this Code or by any other law for the time being in force, which may possibly have produced error or defect in the decision of the case upon the merits:
>
> (c) in a suit relating to immovable property or to any right or interest in immovable property, and in any other suit where the amount or value of the subject matter of the original suit exceeds Rs. 500 any ground which would be a good ground of appeal if it the decree had been passed in an original suit whenever the decree of the appellate Court varies or reverses, otherwise than as to costs, the decree of the original Court.
>
> (2) An appeal may lie under this section from an appellate decree passed *ex pante*.

Regarding the power of the High Court, section 103 sets out that

> [I]n any second appeal, the High Court may, if the evidence on the record is sufficient, determine any issue of fat necessary for the disposal of the appeal which has not been determined by the lower appellate Court or which has been wrongly determined by such Court by reason of any illegality, omission, error, or defect such as is referred to in sub-section(1) of section 100.

To file an appeal to the Supreme court, too, one needs to fulfil the prescribed requirements.[22] Section 109 provides that:

> Subject to such rules as may, from time to time, be made by [the Supreme Court] regarding appeals from [other Courts in the Union on Burma] and to the provisions hereinafter contained, an appeal shall lie to [the Supreme Court] –

[19] Code of Civil Procedure, s 96(2).

[20] ibid, s 96(3).

[21] ibid, s 101. In addition, s 102 stipulates that 'No second appeal shall lie in any suit of the nature cognizable by Courts of Small Causes, when the amount or value of the subject-matter of the original suit does not exceed five hundred rupees.'

[22] Code of Civil Procedure, ss 109–111.

(a) from any decree or final order passed on appeal by the High Court or by any other Court of final appellate jurisdiction;
(b) from any decree or final order passed by the High Court in the exercise of original civil jurisdiction; and
(c) from any decree or order when the case, as hereinafter provided, is certified to be a fit one for appeal to [the Supreme Court].

In the cases in clauses (a) and (b) of section 109,

> the amount or value of the subject-matter of the suit in the Court of first-instance must be ten thousand rupees or upwards, and the amount or value of the subject-matter in dispute on appeal to the Supreme Court must be the same sum or upwards, or the decree or final order must involve, directly or indirectly, some claim or question to or respecting property of like amount or value, and where the decree or final order appealed from affirms the decision of the Court immediately below the Court passing such decree or final order, the appeal must involve some substantial question of law.[23]

It should be noted that notwithstanding anything contained in section 109, no appeal is permitted in certain situations.[24]

V. Foreign Law before Other Authorities

In Myanmar, administrative or non-judicial authorities may recognise or apply foreign law based on documentary evidence issued by a foreign competent authority.

Arbitral tribunals seated in Myanmar may apply foreign law to determine the merits of a case referred to them. Note that Myanmar Arbitration law has different regulations for the law applicable to the substance of disputes. Section 32 of the Arbitration law stipulates that:

(a) If the place of arbitration is the Republic of the Union of Myanmar:

(1) In domestic arbitration, the arbitral tribunal shall decide the dispute which to be settled by arbitration in accordance with the substantive law in force of the Republic of the Union of Myanmar.
(2) In international commercial arbitration:
    (aa) The arbitral tribunal shall decide the dispute in accordance with such rules of law as are chosen by the parties;
    (bb) Any designation of the law or legal system of a given State shall be construed, unless otherwise agreed by the parties, as directly referring to the substantive law of that State and not to its conflict of laws rules;
    (cc) Failing any designation as per subsection clause (AA) by the parties, the arbitral tribunal shall apply the rules of law which it considers applicable.

(b) The arbitral tribunal shall decide the dispute with justice, equity and good conscience if the parties have expressly authorized it to do so.

(c) In all cases, the arbitral tribunal shall decide in accordance with the terms of the contract and shall take into account the usages of the trade applicable to the transaction.

[23] ibid, s 110.
[24] ibid, s 111.

It is evident from the text that disputes in domestic arbitration are always subject to Myanmar law, while disputes in international commercial arbitration may be governed by foreign law. In the arbitration context, there is no rigorous reference system as in Myanmar court proceedings. However, arbitrators typically require the parties to tender evidence of and make submissions on the foreign law applicable to a case, much as judges in Myanmar court proceedings. Parties, therefore, often submit expert reports on the law applicable to their dispute. For other forms of alternative dispute resolutions (ADR), such as mediation, expert determination or adjudication, Myanmar has no specific guidance on whether and how to ascertain and apply foreign law.

VI. Access to Myanmar Law

Most legislation is open to the public on various platforms, such as the Myanmar Law Information System (MLIS) run by the Ministry of Legal Affairs,[25] the relevant ministry websites (the Ministry of Commerce only announces the relevant laws and notifications on their website[26]), the Supreme Court website,[27] and databases (for instance, Myanmar Law Library[28]). The MLIS provides most Myanmar laws in Burmese, including the Constitution, Union Laws, Region or State Laws, and Self-Administered Division or Zone Laws. It also provides English translations of some legislation. In addition, the official website of the Supreme Court and Myanmar Law Library provide law reports and case laws, in addition to relevant laws, rules, regulations and notifications.

It must be borne in mind that no law prescribes how the government makes its laws public. Also, there are no specific criteria to decide whether to make legal information public. In fact, when the State Peace and Development Council was drafting the 2008 Constitution, relevant information was not made public. Furthermore, most government websites do not necessarily provide up-to-date information. Due to the lack of related laws, rules and regulations, it is unclear when the government has to make legal information public. The reality is that the government may make information on law, amendatory and subordinate law public when the law is enacted. Also, the government may announce a draft law to the public at an initial stage before they finalise and announce the final version.

It should be noted that all government departments typically use the Burmese language as it is the official language under section 450 of the 2008 Constitution.[29] However, the ministries dealing with foreign investment-related matters announce relevant legal information in English mostly. In addition to the MLIS, some private databases provide English translations of legislation and case laws and legal information in English on recent developments.[30]

[25] www.mlis.gov.mm/?locale=en_US.
[26] www.commerce.gov.mm/.
[27] www.unionsupremecourt.gov.mm/.
[28] www.myanmar-law-library.org/law-library/.
[29] Constitution of 2008, s 450 reads as 'Myanmar language is the official language.'
[30] Eg, www.myanmar-law-library.org/ (Myanmar Law Library) and www.commonlii.org/resources/239.html (Common LII).

VII. Access to Foreign Law: Future Development in Myanmar and Asia

Myanmar has signed some international treaties such as some Bilateral Investment Treaties (BITs) (including Agreement between the Government of the Republic of Singapore and the Government of the Republic of the Union of Myanmar on the Promotion and Protection of Investments ('Myanmar-Singapore BIT'), Agreement between the Government of the State of Israel and the Government of the Republic of the Union of Myanmar for the Reciprocal Promotion and Protection of Investments ('Israel-Myanmar BIT'), Agreement between the Government of Japan and the Government of the Republic of the Union of Myanmar for the Liberalisation, Promotion and Protection of Investment ('Japan-Myanmar BIT')),[31] The World Trade Organization (WTO) Agreement,[32] Convention on the Elimination of All Forms of Discrimination against Women (CEDAW)[33] and Geneva conventions of 1949 (I–IV).[34] However, on the topic of treatment of and/or access to foreign law, Myanmar is not a party to any international or regional instruments. That said, it seems that the Myanmar courts usually do not have difficulties in ascertaining the contents of foreign law. This is because they are said to follow the common law practice (that is, regarding foreign law as a matter of law), and, therefore, the parties seeking to rely on foreign law need to plead it and prove its contents. As Myanmar's approach is relatively straightforward and simple, there seem to be a few points to be improved in Myanmar (if any).

To the contrary, other states in Asia may have difficulties in ascertaining the contents of Myanmar law because there are scarce materials in English about Myanmar law (including translations). Considering the fact that there is no Asian or international scheme for access to foreign law, the Myanmar Government would have to improve the situation itself. However, it is not an easy task due to a lack of apparently human and financial resources. In light of this situation, from a Myanmar perspective, it would be an attractive and effective way to establish a regional or international institution that can assist national courts in ascertaining the contents of foreign law or establish a regional or international framework that enables national courts to communicate with foreign judges about the contents of foreign law and individual cases. In this regard, the European Convention on Information of Foreign Law[35] might be a good model for us. According to the Convention, a Contracting State may request information from other states' relevant authority.

VIII. Conclusions

It is generally understood that Myanmar belongs to the common law family and follows the common law principles. If this is the case, the treatment of foreign law is relatively straightforward. Foreign law is regarded as a matter of fact. Therefore, the parties seeking to

[31] investmentpolicy.unctad.org/international-investment-agreements/countries/144/myanmar.
[32] www.wto.org/english/thewto_e/countries_e/myanmar_e.htm.
[33] indicators.ohchr.org/.
[34] ihl-databases.icrc.org/applic/ihl/ihl.nsf/vwTreatiesByCountrySelected.xsp?xp_countrySelected=MM.
[35] rm.coe.int/1680072314.

rely on foreign law have to invoke, plead and prove the foreign law and its contents. If the parties fail to prove it to the court's satisfaction, the court will apply Myanmar law. However, there have been no court decisions after the independence in which the Myanmar courts applied foreign law. As a result, it is unclear whether the Myanmar courts, in fact, follow this common law practice. Unfortunately, we need to wait and see how they treat foreign law. That said, from a practical perspective, one is well-advised to consider relevant principles in other common law jurisdictions.

Regarding access to Myanmar law, the Myanmar Government is strongly expected to take measures (for instance, enhancing their existing databases) to make their laws and regulations more easily accessible for foreign courts, business people and investors. The fact that there are some court decisions in other Asian jurisdictions in which local courts were unable to ascertain the contents of Myanmar law[36] clearly speaks for the need.

[36] Judgment of Tokyo District Court, 28 December 2015, 2015WLJPCA12288002.

12

Philippines

LEMUEL DIDULO LOPEZ

I. Introduction: Status of Choice of Laws Rules

A. The Philippine Approach to Choice of Law

The Philippine approach to conflict of laws reflects the civil law and common law influences to its legal system. Hence, conflict of law rules are found in both statutes and cases. For example, while several key choice of law rules are found in the Philippine Civil Code[1] and other legislations,[2] certain rules are also found in case law, like the choice of law rules for torts[3] and on the essential validity of contracts.[4] Furthermore, common law's adversarial system has shaped the Philippine rules of procedure and evidence which in turn explain why courts cannot take judicial notice of foreign law, why foreign law is treated as fact, and why parties need to plead and prove foreign law. Furthermore, key principles of private international law like 'comity, utility and convenience of nations'[5] also guide courts in their approach to foreign law.[6]

The starting point of whether a court would apply a choice of law rule is whether a 'conflicts' situation exists.

> Where the factual antecedents satisfactorily establish the existence of a foreign element … the problem herein could present a 'conflicts' case. A factual situation that cuts across territorial lines and is affected by the diverse laws of two or more states is said to contain a 'foreign element'.[7]
>
> The foreign element may simply consist in the fact that one of the parties to a contract is an alien or has a foreign domicile, or that a contract between nationals of one State involves properties situated in another State.[8]

[1] Eg, Civil Code 1950 (Philippines), Arts 14, 15, 16, 17, 815–817, 1039 ('Civil Code').

[2] Eg, Commonwealth Act No 65 1936 (Philippines), s 2 ('Carriage of Goods by Sea Act'); Family Code of the Philippines 1987, Art 26.

[3] *Saudi Arabian Airlines v Court of Appeals* (1998) 297 SCRA 469,492 ('Saudi Arabian Airlines'); *Alcala Vda de Alcañeses v Alcañeses*, GR No 187847, 30 June 2021.

[4] *Philippine Export and Foreign Loan Guarantee Corporation v VP Eusebio Construction Inc* (2008) 434 SCRA 202, 215.

[5] *Mijares v Ranada* (2005) 455 SCRA 397, 407 ('Mijares').

[6] *Aznar v Garcia* (1963) 7 SCRA 95, 107; *Pilapil v Ibay-Somera* (1989) 174 SCRA 653, 666.

[7] *Saudi Arabian Airlines* (n 3) 484–85.

[8] ibid.

Significantly, even when parties have not pleaded the need to apply a choice of law rule, if the court deems that there is a 'conflicts' situation, it should still be able to apply a choice of law rule. In *Ancheta v Guersey-Dalaygon*, the petitioner, who is the administrator of the deceased's estate, deliberately failed to allege and prove that Maryland laws apply to the probate of Maryland-domicile Audrey Guersey's will.[9] Despite this failure, the Supreme Court proceeded to apply the choice of law rule while pointing out the need to apply the nationality principle to the deceased's testamentary rights.[10] Given that Guersey was domiciled in Maryland, it applied Maryland law not Philippine law.[11]

After a 'conflicts' situation has been determined, the next step is characterisation. '[B]efore a choice [of law] can be made, it is necessary for us to determine under what category a certain set of facts or rules fall. This process is known as "characterization", or the "doctrine of qualification".'[12] 'The purpose of "characterization" is to enable the forum to select the proper law'[13] to resolve the dispute.

After the 'characterisation' of the dispute, the court would now be able to choose the applicable choice of law rule. However, whether the court should apply a certain choice of law rule may depend on whether it is mandatory or not. Unfortunately, in the Philippines, whether or not a certain legal rule is mandatory or discretionary would largely depend on the language of the provision. This is especially true because there is no clear definition or way to distinguish mandatory laws (also known as prohibitory laws) from those which are discretionary or facultative. There is no problem if the language of the provision clearly shows that the application is mandatory. However, it is harder to determine when the language is ambiguous. In these instances, one must resort to the rules of statutory interpretation and case law. For example, words like 'shall' have been interpreted to connote mandatory application.[14] As such, like any legal rule, whether the application of choice of law rules is mandatory or facultative would depend on the language of the particular choice of law rule.

As mentioned, choice of law rules are also found in cases. Because the doctrine of precedents means that subsequent cases should follow the rule established in earlier cases, the practical effect is that these choice of law rules found in earlier cases will be applied in subsequent cases. This may have the effect akin to a statutory mandatory law.

Nonetheless, one must note that even when the language of the choice of law rule appears mandatory, a Philippine court may still end up not applying the rule because of characterisation. In *Gibbs v Government of the Philippine Islands* ('*Gibbs*'),[15] the Supreme Court was faced with the need to characterise the dispute involving real property in the Philippines as either a matter under property law or succession. Based on the facts, if the case would be characterised as a dispute involving property law, given that the land is in the Philippines, Philippine law would apply. On the other hand, if the case is characterised as an issue of succession, the law to be applied is foreign law. One must note that the applicable choice

[9] *Ancheta v Guersey-Dalaygon* (2006) 490 SCRA 140, 155 ('Ancheta').
[10] See Civil Code, Arts 16, 1039.
[11] *Ancheta* (n 9) 152.
[12] *Saudi Arabian Airlines* (n 3) 471.
[13] ibid.
[14] *Codoy v Calugay* (1999) 312 SCRA 333, 342.
[15] *Gibbs v Government of the Philippine Islands* (1933) 59 Phil 293.

of law rules then for both property and succession cases appear to be mandatory. In *Gibbs*, the Court chose to characterise the facts as falling under succession law, thus resolving the dispute using the law of California.

B. Exceptions to the Application of Foreign Law

Even if the choice of law process chooses foreign law, there are several instances when the chosen foreign law would not be applied. First is when the application of the foreign law or its result would be contrary to public order or public policy,[16] or when public interest requires it. 'It is a conflict of law policy that foreign law ordinarily applicable will not be applied if to do so would violate domestic public policy.'[17] In *Pakistan International Airways v Ople* ('*Pakistan Airlines*'), the Supreme Court refused to apply Pakistani law as provided in the choice of law provision in the employment contract. This result is contrary to the choice of law rule that the chosen law of the parties would be the law applicable to the contract. The Court said,

> counter-balancing the principle of autonomy of contracting parties is the equally general rule that provisions of applicable law, especially provisions relating to matters affected with public policy, are deemed written into the contract.[18]

The Court noted, 'employment contracts of overseas Filipino workers is characterised as heavily impressed with public interest'. 'Put a little differently, the governing principle is that parties may not contract away applicable provisions of law especially peremptory provisions dealing with matters heavily impressed with public interest.'[19] This result also follows the rule in contracts that terms and conditions which are contrary to law, morals, good customs, public order or public policy are void.[20] Hence, when the choice of law provision, like any contractual provision, is found to be contrary to public policy, like in *Pakistan Airlines*, the same would be considered void. By voiding the choice of law clause, the court may end up applying domestic law to the contract because public interest requires it.

Similarly, in *Marcaida v Aglubat*, the Supreme Court stressed that since the Philippines follows the nationality principle as regards the 'family rights and duties, or to the status, condition and legal capacity of persons,

> [i]t is quite obvious then that the status of adoption, once created under the proper foreign law, will be recognized in this country except where public policy or the interests of its inhabitants forbid its enforcement and demand the substitution of the *lex fori*.[21]

Likewise, even if the foreign divorce may be valid under foreign law, but 'not being itself valid and enforceable under Philippine law for being contrary to Philippine public policy and public law', like when the divorce was procured by spouses who are both Filipino

[16] Eg, *Tenchavez v Escaño* (1965) 15 SCRA 355, 362; *Mijares* (n 5) 420–1; *Bankruptcy Estate of Mitich v Mercantile Insurance Co, Inc*, GR Nos 238041 & 238502, 15 February 2022 ('Bankruptcy Estate of Mitich').

[17] *Bankruptcy Estate of Mitich* (n 16).

[18] *Pakistan International Airlines Corp v Ople* (1990) 190 SCRA 90, 99.

[19] ibid.

[20] *Civil Code*, Arts 1409,1306.

[21] *Marcaida v Aglubat* (1967) 21 SCRA 1033, 1038.

citizens, the consequences of such foreign divorce, including an agreement to dissolve the conjugal property, would not also be legally valid and enforceable under Philippine law.[22] In that sense, the foreign law allowing divorce and dissolution of conjugal partnership would not be given effect in the Philippines because its application would be contrary to Philippine public policy.

Although the general reason for the non-application of foreign law is based on public policy grounds, the court may nonetheless express such refusal in several ways. For example, the foreign law may be described as a law which 'work(s) undeniable injustice to the citizens or residents of the forum'.[23] Likewise, the court may describe the foreign law as 'obviously unjust [which] negates the fundamental principles of Conflict of Laws',[24] or which is 'noxious to our constitutional values'[25] or 'some of its provisions are contrary to the Constitution and the labor laws of the Philippines'.[26] Similarly, the foreign law may be described as that which 'violates some fundamental principle of justice, good morals, or some deep-rooted tradition of society'.[27]

In the Philippines, foreign law which is contrary to good morals or good customs (ie, *contra bonos mores*) would also be refused. This reflects the general policy in several provisions of the Philippine Civil Code.[28] In Article 17,

> prohibitive laws concerning persons, their acts or property, and those which have for their object public order, public policy and good customs shall not be rendered ineffective by laws or judgments promulgated, or by determinations or conventions agreed upon in a foreign country.

Similarly, whilst parties are given the freedom to stipulate in their contracts, including a choice of law clause in favour of foreign law, when such contractual stipulation is contrary to good morals or good customs, the same shall also be rendered void.[29] In any case, good customs or good morals are often understood to be subsumed within the concept of public policy or public interest since there is no clear distinction between public order, public policy, public interest, good customs or good morals. Hence, a foreign law which is contrary to good customs or morals may not be applied on the ground of being contrary to public order, public policy, or public interest.[30]

Likewise, Philippine law will always apply in property law disputes involving properties within the Philippines. Article 16 of the Philippine Civil Code states: '[r]eal property as well as personal property is subject to the law of the country where it is stipulated.' Nonetheless, in *Laurel v Garcia*, which involves the sale of the Philippine Government's Roppongi property in Tokyo, the Philippine Supreme Court dismissed the possibility of applying Japanese law in determining whether the property could be sold.[31] The Court laid down the requirements of determining a conflict of laws situation when the real property in dispute is located overseas.

[22] *Lavadia v Heirs of Luna* (2014) 730 SCRA 376, 392.
[23] *Bank of America v American Realty Corp* (1999) 321 SCRA 659, 675.
[24] ibid.
[25] *Mijares* (n 5) 372–99.
[26] *Industrial Personnel & Management Services, Inc v De Vera* (2016) 785 SCRA 562, 586.
[27] *Bankruptcy Estate of Mitich* (n 16).
[28] See *Industrial Personnel & Management Services* (n 24) 582–3.
[29] Civil Code, Arts 1409, 1306.
[30] See, eg, *Bankruptcy Estate of Mitich* (n 16); *Arca v Javier* (1954) 95 Phil 579.
[31] *Laurel v Garcia* (1990) 187 SCRA 797, 810.

> A conflict of law situation arises only when: (1) There is a dispute over the *title* or *ownership* of an immovable, such that the capacity to take and transfer immovables, the formalities of conveyance, the essential validity and effect of the transfer, or the interpretation and effect of a conveyance, are to be determined … and (2) A foreign law on land ownership and its conveyance is asserted to conflict with a domestic law on the same matters.[32]

In this case, the Court ruled that there is no conflict of laws situation because the ownership of Tokyo property by the Philippine Government is not in dispute. Rather, the Court characterised the dispute as not involving property law but the government officials' authority to sell state-owned property and the validity of the procedures that they have adopted to effect its sale. Absent a 'conflicts' situation, Philippine law alone would apply.

Philippine courts would also refuse to apply foreign law, which is public law, fiscal or administrative in nature. In *Parado v Republic*, the Supreme Court reminded that no foreign law should be read into the naturalisation laws of the Philippines. 'It would be a brazen encroachment upon the sovereign will and power of the people of this Republic.'[33] As regards matters of taxation, Philippine law would apply including as regards the situs of the asset or activity which is subject to tax. In *Aces Philippines Cellular Satellite Corporation v Commissioner of Internal Revenue*, the Supreme Court emphasised that the fact that

> the main asset is situated in outer space cannot be determinative of the income source and the situs thereof.[34] [T]he Court cannot simply incorporate a foreign law into our legal system …. It is fundamental that the power to determine the nature, object, extent, coverage, and situs of taxation tax rests with [Philippine] Congress.[35]

Although the Supreme Court has yet to decide on this matter, Filipino scholars[36] are also of the opinion that Philippine courts would not apply foreign law which are criminal or penal in nature. These scholars have cited American cases,[37] which Philippine courts have a strong tendency to follow. Furthermore, one must note that penal laws are considered to be imbued with strong public interest such that the accused in criminal proceedings is indicted for a wrong done against the public. In the Philippines, '[t]he test in determining if a statute is penal is whether a penalty is imposed for the punishment of a wrong to the public or for the redress of an injury to an individual.'[38]

Last, Philippine courts would also refuse to apply the foreign procedural laws.

> Ultimately, matters of remedy and procedure such as those relating to the service of summons or court process upon the defendant, the authority of counsel to appear and represent a defendant and the formal requirements in a decision are governed by the *lex fori* or the internal law of the forum.[39]

What is procedural or not, however, may be difficult to determine. In *Cadalin v Administrator, Philippine Overseas Employment Administration* ('*Cadalin*'), the issue was whether to

[32] ibid 810–1.
[33] *Parado v Republic* (1950) 86 Phil 340, 344.
[34] *Aces Philippines Cellular Satellite Corp. v Commissioner of Internal Revenue*, GR No 226680, 30 August 2022.
[35] ibid.
[36] Eg, J Coquia and E Aguiling-Pangalangan, *Conflict of Laws* (Manila, Central Professional Books, 2000) 152; J Salonga, *Private International Law* (San Antoni, Regina Publishing Company, 1995) 129.
[37] Eg, *The Antelope* (1925) 23 US 123.
[38] *Buenaseda v Flavier* (1993) 226 SCRA 645, 652.
[39] *Asiavest Merchant Bankers (M) Berhad v Court of Appeals* (2001) 361 SCRA 489, 502 ('Asiavest').

characterise the foreign law on prescription or statute of limitation as 'substantive' or 'procedural'.[40] The court emphasised that

> [a]s a general rule, a foreign procedural law will not be applied in the forum. Procedural matters, such as service of process, joinder of actions, period and requisites for appeal, and so forth, are governed by the laws of the forum.[41]

Prescription or statute of limitation, however, was described as *sui generis* 'in the sense that it may be viewed either as procedural or substantive, depending on the characterization given such a law'.[42] Unfortunately, in *Cadalin*, the court did not proceed to qualify the Bahrain law as either procedural or substantive because it noted that the Philippines has a 'borrowing statute' which directs the application of the foreign statute of limitations to the pending claims based on a foreign law. Eventually, however, the court refused to enforce the Bahrain law on prescription as it is obnoxious to the Philippines' public policy. Again, this approach strongly reflects the attitude towards the employment contracts of overseas Filipino workers which is deemed as heavily impressed with public interest.

One must also note that foreign law may not be applied because it was not pleaded and proven by the party relying on foreign law. In this instance, the principle of processual presumption may apply, which means that in these instances, Philippine courts would presume that the content of the pleaded foreign law is identical or similar to Philippine law; thus, resulting to courts applying Philippine law to the facts of the case.

II. Foreign Law before Judicial Authorities

A. Nature of Foreign Law

In the Philippines, foreign law is a question of fact. Notably, this law-as-fact treatment of foreign law gives rise to two important requirements: (1) foreign law must be pleaded; and (2) foreign law must be proven in evidence. Under Rule 8, section 1 of the Rules of Court, a party should state '... a plain, concise and direct statement of the ultimate facts, including the evidence on which the party pleading relies for his claim or defense, as the case may be'. Hence, if a party is relying on foreign law for their claim or defence, they have to state this in their pleading. 'A foreign law is considered to be pleaded if there is an allegation in the pleading about the existence of the foreign law, its import and legal consequence on the event or transaction in issue.'[43] Failure to plead the foreign law would allow the court not to apply 'foreign law' even if the choice of law process points to the application of foreign law.[44] Furthermore, the party who is relying on foreign law should provide evidence of foreign law. This is because the party who wants to have a foreign law applied to a dispute or case has the burden of proving the foreign law.[45]

[40] *Cadalin v Administrator, Philippine Overseas Employment Administration* (1994) 238 SCRA 721.
[41] ibid 761.
[42] ibid.
[43] *Wildvalley Shipping Co, Ltd v Court of Appeals* (2000) 342 SCRA 213, 223 ('*Wildvalley*').
[44] ibid.
[45] *ATCI Overseas Corporation v Echin* (2010) 632 SCRA 528, 534 ('*ATCI Overseas Corporation*').

B. Ascertainment of Foreign Law

i. The Need for Parties to Plead and Prove Foreign Law

Significantly, the Philippines does not take judicial notice of foreign laws.[46] Foreign law is not among the matters which the court may admit without the introduction of evidence.[47] As such 'Australian marital laws are not among those matters that judges are supposed to know by reason of their judicial function.'[48] Hence, the '*iura novit curia*' ('the court knows the law') principle does not apply. The Philippine approach stems from the adversarial nature of litigation in the Philippines which requires parties to prove their respective claims or defences. '[T]he party who wants to have a foreign law applied to a dispute or case has the burden of proving the foreign law.'[49] Notably, pursuant to this burden of proof, a party is required to present evidence on the facts in issue necessary to establish their claim or defence by the amount of evidence required by law.[50] Since foreign law is a question of fact, the party who bases their claim or defence is required to present evidence to prove the existence and contents of foreign law.

Nonetheless, despite this rule requiring parties to prove foreign law, there had been instances where the court took judicial notice of foreign law. One must note though that these instances are highly exceptional and should be understood based on the facts and incidents that are peculiar to these cases. In *Testate Estate of C.O. Bohanan v Bohanan* ('*Bohanan*'), the Philippine Supreme Court said that

> we are constrained to hold that the pertinent law of Nevada, especially Section 9905 of the Compiled Nevada Laws of 1925, can be taken judicial notice of by us, without proof of such law having been offered at the hearing of the project of partition.[51]

The Court, nonetheless, noted that in a hearing on a motion filed by one of the defendants, section 9905 of the Compiled Nevada Laws of 1925 was introduced in evidence. This was not objected to by the other party. Hence, although proof of foreign law was not presented at the project of partition itself, it can be argued that the Court allowed judicial notice of foreign law because of the opposing party's failure to object in the motion hearing, which can be interpreted as an implied admission. Likewise, the result is consistent with the nationality principle that applies to matters of succession. In *Bohanan*, the testator was an American citizen, with Nevada as his elected domicile. Hence, it would be contrary to Philippine law for the court to insist the application of Philippine law to the estate of an American citizen.

In *Ancheta v Guersey-Dalaygon*,[52] the Philippine Supreme Court again took judicial notice of the laws of Maryland and applied it to the deceased's will. While the Court has cited *Bohanan* in justifying its action, it nonetheless emphasised the general rule that courts are not allowed to take judicial notice of foreign law.[53] In this case, however, the Court

[46] ibid 535.
[47] Revised Rules on Evidence, r 129, s 1.
[48] *Garcia v Recio* (2001) 366 SCRA 437, 451 ('*Garcia*').
[49] *Del Socorro v Van Wilsem*, GR No 193707, 14 December 2014, 749 Phil 823–40.
[50] Revised Rules on Evidence, r 131, s 1; See also *Garcia* (n 48).
[51] *Philippine Trust Co v Bohanan* (1960) 106 Phil 997, 1002.
[52] *Ancheta* (n 9).
[53] ibid 157.

was motivated to take judicial notice because of the administrator's lack of good faith in executing the will. The Court noted, for instance, that the administrator has deliberately disregarded the foreign law by not presenting any evidence, so as to allow the application of Philippine law.[54] The Supreme Court concluded that this action amounted to the administrator's abject failure to discharge his fiduciary duty.[55] Citing the nationality principle which applies to testamentary disposition, the Court emphasised that applying Philippine law would be a total disregard of the terms of the deceased's will.[56] In that sense, the resort to judicial notice of foreign law was to ensure that the Court's fundamental duty to properly administer justice is dispensed with.

ii. Means of Ascertaining Foreign Law

To prove foreign law, the party invoking it must present a copy thereof and comply with sections 24 and 25 of Rule 132 of the Revised Rules of Evidence. These rules have recently been amended and now reflect the Philippines' accession to the Apostille Convention,[57] which entered into force in the Philippines on 14 May 2019. Prior to the said amended rules, official or certified copies of the foreign law should be authenticated by the Philippine embassy or consulate. Under the current version of the rules, with respect to public documents from countries which are parties to the Apostille Convention, the need for authentication could now be dispensed with.[58] Instead, an apostille may be issued by the designated competent authority of the foreign country.[59] The apostille may be placed on the public document itself or on an allonge.[60] Notably, the apostille only certifies the authenticity of the signature, the capacity in which the person signing the document has acted and the identity of the seal or stamp which the document bears.[61] Hence, proof on how the foreign law is interpreted or applied may therefore still be required by the court.

Nonetheless, for countries which are not parties to the Apostille Convention and those which the Philippines does not recognise as states,[62] the rule in *Nedlloyd Lijnen B.V. Rotterdam v Glow Laks Enterprises* would still apply:

> For a copy of a foreign public document to be admissible, the following requisites are mandatory: (1) it must be attested by the officer having legal custody of the records or by his deputy; and (2) it must be accompanied by a certificate by a secretary of the embassy or legation, consul general, consul, vice-consular or consular agent or foreign service officer, and with the seal of his office. Such official publication or copy must be accompanied, if the record is not kept in the Philippines, with a certificate that the attesting officer has the legal custody thereof. The certificate may be issued by any of the authorized Philippine embassy or consular officials stationed in the foreign country in which the record is kept, and authenticated by the seal of his office. The attestation must

[54] ibid 155.
[55] ibid.
[56] ibid 153.
[57] The Hague Convention Abolishing the Requirement of Legalisation for Foreign Public Document, opened for signature 5 October 1961, 527 UNTS 189 (entered into force 24 January 1965) ('Apostille Convention').
[58] Apostille Convention, Art 2.
[59] Apostille Convention, Art 3.
[60] Apostille Convention, Art 4.
[61] Apostille Convention, Arts 3, 5.
[62] Declaration of the Philippines to the Apostille Convention (12 September 2018).

state, in substance, that the copy is a correct copy of the original, or a specific part thereof, as the case may be, and must be under the official seal of the attesting officer.[63]

The above rules, however, admit exceptions, and do not exclude the presentation of other competent evidence to prove the existence of foreign law. In *Willamette Iron and Steel Works v Muzzal*, for instance, the Supreme Court concluded that the foreign law was sufficiently established by the testimony in open court during trial in the Philippines of a San Francisco lawyer who quoted the particular foreign law sought to be established.[64] Similarly, in *Collector of Internal Revenue v Fisher*, the testimony on the revenue and tax laws of California by a lawyer who is a member of the Californian Bar was admitted to be sufficient proof of the Californian law.[65] In *Manufacturers Hanover Trust Co v Guerrero*, however, a witness affidavit by a New York lawyer was not admitted as proof of New York law because the affidavit was only presented ex parte and the affiant never testified in open court.[66] Moreover, in a number of naturalisation cases, the court dispensed with the need to prove the laws of China which give Filipinos reciprocal rights to naturalise in that country because such laws had already been established in previous cases.[67]

Furthermore, to address the growing number of cases involving foreign divorces, the Office of the Court Administrator of the Supreme Court has produced a compilation of laws of foreign countries on marriage and divorce.[68] This is supposed to dispense with the need to prove and authenticate foreign law on these matters in petitions for recognition and enforcement of foreign decree of divorce. The circular notes that the text of these laws, and/or their English translations were officially transmitted by the foreign ministries or authenticated by competent officials. In short, these copies should comply with the requirements of section 24, rule 132 of the Revised Rules of Evidence.

In *Wildvalley Shipping Co, Ltd. v Court of Appeals*,[69] the Supreme Court distinguished the manner of proving a written and an unwritten foreign law.

> The former falls under Section 24, Rule 132 of the Rules of Court .... Where the foreign law sought to be proved is 'unwritten,' the oral testimony of expert witnesses is admissible, as are printed and published books of reports of decisions of the courts of the country concerned if proved to be commonly admitted in such courts.[70]

iii. Qualifications of Individuals or Institutions that Provide Legal Information

In limited instances where expert witnesses are allowed to provide evidence on foreign law, the rules qualifying an expert witness would apply. Evidence on the witness' possession of special knowledge, skill, experience, training or education, which they are shown to possess

[63] *Nedlloyd Lijnen BV Rotterdam v Glow Laks Enterprises, Ltd*, GR No 156330, 14 November, 747 Phil 170–187 ('*Nedlloyd*').

[64] *Willamette Iron & Steel Works v Muzzal* (1935) 61 Phil 471, 475; see also *Nedlloyd* (n 63).

[65] *Collector of Internal Revenue v Fisher* (1961) 1 SCRA 93, 104.

[66] *Manufacturers Hanover Trust Co v Guerrero* (2003) 397 SCRA 709, 716.

[67] *In re: Yee Bo Mann v Republic* (1949) 83 Phil 749, 750; *Jose Leelin v Republic of the Philippines* (1949) 84 Phil 352, 354; *In re: Go v Anti-Chinese League of the Philippines* (1949) 84 Phil 468, 472–3.

[68] OCA Circular No 157-2022-A (Philippines).

[69] *Wildvalley Shipping* (n 43).

[70] ibid 220.

should be presented in evidence.[71] Hence, in *Yao Kee v Sy-Gonzales*, the testimonies of the plaintiff and his brother, both non-lawyers in China, were not considered as proof of China's law or custom on marriage. '[T]hey are self-serving evidence, but more importantly, there is no showing that they are competent to testify on the subject matter.'[72]

iv. Evidence of Foreign Law Not Conclusive to Court

Like any evidence presented in court, proof of foreign law is not binding upon judicial authorities. The court would use its sound discretion to determine whether the proof presented complies with any legal and procedural requirements, including the Revised Rules of Evidence.

v. Mechanism to examine The Reliability of Legal Information Provided

The adversarial nature of litigation in the Philippines means that the other party should be vigilant on the competence, authenticity and accuracy of the evidence presented before the court. The other party should lodge an objection to evidence,[73] file an application impeaching the evidence presented by the other party on foreign law,[74] or cross-examine the witnesses presented by the opposing party.[75] This mechanism based on the adversarial system ensures that the legal information presented is reliable.

vi. Costs of Ascertaining Foreign Law

The person who relies on foreign law bears the costs of ascertaining foreign law.

C. Interpretation and Application of Foreign Law

i. Conditions for Courts to Apply Foreign Law

The court can only take cognisance of foreign law and apply it to the dispute if the party whose claim is based on foreign law pleads and proves the same in accordance with the Revised Rules of Evidence. In very limited circumstances stated above, however, the court may take judicial notice of foreign law or apply foreign despite failure to properly prove the same.

ii. Interpretation and Application of Foreign Law by Courts

The interpretation and application of foreign law would depend on whether it was successfully pleaded, and the proof provided by the party. Remember that in order to successfully

[71] Revised Rules of Evidence, r 130, s 52.
[72] *Yao Kee v Sy-Gonzales* (1988) 167 SCRA 736, 745.
[73] Revised Rules of Evidence, r 132, s 36.
[74] ibid, r 132, s 11.
[75] ibid, r 132, s 6.

plead foreign law, there should be an allegation in the pleading not just about its existence but also its import and legal consequence on the event or transaction in issue.[76] Hence, if the foreign law should be interpreted in a particular way, the party claiming such should state it in their pleading. If the foreign law's interpretation and application had not been pleaded, the court would not be able to interpret and apply the foreign law. Furthermore, the party whose claim or defence is based on foreign law should present evidence of the foreign law, not just about its existence but also how it should be interpreted and its effects, in accordance with sections 24 and 25, rule 132 of the Revised Rules of Evidence. If the court is convinced that the burden of proving the foreign law has been met, the court will proceed to interpret and apply the foreign law in accordance with the evidence presented. The court cannot take judicial notice of how a particular foreign law is interpreted and applied. In *Crescent Petroleum Ltd. v M/V 'Lok Maheshwari'* ('*Crescent Petroleum*'), the Supreme Court emphasised the two options available when foreign law cannot be ascertained: 'Thus, we are left with two choices: (1) dismiss the case for petitioner's failure to establish a cause of action or (2) presume that Canadian law is the same as Philippine law.'[77] In *Crescent Petroleum*, the Court opted to dismiss the case for failure to establish a cause of action. In instances when the Court presumes that foreign law is the same as Philippine law, the Court may use the rules of interpretation under Philippine law to interpret the foreign law.

Another important point in the application of foreign law is that the remedy to be provided by the Philippine court is necessarily based on Philippine law.[78] For one, the remedy provided under the foreign law may not have a corresponding remedy under Philippine law. Furthermore, remedies like damages including its computation, injunction, appointment of a receiver, etc, may be considered as procedural in nature. Of course, whilst the Philippine Supreme Court has recognised this substance-procedure dichotomy in *Cadalin*, it has not specifically ruled which particular remedies should be considered substantive or procedural.

iii. How Courts Fill Gaps in Foreign Law

Even if sufficient proof has been provided but there remains to be a gap in foreign law, the Philippine court may fill in the gap by resorting to processual presumption. However, it is also possible that the court may dismiss the case for failure to establish a cause of action. If the foreign law, on which the claim is based, does not say anything on a particular matter, necessarily the claim could not be established sufficiently.

D. Failure to Establish Foreign Law

In *Crescent Petroleum*, the Supreme Court emphasised that when foreign law could not be ascertained, courts can either dismiss the case or presume that foreign law is the same as Philippine law.[79] In *Crescent Petroleum*, the Court dismissed the appeal for failure to

[76] *Wildvalley Shipping* (n 43) 223.
[77] *Crescent Petroleum Ltd. v M/V "Lok Maheshwari"* (2005) 474 SCRA 623, 642 ('*Crescent Petroleum*').
[78] See *Asiavest* (n 39) 502.
[79] *Crescent Petroleum* (n 77) 642.

establish a cause of action.[80] The more common option resorted to by courts, however, is the application of the principle of processual presumption, where the content of the foreign law is assumed to be identical or similar as it appears in Philippine law.[81] 'Where a foreign law is not pleaded or, even if pleaded, is not proved, the presumption is that foreign law is the same as ours.'[82]

Nonetheless, if the foreign law has not been pleaded properly and not proven, how then can the court determine the domestic rule that it should apply (ie, the presumed content of foreign law as it appears in Philippine law)? In *Strickland v Ernst & Young LLP* ('*Strickland*'),[83] the court described how the principle of processual presumption is applied. In that case, the alleged applicable foreign law (ie, the Federal Arbitration Act of the US), which determines the interpretation of the contract including the arbitration clause, was not proven. The issue was whether the dispute should be referred to arbitration despite the claim being allegedly based on torts. The Supreme Court agreed with the approach of the Court of Appeals, which after finding that the alleged applicable foreign law was not proven, looked into the issue in dispute – that is, whether or not the dispute should be referred to arbitration. Since the foreign law should have determined that issue, but unfortunately was not available to the Court because the foreign law was not proven, the Court presumed that the American law was the same as the Philippine law. However, since the Philippines has different laws for domestic arbitration and international commercial arbitration, an essential step was the determination of the type of arbitration involved. To determine this, the Court looked into the definition in the UNCITRAL Model Law on International Commercial Arbitration ('UNCITRAL Model Law'), and then concluded that the arbitration involved is an international commercial arbitration. As such the UNCITRAL Model Law as provided in the Alternative Dispute Resolution Act of the Philippines would apply, according to the Court.[84] Therefore, the Court appears to have taken the following steps: (1) to look into the issue in dispute; (2) characterise that issue based on Philippine law; (3) determine which particular domestic law would apply; and (4) apply such domestic law to resolve the dispute. Again, the characterisation of the dispute or issue as falling into a certain category of law appears to be a significant step in applying the principle of processual presumption. This characterisation is notably informed by Philippine law as well.

In *Strickland*, the Supreme Court also used Philippine law to determine whether Strickland's causes of action are indeed based on torts, as this would remove the dispute from the scope of the arbitration agreement. Rebutting Strickland's argument, the Court considered the causes of action as primarily based on contract. Again, the Court arrived at this conclusion by referring to Philippine law, thus, stressing that characterisation of issues is still based on Philippine law.

One important consequence of the use of the processual presumption is that Philippine law would also determine the effects of 'foreign law'. In *Del Socorro v Van Wilsem*, where the defendant pleaded that under Dutch law he had no obligation to support his child and yet had failed to provide evidence of such Dutch law, the court emphasised, after opting to

[80] ibid.
[81] See *Northwest Orient Airlines, Inc. v Court of Appeals* (1995) 241 SCRA 192, 200.
[82] *ATCI Overseas Corporation* (n 45) 534–5.
[83] *Strickland v Ernst & Young LLP*, GR Nos 193782 & 210695, 1 August 2018 ('*Strickland*').
[84] See Alternative Dispute Resolution Act 2004 (Philippines), s 19.

apply the processual presumption, that it would presume that the Dutch law had the same content as the Philippine law.[85] The court said that it would therefore enforce 'the obligation of parents to support their children and penalizing the non-compliance therewith'.[86] In short, if under Philippine law, there are penalties imposed, the party relying on foreign law may also incur such penalties.

In a number of cases involving foreign divorce decrees on their validity and effects, the Supreme Court has opted to remand the case for presentation of further evidence rather than to apply the principle of processual presumption or dismiss the case.[87] This approach in divorce cases is probably because the Philippines has no divorce law which can be used in lieu of the contents of foreign law. The remand would allow the parties to submit evidence and prove foreign law.

Because ascertainment of the foreign law is 'not among those matters that judges are supposed to know by reason of their judicial function',[88] Philippine courts, in dispensing their duties, especially their duty to dispense justice, are necessarily left to either dismiss the case or utilise what is readily available to them (ie, Philippine law) when parties fail to plead and/or prove foreign law. The first option is rarely used, possibly because the courts are trying their best to provide a resolution to the dispute. The use of the principle of processual presumption is more common. This solution is pragmatic because the court proceeds to fulfil its duty of dispensing justice and utilises what judges were trained to use in resolving disputes, that is, Philippine law. Nonetheless, the processual presumption also fulfils one of the goals of private international law, which is harmonised results. This may appear counterintuitive but the process of applying the principle involves the court still applying foreign law to the dispute, albeit its content is considered to be the same or similar to Philippine law, a consequence which is due to the fault of the party relying on foreign law. Nonetheless, this approach is criticised because the assumption that the foreign law has the same content as domestic law is a mere fiction if not arbitrary and has no rational basis in fact.[89]

E. Judicial Review/Appeal

Notably, foreign law may be involved in litigation in any court at any level in the court hierarchy. However, a party should plead (and thus, prove) the foreign law at the earliest occasion. This is because, as a general rule, 'arguments, evidence, causes of action and matters not raised in the trial court may no longer be raised on appeal'.[90] Hence, if during trial at the lower court, foreign law was not pleaded and proven at the earliest opportunity, the party who is relying on foreign law, may not be allowed to plead and present evidence on the foreign law during appeal. They may be considered to have waived their right to raise

[85] *Del Socorro v Van Wilsem* GR No 193707, [December 10, 2014], 749 PHIL 823–40.

[86] ibid.

[87] See, eg, *Garcia* (n 48) 455; *Quita v Court of Appeals* (1998) 300 SCRA 406, 415; *Llorente v Court of Appeals* (2000) 345 SCRA 592, 603; *San Luis v San Luis* (2007) 514 SCRA 294, 314; *Vda de Catalan v Catalan-Lee* (2007) 665 SCRA 487, 498.

[88] *Garcia* (n 48) 451.

[89] Eg, Y Rotem, 'Foreign Law as a Distinctive fact – To Whom Should the Burden of Proof Be Assigned?' (2014) 14 *Chicago Journal of International Law* 625, 630.

[90] *Lagazo v Court of Appeals* (1998) 287 SCRA 18, 28.

an issue about foreign law because a 'judgment or final order is, with respect to the matter directly adjudged or *as to any other matter that could have been missed in relation thereto*, conclusive between the parties and their successors in interest …' (emphasis added).[91] However, if foreign law was properly pleaded and proven at the first instance during trial, albeit there may be alleged errors in the resolution of these issues, a party may raise issues about foreign law during appeal. Curiously, whilst a question about foreign law is technically a question of fact, at no instance did the Supreme Court deny an appeal involving questions about foreign law based on the ground stated in section 1, rule 45 of the Rules of Court that appeals by *certiorari* shall only raise questions of law.[92]

On the other hand, errors involving the choice of law process (eg, the wrong choice of law rule was applied or there was an error in the application of the rule) may be raised during appeal. This is because errors in the choice of law process are questions of law. 'A question of law exists when the doubt or difference centres on what the law is on a certain state of facts.'[93] A pure question of law can be raised even during an appeal to the Supreme Court.[94]

Although not specifically discussing the need to allow appeals on errors involving the choice of law process and the application of foreign law, one can see in *Saudi Arabian Airlines v Court of Appeals* the motivation on why conflict of law issues should be resolved properly – ie, the need to advance both notions of justice and predictability.[95] Furthermore, the court is also conscious of 'comity, utility and convenience of nations'.[96] Hence, courts allow careful review of errors alleged on the application of the choice of law rules and foreign law.

III. Foreign Law in Other Instances

A. Foreign Law before Administrative or Any Other Non-Judicial Authorities

Foreign law may also be involved in disputes heard by administrative and quasi-judicial bodies. Because of the number of Filipinos working overseas, a number of conflict of laws cases have in fact originated from the National Labor Relations Commission, an administrative agency tasked to hear labour disputes. These cases established the general approach usually applied to overseas labour contracts where a Filipino is a party – labour standards set by laws of the Philippines will apply to overseas Filipino workers, such that a foreign law may be refused if they are contrary to these standards. However, in administrative cases, parties only carry the burden of proving their allegations with substantial evidence or 'such relevant evidence as a reasonable mind will accept as adequate to support a conclusion'.

[91] See Rules of Court, r 39, s 47(b).

[92] See PA Manalo, '(Dis)Proving Foreign Law: Understanding Processual Presumption in the Philippines and Arguing for a Confrontational Approach in Dealing with Conflict Cases' (2015) 89 *Philippine Law Journal* 430.

[93] *Microsoft Corp v Maxicorp, Inc* (2004) 438 SCRA 224, 230–1.

[94] Rules of Court, r 45, s1.

[95] *Saudi Arabian Airlines* (n 3) 490.

[96] See *Mijares* (n 5) 407; *Aznar* (n 6) 107.

This much lower burden imposed on parties should also be reflected on the amount of evidence required in proving foreign law. In a recent opinion, the Department of Justice (DOJ), however, emphasised that the applicable foreign law must be proven like any other fact heard by Philippine courts and administrative agencies cannot also take 'judicial notice' thereof.[97] Furthermore, like in cases heard by courts, the decision-maker has three options in disposing conflicts cases: (1) dismiss the case, either because of lack of jurisdiction or refusal to assume jurisdiction over the case; (2) assume jurisdiction over the case and apply the internal law of the forum; or (3) assume jurisdiction over the case and take into account or apply the law of some other state or states.[98]

Evidence of foreign law may also be required by administrative bodies in non-contentious circumstances (eg, as part of documentation in relation to an application for a licence or franchise). In applications for naturalisation, for example, the DOJ has emphasised the need to establish foreign law in accordance with the *Revised Rules of Evidence*.[99] The same rule seems to apply until now given the recent DOJ opinion on online marriages. However, foreign law may also be proven by presenting other documents. In an opinion, the DOJ said that a certificate of legal capacity to contract marriage from the embassy or consular office of his country in the Philippines could be submitted in applying for a marriage licence, since the foreign embassy 'are the ones who know the national law of said foreigner and whether he has capacity to marry under said law'.[100]

B. Foreign Law in Arbitration, Mediation or any Other Alternative Dispute Resolution

The Philippines adopts the UNCITRAL Model Law. Hence, the arbitral tribunal shall decide the dispute in accordance with such rules of law as are chosen by the parties as applicable to the substance of the dispute.[101] Notably, the choice of law rules are excluded from the parties' chosen law or legal system. If parties fail to choose, then the arbitral tribunal shall apply the law determined by the conflict of laws rules which it considers applicable.[102]

IV. Access to Philippine Law

There are a number of database and websites which one can use to access Philippine law and court decisions. The Philippines' official *Gazette*, the Philippine Government's official journal, maintains a website[103] which contains legislations and some administrative issuances.

[97] *Validity of Online Marriages and Marriages Based on Mere Submission of Documents Without Physical or Virtual Appearance Between a Filipino and a Foreign National*, DOJ Opinion No 23, s 2021, 29 July 2021.

[98] *Hasegawa v Kitamura* (2007) 538 SCRA 261, 276–7.

[99] DOJ Opinion No 064 s 1954, 18 March 1954.

[100] *Interpretation of Article 21 of the Family Code on Requirement for Foreigners Applying for a Marriage License*, DOJ Opinion No 064 s 2009, 23 November 2009.

[101] UNCITRAL Model Law, ch VI, Art 28(1).

[102] ibid, Art 28(2).

[103] www.officialgazette.gov.ph/.

The respective websites of the Philippine Senate and House of Representatives also contain copies of legislations, Bills originating from each house, and their respective internal rules. The Supreme Court's website[104] contains the judgments and court resolutions, the Rules of Court, and other court issuances. In addition, there are a number of privately managed websites which contain legislations, court decisions and some administrative issuances. Likewise, there are privately managed databases which provide comprehensive and up-to-date resources on Philippine laws, case decisions, and administrative issuances.[105] Notably, because the Philippines has English as one of its official languages, the laws, cases and administrative issuances are in English.

V. Access to Foreign Law: Future Developments in Asia

A. International or Regional Instruments on Treatment of and/or Information of Foreign Law

The Philippines is not a party to any international or regional instrument on the treatment of and/or information of foreign law.

B. Improving Access to Foreign Law

There is an increasing need to prove and present foreign law in cases before Philippine courts and administrative bodies. The Office of the Court Administrator's circular[106] on foreign divorce laws reflect this increased demand. Hence, there is a need to improve access to foreign law. This would benefit parties litigating before Philippine courts and administrative bodies, the courts themselves, and the Philippine Government in general, oversea Filipino workers and businesses wanting to do business abroad.

Although there is a need to improve access to foreign law, there are considerable obstacles for the Philippines to adopt an international or regional instrument unifying the treatment of foreign law. The adversarial system which gives parties the burden of proving their respective claims and the prohibition imposed against judicial notice would make it difficult for courts to easily subscribe to an agreed set of international rules dealing with the treatment of foreign law. Nonetheless, the removal of the need to legalise foreign documents by acceding to the Apostille Convention, along with the issuance of the OCA Circular[107] establishing a compilation of foreign divorce laws, are developments in the right direction. They both lessen the steps and costs of ascertaining foreign law. Hence, given these experiences, international and regional instruments dealing with the treatment of foreign law, particularly, the ways to prove and ascertain its contents, interpretation and application, would be useful. In addition, the Supreme Court and the Department of Foreign Affairs

[104] sc.judiciary.gov.ph/.
[105] Eg, cdasiaonline.com/; central.com.ph/escra/.
[106] OCA Circular No 157-2022-A (n 68).
[107] ibid.

should continue to establish court-to-court cooperation agreements which can further simplify procedural and evidentiary issues.

VI. Conclusion

Once a 'conflicts' situation has been established, a Philippine court proceeds by characterising the dispute with the goal of determining the proper law which will be used to resolve it. In determining the proper law, the court is aided by the choice of law rules found in both statutory and case law. The court's application of the choice of law rules may result in the application of foreign law, subject to a range of exceptions including the public policy exception. Courts, however, are not allowed to take judicial notice of foreign law as parties should plead and prove the foreign law's existence and contents. A party's failure to properly plead and prove foreign law may result in the court's dismissal of the case or application of the processual presumption, which allows courts to assume that the contents of the foreign law are the same as Philippine law. Errors in the court's choice or application of the choice of law rules could be appealed. Whilst questions involving the treatment of foreign law are technically questions of fact as foreign law is treated as fact under Philippine law, courts still have generally allowed appeals involving issues on foreign law.

This approach in the Philippines emphasises the courts' reliance on parties in arguing and establishing foreign law. Nonetheless, courts have recognised that such heavy reliance means that ascertaining foreign law may depend on the parties' capacity to access and establish proof in accordance with the Revised Rules of Evidence. This may be costly, inefficient, and may even result in injustice, especially when courts have no other option but to dismiss the case or resort to the application of the processual presumption. There is therefore a very real need to improve the manner of ascertaining foreign law before Philippine courts. The Philippine accession to the Apostille Convention and the Office of the Court Administrator's circular compiling foreign divorce laws are steps to the right direction. Nonetheless, there is still much that needs to be done in improving the parties' capacity to prove foreign law or the court's ability to directly ascertain foreign law. Philippine courts and the government, in general, should explore court-to-court cooperation and linkages with foreign governments that could improve access to foreign law.

13

Indonesia

AFIFAH KUSUMADARA,* IDA SUSANTI AND
TIURMA M PITTA ALLAGAN

I. Introduction to the Status of Choice of Laws Rules

A. Application of Choice of Law Rules in Indonesia

In principle, the application of choice of law rules should be mandatory in Indonesia, because the rules are stipulated in Indonesian laws, jurisprudence, and legal doctrines. However, in practice, the courts often do not apply the choice of law rules that are provided in jurisprudence and doctrine, as they are not considered binding. They merely apply the choice of law rules written in statutes and regulations.

General principles of choice of law rules are provided in Articles 16, 17, and 18, paragraph (1) of *Algemene Bepalingen van Wetgeving voor Nederlandsch Indie* ('AB') (General Provisions of Legislation for the Dutch East Indies).[1] Those Articles provide that:

> Statutory provisions governing the status and capacity of persons remain binding for Indonesian citizens during their stay abroad. (Article 16 of the AB)
>
> Concerning immovable property, the law of the country or place where the property is located, applies. (Article 17 of the AB)
>
> Formality of a juridical act is determined by the court in accordance with the law of the country or place where the action is performed. (Article 18 paragraph (1) of the AB)

It means that Indonesian law always applies to govern the status and capacity of Indonesian citizens even if they are outside of Indonesia (Article 16 of the AB); the law of the country in which an immovable property is located shall govern all aspects of that immovable property (Article 17 of the AB); and, the law of the country in which a juridical act is performed shall determine the formal validity of the action (Article 18 of the AB).

* Corresponding author. She and the other authors thank Dr Bayu Seto Hardjowahono, the current Head of the Association of Lecturers and Observers for Indonesian Private International Law (APPIHPI), for his constructive comments and recommendations on the Indonesian chapter.

[1] Although Arts 16, 17, and 18 para (1) of the AB were enacted under the Dutch colonial era, the Articles are still enforced to date under Art I of the Transitional Provisions of the Indonesian Constitution 1945. It stipulates that 'All existing regulations remain effective, as long as the new ones have not yet been provided under this Constitution.' So far, there has been no codified private international law in Indonesia.

The choice of law rules are further provided in other statutes and regulations. Article 18 of the Act No 19 of 2016 concerning electronic information and transactions (the Electronic Information and Transaction Act 2008 as amended in 2016), Article 56, paragraph (2) of the Arbitration and ADS Act 1999, and Article 72 of the Aviation Act No 1 of 2009 require Indonesian courts to apply the law chosen by parties to international contracts. In addition, the statutes require the courts to apply the principles of private international law, such as the connecting factor principle, to determine the applicable law for international contracts to which the parties do not choose any law for their contracts. Theoretically, these statutes make choice of law rules mandatory for Indonesian courts when adjudicating international commercial transactions.

Regarding tort, Indonesian statutes are silent on the choice of law rules on tort with foreign elements. There are several doctrines known in Indonesian private international law to determine the law applicable to tort. The prevailing one is the doctrine of *lex loci delicti commissi* or the law of the place where the tort was committed.[2] The other doctrines are the law of the place of the injury and the law of the place that has the most characteristic territorial connection to tort. However, in practice, Indonesian courts do not apply these doctrines. Instead, they simply apply Indonesian law (*lex fori*) when adjudicating tort with foreign elements, like in the cases of *Richard Bruce Ness v Jane Perlez; et al.*;[3] *Time Inc Asia, et al. v H.M. Soeharto*;[4] and *Sigit Suciptoyono v Singapore Airlines Limited*.[5] As such, the choice of law rules based on these doctrines are not strictly mandatory. The reason for this might be because condemnatory judgments on tort made by Indonesian courts are valid and enforceable only in Indonesia (Article 431 of *Reglement op de Burgerlijke Rechtsvordering* ('Rv')[6]). That leads Indonesian courts to apply Indonesian law because their judgments or decisions are expected to be enforced within Indonesia only.

The law applicable to the formal validity of a will is the law of the place or country where the will is made (*locus regit actum* principle). This choice of law rule is derived from Article 945, paragraph (1) of *Burgerlijk Wetboek voor Nederlandsch-Indie* ('BW') (Dutch East Indies Civil Code and current Indonesian Civil Code). The Article provides that an Indonesian citizen in a foreign country cannot make a will in any manner other than by an authentic deed and by following the applicable formalities in the country in which the deed is made. This choice of law rule shall be mandatory for Indonesian courts. In *Leo Bonady, et al. v Lelly Iskandar, et al.*, the Indonesian courts found that the will made by an Indonesian testator in Singapore was valid in accordance with both the formalities of Singaporean law and the substance of Indonesian law.[7] Unfortunately, in a latter case of *Erlina and Ahmad*

[2] S Gautama, *Hukum Perdata Internasional Indonesia Jilid III Bagian 2 Buku Ke Delapan* (Bandung, Penerbit Alumni, 1987) 191–197.

[3] District Court of Central Jakarta Decision 408/Pdt.G/2007/PN.Jkt.Pst. (25 March 2009).

[4] Supreme Court Extraordinary Appeal 273 PK/Pdt/2008 (16 April 2009).

[5] District Court of South Jakarta Decision 908/Pdt.G/2007/PN.Jak.Sel. (5 February 2008); High Court of Jakarta Decision 611/PDT/2008/PT.DKI (2 February 2009); Supreme Court Decision 1517 K/Pdt/2009 (18 April 2011). Further discussion on each of the cases, see A Kusumadara, *Indonesian Private International Law* (Oxford, Hart Publishing, 2021).

[6] Art 431 of the Rv provides that Indonesian judgments are valid and enforceable only in Indonesia. The Rv is one of Indonesia's civil procedure codes, although initially it was a civil procedure code only for the courts of Dutch and foreign inhabitants during the Dutch colonial era.

[7] District Court of North East Jakarta Decision 158/69/1979 G (not published); High Court of Jakarta Decision 241/1979 (unpublished); affd Supreme Court Decision 148/PK/Perd/1982 (unpublished). See AP Senoadji,

Yuni Nasution, S.H. v Yulia Yusriani Mualim, the Indonesian courts ignored the *locus regit actum* principle. Instead, the courts applied Indonesian law to determine the validity of the will made by an Indonesian testator in Singapore concerning his assets in Singapore.[8] As a result, the courts found the will invalid.

Concerning a marriage, Indonesian choice of law rules adopt the principle of *locus regit actum* to determine the formal validity of a marriage, and the nationality principle to determine the capacity to marriage. Those choice of law rules are provided in Article 56, paragraph (1) of the Act No 1 of 1974 concerning Marriage (the Marriage Act 1974). Since the rules are stipulated in a statute, they become mandatory for Indonesian courts.

Regarding divorce, the nationality principle also applies to the divorce of a foreign couple having domicile in Indonesia, in which both spouses have the same nationalities. An Indonesian court that exercises its jurisdiction over the divorce shall apply the national law of the foreign couple. This choice of law rule is based on the 1953 jurisprudence in which the West-South Jakarta District Court applied the German Civil Code (BGB) to adjudicate the divorce of a German couple who domiciled in Jakarta.[9]

As demonstrated in this section, theoretically, choice of law rules in Indonesia shall be mandatory. However, in practice, the mandatory application of choice of law rules is limited to certain matters. The Indonesian courts usually apply the choice of law rules to the matters that are expressly governed by statutory provisions and ignore the choice of law rules that are only written in doctrine or jurisprudence.

B. Applicability of Foreign Law in Indonesia

As mentioned above, Indonesian courts usually respect the law chosen by parties to international contracts. That is in line with the principles of party autonomy and freedom of contract recognised in several statutory provisions, namely, Article 1338, paragraph (1) of the BW, Article 18 of the Electronic Information and Transaction Act 2008 as amended in 2016, and Article 56, paragraph (2) of the Arbitration and ADS Act 1999. Therefore, the foreign law chosen by the parties to international contracts may lead Indonesian courts to the application of foreign law. In *Marubeni Corporation v P.T. Indokaya Nissan Motors*, the Central Jakarta District Court applied the Japanese law that was the applicable law of the parties' guarantee agreement. Based on the Japanese law, the Court found that the defendant had not performed its obligation to reimburse the plaintiff. The Court also held that the parties' land mortgage and hypothec were valid. In addition, the Court denied the defendant's opinion that the Court should apply Indonesian law.[10]

'Penerapan Legitime Portie (Bagian Mutlak) Dalam Pembagian Waris Menurut Kitab Undang-Undang Hukum Perdata Studi Kasus Putusan Mahkamah Agung Reg No. 148/Pk/Perd/1982' (Master thesis, Universitas Diponegoro, 2007).

[8] District Court of Medan Decision 348/Pdt.G/2009/PN.Mdn (22 June 2010); affirmed by High Court of East Kalimantan Decision 94/PDT/2010/ PT.KT.SMDA (3 March 2011); affirmed by Supreme Court Decision 2562 K/Pdt/2011 (13 March 2012).

[9] S Gautama, *Hukum Perdata Internasional Indonesia Buku Ketujuh Jilid Ke-Tiga (Bagian Pertama)* (Bandung, Penerbit Alumni, 1981) 176.

[10] District Court of Central Jakarta Decision 560/1982 PDT.G. (11 October 1983).

However, in a different case, *PT. Indah Kiat Pulp & Paper Tbk. v Bank America National Trust Company, et al.*, the parties' choice of foreign law in their international contract did not lead Indonesian courts to the application of the foreign law because the plaintiff in that case brought a claim of tort, instead of breach of contract. Since the dispute was based on a tort claim, the courts applied Indonesian law, instead of the foreign law chosen by the parties. In this case, the parties entered into several agreements to fund PT. Indah Kiat Pulp's business expansion. In their indenture agreement, loan agreement, and underwriting agreement, the parties agreed to the laws of the State of New York as the governing law of their agreements. However, the parties' choice of law did not lead the Bengkalis District Court to the application of the State of New York laws. That was because the plaintiff, PT. Indah Kiat Pulp & Paper Tbk ('Indah Kiat'), an Indonesian company, brought a claim of tort, instead of a claim of breach of contracts, against the defendants who were Indah Kiat's bond holders. Indah Kiat argued that their agreements were made in bad faith and misled Indah Kiat; hence, the defendants committed tort. The defendants argued that the merit of their case was a breach of contract by Indah Kiat that did not pay its bonds when they were due. The defendants also argued that the case had to be adjudicated in accordance with the laws of New York State as the choice of law of the parties' agreements. The Bengkalis District Court accepted Indah Kiat's claim of tort and applied Indonesian law concerning tort to adjudicate the case. The Court decided in favour of Indah Kiat and held that all agreements between Indah Kiat and the defendants null and void because the agreements were made based on tort.[11] The decision was upheld by the Riau High Court,[12] and by the Supreme Court as the court of cassation.[13]

The case of *PT. Indah Kiat Pulp & Paper Tbk. v Bank America National Trust Company, et al.* demonstrates that the plaintiff's claim of tort on supposedly a case of breach of contract may cause an Indonesian court not to apply the foreign law that had been chosen by the contracting parties. The plaintiffs' manoeuvring into claims of tort to avoid the application of foreign laws, have become the point of contention among parties in front of Indonesian courts. A similar issue also occurred in *Mitomo Shoji K.K. v Aim Holding, et al.*[14]

The above-mentioned cases demonstrate that in international contracts, Indonesian courts will apply foreign laws that have been mutually agreed by the contracting parties. That is in line with the principles of party autonomy and freedom of contract recognised in several statutory provisions in Indonesia. However, in practice, the courts will apply Indonesian law if the plaintiffs bring the claim of tort, instead of breach of contract, in their international contract cases.

Based on the jurisprudence, the nationality principle applies to the divorce of a foreign couple who have the same nationalities. In 1953 the West-South Jakarta District Court applied the German Civil Code to adjudicate the divorce of a German couple who domiciled in Jakarta.[15] Despite this jurisprudence, Indonesian courts are allowed not to apply the national laws of foreign couples in their divorce in Indonesia based on the *renvoi* doctrine.

[11] District Court of Bengkalis Decision 05/PDT.G./2003/PN-BKS (29 September 2004).

[12] High Court of Riau Decision 40/PDT/2004/PTR (16 June 2005).

[13] Supreme Court Decision 381 K/Pdt/2006 (24 May 2006).

[14] *Mitomo Shoji K.K. v Aim Holding; et al.*, District Court of Central Jakarta Decision 359/Pdt.G/2011/PN. Jkt.Pst (31 July 2012); affirmed High Court of Jakarta Decision 186/PDT/2014/PT.DKI (23 July 2014).

[15] Gautama (n 9) 176.

Indonesian private international law has adopted the remission type of *renvoi* since the Dutch colonial era. That means when the nationality principle leads to a foreign law, and the foreign law – including its conflict of law rules – refers back to Indonesian law, Indonesian courts will apply Indonesian domestic law to adjudicate matters involving personal status. The application of *renvoi* mostly occurs in divorce cases in which the spouses are foreigners who domicile in Indonesia and originate from countries that apply the domicile principle in their private international laws.

Sudargo Gautama, the leading scholar of Indonesian Private International Law, admitted in his writing that

> We are of the opinion that the acceptance of the *renvoi* principle is beneficial to Indonesia. It will result in the application of Indonesian internal law, and consequently, when Indonesian laws are applied, there is greater assurance that the correct law will be applied than when foreign laws are applied. Although we uphold the equality of Indonesian and foreign laws, the Indonesian courts will be more at ease if they can apply their own internal law.[16]

In summary, choice of law rules in Indonesia do not always lead Indonesian courts to the application of foreign law. In breach of contract cases, Indonesian courts usually apply foreign law that has been agreed by the contracting parties based on the principles of party autonomy and freedom of contract enshrined in Article 1338 of the BW. In marriages, Indonesian courts apply foreign laws based on the nationality principle to determine the capacity of foreigners to marriage in Indonesia. Whereas in divorce of foreigners in Indonesia, Indonesian courts usually avoid the application of the national law of the foreigners by applying the remission theory known in the *renvoi* doctrine. In tort containing foreign elements, Indonesian courts do not implement the doctrines that lead to the application of foreign law. Instead, they simply apply Indonesian law to tort cases.

II. Foreign Law before Indonesian Courts

A. Nature of Foreign Law

Under Indonesian private international law, foreign law is an issue of law, not fact. That is based on a 1915 jurisprudence established by the *Hoge Raad* (the Dutch Supreme Court) in its decision on 4 June 1915.[17] As such, the determination and interpretation of foreign law is resolved by a judge. Judges have to find and apply foreign law *ex officio*. As a consequence of being regarded as a matter of law, foreign law could be applied at all levels of court: in trial, appellate, cassation, and extraordinary appellate courts. Since foreign law is an issue of law, the interpretation and application of foreign law by lower courts can be appealed to higher courts, like in the case of PT. *Pelayaran Manalagi v PT. Asuransi Harta Aman Pratama, Tbk.*

[16] S Gautama and H Wiknjosastro, 'Some Aspects of Indonesian Private International Law' (1990) 32(2) *Malaya Law Review* 429, www.jstor.org/stable/24865645 (accessed 31 January 2022).

[17] HR 04-06-1915, NJ 1915/865.

B. Ascertainment of Foreign Law

Indonesian law does not have statutory provisions on how courts ascertain and establish the contents of foreign law. However, based on Article 10, paragraph (1) of the Act No 48 of 2009 concerning judicial authority that obligates the courts to adjudicate cases even if the law is absence or unclear, the principle of *iura novit curia* ('the court knows the law') applies. It is thus the responsibility of the courts to establish the applicable law, including a foreign law, to the merits of a case before them. In terms of determining and applying foreign law, a judge should, to the extent possible, make their own investigations of the foreign law and find out its content. Article 50, paragraph (1) of the Rv provides that judges in their *ex officio* consideration shall include legal grounds that may not be presented by the parties. If this Article is extended to private international law cases, the judges shall also include foreign law in their consideration, even if the foreign law is not presented by the parties.

The above principle was applied in *Marubeni Corporation v P.T. Indokaya Nissan Motors*. This case involved a guarantee agreement between Marubeni Corporation ('Marubeni'), a Japanese company, as a guarantor and creditor, and P.T. Indokaya Nissan Motors ('IKM'), an Indonesian company, as a guarantee and debtor. In their agreement, Marubeni agreed to guarantee and pay IKM's debts to the Bank of Tokyo, and IKM agreed to reimburse Marubeni for that payment. The parties agreed to choose Japanese law to govern their guarantee agreement. When IKM failed to repay Marubeni after Marubeni paid IKM's debts to the Bank of Tokyo, Marubeni sued IKM before the Central Jakarta District Court. IKM asked the court to bring a legal expert from Japan to explain Japanese law to the court. The court rejected IKM's request and stated that the court in Indonesia did not have to summon a legal expert from Japan, and IKM could inform the court about which Japanese law should be applied to the case. However, the court found that both parties in this case failed to provide the court with the relevant Japanese law for their case. Eventually, the Central Jakarta District Court itself had to investigate Japanese law, and determined that Japan's Application of Laws in General (the Horei) promulgated on 15 June 1898 was the appropriate law to govern the case. The court applied Article 10, paragraph (1) and Article 11 of the Horei to the case, and found that the parties' guarantee agreement and the land mortgage to secure the agreement did not infringe the Horei provisions. Therefore, the court decided in favour of Marubeni.[18] The Jakarta High Court and the Supreme Court upheld the decision of the Central Jakarta District Court.[19]

However, despite the Marubeni case in which the court made its own investigation of the foreign law and found out its content, in most cases, Indonesian courts do not fully apply the *iura novit curia* principle to ascertain the contents of foreign law, as they do with domestic law. Instead, the courts usually rely heavily on the assistance of the parties to ascertain and investigate foreign law. However, the parties' information on foreign law is not binding on the judges. Sudargo Gautama said that the judges could employ the assistance of the parties or certain institutions or experts to ascertain and investigate foreign law. In addition, the courts can use documents as evidence *ex officio* if the parties or one of them have

[18] District Court of Central Jakarta Decision 560/1982 PDT.G. (11 October 1983).

[19] High Court of Jakarta Decision 186/PDT/2014/PT.DKI (22 May 1984); Supreme Court Decision 2826 K/PDT/1984 (10 December 1985).

referred to the documents.[20] In other words, Indonesian courts *ex officio* can use all legal means necessary to ascertain foreign law and its content.

That practice was demonstrated in *PT. Pelayaran Manalagi v PT. Asuransi Harta Aman Pratama, Tbk.* This case involved an Indonesian shipping company, PT. Pelayaran Manalagi, that sued PT. Asuransi Harta Aman Pratama ('PT. AHAP'), an Indonesian insurance company, for a breach of their insurance agreement. The applicable law of the parties' marine insurance agreement was the English law and practice. In this case, the plaintiff assisted the Central Jakarta District Court with ascertaining the content of English Law and practice concerning marine insurance. The plaintiff provided the court with the Indonesian translation of the English law and practice written by a sworn translator.[21] The plaintiff also involved a Singaporean average adjuster appointed by both plaintiff and defendant to write an assessment report detailing how the English law would govern the accident and damages suffered by the plaintiff. The judge agreed with the plaintiff and found PT. AHAP had breached the parties' insurance agreement based on the English law and practice.[22] The Jakarta High Court affirmed the decision.[23] In the court of cassation, the parties also assisted the Supreme Court in ascertaining the content of English law and practice. However, the defendant also adduced information about the New Marine Policy Form (MAR 91 Form) that they found in an article published by the Hill Dickinson law firm in the UK. The MAR 91 was the form of the parties' insurance clauses. That article wrote that 'The Institute Clauses remain subject to English law and practice. They are expressed to be used with the New Marine Policy Form. This is now the MAR 91 form which provides for the exclusive jurisdiction of the English Courts.'[24] Eventually, the Supreme Court ruled that the Central Jakarta District Court did not have jurisdiction over the case because the parties' marine insurance agreement (Institute Time Clauses – Hulls/MAR 91) contained a choice of jurisdiction that led to the jurisdiction of English courts. Therefore, the Supreme Court held that PT. Pelayaran Manalagi should have not brought its claim to the Central Jakarta District Court and voided the decision of the Central Jakarta District Court.[25]

In *Erlina and Ahmad Yuni Nasution, S.H. v Yulia Yusriani Mualim*, the defendant invoked the foreign element of the parties' dispute and presented the Medan District Court with the choice of law rule (Article 18, paragraph (1) of the AB) that led to foreign law (Singaporean law). The defendants assisted the court in ascertaining the content of Singaporean law concerning the formal validity of wills. But the Medan District Court simply ignored Singaporean law and applied Indonesian law to the case. Applying Indonesian law, the court

[20] S Gautama, *Hukum Perdata Internasional Indonesia Jilid II Bagian 5 Buku Ke enam* (Bandung, Penerbit Alumni, 1988) 190–94.

[21] A sworn translator in Indonesia is a certified Indonesian translator who is licensed to make a written translation to Indonesian from another language and vice versa. To become a sworn translator, one must take an oath before the Governor of Jakarta or the Governor of East Java. The content of the oath is, among others, to be truthful when making translation (*Staatsblad* No 69 of 1859 and *Staatsblad* No 169 of 1894). After the issuance of the Regulation of the Ministry of Law and Human Rights No 29 of 2016, which has been amended in 2019, the oath is taken before the Minister of Law and Human Rights or the Heads of the Ministry Regional Offices. The written translations provided by sworn translators will usually be accepted by Indonesian courts without the courts having to summon the translators to take oath of truthfulness in front of the courts.

[22] District Court of Central Jakarta Decision 52/Pdt.G/2010/PN.Jkt.Pst. (21 October 2010).

[23] High Court of Jakarta Decision 297/PDT/2011/PT.DKI (24 November 2011).

[24] Supreme Court Decision 1935 K/Pdt/2012 (14 January 2013) 37.

[25] Supreme Court Decision 1935 K/Pdt/2012 (14 January 2013).

found the will made in Singapore invalid and held that the executrix of the will did not have any rights on the testator's assets in Singapore.[26] The East Kalimantan High Court affirmed the decision.[27] In the court of cassation, the defendants once again invoked the foreign element of their case and presented the Supreme Court with the choice of law rule (Article 18, paragraph (1) of the AB) that led to foreign law (Singaporean law). The defendants also presented the Supreme Court with expert witnesses that confirmed the choice of law rule for the case. The Supreme Court dismissed the defendant's appeal of cassation and affirmed the lower courts' decisions.[28]

It could be observed from the above cases that the ways the parties assisted Indonesian courts in ascertaining foreign law become similar to the practices of pleading and proving foreign law by parties in the courts of common law countries. Only in a few cases did the courts not take a passive position in ascertaining foreign law. In *Marubeni Corporation v P.T. Indokaya Nissan Motors*, the Central Jakarta District Court investigated the contents of Japanese law. In *Leo Bonady, et al. v Lelly Iskandar, et al.*, the Jakarta High Court also made its own investigation of the procedure of making a testament under Singaporean law to determine the formal validity of a testament made by an Indonesian in Singapore.

To implement the *iura novit curia* principle, Indonesian courts can employ all legal means or methods to investigate and ascertain foreign law. In practice, the courts usually rely heavily on the assistance of the parties to do this. The parties need to invoke the foreign elements of their cases and assist the judges with the choice of law rules; provide judges with sufficient information on the content of foreign law; submit an Indonesian translation of the foreign law; and adduce documents related to the foreign law. Usually, the parties' lawyers and legal experts provide the courts with information on foreign law. There is no specific mechanism that must be employed by the courts to check the reliability of their information on foreign law. Judges can use whatever means or methods to examine and assess the reliability of the legal information provided to them.

Although, in principle, the courts (or the state) shall bear the costs of ascertaining foreign law because the courts must apply foreign law *ex officio*, in most cases, the costs for ascertaining foreign law are borne by parties who assist the courts. Therefore, it becomes part of their litigation costs.

C. Interpretation and Application of Foreign Law

i. *The Application of Foreign Law before Indonesian Courts*

Foreign law is applied before Indonesian courts when a choice of law rule leads to foreign law. As written above, following the *iura novit curia* principle, Indonesian courts apply foreign law *ex officio*. Besides being required by choice of law rules, there are other conditions under which the Indonesian courts apply foreign law. One such condition is when the courts implement international conventions that have been ratified by Indonesia, for

[26] District Court of Medan Decision 348/Pdt.G/2009/PN.Mdn (22 June 2010).
[27] High Court of East Kalimantan Decision 94/PDT/2010/ PT.KT.SMDA (3 March 2011).
[28] Supreme Court Decision 2562 K/Pdt/2011 (13 March 2012).

example, the Paris Convention for the Protection of Industrial Property.[29] In *CBS Interactive Inc. v Lie Jong Wei (Jong Wei Rusli)*,[30] the Indonesian Supreme Court applied the Paris Convention for the Protection of Industrial Property (Paris Convention) and the Agreement on Trade-Related Aspects of Intellectual Property Rights (TRIPS Agreement)[31] that have been ratified by Indonesia to revoke a trademark registered in Indonesia. By revoking the registered trademark, the court protected a foreign well-known trademark owned by the claimant according to the Paris Convention and TRIPS Agreement.

Another condition for the application of foreign law is that Indonesian courts implement international trade usages agreed by the parties, such as, the Uniform Customs and Practice for Documentary Credits (UCP) and the International Commercial Terms (INCOTERMS) – both are published by the International Chamber of Commerce. In several cases in which both the contracting parties were Indonesians but agreed to the UCP and INCOTERMS, Indonesian courts would apply the UCP and INCOTERMS.[32]

Foreign law is also applied *ex officio* by Indonesian courts when the parties invoke the foreign elements of their case and present the courts with the choice of law rules that lead to foreign law.[33]

ii. The Ways Indonesian Courts Interpret and Apply Foreign Law

Sudargo Gautama wrote that Indonesian courts must interpret and apply foreign law in the same way as the courts of the country of origin. He explained foreign law, including statutes, jurisprudence, legal doctrines, and custom, must be interpreted and applied in the same manner in the country of origin.[34] This doctrine supports the purpose of private international law, which is to provide legal certainty for the parties and international harmony.

iii. Filling a Gap in Foreign Law by Indonesian Courts

Both Indonesian law and doctrine are silent on how Indonesian courts should fill a gap in foreign law. There is also no case law in Indonesia in this regard. Sudargo Gautama, who wrote extensively about Indonesian private international law, has never dealt with this issue in his books either. That indicates that Indonesian courts have never practised gap-filling of foreign law. There are some possible reasons for this situation; for instance, it is not easy for Indonesian judges to obtain foreign law, the relevant foreign law might not be

[29] World Intellectual Property Organization, Paris Notification No 177, Paris Convention for the Protection of Industrial Property Ratification by the Republic of Indonesia of Articles 1 to 12 of the Stockholm Act (1967). Ratification date: 5 June 1997. www.wipo.int/treaties/en/notifications/paris/treaty_paris_177.html (accessed 6 May 2022).

[30] Supreme Court Decision 696 K/PDT.SUS/2011 (23 February 2012).

[31] World Trade Organization, Indonesia and the WTO. Ratification date: 1 January 1995. www.wto.org/english/thewto_e/countries_e/indonesia_e.htm#stcsHeading (accessed 6 May 2022).

[32] *PT Petrobas v PT. Cosmic Indonesia, et al.*, District Court of Central Jakarta Decision 41/Pdt.G/2012/PN.Jkt. Pst (21 November 2012); *Dody Soehardy v PT. Venture Technology Indonesia, et al.*, District Court of Batam Decision 191/Pdt.G/2012/PN.Btm (9 July 2014); J Junaiding, 'Soft Law Sebagai Sumber Hukum Kontrak Dalam Perdagangan Internasional' (2021) 1(3) *Dharmasisya* 1293–95: scholarhub.ui.ac.id/dharmasisya/vol1/iss3/15 (accessed 19 January 2022).

[33] See the cases presented earlier.

[34] Gautama (n 20) 187.

easily accessible, and its sources are vague. Hence, it is also difficult for them to determine whether such a gap actually exists in the relevant foreign law. If the gap does exist, it will be even more difficult for the judges to understand how to fill the gap according to the criteria and methods in the country of origin. Therefore, Sudargo Gautama, the leading scholar of Indonesian Private International Law, never wrote about filling a gap in foreign law under Indonesian private international law. Instead, he preferred to write on what the courts should do when they fail to establish foreign law. The practical solution for this issue, in the authors' opinion, would be that Indonesian courts apply their own gap filling method, and that gaps in foreign law are resolved by reference to forum law.

D. Failure to Establish Foreign Law

Indonesian law is silent on what the court must do when it cannot establish the content of foreign law. There are also no court judgments in Indonesia in which the courts openly stated that they had failed to establish the content of foreign law and explained what they did as a result of the failure.

The most obvious solution would be that the courts simply apply the *lex fori* to substitute the foreign law. This solution is also mentioned by Sudargo Gautama in his book. He wrote that the application of the *lex fori* is a practical solution for judges because they are familiar with their own law.[35] The *lex fori* application could also mean that the courts make rebuttable presumption that foreign law is the same as *lex fori*, unless the parties can prove otherwise. If the parties cannot prove otherwise, *lex fori* will be applied by the courts.[36]

Another solution offered by Sudargo Gautama was to apply different sources of foreign law presumed to be most similar to the foreign law.[37] For example, an Indonesian court could apply a French law that belongs to the same legal system as the Mali law that its content cannot be established, because Mali's legal system derives from French civil law and Mali was a French colony until 1960.

Finally, the courts can dismiss the claim allegedly governed by foreign law that the parties or the courts cannot establish its content. However, Sudargo Gautama suggested that to apply *lex fori* be better than to dismiss the parties' claims.[38]

E. Judicial Review

i. Erroneous Application of Choice of Law Rules

There have been several cases in which Indonesian lower courts erroneously applied choice of law rules, and the higher courts, including the Supreme Court as either the court of cassation or the court of extraordinary appeal, corrected the erroneous application. In those cases, the lower courts had ignored the international aspects of the case and applied

[35] Gautama (n 20) 196.
[36] ibid 197.
[37] ibid 198–99.
[38] ibid 199–200.

Indonesian law instead of the foreign law designated by Indonesian choice of law rules. So far, there have been no cases in which the courts erroneously applied the foreign law designated under the relevant choice of law rules. That means the erroneous application of choice of law rules in Indonesia only involves the application of Indonesian law instead of foreign law. In *Leo Bonady, et al. v Lelly Iskandar, et al.* the North East Jakarta District Court did not apply the choice of law rules to determine the validity of a testament made by an Indonesian testator in Singapore.[39] The defendants appealed to the Jakarta High Court. The High Court rendered a new judgment that corrected the lower court's judgment and applied Singaporean law to determine the formal validity of the testament. The Supreme Court affirmed the decision of the Jakarta High Court.[40]

In *PT. Indah Kiat Pulp & Paper Tbk. v Bank America National Trust Company, et al.*, the Bengkalis District Court, Riau High Court, and Supreme Court as the court of cassation, erroneously applied Indonesian law, instead of the laws of the New York State, to determine the contractual dispute. The courts ignored the laws of the State of New York that the parties had chosen as the governing law of their contracts.[41] The defendants made an extraordinary appeal to a different panel of the Supreme Court and argued, among others, that the lower courts had ignored the choice of law rules that led to the laws of the State of New York. The justices in the extraordinary appeal annulled the lower courts' decisions, including the previous cassation decision by the Supreme Court, and agreed with the defendants that the previous courts should have determined the case by applying the law of the New York State. However, the justices also ordered the parties to bring and settle their dispute before a New York State court in accordance with the parties' choice of jurisdiction agreement.[42]

In *Erlina and Ahmad Yuni Nasution, S.H. v Yulia Yusriani Mualim*, the defendants filed an appeal to the Supreme Court to argue that the lower courts had ignored the international aspects of the case and applied Indonesian law instead of Singaporean law. Unfortunately, the Supreme Court dismissed the defendant's cassation request and affirmed the lower courts' decisions.[43]

These cases show that when a court erroneously applies or disregards a choice of law in Indonesia, one can appeal to higher courts including the Supreme Court. The parties can appeal under the same conditions as domestic law. The appeal to the highest court against the lower courts' erroneous application of choice of law rules is possible in Indonesia because it is part of the Supreme Court's responsibility to process the appeal. Pursuant to Article 32, paragraph (1) of the Act No 3 of 2009 concerning second amendment to Act No 14 of 1985 on Supreme Court (the Supreme Court Act 2009), the Supreme Court has a responsibility to supervise all lower courts concerning their conduct in exercising their judicial authority.

[39] District Court of North East Jakarta Decision 158/69/1979 G (not published). See AP Senoadji, 'Penerapan Legitime Portie (Bagian Mutlak) Dalam Pembagian Waris Menurut Kitab Undang-Undang Hukum Perdata Studi Kasus Putusan Mahkamah Agung Reg No. 148/Pk/Perd/1982' (Master thesis, Universitas Diponegoro, 2007).

[40] High Court of Jakarta Decision 241/1979 (unpublished); affd Supreme Court Decision 148/PK/Perd/1982 (unpublished). See Senoadji (n 7).

[41] District Court of Bengkalis Decision 05/PDT.G./2003/PN-BKS (29 September 2004); affd High Court of Riau Decision 40/PDT/2004/PTR (16 June 2005); affd Supreme Court Decision 381 K/Pdt/2006 (24 May 2006).

[42] Supreme Court Extraordinary Appeal 445 PK/Pdt/2007 (19 August 2008).

[43] Supreme Court Decision 2562 K/Pdt/2011 (13 March 2012).

ii. Erroneous Application of Foreign Law

Like erroneous application of choice of law rules, one can appeal up to the highest court – the Supreme Court – either by a cassation proceeding or by an extraordinary appeal, when a court erroneously applies foreign law. In *PT. Pelayaran Manalagi v PT. Asuransi Harta Aman Pratama, Tbk*, the Central Jakarta District Court applied the English law and practice that were the applicable law of the parties' marine insurance agreement (Institute Time Clauses – Hulls), holding that the defendant, PT. AHAP, had breached the parties' insurance.[44] The Jakarta High Court affirmed the decision.[45] PT. AHAP appealed to the court of cassation on the ground that the Central Jakarta District Court did not have jurisdiction over the case. The Supreme Court found that the MAR 91 Form used in the parties' Institute Time Clauses – Hulls gave exclusive jurisdiction to English courts. The MAR 91 Form stipulates that 'This insurance shall be subject to the exclusive jurisdiction of the English Courts, except as may be expressly provided herein to the contrary.' Eventually, the Supreme Court corrected the erroneous application of English law and practice by the lower courts that ignored the practice written in the MAR 91 Form and decided that the plaintiff should not have brought its claim to the Central Jakarta District Court. The Supreme Court also voided the decision of the Central Jakarta District Court.[46]

This case demonstrates that when foreign law is not applied in accordance with the interpretation followed in the foreign country, the interpretation and application of foreign law is appealable. The interpretation and application of foreign law can even be reviewed by the highest judiciary in the ultimate proceeding of extrajudicial appeal. The parties can appeal the erroneous application of foreign law under the same conditions as the erroneous application of domestic law. The erroneous interpretation and application of foreign law is appealable up to the highest court in Indonesia because pursuant to Article 32, paragraph (1) of the Supreme Court Act 2009, the Indonesian Supreme Court is in charge of ensuring the proper administration of justice in the Indonesian legal system.

III. Foreign Law in Other Instances

A. Administration and Non-judicial Authorities

Based on Article 16 of the AB, civil registry offices in Indonesia shall apply the national law of foreigners to determine their civil status, capacity and issues related to their family matters. Influenced by the civil law traditions, civil registry officers in Indonesia apply foreign law *ex officio*. They do not require the foreign parties to prove the content of their law.

To ascertain foreign law related to a foreigner's civil status, capacity and family matters in Indonesia, an Indonesian civil registry office can require the foreigner's assistance to provide the office with certain legal documents from their country of origin. Furthermore, to determine the capacity of foreigners to marry in Indonesia, Indonesian civil registry offices can also require foreigners to obtain Certificates of No Impediment to Marriage issued by the

[44] District Court of Central Jakarta Decision 52/Pdt.G/2010/PN.Jkt.Pst. (21 October 2010).
[45] High Court of Jakarta Decision 297/PDT/2011/PT.DKI (24 November 2011).
[46] Supreme Court Decision 1935 K/Pdt/2012 (14 January 2013).

foreigners' embassies in Indonesia. The certificates from the embassies will determine the foreigners' capacity to marriage in Indonesia based on their national laws. Such certificate with its Indonesian translation helps the civil registry office ascertain foreign law that governs a foreigner's capacity to marriage.

B. Arbitration and Alternative Dispute Resolutions

i. Arbitration

Act No 30 of 1999 concerning arbitration and alternative dispute settlement (the Arbitration and ADS Act 1999) is silent on how arbitral tribunals seated in Indonesia shall ascertain and apply foreign law. The Arbitration and ADS Act 1999 only governs the arbitrators to settle the parties' dispute by applying the law chosen by the parties, or in case the parties do not make a choice of law agreement, the law where the arbitration takes place (Article 56, paragraph (2)).

No provision in the Arbitration and ADS Act 1999 requires the arbitrators to ascertain and apply the law *ex officio*. That means arbitrators in Indonesia are free to use both the civil law approach and common law approach when ascertaining and applying foreign law chosen by the parties. The arbitrators can ascertain and apply the foreign law *ex officio*, and they are also allowed to require the parties to prove the foreign law. Arbitrators are free to employ all legal means or methods to investigate foreign law. They can ask the parties to provide materials for ascertaining foreign law. They can also ask the parties to obtain expert opinions[47] and make submissions on the content of foreign law. Pursuant to Article 50 of the Arbitration and ADS Act 1999, arbitrators are allowed to request assistance of expert witnesses to provide the arbitrators with a written or oral statement concerning a specific matter which is related to the merits of the dispute. This provision indicates that arbitrators can ascertain the content of foreign law *ex officio* by inviting expert witnesses who provide information concerning the foreign law chosen by the parties. After obtaining the statement or affidavit from an expert witness, the arbitrators shall pass the statement to the parties and invite the parties to comment on the expert witness' statement (Article 50, paragraphs (1), (3), (4)).[48]

[47] Art 49 of the Arbitration and ADS Act 1999 provides that:

(1) Upon order from the arbitrator or arbitral tribunal or based on request of both parties, one or more witness or expert witness can be summoned to be heard.
(2) The costs associated with the summon and travel expenses of the witness or expert witness shall be borne by the party who requests it.

[48] Art 50 of the Arbitration and ADS Act 1999 provides that:

(1) Arbitrator or arbitral tribunal may request assistance of one or more expert witnesses to provide written statement concerning a specific matter which is related to the merits of the dispute.
(2) Both parties must provide information which is required by expert witnesses.
(3) Arbitrator or arbitral tribunal shall forward the copy of the expert witness' statement to both parties so that it can be responded in writing by both parties.
(4) If there is an unclear matter, upon request from the party who has interest on it, the relevant expert witness may be summoned and heard before the arbitration tribunal with the presence of both parties or their attorneys.

ii. Mediation

With regard to mediators, they do not usually advise the parties about the law. The Arbitration and ADS Act 1999 also does not require the mediators to settle the parties' dispute by applying the law chosen by the parties. The Supreme Court Regulation No 1 of 2016 concerning mediation procedures in courts appoints judges, court officials, or certified mediators to mediate the disputing parties before their dispute is heard by the courts (Articles 3(1), 4, and 8). Pursuant to the Regulation, disputes in civil matters, save for certain cases, shall go through the mediation process to enable out of court settlements between the parties, hence reducing the burden of the courts. Although the mediators could be judges or court officials, they, as mediators, do not advise the parties about the law, and they are not authorised to make any judgment. The amicable settlement mediated by a mediator shall be based on the negotiation and agreement reached by the disputing parties, not necessarily based on the foreign law designated by choice of law rules.[49] Accordingly, mediators are not required to apply and ascertain any foreign law.

iii. Conciliation

As for another alternative dispute resolution, namely, conciliation, the Arbitration and ADS Act 1999 mentioned it as one of the alternative dispute settlements (Article 1, no 1). However, the Act does not govern further the procedure of conciliation beyond Article 1, no 1. The only law that regulates the conciliation procedure is Act No 2 of 2004 concerning Industrial Relation Dispute Settlements (the Industrial Relation Dispute Settlements Act 2004). Pursuant to Article 1, no 13 of the Act, industrial relation conciliation refers to the settlement of dispute of rights, dispute over employment termination or dispute among worker unions/labour unions within a company through a consultative meeting which is moderated by one or more neutral conciliators. One of the requirements of being a conciliator of industrial relations is to have a knowledge of laws and regulations concerning employment (Article 19, paragraph (1)h of the Industrial Relation Dispute Settlements Act 2004). The conciliator is also obligated to provide written recommendations of solutions to the disputing parties to resolve their dispute (Article 1, no 14). Following these provisions, the principle of 'conciliator knows the law' applies. The conciliator is responsible for establishing the applicable law to the facts furnished by the parties to recommend solutions.

However, based on the established doctrine in Indonesia, Indonesian employment law is categorised as one of the mandatory rules. Sudargo Gautama wrote that Indonesian agrarian law, consumer protection law, employment law, and laws concerning export and import prohibitions, rental or lease, and exchange regulations are categorised as part of the mandatory rules because they relate to Indonesian social and economic interests.[50] In fact, the Industrial Relations Court is the only court having jurisdiction over disputes arising out of employment contracts in Indonesia and only applies Indonesian law.[51] Against this backdrop, conciliators of industrial relations in Indonesia shall apply only Indonesian law when

[49] Opinion given by Lita Arijati, a certified mediator trainer and a senior law lecturer in the subject of Mediation at the Faculty of Law, Universitas Indonesia.

[50] S Gautama, *Pengantar Hukum Perdata Internasional Indonesia* (Jakarta, Binacipta, 1985) 170, 205.

[51] Kusumadara (n 5) 112.

determining any dispute irrespective of the parties' choice of foreign law. That means they do not have to apply and ascertain foreign law in handling the disputes.

In conclusion, in arbitration in Indonesia, the arbitrators are free to use both the civil law approach and common law approach when applying and ascertaining foreign law, provided that they do it under the fundamental principles of due process, fairness, and respect relevant mandatory rules. As for mediation in Indonesia, the mediators prioritise amicable settlement based on the negotiation and agreement reached between the parties, rather than applying and ascertaining foreign law. With regard to conciliation, particularly industrial relation conciliation, the conciliators only apply Indonesian law. This is because employment law is considered part of the body of mandatory rules. Hence, they do not apply foreign law to deal with employment or labour union disputes.

IV. Access to Indonesian Law

There are several official databases in Indonesia that provide English translations of Indonesian legislation and case laws. The official databases are managed by Indonesian ministries, other government agencies and Indonesia's Constitutional Court. One of the databases is also provided by the International Labour Organization (ILO). Since the state and an international organisation provide those databases, the databases are accessible for free without any password.

The official databases are, among others:

(a) *Peraturan | Terjemah*, which is a database managed by Indonesia's Ministry of Law and Human Rights. It contains official English translations of many, but not all, Indonesian legislation and regulations. It does not include case laws. This database itself is available only in Indonesian; hence, the user must know first the original Indonesian titles to search for a specific law or regulation within the database. When the search yields a matched legislation or regulation, the user will find its English translation (*terjemah*) next to the relevant legislation or regulation.[52]

(b) *The Bank of Indonesia | Regulation*, which is a database managed by Indonesia's Central Bank, Bank Indonesia. It contains official English translations of the Bank Indonesia's regulations.[53]

(c) *List of Unofficial English Translation of Laws and Regulations on Communications and Informatics 1999*, which is a database of unofficial English translations of laws and regulations on communications and informatics that is managed by Indonesia's Ministry of Information and informatics.[54]

(d) *NATLEX*, which is a database managed by ILO. It contains unofficial English translations of Indonesia's legislation on labour, social security and human rights.[55]

(e) *MKRI*, which is a database managed by Indonesia's Constitutional Court.[56] It provides English translations of many, but not all, Constitutional Court's judgments. Court

[52] See peraturan.go.id/peraturan/terjemahan.html (accessed 13 February 2022).
[53] See bi.go.id/en/publikasi/peraturan/Default.aspx (accessed 13 February 2022).
[54] See jdih.kominfo.go.id/produk_hukum/inventarisasi-terjemahan (accessed 13 February 2022).
[55] See ilo.org/dyn/natlex/natlex4.countrySubjects?p_lang=en&p_country=IDN (accessed 13 February 2022).
[56] See en.mkri.id/court/ (accessed 13 February 2022).

decisions rendered by other courts are compiled in a different database, run by Indonesia's Supreme Court.[57] However, this database does not provide any English translation of those court decisions.

In addition, there are private services that provide unofficial English translations of and information on Indonesian legislation. The service providers also have their own databases. Since the databases belong to private companies, the databases are not free. Users are required to pay a subscription fee to access their databases. However, as part of their societal services, these private companies regularly provide, for free, information on some Indonesian legislation and case laws. They provide some information in English. The private database and services are, among others:

(a) *Hukum | Regulation* is a database managed by an Indonesian private company, PT Justika Siar Publika. It contains the English translations of Indonesian legislation and regulations.[58] The company also runs a huge database of Indonesian case laws, but it is only available in Indonesian language.[59]
(b) Hukum | *Data* contains the latest report on and analysis written in English of legislation, regulations and bills.[60]
(c) *ICLG* provides information in English on some legal matters in Indonesia. The website is managed by Global Legal Group, a London-based media company.[61]

V. Access to Foreign Law: Future Developments in Indonesia and ASEAN

To date, Indonesia is not a party to any international or regional instruments that attempt to harmonise the treatment of foreign law. Neither is Indonesia any party to international or regional instruments on the information of and access to foreign law. In fact, there is no such kind of legal instruments within the Association of South-East Asian Nations (ASEAN).[62] The 1978 Agreement on Judicial Co-operation between the Republic of Indonesia and the Kingdom of Thailand[63] also does not govern cooperation related to the treatment of and information on foreign law.

Given the mandatory application of foreign law in Indonesia, judges in Indonesia need more access to foreign law. Based on the cases presented in the previous sections, it is evident that judges require a more easily-accessible method of access to foreign law to avoid its erroneous application. Therefore, administrative and judicial cooperation, either at the regional or international level, to enable Indonesian judges easily to access foreign

[57] See putusan3.mahkamahagung.go.id/beranda.html (accessed 13 February 2022).
[58] See pro.hukumonline.com/regulation accessed (13 February 2022).
[59] See www.hukumonline.com/pusatdata/view/npts/lt49f14ead411d0 (accessed 13 February 2022).
[60] See pro.hukumonline.com/home (accessed 13 February 2022).
[61] See iclg.com/jurisdictions/indonesia (accessed 13 February 2022).
[62] See agreement.asean.org/ (accessed 13 February 2022).
[63] Ratified by the Indonesian Government on 13 December 1978 and by the Thai Government on 25 December 1978.

law should be established. In addition, the existing judicial cooperation network between the ASEAN Member States should be expanded to include judicial assistance, access to foreign law, and the exchange of information on foreign law. The ASEAN Senior Law Officials Meeting (ASLOM) under the ASEAN Law Ministers' Meeting (ALAWMM) shall discuss establishing an administrative and judicial assistance network that enables judges in ASEAN to access and obtain information on foreign law. So far, there has been no discussion in ASLOM and ALAWMM about this issue.[64]

In addition, courts, arbitration institutions, and civil registry offices should establish their own units within their institutions to provide judges, arbitrators, civil registry officers, and notaries with information on foreign law swiftly and efficiently. The units can obtain information on foreign law from the Internet, libraries, and other sources, including foreign embassies. The units should employ staff that can obtain an Indonesian translation of foreign law and how the foreign law is applied in the country of origin. For courts located in remote and small districts in Indonesia that lack human resources, the Supreme Court, as the supervising body of Indonesian courts, shall help provide them with access to foreign law.

When Indonesia accedes to the Hague Conventions that govern family matters, such as the 1980 Hague Child Abduction Convention and the 1996 Hague Child Protection Convention, Indonesia should join the International Hague Network of Judges that helps facilitate direct judicial communications among judges in family matters.

Regarding the international or regional instrument unifying the treatment of foreign law, although it might be useful to achieve international harmony of judgments, one must remember that the instrument will require a fundamental revision of procedural rules, such as the revision of the Member States' Civil Procedure Codes. This could make the instruments infeasible and not practical.

Therefore, the authors suggest that it be more important and urgent to provide an easily-accessible method of access to foreign law for judges and other non-judicial authorities, either at the national, regional, or international level than to establish instruments unifying the treatment of foreign law. One possible way to achieve this purpose is the Indonesian Supreme Court establishing a cooperation on information on foreign law in civil and commercial matters, with Supreme Courts of other countries. Another way is by establishing the ASEAN Judicial Network to help courts in ASEAN Member States obtain information on the national law of other Member States via a certain website or direct judicial communications facilitated by liaison judges.

VI. Conclusion

Based on the civil law traditions to which Indonesian private international law belongs, foreign law is an issue of law, not fact. As such, the determination and/or interpretation of foreign law is resolved by judges. Judges have to find and apply foreign law *ex officio*. That has been jurisprudence since 1915. Nevertheless, Indonesian judges usually rely heavily on

[64] See asean.org/our-communities/asean-political-security-community/rules-based-people-oriented-people-centred/legal-matters-and-judicial-cooperation/ (accessed 13 February 2022).

the assistance of the parties to investigate and ascertain foreign law. In addition, the parties need to invoke the foreign elements of their cases and assist the judges with many things related to foreign law. It is concluded that the ways the parties assisted Indonesian courts are similar to the practice in the common law jurisdiction, namely, the parties must invoke, plead and prove the foreign law and its contents. Only in a few cases have courts taken an active position in ascertaining foreign law.

Given the mandatory application of foreign law, Indonesian judges need more access to foreign law. However, it is evident from the case law that ascertaining the content of foreign law is quite challenging for Indonesian judges. Therefore, the international or regional instruments on the information on foreign law and an administrative and judicial cooperation network that enable Indonesian judges easily to access foreign law should be established. That is more important than establishing instruments unifying the treatment of foreign law.

14

Thailand

POOMINTR SOOKSRIPAISARNKIT AND
KRISDA SAENGCHAROENSAP

I. Introduction

In the globalised world where virtually citizens of every country on earth, being natural or juristic persons, are linked or connected, it is inevitable that courts in every country will see increasing cases involving foreign elements. Thai courts will see no exception in this respect. In Thailand, the main source of the conflict of law rules is contained in a statute, namely the Act on Conflict of Laws, B.E. 2481.[1] This piece of legislation identifies relevant connecting factors and hence stipulates choice of law rules which in turn lays down instances when Thai courts need to apply foreign laws. However, in terms of the treatment of foreign laws, this legislation only broadly states in section 8: 'Whenever the law of a foreign country which is to govern is not proved to the satisfaction of the Court, the internal law of Siam shall apply.'[2] However, this legislation does not set out rules on how foreign law is to be proved. This necessitates further exploration into domestic civil procedure laws.

In line with the theme of the book, in this chapter, the authors examine the treatment of foreign law in Thailand. With rather scant primary sources on the conflict of laws in Thailand, in addition to primary sources including the statute and the cases decided by the Supreme Court of Thailand, and the secondary sources, that is, academic works of literature, to ensure accuracy and contemporaneity of information, the authors also interviewed two judges so to gain perspectives on the courts' practices, to which we acknowledged here.[3] This chapter is split into six parts. After this Introduction (I), in the second part (II), instances when the courts will apply a foreign law will be outlined. Afterward, in the third part (III), how a foreign law is to be proved will be explored. In the fourth part (IV), how Thai courts apply and construe foreign law and, if necessary, fill the gaps created by such application will be discussed. The fifth part (V) then looks into the application of foreign law in the context

[1] Office of the Council of State, 'Act on the Conflict of Laws, B.E. 2481', available online: web.krisdika.go.th/data/outsitedata/outsite21/file/Act_on_Conflict_of_Law,_B.E._2481.pdf. Thailand uses the Buddhist era calendar which is 543 years ahead of the Gregorian year.

[2] Siam was the former name of Thailand. The country has been re-named since 23 June 1939.

[3] The authors are indebted to Mr Watcharapon Suntrasantik, Vice Presiding Judge of the Central Intellectual Property and International Trade Court (former Secretary of the Court, Central Intellectual Property and International Trade Court), and Miss Jarimjit Pantawee, Judge of the Office of the President of the Supreme Court, for their valuable input.

of practices in arbitration. Finally, in the sixth part (VI), the authors then discuss the future with respect to the treatment of foreign law in Thailand.

II. Instances when Thai Courts will Apply Foreign Law

As mentioned earlier, the Act on Conflict of Laws B.E. 2481 stipulates connecting factors relevant to each instance. If a connecting factor points to a foreign law, this will lead to the application of the foreign law by the courts. The general principles are laid down in section 3 which is in itself delineating the hierarchy of law to be applied as well as providing for a gap-filling method (to be discussed further in part IV). This section provides: 'Whenever there is no provision in this Act or in any other laws of Siam to govern a case of conflict of laws, the general principles of private international law shall apply.' In certain specific situations, the courts may come to apply foreign law or even a foreign conflict of law rules through the *single renvoi*.[4] This is because of the language of section 4 provides: 'Whenever the law of a foreign country is to govern and under that law it is the law of Siam which shall be applied, the internal law of Siam governs, and not the Siamese rules on conflict of laws.' This provision leads to more contentious issues. First, when latter provisions in the same statute refer to the law, for example, the law of nationality of a person (as per section 10), the law of the place where the property is situated (as per section 16), whether such reference is made to the substantive law of such country or the conflict of law rules of such country? In other words, when or in which instance do Thai private international law rules provide for the application of the doctrine of *renvoi*? Second, and this is a point which remains contentious among Thai private international law scholars, whether the Thai courts will apply the law of the third country if, for example, by private international law rules in Thailand, the courts are to apply the choice of law rules of state X and the choice of law rules of state X provides for the substantive law of state Y? This is contentious since the language of section 4 addresses remission only.

Concerning the first point, it appears that the term 'the law of a foreign country' in section 4 encompasses that country's private international law rules.[5] A scholar explained this point that it was not a drafting mistake that the language of this provision uses first the term 'the law of a foreign country' and almost immediately refers to it again with the pronoun 'that'. This demonstrated an intention to import the *renvoi* mechanism into the conflict of law rules of Thailand.[6] However, there are certain exceptions to the application of the doctrine of *renvoi* too.[7] The first is a recognition of the party autonomy in respect of

[4] K Prokati and A Laowonsiri, 'Thailand' in J Basedow, G Rühl, F Ferrari and PM Asensio (eds), *Encyclopedia of Private International Law* (Cheltenham, Edward Elgar Publishing, 2017) 2569, 2571. The *single renvoi* technique is seen mostly in civil law systems. It refers to the situation when the forum courts 'take account of the foreign choice-of-law rules, but on the basis that the reference by the foreign system back to the law of the forum, or on to the law of a third country, is a reference to the domestic law of the forum, or of the third country respectively'. M Davies, A Bell, PLG Brereton, and M Douglas, *Nygh's Conflict of Laws in Australia*, 10th edn (Chatswood, LexisNexis Butterworths, 2020) para 15.4.

[5] K Luchai, *Explanation on the conflict of laws*, 9th edn (Bangkok, October Publishing House, 2021) 35.

[6] K Chunchaemsai, *Private International Law Book 1: Conflict of Laws* (Bangkok, Thammasat University Faculty of Law, 2021) 256.

[7] ibid 260.

the choice of law in contract enshrined in the first paragraph of section 13 of the Act on Conflict of Laws, B.E. 2481: 'The question as to what law is applicable in regard to the essential elements or effects of a contract is determined by the intention of the parties to it ….'[8] It is a matter of general recognition that when the parties to a contract expressly or tacitly choose a law of a country to govern their contract, their intention is for the substantive law of that country to apply.[9] The second exception is in the law of arbitration which likewise reflects the concept of party autonomy.[10] The first paragraph of section 34 of the Arbitration Act B.E. 2545 reads:

> The arbitral tribunal shall decide the dispute in accordance with the governing law chosen by the parties. Any designation of law or legal system of a country shall be construed, unless otherwise expressed, as directly referring to the substantive law of the country and not to its conflict of laws rules.[11]

So, in effect, the consequence of adopting the *single renvoi* approach can be demonstrated in an example given by a Thai scholar. Suppose that the Thai conflict of law rules the legal capacity of A is to be determined by the law of Malaysia (as the law of A's nationality as per section 10). The courts have to look into the conflict of law rules of Malaysia. According to the conflict of law rules of Malaysia, the legal capacity of a person is determined by the law of their domicile. A's domicile is in Malaysia. In this case, the Thai courts will directly apply the substantive law of Malaysia dealing with the legal capacity of a person.[12] The problem arises, and this leads to the second point mentioned earlier, what if the foreign conflict of law rules do not result in the application of that foreign substantive law or do not result in remission?

One way which one may read into section 4 is that it aims at preventing the problem of *circulus inextricabilis*.[13] If anything, this provision is silent on transmission. An alternative understanding is that since, as in the example given above, when the conflict of law rules of Malaysia points to the substantive law of Malaysia, the Thai courts have to apply that law, by the same token, if the foreign conflict of law rules point further to the law of another foreign country, there is no sensible reason why Thai courts will not apply the law of that third country. In other words, there is no logical reason why only the remission, but also not the transmission, is recognised.[14] Since the statute sought to import the concept of *single renvoi*, the concept should be adopted as a whole. The narrow interpretation of section 4 to the event of remission only seems to suggest partial importation of the concept.[15] This is also in line with the idea that the parties should be able to expect a similar outcome in terms of the application of the law whether they sue before the Thai courts or before the courts of a foreign country.[16] The records of the meetings leading to the drafting

[8] ibid.
[9] ibid 332.
[10] ibid 260.
[11] The Arbitration Institute, Office of the Judiciary, 'Arbitration Act B.E. 2545', available online: tai.coj.go.th/th/file/get/file/20190328ecac5333356ffad0331bd601151db9f4142557.pdf.
[12] Luchai (n 5) 35.
[13] Chunchaemsai (n 6) 258.
[14] Luchai (n 5) 36.
[15] ibid.
[16] ibid.

of the Act on the Conflict of Laws B.E. 2481 were not of much assistance since some were in support of the recognition of the *single renvoi* doctrine while others supported the rejection of the concept of *renvoi* in its entirety.

To the extent that the choice of law rules in Thailand accommodates the *single renvoi* approach, this is at odds with international developments. In English law, the doctrine of *renvoi* is applied only in very limited circumstances.[17] The exclusion of *renvoi* is also reflected in Article 4 of the Asian Principles of Private International Law.[18] This is also the position in Article 8 of the Hague Principles on Choice of Law in International Commercial Contracts.[19] This is perhaps one of the areas which can be considered for any potential reform of the Act on the Conflict of Laws B.E. 2481 which has come of age after over 80 years of application without even a single amendment.

Bearing in mind the general application of the *single renvoi* doctrine in Thai private international law, any foreign law to which the relevant connecting factors point to needs to be read as encompassing also that country's private international law rules. Connecting factors in use may be quickly summarised here. As far as contracts are concerned, in the absence of express or tacit choice as per the first paragraph of section 13, then the law of the common nationality of the parties is to be applied. If the parties have different nationalities, then the law of the place where the contract is made is to be applied. For the legal capacity of an individual, as mentioned earlier, section 10 provides for the law of nationality of such person. For a juristic person, the law of nationality is taken to be that of the place where such a company or organisation has its principal office as per section 7. In the case of torts, Thai private international law adopts the 'double actionability' rules as reflected in section 15.[20] For the property, whether movable or immovable, this is a matter for the *lex situs* per section 16. As far as family law is concerned, the capacity to enter betrothal depends on the law of nationality of each party. Effects of such betrothal depend on the *lex fori* as per section 18. Likewise, the conditions for marriage depend on the law of nationality of each party as per section 19 but the formal validity of marriage depends on the *lex celebrationis* as per section 20.

In terms of the relationship between husband and wife, that depends on the law of the common nationality. Where they do not have the same nationality, however, the law of the husband's nationality shall govern as per section 21. In terms of the property of the husband and wife where there is no antenuptial agreement, that depends on the law of the common

[17] See J Fawcett and JM Carruthers, *Cheshire, North & Fawcett Private International Law*, 14th edn (Oxford, Oxford University Press, 2008) 71–72.

[18] 'Where the choice of law rules of an APIL-Jurisdiction refer to the legal system of a foreign country, the reference is limited to the substantive rules of that foreign legal system in exclusion of its choice of law rules as well as procedural rules.' W Chen and G Goldstein, 'The Asian Principles of Private International Law: objectives, contents, structure and selected topics on choice of law' (2017) 13(2) *Journal of Private International Law* 411, 423.

[19] 'A choice of law does not refer to rules of private international law chosen by the parties unless the parties expressly provide otherwise.' The Hague Conference on Private International Law, '40: Principles on Choice of Law in International Commercial Contracts', available online: www.hcch.net/en/instruments/conventions/full-text/?cid=135.

[20] 'An obligation arising out of a wrongful act is governed by the law of the place where the facts constituting such wrongful act have taken place.

The foregoing provision does not apply to facts which, having taken place in a foreign country, are not wrongful according to the Siamese law.

In no case can the injured party claim compensation or remedies other than those allowed by the Siamese law.'

nationality, or else the husband's nationality. If that property is immovable, then it depends on the *lex situs* as per section 22. The capacity to enter an antenuptial agreement is determined by the law of nationality of each party following section 24. Elements and effects of an antenuptial agreement depend on the law of common nationality. Otherwise, it depends on the law of the place where 'the parties intended or may be presumed to have intended to submit themselves …'. Where no such intention can be gleaned, then it will depend on the law of the first matrimonial domicile. But, for the immovable property, this still depends on the *lex situs* as per section 25. In respect of the divorce, if it is one by mutual consent, its validity depends on the law of each party's nationality as per section 26. The same can be said in respect of the divorce with no mutual consent but the grounds for divorce will depend on the *lex fori* as per section 27. The question of the legitimacy of a child is determined by the law of the nationality of the husband of the mother at the time the child was born. Or the nationality of the husband at the time of his death if he died before the birth. This is per section 29.

As to the rights and duties between parents and the child, according to section 30, this is the matter of the law of nationality of the father. However, the law of nationality of the mother may be applicable if the mother was not married. The law of nationality of the father is relevant again in the event of the legitimation of a child following section 31. Where the minor is placed under guardianship, the law of the nationality of the minor governs the duties and powers of the guardian along with the termination of the guardianship. However, the powers of the guardian to deal with immovable properties are matters for the *lex situs*. This is laid down in section 32. There is also an exception to this. Even if the minor is of foreign nationality, they may be placed on guardianship according to Thai law 'if it appears that, under the circumstances of the case, the interests of such minor cannot be efficiently protected by the organisation and management of guardianship under the foreign law.'[21] It is the law of the court ordering such deprivation which governs the deprivation of parental powers, according to section 33. Whether action can be initiated against the ascendants depends on the law of the nationality of the descendant as provided for in section 34.

As to the matter of adoption, in general, it will be governed by the law of the common nationality of the adopter and the adopted. However, if they are not of the same nationality, then the capacity and conditions for adopting will depend on the law of nationality of each. In such a case, the effects of adoption will be a matter for the law of the adopter's nationality. All of these are set out in section 35. As to the maintenance, while this depends on the law of nationality of the person whom the maintenance claim is made against, in any event, the said claim cannot exceed the amount provided for under Thai law. This is according to section 36.

As far as succession is concerned, if the property is an immovable one, again that is a matter for the *lex situs* according to section 37. In the case of the movable property, this will depend on the law of the domicile of the deceased at the time of the death as per section 38. The capacity to make a will depends on the law of nationality of the person who makes the will at the relevant time, according to section 39. The form of the will, according to section 40, can either follow the law of nationality of the person who makes it or the law

[21] The Act on the Conflict of Laws, B.E. 2481, s 32.

of the place where the form is made. Effects and interpretation of the will along with the question of validity and effectiveness are matters for the law of the domicile of the testator at the time of their death, according to section 41. Likewise, according to section 42, the law of the domicile of the testator at the time of the revocation of the will governs the matter of revocation. This same provision also provides that the law of the domicile of the testator at the time of their death is what is to be referred to in respect of the lapse of the will.

All connecting factors as outlined above are rigid in the sense that it is fixed in the statute which does not allow courts to exercise discretion otherwise.[22]

Aside from the stipulation of connecting factors relevant to each instance as in the Act on Conflict of Laws B.E. 2481 which can point the courts to the application of foreign law, outside of the context of this statute, the courts may be bound as a matter of Thailand's obligations in public international law to apply foreign law. These international conventions which Thailand became a State Party to may lead the courts to apply foreign law:[23] The Convention on the Rights of the Child, 20 November 1989; Convention of 25 October 1980 on the Civil Aspects of International Child Abduction; Convention of 29 May 1993 on Protection of Children and Co-operation in Respect of Intercountry Adoption; The Berne Convention for the Protection of Literary and Artistic Works of 9 September 1986 (with subsequent amendments); Convention of Paris for the protection of industrial property of 20 March 1983 (with subsequent revisions and amendments); and The United Nations Convention on the Recognition and Enforcement of Foreign Arbitral Awards (New York, 10 June 1958).

Despite Thai courts being bound to apply foreign law where connecting factors point to that law, an exception exists in section 5 of the Act on the Conflict of Laws B.E. 2481: 'Whenever a law of a foreign country is to govern, it shall apply in so far as it is not contrary to the public order or good morals of Siam.' There is a rather dated case decided by the Supreme Court on this point cited in academic commentaries.[24] In Supreme Court Case No 1583/2511, the case involved a carriage of goods by sea from Denmark and Norway to Thailand. In the year 1968 or earlier when this carriage of goods occurred, Thailand had no law as to the carriage of goods by sea. The choice of law clause in the bills of lading stipulating that Danish law would apply to the disputes between the parties but was found inapplicable so far as it related to the time bar aspect since the law relating to the time bar is the one which is about the public policy of Thailand. This decision has been criticised by scholars who abandoned it as no longer a good authority since no reason was provided why the application of the Danish law on time-bar would be repugnant to the public policy of Thailand.[25] This decision is also no longer good law because Thailand has since enacted the Carriage of Goods by Sea Act, B.E. 2534 where the first paragraph of section 4 provides:

> This Act shall apply to the carriage of goods by sea from one place within the Kingdom to another place outside the Kingdom or from one place outside the Kingdom to another place within the Kingdom except that, in the case where it is indicated in the bill of lading that the law of another

[22] Chunchaemsai (n 6) 227.
[23] Prokati and Laowonsiri (n 4) 2570.
[24] Luchai (n 5) 43; Chunchaemsai (n 6) 273.
[25] Luchai (n 5) 43; Chunchaemsai (n 6) 273.

country or international law shall apply, such law shall apply, provided that notwithstanding such indication, the Act shall apply if it is apparent that any party is of Thai nationality or is a juristic person established under the law of Thailand.[26]

An example on the possible application of section 5 was given by scholars considering the situation of a marriage, where both partners did not reach the minimum age to be able to marry according to Thai law even though they had the capacity to marry under their respective laws of nationality might be found to be against the public policy of Thailand.[27] However, in Supreme Court Case No 45/2524, where the marriage happened in the People's Republic of China between the plaintiff and the girl – both were Thais. At the time, the plaintiff was 10 years of age and the girl was 12 years of age, and the Supreme Court held that as there was no Chinese law at the time which prohibited such a marriage, the marriage was lawful according to section 20 of the Act on the Conflict of Laws, B.E. 2481 and this was not against the public policy of Thailand. This decision is questionable to the extent that the Supreme Court should have classified the matter as substantive validity and applied section 19 of the Act on the Conflict of Laws, B.E. 2481, instead of section 20.[28] Scholars assumed the Court wanted to give effect to the acquired rights of the parties under the foreign law.[29] It was unfortunate that published decisions in Thailand, as is the case in most civil law jurisdiction countries, tend to be short since the courts do not always elaborate on their reasoning.

Provided that relevant connecting factors point to the law of a foreign country, Thai courts will be bound to apply that foreign law so far as it can be proved, according to section 8, so far as that foreign law is not repugnant to the public policy of Thailand which will render that relevant part inapplicable as per section 5. If foreign law is inapplicable in whole or in part on the basis that it is repugnant to the public policy of Thailand, then Thai courts will apply Thai law to that case or that part of the case instead.[30] So, the matter of how foreign law is to be proved becomes crucial and it is the issue that will be discussed in the following part.

III. Proving Foreign Law in Thai Courts

In Thailand, judges take a passive role. The duty to ascertain the contents of foreign law rests upon the party.[31] The question of foreign law is taken to be a question of fact.[32] While treating the question of foreign law in this way places Thailand at odds with other civil law countries, this practice can be explained on the basis of the evolution of the Thai judicial system. As Darling correctly observed, Thai judicial procedure 'is an amalgam drawn

[26] Office of the Council of State, 'Carriage of Goods by Sea Act, B.E. 2534 (1991), available online: www.krisdika.go.th/data//document/ext809/809771_0001.pdf.
[27] Prokati and Laowonsiri (n 4) 2571.
[28] ibid 2574.
[29] ibid.
[30] Chunchaemsai (n 6) 272.
[31] Prokati and Laowonsiri (n 4) 2572.
[32] Chunchaemsai (n 6) 262.

somewhat equally from British and continental practices' and both common law and civil law techniques are utilised.[33] While Thailand (or referred to in history as Siam) has never been a colony of any western countries, there were increased interactions with foreign countries in terms of international trade. As part of the opening up process, Siam at the relevant time, in particular the kings, were under immense pressure to agree to what can be regarded as one-sided and unfair treaties. As early as 1855, Siam entered into what became known as the 'Bowring Treaty' with Britain.[34] This was then followed by 14 similar treaties with other western countries.[35] The essence of these treaties was that citizens of those foreign countries would not be subject to the jurisdiction of the Siamese courts even if they did wrong or committed a crime in Siam. All cases involving them would be heard and tried in the consuls of the respective countries applying their own laws.[36] To take control of its jurisdiction and to negotiate for the abolition of these unfair treaties, as part of efforts to modernise Siamese laws and its legal system, western legal advisors were appointed. At the same time, King Rama V launched the programme for Thai students to receive legal education overseas.[37] Between 1910–41, a British judge was always appointed to sit in the Supreme Court of Siam.[38] Hence, these British judges and those Thai graduates from the common law legal tradition helped shape and influenced the Thai legal procedure.

According to section 84/1 of the Civil Procedure Code B.E. 2477[39] (with subsequent amendments), the party who alleges any fact in support of their plaint or answer has the burden of proof. When a party wants to submit documentary evidence to prove the foreign law, such party must ensure that a certified translation into Thai of such document is submitted to the courts. This is so even though many Thai judges nowadays receive overseas education and are well fluent in English language. This is according to section 46 of the Civil Procedure Code which provides:

> All proceedings carried out by a Court relating to the trial and adjudication of civil cases shall be in the Thai language.
>
> All pleadings and all documents or papers whatsoever, whether made by a party or by the Court or an officer of the Court and constituting the file of the case shall be drawn up in Thai and written in ink, typewritten or printed. If any mistake occurs, it shall not be erased, but merely crossed out and rewritten and the writer shall sign his name in the margin. Any addition made shall be signed or initialled by the person making it.
>
> Where the original of any document or paper whatsoever filed with the Court is in a foreign language, the Court shall order the party who filed it to submit a certified translation of the whole or of any material part thereof to be attached the original.

[33] FC Darling, 'The Evolution of Law in Thailand' (1970) 32(2) *The Review of Politics* 197, 215.

[34] S Reekie and A Reekie, 'British Judges in the Supreme Court of Siam' in A Harding and M Pongsapan (eds), *Thai Legal History: From Traditional to Modern Law* (Cambridge, Cambridge University Press, 2022) 103, 105. This treaty was named after Sir John Bowring, the 4th Governor of Hong Kong between 1854–59.

[35] ibid.

[36] ibid.

[37] Darling (n 33) 206.

[38] Reekie and Reekie (n 34) 108.

[39] International Money Laundering Information Network, 'The Civil Procedure Code', available online: www.imolin.org/doc/amlid/Thailand_The%20Civil%20Procedure%20Code.pdf. While this website provides only a source where the English-translated version of the Civil Procedure Code can be found, the version is no longer up to date. Where subsequent amendments were made, the authors replaced the provision numbering in line with the current version of the Code, and, where relevant, the authors supplied their own English translation.

> Where any party or person appearing in Court does not understand the Thai language, or is deaf or dumb or illiterate, the services of an interpreter shall be provided by the party concerned.

Since it is the duty of the concerned party, associated costs for translation must also be borne by that party. A scholar opined that it is also possible for the party to submit an explanation of such foreign law, an example of how such foreign law is applied, an explanatory report leading to the enactment of that law, and other documents which may assist Thai courts in construing and applying such foreign law.[40] The language of section 8 of the Act on the Conflict of Laws, B.E. 2481, indicated that the foreign law must be proved 'to the satisfaction of the court'. It has been explained that this does not mean that the party needs to prove it to the extent that the court understands the foreign law clearly as if it is the court located in that foreign country.[41] But, at the same time, the party needs to prove to the extent that it enables the court to be able to apply that foreign law in a reasonable manner sufficient to each instance of the case.[42] Of course, in a civil litigation, the other party may argue the position of the foreign law otherwise. Section 104 of the Civil Procedure Act B.E. 2477 provides then that: 'The Court shall have full power to decide whether the evidence as adduced by the parties is relevant to the issue and is sufficient to be taken as conclusive or not and then give judgment accordingly.' In all civil cases (including those involving family and personal status), in practice, the courts will weigh evidence according to the standard of the balance of probability. Still, some scholars think that the applicable standard should be higher than that of the mere balance of probability. It should go to the extent of 'proof by the clear and convincing evidence'. They maintained that a foreign law represents a specific type of fact, different from other factual circumstances or evidence in the case.[43] There has been no conclusive legal precedent that suggests that the proof of a foreign law requires any higher standard than establishing other facts in civil cases.

Aside from the documentary evidence, the parties can also adduce expert witnesses. According to section 98 of the Civil Procedure Code B.E. 2477,

> Any party may cite as a witness on his behalf any person having expert knowledge in art, science, work or skill, trade or practical work, or in foreign law and whose opinion may be of value in setting points in issue, irrespective of whether such witness is engaged in that particular occupation or not.

There is no specific requirement on the qualifications of expert witnesses in foreign law. The party who adduces that expert witness needs to prove their qualifications and experiences pertinent to that foreign law. That party has a burden to convince the court on the reliability of the expert witness. The other party can also adduce its own expert witness to prove otherwise, and each party can cross-examine the other party's expert witness in the course of the proceedings. There is a frequently cited Supreme Court case on this point.[44] In the Supreme Court Case No 1687/2498, the plaintiff tried to prove Chinese law by bringing the Secretary-General of the Office of the Council of State who obtained qualifications in

[40] Chunchamsai (n 6) 263.
[41] ibid 265.
[42] ibid.
[43] Y Nitiruchirot and T Wongyai, 'Problem arising from applying foreign laws in Thai courts' (July–August 2015) *Chulaniti* 73, 85.
[44] ibid 81; Chunchaemsai (n 6) 264.

Thai laws and graduated with a doctorate from Germany to explain the Chinese law. This expert, through the Ministry of Foreign Affairs, obtained that piece of legislation from the Chinese Consulate. The Court declined to recognise him as an expert on Chinese law. In another oft-cited case,[45] the Supreme Court Case No 3537/2546, the Court explained that it is the duty of the party who pleaded the Singaporean law to prove the contents of the same. To do so, the Court emphasised that the party must bring an expert witness who really has relevant knowledge of law of *that* country to prove to the satisfaction of the courts. Since in this case, the defendants failed in their burden of proof, the Court applied Thai law as per section 8 of the Act on the Conflict of Laws, B.E. 2481. Aside from adducing the expert witness, there is nothing to prevent a party from adducing documentary evidence in the form of a legal opinion from respectable institutions since the Civil Procedure Code B.E.2477 allows for documentary evidence in section 93.

While Thai courts adopt the adversarial system where judges take a more passive role, in practice, where judges are in doubt of the veracity of the evidence as to the foreign legal position adduced before them, international databases such as Westlaw and LexisNexis are subscribed to by Thai courts and judges can have access to these. This is part of the process to weigh the evidence. The fact remains that judges have no active role whatsoever to research to ascertain the foreign legal position. In other words, the principle *iura novit cura* has no place in the context of the Thai judicial system. The courts tend to take the foreign legal position adduced by a party as conclusive where there is no argument otherwise.

In light of the absence of any authority from the Supreme Court of Thailand addressing the point and the absence of any opportunity for private international law-related issues to be raised before the Thai courts, the authors submitted that proving foreign law before the Thai courts presents an almost insurmountable task for the party. This is so because the burden of proof becomes two-fold. First, the party needs to prove the private international law rules of the relevant country. Second, and subsequently, the party needs to prove the substantive law of the country where such private international law rules lead to. For example, in the case involving a contract where there is no express choice of law and where the parties to the contract do not have the same nationality, the party needs to prove the private international law rules of the country where the contract was made as per section 13 of the Act on the Conflict of Laws, B.E. 2481. Suppose the party can ascertain that the country where the contract was made in the People's Republic of China, the party will then need to prove the law of the country where the party who effects the characteristic performance of the contract has their habitual residence.[46] As part of the process to do so, the party also needs to prove how the courts in the People's Republic of China apply the characteristic performance concept, something which does not seem to exist in Thai law. Then, that party needs to prove the contract law of the place of the party effecting the characteristic performance. This will bring complexity at the expense of the party who pleads foreign law as,

[45] Nitiruchirot and T Wongyai (n 43) 81.

[46] Art 41 of the Law of the People's Republic of China on the laws applicable to foreign-related civil relations (Adopted at the 17th session of the Standing Committee of the 11th National People's Congress, 28 October 2010): 'The parties may by agreement choose the law applicable to their contract. Absent any choice by the parties, the law of the habitual residence of a party whose performance of the obligation is most characteristic of the contract or the law that most closely connected with the contract shall be applied', available online: conflictoflaws.net/News/2011/01/PIL-China.pdf.

from the example, the party will perhaps need to bring in two expert witnesses, namely the expert on Chinese private international law and the expert on the contract law of the place of the party effecting characteristic performance. Provided that the party can prove these two aspects, it will be for the courts to seek to construe and apply the foreign law, the issue of which will be discussed in the next section.

IV. Thai Courts Construing and Applying Foreign Law and the Gap-Filling Method

Since Thai courts adopt the adversarial system with judges taking a passive role, the answer is apparent that it is unlikely that Thai courts will be able to construe and apply foreign law as if they are courts in that foreign country. This is so because the courts only rely on the evidence adduced by the party, upon which they weigh and apply. Where there is a gap in the foreign law, either the party fails to prove it or otherwise, the answer derived from the combined reading of section 8 and section 3 of the Act on the Conflict of Laws, B.E. 2481, is that the courts will apply the relevant Thai laws. At the last resort when the courts cannot find Thai laws relevant to the matter, then section 3 provides for the courts to apply 'the general principles of private international law'. But what does this term mean exactly?

It appears that this term may be understood in two ways. First, the said general principles of private international law may be gleaned from the overall purpose of the conflict of laws statute itself.[47] In this way, the reasoning for the drafting of the conflict of laws statute is considered. In drafting this statute, the drafters deduced the general principles of private international law into each provision, for example, the status of a person is according to their nationality or matters relating to properties will be governed by the *lex situs*.[48] The problem with this approach is that it remains unclear how the purported general principles of private international law came about. For example, in some jurisdictions, the matters relating to the status of the person may be governed by the law of the domicile of that person. How can one say the use of nationality as a connecting factor is in accordance with the general principles of private international law? In the second sense, by reference to this terminology, the courts may be allowed to import and apply broader ranges of laws such as treaties, international customs, and general principles of international law.[49] There are a couple of problems with adopting this second sense of understanding. First, judges will in effect be as flexible as arbitrators. Second, it may mean judges will give effect to some treaties or international conventions which Thailand does not become a State Party to. Third any reference to international customs or general principles of international law is the methodology in public international law. The only case before the Supreme Court which has been cited by academic commentators[50] is Supreme Court Case No 4027/2545. In this case, the

[47] N Pluajinda (Kiatwatcharachai), 'Filling the gaps in the conflict of laws' in Luchai (n 5) 194.
[48] ibid 195.
[49] ibid.
[50] ibid 196; Chunchaemsai (n 6) 285–86.

Supreme Court had to consider the power of the trustee of the estate of the deceased. The deceased is of English nationality. The trustee was appointed by the English court. The Supreme Court held that the Act on the Conflict of Laws, B.E. 2481 did not stipulate the applicable law relating to the power of the trustee. As such, the general principles of private international law according to section 3 of the Act on the Conflict of Laws, B.E. 2481 had to be referred to. According to this, the applicable law may be either the law of nationality or the law of domicile. Since the plaintiff (trustee) held English nationality and her domicile was also in the UK, as such, either by way of applying the law of nationality or the law of domicile, the applicable law was English law. Since the plaintiff failed to prove the contents of the English law on this matter, the case would be resolved according to section 8 of the Act on the Conflict of Laws, B.E. 2481 which led to the application of the relevant provision in the Thai Civil and Commercial Code. This case has been criticised by an academic commentator on the basis that the Supreme Court was not clear in its reasoning of whether the general principles of private international law in this instance could be taken as the law of nationality or the law of domicile exactly and for what reason.[51] This case represents the gap-filling in the absence of specific private international law rules applicable to the matter. However, the judgment failed to provide clarity on the application of section 3.

Among the two alternative senses in which the general principles of private international law may be understood, the first sense has gained support from an academic commentator who sought to explain the step-by-step process. First, the starting point of all should be the provisions within the Act on the Conflict of Laws, B.E. 2481 itself. Specific provisions along with connecting factors they stipulated need to be analysed to gain or understand by way of the inductive reasoning the general tendency of the statute. For example, in matters relating to the person, the likelihood is that the law of nationality is likely to be applicable.[52] Once the overall tendency relevant to the particular matter is observed, there might be a direct application of the law which that connecting factor leads to, or the application may be by way of analogy.[53] Third, the process of analysis as per the two steps mentioned earlier has to be done in a very careful manner considering differences between specific provisions and general provisions along with their exceptions. This is because, for example, while under the Act on the Conflict of Laws, B.E. 2481, the tendency is that the law of nationality is a connecting factor in the matters relevant to a person while the *lex situs* is a connecting factor in the matters relating to properties, however, in the matters relevant to succession, the statute tends to favour the law of the domicile of the deceased as a connecting factor.[54] The problem with limiting the analysis within the confine of the statute is that this statute was drafted over 80 years ago so it necessarily lacks provisions applicable to newly emerging instances. Thailand does not use the common law legal system so the courts are not in the position to create new connecting factors applicable to such instances. While one may say that the process of deriving the general principles may in itself be considered the process of creating an unwritten choice of law rule, this may take the matter too far. After all, the general principles are ascertained within the limit or the confine of what can be gleaned from the language of different

[51] Chunchaemsai (n 6) 285.
[52] ibid 284.
[53] ibid.
[54] ibid 285.

provisions of the statute. Even if the court in one case purportedly ascertains the general principles, the courts in subsequent cases do not need to follow because in Thailand the judicial precedent 'is not rigid and each case is judged on its own merits'.[55]

What the authors discussed above is the method of gap-filling in the absence of a specific choice of law rules applicable to the matter. However, where the foreign substantive law does not provide for a matter is more straightforward under the Thai private international law mechanism. As mentioned earlier, the combined reading of sections 3 and 8 of the Act on the Conflict of Laws, B.E. 2481 only suggests that in that case, the applicable law will be that of Thailand. The chance that the courts will not be able to find Thai law to govern the matter is highly unlikely given that section 4 of the Civil and Commercial Code, B.E. 2468 also provides for a gap-filling mechanism in the absence of the specific substantive law:

> The law must be applied in all cases which come within the letter or spirit of any of its provisions.
>
> Where no provision is applicable, the case shall be decided according to local custom.
>
> If there is no such local custom, the case shall be decided by analogy to the provision most nearly applicable, and, in default of such provision, by the general principles of law.[56]

With rather fixed connecting factors provided for different instances in different provisions of the Act on Conflict of Laws, B.E. 2481, one would think the chance the courts will apply the statute incorrectly is unlikely. In reality, there might be the case that the judge incorrectly characterised the issue which led to the application of the wrong provision of the statute. Or it might be the case that the parties disagree with how the judge derived the connecting factor (and hence the applicable law) via the method in section 3. In these instances, the parties can appeal the judgment as to the matter of the question of law. This is per section 225 of the Civil Procedure Code B.E. 2477 (and subsequent amendments), which provides:

> A question of fact or of law can be relied upon by the parties presenting appeal only if such question has been expressly stated in the appeal or has arisen in the Court of First Instance, and it shall be the essential matter of the case so as to worthy of a decision.
>
> If any party has failed to raise in the Court of First Instance a question involving public order, or where any party was unable to raise any question of law in the Court of First Instance owing to circumstances not admitted chance as doing an act or because it relates to non-compliance with the provision of this Code governing the appeal proceedings, the party concerned shall be allowed to rely upon such question.[57]

Where, however, in the opinion of the parties or one of the parties, the judge applied the foreign conflict of law rules or the foreign substantive law incorrectly, this will be an appeal on the question of fact. The detailed procedure is provided for in section 224 of the Civil Procedure Code, B.E. 2477:

> In the cases where value of the property or the amount in dispute in the Appeal Court does not exceed fifty thousand baht or the amount as prescribed by the Royal Decree, no appeal shall lie on questions of fact, unless a judge of the Court of First Instance trying such case has given a dissenting opinion or has certified that there are reasonable grounds for appeal or, in the absence of any such dissenting opinion or certification, unless permission to appeal is given in writing by

[55] Darling (n 33) 216.
[56] 'Civil and Commercial Code, B.E. 2468, Book 1', available online: thailaws.com/law/t_laws/TCCC-book1.pdf.
[57] International Money Laundering Information Network (n 39).

> the Chief Judge of the Court of First Instance or by the competent Chief Judge of the Region, as the case may be.
>
> The provisions of the first paragraph shall not apply to the cases relating to the rights pertaining to personal status or family rights and the cases where the relief applied for cannot be computed in terms of money, unless the cases for the eviction of any person from an immovable property shall have or may be hired a monthly rental value not exceeding four thousand baht or not exceeding the amount as prescribed by the Royal Decree at the time of entering the case.
>
> In the application shall be certified by the judge sitting the trial of the case in the Court of First Instance that there are reasonable grounds for appeal, the applicant shall file to such judge the motion together with the petition of appeal to the Court of First Instance. When the Court of First Instance has accepted such motion, the Court of First Instance shall forward such motion together with the file to the aforesaid judge for trying the certification.[58]

This has to be read along with subsequent provisions (from sections 226–246).

If one of the parties remains unsatisfied with the approach taken by the Court of Appeal in respect of foreign law and still wants to appeal further to the Supreme Court, such party may be able to do so. However, there are limited grounds on which the Supreme Court will allow the appeal. As per section 249:

> The Supreme Court may consider granting permission to appeal as per section 247 if it considers the issue on appeal to be a significant one which the Supreme Court should consider.
>
> The significant issue as mentioned in the first paragraph includes:
>
> (1) That legal issue is relating to public interests or public order;
> (2) When the Court of Appeal in its judgment or order determined a significant legal issue in contradiction with its own earlier judgment or contradiction with the legal precedent laid down in the Supreme Court's judgment or order;
> (3) When the Court of Appeal in its judgment or order determined a significant legal issue which there is no existing legal precedent from the Supreme Court;
> (4) When the judgment or order of the Court of Appeal is in contradiction with the final judgment of other courts;
> (5) When determining that issue will help develop the legal interpretation;
> Other important legal issues under the rules set out by the President of the Supreme Court … .

So, any appeal on the question of law relating to the application of the Act on the Conflict of Laws, B.E.2481 may fall within the ambit of section 249(3) or (5) above. Yet, it will be more complicated how the party will convince the Supreme Court that any determination on the application of foreign law will fall into one of the grounds stated in section 249.

V. Arbitration Practices Relating to Foreign Law

In Thailand, arbitration practices are governed by the Arbitration Act B.E. 2545,[59] which is based on the UNCITRAL Model Law on International Commercial Arbitration.[60]

[58] ibid.

[59] Thai Arbitration Institute, Office of the Judiciary (n 11).

[60] International Bar Association, 'Arbitration Guide: THAILAND', available online: www.ibanet.org/MediaHandler?id=AF819767-C572-4B20-97AD-448D3CE1EFFD.

As in other countries, the arbitration procedure allows for more flexibility. Again, section 34 should be revisited here in full:

> The arbitral tribunal shall decide the dispute in accordance with the governing law chosen by the parties. Any designation of law or legal system of a country shall be construed, unless otherwise expressed, as directly referring to the substantive law of the country and not to its conflict of laws rules.
>
> Failing any designation by the parties, the arbitral tribunal shall decide the dispute in accordance with Thai laws, save where there is a conflict of laws, the arbitral tribunal shall apply the law determinated by the principle of conflict of laws it considers appropriate.
>
> The parties may expressly stipulate that the arbitral tribunal shall determine the dispute *ex aequo et bono*.
>
> The arbitral tribunal shall decide in accordance with the terms of the contract and shall take into account the trade usage applicable to the transaction.

So, the arbitral tribunal will have to apply foreign law in light of the express choice of law indicated by the parties. In the absence of such express choice, unlike the courts, the arbitral tribunal is not bound by the rules and methods contained in the Act on the Conflict of Laws, B.E. 2481. There is nothing in the Arbitration Act B.E. 2545 that suggested that the arbitral tribunal has to take a passive role and cannot take an active role in acquiring knowledge of the foreign law and applying it to the case. Unlike the constraint set out in the Civil Procedure Code, B.E. 2477, the arbitral tribunal can consider primary sources of the foreign law which is in the English language (or indeed in any other language). There is no compulsory rule that the parties need to supply the certified Thai translation. This is in line with section 28 of the Arbitration Act B.E. 2545 which provides:

> The parties are free to agree on the language or languages to be used in the arbitral proceedings. Failing such agreement, the arbitral tribunal shall determine the language or languages to be used in the proceedings. This agreement or determination, unless otherwise specified therein, shall apply to any statement of claim, statement of defense, any written statement by a party, any hearing, and any award, decision or other communications by or to the arbitral tribunal.
>
> The arbitral tribunal may order that any documentary evidence shall be accompanied by a translation into language or languages agreed upon by the parties or determined by the arbitral tribunal.

Of course, in ascertaining the contents of the foreign law, the arbitral tribunal may as well seek guidance from experts. This is following the Arbitration Act B.E. 2545, section 32:

> 'Unless otherwise agreed by the parties, the arbitral tribunal may proceed as follows:
>
> (1) Appoint one or more experts to report to it on specific issues to be determined by the arbitral tribunal;
> (2) Require a party to give the expert any relevant information or to produce, or to provide access to, any relevant documents, materials or places for his inspection.
>
> Unless otherwise agreed by the parties, if a party so requests or if the arbitral tribunal considers it necessary, the expert shall, after delivery of his written or oral report, participate in a hearing in order that the parties may have an opportunity to ask questions or to present his own expert witnesses.'

Like any civil litigation, in the case of the conflicting opinions of the expert witnesses, the arbitral tribunal may weigh the given information based on the balance of probability.

However, there is nothing in the arbitration mechanism to bar the tribunal from seeking to verify the foreign legal position through its own sources. The language of section 34 of the Arbitration Act B.E. 2545, as in the UNCITRAL Model Law, is so flexible that the arbitration tribunal may consider applying soft law, something which is not feasible under the formal court procedure.

As in the UNCITRAL Model Law, the Arbitration Act B.E. 2545 does not provide for an appeal mechanism from the arbitral award. It only indicates limited grounds when such an arbitral award can be challenged. However, an arbitral tribunal mistakenly applying the foreign law does not constitute one of such grounds.[61]

VI. Treatment of Foreign Law – The Future: Perspectives of Thailand

So far in this chapter, the authors examined how the courts and the arbitral tribunal deal with foreign law. The Civil Procedure Code, B.E. 2477 led the Thai courts to be rather conservative in that any document submitted to prove the foreign law must be in a certified translation in the Thai language. Any translation risks misunderstanding. Technical jargons specific to a particular judicial system are unlikely to find equivalent words elsewhere. The need for a two-step proof of both the foreign private international law rules and the foreign substantive law leads to further complications and increases expenses and burdens on the party who wants to plead the foreign law.

Recently, there has been at least an initiative on the part of the Central Intellectual Property and International Trade Court in Thailand to attempt to modernise the procedure even though whether this attempt will be implemented in practice remains to be seen. This is in the form of the 'draft Directive on intellectual property and international trade cases B.E …'. According to this draft:

> 32/1 When the Court deems it beneficial for the preparation of the judgment or the order in the event the defendant fails to provide a statement as per the scheduled date or any party fails to appear in the trial, when the party who appears in Court requests for the submission of documents in English without the need to provide a certified English translation or to provide only a partial translation, if the Court deems those documents not to be pieces of evidence relating to the main issues of the case, the Court can allow those documents to be submitted as pieces of evidence without the need to provide the certified translation;
>
> 32/2 When the Court, taking into account the overall justice, deems it beneficial to consider documentary evidence in the English language relating to an issue in the case, whether a party or both parties provide a certified translation in whole or in part or not, the Court may consider taking the following procedure:
>
> (1) The Court may consider the information available in international agreements, international law, foreign law, rules, and directives or announcements relating to the intellectual property or international trade or arbitration or customary practices relating to international trade in the English language, instead of the translated version submitted by a party;

[61] See s 40 of the Arbitration Act B.E. 2545.

(2) The Court may use international conventions, international agreements; guidelines on the application of a treaty, or model laws to assist in interpretation and explanation and preparation of the judgment or order determining the case or any issue in the case, provided that those documents are in the English language and Thailand is a State Party, if that a party or both parties raised these as issues in the case;

(3) The Court may use international conventions, international agreements, international law, foreign laws, rules, directives, or announcements on intellectual property or international trade or arbitration or customary practices in international trade as pieces of evidence in preparation for the judgment or order determining the case or any issue in the case once the Chief Justice of the Central Intellectual Property and International Trade Court enlisted them to be admissible pieces of evidence which the Court can take judicial notice of.

However, this is only a draft and, if any, its application will be confined to that of the Central Intellectual Property and International Trade Court because of the separate statutory regime from that of other courts in Thailand. Under section 30 of the Act for the Establishment of and Procedure for Intellectual Property and International Trade Court, B.E. 2539,

> In order to ensure convenience, expediency and fairness in proceedings, the Chief Judge of the Central Intellectual Property and International Trade Court shall be empowered, subject to the approval of the President of the Supreme Court, to issue Rules on proceedings and hearing of evidence in the intellectual property and international trade courts provided that such provisions shall not impair the right of defense of an accused in a criminal case.
>
> Such Rules shall come into force after their publication in the Royal Gazette.[62]

Other courts in Thailand may not be able to adopt a similar Directive without entailing the legislative amendment to the Civil Procedure Code, B.E. 2477. Any parliamentary process is likely to be time-consuming and success cannot be ensured. Nevertheless, this is in line with what scholars suggested that there should be amendments to the Civil Procedure Code, B.E. 2477 to clarify matters of evidence and proof of foreign law. They also recommended that the law should be amended such that more powers are given to judges to prove and verify foreign law.[63]

The fact that all the judicial processes must be conducted in the Thai language with all judgments published in Thai having no English translation, renders information on Thai laws mostly inaccessible to foreign lawyers. The Office of the Council of State does, rather selectively, provide the English translation of some statutes. There is a serious lack of databases in the English language to provide access to primary legal materials of Thailand. There have been some concerns over any inaccuracy in the translation of sources into the English language and which organisation should bear ultimate responsibility if such imprecision occurs. However, Thailand cannot evade the reality of globalisation with the increasing connectivity of citizens and juristic persons globally. While there has been a feeling among judges in Thailand that private international law is a matter far removed from Thai courts since there are rarely any cases involving conflict of laws that are raised before the courts,

[62] The Central Intellectual Property and International Trade Court, 'Act for the Establishment of and Procedure for Intellectual Property and International Trade Court, B.E. 2539 (1996)', available online: ipitc.coj.go.th/th/content/page/index/id/191335.

[63] Nitiruchirot and Wongyai (n 43) 88.

this trend is likely to shift following globalisation. Thai courts will likely find themselves having to consider private international law issues and having to apply foreign law. By the same token, courts in other countries will find themselves having to apply Thai substantive laws too. The lack of reliable sources of Thai laws in the English language will create many difficulties. This is an area that requires improvement. Scholars suggested that it might be worthwhile to establish an institution along the line of 'The Institute for Foreign Law and Private International Law' in Thailand. Along with this, they also recommended the establishment of the 'Foreign Law Translation Institute of Ministry of Justice.'[64] However, the authors are inclined to think that these matters will rank lowly among the priorities of Thai politicians.

Following this trend of globalisation, any attempt at developing harmonised rules on the treatment of foreign laws will only promote certainties. Thailand will likely be influenced if such harmonised rules are developed by an international organisation, especially the Hague Conference on Private International Law, in which Thailand became its 88th Member State on 8 March 2021.[65] Currently, there have been some discussions about whether Thailand will consider acceding to the 'Convention on the Service Abroad of Judicial and Extrajudicial Documents in Civil or Commercial Matters, 15 December 1965.' However, any change of the current laws or rules relating to the treatment of foreign laws in Thailand so as to follow the harmonised rules (if any) is likely to face significant delays considering such change may involve legislative amendments to the Civil Procedure Code, B.E. 2477 and possibly the Act on the Conflict of Laws, B.E. 2477. Frequent dissolution of Parliament and cabinet forming and reshuffling will bring uncertainty as to who the exact driving persons are behind each legislative amendment. Nevertheless, any move on the international level will likely be an effective push behind any likely change in Thailand.

[64] ibid.

[65] Ministry of Foreign Affairs, Kingdom of Thailand, 'Thailand Became the 88th Member of the Hague Conference on Private International Law (HCCH) to Develop Rules of Private International Law and Efficiently Facilitate Cross-Border Activities', available online: www.mfa.go.th/en/content/thailand-member-hague-conference-hcch?cate=5d5bcb4e15e39c306000683e.

15

Sri Lanka

RAMESH FERNANDO

I. Introduction

Sri Lanka is considered to be a mixed legal system, comprised of elements from the Roman Dutch law, English Common law, and the local customary laws. For a reader unfamiliar with Sri Lanka's historical background, the key to understanding why certain things are the way they are in our legal system is by getting a reasonably sufficient insight into, and appreciation of, the myriad of sources upon which its legal system is based. The legal system of Sri Lanka, often likened to a coloured mosaic,[1] is reflective of its multicultural, multi-ethnic and multi-religious populous, with laws that have their roots from sources as diverse and distinctive as England, Rome, the Netherlands, and, indigenous customs. As a Supreme Court judge once commented on Sri Lanka's legal system, 'Law, like race, is not a pure-blooded creature.'[2]

Sri Lanka's recorded history dates back to about 500 BC when Prince Vijaya and his turbulent companions, 700 in number, are said to have arrived on the shores of Sri Lanka upon banishment from the Kingdom of Sinhapura in Northern India by Sinhabahu, Vijaya's father.[3] Through the ages, the local inhabitants belonging to the different ethnicities developed and followed their respective customary laws. The Sinhalese followed the Sinhalese law, the Tesawalamai law was administered to the Tamils residing in the Northern Kingdom of Sri Lanka, the Muslim community conducted their private and social affairs according to the Muslim laws and custom, and, the Mukkuvars, Chetties, Parsees and Paravars preserved their own laws and customs.

Sri Lanka fell under the consecutive rule of three western colonial powers. The Portuguese dominated parts of Sri Lanka from 1505 to 1656, and the Dutch ruled a part of it from 1656 to 1796. The British took over the island in 1796 and went on to rule the whole of the island until Sri Lanka gained its independence in 1948. From the three colonial powers that ruled Sri Lanka, it was the Dutch and the British who left a lasting influence on Sri Lanka's legal system. The Dutch, who introduced an elaborate court system in the areas under their rule, applied the Roman Dutch law as a residuary law which was resorted to where the local

[1] CG Weeramantry, *The Law of Contracts* (Vol I), (Pannipitiya, Stamford Lake Publications, 1967) 21.
[2] Per Tambiah J., *Kamalawathie v de Silva* 64 N.L.R. 252 at 259.
[3] K Muthumuni de Silva, *A History of Sri Lanka* (Colombo, Vijitha Yapa Publications, 2005) 6.

customary laws were silent or the Dutch considered them unsuitable.[4] The influence of the Roman Dutch law persists to this day, albeit insubstantial, particularly in the laws relating to succession, persons, property and obligations. However, the sphere of influence of the Roman Dutch law even in these areas has been restricted in recent times by statute, some of which are based on English principles or judicial decisions.

The English law, legal principles, and its legal system, has had the most far-reaching impact on the local law and system of legal administration. Even though Lord Mansfield in *Campbell v Hall*[5] proclaimed that 'the laws of a conquered country continue to be in force until they are altered by the conqueror', a principle given effect in Sri Lanka through the Proclamation of 23 September 1799 by Governor Sir Francis North and the Proclamation of 2 March 1815, the British found it difficult to abide by this principle in practice. Whilst the English did not apply English law in Sri Lanka in toto, there was significant and gradual encroachment by English law through legislation and judicial activism, particularly because the British judges and lawyers administering justice in Ceylon, as it was known at the time, were unfamiliar with the Roman Dutch law, the sources of which were written in Dutch or Latin.[6]

Important and relevant to the topic of treatment of foreign law in Sri Lankan courts, English legal principles on areas of law such as criminal law, the law of trusts and especially the law of evidence, codified into statute form in India, have been reproduced with slight modifications in Sri Lanka. These include the Penal Code, 1883, the Trusts Ordinance, 1917 and the Evidence Ordinance, 1895.[7] Some of these statutes,[8] including the Evidence Ordinance, contain *casus omissus* provisions, which direct the application of English law where the respective statutes are not complete.

Even though Sri Lanka is an island strategically located on the Indian ocean, rich in natural beauty and resources, including international ports and harbours, its economy and legal system have been lagging behind due to several turbulent events and political and social problems that it has experienced since its independence. Sri Lanka does not have a codified or developed private international law regime, particularly because its courts do not often deal with litigation involving cross-border issues, such as the application or interpretation of foreign law. As discussed below, the Evidence Ordinance, 1895, provides for the proof of foreign law by experts. However, the number of reported cases in which this provision has been resorted to is limited, and therefore it is difficult to state with exactness the manner in which a question of foreign law will be addressed by local courts. However, in light of the fact that the Evidence Ordinance provides for the application of English law in the event of a *casus omissus*,[9] and, English judgments on this area will be of persuasive authority, it would be quite safe to assume that local courts will follow English law and practice in the event an issue of foreign law arises before it.

[4] LJM Cooray, *An Introduction to the Legal System of Sri Lanka*, 2nd edn (Pannipitiya, Stamford Lake Publications, 2003) 4.

[5] *Campbell v Hall* (1774) 1 Cowp 204–10, 98 ER 1045, 1047.

[6] Cooray (n 4) 38.

[7] Cooray (n 4) 31–32.

[8] Section 58(2) of the Sale of Goods Ordinance, 1896, s 2 of the Trusts Ordinance, 1917 and s 98(2) of the Bills of Exchange Ordinance, 1927.

[9] Section 100 of the Evidence Ordinance.

II. Foreign Law before Judicial Authorities

A. Nature of Foreign Law in Sri Lanka

Under section 57(1) of the Evidence Ordinance, courts can *inter alia* take judicial notice of 'all laws, or rules having the force of law, now or heretofore in force or hereafter to be in force in any part of Sri Lanka'. However, foreign law is excluded from this provision, therefore judges cannot take judicial notice of any foreign law. Foreign law is considered to be a question of fact,[10] which has to be proved by witness evidence. The general rule is that a witness will only be allowed to testify orally and produce documents in order to establish facts, but will not be permitted to express their opinion on any matter.[11] The principle underlying this rule is that it is for the judge or the jury[12] to form opinions or draw inferences from the relevant facts established. However, expert opinion on foreign law, in some ways, is an exception to this rule, as the Evidence Ordinance considers such third-party opinion to be relevant facts:

> **Section 45 of the Evidence Ordinance**
>
> When the court has to form an opinion as to foreign law, or of science, or art, or as to identity or genuineness of handwriting or finger impressions, the opinions upon that point of persons specially skilled in such foreign law, science, or art, or in questions as to identity or genuineness of handwriting or finger impressions, palm impressions or foot impressions, are relevant facts.
>
> Such persons are called experts.

The general rule in English law is that knowledge of foreign law is not to be imputed to an English judge.[13] This approach has been adopted in Sri Lanka through the Evidence Ordinance. Accordingly, the onus of proving that the foreign law pleaded is different from Sri Lankan law, and of proving its contents, lies on the party relying on such difference.

B. Ascertainment of Foreign Law

There are a number of ways in which foreign law can be proved before a Sri Lankan court.

i. By Expert Evidence

Section 45 of the Evidence Ordinance provides for proof of foreign law by leading expert evidence. An expert providing evidence under this section must give evidence to court in-person or by way of an affidavit, and must allow themselves to be cross-examined by the

[10] *Kandasamy v Bandaranayake* 48 NLR 449 at 451, *The Attorney General v V. Ramaswami Iyengar et al* 55 NLR 481 at 486.

[11] ERSR Coomaraswamy, *A Text Book of The Law of Evidence in Ceylon*, 1st edn (Colombo, NE Hamer, 1955).

[12] In England, s 69(5) of the Supreme Court Act 1981 now provides that any question as to the effect of the evidence given with respect to any foreign law shall be decided by the judge alone, and not be submitted to the jury.

[13] P Torremans and others (eds), *Cheshire, North & Fawcett Private International Law*, 15th edn (Oxford, Oxford University Press, 2017) 105.

party against whom the evidence is to be led.[14] Under English law, foreign law cannot be proved by arguably more expeditious and cost-effective methods such as citing a previous decision of an English court in which the same foreign rule was in issue,[15] or by presenting the judge with the text of the foreign law and leaving them to draw their own conclusions,[16] or by referring to a decision in which a court of the foreign country has stated the meaning and effect of the law in question.[17] Sri Lankan courts consider the right of the opposing party to cross-examine expert evidence as sacrosanct.

Evans LJ in *MCC Proceeds Inc v Bishopsgate Investment Trust plc*[18] identified three principal functions of an expert witness on foreign law:

(a) to inform the court of the relevant contents of the foreign law, identifying statutes or other legislation and explaining where necessary the foreign court's approach to their construction;
(b) to identify judgments or other authorities explaining what status they have as sources of the foreign law; and
(c) where there is no authority directly on point, to assist the English judge in making a finding as to what the court's ruling would be if the issue was to arise for decision there.

The provision requires experts giving evidence on foreign law to be persons 'specially skilled in such foreign law'. The Ordinance does not provide further guidance on the qualifications required from such witness. In English law, courts have generally only considered the following types of persons to be expert witnesses on foreign law:

i. a practising lawyer in the particular legal system; or
ii. a person who occupies a position wherein they would necessarily acquire a practical working knowledge of the relevant foreign law.[19]

English courts used to be of the general view that academic knowledge by itself is not a sufficient qualification to be an expert witness on foreign law. In *Bristow v Sequeville*, a case which concerned the law in force at Cologne, a witness who was a jurisconsult who had acquired his knowledge solely from study at Leipzig University but never actually practiced in Prussia, was not considered a competent witness. However, this view was not applied consistently. For instance, the evidence of a Reader in Roman-Dutch law to the Council of Legal Education, who had studied that law for his lectures, was admitted,[20] and, an English barrister who in the course of his practice had researched into the marriage laws of Malta, was held to be competent to prove the validity of a marriage solemnised at Valetta.[21]

[14] Coomaraswamy (n 11) 164.
[15] *Lazard Bros & Co v Midland Bank Ltd* [1933] AC 289, *McCormick v Garnett* (1854) 24 LJ Ch 777.
[16] *Beurger v New York Life Assurance Co* (1927) 96 LJKB 930 at 940.
[17] *Beatty v Beatty* [1924] 1 KB 807 at 814–15, *Guaranty Trust Co of New York v Hannay & Co* [1918] 2 KB 623 and 638, 667.
[18] [1999] CLC 417 (CA), at [23].
[19] *The Sussex Peerage Case* (1844) 11 Cl. & Fin/ 85, *R v Savage* (1876) 13 Cox. C.C. 178.
[20] *Brailey v Rhodesia Consolidated Ltd* [1910] 2 Ch 95.
[21] *Wilson v Wilson* [1903] P 157.

Expert witnesses can produce works of authority to the court, and the court, having received the necessary explanation, may construe them for itself.[22] If the experts refer to a Code, the court at its discretion may examine it.[23] An opinion provided by an expert witness is not binding on the court.[24] It is the court's responsibility to examine and criticise the evidence.[25] In the event of a conflict between the expert witnesses on either side, the court must apply its own interpretation on the points of foreign law based on all the evidence provided.[26] But it would be irregular for a judge to lightly disregard such opinion without expressing justifiable reasons for so doing. Failure to provide such justifiable reasons could be grounds for an appeal.

ii. Books and Reports

Section 38 of the Evidence Ordinance makes provision for courts to take cognisance of statements of foreign law in law books and law reports:

> When the court has to form an opinion as to a law of any country, any statement of such law contained in a book purporting to be printed or published under the authority of the Government of such country, and to contain any such law, and any report of a ruling of the courts of such country contained in a book purporting to be report is such rulings, is relevant.

The abovementioned section has to be read with section 84 of the Ordinance which makes it obligatory on the court to presume the genuineness of every book purporting to be printed or published under the authority of the government of any country, and to contain any of the laws of that country, and of every book purporting to contain reports of decisions of the courts of such country. Section 86 also provides that a court provided with any document purporting to be a certified copy of a judicial record of any foreign country, may presume that it is genuine and accurate, if the document is certified in a manner which is commonly in use in that country for the certification of copies of judicial records.

According to section 122 of the Civil Procedure Code, the party applying for a witness summons must pay into court, or provide security for payment of, such a sum of money as appears to the court to be sufficient to defray the travelling and other expenses of the person summoned. Section 124 enables the court to order further sums to be paid to the witness summoned if it appears to the court that the sum paid into court is insufficient to cover the expenses of the witness. The proviso to section 122, however, states that, no such payment shall be made in the case of a witness residing within four miles of the court at which their attendance is required. Therefore, it appears that these sections solely or primarily contemplate compensating witnesses for their travelling expenses. As is the case in other jurisdictions, in the case of expert witnesses, as opposed to regular witnesses, the party seeking to adduce expert evidence will be required to provide remuneration that goes beyond compensation for travelling expenses. In practice, the costs of summoning an

[22] *Baron de Bode's Case* 8 QB 250, *Castriqua v Imrie* LR 4 e. & I. App. 434.
[23] *Concha v Murieta* 40 Ch. D. 543.
[24] Coomaraswamy (n 11) 166.
[25] *Tallinna Laevaushisus (A/S) v Estonian State Steamship Line* (1947) 80 Lloyd's Rep 99 at 108.
[26] *Shiblaq v Sadikoglu* [2004] EWHC 1890 (Comm) at [10].

expert witness are borne by the party calling such witness, pursuant to a private arrangement between them.

iii. Commissions

Section 422 of the Civil Procedure Code enables the court to issue a commission to any court situated outside the local limits of the jurisdiction of the court issuing the commission to examine any person resident within the jurisdiction of such court. Coomaraswamy states that this provision is often relied upon in order to obtain expert evidence on a question of foreign law.[27] This type of provision would be particularly useful where it is necessary to obtain evidence from an expert who is unable to present themselves before the court. One main distinction between leading of expert evidence in court and obtaining evidence on commission is that the witness giving evidence on commission cannot be subjected to cross-examination by the opposing party. In *Ameresekere v Cannangara*,[28] the Supreme Court considered an appeal against an order of the District Court refusing to issue a commission for the examination of the defendant and of certain witnesses, all of whom were resident in England. The Court was of the view that such applications should not be granted unless they were supported by affidavits clearly stating that the commission would be conducive to the administration of justice. The Court insisted on this 'stringent rule' for fear that the absence of such a rule would lead to the pernicious practice of parties going abroad to avoid the risk of cross-examination in open court. However, the Court decided to set aside the order of the district judge dismissing the application and directed that a commission be issued at the expense of the defendant to such a court or person as the trial judge deemed fit for the evidence to be taken on commission. The Supreme Court was of the view that in such a case, the interests of justice will not suffer by the evidence being taken on commission, particularly because the trial judge, in adjudicating the case, would bear in mind that the evidence for the defence was placed before him in such manner, and the plaintiff had not had the advantage of subjecting those witnesses to cross-examination.

iv. British Law Ascertainment Act, 1859

By virtue of the abovementioned Act of the UK, if in any action pending in any court within the UK's dominions, it becomes necessary to ascertain the law applicable to the facts of the case as administered in any other dominion of the UK, the court is able to prepare a case and remit the case for the opinion of a superior court of such other dominion seeking its opinion on the matter.[29] Whilst Sri Lanka remained a dominion of England despite gaining independence on the 4 February 1948, it emerged from this status to become a fully independent Republic in May 1972. Therefore, the British Law Ascertainment Act, 1859 would no longer be applicable in Sri Lanka.

[27] Coomaraswamy (n 11) 166.
[28] *Ameresekere v Cannangara*, 41 N.L.R. 333, per Soertsz S.P.J.
[29] British Law Ascertainment Act, 1859 (UK), s 1.

v. *Appointment of amicus curiae*

Though not often resorted to, it is open to the courts to seek the assistance of an amicus curiae when deemed necessary. An amicus curiae is a friend of the court, who is not a party to a particular litigation, but is permitted or invited by the court to advise it in respect of some matter of law that directly affects the case in question. For instance, in *Natalie Abeysundere v Christopher Abeysundere and Anor*,[30] a seminal case on family law, the Supreme Court invited RKW Goonesekera, a legal expert, to assist the Court in the case. Therefore, should the Court deem it necessary, it may invite experts on foreign law to assist the Court as amici curiae if a question of foreign law arises before it. However, such an invitation would only be made at the Court's discretion, and such discretion is rarely exercised.

C. Interpretation and Application of Foreign Law

As discussed in the preceding parts of this chapter, courts in Sri Lanka apply foreign law on an application to such effect being made by a party. As in England, the pleading of foreign law is generally voluntary.[31] Fentiman, analysing the English context, states that in practice, a party is likely to plead foreign law only in three circumstances: where English law offers no equivalent claim or defence; where foreign law is significantly more advantageous than English law; and, where the pleading of foreign law is mandatory (such as in cases involving immovable property). The same rings true for Sri Lanka. There have also been instances where Sri Lankan nationals residing overseas plead Sri Lankan law, particularly the Sri Lankan personal laws such as Tesawalamai law, in litigation overseas, particularly in cases involving family disputes. Such laws are resorted to primarily because in certain instances these personal laws are more advantageous to the husband or wife than the *lex fori*.

There are two principles which define the role of a judge in an English court when deciding on a matter of foreign law.[32] First, the judge's task in such an instance is predictive. This means that the judge's role is not to determine what the foreign law is or ought to be, but to predict how the relevant foreign court would conclude if a similar matter came before it. Second, application of foreign law is a decision based on fact, based on evidence, not a question of law based on argument. The courts have taken as guiding principles, the restatement of the law by Moses J on the treatment of such evidence in *City of Gotha and the Federal Republic of Germany v Sotheby's and Colbert Finance SA*[33] (citing *Bumper Development Corporation v Commissioner of Police of the Metropolis*[34]):

i. when faced with evidence conflicts, judges are bound to look at the effect of the foreign sources on which the experts rely as part of their evidence in order to evaluate and interpret that evidence and decide between the conflicting testimony;

[30] (1998) 1 Sri L.R. 185.

[31] R Fentiman, *International Commercial Litigation*, 2nd edn (Oxford, Oxford University Press, 2015), 666.

[32] ibid 672.

[33] *City of Gotha and the Federal Republic of Germany v Sotheby's and Colbert Finance SA* Judgment 9 September 1998 (unreported), summarised in *Islamic Republic of Iran v Barakat Galleries Ltd* [2007] EWHC 705 (QB) at [14]; *Harley v Smith* [2010] EWCA Civ 78.

[34] *Bumper Development Corporation v Commissioner of Police of the Metropolis* [1991] 1 WLR 1362, 1368G.

ii. judges should not consider passages contained within foreign sources of law produced by the experts to which those experts have not themselves referred;
iii. it is not permissible to reject uncontradicted expert evidence unless it is patently absurd;
iv. in considering foreign sources of law, judges should adopt those foreign rules of construction of which the experts have given evidence (the underlying principle here is that an English court must not conduct its own researches into foreign law);
v. an expert may not interpret the meaning of a foreign document, it is the responsibility of the court to construe such document. The role of the experts is limited to providing evidence on the proper approach according to the relevant foreign rules of construction to that document.

D. Failure to Establish Foreign Law

In England, where the evidence of foreign law is unsatisfactory, or where no evidence is tendered, an English court generally applies English law in default.[35] Where foreign law was not proved, there was a presumption that the foreign law was the same as English law. As Lord Dunedin in *Dynamit AG v Rio Tinto Co*[36] stated,

> But were it necessary to so decide, I am clear that it is for those who say that the German law is different from the English law to aver it as a fact and to prove it. This they have not done, and that being so, the German law must be presumed to be the same as the English.

However, in *Shaker v Al-Bedrawi*, quite significantly, the court recognised the difficulties in applying the aforementioned presumption in a case which involved a principle of law derived from civil law systems of the European Community, to the law of Pennsylvania, a common law jurisdiction. Instead of applying the presumption, the court accepted that the correct position was for an English court to apply English law where foreign law is not proved. In effect, the Court of Appeal rejected the fictitious presumption that foreign law was the same as English law, and instead, considered English law the *lex causae* in such situations.[37] Although Sri Lanka does not have reported decisions relevant to this type of scenario, it is likely that the decisions of the English courts, such as the one in *Shaker*, will have a persuasive effect on the Sri Lankan judges in the event that this type of issue materialises before them.

E. Appeals

In England, although decisions on points of foreign law are regarded as findings of fact, appeals against such findings are permitted. In the same manner, it would be possible for a party before a court of first instance in Sri Lanka to appeal against an order or judgment

[35] *Dynamit AG v Rio Tinto Co* [1918] AC 260, *Royal Boskalis Westminster NV & Ors. v Trevor Rex Mountain and Ors.* [1999] QB 674.
[36] Fentiman (n 31).
[37] Fentiman (n 31) 693.

on a point of foreign law to an appellate court possessing the necessary jurisdiction. The characterisation of whether findings on foreign law are findings of fact or of law, is significant, because, if they are treated as findings of law, am appellate court is able to review such findings and reach its own conclusions. As Evan LJ stated in *MCC Proceeds Inc v Bishopsgate Investment Trust Plc & Ors*,[38] 'An appeal to the Court of Appeal is by way of re-hearing (R.S.C. Order 59 rule 3). The Court exercises its own judgment, independently, of, though not uninfluenced by the views of the trial judge.' On the other hand, if they are treated as pure findings of fact, the scope of the court's appellate powers are restricted, as in such case, an appellate court would be reluctant to reverse a finding of fact made by a trial judge after hearing and seeing witnesses. The English courts regard issued of foreign law as factual issues of a peculiar kind for appeal purposes.[39] The reasoning behind this seems to be that 'Where the inference of fact depends on the consideration of written material, an appellate court is at no particular disadvantage compared to a trial court and will regard itself as freer to review the decision of the trial court.'[40] In *MCC Proceeds Inc v Bishopsgate Investment Trust & Ors*[41] the Court of Appeal treated the issue of foreign law as if it were a question of law, and not fact, and revisited the interpretation afresh.

In Sri Lanka, the District Court within its particular judicial district, exercises unlimited first instance jurisdiction in all civil, revenue, trust, insolvency and testamentary matters,[42] and it also functions as the Family court. The High Court of the Provinces (Special Provisions) Act No 19 of 1990, section 5A, as amended by the High Court (Special Provisions) (Amendment) Act No 54 of 2006, created the provincial High Courts of Civil Appeal with appellate and revisionary jurisdiction for the correction of all errors in fact or law pertaining to any judgment or order delivered by a District Court within its jurisdiction. A further and final appeal lies to the Supreme Court from any judgment, decree or order of a High Court of Civil Appeal, with leave of the Supreme Court first had and obtained.[43] Therefore, a party aggrieved by a judgment, order, or decree, of a District Court, pertaining to a question of foreign law, would have an initial right of appeal to the High Court of Civil Appeal, and another appeal finally to the Supreme Court therefrom. The High Court of the Provinces (Special Provisions) Act No 10 of 1996 established a High Court with specialised and exclusive jurisdiction to hear and determine commercial disputes (referred to as the Commercial High Court) which fall within the First Schedule of the Act where the debt, damage or demand is for a sum exceeding 20 million rupees.[44] Additionally, the Commercial High Court in Colombo has jurisdiction over actions filed under the Intellectual Property Act No 36 of 2003, where the defendant resides, or, the cause of action has arisen, or, the contract sought to be enforced was made, within the Western Province.[45] Currently, only one such High Court has been established, in

[38] *MCC Proceeds Inc v Bishopsgate Investment Trust Plc & Ors* [1999] CLC 417 (CA).

[39] Fentiman (n 31) 703.

[40] *Parkasho v Singh* [1968] P 233.

[41] See (n 38).

[42] Judicature Act, s 19.

[43] High Court of the Provinces (Special Provisions) (Amendment) Act No 54 of 2006, s 2, adding s 5C to the Act.

[44] The threshold sum was raised to 20 million Sri Lankan rupees by Gazette Extraordinary No 2112/33 (28 February 2019), and can be changed from time to time by the Minister of Justice.

[45] Intellectual Property Act No 36 of 2003, s 212.

Colombo. A party aggrieved by a judgment or order of the Commercial High Court may prefer an appeal to the Supreme Court, for any error in fact or in law, with leave of the Supreme Court first obtained where the appeal is against an order (not a final judgment) of the Commercial High Court.[46]

III. Foreign Law before Other Instances

A. Foreign Law before Administrative or Other Non-Judicial Authorities

There is no law specifically enabling persons to rely on foreign law before administrative or other similar public bodies in Sri Lanka. Whilst it may be possible to provide public authorities with evidence of applicable foreign law, authorities would in general be reluctant to depart from local laws and regulations and apply a foreign law. However, a party aggrieved by the failure of or refusal by a public body or official to take due cognisance of a point of foreign law, where such foreign law is applicable, may make an application to the Court of Appeal for writs of *certiorari*, *prohibition*, *procedendo* and or *mandamus* against such public body or public official.[47] A citizen of Sri Lanka may also make an application to the Supreme Court urging a violation of their fundamental rights guaranteed under the Constitution, and seek to obtain an appropriate order against such public body or public official. It must be noted that whilst marriages contracted in foreign jurisdictions involving Sri Lankan parties are considered valid if contracted in accordance with the law of the relevant jurisdiction, in 2021 the Registrar General, on the initiative of the Ministry of Defence, issued Circular No 18/2021, which requires the registration of marriages between foreigners and Sri Lankans, citing security concerns. However, this is only a precondition for registering such a marriage in Sri Lanka and is silent on such marriages contracted and registered overseas. A writ application has been filed in the Court of Appeal challenging the validity of this Circular.

B. Foreign Law in Arbitration

Sri Lanka's Arbitration Act No 11 of 1995 was greatly influenced by the UNCITRAL Model Law on International Commercial Arbitration (1985). In terms of section 24(1) of the Act, the parties are free to choose the law to be applicable to the substance of the dispute, and in the absence of such choice, the arbitral tribunal is to apply the law determined by reference to the conflict of laws rules which the arbitral tribunal considers applicable. Section 17 leaves it open to the parties to agree on the rules of procedure to be followed by the arbitral tribunal in conducting the proceedings. Therefore, in common practice, parties to

[46] High Court of the Provinces (Special Provisions) Act No 10 of 1996, s 5(1), (2).
[47] Art 140 of the Constitution.

arbitration proceedings opt to conduct the arbitral proceedings under specific institutional rules, and accordingly, ascertainment of any applicable foreign law would be done following the applicable institutional rules. Parties are generally able to provide expert evidence on points of foreign law, leaving it to the arbitral tribunals to make their determinations. The provisions of the Arbitration Act would apply to ad hoc arbitrations, where the parties have not agreed to abide by or adopt a particular set of procedural rules. Section 22(1) provides that evidence before an arbitral tribunal may be provided orally, in writing, or by affidavit. Furthermore, section 22(3) provides that an arbitral tribunal shall not be bound by the provisions of the Evidence Ordinance, unless otherwise agreed.

IV. Access to Sri Lanka Law: Legal Databases

The Ministry of Justice maintains an official website which provides free access to, among others, legislation, reported case law, and, agreements to which Sri Lanka is a party.[48] All of the aforementioned are available in English. Furthermore, the Supreme Court[49] and the Court of Appeal[50] maintain websites which publish all of the judgments passed by the respective courts, and these websites are updated on a day-to-day basis. The website of the Parliament of Sri Lanka[51] also publishes Parliamentary Bills and enacted legislation in Sinhala, Tamil and English, and also provides access to the *Hansard*. Additionally, there are other privately maintained legal databases providing access to legislation and reported and unreported judgments for which paid subscription must be obtained.[52]

V. Access to Foreign Law: Future Developments

Sri Lanka, being a dualist state, requires parliamentary approval before any international treaty, convention, or agreement, can have the force of law within Sri Lanka. Article 157 of the Constitution sets a high threshold and requires Parliament to approve such international treaties or agreements by no less than a two-thirds majority. For this reason, and others such as administrative delays, little or no steps have been taken to enact the necessary enabling legislation to give effect to a large number of international instruments, although Sri Lanka is a ratifying party to many. Sri Lanka has ratified several Private International Law conventions, including the Hague Convention on the Service Abroad of Judicial and Extrajudicial Documents in Civil or Commercial Matters[53] and the Hague Convention on the Taking of Evidence Abroad in Civil or Commercial Matters.[54] As a rare exception, the

[48] www.lawnet.gov.lk.
[49] www.supremecourt.lk.
[50] www.courtofappeal.lk.
[51] www.parliament.lk.
[52] Eg, www.lawlanka.com.
[53] (Hague, 15 November 1965).
[54] (Hague, 18 March 1970).

aforesaid treaties have been incorporated into the law of Sri Lanka through the enactment of the Mutual Assistance in Civil and Commercial Matters Act.[55]

Whilst there are international instruments relating to the discernment of, or enabling access to, foreign law, such as the European Convention on Information on Foreign Law,[56] to date, Sri Lanka is not a party to any such instrument. However, with the world growing ever closer to, and dependent on, each other, it is important for Sri Lanka to be a part of an international instrument which facilitates the easy mutual exchange of information relating to domestic law where necessary. This is particularly important to Sri Lanka in the background of the limited resources of both the government and private parties, especially the prevailing dearth of foreign exchange reserves, which makes the engagement of foreign legal experts in domestic litigation an unaffordable luxury to many.

A conference organised jointly by the European Commission and the Hague Conference on Private International Law, with the participation of many states, particularly a number of non-European countries, as well as international organisations, unanimously identified the need to improve access to foreign law as a result of inter alia increased globalisation and growing cross-border movement of persons, goods, services and investment. Significantly, it was identified that access to foreign law is an essential component of access to justice, strengthening the Rule of Law, and the proper administration of justice. In light of the foregoing, it is observed that an international agreement which unifies the treatment of foreign law would be useful and, in the future, may be necessary. However, as the conference under reference recognised, any global instrument in this field should focus on the facilitation of access to foreign law only and should not attempt to harmonise the status of foreign law in national processes.

VI. Conclusion

The foregoing sections will indicate that Sri Lanka has limited material on the treatment of foreign law and, indeed, on Private International Law. This is true and is a result of a number of unfortunate factors. Sri Lanka's economy and other sectors, such as the legal system, have faced a number of challenges over the past few decades, particularly in the background of the brutal internal armed conflict that ravaged the country for nearly three decades. Furthermore, at the time of writing this chapter, Sri Lanka is facing its worst economic crisis in its long history, having defaulted on external debt repayments for the first time. A result of grave economic mismanagement, short sightedness on the part of policy-makers, and corruption, exacerbated by the Covid-19 pandemic. In light of these consistent challenges, Sri Lanka continues to lag behind on development, economically and otherwise, with a direct bearing on the legal system. Whilst other countries in the South Asian region, particularly India and Bangladesh, have experienced rapid economic development in recent years, Sri Lanka has not been a partaker in this success. Accordingly, due to these economic limitations, Sri Lanka has not had a high volume of cases which involve cross-border issues and reference to Private International Law. Whilst

[55] Mutual Assistance in Civil and Commercial Matters Act No 39 of 2000.
[56] (London, 7 June 1968).

the Ministry of Justice took certain steps towards the revamping of Sri Lanka's commercial laws in anticipation of future economic growth, which included the drafting of a new Arbitration Bill and the setting up of a specialised Investor Disputes High Court, these have now come to a standstill in light of the prevailing economic, political and social instability.

Even though Sri Lanka does not have a developed Private International Law regime, with lacunas in areas such as the recognition and enforcement of foreign judgments, a Sri Lankan court faced with a Private International Law issue, such as the necessity to interpret and apply foreign law, will be very likely to consider and follow accepted practice in other jurisdictions such as the UK, especially since the consideration of foreign law is allowed under the Evidence Ordinance.

16

India

SAI RAMANI GARIMELLA AND WASIQ ABASS DAR

I. Introduction

The year 1947, when India became independent from the colonial rule of the British crown, and three years later, when India declared itself as a Republic with a constitutional form of government, is a definitive indicator of India's legal history. That said, India's legal history dates much earlier than 1947, and its law and institutions, in many aspects of governance, also pre-date the independence. India's domestic jurisprudence resonates from the amalgamation of cultures, peoples and the laws that interacted with the subcontinent prior to independence. Such cultural impact on the legal system was expansive enough to include the early Hindu kingdoms that ruled various parts of India that are much different from the political map of India today. It also included Mughals, whose Muslim code remains a part of the fabric of modern Indian law, and the French, whose impact extended far beyond their officially minimal possessions that existed for a limited period in the southern part of India. The multifarious past makes modern, domestic Indian law construction of domestic and non-domestic processes and precedents.[1] A significant chronological era impacting the construction of domestic jurisprudence was the colonial era that witnessed extensive resort to Privy Council decisions, with the pre-1947 judiciary both bringing Indian cases to the body and referring to decisions of the body for persuasive and binding precedent. The corpus of transnational common law created through this process was explicitly kept alive through the Indian Constitution's Article 372, holding that all laws in place prior to the Constitution's passage were to remain in place unless repealed.[2]

[1] AM Smith, 'Making Itself at Home: Understanding Foreign Law in Domestic Jurisprudence – the Indian Case' (25 May 2005) 25. Available at ssrn.com/abstract=729946; RD Baird, 'Traditional Values, Governmental Values, and Religious Conflict in Contemporary India' [1998] *Brigham Young University Law Review* 337; P Diwan, *Muslim Law in Modern India* (ALA, 1977).

[2] Constitution of India, 1950. Art 372 – Continuance in force of existing laws and their adaptation.

(1) Notwithstanding the repeal by this Constitution of the enactments referred to in Article 395 but subject to the other provisions of this Constitution, all the laws in force in the territory of India immediately before the commencement of this Constitution shall continue in force therein until altered or repealed or amended by a competent Legislature or other competent authority.

(2) …

Modern Indian law's content, therefore, includes local (domestic law) as well as foreign law. The foreign law includes international law of the pre-colonial and the colonial periods in the form of trade-related treaties and covenants[3] as well as customary international law.[4] It also includes the national laws of the colonisers (Portuguese,[5] French[6] and the English[7] – note that while the Dutch held colonies on the Indian subcontinent,[8] there is no documentation related to the introduction of the Dutch law in such colonies, with the exception of Dutch Ceylon) which to a large extent replaced the prevailing local law on matters related to trade and commerce, and in certain aspects of family and personal laws. Foreign law for the purposes of this chapter would address the second part, that is, the reception of foreign law in India. It needs to be noted that in very many subjects, the colonial law continues to exist[9] via the legislation on continuation of laws in the successor state.[10] Thus, familiarity with the colonisers' legal systems has ensured that Indian courts as well have referenced foreign law and jurisprudence in their decisions. The interpretation of such foreign precedent (not in the form of precedent *in strictu sensu*) has been either for reinforcement of the Indian court's opinion or for demonstrating a different legal position.

(3) …

Explanation I. – The expression 'law in force' in this article shall include a law passed or made by a Legislature or other competent authority in the territory of India before the commencement of this Constitution and not previously repealed, notwithstanding that it or parts of it may not be then in operation either at all or in particular areas.

….

[3] See generally, J Shaw, *Charters Relating to the East India Company from 1600 to 1761* (Madras, Madras Government Press, 1887); AC Patra, 'Historical Background of the Indian Contract Act, 1872' (1962) 4(3) *Journal of the Indian Law Institute 373.*

[4] CH Alexander, 'International Law in India' (1952) 1(3) *ICLQ* 289, 291.

[5] The Portuguese had a continuous presence in India for more than 450 years and only ceded its possessions – Goa, Daman and Diu, Dadra and Nagar Haveli – in 1961, more than a decade after Indian independence. See generally, MN Pearson, *The Portuguese in India* (Cambridge, CUP, 1988); see, Smith (n 1) 26.

[6] For an extensive discussion on the French law in India, see SC Jain, 'French Legal System in Pondicherry: An Introduction' (1970) 12(4) *Journal of the Indian Law Institute* 573. The French territories were subjected to a de facto transfer of power to the Government of India following an Agreement effective 1 November 1954. Art X of the Agreement allowed the continuation of the proceedings in disputes that were in existence on the effective date to be administered by the courts under the French law. It further stated 'The interested parties shall be entitled, if so they decide by common agreement, to transfer to the competent Indian Courts, the said proceedings as well as proceedings which, though already open, are not yet entered with the Registrars of the French Courts, and also proceedings which constitute an ordinary or extraordinary appeal. Judgments, decrees and orders passed by the French Courts, prior to the de facto transfer, which are final or may become so by expiration of the delays of appeal, shall be executed by the competent Indian authorities. Judgments, decrees and orders passed after the date of the de facto transfer in conformity with the first paragraph of the present article shall be executed by the competent Indian authorities, irrespective of the Court which exercised the jurisdiction. Acts or deeds constitutive of rights established prior to the date of the de facto transfer in conformity with French law shall retain the value and validity conferred at that time by the same law.'

[7] The Charter of 1600 granted by Queen Elizabeth to the East India Company gave the company extensive and exclusive trading rights. The subsequent charters expanded these powers to include establishment of settlements, dispute resolution and entering into trade covenants. See Shaw (n 3).

[8] The Dutch East India Company established their first factory at Masulipatnam (Andhra Pradesh) in 1605. See FN Zaal, 'Roman Law and the Racial Policies of the Dutch East India Company: An Exploration of Some Historical Inter-connections' (1996) 29(1) *The Comparative and International Law Journal of Southern Africa* 31.

[9] Adaptation of Laws Order, 1950, available at legislative.gov.in/sites/default/files/legislative_references/A.O%20 PtII_0.pdf.

[10] Note that India of 1947 was carved as a successor state to the British India via the Indian Independence Act, 1947, wherein the British Parliament legislated upon the creation of two independent states – India and Pakistan.

But while referencing such foreign law, Indian courts have avoided the traditional division of interpretation of the precedent – the distinction between ratio decidendi and obiter dicta and referenced the portions of the judgment that suited their averments.[11]

India's position on customary international law is influenced by the colonial practice. It is, therefore, necessary to state, albeit in brief, the British practice on customary international law as was known in the Indian territory.[12]

1. Customary principles of international law form part of the law of the land (Blackstone's incorporation doctrine).
2. Binding treaties which are part of international law do not form part of the law of the land unless expressly made so by the legislature.[13]
3. In case of a direct conflict between a treaty and a law enacted by the Parliament, it has been decided that if a treaty had been enforced through law enacted by Parliament, then such a law would prevail over the earlier inconsistent British law and not otherwise.[14]

On the constitutional scheme regarding international law in independent India, the drafters of the Indian Constitution have been extremely vague in defining the status of international law in the municipal sphere.[15] Further, there is little guidance as to the relationship between international law and municipal law. However, Article 51(c)[16] (which falls within the realm of the Directive Principles that are non-justiciable in character) of the Constitution specifically mentions international law and imposes a duty on the state to respect it.[17]

The entry of foreign law into the Indian law was first sanctioned within the Regulating Act 1873, which directed all courts in India to act in accordance with 'equity, justice and good conscience'. On the basis of this principle, Common Law rules (including rules regarding international law) were transplanted into the Indian municipal law.[18] There has been

[11] For instance, in *Central Bureau of Investigation, Bank Securities & Fraud Cell v Ramesh Gelli* (2016) 3 SCC 788, the Supreme Court of India referenced the opinion of Lord Denning in where the Lordship referred to extensive powers of the court to fill in the gaps of the legislation by reading its preamble. While the English court's decision itself did not subscribe to this opinion, the Indian court famously quoted Lord Denning and also adopted the methodology of gap-filling as suggested by him in the English court order.

[12] See generally, AD McNair, 'The Method Whereby International Law is made to Prevail in Municipal Courts on An Issue of International Law' (1944) 30 *Transaction of the Grotius Society* 88; NK Singh, 'The Indian Constitution and Customary International Law' (2000) 12 *National Law School of India Review – Student Advocate* 81, 85–86.

[13] FA Mann, 'The Enforcement of Treaties by English Courts' (1958–59) 44 *Transaction of the Grotius Society* 29. See also, H Lauterpacht, 'Is International Law As Part of The Law of The England?' (1939) 30 *Transactions of the Grotius Society* 51.

[14] *Ostime v Australian Mutual Provident Fund Society* (1959) All ER 345.

[15] See generally, BS Rao, *The Framing of Indian Constitution-Select Documents* (Indian Institute of Public Administration, 1968).

[16] Art 51 of the Constitution finds similarity with: (I) Art 29 of the Constitution of Eire, 1937; (II) Article 28, 29, 30 of the USSR, 1977 and (III) Article VI Cl.(2) of the Constitution of the United States. Apart from this it has close similarity to some of the International Charters and Covenants such as: (I) Arts 28, 29 of the Universal Declaration of the Human Rights, 1948; (II) Arts 1 and 2 of the International Covenant on Economic, Economic, Social and Cultural Rights 1966; and (III) Arts 1, 4 and 22 of the International Covenant Civil and Political Rights, 1966.

[17] Alexander (n 4).

[18] See TSR Rao, 'Some of the Problems of the International Law in India' (1957) 6 *Indian Yearbook of International Affairs* 3.

little change from this pre-constitutional position in the matters of basic canons governing the principles of international law and municipal law. While the Constitution thus imposed a positive non-justiciable obligation in the context of international law, the court continues to observe the common law if it is not inconsistent with enacted law. Neither would it disregard the usual presumptions which safeguard international law, and thus it is fair to assume that Article 51(c) is not derogatory from the common law doctrine to which Blackstone gave early expression in English law.[19] The jurisprudence of the Indian courts, early on into the constitutional republic,[20] shows that the allegiance to the common law principles, including those related to international law, remains unchanged.

The reader is made aware of the position of normative content that governs Private International Law disputes in India. There is precious little in the form of normative content, only in the context of rules related to jurisdiction. Indian courts have contributed with their jurisprudence, although it is largely founded upon the common law principles. Interpersonal conflicts, especially those related to contractual obligations and tortious liability, are subjected to a *de minimis* regime that includes legislative provisions on the recognition and enforcement of foreign judgments[21] and the law related to limitation.[22] Much of the jurisprudence related to the law on obligations involving a foreign element is a derivation from the judicial decisions. It has been a stated part of the early literature on the subject[23] that the common law principles have had a significant impact on the handling of a foreign element within a dispute.

Success with the United Nations Convention on Recognition and Enforcement of Foreign Arbitral Awards (New York Convention)[24] notwithstanding, membership with international organisations working in the private law space, such as the Hague Conference on Private International Law (HCCH) and the International Institute for the Unification of Private Law (UNIDROIT), could not, as yet encourage an address to substantive legal issues in disputes with a foreign element.

The following narrative will try to analyse the position of foreign law – the law and jurisprudence of another nation and harmonised law – regarding the manner of its reception in disputes before Indian courts.

II. Status of Choice of Laws Rules

The principle of party autonomy, applicable as it is to the parties conferring exclusive jurisdiction on any court of choice, extends to the freedom of the parties to choose the governing law applicable to their contract. Inspired by the Privy Council's decision in

[19] Alexander (n 4) 298.

[20] *Birma v The State* [1951] A.I.R. (38) Raj. 127. Vide also a similar case: *Nanka v Gov. of Rajasthan* [1951] A.I.R. (38) Raj. 15.

[21] Code of Civil Procedure, 1908, ss 13, 44A.

[22] The Limitation Act 1963.

[23] See, eg, PV Rajamannar, 'The Future of Private International Law in India' (1952) 1 *The Indian Yearbook of International Affairs* 20; VK Thiruvenkatachari, 'Developments in the field of Private International Law' (1953) 2 *The Indian Yearbook on International Affairs* 195.

[24] United Nations Convention on the Recognition and Enforcement of Foreign Arbitral Awards (New York, 10 June 1958) 330 UNTS 3.

Vita Food Product Inc v Unus Shipping,[25] Indian courts delineated the law on express, implied and objective choice of law applicable to a commercial contract.

In *Dhanrajamal Gobindram v Shamji Kalidas and Co*,[26] the Court held that choice between the *lex loci contractus* or *lex loci solutionis* for the decision on a proper law of the contract is a matter of presumption.[27] The determination is, however, to be founded upon accepted rules. An expressed intention of the parties regarding the choice of law overrides any presumption. In the absence of an express intention regarding the choice of law, the applicable law is to be inferred from the terms and nature of the contract and from the general circumstances of the case.

The determination of the proper law of the contract has moved away from any presumptions and founded itself upon the consideration of all relevant factors. In *Delhi Cloth and General Mills v Harnam Singh*,[28] the grouping of elements test was applied in order to ascertain the proper law of contract, thus, endorsing the objective approach.

In *Rabindra N. Maitra v Life Insurance Corporation of India*,[29] the Supreme Court listed the factors to be considered while imputing the objective choice of law by the court – the place where the contract was made; place of performance; place of domicile; residence or business of the parties; national character of corporation; subject matter of contract; and all other facts that help localise the contract. Amongst these, the Court underscored the importance of the law of the place of performance of the contract as a determinant factor because of the contract's closer connection with *that* law than any other.

In *British India Steam Navigation Co., Ltd. v Shanmughavilas Cashew Industries and Ors*,[30] the Court ruled on the 'fixed' nature of the proper law of the contract and explained that there cannot be a 'floating' proper law.[31] Choice of law, founded upon the freedom of the parties, ought to be bona fide legal and not impinge upon public policy.[32] Courts in India possess the residual power to strike down the wholly unconnected choice of law clauses.

The Supreme Court in *National Thermal Power Corporation v Singer Company and Ors*[33] explained that an express choice of law, to be considered valid, ought to be explicit, emphatic, unambiguous, bona fide legal, and not opposed to public policy. The term 'proper law of a contract' refers to the system of law by which the parties intended the contract to be governed. This intention is either expressed or to be inferred from the circumstances of the case. In the absence of such choice of the proper law, the courts could impute an intention by applying the objective test to determine what the parties would have intended as regards the applicable law had they applied their minds to the question. Relevant factors for the objective test could be the place, form and object of the contract, place of performance, the

[25] *Vita Food Product Inc v Unus Shipping UKPC* 7, A.C. 277 (P.C.), (1939) 63 Ll L Rep 21.

[26] [1961] 3 SCR 1029.

[27] ibid [37]. See SR Garimella, 'OBOR and the Syncretic Private International Law Rules in India: Time for Accession to Harmonised Legal Regimes' in P Sooksripaisarnkit and SR Garimella (eds) *China's One Belt One Road Initiative and Private International Law* (London, Routledge, 2018).

[28] AIR 1955 SC 590.

[29] AIR 1964 Cal 141.

[30] (1990) 3 SCC 481.

[31] ibid [29].

[32] ibid [31].

[33] [1992] 3 SCR 106.

place of residence or business of the parties, and reference to courts having jurisdiction play an important role for the courts to determine the system of law with which the transaction has its closest and most real connection.

> Rule 180 – The term 'proper law of a contract' means the system of law by which the parties intended the contract to be governed, or, where their intention is neither expressed nor to be inferred from the circumstances, the system of law with which the transaction has its closest and most real connection. (Dicey & Morris, The Conflict of Laws (Vol.11) pp 1161–62)
>
> The expression 'proper law of a contract' refers to the legal system by which the parties to the contract intended their contract to be governed. If their intention is expressly stated or if it can be clearly inferred from the contract itself or its surrounding circumstances, such intention determines the proper law of the contract.
>
> ....
>
> Where, however, the intention of the parties is not expressly stated and no inference about it can be drawn, their intention as such has no relevance. In that event, the courts endeavour to impute an intention by identifying the legal system with which the transaction has its closest and most real connection.[34]

In the absence of an express choice of law as the proper law of the contract, the same could be inferred by applying sound ideas of business, convenience, and sense to the language of the contract itself.

> Where the parties have not expressly or impliedly selected the proper law, the courts impute an intention by applying the objective test to determine what the parties would have as just and reasonable persons intended as regards the applicable law had they applied their minds to the question. The judge has to determine the intention of the parties by asking himself 'how a just and reasonable person would have regarded the problem,' *The Assunzione (1954) P. 150; Mount Albert Borough Council v. Australasian Temperance and General Mutual Life Assurance Society Ltd.* (1938) A.C. 224.[35]

The *NTPC v Singer* ratio related to an arbitration issue with a designated proper law of the contract – the Indian law. Hence, much of the import of the decision on the proper law is an obiter. Nevertheless, the decision addressed an important issue in private international law – the choice of the forum and its impact on the tacit choice of law. In the absence of an expressed choice of law, such choice may be clearly inferred based on the contract and the surrounding circumstances.[36] The Court observed that if the contract did not have a choice of law, the law of the 'closest and real connection' must be applied to the proper law.[37] Neels commented that a choice of forum provision may nevertheless be seen as one of the *indicia* of a tacit choice of law, corroborated by other factors indicating to such an intention.[38] While the decision accepted only a rebuttable presumption with regard to a choice of forum

[34] ibid [13].
[35] ibid [16].
[36] JL Neels, 'Choice of Forum and Tacit Choice of Law: The Supreme Court of India and the Hague Principles on Choice of Law in International Commercial Contracts (An Appeal for an Inclusive Comparative Approach to Private International Law)' in *Eppur si Muove: The Age of Uniform Law Essays in honour of Michael Joachim Bonell to celebrate his 70th birthday* (UNIDROIT, 2016) 358, 366.
[37] (n 33) [13] and [17].
[38] (n 36) 367.

indicating a tacit choice of law, the Court clearly indicated that such choice of forum would not, on its own, be sufficient to deduce a choice of law. It shall only serve as a rebuttable presumption.[39]

In *Shreejee Traco (I) Pvt Ltd. v Paperline International Inc.*,[40] the Supreme Court, in a matter related to arbitrator appointment, referred to the *NTPC v Singer* decision and ruled in favour of a presumption of linkages between the choice of forum and a tacit choice of law. It is commented that the instant decision made a mistaken reading of a presumptive linkage, where the precedent only recommended a casual linkage and a possible factor for consideration. It is hoped that in an appropriate dispute before it, the apex court will make an authoritative precedent, drawing upon the international practice, and especially the import of Article 4 of Hague Principles on Choice of Law in Commercial Contracts, 2015.[41]

In retrospect, the position on choice of law rules in India could be stated as follows. The cases of *Delhi Cloth and General Mills v Harnam Singh*, *British India Steam Navigation v Shanmughavilas cashew Industries* and *Rabindra Maitra v Life Insurance Corporation of India* brought about a restrictive approach in dealing with private international law.[42] The Court in these cases held that the 'unconnected' laws cannot be chosen by international parties unless such law is also the proper law. This restrictive position when it comes to the application of 'choice of law' is considered to have been deserted by the Supreme Court in recent times. In *NTPC v Singer Company*,[43] the Court allowed the parties to choose the law that would govern them despite it being unconnected to the contract. The permission to make a choice of law did not depend on the geographical nexus between the chosen laws and the obligation the contract created. In the case of *Modi Entertainment v WSG Cricket Ltd*,[44] the Supreme Court elucidated the emerging stance of a connection of the chosen legal system with the contractual obligation not being necessary.

In a recent decision of the Delhi High Court,[45] of importance to party autonomy articulation in the context of choice of law, it was specified in clear terms that parties have the unquestionable right to choose a governing law for their arbitration agreement/clause including the choice of a foreign law as such governing law. The Court referred to the Supreme Court's decisions in *Centrotrade Minerals and Metal Inc. v Hindustan Copper Ltd.*,[46] which stressed on party autonomy in arbitration and held that it is a virtual backbone that allows parties to choose foreign law as proper law for arbitration, and *Technip SA v SMS Holding Pvt. Limited & Ors.*,[47] wherein it was held that applicability of foreign law can be objected to only in cases where the law amounts to flagrant or gross breach of morality and justice, and that foreign law cannot be discarded only because it is contrary to Indian statute, as the same would defeat the basis of private international law.

[39] (n 33), headnote [5].
[40] (2003) 9 SCC 79.
[41] India was represented at the HCCH on the Choice of Law Principles, and at the adoption on 19 March 2015.
[42] (n 28, 30, 29).
[43] (n 33).
[44] *Modi Entertainment Network and another v WSG Cricket Pte. Ltd* (2003) 4 SCC 341.
[45] *Dholi Spintex Pvt. Ltd. v Louis Dreyfus Company India Pvt. Ltd.*, 2020 SCC OnLine Del 1476.
[46] (2017) 2 SCC 228.
[47] (2005) 5 SCC 465.

A. Foreign Law before Judicial Authorities

As discussed earlier, foreign law has had and continues to find an important place before the judicial authorities in India. Such foreign law included not just the law of the colonisers, but Indian courts are known to have found inspiration elsewhere as well. For instance, the American constitutional jurisprudence on the due process has and continues to impact the constitutional and other jurisprudence in this country. Other sources include references to the South African, Irish, and Australian jurisprudence, amongst others.

B. A Brief Note on the Structure of Judiciary in India

The judiciary is vertically structured with the Supreme Court at the apex. The Supreme Court exercises appellate jurisdiction for final appeals in civil, criminal and administrative matters, as well as original jurisdiction in constitutional matters.[48] The state judiciary, that is, at the regional or federal unit level, consists of a high court and lower courts. The high courts have the appellate jurisdiction for the lower courts in the respective state or assigned union territory.[49] They establish the administrative procedures for the lower courts and, through precedent, outline standards the interpretation of the Code of Civil Procedure and the Indian Evidence Act for civil and administrative cases and the Code of Criminal Procedure for criminal cases.

III. Nature of Foreign Law

Foreign law is seen as a matter of 'fact' in India, its proof depends on expert evidence as laid down in section 45 of the Indian Evidence Act, 1872.[50] The provision is as follows:

> When the Court has to form an opinion upon a point of foreign law or of science or art, or as to identity of handwriting [or finger impressions], the opinions upon that point of persons specially skilled in such foreign law, science or art, [or in questions as to identity of handwriting] [or finger impressions] are relevant facts. Such persons are called experts.

There are two prerequisites for the reception of such expert testimony and its consideration as evidence.

1. the subject is such that expert testimony is necessary, and
2. the person called in for such testimony has demonstrable expertise in such subject. It must be proved that the witness is competent enough to give the evidence and that

[48] The original jurisdiction of the Supreme Court also extends to any dispute between the Union and the states or between the states. See, Arts 131–134 and 136 of the Constitution of India.

[49] Only six of the high courts (the high courts of Madras, Delhi, Himachal Pradesh, Jammu and Kashmir, Calcutta, and Bombay) exercise ordinary original civil jurisdiction, i.e., they function as the courts of first instance for civil suits, a per the pecuniary jurisdiction rules.

[50] The Indian Evidence Act 1872, No 1, Acts of Parliament 1872, s 45; *Technip SA v SMS Holding (P) Ltd. & Ors.*, (2005) 5 SCC 46.

> the fact to be proved is a point of science or art of which the witness is an expert in, before the opinion of a person can be admitted in evidence.

Further, any other fact, which was otherwise irrelevant, will become relevant if it either supports or contradicts the opinion of the expert.[51] Expert testimony is only corroborative in nature. In other words, it is used as a supplement to the direct or ocular evidence in a case. Moreover, it is a mere advisory and thus, not binding on the Court.

A. *Jura Novit Curia* – The Position in the Indian Law

Jura novit curia – the court knows the law – encapsulates the distinction between facts and the law. The parties to the dispute present the facts of the case, and it is up to the judge to decide the dispute by applying the laws to the facts. The concept emerges as a prerequisite in making the right of access to courts meaningful enough for the parties – right to appear in court and plead in the proceedings, right to be represented, the right to equal protection in the proceedings, due application of law, amongst others. Importantly, the concept acts as a bar against abuse of law by the judiciary by acting as a limit on the discretionary powers of the court. Thus, the concept acts a limit on the fact-trier's discretion. In India, all these features are assured constitutional rights[52] for the parties to the dispute.

Section 37 of the Indian Evidence Act specifies that the courts in India when required to form an opinion on the existence of any fact of a public nature (relating to the contents of the law) shall refer to any statement of such law found in any legislation either of the British Parliament or of its constituent units, or in a government/crown representative's notification or in the Official Gazette thereof. A related provision, section 39 of the same legislation, states that when the court has to form an opinion as to a law of any country, any statement of such law contained in a book purporting to be printed or published under the authority of the government of such country and to contain any such law, and any report of a ruling of the courts of such country contained in a book purporting to be a report of such rulings, is relevant. The Law Commission of India in its 69th Report explained the relevance of these two provisions, and also suggested revisions/amendments to the same. In this context, the Report also touched upon the relevance and expanse of *jura novit curia* in the Indian law.

> The first observation which we would like to make is, that a question of Indian law is not a matter of evidence, and therefore the terminology of 'relevant fact' is not appropriate for such questions. It is well established that evidence cannot be given of the general law, although evidence can be given of customs which derogate from the general law. Even if it be assumed, for the sake of argument, that what has been stated officially on a matter of law can be used for persuading the court, it is obvious that official expression of views on a matter of Indian law can have no binding effect.

[51] The Indian Evidence Act, s 46.

[52] Part III, especially Arts 14, 19 and 21, of the Constitution of India, 1950 and its amendments.

> Foreign law is a question of fact, and therefore, a matter for evidence. [...] But it cannot be denied that a question of Indian law is a question to be decided by the judge, 'Jura novit curia' (The Judge knows the law).[53]

It could therefore be said that the concept is prevalent in India only in the context of local law and not applicable to foreign law.

B. Ascertainment of Foreign Law

In India, foreign law is seen as a matter of fact, for which expert evidence is used to ascertain foreign law. However, the actual application of the law lies with the discretion of the court; only the proof of the foreign law, its ambit and pertinence to the case is a matter of fact, its eventual interpretation is a matter of law. Explaining the significance of the expert evidence in *State of Himachal Pradesh v Jai Lal and others*,[54] the court observed,

> The duty of an expert witness is to furnish the Judge with the necessary scientific criteria for testing the accuracy of the conclusions so as to enable the judge to form his independent judgment by the application of this criteria to the facts proved by the evidence of the case.[55]

In *Rhodia Ltd v Neon Laboratories Ltd*,[56] the Bombay High Court heard an application relating to the enforcement of a foreign jurisdiction clause. The Court ordered that evidence about the governing foreign law ought to be adduced to enable it to decide whether the jurisdiction clause should be over-ridden. The *Rhodia* dictum is an important guide to understanding the legal position with regard to proving foreign law before forum courts.[57] A brief note on the dispute and the jurisprudence that it was referenced upon is presented here. The foreign element in this dispute related to a jurisdiction clause that vested dispute resolution with a foreign court. The dispute related to a distribution agreement between an English company and an Indian company, which retained the right to distribute the former's products in India and Sri Lanka. The governing law of the contract was agreed to be English law, and the choice of forum for dispute resolution was agreed to be the English courts. The Indian company approached the trial court for relief against the English company. In its reply to the interim application, the English company, inter alia, stated that the trial court had no territorial jurisdiction to entertain the suit for the reason that the parties to the agreement had agreed by choice to be governed by English law and had submitted themselves to the jurisdiction of English courts alone. The trial court held that, as the Indian company's plant was situated within its jurisdiction, then under section 20(c) of the CPC, the suit could be filed in that court. On appeal, the pleadings at

[53] Law Commission of India, 69th Report on the Indian Evidence Act 1872 (1977) [14.46]–[14.47] lawcommissionofindia.nic.in/51-100/Report69.pdf.

[54] (1999) 7 SCC 280.

[55] ibid [18].

[56] *Rhodia Ltd v Neon Laboratories Ltd* AIR [2002] Bom 502.

[57] For a detailed discussion on *Rhodia* dictum, see P Sooksripaisarnkit and SR Garimella, 'Choice of Court Agreements: Selected Common-Law Jurisdictions and Indian Laws Compared – Time for the Convention of 30 June 2005 on Choice of Court Agreements?' (2021) 30 *Journal of Transnational Law and Policy* 1.

the Bombay High Court addressed the following aspects related to enforcement of a choice of court clause:

- validity of contracts with a foreign choice of law clause within the Indian law, and whether foreign law can be relied upon to assess whether an Indian court has jurisdiction in the matter;
- jurisdiction of Indian courts to entertain a suit arising out of an agreement specifying a foreign court as having exclusive jurisdiction, were the cause of action to arise in India.

Since *Rhodia* involved an interpretation founded upon foreign law, the Bombay High Court, referring to a Supreme Court decision in *Harishankar Jain v Sonia Gandhi*,[58] explained the necessity of proving foreign law as a question of fact before the Indian court and ordered that the trial court ensure that evidence is adduced regarding the same. Foreign law, therefore, ought to be proved by adducing expert evidence regarding the same, as per section 45 of the Evidence Act 1872. Courts can also take judicial notice of a publication on such foreign law, were such publication is sanctioned by a governmental authority. The court can approve the law as set out in such publication. It should be noted that when such a publication is relied upon as evidence of foreign law, then the publication is not the proof that it incorporates all the law and expert testimony may still be necessary.[59] In *Shin Etsu Chemical Co. Ltd. v Aksh Optifibre Ltd.*,[60] the Supreme Court held that foreign law (the Japanese law in the instant case) could not be established via affidavit testimony, and proof ought to be led as in a trial dispute. Commenting upon the role of Indian courts on the ascertainment of foreign law, TS Rama Rao was of the view that judges need not be restricted to the means of evidence submitted by the parties, they can consult reports, textbooks and other secondary sources on their own,[61] unlike the English law that viewed the judge's role vis-à-vis the foreign law as a passive one, or as Sass explained,

> the English judge cannot avail himself of his eventual knowledge of the applicable foreign law just as he cannot take account of his personal knowledge of facts, nor is he allowed to engage in his own research of that law just as he cannot search for relevant facts on his own.[62]

C. The Expert Opinion: Evidentiary Value

The significance attached to an expert opinion and especially to its evidentiary value is determined by two aspects:

(a) it depends on the facts upon which it is based, and
(b) depends on the 'validity of the process' to reach the conclusion.[63]

[58] *Harishankar Jain v Sonia Gandhi*, AIR 2001 SC 3689.
[59] *Jagdish Chandra v Commissioner of Income Tax, West Bengal*, AIR 1956 Cal. 48.
[60] (2005) 7 SCC 234.
[61] TS Rama Rao, 'Conflict of Laws in India' (1958) 23 *Rabels Zeitschrift für ausländisches und internationals Privatrecht* 276.
[62] SL Sass, 'Foreign Law in Civil Litigation: A Comparative Survey' (1968) 16(3) *American Journal of Comparative Law* 332, 340.
[63] *Ramesh Chandra Agarwal v Regency Hospital Ltd.*, (2009) 9 SCC 709.

Expert evidence, being of corroboratory value, should be in consonance with the direct or ocular evidence. Where inconsistencies appear in between the expert opinion and the ocular evidence, the latter shall prevail.[64]

The court can approve the law that is set out in such publications as specified in section 38 of the Indian Evidence Act. However, if such a publication is used as evidence to ascertain the foreign law, it may not be the proof that it consists of all the law and expert evidence may still be required in such a case.[65]

Judges of the Supreme Court consult the relevant scholarly works as well. There is no Indian system which deals with resolution of inter-territorial issues which have cross-border implications.[66] Section 38 of the Indian Evidence Act[67] also states that any statement regarding foreign law in a book that is published or printed under the government of such a country is relevant. It also cites reports of a ruling of the courts of the country contained in a book purporting to be a report of such rulings as relevant sources.

While the Indian Evidence Act does not define who an expert is, it is understood that such a person has superior knowledge and practical experience in the field. It needs to be ensured that the person is an expert under law.[68] If this cannot be proved then their opinion is not regarded by the court. The expert must be examined and cross-examined to gauge their expertise.[69]

In the case of *Malay Kumar Ganguly v Dr. Sukumar Mukherjee*,[70] the Supreme Court held that the expert evidence is merely advisory in nature and that a Court is not bound by it.

> The purpose of an expert opinion is primarily to assist the Court in arriving at a final conclusion. Such report is not binding upon the Court … the Court will be well within its jurisdiction to discard the expert opinion.[71]

In the case of *Standard Chartered Bank & DBS Bank Ltd v Ruchi Soya Industries Ltd.*,[72] the court stated that foreign law cannot be binding upon it if there is an 'express prohibition' to do so under Indian law. Further, if a non-reciprocating country's judgment is brought in front of the court, it cannot be enforced in India and is seen as having merely persuasive value.[73]

There is no standardised mechanism provided specifically for foreign law. However, as has been indicated, the onus is upon the parties to prove legal information by using

[64] *Darbara Singh v State of Punjab*, (2012) 10 SCC 476; see generally, G Singh, 'Evidentiary Value of Expert Opinion under the Indian Evidence Act: A Critical Analysis of Section 45' (2020) 2 *International Journal for Legal Science and Innovation* 552.

[65] *Jagdish Chandra v Commissioner of Income Tax, West Bengal*, AIR 1956 Cal. 48.

[66] VC Govindraj, *Private International Law: A Case Study 1–20* (Oxford Scholarship Online 2018) oxford.universitypressscholarship.com/view/10.1093/oso/9780199489282.001.0001/oso-9780199489282.

[67] The Indian Evidence Act 1872, s 38.

[68] *Ramesh Chandra Agarwal v Regency Hospital Ltd.* (2009) 9 SCC 789.

[69] *Balkrishna Das Agarwal v Smt. Radha Devi* AIR 1989 All 133.

[70] *Malay Kumar Ganguly v Dr. Sukumar Mukherjee* AIR 2010 SC 1162.

[71] *Dayal Singh and others v State of Uttaranchal* [2012] INSC 425 [32].

[72] *Standard Chartered Bank & DBS Bank Ltd v Ruchi Soya Industries Ltd* CP 1371 & CP 1372/I&BP/NCLT/MAH/2017.

[73] N Chada and S Arora, 'India' in P Doris (eds), *Enforcement of Foreign Judgements 2020* (Law Business Research, Aug 2019) 59–63.

trustworthy means. Also, as per the ratio in *Kishan Chand v Sita Ram and others,*[74] if there is a conflict in the opinion of experts, the court is competent to form its own opinion given the specifications of the case. This means that the court can conduct an inquiry in its own right to examine the veracity/pertinence of expert claims.

The 89th Report of the Law Commission of India[75] was of the view that ascertaining foreign law could be an onerous task for Indian courts. The Report recommended that the courts could bear the burden of paying the fees of foreign experts.[76] An alternative method could be that Indian courts adopt the much prevalent[77] practice of 'costs follows the event' rule, which directs the losing party to pay the costs that the winning party has incurred. Such practice would shift the burden of the costs related to the expert testimony as part of the general costs related to the dispute resolution that are otherwise borne by the party(s), depending upon the costs-related orders. With no codified law being present, the court holds the discretion of awarding such costs with reason and justice and not arbitrarily.[78]

D. Interpretation and Application of Foreign Law

An Indian court will, in accordance with the prevalent choice of law rules, apply the appropriate foreign law even if the acceptance and application of a foreign law under the circumstances of the case may prove to be contrary to a policy of Indian law which the court would ordinarily apply in a purely domestic case.[79] Such application of foreign law is excluded in the case of foreign penal laws, on grounds of public policy,[80] foreign revenue laws (though recognised on grounds of comity) and foreign public law.[81] However, Indian courts have referenced foreign precedents extensively, within their ratio as well as obiter, as exemplified in the following decision. In *Central Bureau of Investigation & Others v Ramesh Gelli,*[82] the court extensively referenced to the dicta from English jurisprudence including the opinion of Lord Denning (otherwise subjected to criticism in England). It borrowed and adapted the law-finding method given in such decisions of the British courts to develop new and expansive content to the legislative provisions of the Prevention of Corruption Act. This example is proof enough to demonstrate the penchant of Indian courts for inspiration from foreign precedent.

[74] AIR 2005 P&H 156.

[75] Law Commission of India, 89th Report on The Limitation Act 1963 (1983) 25. lawcommissionofindia.nic.in/51-100/Report89.pdf.

[76] ibid [11.14].

[77] See, generally, SR Garimella, 'Arbitral Reforms in India – The Case for Third Party Funding of Arbitral Claims' (2018) 15(2) *Transnational Dispute Management* 1, 19; B Srinivasan, 'Appeal against the Order of the Chief Justice under Section 11 of the Arbitration and Conciliation Act, 1996: An Empirical Analysis' (2012) 1 *Indian Journal of Arbitration Law* 21. This category also included cases where the court would not have awarded costs for justifiable reasons recorded in the judgment.

[78] Law Commission of India, 240th Report, Costs in Civil Litigation (2012).

[79] VC Govindraj, *Conflict of Laws in India: Inter-territorial and Inter-personal Conflict* (Oxford, OUP, 2019) 1, 17; *(Gummideli) Anantapadmanabhaswami v Official Receiver of Secunderabad*, AIR 1933 PC 134, 142 IC 552, (1933) All LJ 645, (1933) 37 CAL WN 553; *Lakhpat Rai Sharma v Atma Singh*, AIR 1962 PUNJ 228, (1961) ILR PUNJ 166.

[80] Indian Contract Act 1872, s 23.

[81] Govindraj (n 78) 19.

[82] (2016) 3 SCC 788.

Regarding the method of interpretation of foreign law, there is not much clarity from Indian law, neither has the jurisprudence indicated a standardised method for application of foreign law by the Indian courts and the scrutiny of the same. There is, however, an indication with regard to the interpretation rule in the context of section 45 of Indian Evidence Act, wherein foreign law has been mentioned. The Kerala High Court in *Law Society of India v Fertilizers and Chemicals Travancore Ltd.*,[83] stated the interpretation rule for section 45 as follows:

> […] if the court finds that the conclusions reached by the experts are unsatisfactory, the court is not bound to accept the reports […].[84]

It, therefore, leads to the understanding that the Indian courts retain the discretion to form their own opinion upon a point of foreign law based upon the evidence and testimony of the experts.

E. Failure to Establish Foreign Law

There is, as of now, no jurisprudential direction on the consequences of failure to prove foreign laws from the Indian courts. However, since the rules of burden of proof regarding foreign law are similar to those of the English law, it could be said that the Indian courts may consider the approach adopted by the English courts. Indian courts, on numerous occasions, have relied on the scholarship of authors such as Dicey. In the book, 'The conflict of Laws' by Dicey, Morris & Collins, rule 25(2) specified that 'in the absence of satisfactory evidence of foreign law, the court will apply English law'.[85] Indian courts could consider a similar course in situations where the foreign law cannot be ascertained or where there is a gap in foreign law.

In the case of *FS Cairo LLC v Brownlie*,[86] this principle of 'presumption of similarity' was applied. The Supreme Court held it could be presumed that Egyptian law was materially similar to English law and so the latter could be applied. In some countries, parochial reasons seem to have guided courts to apply local law if the foreign law could not be proved to a 'satisfactory standard'. There is, at least, one example of an American court dictum that held that that local law will be applied if the injury occurred in an 'uncivilized place that has no law or legal system'.[87]

[83] AIR 1994 Ker. 308.

[84] ibid [185].

[85] Dicey, Morris & Collins, *Conflict of Laws*, 15th edn (London, Sweet & Maxwell, 2018); G Sitaraman, 'The Use and Abuse of Foreign Law in Constitutional Interpretation' (2009) 32 *Harvard Journal of Law & Public Policy*. 653. See, for instance, the decision in *State of west Bengal v B.K. Mondal and Sons*, AIR 1962 SC 779 wherein the court reiterated that the assistance of such decisions is subject to the qualification that prime importance is always to be given to the language of the relevant Indian Statute, the circumstances and the setting in which it is enacted and more importantly the Indian conditions. Further, in *Mohideen Mohamed Sheik Dawood v Sovfracht Jsc And Anr*, (INTERIM APPLICATION (l) NO 18323 OF 2021in SUIT (L) NO 18314 OF 2021) the Bombay High Court held against application of foreign court orders and processes that seem vexatious, while referencing Dicey, Morris and Collins' commentary on the same.

[86] *FS Cairo LLC v Brownlie* UKSC 2020/0164.

[87] *Walton v Arabian American Oil Co.*, 233 F.2d 541 (2nd Cir. 1956); See also A Nussbaum, 'The Problem of Proving the Foreign Law' (1941) 50 *Yale Law Journal* 1018.

F. Judicial Review

No special provisions or restrictions exist in Indian law to deal with appellate proceedings in matters that involve foreign law. However, the standard understanding that a judicial decision can be contested by the way of an appeal by parties, unless specifically excluded by the laws does exist. In a situation where the choice of law rules has been applied erroneously, the parties can turn to the standard conditions laid down in the Indian Civil Procedure Code. Part VII of CPC[88] describes the different conditions in which an appeal can be filed. In such a situation, a party can either file a first appeal or a second appeal.

Regarding the appeals to the Supreme Court, the High Court has to grant a certificate under Articles 132(1), 133(1) or 134 of the Indian Constitution.[89] In civil cases, the appeal application should be founded upon a substantial question of law of general importance.[90] Further, the Supreme Court of India, as per Article 136,[91] is vested with the discretionary power to decide upon any judgment related to a dispute via allowing an appeal to it, from such judgment, decree, sentence or order passed or made by any court or Tribunal of India. The non obstante clause emphasises that the power overrides the limitations on the court's power to entertain appeals.

The concept of Special Leave Petition (SLP) is governed under the rules mentioned in Order XVI of the Supreme Court Rules 1996 under either which the SLP is filed upon refusing the Certificate of fitness by the High Court or when there is a need to interfere by the Supreme Court to. However, it must be remembered that Article 136 does not confer a 'right to appeal' but only a 'right to apply' for special leave which, if granted, confers a right to appeal so long as the leave is not revoked.

G. The Rationale Explaining the Appeal Mechanism in India

The law ensures an unrestricted right of appeal to the Supreme Court of India, of any judgment, decree or final order in a civil dispute, if the dispute involved a substantial

[88] The Code of Civil Procedure, 1908, No 5, Acts of Parliament, 1908, Part VII.

[89] Constitution of India 1950, Arts 132(1), 133(1), 134.

[90] Article 133. Appellate jurisdiction of Supreme Court in appeals from High Courts in regard to civil matters.

(1) An appeal shall lie to the Supreme Court from any judgment, decree or final order in a civil proceeding of a High Court in the territory of India if the High Court certifies under article 134A-

  (a) that the case involves a substantial question of law of general importance; and
  (b) that in the opinion of the High Court the said question needs to be decided by the Supreme Court.

(2) Notwithstanding anything in article 132, any party appealing to the Supreme Court under clause (1) may urge as one of the grounds in such appeal that a substantial question of law as to the interpretation of this Constitution has been wrongly decided.

(3) Notwithstanding anything in this article, no appeal shall, unless Parliament by law otherwise provides, lie to the Supreme Court from the judgment, decree or final order of one Judge of a High Court.

[91] Article 136. Special leave to appeal by the Supreme Court

(1) Notwithstanding anything in this Chapter, the Supreme Court may, in its discretion, grant special leave to appeal from any judgment, decree, determination, sentence or order in any cause or matter passed or made by any court or tribunal in the territory of India.

(2) Nothing in clause (1) shall apply to any judgment, determination, sentence or order passed or made by any court or tribunal constituted by or under any law relating to the Armed Forces.

question of law requiring interpretation by the apex court. In the case of *Technip SA v SMS Holding (P) Ltd. & Ors*,[92] the Supreme Court held that the dispute regarding the application of two different systems of law is a 'question of law'. Thus, if any appeal is made against the application of choice of law rules erroneously, it should be looked as a 'question of law.' First appeals can be filed on the grounds of both question of fact and that of law. However, the second appeal can only be on the point of a 'substantial question of law'.[93]

Wherein courts have erroneously applied foreign law, the parties can appeal to higher courts including the apex court, the abovementioned appellate procedure can be resorted to by the aggrieved party(s). It is doubtful if there would lie a second appeal to the Supreme Court, as forum courts may not necessarily appreciate the content of foreign law and hence cannot certify that the dispute involved a substantial question of law requiring interpretation by the highest court. Determination or interpretation of foreign law is seen as a 'question of fact'[94] in India and as mentioned above only substantial questions of 'law' can be a ground to admit second appeals. The High Court can only certify a case to be appealed before the Supreme Court when it is a question of law.

IV. Foreign Law before Other Instances

There is no information about how administrative or non-judicial bodies ascertain and apply foreign law. It is inevitable that such bodies may have to adjudicate private matters which involve the application of foreign law. However, there are not any direct legal grounds upon which such bodies can rely on to apply foreign law. A possible approach adopted by such bodies could be to seek guidance from relevant judicial discourse, especially on matters related to interpretation of foreign law, and the methods of such interpretation.[95]

A. Ascertaining Foreign Law in Arbitration and ADR Mechanisms

Indian courts have upheld party autonomy when it comes to arbitration agreements. In the case of *PASL Wind Solutions (P) Ltd. v GE Power Conversion (India) (P) Ltd.*,[96] the court strengthened the power of parties to choose a foreign seat of arbitration, specifying that two Indian parties to a dispute retain the autonomy to attribute foreign law as the governing law of the arbitration agreement and locate their arbitration to a foreign seat, thus reiterating the seat-centric nature of Indian arbitration law.

> It can be seen that section 28(1)(a) of the Arbitration Act makes no reference to an arbitration being conducted between two Indian parties in a country other than India, and cannot be held, by

[92] *Technip SA v SMS Holding (P) Ltd. & Ors.*, (2005) 5 SCC 46.
[93] The Code of Civil Procedure 1908, s 100.
[94] (n 91).
[95] KG Balakrishnan, 'The Role of Foreign Precedents in a Country's Legal System' (2010) 22(1) *National law School of India Review* 1.
[96] *PASL Wind Solutions (P) Ltd. v GE Power Conversion (India) (P) Ltd.*, 2021 SCC Online SC 331.

some tortuous process of reasoning, to interdict two Indian parties from resolving their disputes at a neutral forum in a country other than India.[97]

While the Indian Arbitration Act does not lay down how exactly foreign law must be ascertained, Part II of the Act does deal with how foreign awards must be dealt with. Section 47 of the Act[98] requires sufficient proof of a foreign award from the parties. It needs to be 'duly authenticated in the manner required by the law of the country in which it was made'. Section 47(2) also requires the party to produce the award or agreement to be translated in English and to be certified as correct by a diplomatic or consular agent. This indicates that the judges can call upon a similar procedure to be administered while dealing with foreign law. Similarly, in matters concerning resistance to enforcement of foreign arbitral awards under section 48 of the Act, determination of applicable law by arbitral tribunals or otherwise is considered as a question of fact.[99]

Section 26(1)(a)[100] of the Act allows the arbitral tribunal to appoint expert(s) to assist it with specific issues. They could utilise this provision to ascertain and apply foreign law.[101]

Section 27 of the Act[102] allows the arbitral tribunal or even a party with the approval of the tribunal to take assistance of the court in taking evidence. Therefore, courts can facilitate the availability of relevant witnesses and documents that would help in ascertaining and applying foreign law.

Section 28 of the Act suggests that parties enjoy the autonomy with respect to choice of law and procedure in international commercial agreements and that the tribunals are under an obligation to abide by the choice of parties.[103]

V. Access to Indian Law

In India, legislations and case laws are widely available in the English language as it is one of the official languages. The Constitution of India through Article 348(1)[104] recognises English as the primary language that is to be utilised by the Supreme Court and High

[97] ibid [52].

[98] The Arbitration and Conciliation Act 1996, No 26, Acts of Parliament, 1996, s 47.

[99] See, eg, *Pari Agro Exports v Soufflet Alimentaire & Anr*, (2019) 08 P&H CK 0018.

[100] The Arbitration and Conciliation Act 1996, s 26(1)(a).

[101] See generally, M Hunter, S Garg, et al., 'Chapter 7: The Conduct of Arbitral Proceedings in India' in D Dave, M Hunter, F Nariman and M Paulsson (eds), *Arbitration in India* (Alphen aan den Rijn, Kluwer Law International, 2021) 135–36.

[102] The Arbitration and Conciliation Act 1996, s 27.

[103] See generally, N Dewan, 'Chapter 6: The Laws Applicable to an Arbitration' in D Dave, M Hunter, F Nariman and M Paulsson (eds), *Arbitration in India* (Alphen aan den Rijn, Kluwer Law International 2021) 103–22.

[104] Constitution of India, Art 348. Language to be used in the Supreme Court and in the High Courts and for Acts, Bills, etc. – (1) Notwithstanding anything in the foregoing provisions of this Part, until Parliament by law otherwise provides – (a) all proceedings in the Supreme Court and in every High Court, (b) the authoritative texts – (i) of all Bills to be introduced or amendments thereto to be moved in either House of Parliament or in the House or either House of the Legislature of a State, (ii) of all Acts passed by Parliament or the Legislature of a State and of all Ordinances promulgated by the President or the Governor of a State, and (iii) of all orders, rules, regulations and bye-laws issued under this Constitution or under any law made by Parliament or the Legislature of a State, shall be in the English language.

[..].

Court. Further, the legislations are made available in the other listed official languages as mentioned in the Eighth Schedule of the Constitution.

India has several legal databases that can help with legal research.[105] Further, the New York University has put together a list of Indian law databases, consisting of both official and unofficial databases.[106]

VI. Access to Foreign Law: Future Developments in Asia

India is not a party to the Convention on the Recognition and Enforcement of Foreign Judgments in Civil and Commercial matters. However, India does have bilateral treaties in place with various countries which ensure reciprocity when it comes to the enforcement of decrees and judgment. India is a member of the following international conventions dealing with Private International Law:

Subsequent to India becoming a party to the Hague Convention on Inter-Country Adoptions, 1993, with effect from 1 October 2003, India embraced three other Hague Conventions on Private International Law, namely the Convention Abolishing the Requirement of Legalisation of Foreign Public Documents, 1961, the Convention on the Service Abroad of Judicial and Extra-Judicial Documents in Civil or Commercial Matters, 1965, and the Convention on the Taking of Evidence Abroad in Civil or Commercial Matters, 1970.

Having an international or regional instrument that unifies the treatment of foreign law would significantly help jurisdictions like India. In India, there has been a trend of adopting traditional common law principles blindly. This has led to ambiguities in Indian Private International law. Having a uniform instrument to turn to could resolve some of these ambiguities.

VII. Conclusion

As demonstrated via the foregoing narrative, there is sparse regulatory activity on the treatment of foreign law in India, leading to whimsical approaches on the reading of foreign precedent. The Indian state would do well to bring in much needed clarity through legislative activity rather than wait for jurisprudential developments to unravel the maze around this aspect. Importantly, India should consider participation in harmonised legal platforms that would ensure clarity of the law and its interpretation.

[105] See, eg, www.indiacode.nic.in/, https://main.sci.gov.in/, www.advocatekhoj.com/library/index.php, https://indiankanoon.org/, https://prsindia.org/.

[106] NYU Law, Foreign Law by Jurisdiction: India, NYU LAW LIB (20 January 2021) nyulaw.libguides.com/c.php?g=773850&p=5552110.

17

Conclusion

KAZUAKI NISHIOKA

I. Introduction

The Introduction to this book described the purpose of this project and posed selective key issues to be considered in the respective chapters. The closing chapter will tease out the similarities and differences in the approaches taken by the 15 Asian states, with a view to assessing the extent to which those approaches are consistent with or different from each other. It will also consider what the future might hold with regard to the treatment of and access to foreign law by way of a beneficial initiative to improve systems in Asia and cater for the interests of not just judges but also concerned parties.

II. Current Challenges, Obstacles, and Solutions in Asia

When a foreign law is to be applied to determine some question in a case having foreign elements, national courts and other bodies will be called upon to ascertain, interpret and apply a particular foreign law(s). The treatment of foreign law is grounded on different theoretical foundations and practical considerations in different legal systems. As anticipated, some notable differences in approach between common law and civil law jurisdictions remain. In common law jurisdictions (plus the Philippines and Thailand), courts will not introduce foreign law *ex proprio motu*. Therefore, a party wishing to rely on foreign law must plead it and prove its contents. In most civil law countries in Asia, courts need to apply choice of law rules whether or not raised by the parties and, if a relevant choice of law rule points to a particular foreign law, the judge must *ex officio* ascertain its contents and apply the same. In addition to these typical approaches, some countries (eg, Cambodia and Vietnam) adopt a hybrid approach to foreign law. According to this, although foreign law is considered a matter of law, parties seeking the application of foreign law are obliged (or at least urged) to adduce evidence to prove the contents of a particular foreign law. In other words, foreign law is categorised as law, but does not have the same value as 'domestic law'.

As shown, there are several approaches in Asia. In terms of the actual process of ascertaining foreign law, however, there seem to be few significant differences among states. In particular, parties play an essential role in ascertaining the contents of foreign law by adducing evidence or simply submitting written documents on foreign law in both common law and civil law states. Nevertheless, there are critical issues which the common law and civil law families approach differently. Further, there remain some practical difficulties for judges in most civil law countries surveyed and parties everywhere in ascertaining the content of foreign law. This seems to be a key underlying cause of the unsatisfactory situation in Asia.

A. Status of Choice of Law Rules

The civil law and common law treat choice of law rules differently. It comes as no surprise that this is the case in Asia, where common law jurisdiction and civil law jurisdiction co-exist. In civil law countries (except for Thailand), it is mandatory for courts to apply choice of law rules as those rules are part of domestic law and must be applied under the *iura novit curia* principle. However, there is no explicit provision requiring this to be so in many of those countries.[1] To the contrary, courts in common law jurisdictions (plus Thailand) treat foreign law as a matter of fact and courts will not introduce foreign law on their own initiative. Consequently, a party wishing to rely on foreign law needs to plead it much as the party must plead all material facts supporting its cause of action. This distinction between the common law and civil law also exists in Asia and is the split-off point for the treatment of foreign law.

As for the applicability of foreign law, all the states surveyed recognise the applicability of foreign law. However, some states deny the relevance of foreign law in certain legal areas.[2] Further, due to a dearth of court decisions, it is unclear whether the national courts of a few states apply foreign law in practice. For instance, it is generally accepted that Myanmar was and remains a member of the common law family even after independence. If so, the relevant choice of law rules and principles of the common law should apply in theory. Yet, it is not apparent that the Myanmar courts apply the same rules and principles leading to the application of foreign law.[3] Therefore, one should be alive to the reality that a court may refuse to apply foreign law for no good jurisprudential reason. The judge may simply apply the *lex fori* by default, on the basis that the applicable foreign law is difficult to ascertain, the judge is more familiar with domestic law, and there are no analogous case precedents in which foreign law has been applied.

B. Foreign Law before Judicial Authorities

From a state's choice of law rules, one should be able to determine what law will be applicable. However, the process by which Asian courts decide that foreign law is applicable and then ascertain, interpret, and apply that foreign law to the facts of a case, is rarely transparent.

[1] Some states (eg, Indonesia) recognise the mandatory application of choice of law rules in theory, but their courts often do not apply or even consider foreign law in practice.

[2] Eg, ch 13 in this volume. Several choice of law doctrines in tort are known in Indonesian private international law, but Indonesian courts simply apply Indonesian law.

[3] See ch 11 in this volume. One author observes that, although at the substantive law level, Myanmar courts do not necessarily follow common law rules and principles but instead deal with cases differently.

In Asia, one can see the traditional difference between common law and civil law, that is, whether to regard foreign law as a matter of law or fact, though only a few countries have black-letter rules or case law in this regard. In common law jurisdictions, national courts regard foreign law as a matter of fact, and the parties wishing to rely on a foreign law need to plead it and prove its contents.[4] Courts in civil law jurisdictions consider foreign law to be a matter of law with the result that, under the *iura novit curia* principle, courts are called upon to ascertain and apply *ex officio* a particular foreign law applicable to disputes. In other words, the onus ascertaining the contents of foreign law lies with the courts. The courts in civil law jurisdictions are expected to make reasonable efforts to ascertain the contents of foreign law through the materials and channels available to them. But it does not mean that the parties are prohibited from submitting written documents regarding foreign law. Instead, as Article 18 of the Korean Private International Law Act provides, courts may request a party's cooperation in ascertaining the contents of foreign law. Many contributions observe that parties often submit written documents, such as expert opinions, to assist the court in determining and interpreting the contents of foreign law. Courts then make a final decision based on the opinions provided by the parties.[5] Courts, if needed, may ask the parties to clarify points relevant to an issue (including foreign law) by exercising their discretion per domestic procedural rules. Consequently, the parties to court proceedings often play an important role in ascertaining the content of foreign law, even under the civil law approach.

Going a step further, through legislation, some civil law states have shifted all or part of the burden of ascertaining the content of foreign law on the parties. For example, under Article 481 of the Vietnamese Civil Procedure Code, the parties are responsible for pleading foreign law and proving its contents to the courts' satisfaction in cases where the parties have designated a foreign law as applicable. The reason behind this shift is that 'the application of foreign law is ultimately to ensure the interests of the litigants, and they cannot stand aside from this work for their sake'.[6] The author of the Cambodia chapter has commented that 'foreign law, local government ordinances and customs are not always clear and unambiguous to judges, so the contents of these norms may have to be identified based on evidence'.[7] Accordingly, if foreign law is unknown to judges, they may only have the authority to investigate and apply it based on evidence adduced by the parties. Judges are trained under their local law and are unlikely to be versed in foreign law. So, it would be unrealistic to place the burden of investigating and ascertaining foreign law on judges. Furthermore, placing such burden on the parties relying on foreign law would ensure procedural efficiency and economy. In this light, the hybrid approach may be regarded as practical and realistic. In short, although there are some notable theoretical differences between the common law and civil law on who bears the legal burden of establishing foreign law, it is the parties in both regimes who play a crucial part in the ascertainment of foreign law at the end of the day.

[4] National courts in some common law jurisdictions may take judicial notice of foreign law. The courts in India are by legislation allowed to take judicial note of the contents of foreign law, while the courts in Sri Lanka or the Philippines cannot do so.

[5] In some jurisdictions, it is a de facto requirement to have documents certified before submitting them to the court.

[6] See ch 9 in this volume.

[7] See ch 10 in this volume.

The courts in some of civil law states surveyed here have had difficulties in accessing and ascertaining foreign law for various reasons, such as a lack of effective or functional methods and channels. The reality is that, due to a lack of useful channels and methods for accessing foreign law, the courts will inevitably rely on the legal information provided by the parties, subject only to a reliability check (possibly only cursory) by the courts. If so, there would not be much difference between common law and civil law jurisdictions regarding the actual process of ascertaining the content of foreign law.

Once the content of foreign law has been ascertained, courts must interpret and apply it. In this regard, the 15 Asian states examined in this book are basically on the same page. They apply foreign law in the same way as courts of the country of origin would do. This is likewise the position in the major jurisdictions surveyed by Professor Nishitani.[8] Nevertheless, some contributors have expressed concern about courts being unable to follow this principle strictly due in part to their unfamiliarity with foreign law.[9] Unfortunately, this might be the current situation in certain countries. However, those countries have taken initiatives to tackle the issue by building capacity through judicial training programs. International or regional support[10] would undoubtedly be helpful in accelerating such improvement.

When it comes to a court or the parties failing to establish the content of foreign law, various approaches have been adopted or proposed. In today's legally developed and highly-digitalised world, it is probable that courts and parties will successfully ascertain the contents of foreign law in most cases. But there have been reported cases where judges or parties failed to establish foreign law. Courts would then need to determine the merits of a case without reference to foreign law. Common law jurisdictions and some civil law states in Asia (for instance, Thailand and Vietnam) follow the traditional common law approach (that is, assuming that foreign law is the same as the *lex fori*) and directly apply the *lex fori* to determine the disputes. Other states in the civil law family have adopted or proposed alternative approaches (including recourse to the *lex fori*) based on different considerations. As many contributors suggest, however, judges should not immediately adopt a parochial approach. Instead, courts in civil law jurisdiction should first ascertain the content of foreign law and only fall back on the *lex fori* as a last resort if they genuinely cannot find out the content of foreign law within a reasonable time[11] at a proportionate cost. In modern society which is replete with easily-accessible online legal information, it is likely that courts will be able to ascertain the content of foreign law in many cases.

[8] Y Nishitani, 'Treatment of Foreign Law: Dynamics Towards Convergence? – General Report', in Y Nishitani (ed), *Treatment of Foreign Law – Dynamics towards Convergence?* (Cham, Springer, 2017) 31.

[9] See ch 10 in this volume.

[10] For instance, support by Japan International Cooperation Agency (JICA). See ch 10 in this volume.

[11] *Cf* Art 481(4) of the Vietnamese Code of Civil Procedure which explicitly sets up a limit of 6 months for the provision of information on foreign law by parties or the requested agencies. If the parties fail to do so, the courts will apply Vietnamese law to determine their dispute. It is hard to define what would be a reasonable time for an Asian court because their capacity differs significantly. Considering the latest technological progress, a period of 3 to 6 weeks seems reasonable. With a regional or international judicial network, a reasonable time could be much shortened.

In ascertaining the contents of foreign law, due process must be ensured. However, domestic procedural rules have no direct or specific regulation in most states examined in this book. In the common law approach, the evidence adduced by the parties, particularly expert opinions, is subject to cross-examination, which will offer the parties opportunities to tackle the reliability of submitted evidence and experts' credentials. On the other hand, since foreign law is regarded as a matter of law in civil law, information on foreign law provided by the parties is merely their assertion and has no binding effect on courts at all. Courts are free to assess the reliability of provided information and can form their view on the contents of foreign law. However, judges should present their views on the matter to the parties early enough to ensure the parties' opportunities to express their opinions (that is, at least before the parties make closing submissions). The fairness of the trial and parties' opportunities to defend their cases can be ensured only this way.

Concerning judicial review as to the treatment of foreign law, there are two conceivable situations: (i) when national courts erroneously applied choice of law rules (that is, they applied the law of state A instead of the law of state B; and (ii) when national courts erroneously applied a designated foreign law. For the first scenario, the 15 states surveyed do not see any problem in accepting that an erroneous application of choice of law rules is amenable to judicial review (mostly up to the apex court) insofar as the requirements in the domestic procedural rules are met. To the contrary, although there is not much discussion in the examined 15 states, their national courts may take different positions in the second scenario. In common law jurisdiction (plus Thailand), findings of fact are binding on upper courts, and their courts tend to be slow to re-assess and reverse findings of fact as they typically recognise that the lower court is in a better position to assess evidence regarding foreign law. However, with a higher standard than one for the ordinary appeal, their courts may allow an appeal against an erroneous application to judicial review.[12] The civil law family members in this region are likely to adopt a straightforward approach accepting judicial review (including by the apex court) of an appeal against an erroneous application of foreign law (possibly with certain qualifications) on various grounds, for instance, that such an application would have a significant impact on their jurisprudence.[13]

C. Foreign Law before Other Instances

In the surveyed states, there is little regulation[14] or even less discussion concerning how administrative or quasi-judicial authorities, arbitrators and mediators treat foreign law. It is thus unclear how they approach the issue. Although administrative or quasi-judicial

[12] Nevertheless, a second appeal to the highest court will not necessarily be available. For instance, the Indian High Court can only certify a case to be appealed before the Supreme Court when it is a question of law.

[13] Eg, ch 6 in this volume. To the contrary, some European civil law countries restrict judicial review by the highest court to an erroneous application and interpretation of foreign law. See Nishitani (n 4) 37–38.

[14] Among the examined states, only China has a specific regulation on this (ie, Art 10 of the 2010 Conflicts Statute), requiring that the content of foreign law be ascertained by 'arbitral authority or administrative organ'.

authorities are governmental organisations, they have a tendency over time to mimic the approaches taken by courts. Arbitrators may be similar. They are likely to take more and more formal steps and measures with the passage of time, rather than simply basing themselves on robust broad-brush guidelines.[15] This tendency to become more technical is at the heart of what has been called 'due process paranoia' whereby arbitral tribunals conduct proceedings in an even more legalistic manner than the courts. Proof of foreign law in arbitration is an example. Arbitrators from the common law tradition, for example, may be unwilling for foreign law to be proved differently from the way it is proved in court through the examination of foreign law experts. That unwillingness is despite there being no rule requiring arbitrators to stick to the common law method for proving foreign law. It would be open (and less expensive) for arbitrators simply to hear submissions on foreign law directly from the parties' lawyers. But many common law arbitrators are reluctant to do this. In commercial mediation, the notion of a governing law typically does not play an important role, as legal evaluation is not usually required to settle a dispute. Nevertheless, a legal analysis may be the key to effective mediation in complex commercial disputes. In such a case, mediators may behave in a similar way to arbitrators.

D. Access to Local or Foreign Law

As reported in many chapters, unsurprisingly, legislation and court decisions are typically rendered only in non-English local languages in most Asian jurisdictions (except for English-speaking jurisdictions such as Hong Kong, India, Malaysia and Singapore). The result is that there are not many English legal materials in those jurisdictions. The judiciary and other governmental organisations in many Asian states provide English translations of major legislation on their websites. But the English translations provided are not necessarily up-to-date, final, comprehensive or even correct. Users will need to check their accuracy by referring to their original versions. In addition, a few jurisdictions provide English translations and summaries of selective court decisions, whether official or unofficial.[16] Private databases, too, are available in some jurisdictions, but they typically provide court decisions only in local languages. Due to this language barrier and a lack of English materials, it was and remains difficult for outsiders to access and understand existing laws in most states in the Asian region. This is one of the reasons why national courts in civil law jurisdiction have had difficulty in accessing and ascertaining the content of foreign law. There is a need for future improvement in this regard. Besides domestic measures (eg, building judges' investigative capacity in civil law jurisdictions and setting up liaison departments), an international mechanism enabling judges and citizens to access foreign law easily will improve the current situation.

[15] Eg, F De Ly, MW Friedman and LG Radicati di Brozolo, 'International Law Association International Commercial Arbitration Committee's Report and Recommendations on "Ascertaining the Contents of the Applicable Law in International Commercial Arbitration"' (2010) 26(2) *Arbitration International* 193.

[16] In some jurisdictions, academics, law firms and journals offer updates on recent legal developments in English and other foreign languages on a regular basis. See ch 5 in this volume.

III. A Glimpse into the Future: A Potential Way Ahead in Asia

As mentioned above, the system and actual practice on the treatment of and access to foreign law in not all but most Asian states surveyed is unsatisfactory for various reasons, such as still-developing legal systems, little discussion, and a dearth of court decisions. How can we improve the situation? This section will consider three ways:

(a) establishing an international or regional convention unifying the treatment of foreign law;
(b) concluding memorandums of understanding; and
(c) creating an international or regional institution that can assist national courts or parties in ascertaining the content of foreign law.

A. An International or Regional Convention?

A game-changer might be to unify the domestic rules on the treatment of foreign law in the region. On this, the HCCH and its invited experts concluded that 'it would be pointless to attempt to comprehensively harmonise the different approaches to the treatment of foreign law, as there is no need or likelihood of success for harmonisation'.[17] Is this observation correct about Asia? If Asia can adopt a unified approach to the treatment of foreign law, whether common law, civil law or hybrid style, there would be consistency across Asia.[18] This would appeal to some (particularly developing) states because they could implement the ready-made system. There would be a dramatic improvement. The reality, however, is that it would be unrealistic and almost impossible to unify the domestic rules on the treatment of foreign law as the HCCH concluded.

Unifying the rules on the treatment of foreign law would entail changes to domestic procedural laws.[19] The region would need to choose a single approach, with the result that states would be required to abandon current approaches and engineer a transformation in theoretical and practical aspects. Suppose that Asian courts follow the typical common law or hybrid approach. Parties seeking the application of a particular foreign law will need to plead foreign law and prove its content. If they fail, courts will apply the law of the forum. The legal burden that courts in civil law jurisdiction presently bear would shift to the parties. On the other hand, if the traditional civil law approach is adopted, Asian courts would need to ascertain the contents of foreign law *ex officio*, albeit mostly with the parties' assistance. This will then place the burden of identifying a foreign law and

[17] See section II of the Introduction to this book. Preliminary Document No 21 A of March 2007, 'Feasibility Study on the Treatment of Foreign Law: Report of the Meeting of 23–24 February 2007', 3; Preliminary Document No 11 A of March 2009 – Accessing the Content of Foreign Law and the Need for the Development of a Global Instrument in this Area – A Possible Way Ahead', para 1. Available at assets.hcch.net/docs/ec2804c3-f55c-427d-9761-e0fa4eac41a7.pdf.

[18] There will remain practical differences. For instance, under the common law approach, courts need to assess evidence adduced by the parties to decide whether the content of a particular foreign law has proved to its satisfaction. The extent to which parties need to prove the contents of a particular foreign law might vary depending on judges' skill.

[19] Many contributors express the same concern. See, eg, ch 13 in this volume.

proving its content on the courts. This will also still impact domestic rules in theoretical and practical aspects. In a region where there co-exist common law and civil law jurisdictions and there is no regional organisation or union (in contrast to the EU) to which Member States have delegated at least some sovereignty,[20] such a change will be unrealistic. Even if possible, it would take time. Such reform has never been achieved, even in the EU or elsewhere. Further, assume a unified approach has been adopted, there would remain problems of accessing foreign law. In many Asian states, not only courts but also citizens have found it hard to access foreign law for various reasons, including for want of judicial and financial resources.[21] Introducing a uniform regime on the treatment of foreign law will not improve the situation in Asia until access to foreign law is enhanced. As the HCCH suggested, the focus should be on facilitating access to foreign laws. The priority must be to set up mechanisms to enable courts and parties conveniently and cost-effectively to access foreign law.

B. A Memorandum of Understanding?

Some states examined in this book reported that they have concluded legally binding instruments[22] and memorandums of understanding (MOU) on: (1) references of questions of law; (2) cooperation on information on foreign law; or (3) judicial cooperation.[23] Instruments and MOUs on (1) and (2) can help ascertain the content of foreign law. An MOU on (3) may be less helpful as far as access to foreign law in court proceedings is concerned. Under the latter, states usually undertake to cooperate on matters of mutual interest, including exchanging legal publications and holding meetings, conferences and dialogues.[24] Such arrangements do not typically directly cover access by the public to foreign law. In addition, states or authorities are generally obliged to keep the information and knowledge obtained through the MOU confidential.[25] The MOUs will not by themselves facilitate access to foreign law. To facilitate access to foreign law, further concrete measures will be needed. Given the spirit, scope and mode of cooperation envisaged in type (3) MOUs, states must take a further step to assist their courts in ascertaining the contents of foreign law. The MOUs usually have no legally binding effect and impose no obligation on states to implement whatever measures judiciaries or concerned parties seek.[26] In addition, most citizens are unaware of those arrangements.

[20] Even in ASEAN, there is no legislative body to which each Member State has delegated some sovereignty. It consequently will be difficult to unify domestic rules on the treatment of foreign law within the region, unless a special arrangement is set up.

[21] For instance, the author for the Sri Lanka chapter states that '[t]his is particularly important to Sri Lanka in the background of the limited resources of both the government and private parties, especially the prevailing dearth of foreign exchange reserves, which makes the engagement of foreign legal experts in domestic litigation an unaffordable luxury to many.'

[22] See chs 6 and 7 in this volume.

[23] See chs 2, 5, 7 and 9 in this volume.

[24] Eg, para 2 of the memorandum between Japan and Singapore.

[25] Eg, para 6 of the memorandum between Japan and Singapore.

[26] For instance, para 10 of the Memorandum of Cooperation between Singapore and Japan provides that '[n]othing in this MOC creates or is intended to create any legally enforceable rights or obligations under national or international law on any person or either Participant'.

These circumstances present a critical question: How beneficial are MOUs to courts and the parties concerned? MOUs are a valuable addition to relevant states' toolboxes in the sense that they are better than nothing. However, what would they bring to actual practice? They may or may not improve the current situation in respect of the treatment of foreign law. It is too early to answer this question. The critical consideration will be how states implement MOUs to enhance their infrastructure for accessing foreign law. A potential measure might be to set up a special reference department to liaise with counterparties to provide the legal information applicable to a dispute. One still needs to wait and see how matters develop in relevant states. Having MOUs on judicial cooperation is a simple and attractive first step to making a breakthrough in the current unsatisfactory situation. However, it must be borne in mind that an MOU by itself does not per se facilitate access to foreign law, concrete measures will need to be implemented simultaneously or subsequently.

C. An International or Regional Network or Institution?

As many contributors from civil law jurisdiction have pointed out, there is a great need (an urgent one in some states) to improve the availability of information on foreign law to ensure legal certainty and provide citizens with access to sound justice. An effective way to cater for this need would be to establish a regional or international institution or network that can assist not only national courts but also citizens in ascertaining the contents of foreign law by providing information in English and (ideally) other major languages.[27] China has established a network within its judiciary to investigate and collect information on foreign law.[28] Presumably, other Asian states could do the same. Nevertheless, capacity to establish an institution or network may vary for various reasons, such as a want of human or financial resources. By the same token, a single state's efforts will have a limitation in its capacity to collect and keep updating information on foreign law. Bare legislative texts will not necessarily offer a clearcut answer to a legal question. Instead, one may need to look into court decisions or academic materials to ascertain actual practice in a jurisdiction. This may in turn require familiarity with a relevant local language. Under these circumstances, establishing a regional institution as a 'link' with physical and financial support from more developed states, would be an ideal solution.[29] With such a mechanism, judges could access foreign law more readily. Furthermore, if such a link, whether an institution or an online database, is open to the public, it will provide citizens with an accessible platform to collect information on foreign law. As reported in some contributions, it can be costly for citizens

[27] National courts in common law jurisdictions usually do not have difficulty in ascertaining foreign law because the parties relying on foreign law are obliged to prove it. To improve the situation regarding access to foreign law in Asia as a whole where common law and civil law jurisdictions co-exist, an institution or network would need to be available to both courts and citizens.

[28] See ch 2 in this volume. Other regions have similar public or private institutions, for instance, the Swiss Institute of Comparative Law and the Dutch International Juridisch Instituut.

[29] To establish a robust system, it is preferable to set up a multilateral convention. An institution (should be) established in an Asian city with developed infrastructure and transport accessibility. Candidate cities could be Bangkok, Hong Kong, Seoul, Shanghai, Singapore and Tokyo.

to obtain information on foreign law.[30] With a collective database of legislation and court decisions of the member states of a network, this problem could be resolved.

To establish such a mechanism, each Member State will be required to provide and keep updating its legal information in timely fashion. This could entail great cost, especially in connection with translation. Most countries have already been equipped with English databases of their legislation and court decisions, although these may not be comprehensive. It is conceivable that there would be attractive incentives for countries in embarking upon such a project. For instance, a country could attract foreign investment within its territory by providing reliable and up-to-date legal information on its database. An institution may also form a network similar to the IHNJ and offer Member States an opportunity (through conferences, seminars, and roundtables) to gain a better understanding of each other's laws and practices. This would enhance judicial capacity. It would improve access to foreign law not only in a single state but in Asia as a whole.

[30] Eg, ch 15 in this volume.

BIBLIOGRAPHY

Chapter 1. Introduction

A Kusumadara (ed), *Indonesian Private International Law* (Oxford, Hart Publishing, 2021).

A Reyes, W Lui and K Nishioka (eds), *Choice of Law and Recognition in Family Law* (Oxford, Hart Publishing, forthcoming).

A Reyes and W Lui (eds), *Direct Jurisdiction: Asian Perspectives* (Oxford, Hart Publishing, 2021).

A Reyes (ed), *Recognition and Enforcement of Judgments in Civil and Commercial Matters* (Hart Publishing, 2019).

C Esplugues and G Palao, 'Foreign Law, Application and Ascertainment' in J Basedow, G Rühl, F Ferrari and P de Miguel Asensio (eds), *Encyclopedia of Private International Law* (Cheltenham, Edward Elgar, 2017) 769–78.

C Esplugues, JL Iglesias, and G Paolo (eds), *Application of Foreign Law* (Munich, Sellier, 2011).

CE Mota, 'Harmonization of Private International Law in Europe and Application of Foreign Law: the "Madrid Principles" of 2010' (2011) 13 *Yearbook of Private International Law* 273.

F De Ly, MW Friedman and LG Radicati di Brozolo, 'International Law Association International Commercial Arbitration Committee's Report and Recommendations on "Ascertaining the Contents of the Applicable Law in International Commercial Arbitration"' (2010) 26(2) *Arbitration International* 193.

HCCH 'Preliminary Document No 21 A of March 2007, 'Feasibility Study on the Treatment of Foreign Law: Report of the Meeting of 23–24 February 2007'.

HCCA 'Preliminary Document No 11 A of March 2009 – Accessing the Content of Foreign Law and the Need for the Development of A Global Instrument in this Area – A Possible Way Ahead', para 1. https://assets.hcch.net/docs/ec2804c3-f55c-427d-9761-e0fa4eac41a7.pdf.

HCCH, 'The Conclusions and Recommendations on Access to Foreign Law in Civil and Commercial Matters.' https://assets.hcch.net/docs/b093f152-a4b3-4530-949e-65c1bfc9cda1.pdf).

K Nishioka and Y Nishitani, *Japanese Private International Law* (Oxford, Hart Publishing, 2021).

Lord Collins of Mapesbury and others (eds), *Dicey, Morris and Collins on Conflict of Laws* 15th edn, vol 1 (London, Sweet and Maxwell, 2012).

P Lortie and M Groff, 'The Evolution of Work on Access to Foreign Law at the Hague Conference on Private International Law' in Y Nishitani (ed), *Treatment of Foreign Law – Dynamics towards Convergence?* (Cham, Springer, 2017) 615–38.

R Fentiman, *Foreign Law in English Courts: Pleading, Proof and Choice of Law* (Oxford, Clarendon Press, 1998).

Swiss Institute of Comparative Law (ed), *The Application of Foreign Law in Civil Matters in the EU Member States and its Perspectives for the Future* (JLS/2009/JCIV/PR/0005/E4, 2011. http://ec.europa.eu/; Part I: Legal Analysis; Part II: Empirical Analysis; Synthesis Report with Recommendations.

S Jolly and S Khanderia, *Indian Private International Law* (Oxford, Hart Publishing, 2021).

X Liu and Z Zhang (eds), *Chinese Private International Law* (Oxford, Hart Publishing, 2021).

Y Nishitani (ed), *Treatment of Foreign Law – Dynamics towards Convergence?* (Cham, Springer, 2017).

Chapter 2. China

H Wang and W Shen, 'Fixing the Failure of Ascertainment of Foreign Law An Empirical and Economics Study' (2016) 5 *Journal of the University of International Business and Economics* 135–49.

J Gu, 'Study on the Legal Aspects of the Free Trade Area (II): Ascertaining Recent Practices in Foreign Laws – Cross-border Guardianship' (*Tiantong Law Firm*, 24 April 2020). www.sohu.com/a/390883403_159412.

J Zhong, 'A Study on the Identification of Foreign Law in the Practice of Civil and Commercial Judgment in China – Taking Article 10 of the Law of Application of Law as the Analytical Object' [2021] *Guilin University of Electronic Science and Technology* 5.

J Hu, J Xu and L Wang, 'Research and Analysis over Discerning and Applying Foreign Law – from the Perspective of Judicial Practice of Ningbo Maritime Court' (2019) 1 *Chinese Journal of Maritime Law* 42.

J Deng, 'The Practical Dilemma of Foreign Law Ascertainment in China and the Path of Breaking it – An Empirical Analysis Based on 43 Maritime Cases' (2021) 2/2021 *Jiangxi Social Science* 182.

J Tan, 'The Predicament and Perfection of China's Foreign Laws' Ascertainment System' (2021) *Beijing Jiaotong University* 2021.

L Zhu, 'Conflict of laws in the People's Republic of China' (2017) 25 *Asia Pacific Law Review* 199.

S Zhu, *Chinese Conflicts of Law: A Restatement and Legisprudence Proposal*, (2017) SJD Dissertations.

T William, *International Conflict of Laws: Common Civil and Maritime* (Montreal, Blais, 1994) 512–521.

W Xu and J Yao, 'The Improvement of the System of Ascertainment of Foreign Laws by Experts under the Belt and Road Initiative – an Empirical Analysis of 134 Cases in China since the Implementation of the Law on the Legal Application of Foreign-related Civil Relations ("一带一路"倡议下专家查明外国法制度的完善 —— 基于《涉外民事法律关系适用法》施行以来全国134件案件的实证分析)' (2019) *A Study on Comprehensive Reform of the Judicial System and Criminal Trials*.

World Trade Organization, *Word Trade Statistical Review 2021*, (World Trade Organization, 22 July 2022). www.wto.org/english/res_e/statis_e/wts2021_e/wts2021chapter05_e.pdf.

X Song, 'Foreign Law: The Difference between "Fact" and "Law"' (2010) 1 *Global Law Review* 14.

Y Jiao, 'A Review of the New Regulations on the Ascertainment of Foreign Laws in China: A Review of Article 10 of the Law of the People's Republic of China on Choice of Law for Foreign-related Civil Relationships' (2013) 2 *Tsinghua University Law Journal* 163.

Y Lin and Y Huang, 'Why Foreign Laws is Difficult to Ascertain an Empirical Analysis Based on Article 10 of the Law of the People's Republic of China on Choice of Law for Foreign-related Civil Relationships' (2014) 10 *Law Science Monthly* 116.

Y (Lee) Li and W Yan, 'PRC Law on the Application of Laws to Foreign-Related Civil Relationships' (*Faegre Drinker*, 1 February 2011). www.faegredrinker.com/en/insights/publications/2011/2/prc-law-on-the-application-of-laws-to-foreignrelated-civil-relationships.

Y Zou, *Dictionary of Jurisprudence* (China University of Political Science and Law Press,1991).

Y Guo, 'The Theory and Practice of Ascertainment and Application of foreign law in China in Recent Years' (2007) 2 *Wuhan University International Law Review* 1.

Chapter 3. Hong Kong

A Briggs, *Private International Law in English Courts* (Oxford, Oxford University Press, 2014).

A Briggs, *Private International Law in English Courts*, 2nd edn (Oxford, Oxford University Press, 2023).

A Mills, 'Arbitral Jurisdiction and the Mischievous Presumption of Identity of Foreign Law' [2008] *Cambridge Law Journal* 25-27.

A Gray, 'Choice of Law: The Presumption in the Proof of Foreign Law' (2008) 31(1) *UNSW Law Journal* 136–57.

G Ma and D Brock (eds), *Arbitration in Hong Kong: A Practical Guide*, 5th edn (Hong Kong, Sweet and Maxwell, 2021).

G Johnston and P Harris, *The Conflict of Laws in Hong Kong*, 3rd edn (Hong Kong, Sweet and Maxwell, 2017).

G Tu, 'Inter-regional Private Law among Mainland China, Hong Kong and Macau after the Handovers: Achievements, Reflections and Prospects' (2021) 8(2) *Chinese Review of International Law* 115–28.

HM Courts & Tribunals Service, *The Commercial Court Guide*, 11th edn (2022) www.judiciary.uk/wp-content/uploads/2022/06/Commercial-Court-Guide-11th-edition-1.pdf.

I Fletcher, 'Review of Forum Law in English Courts' (1999) 115 *LQR* 518–20.

JH Baker, 'Ascertainment of Foreign Law: Certification to and by English Courts Prior to 1861' (1979) 28(1) *International and Comparative Law Quarterly* 141–51.

J Huang, *Interregional Conflict of Laws* (Taipei, Perennial Culture Publishing Inc, 1996).

JJ Spigelman, 'Proof of Foreign Law by Reference to the Foreign Court' (2011) 127 *Law Quarterly Review* 208–16.

J Hogan-Doran and D Hogan-Doran, 'New and Alternative Approaches to Proof of Foreign Law: A Practitioners' Perspective' in M Douglas and others (eds), *Commercial Issues in Private International Law: A Common Law Perspective* (Oxford, Hart Publishing, 2019) 231–56.

L Collins and others (eds), *Dicey, Morris and Collins on the Conflict of Laws*, 13th edn (London, Sweet and Maxwell, 2000).

Lord Collins of Mapesbury and others (eds), *Dicey, Morris and Collins on the Conflict of Laws*, 15th edn (London, Sweet and Maxwell, 2012).

—— *Dicey, Morris and Collins on the Conflict of Laws*, 16th edn (London, Sweet and Maxwell, 2022).

N Blackaby, C Partasides and A Redfern, *Redfern and Hunter on International Arbitration*, 7th edn (Oxford, Oxford University Press, 2022).

R Fentiman, *Foreign Law in English Courts* (Oxford, Oxford University Press, 1998).

—— 'Foreign Law in National Courts: A Common Law Perspective' in M Andenas and D Fairgrieve (eds), *Courts and Comparative Law* (Oxford, Oxford University Press, 2015) 79–101.

—— *International Commercial Litigation*, 2nd edn (Oxford, Oxford University Press, 2015).

—— 'Laws, Foreign Laws, and Facts' (2006) 59(1) *Current Legal Problems* 391–426.

W Day, 'Pleading and Proving Foreign Law' (2022) 81(1) *Cambridge Law Journal* 24–27.

W Lui, 'Hong Kong' in A Reyes, W Lui and K Nishioka (eds), *Choice of Law and Recognition in Asian Family Law* (Oxford, Hart Publishing, 2023) 51–80.

—— 'Researching and Teaching Asian and Hong Kong Private International Law' (2023) 20(2) *Indonesian Journal of International Law*, Article 2.

W Lui and A Reyes, *Hong Kong Private International Law* (Oxford, Hart Publishing, 2024).

Chapter 4. Taiwan

A Mazahéri, La Route De La Soei 315 (Sheng Geng tr, China Tibetology Publishing House, 2014).

En-Wei Lin, 'Wai Guo Fa Shi Yong Wen Ti Zhi Yan Jiu: Tai Wan Si Fa Shi Wu Pan Jue Yu Bi Jiao Fa Shang De Yi Xie Si Kao' ['A Study on the Application of Foreign Law: Some Reflections on Taiwan Judicial Practice Judgment and Comparative Law'] (2019) 58 *Tunghai University Law Review* 103.

Guan-Ping Wu, 'Fa Guan Ying Yi Zhi Quan Shi Yong She Wai Min Shi Fa Lu Shi Yong Fa' [Should the Courts Apply the "Statute Governing the Application of Laws to Civil Matters" Ex Officio?] in *Er Shi Yi Shi Ji Fa Xue Fa Zhan Xin Jing Jie - Ke Ze Dong Jiao Shou Qi Zhi Hua Dan Zhu Shou Lun Wen Ji [Collected Papers for Professor Tse-Tung Ke's 70th Birthday Celebration (2008)]* (Taipei, Angle Publishing, 2008) 415.

Han-Je Pak, *Da Tang Di Guo De Yi Chan: Hu Han Tong He Ji Duo Min Zu Guo Jia De Xing Cheng [Legacy of the Great Tang Empire: Han-barbarian Integration and the Form of Multi-ethnic State]* (Taipei, Gūsa Press, 2020).

Han-Pao Ma and Chun-Liang Lai, *Guo Ji Si Fa: Zong Lun Ge Lun [Private International Law: General Principles and Special Provisions]*, 4th edn (Taipei, self-publishing, 2022).

—— *Xi Yang Fa Lu Si Xiang Lun Ji [Essays on Western Legal Thoughts]* (Taipei, Han Lin Publishing, 1977).

H Prütting and M Gehrlein (eds), *ZPO Kommentar*, 5th edn (Köln, Luchterhand Verlag, 2013).

Hua-Kai Tsai, *Guo Ji Si Fa Shi Li Yan Xi [Case Study on Private International Law]* (Taipei, San Min Book, 2018).

J Austin, *The Province of Jurisprudence Determined* (Xing Liu tr, China Legal System Publishing House, 2002).

Ju-Hui Yen, 'Lun "Hua Wai Ren" Yu Wen Hua Ren Tong - Yi Ba Shi Ji De Du Tang Ri Ben Ren Wei Li' ['A Study on "Persons beyond the Pale of Civilization" and Their Cultural Identification: Using Japanese Who Went to China in the 8th Century as Example'] in Ming-Shih Kao (eds), *Tang Lu Yu Guo Jia Zhi Xu [Tang Code and National Order]* (Taipei, New Sharing Culture Enterprise, 2013) 312.

K O'Shaughnessy, *Gender, State and Social Power in Contemporary Indonesia: Divorce and Marriage Law* (New York, Routledge, 2009).

K Zweigert and H Kötz, *Einführung in die Rechtsvergleichung*, 3rd edn (Türbingen, Mohr Siebeck, 1996).

Kuan-Ling Shen, 'Cheng Xu Bao Zhang Yu Dang Shi Ren' ['Procedural Guarantees and Parties'] in *Min Shi Su Song Fa [Civil Procedure]* (Taipei, Angle Publishing, 2012) 39.

Shih-Ming Chiang, *Fei Song Shi Jian Fa Xin Lun [New Theory of Non-Contentious Matter Law]*, 2nd edn (Taipei, New Sharing Culture Enterprise, 2013).

Tie-Zheng Liu and Jung-Chuan Chen, *Guo Ji Si Fa [Private International Law]*, 6th edn (Taipei, San Min Book, 2018).

Tse-Tung Ke (Guan-Ping Wu ed.), *Guo Ji Si Fa [Private International Law]* (Taipei, Angle Publishing, 2020).

Wei-Hua Tang and Yu Huang, *Qing Dai Guang Zhou She Wai Si Fa Wen Ti Yan Jiu 1644–1840 [Research on Juridical Questions Involving Foreign Elements in Guangzhou in Qing Dynasty 1644-1840]* (Beijing, China Social Sciences Press, 2009).

Yuan-Cheng Su, *Guo Ji Si Fa [Private International Law]*, 5th edn (Taipei, Wu-Nan Book, 2008).

Yuan-Sheng Huang, *Zhong Guo Fa Shi Dao Lun [The Introduction of the Legal History of China]* (Taipei, New Sharing Culture Enterprise, 2012).

Z Kitagawa, 'Development of Comparative Law in East Asia' in M Reimann and R Zimmermann (eds), *The Oxford Handbook of Comparative Law* (Oxford, Oxford University Press, 2006) 259.

Chapter 5. Japan

A Mikazuki, 'Gaikokuho no Tekiyo to Saibansho' in T Sawaki and Y Aoyama (eds), *Kokusai Minji Soshoho no Riron* (Tokyo, Yuhikaku, 1987) 252.

B Huber and H Nakamura, *Die japanische ZPO in deutscher Sprache* (Köln, Heymanns Verlag, 2006).

H Kansaku, A Kimura, G Koziol, M Lentz, F Nagano, M Nakamura, T Spiegel, A Katharina Suzuki-Klasen, H Tanaka, and K Wada, 'Übersetzung des novellierten Zivilgesetzes 2020' 23 (2018) *Journal of Japanese Law (Zeitschrift für Japanisches Recht)* 183.

H Matsuoka, 'Gaikoku Ho no Tekiyou to Saibansho' in A Takakuwa and M Dogauchi (eds), *Shin Saiban Jitsumu Taikei 3 (Kokusai Minji Sosho Ho (Zaisan Ho kankei))* (Tokyo, Seirin Shoin, 2002) 280).

H Sakai et al., *Kokusai Minji Tetsuzukiho*, 2nd edn (Tokyo, Yuhikaku, 2012).

H Sano, 'Nin'i-teki Teishokuho no Riron' (2000) 49 (3–4) *Okayama Law Journal* 781.

J Yokoyama, *Private International Law in Japan*, 2nd edn (Alphen aan den Rijn, Kluwer Law International, 2020).

K Anderson and Y Okuda, 'Japan's Private International Law: Act on the General Rules of Application of Laws [Ho no Tekiyo ni Kansuru Tsusokuho], Law No 10 of 1898 (as newly titled and amended 21 June 2006)]' (2006) 8(1) *Asian-Pacific Law & Policy Journal* 160.

K Nishioka and Y Nishitani, *Japanese Private International Law* (Oxford, Hart Publishing, 2021).

K Takahashi, 'Japan's Newly Enacted Rules on International Jurisdiction: with a Reflection on Some Issues of Interpretation' (2011) 13 *Japanese Yearbook of Private International Law* 146.

K Yamamoto, 'Gaikokuho no Tekiyo' in Y Sakurada and M Dogauchi (eds), *Chushaku Kokusai Shiho Vol 2* (Tokyo, Yuhikaku, 2011) 352.

—— 'Renketsuten no Shucho Rissho' in Y Sakurada and M Dogauchi (eds), *Chushaku Kokusai Shiho Vol 2* (Tokyo, Yuhikaku, 2011) 369.

M Bälz, M Dernauer, C Heath, and A Petersen-Padberg (eds), *Business Law in Japan – Cases and Comments: Intellectual Property, Civil, Commercial and International Private Law* (Alphen aan den Rijn, Kluwer, 2012).

M Dogauchi, 'Historical Development of Japanese Private International Law' in J Basedow et al. (eds), *Japanese and European Private International Law in Comparative Perspective* (Tübingen, Mohr Siebeck, 2008) 23.

S Nakano, 'Japan: Proof of and Information About Foreign Law in Japan' in Y Nishitani (ed), *Treatment of Foreign Law – Dynamics towards Convergence?* (Cham, Springer, 2017) 530.

T Sawaki and M Dogauchi, *Kokusai Shiho Nyumon*, 8th edn (Tokyo, Yuhikaku, 2018) 11.

Y Nakanishi et al., *Kokusai Shiho*, 2nd edn (Tokyo, Yuhikaku, 2018).

Y Okuda, 'Translation of New Rules on International Jurisdiction of Japanese Courts in Family Matters' 25 (2020) *Journal of Japanese Law (Zeitschrift für Japanisches Recht)* 235–46.

Y Sakurada, 'The Origin and Evolution of Private International Law in Japan' (2013) 56 *Japanese Yearbook of International Law* 164.

—— *Kokusai Shiho*, 7th edn (Tokyo, Yuhikaku, 2020) 25.

Z Kitagawa, *Doing Business in Japan* (London, LexisNexis, 1980).

Chapter 6. South Korea

Ae Ra Han, 'Jun-ge-bub-in Eo-guk-bub-ui Jo-sa-e Gwan-han So-go' ['A Study on the Investigation of the Foreign Law as the Governing Law'] (2019) *Guk-je-sa-bub-yeon-gu [Korea Private International Law Journal]* 33.

Il Young Min, 'Ju-seok Min-sa-so-song-bup' ['Commentary on Civil Procedure Act'] (2018) *Han-guk-sa-bub-haeng-jong-hak-hoi [Korea Private Law Administration Academy]* 196.

J Han Kim, 'Jeung-geo-jae-pan-ju-ui-ui ui-mi-wa um-gyuk-han jeung-myung, ja-yu-ro-un jeung-myung' ['The Reconsideration of "Principle of Trial by Evidence", and Strict Proof, Free Proof'] (2010) 17(1) *Chosun-dae-bup-hak-non-chong [The Legal Studies Institute of Chosun University]* 459.

K Hyun Suk, *Guk-je-min-sa-so-song-bub [International Civil Litigation Law]* (Seoul, Pakyoungsa, 2012) 326.

—— *Guk-je-sa-bub Hae-sol [Commentary on Private International Law]* (Seoul, Pakyoungsa, 2013) 128.

—— *Guk-je-sa-bub-gwa Guk-je-so-song Je-6-kwon [Private International Law and International Litigation Vol 6]* (Seoul, Pakyoungsa, 2019) 93.

—— 'Han-guk-bub-won-e-seo je-gi-deon joong-guk-bub-ui jaeng-jum – gye-yak-bub, bul-bup-haeng-wi-bup, hon-in-bup-gwa oi-guk-pan-gyul-ui seung-in jip-haeng-eul joong-sim-ui-ro' ['Several Chinese Law Issues raised before Korean Courts: With Emphases on Laws on Contract, Tort, Marriage and Recognition and Enforcement of Foreign Judgments'] (2010) 51(3) *Seoul-dae-hak-kyo-bup-hak [Seoul Law Journal]* 181.

San-up-tong-sang-ja-won-bu [Ministry of Trade, Industry and energy] '2021-nyun soo-chool-aek, moo-yuk-aek 'sa-sang choi-dae" (Dae-han-min-guk Jeong-chaek-briefing [Korea Policy Briefing] 4 January 2022), available online: www.korea.kr/news/visualNewsView.do?newsId=148897615 (accessed 10 February 2022).

S Yoon Lee, *Shin-min-sa-so-song-bub [New Civil Procedure Act]*, 12th edn, (Seoul, Pakyoungsa, 2018) 326.

Chapter 7. Singapore

A Staehelin, D Staehelin, P Grolimund and E Bachofner, *Zivilprozessrecht, Unter Einbezug des Anwaltsrechts und des internationalen Zivilprozessrechts*, 3rd edn (Baden, Baden, Schulthess, 2019), ch 10 para 18.

A Yeap, K Poon and A Pang 'The rise of arbitration in the Asia-Pacific' in *The Asia-Pacific Arbitration Review 2022* (Global Arbitration Review, 2022) 29.

D Girsberger and N Voser, *International Arbitration: Comparative and Swiss Perspectives*, 4th edn (Baden-Baden, Schulthess, 2021) para 1419.

GS Teo and HD Wong, 'Referring Questions of Foreign Law to the Court of the Governing Law: No Longer Lost in Translation' (2011) 23(1) *Singapore Academy of Law Journal* 227, *passim*.

Halsbury's Laws of Singapore (2021) 4 LexisNexis, accessed 29 March 2023, 50.394.

Halsbury's Laws of Singapore (2021) 6(2) LexisNexis, accessed 29 March 2023, 75.255.

J Landbrecht, 'The Singapore International Commercial Court (SICC) – an Alternative to International Arbitration?' (2016) 34(1) *ASA Bulletin* 112, 112–25.

J Choong, M Mangan and N Lingard, *A Guide to the SIAC Arbitration Rules*, 2nd edn (Oxford University Press, 2018) para 5.20.

K Ching, 'A Theoretical Perspective of the Public Policy Doctrine in the Conflict of Laws', (2018) 14(1) *Journal of Private International Law* 130.

L Kirchhoff, *Constructive Interventions: Paradigms, Process and Practice of International Mediation*' (Alphen aan den Rijn, Kluwer Law International, 2008) 122.

LV Chan, 'Taming the Unruly Public Policy Horse in Private International Law in Family Law: A Pragmatic Singaporean Approach to the Recognition of Foreign Same-Sex Marriages and Divorces' (2021) 35(1) *International Journal of Law, Policy and the Family* 1, 4.

N Alexander and S Chong, *The Singapore Convention on Mediation: A Commentary* (Alphen aan den Rijn, Wolters Kluwer, 2019) paras 0.41–0.52.

N Blackaby, C Partasides, A Redfern and M Hunter, *Redfern and Hunter on International Arbitration*, 6th edn (Oxford, Oxford University Press, 2015) paras 3.128–3.130.

Queen Mary University of London and White & Case LLP, '2021 International Arbitration Survey, Adapting Arbitration to a Changing World', 6, https://arbitration.qmul.ac.uk/media/arbitration/docs/LON0320037-QMUL-International-Arbitration-Survey-2021_19_WEB.pdf

W Lui, '*Singapore*' in A Reyes and W Lui (eds), *Direct Jurisdiction, Asian Perspectives* (Oxford, Hart Publishing, 2021) 127.

World Justice Project, 'Rule of Law Index 2020', 28; https://worldjusticeproject.org/sites/default/files/documents/WJP-ROLI-2020-Online_0.pdf.

Chapter 8. Malaysia

A Fiorini, 'Rome III – Choice of Law in Divorce: Is the Europeanization of Family Law Going Too Far?' (2008) 22 *International Journal of Law, Policy and the Family* 178.

A Mills, 'Private International Law and EU External Relations: Think Local Act Global, or Think Global Act Local?' (2016) 65 *ICLQ* 541, 549–50.

A Phang BL, 'Of "Cut-Off" Dates and Domination: Some Problematic Aspects of the General Reception of English Law in Singapore' (1986) 28 *Malaya Law Review* 242.

B Premaraj, 'The Choices of Law – Better Safe Than Sorry: The Malaysian Arbitration Perspective' 15–16. https://beldenlex.com/training/publications/The%20Choices%20of%20Law%20-%20Better%20Safe%20Than%20Sorry.pdf.

CN Chen, 'Recovery of Gambling Debts in Malaysia and Singapore' (2001) 1 *Malayan Law Journal* i.

D McClean and V Ruiz Abou-Nigm, *Morris on The Conflict of Laws*, 9th edn (London, Sweet & Maxwell, 2016) para 1-004.

DP Stewart, 'New Directions in Private International Law' [2009] *Agenda Internacional* 255, 256.

G Dhillon and SL Lee, 'Alternative Dispute Resolution Methods and Processes in Malaysia – A Review' (2015) 2 *Malayan Law Journal* viii, xii–xiii.

GS Teo and HD Wong, 'Referring Questions of Foreign Law to the Court of the Governing Law: No Longer "Lost in Translation"' (2011) 23 *Singapore Academy of Law Journal* 227.

H Omar, SB Marimuthu, and M Mahali, *Law of Evidence in Malaysia*, 2nd edn (London, Sweet & Maxwell 2018) para 1.030.

Hamid Sultan bin Abu Backer, *International Arbitration with Commentary to Malaysian Arbitration Act 2005* (Kuala Lumpur, Amirudeen bin Hamid Sultan ed, Janab 2016) 308.

KPK Foo and S Lee, *Companies Act 2016: The New Dynamics of Company Law in Malaysia* (Selangor, CLJ Publication, 2017) 519–20.

L Turner, 'Buried Treasure: Excavating Foreign Law from Civil Pleadings Filed in US Federal Courts' (2019) 47 *International Journal of Legal Information* 22, 40–41.

M Mohamad, 'The Islamic Divorce Contract and a Flawed Axiom of Masculine Protectionism' (2011) 39 *Asian Journal of Social Science* 821, 828.

MF Rutter, 'The Applicable Law in Singapore and Malaysia' [1989] *Malayan Law Journal* pt II.

N Blackaby et al, *Redfern and Hunter on International Arbitration*, 6th edn (Oxford OUP, 2015) paras 6.143–6.145.

N Ibrahim, 'The Right of Wife to Apply for the Division of Matrimonial Property on Dissolution of Marriage: The Malaysian Perspective' [2007] *The Law Review* 13.

NM Zin et al, *Islamic Family Law in Malaysia* (London, Sweet & Maxwell, 2016) 43–46.

N Pathmanathan JCA, 'Managing and Enhancing Quality in Judicial Performance and the Writing of Judgments' (2015) paras 38–41: www.kehakiman.gov.my/sites/default/files/YA-Datuk-Nallini-1.pdf.

NV Nadkarni and WF Teh, 'Malaysia' in A Reyes and W Lui (eds), *Direct Jurisdiction: Asian Perspectives* (Oxford, Hart Publishing, 2021) 162–63.

Pejabat Ketua Pendaftar Mahkamah Persekutuan Malaysia, 'EJudgment Management System': cms2.kehakiman.gov.my/CommonWeb/ejudgment/SearchPage.aspx?JurisdictionType=ALL.

Percetakan Nasional Malaysia Berhad, 'About Us' (*LawNet*) www.lawnet.com.my/home/aboutus.

—— 'Welcome to Malaysia's National Printer' (*Percetakan Nasional Malaysia Berhad*) www.printnasional.com.my/.

PJ Omar, 'Cross-Border Jurisdiction and Assistance in Insolvency: The Position in Malaysia and Singapore' [2008] *Potchefstroomse Elektoniese Regsblad* 1.

R Daw, 'Some Problems of Conflict of Laws in West Malaysia and Singapore Family Law' (1972) 14 *Malaya Law Review* 179, 183–84 and 191–92.

R Fentiman, *Foreign Law in English Courts* (Oxford, OUP, 1998) 70–76.

RH Hickling and MA Wu, *Conflict of Laws in Malaysia* (Singapore, Butterworths Asia, 1995) 1–16.

R Powell and A Hashim, 'Language Disadvantage in Malaysian Litigation and Arbitration' (2011) 30 *World Englishes* 92.

R Reddy, 'Marriage and Divorce Regulation and Recognition in Malaysia' (1995) 29 *Family Law Quarterly* 613, 619.

R Ward, 'Building Free Access to Law in Africa: Some Examples of Successful Projects' (2014) 14 *Legal Information Management* 290, 291.

SA Aziz, 'The Malaysian Legal System: The Roots, The Influence and The Future' (2009) 3 *Malayan Law Journal* xcii.

S Atkins and J Martin, 'The Model Law on Cross-Border Insolvency Turns 25' (*Norton Rose Fulbright*, May 2022).

SC Mohan, 'Cross-Border Insolvency Problems: Is the UNCITRAL Model Law the Answer?' (2012) 21 *International Insolvency Review* 199.

S Lee, 'The National Language in the Courts' (*Of Counsel*, 20 April 2008) leeshih.com/2008/04/20/the-national-language-in-the-courts/.

SS Lee (ed), *Law and Practice of Family Law in Malaysia* (London, Sweet & Maxwell, 2019) 62–66.

SS Faruqi, *Our Constitution* (London, Sweet & Maxwell, 2019) 40–41.

Singapore Courts, 'References of Questions of Law between Singapore and Foreign Courts' www.judiciary.gov.sg/who-we-are/references-questions-of-law-singapore-foreign-courts.

S Selvaratnam, 'Maritime Reform: Arrest for Arbitration' (2005): www.tommythomas.net/upload/staticpage/download/Maritime%20Reform%20-%20Arrest%20for%20Arbitration.pdf.

—— 'The Right of Arrest – Are We Making It Too Difficult? A Common Law Perspective' paras 15, 33 www.aiac.world/news/209/Sitpah-Selvaratnam:-The-Right-of-Arrest-%E2%80%93-Are-we-making-it-too-difficult-?-A-Common-Law-Perspective.

S Subramaniam, 'Determining the Law to Govern an Arbitration Agreement' (2020) 47 *Journal of Malaysian and Comparative Law* 1, 15.

T Moustafa, 'Liberal Rights versus Islamic Law? The Construction of a Binary in Malaysian Politics' (2013) 47 *Law & Society Review* 771.

Tan Sri Dato' C Abraham and AA Amirudin, 'Interaction of Laws in International Arbitration' in Tun Arifin Zakaria, Datuk Professor S Rajoo and P Koh (eds), *Arbitration in Malaysia: A Practical Guide* (London, Sweet & Maxwell, 2016) para 3.019.

TAG Beazley, 'Jurisdiction and Choice of Law in Tort Conflicts: Chan Kwon Fong & Anor v Chan Wah' (1977) 19 *Malaya Law Review* 391.

TAH Mohamad and A Trakic, 'The Reception of English Law in Malaysia and Development of the Malaysian Common Law' (2015) 44 *Common Law World Review* 123.

Tun Tengku Maimun Tuan Mat and GS Ram (eds), *Malaysian Civil Procedure 2021* (London, Sweet & Maxwell, 2021) para 40/0/2.

YN Foo and K Dhaliwal, 'Dissolution of Marriage: Jurisdiction and Forum' in SS Lee (ed), *Law and Practice of Family Law in Malaysia* (London, Sweet & Maxwell, 2019) 62–66.

YN Lim, 'Towards a Uniform Conflict of Laws Regime in ASEAN Governing International Commercial Transactions: Uniformization of Choice of Law Rules in Contract and Tort' (Montreal, McGill University 2000).

Chapter 9. Vietnam

BQ Tuan, 'Áp dụng và giải thích pháp luật nước ngoài trong tư pháp quốc tế [Application and Interpretations of Foreign Law in Vietnamese Private International Law]' 3 (2017) *Tạp chí Nghiên cứu lập pháp [Journal of Legislative Reseach]* 3.

Báo cáo Thường niên VIAC và VMC 2021 [Annual Report of VIAC and VMC 2021] www.viac.vn/…/VIAC_Bao-cao-thuong-nien-2021.pdf.

CE Mota, 'Application of Foreign Law – Harmonisation of Private International Law in Europe and Application of Foreign Law: "The Madrid Principles" of 2010' 13 (2011) *Yearbook of Private International Law* 273, 294.

DM Tuan, 'Xác định nội dung pháp luật nước ngoài để giải quyết tranh chấp dân sự quốc tế bởi tòa án [Ascertaining the content of foreign law for resolving international civil disputes by courts]' 40 (2014) *Tạp chí Kinh tế Đối ngoại [Journal of International Economics and Management]* tinyurl.com/2p9ec3ds.

DV Dai, Pháp luật trọng tài thương mại Việt Nam [Arbitration law in Vietnam] 1 (2018) Nhà xuất bản Hồng Đức [Hong Duc Publishing House] 582.

DV Dai and MH Quy, *Tư pháp quốc tế Việt Nam* [*Vietnamese Private International Law*] (Hanoi, Nhà xuất bản chính trị quốc gia [National Political Publishing House], 2010) 228.

D Nang, *Một số vấn đề lý luận cơ bản về Tư pháp quốc tế [Some Basic Theoretical Issues about Private International Law]* (Nhà xuất bản Chính trị quốc gia [Vietnamese National Political Publishing House] 2001).

Hanoi Law University, *Giáo trình Tư pháp quốc tế [Textbook on Private International Law]* (Hanoi, Nhà xuất bản Công an Nhân dân [People Police Publishing House], 2013), 61–62.

Institute of Legal Science (Ministry of Justice), Special Issue of Legal Information and Sciences 'Some issues in the application of foreign law in civil trials at Vietnamese Courts', (2020).

LM Hung, 'Vấn đề áp dụng pháp luật nước ngoài trong giải quyết các vụ việc dân sự tại Tòa án Việt Nam [The application of Foreign Law in civil cases in Vietnamese courts]' (2021) *Tạp chí Tòa án điện tử [Online People's Court Journal]* tinyurl.com/4e7xkv9n.

NQ Chien and NH Anh, 'Trọng tài thương mại quốc tế và vấn đề luật áp dụng [International Commercial Arbitration and applicable law]' 1 (2021) *Tạp chí Nghiên cứu lập pháp số [Journal of Legislative Research].*

NN Dien, 'Chế định Ly hôn trong Tư pháp quốc tế' [Divorce in Vietnamese Private International Law] in Bernard Audit (ed) *Material of Conference on Private International Law* (Hanoi, Vietnamese – French Publishing House, 2005) 70.

NV Cuong, 'Tranh chấp của người lao động và công ty xuất khẩu lao động [Dispute of Employees with Labor Export Companies]' 11 (2006) *Tạp chí Tòa án nhân dân [The People's Court Journal]* 18.

PH Huong and HN Bich, 'An Overview of Vietnamese Private International Law' 18 (2016/2017) *Yearbook of Private International Law* 341, 344.

PT Dat (Vice Chief Secretary of VIAC), 'Áp dụng CISG trong Trọng tài thương mại quốc tế [Application of CISG in international Commercial Arbitration]' Power Point Presentation at Conference on CISG (2020).

TN Quang, *Pháp luật về Hợp đồng [Laws on Contracts]* (Nhà xuất bản Dân Trí [Dan Tri Publisher], 2020) 765.

Chapter 10. Cambodia

A Ito, 'Legal Education and Professional Legal Training in Laos: Towards the Birth of Lao Jurisprudence [in Japanese]' (2020) *ICD News* 40.

A Kamiki, 'Report on the Investigation of Cambodian Court Judgements [in Japanese]' (2011) *ICD News* 25.

A Mikazuki, 'The Application of Foreign Law and the Court [in Japanese]' in Takao Sawaki and Yoshimitsu Aoyama (eds), *Theories of International Civil Procedure Law* (Tokyo Yuhikaku Publishing, 1987) 239-83.

A Misawa, 'Supporting the Training of Judges and Prosecutors in Cambodia [in Japanese]' (2004) 18 *ICD News* 1.

Bun & Associates, 'Governing Law and Dispute Resolution [in Japanese]', (*Bun & Associates Newsletter*, August 2017).

C Azcárraga Monzonís, 'Spain: The Application of Foreign Laws in Spain – Critical Analysis of the Legal Novelties of 2015' in Yuko Nishitani (ed), *Treatment of Foreign Law – Dynamics towards Convergence?* (Cham, Springer, 2017) 329-46.

C Huot and S Rith, 'Hope of Justice Lies in School for Judges', (*The Phnom Penh Post*, 21 November 2003).

CCF Director-General, 'Laws & Regulations: Laws, Regulations and Other Legal Documents Related to the Roles and Functions of the CCF Directorate-General' (2021) www.ccfdg.gov.kh/en/laws-regulations/.

CDC, 'Laws and Regulations' (2017) www.cambodiainvestment.gov.kh/why-invest-in-cambodia/laws-regulation.html.

CP Alberti and DM Bigge, 'Ascertaining the Content of the Applicable Law and Iura Novit Tribunus: Approaches in Commercial and Investment Arbitration' (2015) 70 *Dispute Resolution Journal* 1.

DA Donovan, 'Cambodia: Building a Legal System from Scratch' (1993) 27 *The International Lawyer* 445.

E Gaillard, *Legal Theory of International Arbitration* (Leiden, Martinus Nijhoff Publishers, 2010).

European Commission and Hague Conference on Private International Law, 'Access to Foreign Law in Civil and Commercial Matters: Conclusions and Recommendations' (2012) assets.hcch.net/docs/b093f152-a4b3-4530-949e-65c1bfc9cda1.pdf.

F De Ly, MW Friedman and LG Radicati di Brozolo, 'International Law Association International Commercial Arbitration Committee's Report and Recommendations on Ascertaining the Contents of the Applicable Law in International Commercial Arbitration" (2010) 26 *Arbitration International* 193.

G Kaufmann-Kohler, 'The Arbitrator and the Law: Does He/She Know It? Apply It? How? And a Few More Questions' (2005) 21 *Arbitration International* 631.

G Tu, 'Macau: Proof and Information About Foreign Law in Macau' in Yuko Nishitani (ed), *Treatment of Foreign Law – Dynamics towards Convergence?* (Cham, Springer, 2017) 541–48.

GB Born, *International Commercial Arbitration* 3rd edn (Alphen aan den Rijn, Wolters Kluwer, 2020).

H Brander, 'Fake or Fact? (1) Digital Docs Manipulation and How to Spot It', (*Counsel*, 15 January 2021). www.counselmagazine.co.uk/articles/fake-or-fact-digital-docs-manipulation-how-to-spot-it-(1).

I Sakano, 'Reflection on the Legal and Judicial Development Project for Drafting the Civil and Civil Procedure Codes of Cambodia [in Japanese]' (2003) *ICD NEWS* 91.

Industrial Development and Public Policy Department at JICA, *Legal Technical Assistance for Cambodia: The History and Methodology of the Assistance of JICA in Drafting the Civil Code and the Civil Procedure Code [in Japanese]* (2012).

J Menzel, 'Cambodian Law: Some Comparative and International Perspectives' in H Peng, K Phallack and J Menzel (eds), *Introduction to Cambodian Law* (Phnom Penh, Konrad-Adenauer-Stiftung, 2012) 477–93.

J Waincymer, 'International Arbitration and the Duty to Know the Law' (2011) 28 *Journal of International Arbitration* 201.

JICA, 'Commentary on Cambodian Code of Civil Procedure: Judgment Procedure [in Japanese]' (n.d.). www.moj.go.jp/content/000122394.pdf.

K Phallack, 'Overview of Contemporary Civil Procedures of Cambodia' in H Peng, K Phallack and J Menzel (eds), *Introduction to Cambodian Law* (Phnom Penh, Konrad-Adenauer-Stiftung, 2012) 155–80.

—— 'Overview of the Cambodian Legal and Judicial System and Recent Efforts at Legal and Judicial Reform' in H Peng, K Phallack and J Menzel (eds), *Introduction to Cambodian Law* (Phnom Penh, Konrad-Adenauer-Stiftung, 2012) 5–22.

M Ito, 'The History of JICA's Legal Technical Assistance in Cambodia [in Japanese]' (2021) 87 *ICD News* 47.

—— 'Professional Legal Education at the Royal School for Judges and Prosecutors (Cambodia)' [in Japanese] (2022) 90 *ICD* News 47, 49.

M Vickery, *Kampuchea: Politics, Economy and Society* (Frances Pinter, 1986).

N Blackaby and others, *Redfern and Hunter on International Arbitration*, 6th edn (Oxford, Oxford University Press, 2015).

N Chheng, 'Courts' Decisions Now Published as Reference Source', (*The Phnom Penh Post*, 4 January 2021). www.phnompenhpost.com/national/courts-decisions-now-published-reference-source.

N Sakai and S Kamata, 'The Doctrine of Precedent in Vietnam [in Japanese]' (2017) *ICD News* 29.

N Teramura, 'Cambodia' in A Reyes and W Lui (eds), *Direct Jurisdiction* (Oxford, Hart Publishing, 2021) 201–19.

—— 'Ex Aequo et Bono and Arbitration Theories: an Arbitrator's Subjective Perspective of Fairness as the Final 'Gap-Filler" (2020) 38 *ASA Bulletin* 350.

—— 'Japan as a Source of Legal Ideas: A View from the Mekong Subregion of ASEAN' (2021) 13 *New Voices in Japanese Studies* 19.

—— *Ex Aequo et Bono as a Response to the 'Over-Judicialisation'of International Commercial Arbitration* (Alphen aan den Rijn, Wolters Kluwer, 2020).

O Remien, 'Germany: Proof of and Information about Foreign Law – Duty to Investigate, Expert Opinions and a Proposal for Europe' in Y Nishitani (ed), *Treatment of Foreign Law – Dynamics towards Convergence?* (Cham, Springer 2017) 183–220.

P Baysal and M Atar, 'A Comparative Analysis of Content-of-Laws Inquiry and Its Importance for International Commercial Arbitration', (*Kluwer Arbitration Blog*, 25 January 2020). arbitrationblog.kluwerarbitration.com/2020/01/25/a-comparative-analysis-of-content-of-laws-inquiry-and-its-importance-for-international-commercial-arbitration/.

P Nicholson and T Kuong, 'Japanese Legal Assistance: An East Asian Model of Legal Assistance and Rule of Law?' (2014) 6 *Hague Journal on the Rule of Law* 141.

R Yamada, *Lectures on Private International Law [in Japanese]* 3rd edn (Tokyo, Yuhikaku Publishing, 2004).

S Corneloup, 'France – The Evolving Balance Between the Judge and the Parties in France' in Y Nishitani (ed), Treatment of Foreign Law – Dynamics towards Convergence ? (Cham, Springer, 2017) 157–183

S Ikehara, H Egawa and R Yamada, *The General Theory of Private International Law and Nationality Law [in Japanese]* (Yuhikaku Publishing, 1973).

S Leng, 'Problems in Translating Cambodian Civil Code and Civil Procedure Code and Future Prospects [in Japanese]' (2016) *ICD NEWS*. www.moj.go.jp/content/001298242.pdf.

S Loizou, 'Revisiting the "Content-of-Laws" Enquiry in International Arbitration' (2018) 78 *Louisiana Law Review* 811.

S Nakano, 'Japan: Proof of and Information about Foreign Law in Japan' in Y Nishitani (ed), *Treatment of Foreign Law – Dynamics towards Convergence?* (Cham, Springer, 2017) 529–40.

S Sarath, 'Arbitration Rules Under Review', (*Khmer Times*, 28 July 2020) www.khmertimeskh.com/50749327/arbitration-rules-under-review/.

S Tamagaki, 'The Arbitration Council in Cambodia: Impacts of the 2016 Law on Trade Unions and Prakas No. 303 by the Ministry of Labour and Vocational Training [in Japanese]' (2019) *ICD NEWS:* www.moj.go.jp/content/001306610.pdf.

V Phun, 'Country Factsheet 2: Judicial Training in Cambodia' in Aviva Nababan and others (eds), *Judicial Training in ASEAN: A Comparative Overview of Systems and Programs* (Phnom Penh, Konrad-Adenauer-Stiftung, 2014) 31–34.

Y Kaneko, 'Japan's Civil Code Drafting Support for Socialist Reform Countries: Diversity of Normative Choice' in Y Kaneko (ed), *Civil Law Reforms in Post-Colonial Asia: Beyond Western Capitalism* (Cham, Springer, 2019) 155–76.

Y Nishitani, 'Treatment of Foreign Law: Dynamics Towards Convergence? – General Report' in Y Nishitani (ed), *Treatment of Foreign Law – Dynamics towards Convergence?* (Cham, Springer, 2017) 3–60.

—— 'Treatment of and Access to Foreign Law in Japan' (2018) 23 *Journal of Japanese Law* 69.

Y Shinoda, 'Report on the Investigation of Cambodian Court Judgments (1) [in Japanese]' (2019) *ICD NEWS* 60.

Y Tameike, *Lecture on Private International Law [in Japanese]* (Tokyo, Yuhikaku Publishing, 2005).

Chapter 11. Myanmar

A Briggs, *Private International Law in Myanmar* (Oxford, Oxford University Press, 2015) 11.

Dicey, Morris and Collins, Conflict of Laws Vol. 1, 14th edn (London, Sweet and Maxwell, 2006) 255.

N Yin Kham, 'An Introduction to the Law and Judicial System of Myanmar' CALS Myanmar Working Paper, No. 1 March 2014. law1.nus.edu.sg/pdfs/cals/working_papers/Myanmar/MWPS001.pdf.

Z Thura, 'Myanmar' in A Reyes (ed), *Recognition and Enforcement of Judgments in Civil and Commercial Matters* (Oxford, Hart Publishing, 2019).

—— 'Myanmar' in A Reyes and W Lui (eds), *Direct Jurisdiction: Asian Perspectives* (Oxford, Hart Publishing, 2021).

Chapter 12. Philippines

J Coquia and E Aguiling-Pangalangan, *Conflict of Laws* (Manila, Central Professional Books, 2000) 152.

J Salonga, *Private International Law* (San Antoni, Regina Publishing Company, 1995) 129.

PA Manalo, '(Dis)Proving Foreign Law: Understanding Processual Presumption in the Philippines and Arguing for a Confrontational Approach in Dealing with Conflict Cases' (2015) 89 *Philippine Law Journal* 430.

Y Rotem, 'Foreign Law as a Distinctive fact – To Whom Should the Burden of Proof Be Assigned?' (2014) 14 *Chicago Journal of International Law* 625.

Chapter 13. Indonesia

A Kusumadara, *Indonesian Private International Law* (Oxford, Hart Publishing, 2021).

AP Senoadji, 'Penerapan Legitime Portie (Bagian Mutlak) Dalam Pembagian Waris Menurut Kitab Undang-Undang Hukum Perdata Studi Kasus Putusan Mahkamah Agung Reg No. 148/Pk/Perd/1982' (Master thesis, Universitas Diponegoro, 2007).

J Junaiding, 'Soft Law Sebagai Sumber Hukum Kontrak Dalam Perdagangan Internasional' (2021) 1(3) *Dharmasisya* 1293–95. scholarhub.ui.ac.id/dharmasisya/vol1/iss3/15.

S Gautama and H Wiknjosastro, 'Some Aspects of Indonesian Private International Law' (1990) 32 (2) *Malaya Law Review* 429. www.jstor.org/stable/24865645.

S Gautama, *Hukum Perdata Internasional Indonesia Buku Ketujuh Jilid Ke-Tiga (Bagian Pertama)* (Bandung, Penerbit Alumni, 1981) 176.

—— *Pengantar Hukum Perdata Internasional Indonesia* (Jakarta, Binacipta, 1985) 170, 205.

—— *Hukum Perdata Internasional Indonesia Jilid III Bagian 2 Buku Ke Delapan* (Bandung, Penerbit Alumni, 1987) 191–97.

—— *Hukum Perdata Internasional Indonesia Jilid II Bagian 5 Buku Ke enam* (Bandung, Penerbit Alumni, 1988) 187, 190–194, 196–200.

World Trade Organization, Indonesia and the WTO. Ratification date: 1 January 1995. www.wto.org/english/thewto_e/countries_e/indonesia_e.htm#stcsHeading.

Chapter 14. Thailand

FC Darling, 'The Evolution of Law in Thailand' (1970) 32(2) *The Review of Politics* 197, 215.

J Fawcett and JM Carruthers, *Cheshire, North & Fawcett Private International Law*, 14th edn (Oxford, Oxford University Press, 2008) 71–72.

K Chunchaemsai, *Private International Law Book 1: Conflict of Laws* (Bangkok, Thammasat University Faculty of Law, 2021) 256.

K Luchai, *Explanation on the conflict of laws*, 9th edn (Bangkok, October Publishing House, 2021) 35, 194.

K Prokati and A Laowonsiri, 'Thailand' in J Basedow, G Rühl, F Ferrari and PM Asensio (eds), *Encyclopedia of Private International Law* (Cheltenham, Edward Elgar Publishing, 2017) 2569, 2571.

M Davies, A Bell, PLG Brereton, and M Douglas, *Nygh's Conflict of Laws in Australia*, 10th edn (Chatswood, LexisNexis Butterworths, 2020) para 15.4.

S Reekie and A Reekie, 'British Judges in the Supreme Court of Siam' in A Harding and M Pongsapan (eds), *Thai Legal History: From Traditional to Modern Law* (Cambridge, Cambridge University Press, 2022) 103, 105.

The Hague Conference on Private International Law, '40: Principles on Choice of Law in International Commercial Contracts', www.hcch.net/en/instruments/conventions/full-text/?cid=135.

W Chen and G Goldstein, 'The Asian Principles of Private International Law: objectives, contents, structure and selected topics on choice of law' (2017) 13(2) *Journal of Private International Law* 411, 423.

Y Nitiruchirot and T Wongyai, 'Problem arising from applying foreign laws in Thai courts' (July–August 2015) *Chulaniti* 73, 85.

Chapter 15. Sri Lanka

CG Weeramantry, *The Law of Contracts* (Vol I), (Pannipitiya, Stamford Lake Publications, 1967) 21.

ERSR Coomaraswamy, *A Text Book of The Law of Evidence in Ceylon*, 1st edn (NE Hamer, 1955).

K Muthumuni de Silva, *A History of Sri Lanka* (Colombo, Vijitha Yapa Publications, 2005), 6.

LJM Cooray, *An Introduction to the Legal System of Sri Lanka*, 2nd edn (Pannipitiya, Stamford Lake Publications, 2003) 4.

P Torremans and others (eds), *Cheshire, North & Fawcett Private International Law*, 15th edn (Oxford, Oxford University Press, 2017) 105.

R Fentiman, *International Commercial Litigation*, 2nd edn (Oxford, Oxford University Press, 2015), 666.

Chapter 16. India

AC Patra, 'Historical Background of the Indian Contract Act, 1872' (1962) 4(3) *Journal of the Indian Law Institute 373.*

AD McNair, 'The Method Whereby International Law is made to Prevail in Municipal Courts on An Issue of International Law' (1944) 30 *Transaction of the Grotius Society* 88.

AM Smith, 'Making Itself at Home: Understanding Foreign Law in Domestic Jurisprudence – the Indian Case' (May 25, 2005), 25. ssrn.com/abstract=729946.

A Nussbaum, 'The Problem of Proving the Foreign Law' (1941) 50 *Yale Law Journal* 1018.
B Srinivasan, 'Appeal against the Order of the Chief Justice under Section 11 of the Arbitration and Conciliation Act, 1996: An Empirical Analysis' (2012) 1 *Indian Journal of Arbitration Law* 21.
BS Rao, *The Framing of Indian Constitution-Select Documents* (Indian Institute of Public Administration, 1968).
CH Alexander, 'International Law in India' (1952) 1(3) *ICLQ* 289, 291.
D Dave, M Hunter, F Nariman and M Paulsson (eds), *Arbitration in India* (Alphen aan den Rijn, Kluwer Law International 2021) 135–36.
Dicey, Morris & Collins, Conflict of Laws, 15th edn (London, Sweet & Maxwell, 2018).
FA Mann, 'The Enforcement of Treaties by English Courts' (1958–59) 44 *Transaction of the Grotius Society* 29.
FN Zaal, 'Roman Law and the Racial Policies of the Dutch East India Company: An Exploration of Some Historical Inter-connections' (1996) 29(1) *The Comparative and International Law Journal of Southern Africa* 31.
G Singh, 'Evidentiary Value of Expert Opinion under the Indian Evidence Act: A Critical Analysis of Section 45' (2020) 2 *International Journal for Legal Science and Innovation* 552.
G Sitaraman, 'The Use and Abuse of Foreign Law in Constitutional Interpretation' (2009) 32 *Harvard Journal of Law & Public Policy* 653.
H Lauterpacht, 'Is International Law As Part of The Law of The England?' (1939) 30 *Transactions of the Grotius Society* 51.
JL Neels, 'Choice of Forum and Tacit Choice of Law: The Supreme Court of India and the Hague Principles on Choice of Law in International Commercial Contracts (An Appeal for an Inclusive Comparative Approach to Private International Law)' in *Eppur si Muove: The Age of Uniform Law Essays in honour of Michael Joachim Bonell to celebrate his 70th birthday* (UNIDROIT, 2016) 358, 366.
J Shaw, *Charters Relating to the East India Company from 1600 to 1761* (Madras, Madras Government Press, 1887).
KG Balakrishnan, 'The Role of Foreign Precedents in a Country's Legal System' (2010) 22(1) *National law School of India Review* 1.
Law Commission of India, 89th Report on The Limitation Act, 1963 (1983) 25. lawcommissionofindia.nic.in/51-100/Report89.pdf.
Law Commission of India, 240th Report, Costs in Civil Litigation (2012).
MN Pearson, *The Portuguese in India* (Cambridge, CUP, 1988).
N Chada and S Arora, 'India' in P Doris (eds), *Enforcement of Foreign Judgements 2020* (Law Business Research, Aug 2019) 59–63.
NK Singh, 'The Indian Constitution and Customary International Law' (2000) 12 *National Law School of India Review - Student Advocate* 81, 85–86.
RD Baird, 'Traditional Values, Governmental Values, and Religious Conflict in Contemporary India' [1998] *Brigham Young University Law Review* 337.
P Diwan, *Muslim Law in Modern India* (ALA, 1977).
P Sooksripaisarnkit and SR Garimella, 'Choice of Court Agreements: Selected Common-Law Jurisdictions and Indian Laws Compared – Time for the Convention of 30 June 2005 on Choice of Court Agreements? (2021) 30 *Journal of Transnational Law and Policy* 1.
PV Rajamannar, 'The Future of Private International Law in India' (1952) 1 *The Indian Yearbook of International Affairs* 20.
SC Jain, 'French Legal System in Pondicherry: An Introduction' (1970) 12(4) *Journal of the Indian Law Institute* 573.
SL Sass, 'Foreign Law in Civil Litigation: A Comparative Survey' (1968) 16(3) *American Journal of Comparative Law* 332, 340.
SR Garimella, 'Arbitral Reforms in India – The Case for Third Party Funding of Arbitral Claims (2018) 15(2) *Transnational Dispute Management* 1, 19.
—— 'OBOR and the Syncretic Private International Law Rules in India: Time for Accession to Harmonised Legal Regimes' in P Sooksripaisarnkit and SR Garimella (eds) *China's One Belt One Road Initiative and Private International Law* (London, Routledge, 2018).
TSR Rao, 'Some of the Problems of the International Law in India' (1957) 6 *Indian Yearbook of International Affairs* 3.
—— 'Conflict of Laws in India' (1958) 23 *Rabels Zeitschrift für ausländisches und internationals Privatrecht* 276.

VC Govindraj, *Private International Law: A Case Study 1–20* (Oxford Scholarship Online 2018) oxford.universitypressscholarship.com/view/10.1093/oso/9780199489282.001.0001/oso-9780199489282.
—— *Conflict of Laws in India: Inter-territorial and Inter-personal Conflict* (Oxford, OUP, 2019) 1, 17.
VK Thiruvenkatachari, 'Developments in the field of Private International Law' (1953) 2 *The Indian Yearbook on International Affairs* 195.

Chapter 17. Conclusion

F De Ly, MW Friedman and LG Radicati di Brozolo, 'International Law Association International Commercial Arbitration Committee's Report and Recommendations on "Ascertaining the Contents of the Applicable Law in International Commercial Arbitration"' (2010) 26(2) *Arbitration International* 193.
Y Nishitani, 'Treatment of Foreign Law: Dynamics Towards Convergence? – General Report', in Y Nishitani (ed), *Treatment of Foreign Law – Dynamics towards Convergence?* (Cham, Springer, 2017) 31.

INDEX